Ancient Greece and China Compared

Ancient Greece and China Compared is a pioneering, methodologically sophisticated set of studies, bringing together scholars who all share the conviction that the sustained critical comparison and contrast between ancient societies can bring to light significant aspects of each that would be missed by focusing on just one of them. The topics tackled include key issues in philosophy and religion, in art and literature, in mathematics and the life sciences (including gender studies), in agriculture, city planning and institutions. The volume also analyses how to go about the task of comparing, including finding viable comparanda and avoiding the trap of interpreting one culture in terms appropriate only to another. The book is set to provide a model for future collaborative and interdisciplinary work exploring what is common between ancient civilisations, what is distinctive of particular ones, and what may help to account for the latter.

G. E. R. LLOYD is Emeritus Professor of Ancient Philosophy and Science at the University of Cambridge, Former Master of Darwin College, Cambridge, and Senior Scholar in Residence at the Needham Research Institute, Cambridge. He is the author of twenty-two books and editor of four, and was knighted for 'services to the history of thought' in 1997.

JINGYI JENNY ZHAO is Lloyd-Dan David Research Fellow at the Needham Research Institute and at Darwin College, Cambridge.

QIAOSHENG DONG is currently affiliated to the Cambridge Peking University China Centre at Jesus College.

Ancient Greece and China Compared

EDITED BY G. E. R. LLOYD AND JINGYI JENNY ZHAO

In collaboration with Qiaosheng Dong

CAMBRIDGE
UNIVERSITY PRESS

University Printing House, Cambridge CB2 8BS, United Kingdom

One Liberty Plaza, 20th Floor, New York, NY 10006, USA

477 Williamstown Road, Port Melbourne, VIC 3207, Australia

314-321, 3rd Floor, Plot 3, Splendor Forum, Jasola District Centre, New Delhi - 110025, India

79 Anson Road, #06-04/06, Singapore 079906

Cambridge University Press is part of the University of Cambridge.

It furthers the University's mission by disseminating knowledge in the pursuit of education, learning and research at the highest international levels of excellence.

www.cambridge.org
Information on this title: www.cambridge.org/9781107086661
DOI: 10.1017/9781316091609

© Cambridge University Press 2018

This publication is in copyright. Subject to statutory exception and to the provisions of relevant collective licensing agreements, no reproduction of any part may take place without the written permission of Cambridge University Press.

First published 2018

A catalogue record for this publication is available from the British Library

ISBN 978-1-107-08666-1 Hardback
ISBN 978-1-107-45159-9 Paperback

Cambridge University Press has no responsibility for the persistence or accuracy of URLs for external or third-party internet websites referred to in this publication, and does not guarantee that any content on such websites is, or will remain, accurate or appropriate.

Contents

List of Figures [*page* vii]
Acknowledgements [x]
Notes on Editions [xi]
List of Contributors [xiii]

Introduction: Methods, Problems and Prospects [1]
G. E. R. LLOYD

    PART I   METHODOLOGICAL ISSUES AND GOALS [31]

1 Why Some Comparisons Make More Difference than Others [33]
NATHAN SIVIN

2 Comparing Comparisons [40]
WALTER SCHEIDEL

3 On the Very Idea of (Philosophical?) Translation [59]
ROBERT WARDY

    PART II   PHILOSOPHY AND RELIGION [81]

4 Freedom in Parts of the *Zhuangzi* and Epictetus [83]
R. A. H. KING

5 Shame and Moral Education in Aristotle and Xunzi [110]
JINGYI JENNY ZHAO

6 Human and Animal in Early China and Greece [131]
LISA RAPHALS

7 Genealogies of Gods, Ghosts and Humans: The Capriciousness of the Divine in Early Greece and Early China [160]
MICHAEL PUETT

v

PART III ART AND LITERATURE [187]

8 Visual Art and Historical Representation in Ancient Greece and China   [189]
JEREMY TANNER

9 Helen and Chinese Femmes Fatales   [234]
YIQUN ZHOU

PART IV MATHEMATICS AND LIFE SCIENCES [257]

10 Divisions, Big and Small: Comparing Archimedes and Liu Hui   [259]
REVIEL NETZ

11 Abstraction as a Value in the Historiography of Mathematics in Ancient Greece and China: A Historical Approach to Comparative History of Mathematics   [290]
KARINE CHEMLA

12 Recipes for Love in the Ancient World   [326]
VIVIENNE LO AND ELEANOR RE´EM

PART V AGRICULTURE, PLANNING AND INSTITUTIONS [353]

13 From the Harvest to the Meal in Prehistoric China and Greece: A Comparative Approach to the Social Context of Food   [355]
XINYI LIU, EVI MARGARITIS AND MARTIN JONES

14 On Libraries and Manuscript Culture in Western Han Chang'an and Alexandria   [373]
MICHAEL NYLAN

Afterword   [410]
MICHAEL LOEWE

Index   [420]

Figures

2.1 Comparative ancient East/West publications. [*page* 49]

8.1 Tyrannicides: Harmodius and Aristogeiton. Roman marble copy of bronze statues by Kritios and Nesiotes, 476 BCE. Photo: Permission of the Ministero dei Beni e delle Attività Culturali e del Turismo – Museo Archeologico Nazionale di Napoli. [190]

8.2 Wu Liang Shrine, West Wall. Second century CE. Rubbing after the original stone engravings. Image: Courtesy of the C.V. Starr East Asian Library, University of California, Berkeley. [191]

8.3 (a) *He zun*, eleventh century BCE. (b) Rubbing of the inscription from the interior of the *He zun*. Photos: © Baoji Bronze Ware Museum, 宝鸡青铜器博物院. [195]

8.4 Shi Qiang bronze *pan* vessel, tenth century BCE. Zhuangbai, Fufeng, Shaanxi Province. Photo: Zhang Yawei. © Zhouyuan Museum. [196]

8.5 Croesus, Anavyssos *kouros* (NM Inv. 3851), c. 540 BCE. National Archaeological Museum Athens (photographer: V. v. Eickstedt). © Hellenic Ministry of Culture and Sports/ Archaeological Receipts Fund. [200]

8.6 Stoa Poikile, Athens, c. 460 BCE. Restored perspective by W. B. Dinsmoor. Courtesy of the American School of Classical Studies at Athens: Agora Excavations. [203]

8.7 Reconstruction of compositional scheme of the Battle of Marathon Painting in the Stoa Poikile. After E. Harrison (1972), ill. 1; courtesy Archaeological Institute of America and *The American Journal of Archaeology*. [204]

8.8 Greek battles fleeing Persian. Attic red-figure Nolan amphora. New York, Metropolitan Museum of Art, Rogers Fund. 1906.06.1021.117. © Photo: SCALA, Florence, 2016. [206]

8.9 South frieze from the Temple of Athena Nike, Athens. Slab G, British Museum. Photo: © British Museum. [207]

List of Figures

8.10 (a) Temple of Athena Nike, Athens, c. 425 BCE. Photo: American School of Classical Studies at Athens, Archives, Alison Frantz Photographic Collection. (b) Reconstruction of bastion of the Temple of Athena Nike, with shields attached. Drawing: David Scahill. [211]

8.11 (a) Reconstruction of shrine from Songshan, second century CE. After Wu Hung 1989, figure 42. (b) West wall of shrine from Songshan, second century CE. Rubbing after engraved stones in Shandong Provincial Museum. Image: with permission of the Royal Ontario Museum © ROM. [215]

8.12 Jing Ke and the King of Qin (top register). Rubbing after engravings on the south wall of Shrine 1, Wu Family Cemetery. Second century CE. Image: Courtesy of Harvard University Fine Arts Library, Special Collections. [217]

8.13 Rubbing after engraving from Eastern Han shrine, Songshan, Shandong Province. Image: with permission of the Royal Ontario Museum © ROM. [218]

8.14 The First Emperor fails to recover the Zhou Tripods. Rubbing after engravings on the East Wall, Chamber 2, Wu Family Cemetery, Shandong. Image courtesy of Harvard University, Fine Arts Library Special Collections. [219]

10.1 The 'Box-Lid'. [260]

10.2 Archimedes' *Method* 14 supplemented by a three-dimensional extension above the base. [262]

10.3 Proof of properties in Figure 10.2. [263]

10.4 Bicylinder and circumscribed sphere. [266]

10.5 Figure 10.4 with added plane parallel to the base of the cube. [267]

10.6 Box-Lid decomposed. [268]

10.7 Illustration of use of Cavalieri's principle. [272]

11.1 The rectangular cropland in the first problem in chapter 4. [310]

11.2 The representation of a quantity of area of 240 *bu* using measurement units for length. [311]

11.3 Interpreting the expression 'Reducing the Width' using the geometrical representation of the value of areas. [317]

12.1 Red-figure *pelike*, attributed to the Hasselmann Painter, BM1865, 1118.49. [327]

12.2 Double phalli from Tomb M1 Mancheng, Hebei. [328]

12.3 A chart of the vulva, Mawangdui tomb 3. [329]
13.1 Locations of key sites mentioned in the text. [369]
14.1 The Tianlu ge library site. [382]
14.2 Han roof-tile end bearing the legends 'Shiqu qianqiu'. [383]
14.3 Western Jin scholars collating texts. [385]

Acknowledgements

This book originated in a conference entitled Comparing Ancient Worlds: Greece and China that marked the celebration of G. E. R. Lloyd's eightieth birthday on 25 January 2013. The idea for such a conference came from Qiaosheng Dong and Jenny Zhao, who jointly organised the whole proceedings, and it could not have taken place without the generous support of the Needham Research Institute, the Centre for Research in the Arts, Social Sciences and Humanities, the Classics Faculty at Cambridge and above all the Chiang Ching-kuo foundation. Our thanks go to all these organisations and especially to the staff of CRASSH, Catherine Hurley and Michelle Maciejewska, and at the NRI, Sue Bennett and John Moffett. Not all the original talks held at the conference have been included and some have been added to cover subjects that were not part of our original discussions, but every chapter has been extensively revised in the light of comments at the original conference and from external reviewers. Given Qiaosheng Dong's other commitments, the bulk of the editorial work was undertaken by G. E. R. Lloyd and Jenny Zhao.

Notes on Editions

Unless otherwise specified

For Greek and Latin texts

References to Plato are to Burnet's Oxford edition.
    References to Aristotle are to Bekker's Berlin edition; translations to J. Barnes (ed.) (1991) *The Complete Works of Aristotle* (revised edn). Princeton.
    The Presocratic philosophers are cited according to H. Diels and W. Kranz (1952) *Die Fragmente der Vorsokratiker* (6th edn). 3 vols. Berlin.
    The following is cited according to the Loeb Classical Library: Homer (1919) *Odyssey*. Trans. A. T. Murray. Cambridge, MA.

For Chinese texts

The following editions are used:
Huainanzi 淮南子 (1926; reprint 1989) Liu An 劉安. Liu Wendian 劉文典 ed. *Huainan Honglie jijie* 淮南鴻烈集解. 2 vols. Beijing.
Lienü zhuan 列女傳 (1936) Liu Xiang 劉向. Sibu beiyao ed. Shanghai.
Lunheng 論衡 (1990) Wang Chong 王充 (27-97). Liu Pansui 劉盼遂 ed. *Lunheng jiao shi* 論衡校釋. Beijing.
Suanjing Shishu 算經十書 (1963) Qian Baocong 錢寶琮 ed. Beijing.
Zhuangzi 莊子 (*Zhuangzi jishi* 莊子集釋) (1961) Guo Qingfan 郭慶藩 ed. Beijing.
Zuozhuan 左傳 (*Chunqiu Zuozhuan zhu* 春秋左傳注) (1990) Annotated by Yang Bojun 楊伯峻 (revised edn). 4 vols. Beijing.
    References to the dynastic histories are to the Beijing Zhonghua shuju editions, as follows:
Shiji 史記 (1959) Sima Qian 司馬遷. 10 vols.
Hanshu 漢書 (1962) Ban Gu 班固, et al. 8 vols.
Hou Hanshu 後漢書 (1965) Fan Ye 范曄, et al. 12 vols.

Citations are made in accordance with the Ancient Chinese Text Concordance Series (Institute of Chinese Studies, Chinese University of Hong Kong) for the *Daodejing, Liji* and *Lunyu*, and in accordance with the Harvard Yenching Concordances for the *Xunzi*.

Details of the editions used for other texts that are cited in only one chapter appear in the separate bibliography for the chapter in question.

Contributors

Karine Chemla is Senior Researcher at the French National Center for Scientific Research (CNRS), in the laboratory SPHERE (CNRS & University Paris Diderot). She co-edited recently *The Oxford Handbook of Generality in Mathematics and the Sciences* (with R. Chorlay and D. Rabouin, 2016) and *Cultures without Culturalism: The Making of Scientific Knowledge* (with Evelyn Fox Keller, 2017).

Qiaosheng Dong is currently affiliated to the Cambridge Peking University China Centre at Jesus College.

Martin Jones is George Pitt-Rivers Professor of Archaeological Science at the University of Cambridge, and a fellow of Darwin College. Recent publications include M. K. Jones, H. V. Hunt, C. J. Kneale, E. Lightfoot, D. Lister, X. Liu and G. Motuzaite-Matuzeviciute (2016) 'Food globalisation in prehistory: the agrarian foundations of an interconnected continent', *Journal of the British Academy* 4: 73–87, and E. Lightfoot, X. Liu and M. K. Jones (2013) 'Why move starchy cereals? A review of the isotopic evidence for prehistoric millet consumption across Eurasia', *World Archaeology* 45.4: 574–623.

R. A. H. King is Professor of the History of Philosophy in the Institute of Philosophy at the University of Berne. He has co-edited with Dennis Schilling one collection of papers, *How Should One Live? Comparing Ethics in Ancient China and Graeco-Roman Antiquity* (2011), and edited another, *The Good Life and Conceptions of Life in Early China and Graeco-Roman Antiquity* (2015).

Xinyi Liu is Assistant Professor at the anthropology department, Washington University in St. Louis. He has published extensively in archaeology, Quaternary geology and scientific journals.

G. E. R. Lloyd is Emeritus Professor of Ancient Philosophy and Science in the University of Cambridge and Senior Scholar in Residence at the Needham Research Institute. The most important of his comparative studies of ancient Greek and Chinese thought is the book he wrote with Nathan Sivin, *The Way and the Word: Science and Medicine in Early China and Greece* (2002).

Vivienne Lo is Senior Lecturer at University College London and Director of the China Centre for Health and Humanity there. She was the founder editor of the journal *Asian Medicine: Tradition and Modernity*, and publications include *Perfect Bodies: Sports Medicine and Immortality* (2008), *Medieval Chinese Medicine* (2005, with Christoper Cullen ed.) and *Imagining Chinese*

Medicine (2017). Her forthcoming monograph is *Potent Substances: A History of Nutrition in China*.

Michael Loewe was University Lecturer in Chinese Studies, Cambridge, 1963–90. Publications include *Records of Han Administration* (1967), *Crisis and Conflict in Han China* (1974), *A Biographical Dictionary of the Qin, Former Han and Xin Periods* (2000) and *Problems of Han Administration* (2016).

Evi Margaritis is Assistant Professor at the Science and Technology for Archaeology Research Center, the Cyprus Institute, Nicosia, Cyprus. She has published extensively in the field of Mediterranean archaeobotany.

Reviel Netz is Patrick Suppes Professor of Greek Mathematics and Astronomy at Stanford University. He has published widely on Greek mathematics, and in particular he is among the co-editors of *The Archimedes Palimpsest* (2011).

Michael Nylan is Professor of History at the University of California at Berkeley. She is the author of *Chang'an 26 BCE* (2014) and *The Five 'Confucian' Classics* (2001).

Michael Puett is the Walter C. Klein Professor of Chinese History and Anthropology, and Chair of the Committee on the Study of Religion, at Harvard University. He is the author of *The Ambivalence of Creation: Debates Concerning Innovation and Artifice in Early China* (2001) and *To Become a God: Cosmology, Sacrifice, and Self-Divinization in Early China* (2002), as well as the co-author, with Adam Seligman, Robert Weller and Bennett Simon, of *Ritual and its Consequences: An Essay on the Limits of Sincerity* (2008).

Lisa Raphals is Professor of Chinese and Comparative Literature at the University of California, Riverside. Among her most important books are *Knowing Words: Wisdom and Cunning in the Classical Traditions of China and Greece* (1992), *Sharing the Light: Representations of Women and Virtue in Early China* (1998) and *Divination and Prediction in Early China and Ancient Greece* (2013).

Eleanor Re'em is a Classics graduate of King's College, Cambridge and has an MA in History of Art from the Warburg Institute. She now works in software design and coding, and with Vivienne Lo is working on an animated series for children called *Granny and the Wolf*.

Walter Scheidel is Dickason Professor in the Humanities, Professor of Classics and History, and Kennedy-Grossman Fellow in Human Biology at Stanford University. His research covers ancient social and economic history and the comparative history of population, state formation, labour regimes and inequality, and includes comparative studies of ancient Rome and early China.

Nathan Sivin is Emeritus Professor of Chinese Culture and the History of Science in the Department of the History and Sociology of Science at the University of Pennsylvania. Among his most influential studies of ancient

China are his two collections of essays, *Science in Ancient China: Researches and Reflections* (1995) and *Medicine, Philosophy and Religion in Ancient China: Researches and Reflections* (1995), and (with G. E. R. Lloyd) *The Way and the Word: Science and Medicine in Early China and Greece* (2002). His most recent book is *Health Care in Eleventh-Century China* (2015).

Jeremy Tanner is Professor of Classical and Comparative Art at the Institute of Archaeology, University College London, where he coordinates the MA programme in Comparative Art and Archaeology. Recent publications include 'Portraits and politics in classical Greece and early imperial China' (*Art History* 2016) and 'Narrative, naturalism and the body in classical Greek and early imperial Chinese art' (in J. Elsner, ed., *Comparativism in Art History*, 2017).

Robert Wardy is Reader in Ancient Philosophy at the University of Cambridge and a fellow of St Catharine's College. *Aristotle in China: Language, Categories and Translation* (2000) is one of his books.

Jingyi Jenny Zhao is Lloyd-Dan David Research Fellow at the Needham Research Institute, and at Darwin College, University of Cambridge. She works on ancient Greek and early Chinese philosophy from a comparative perspective, with a special interest in shame and the emotions, and representations of infancy and childhood.

Yiqun Zhou is Associate Professor in the Department of East Asian Languages and Cultures, Stanford University. Her book *Festivals, Feasts, and Gender Relations in Ancient China and Greece* was published in 2010.

Introduction: Methods, Problems and Prospects

G. E. R. LLOYD

This volume brings together a collection of essays by scholars who are united in their conviction that the critical comparative study of ancient civilisations offers notable opportunities to advance our understanding, in particular by drawing attention to questions and problems that will not readily occur to those who concentrate their efforts on just one civilisation. Traditionally, ancient historians have done just that, all too aware, in many cases, of the complexities and difficulties in investigating a single society over an extended period of time. Yet it is only if, working on our own or in collaboration, we engage in cross-cultural analysis, that we can be in a position more confidently to identify what is distinctive and what is common across ancient civilisations. Claims for uniqueness can sometimes be sustained, but rather less often than advocates of the superiority of one culture over all others are prone to assert. If we limit ourselves to just one ancient society, we might assume that what happened in it was somehow inevitable. Consideration of others can show how mistaken this may be, thereby raising the fundamental question of why things turned out in the ways they did in each case, difficult though it may be to attempt any satisfactory explanatory account on that subject.

That is just a bare statement, in very general terms, of the comparative project. Yet all our contributors are very well aware that comparing can be anything but fruitful. It is easy to see why comparing has so often got a bad reputation. In principle it is possible to compare anything with anything else. In practice many comparative studies seem to engage in an arbitrary juxtaposition of widely different objects without any concern for context or for what may validate the exercise. Nathan Sivin's chapter at the outset of this volume takes up just this question as does Walter Scheidel's examination of the 'how' and 'why' of comparative history, while Michael Loewe reflects on the problems in retrospect at the end. So if comparison is to generate valuable new insights, it is essential that we have a clear idea of why the project should be undertaken, what criteria we should adopt for a worthwhile comparison and how we can test whether our results are sound. I construe my task in this introductory chapter to be to outline the principles that guide our project and to draw attention to the major problems it faces, though I shall not limit myself to the particular topics that will be the focus of the subsequent chapters of this book.

In the present volume our targets are ancient Greece (including what it bequeathed to the Roman world) on the one hand, and ancient China on the other, and we restrict ourselves to the period down to the end of the third century CE. That cut-off point is, to some extent, an arbitrary one, but it means that in both cases we are studying civilisations not yet fundamentally affected by the major transformations brought about on the one hand by the Christianisation of the Roman Empire, and on the other by the emergence of Buddhism as a dominant influence in China. We should not underestimate the variety and diversity that existed in both the Greco-Roman world and China even before those religious upheavals: but certainly once they had occurred, the complexities of the problems of comparison increase very considerably.

We happen to have particularly rich evidence for both ancient civilisations in the periods concerned, but the comparative approach can and, we hope, will be adopted to advance the study of other societies too, not confined to the ancient world. Ancient history has much in common with, and much to learn from, social anthropology. We may suffer from the disadvantage of not having direct access to our witnesses: obviously we cannot question them. But we have advantages too, in the ability to track changes across many generations, giving our account a diachronic dimension that is much harder to achieve in ethnography.

The possible subjects for comparison between ancient civilisations vary enormously and there is no reason to suppose that the methodological questions I have raised should be answered in identical ways across different fields. One major recurrent issue relates to the concepts we use in discussing what we compare, where there is an obvious danger in any assumption that those we are used to, in whatever happens to be our own mother tongue, will be fit for purpose. The dilemma we face is clear: if we use our own conventional conceptual categories, will that not be bound to lead to us distorting those used by those whom we are trying to understand? And yet how can we fail to employ those categories of ours, since they are the only ones we have?

Evidently there is no entirely neutral vocabulary that we can use. But provided that we allow, as we surely must, that our concepts are revisable, that dilemma can be avoided. Indeed one of the benefits of cross-cultural studies is precisely to enable us to expand our views and to modify our preconceptions on certain fundamental questions. The recurrent difficulty we have to overcome can be expressed like this. If we talk about agriculture, say, or medicine, or mathematics, or philosophy, or law, or bureaucracy, or slavery, or religion, or warfare, we have to question, in each case, just where such terms are appropriate or inappropriate to our studies of different ancient societies.

On the one hand, then, we cannot export our own categories and expect them to be applicable to any and every other society. On the other, where we find mismatches and discrepancies, that does not mean that comparison is ruled out. We have to avoid both kinds of mistake, both the imposition of our concepts, and the assumption that others are strictly incomparable, if not totally unintelligible (cf. Robert Wardy's chapter below). How are we to steer a course between those two extremes? This is where the chief difficulties, but also the greatest opportunity, of comparative studies lie. Let me take some time now to give some examples, going back to the items in the check-list of possible comparanda I gave just now, to show how, as we proceed, our understanding of the very subjects we are investigating is subject to modification, as we learn from the very variety that our investigations throw up.

I shall first illustrate this with two of the most important categories that we use in the West to classify certain intellectual activities, namely 'philosophy' and 'mathematics'. I shall then widen the field to cover also practical matters where there is a more obvious sense in which these relate to common human concerns, where I shall focus on food-supply, housing and health. In a third phase of my discussion I shall broaden the net still further with some admittedly programmatic remarks about other aspects of inquiries, social institutions and practices, including attitudes towards the past, law, education, religion, music and art.

It would clearly be rash to assume that what 'philosophy' comprises is agreed even among the speakers of languages that appear to have a term derived from the Greek *philosophia* that appears to refer to it, 'philosophie' in French and 'Philosophie' in German, 'filosofia' in Italian and so on. Already striking differences appear within different European traditions, both as regards the subjects investigated and in how to investigate them, as between so-called continental philosophy and the mainly English-speaking (but partly German) analytic tradition, each with its paradigmatic philosophical heroes, Hegel, Nietzsche and Heidegger it may be on the one hand, Quine, Kripke and Bernard Williams on the other. Where some positivist adherents of the analytic approach tended to argue that many standard metaphysical questions rest on confusions which could and should be removed by careful linguistic analysis, in the continental tradition such questions were fundamental to the whole philosophical endeavour.

So given that there is no universal agreement, in the West, on what philosophy should include, many studies that purported to survey Chinese philosophy, and in particular several that claimed that there was no such thing (the Chinese did not have philosophy, they only had wisdom[1]) were alike based on a confusion or at least oversimplified the problems. Yet to go to the opposite extreme and say that any such study is simply impossible is also to fall into a mistake. Even though 'philosophy' itself is contentious, there are some areas of reasonable agreement about some elements of what should be included. The discussion of questions of morality and right and wrong would surely be accepted as such, and such questions are evidently the subject of concerned debate in China just as much as in Greece, or Rome, or modern Europe. There is, for example, the famous dispute between Mencius, Gaozi and Xunzi in the fourth and third centuries BCE over whether human beings are naturally good, bad or indifferent. So that provides us with a starting point from which we can compare both the positions adopted, and the manner in which they were defended, as between ancient Greece and China.

Further questions concerning other areas that might be included in 'philosophy', such as philosophy of language, logic, epistemology, and indeed metaphysics itself, present greater challenges, but also offer prospects for interesting reflection. Thus the topic of the relation between words and objects is pursued in classical Chinese texts although not with the same problems in mind as those of Plato's *Cratylus*. The Chinese discussion focuses on the proper relations between humans and the maintenance of social roles, and this certainly suggests that the social implications of this study were seen as more important than the purely intellectualist ones.

Two further issues will illustrate both the complexities and the possible pay-offs of comparison in this domain, first how the individuals in question saw themselves and were seen by others – how they were categorised indeed – and, secondly, how they saw their chief goal. The origin of the Greek term *philosophos* is disputed and some early uses of that term and cognates are very general and appear to refer to any mode of curiosity.[2]

---

[1] Such a view goes back to Hegel, but for a relatively recent survey of the *status quaestionis* see Cheng 2005, and cf. Deleuze and Guattari 1994: 93–5.

[2] See for example Herodotus 1.30 on Solon and Thucydides 2.40 on the Athenians in general. For several divergent views on what 'philosophy' stood for in the period before Plato, see Laks and Louguet 2002.

There are some late sources that ascribe the word to Pythagoras.[3] But in any event those whom we conventionally label the 'Presocratic philosophers' would not all have seen themselves as belonging to a single unified group with a clearly defined goal. 'Philosophy' only becomes a recognisable activity in the late fifth and early fourth centuries, especially with Plato's adoption of Socrates as his model. Aristotle considered the investigations he associated with philosophy (*theōrein*) as the highest activity of which humans are capable and a major contribution to happiness.

Thereafter Greek philosophers achieved a certain recognisability, if not notoriety. Many were figures of fun, exposed as pretentious hypocrites in comedy. But many saw themselves as serious seekers after the truth and concerned in the process to find personal happiness. Some (Epicureans and Sceptics) considered that that was incompatible with engagement in public life, though others, among the Stoics especially, saw their responsibilities as extending into the political domain and were indeed notable statesmen or advisers to rulers.

In China, however, the balance between the personal aspirations and the public involvement of those I have already identified as interested in moral questions is rather different. Of course there are Chinese thinkers who turned their backs on life at court and lived more or less as recluses. Zhuangzi is one such who refused to take office when there were those who tried to persuade him to do so.[4] However, another who retired from public life, Wang Chong, at the turn of the millennium, still saw fit to compose a notable treatise, the *Lun Heng*, in which he criticised many others for their wrong beliefs contributing to disorder.

Nevertheless a large number of prominent Chinese thinkers were centrally involved with good government. In the Warring States period these were often known as *you shui*, wandering advisers or persuaders, or alternatively *you shi*, wandering 'knights'.[5] The rulers of Warring States kingdoms surrounded themselves with experts of many different kinds, including those who, precisely, claimed to be able to offer advice on how to govern the country. Many such experts moved from one state to another, as opportunities arose: we know that Confucius visited several, hoping, against hope, to find a ruler worthy enough to accept his advice. Of course these advisers attracted followers who saw it as their duty to preserve the

---

[3] See for example Diogenes Laertius 1.12. This issue is discussed by several contributors to Huffman 2014.
[4] See for example *Zhuangzi* 17: 81–4. I use the Harvard Yenching editions for *Xunzi* and *Zhuangzi* (cited by *pian* and line number).
[5] The shifts in the sense and reference of the term *shi* are discussed in Lloyd and Sivin 2002: 18.

teachings of the master – a process that continued and was strengthened with the creation of canonical texts after the unification of China. But when that occurred, the relation between teachers and rulers generally remained strong, and the main concern of the former was to provide useful advice to the latter.

If we ask what goals the majority of Chinese thinkers set themselves, the answer is of course very different from some Aristotelian ideal of *theōrein*. The Chinese aim was less a matter of learning or of understanding than of being, that is of embodying the way, the *dao*. To be sure the *dao* could take many forms: there is a *dao* of cooking and of butchery, and even a mockery of a *dao* of robbery.[6] But the ideal was set by the *dao* that the Sage Kings of antiquity embodied, a matter of being in tune with the universe, with 'Heaven', *tian*, as the Chinese generally put it.

I shall have more to say about the *dao* in my next section, on mathematics, but for now may conclude this first discussion by stressing four points. First 'philosophy' can certainly not be considered a well-defined cross-cultural category. Yet secondly we can investigate thinkers in both the Greco-Roman and the Chinese worlds who engaged in one or other study that for us falls into one or other of the components of philosophical inquiry. When we do so, thirdly, we find that the circumstances under which they worked and the goals they set themselves differ, both as between different periods, and as between our two societies, and this in turn, fourthly, helps to shed light on the values of the groups concerned. Crudely stated, the balance between personal self-cultivation and public involvement varies. Both goals are represented in both ancient civilisations, but thanks to the greater concern with advice on public affairs that we find in China, there that interest tends to outweigh personal, intellectual, ambitions.

My second example, 'mathematics', poses a similar set of problems. We cannot assume that everywhere there will be an equivalent intellectual inquiry to the one we call mathematics, which in any case in the West comprises a number of sub-fields, including those we distinguish as 'pure' and 'applied'. The Greeks did talk of *mathēmatikē* for sure, from which our own term is derived, but the Greek word is cognate to the most general word for learning, namely *mathēma*. We should not approach the ancient Chinese texts expecting to find an equivalent concept, but they spoke of *suan shu* and *shu shu*, roughly 'calculations and methods', and certainly engaged in detailed studies of numbers and shapes, and thought about the

---

[6] Cf. Lloyd and Sivin 2002: 200.

ways in which they might be applied to achieve understanding of other problems.

But while that secures some common ground that we can use to get our comparison started, we should not assume that the manner in which 'mathematical' studies were pursued was uniform in all ancient societies and in particular in the two we are most concerned with, as the chapters by Karine Chemla and Reviel Netz will illustrate. As I have pointed out on other occasions, the pursuit of axiomatic-deductive demonstrations is not only distinctive of some (not all) Greek mathematics, but unparalleled in any other ancient civilisation.[7] So far from the search for such demonstrations being a natural or normal or even inevitable development once mathematical inquiries were established, it is quite exceptional and we have to ask why.

That Greek ambition owes much to the work of Aristotle who was after all the first to define strict demonstration in terms of the combination of self-evident primary premises and valid deductive arguments leading to incontrovertible conclusions.[8] But if we ask in turn what may have stimulated his exploration of this possibility, then over and above a no doubt laudable sense of the value of rigour in argument, we should bear in mind that, like Plato before him, he was profoundly dissatisfied with what he considered the merely plausible or persuasive arguments used by his fellow Greeks in such contexts as the law-courts and political assemblies, where indeed decisions were taken by the audience themselves, generally by majority vote. Given that neither in China nor elsewhere in ancient societies was there any real equivalent to such debates held in public and settled by taking a vote, it may be less surprising that we find no urge to develop an alternative style of argumentation that would be immune to error.

That does not mean that the Chinese had no sense of the need to check their results. On the contrary they do so regularly, verifying that the algorithms that they used are correct.[9] But once they assured themselves that they were, they got on with the next problem without attempting to produce demonstrations based on self-evident axioms. Comparison, here,

---

[7] I first developed this argument in 1990. In some histories of Greek mathematics it tends to be assumed that the development of mathematical proof was purely internal to mathematics itself. But the ideal of incontrovertibility was first made explicit in Aristotle, as indeed was the notion of self-evident axioms.
[8] Aristotle, *Posterior Analytics* 1.1–2 and 1.10.
[9] On Chinese techniques of proof and verification in mathematics, see Chemla 2012 and cf. Netz's Chapter 10 below.

between ancient societies reveals that there was no one route by which mathematics could, let alone had to, develop.

But we can go further. The idea that Chinese mathematics is practical in orientation has been grossly exaggerated, since it leaves out of account considerable theoretical interests, in determining the circle–circumference ratio for example, or what we call π.[10] But there is a further interesting point of comparison and contrast in the ways in which Chinese and Greeks saw the possibilities of using their mathematical skills to resolve problems beyond those suggested by mathematics itself. Some Greeks in the Pythagorean tradition held that numbers are the key to understanding everything in nature, but the way that idea worked out in practice ranged from the manipulation of number symbolism to the mathematical analysis of harmonic ratios. In China too there was a fascination with number symbolism, but again an interest in such matters as the numerical analysis of musical harmonies and the use of similar right-angled triangles to determine the height and distance of remote objects – the sun itself included.[11]

One text that mentions that last possibility is particularly interesting for the way in which mathematical skills are represented. In the *Zhoubi suanjing* (23–5) a pupil praises his teacher for his ability to tackle a whole list of obscure problems, but he puts all this down to the teacher's *dao*. When the pupil asks how to get similar results, he is told that he will do so if he tries hard enough, and several abortive attempts occur before the teacher relents and gives the pupil more detailed instructions on how to do it. Learning mathematics through Euclid was a matter simply of understanding the proofs with which you were presented. Learning mathematics, in some cases in China, is a matter of internalising the skills. Moreover the invocation of the *dao* links mathematics to the most important and prized activity of all. Indeed mathematics is claimed to have been the invention of Sage Kings in remotest antiquity. 'Mathematics' was no mere intellectual pursuit but an aspect of wisdom.

'Philosophy' and 'mathematics' are both particularly problematic areas for comparative study. But other topics seem to be more straightforward since they correspond to basic needs that humans always have to meet, such as the provision of food and shelter, to which we may add securing health or well-being however these are construed. However, in each of

---

[10] One of the most sustained early investigations of the circle–circumference comes in Liu Hui's commentary to the *Jiuzhang suanshu* 1.104–6.
[11] See, for example, *Zhoubi suanjing* 23, and cf. *Huainanzi* 3.

these areas there is, potentially, much more to investigate than might appear at first glance.

Thus where food is concerned, we may first note the symbolic, ideological, even religious, significance of agricultural activities, carried on under the auspices of tutelary deities, Demeter in Greece, Ceres in Rome, Shennong in China (cf. Sterckx 2010; Lloyd 2002: ch. 4). Then we must ask who actually produced the food and how far they enjoyed the benefits of their labour themselves or were compelled to work for others. This introduces the topic of slavery, again a difficult concept to apply cross-culturally since we encounter many different types of unfree labour across the world. Who controlled the agricultural surpluses produced is a question that leads into social and political organisation more generally. How far is it possible to test Finley's argument that the institutions of the Greek city-state depended crucially on the existence of considerable numbers of slaves?[12] Certainly many of those institutions – the law-courts and assemblies – could not have functioned if the citizen body, or a large proportion of it, had not enjoyed considerable leisure. This is a point that Greek political theorists themselves draw attention to when considering which kinds of activities – including trade, crafts and agriculture – were or were not compatible with fulfilling the responsibilities of citizenship.[13] In China too officials had the usufruct of considerable estates and yet the existence of those agricultural surpluses did not there lead to comparable political institutions. Evidently the particular mode by which surpluses were extracted and used in the Greco-Roman world – slavery especially – provided in no sense a sufficient condition for the particular institutions we find there, though some surplus production was undoubtedly a necessary condition for those institutions.

A second controversial issue here relates to the extent to which in either Greece or China efforts were devoted to improving efficiency whether in agriculture or in any other aspect of technology.[14] The negative effects of the existence of slaves in the Greco-Roman have often been held to have been a prime cause of a supposed technological stagnation there. But first, that stagnation has often been exaggerated: I addressed the question and summarised the chief data in Lloyd 2002: ch 4. Secondly, where China is concerned the experience is mixed. There were extraordinary and extraordinarily successful engineering undertakings in connection with schemes of irrigation, notably Li Bing's division of the river Min at

---

[12] See Finley 1983 especially.   [13] As discussed at length, for example, by Aristotle, *Politics* 7.9.
[14] See, for example, Finley 1965; Pleket 1973.

Guanxian, using corvée labour. This at one stroke solved the problems of flooding and provided water to irrigate large tracts of what is now Sichuan province, turning one uncontrolled river into two manageable ones. Yet in China members of the literate elite were generally as reluctant to involve themselves directly in agricultural activity as were some of their Greek counterparts (cf. Lloyd 2002: 80–1).

As for shelter, it may seem that there is nothing interesting to say about houses of different kinds. But again we must be careful. We do not have enough evidence concerning Greek and Chinese domestic buildings to be able to match the sophisticated analyses that such anthropologists as Tambiah and Humphrey have given of the symbolism of the organisation of the space of houses in the societies they studied, where the house serves as a microcosm mirroring the cosmos as understood by the peoples concerned and serving to reinforce beliefs about the place of humans in the order of things.[15] Yet in both Greco-Roman and Chinese houses there was space reserved for ritual functions. A house was not just a place of shelter but one for worship.

Much more obviously when we are dealing with town or city agglomerations, considerable attention was paid not just to defensibility but to symbolic appropriateness. The siting of cities, palaces and tombs in China called upon elaborate procedures of geomancy. The privileged south-facing position associated with the Emperor was a simple rule to apply: but when it came to the position of tombs for members of the imperial family, the relations that had to be taken into account were extremely complex.[16] In the classical Greek world there were no tombs of emperors to worry about, but there were arguments about how best to adapt the planning of a city to the democratic ideology of equality among citizens.[17] That points to an obvious difference with China but we encounter similarities again in those texts, in the Hippocratic Corpus and in the Chinese medical writings, that concern themselves with the relative healthiness of different orientations. So once again a comparative approach can help one to identify both recurrent cross-cultural interests and divergent ideological concerns.

That takes me to the third topic I mentioned among basic human needs, namely health, where perhaps the temptation is particularly strong to

---

[15] See Tambiah 1969; Humphrey 1974, 1988; and the essays collected in Carsten and Hugh-Jones 1995.
[16] See, for example, Loewe 2010a.
[17] Some of these ideological factors are discussed by Lévêque and Vidal-Naquet 1964 and by Vernant 1965/1983.

assume that the biomedicine we are today familiar with in the West provides the yardstick by which to evaluate other traditions and practices and that those that fail that test can be dismissed as mere popular superstition. That, of course, is to fall straight into the trap of anachronism. We may certainly start with the observation that practically everyone has sought to be healthy, but that masks the very different ideas that have been entertained about what precisely that consists in, as also on the nature and causes of diseases and illnesses (that is, not feeling well). We indeed continue to be concerned with the question of the relation between mere physical fitness and a more comprehensive sense of well-being.

One important point of similarity between ancient China and Greece is that both societies have rival groups of practitioners competing for clients and offering very different types of medical and indeed spiritual or psychological care. Indeed this is not just the case in the two ancient societies with which we are primarily concerned but a feature that can also be found elsewhere, in Mesopotamia for instance, in ancient Egypt and in India, where in each case we can draw on considerable bodies of extant medical texts.[18]

One question that naturally arises, then, is how the various rival groups, often clearly distinguished by the names that they went by, justified their claims to effectiveness, let alone superiority, in the matter of the care they provided. Part of the answer in the case of the medical elites we find in both China and Greece is clear. Membership of those elites depended on mastery of a body of learned texts. In China the core of elite medical education came to consist in the various recensions of the *Huangdi neijing*. Yet in the biography of the doctor Chunyu Yi which is reported in the first dynastic history, the *Shiji*, he mentions a variety of other texts and recipes that he obtained from his teachers, and some of this lore is represented as secret, passed on to him under oath of confidentiality. In the Greco-Roman world, similarly, first the Hippocratic Corpus and eventually the Galenic one came to dominate medical education, although again other texts also competed for the attention of would-be practitioners. However, a very different tactic, as I shall be mentioning shortly, was to claim the support of divine, or demonic, in other words supernatural, agencies.

But neither in Greece nor in China was access to common remedies restricted to members of some elite or those who claimed privileged access to the divine. In both ancient societies the first line of medical defence, as

---

[18] Thus for Ayurvedic medicine we have the two great compendia, the *Caraka-saṃhitā* and the *Suśruta-saṃhitā*, on which see, for example, Zysk 1991.

one might put it, was self-help or the help of those in one's immediate household, where knowledge of remedies of different types was passed on from one generation to the next without being mediated by imposing learned disquisitions. In any case we know from the medical texts unearthed at Mawangdui and elsewhere that two common Chinese practices, acupuncture and moxibustion, antedated the standardisation of medical knowledge in the *Huangdi neijing*.[19] The particular factors that led to the adoption of those techniques are still the subject of controversy, but certainly they have proved their longevity, for they both continue to be practised today.

In Greece, apart from the learned doctors, we hear of root-cutters and drug-sellers who made available herbal and mineral remedies to a wide clientele. Importantly, it is clear that women's complaints were generally treated by women practitioners. The usual term for these, *maiai*, is conventionally translated 'midwives' but they certainly dealt with other cases apart from those connected with child-birth. It is obvious from certain Hippocratic texts that the question of whether women suffered from different types of diseases from men and how far they should be treated differently baffled the male writers of those texts and remained controversial.[20]

Medical treatment always reflects ideas about the human body and the causes of diseases, where very considerable divergences exist both within each of our two civilisations and between them. Once again we may start with a similarity, though it is one that should not be allowed to mask underlying divergences. For both Greeks and Chinese the key to health is a balance between opposing factors in the body, but the factors in question were construed quite differently. Greek doctors tended to assume that the primary constituents of the body were either elements, such as earth, water, air and fire, or opposites, hot and cold, wet and dry, sweet and bitter, or again humours such as bile and phlegm. It was only after Galen's adoption of the four humour theory that he found in the Hippocratic treatise *On the Nature of Man* that the theory in that form (adding blood and black bile) came to be standardised throughout the European Middle Ages.

But these constituents were all substances. The interactions the Chinese were interested in were between processes or vital functions. They associated various of these with certain organs or depots but the focus of attention was not so much with these as anatomical structures as with

---

[19] See, for example, Harper 1998 and Lo and Li 2010.
[20] See, for example, Dean-Jones 1994; King 1998; and cf. Lloyd 2003: 50–1 on the Hippocratic treatise *On the Eighth Month Child*.

the associated functions, the heart function, the kidney function and so on.[21] The ideal for health was here not so much a static equilibrium between substances as rather one of the proper, unimpeded interaction between vital functions and the free flow or circulation of the *qi* (breath or energy) throughout the body. The aim of acupuncture and moxibustion treatment, too, was, of course, to facilitate such free flow, to remove blockages and obstacles and to repel invasive pathogenic *qi*.

It would be extravagant to claim that we are in any position to explain why these different pictures of how the body worked were developed in China and the Greco-Roman world, but we can see that in both cases the models adopted carried more general significances. In both ancient societies the way the body was imagined served as a model for how the political state and even the cosmos as a whole should be. Whether or not the medical writers in question consciously manipulated the analogies (and in some cases it seems they did) it was scarcely possible to ignore the wider political repercussions of medical theories of health and disease. In Greece the notion of the need to maintain the health of the body politic was a *topos* used to justify dealing with those you disagreed with as if they were pathogens, that had to be 'cured', that is punished, if necessary by being excised, that is expelled, from the state.[22]

In China the medical and political analogies worked both ways. The drugs used in treatment were regularly classified in three grades, 'monarchs', 'ministers' and 'assistants'.[23] More tellingly, perhaps, the ideal of the free flow of *qi* in the body was used as a model to advocate that within the state there should be free flow of communication between the ruler and those who advised him. Such an analogy served a double function. They could be used to justify a particular view of the relationship between ruler and ministers. But when medical writers elaborated the parallelism, that served to bolster the claims to prestige and influence that those writers implicitly made. The covert message was that they were in a position, not just to guide patients on questions to do with health, but also to advise statesmen about good government. There is, we may say, a mutually corroborating effect in these analogies, where the plausibility of the initial model gains from its possible applicability in the analogous context.

But now let me return to the topic of supernatural agency. In both Greece and China the belief that diseases may be caused by demons or

---

[21] See *Huangdi neijing suwen* 8.1–2, 28, on which see Sivin 1995b: ch. 1; Lloyd and Sivin 2002: 221–2.
[22] See Lloyd 2003: ch. 6 on Plato's particularly striking uses of this *topos*.
[23] See *Bencao jing* preface, 1: 2–4, on which see Sivin 1987: 181 and Ma 1995: 540–600.

gods or spirits of one kind or another is found together with a corresponding claim that they can be treated and cured by prayers, spells, incantations, purifications or offerings to the gods. In China, for instance, those called *wu* (sometimes translated 'shamans' but more correctly thought of as 'mediums') were consulted not just to treat diseases, but to bring or stop wind and rain (cf. Lewis 2007: 179–81, Sterckx 2010: 416). In both ancient societies such a complex of beliefs comes to be challenged, but in interestingly different ways. Sometimes, in Greece, that challenge comes from medical practitioners who set out to show not just that all diseases have a physical natural cause – and can be cured by physical means – but also that those who purveyed those ideas about divine agencies were charlatans, ignoramuses, out to exploit a gullible clientele for personal profit. The most famous tract that launches such criticisms is the Hippocratic *On the Sacred Disease* which further attacks its opponents on religious grounds. So far from being particularly pious, the purifiers, as he calls them, are positively impious, quite mistakenly attributing maleficent actions to the gods.[24]

But in both Greece and China criticisms of the notion that there are divine causes of diseases also came not from those who considered themselves healers, but from members of the literate elite: Plato, for instance, in Greece, and Xunzi, Huan Tan and Wang Chong in China.[25] One might wonder what motivated them, since they in no sense purported to be medical practitioners themselves. But that would be to ignore that – as we said – knowing about medical matters was an important aspect of knowledge or wisdom in general. Plato even produces a theory of diseases both of the body and of the soul in his cosmological treatise the *Timaeus*, and I have noted before that notions about health and well-being are closely intertwined and therefore a proper subject for an adviser (or philosopher) to advise about.

The Greek attack on divine causation was not confined to medicine but spilled over into causal accounts more generally. The key move was to make explicit a notion of 'nature' (*phusis*). When natural causes could be assigned to phenomena there was no need to invoke divine or demonic agencies – indeed to do so was to make a category mistake. So not only diseases, but earthquakes, eclipses, lightning and thunder and the like – which had often been considered to be the work of gods – were rather to be

---

[24] On the polemic conducted by the author of *On the Sacred Disease* against those he dubs 'mages', 'purifiers', 'vagabonds' and 'charlatans', see Lloyd 1979: ch. 1.

[25] See, for example, Plato, *Republic* 364b, and cf. *Xunzi* 21: 74–8, Huan Tan fragments 133 and 146 in Pokora 1975, and Wang Chong, *Lun Heng* 71, among other expressions of scepticism of traditional beliefs in China.

seen as having regular natural causes (even though the actual explanations these Greek thinkers offered were generally pretty speculative).

There is no exact equivalent to that explicit notion of nature in China.[26] They certainly recognised the regularities in many phenomena; they identified the characteristics of different kinds of objects as their *xing*; they used the terms Heaven, *tian*, or Heaven and Earth, *tiandi*, to speak of the cosmos as a whole, and they used the notion of the spontaneous, *ziran*, to speak of what happens without external intervention and so is 'natural' in that sense. But they did not assume that all those issues related to a single problem, that of 'nature', as the Greeks thought of that. The conclusion we may draw is that so far from this explicit concept of nature being natural or inevitable, it is anything but so. Rather, the circumstances in which such a notion was originally forged in ancient Greece were indeed quite distinctive. It was the product of the ambition of a group of people, who styled themselves 'naturalists' (*phusikoi*) or were so styled by others, to define a domain over which they were to be the unchallenged experts.

This tells us something about the particularly hard-hitting polemics that rival Greek claimants to prestige sometimes engaged in. Their opponents, they claimed, must be wrong since their fundamental assumptions (about divine intervention) were mistaken. Yet where we might think that the battle against the notion of the gods intervening in disease would have been won by those who insisted on purely natural causes, that was evidently not the case. Quite the contrary. We might feel surprised that at the very same time as certain medical practitioners were presenting this naturalistic account, the practice of healing in shrines dedicated to Apollo and Asclepius was also growing, but such was the case. Temple medicine, as we call it, so far from declining in popularity, enjoyed spectacular success. The imposing remains of the precincts at Epidaurus and at Pergamum testify to this phenomenon lasting from the fifth century BCE until the second century CE and well beyond.[27]

Some have argued that this popularity owed not a little to the apparent failures of ordinary doctors faced with such epidemics as the plague at Athens which broke out during the Peloponnesian War. But there is undoubtedly more to it than that. If we consider what was on offer in Greek temple medicine, the surprise is not so much that it flourished in Greece as that in China there were no equivalently ostentatiously successful institutions purveying healing under the auspices of the gods. Let me

---

[26] I developed this argument in Lloyd 1996: ch. 1, though it remains controversial.
[27] On the success and resilience of Greek temple medicine, see, for example, Lloyd 2003: chs. 3 and 8.

explain this argument. In Greece patients came to the shrines and slept in them overnight. They were expected to have a dream, and if they did not awake already cured, the dream could be interpreted by the priests to indicate how they were to be treated. Those treatments included some – advice about diet and herbal medicines for instance – that are similar to those found in the Hippocratic writers. But what the shrines offered in addition – to those with faith at least – was the assurance that god was on their side. In many situations where most ordinary doctors were at a loss to secure any improvement, let alone a cure (and many Hippocratic writers honestly testify to their failures in that regard[28]) there was considerable psychological comfort to be had from the belief that divine help was at hand. We can see this factor at work in the writings of Aelius Aristides, a famous orator of the second century CE and a fervent devotee of Asclepius.[29] He tells us in person of the many terrible afflictions he suffered from. No sooner was he cured of one complaint – thanks to the god – than he was struck down by another. Yet despite his awful medical misfortunes his faith in Asclepius, and his conviction of the superiority of divine to merely mortal healers, remained unshaken.

In the Greco-Roman world the strong contrast drawn between naturalistic and divine agencies may have led paradoxically to the simultaneous growth of both, for each had to develop the rationale for their rival models of healing. In China there was less of a clear-cut distinction between two alternative paradigms. Of course those who frequented the shrines of Asclepius in Greece did not go there just for what we would call psychological comfort: they went to be cured of their physical ailments, and the inscriptions claim such, including conditions such as blindness, and some that involved miraculous surgical interventions.[30] But in China some talk of demons sometimes appears alongside mention of the imbalance of vital functions in the body. That juxtaposition gave no clear indication that these were thought of as alternative causal paradigms.

Thus far I have taken a number of fields to illustrate the varying circumstances in which comparison is possible within certain limits and observing due cautions. Sometimes the concepts we bring to the study suffer from a debilitating parochialism, not to say ethnocentricity, and so

---

[28] As has often been remarked, some 60 per cent of the individual case histories reported in the first and third books of the Hippocratic *Epidemics* end in the death of the patient, and there are many texts throughout the Corpus where the writers confess that they were unable to help their patients, let alone to cure them. Cf. Lloyd 2003: ch. 3.
[29] For Aelius Aristides *Sacred Tales*, see Behr 1968 and cf. Lloyd 2003: ch. 8.
[30] See Edelstein and Edelstein 1945.

have to be overhauled for comparison to be fruitful. We have to retreat from the overall concepts of 'philosophy' and 'mathematics' to component elements of each inquiry. On other occasions the problem is not so much the conceptual framework: but the hard work of exploring the implications of comparison remains. We have always to examine why the problems were resolved in similar or in different ways by different groups at different periods and we must often admit that we cannot provide robust solutions.

The field of possible comparanda can thus grow to include just about every aspect of the life and thought of each ancient society, always guarding against the dangers of unduly assimilating one society's experience to that of another. Thus every society produces its own more or less self-conscious self-representation and will use ideas or beliefs about its past to construct an image or images of itself. Every society makes provision to secure good order in the state. Both 'historiography' and the 'law' are well documented in both China and the Greco-Roman world and can provide further areas in which to use the comparative method to throw light on features of both ancient societies which we might otherwise take for granted.

As plenty of other societies show, the ways in which what was recognised as myth or as unverifiable stories of the remotest times is related to what is thought of as reliable accounts of experience within living memory vary: indeed those differences include differences on the very question of whether such a distinction can be drawn. Remote ancestors are of course regularly invoked to legitimate some aspect of the present order, not without a certain tension, on occasions, in the working out of such an invocation. Thus reconciling the figure of the founder of Athens King Theseus with the democratic ideology involved some ingenuity on the part of various Athenian writers.[31] One distinctive feature of Chinese stories about the past and even the present is the acceptance of the inevitability of dynastic change.

But in both ancient societies there were those who took seriously their responsibilities to give an accurate account of at least the less remote past. Both the Greco-Roman world and China produce a series of historians, as we call them, though their positions in contemporary society, and the aims they set themselves, vary. On the first question, some Greek and Roman historians were commissioned to produce an account covering a particular period, and that was more regular a feature of Chinese authors of dynastic histories. Yet although the authors of the first great general Chinese history, the *Shiji* composed by Sima Tan and Sima Qian around 90 BCE,

---

[31] See most recently Atack 2014.

held the office of *Tai Shi*, or Grand Scribe,[32] neither was directly appointed to write an official history. Nor did either of the founders of Greek historiography, Herodotus and Thucydides, hold any official position. These early historians, unlike some of their successors, all acted on their own personal initiative. While the Simas did not claim to produce a Thucydidean 'possession for always', *ktēma eis aei*, they certainly claimed their work was a valuable resource from which later generations could learn.

Moreover they did not limit their instruction to catalogues of events, often followed by comments from one or other of them. As later Chinese dynastic histories were also to do, they included treatises on subjects ranging from the calendar to agriculture – all useful information for anyone interested in good government, as most of the Chinese literate elite certainly were. Herodotus, for his part, also regales his reader with information about non-Greek peoples, or if not information, at least what he believed about them or imagined them to be. So these texts are precious resources for us to examine not just how some Chinese and Greeks constructed their past, but also how they saw themselves in relation to the other peoples by whom they were surrounded. Most of these were generally despised as barbarians of one sort or another, but not all equally. Unlike the Chinese, the Greeks had two impressive cultures on their doorsteps, in Egypt and the Persian Empire. Those peoples were difficult or rather impossible simply to dismiss, so different types of barbarian had to be admitted, just as later the Romans had to make room for Greek exceptionality. However, one of the important lessons for us, in this area, is that what we may think of as 'history' included interventions on many other topics besides recounting the events of the past.

The historians are one of our chief sources for laws and in the Greek case for distinct political constitutions. In China that information can be supplemented by considerable bodies of texts dealing with legal matters that have been unearthed from the tombs at Zhangjiashan.[33] These materials thus open up general questions to do with how the law was administered, the status of the laws to which appeal could be made to determine judgement, the range of types of case, civil and criminal, that came before the magistrates or the law-courts, and the varying rights or privileges of different members of society, nobles or commoners, men and women,

---

[32] The post of Tai Shi originally involved overseeing ritual, but it evolved into that of chief palace scribe, combining duties as historian, diviner and astronomer. See Lloyd and Sivin 2002: 26.

[33] There is a detailed analysis of these in Loewe 2010b, and cf. more generally Loewe 1967 and 2004.

citizens or freedmen or slaves (to name some categories that do and others that do not have cross-cultural validity).

In Chinese texts there are complaints about the proliferation of legal precedents. They were so complex, according to some, that they made their application unworkable. Confucius is even represented as regretting the very fact that the laws were written down, for that, he thought, distracted people's attention from the business of internalising standards of good conduct.[34] But the opposite school of thought insisted that order can only be maintained by the strict application of the severest punishments. The similarities and differences in the Greek situation include on the one hand Aristotle's recognition at the end of his treatise, the *Nicomachean Ethics*, that what keeps most people from criminal activity is not an intellectual grasp of the considerations he has set out in that treatise, but simply the threat of punishment if found out. Yet to a quite unprecedented degree the citizens of Athens engaged in litigation, and had extensive experience not just of bringing others to court, but on other occasions of serving as 'dicasts' (who combined the duties of both judges and jurors) in those very courts. As already noted, many Greek citizens enjoyed considerable leisure, and to ensure that even the poorer citizens, those engaged in trade for instance, could participate, from Pericles onwards the dicasts were paid for their jury service.[35]

It is obvious that generalising about 'the' Chinese or 'the' Greek attitude towards the law is foolish since in both ancient societies a spectrum of positions is found, from a minimalist acceptance of the need for law to a maximalist engagement. Comparison here serves to highlight the diversity of experience, pointing up the idiosyncrasies of the diverse provisions made in the shifting and disputed political scene. While the Athenian penchant for litigation clearly depended on the leisure of those involved, and there is evidently a correlation between broadly economic factors and the degree of engagement in legal activity, we have in China no clear-cut interdependence of attitudes towards the law and political regimes. The attitudes vary from the view that the law is essential, to the optimistic idea that it should be dispensable. But while particular rulers with their particular policies on the subject came and went, in China the ideal of monarchic government remained a constant.

---

[34] See *Zuozhuan*, Zhao 29 and cf. *Daodejing* 57. The proliferation of legal precedents is the subject of critical comment in the *Hanshu* 23: 1101, cf. Hulsewé 1955: 338.
[35] At Athens payment for the dicasts was introduced by Pericles, and was seen as a key institution of democracy.

My remark about Aristotle's recognition that only a small proportion of his audience will learn from the advice he dispensed on ethical matters takes me to the next especially thorny topic, education. Outside the circles of the literate elite in the Greco-Roman world and China, schooling was minimal. A child picked up how to behave and how to fulfil his or her assigned role in the household without any formal instruction. In classical Greece a male child in a well-to-do family had a teacher who taught him letters and 'music' (more on that later) and some basic instruction in 'mathematics' seems to have been common, although in the *Laws* (820ab) Plato is led to complain how ignorant his fellow Greeks are in that they do not even know that the side and the diagonal of a square are incommensurable.

The two most important questions here concern (1) the technology of communication and the level of literacy on the one hand and (2) the nature and institutions of what we may call 'higher education' on the other. In both, important differences emerge between our two ancient civilisations, and once again we can learn about the situation in one of them by considering the situation that obtained in the other.

Goody argued that the spread of literacy was crucial to the process he dubbed the 'domestication of the savage mind', that is the transition from what Lévi-Strauss dubbed the science of the concrete to more recognisable modern modes of abstract thought, and Goody further insisted on the superiority of the alphabetic to every other script.[36] As to the second point, there is some empirical evidence that syllabic scripts, such as the Japanese kana, are easier to learn than kanji (the Japanese adaptation of Chinese pictographic writing).[37] Yet in Japan, where both systems are used, the former has in no sense led to the demise of the latter. As for ancient Greece, citizens were expected to be minimally literate, but perhaps the emphasis should be on 'minimally'. Two Athenian institutions presuppose a certain level of literacy. The first was ostracism, the procedure whereby citizens wrote down on a shard (*ostrakon*) the name of the statesman they wished to see expelled temporarily from the state. But we know hoards of pre-prepared shards all with the same name Themistocles written in the same

---

[36] See Goody 1977, criticising Lévi-Strauss 1962/1966. These remain important theses in Goody's later work even though that modified some of the arguments of his earlier book: see Goody 1986 and 1987.

[37] See Sakamoto and Makito 1973, and cf. Olson and Torrance 1991; Olson 1994.

hand.[38] That does not prove that those who used them could not write, but it certainly shows that some citizens cut corners.

The second institution is the setting up of laws and other memorial inscriptions in public places. That certainly gave them public accessibility, though the question of how many citizens could read them with any fluency is a moot point. It is of course impossible to attempt anything but a guess at the level of literacy in classical Athens. But the crucial reservation that has to be expressed concerning the increased access to reading and writing that may have been afforded by the use of an alphabetic script resides in the fact that classical Athens was still very much an oral, face-to-face, society. It was only in Hellenistic times that the written word became increasingly prominent in the formation of a literate elite, just as it did in China, as Michael Nylan's detailed comparative analysis of the libraries of Han Cheng Di and of the Ptolemies at Alexandria shows.

Conversely whether the use of a different script would have made an appreciable difference to Chinese levels of literacy is an issue on which we can do no more than speculate. What is clear is that among those who aspired to join the ranks of the Chinese literate elite (the *ru*) there were key texts to master, indeed in many cases to be learned by heart, though here too the usual medium of transmission was oral, not by the written mode. We know from the evidence from the tombs that texts such as the *Changes* and the *Daodejing* existed in different versions, each handed down by a particular group of scholars, a *jia* or lineage, responsible for its preservation.[39] But the role and status of canons came to be transformed in the Han dynasty with the founding of the Imperial Academy by Han Wu Di. He laid down by edict in 136 BCE the core curriculum, the so-called five classics, the *Odes* (*Shi*), *Documents* (*Shu*), *Changes* (*Yi*), *Spring and Autumn Annals* (*Chunqiu*) and *Rites* (*Li*).[40]

Those five texts did not include such general surveys of useful knowledge as the *Lüshi Chunqiu*, nor the medical and mathematical classics, the *Huangdi neijing*, the *Jiuzhang suanshu* and the *Zhoubi suanjing*, such as we have already mentioned. Access to the latter generally depended on being accepted as a pupil by an acknowledged master. Such apprenticeships also occurred in Greece but we may note something of a contrast in the extent of interest shown in such subjects as medicine and mathematics in the

---

[38] See Vanderpool 1973: 225–6; Lang 1990: 142. On the levels of literacy in classical Athens, see Thomas 1989.
[39] See Boltz 1993. The earliest extant MS of this text, found at Mawangdui, puts the *de* section before the *dao* one, so a *Dedaojing* rather than a *Daodejing*.
[40] See Nylan 2001: 33ff.

Greco-Roman world by individuals who had no intention of becoming practitioners or professionals in the field. Again as we noted before, in the Warring States ambitious rulers and ministers gathered around them experts of every kind, and the more successful among the latter received considerable patronage. While such patronage also existed in Greece and more especially in Rome, other experts earned a living from the general public.[41]

This takes me to the chief general difference between the Greco-Roman world and China where 'higher' learning is concerned. This relates to the degree of what we may call governmental control or at least influence. I have remarked that the curriculum of the Imperial Chinese Academy was settled by imperial edict. Excellence in the classics there led to a career in the imperial civil service, so the Academy was a crucial way of recruiting those who were to run the Empire. Plato's Academy also produced individuals who aspired to a political career, but it was a private institution, as were Aristotle's Lyceum and the schools founded by Epicurus and Zeno the Stoic. In each what was taught was in the hands of the head of the school and his senior colleagues. We have mentioned Chinese wandering advisers, some of whom have been labelled 'sophists' thanks in part to their interests in paradox. But that is rather a misnomer.[42] The chief difference from their Greek counterparts who went by that name was that the latter were prepared to teach anyone for a fee. Their targeted audience was not the ruler and his courtiers, but any interested citizen, and those fees provided the sophists with an alternative livelihood to courtly patronage.

I have already mentioned the belief in divine intervention in diseases and their cures, but my next main topic, religion, has undoubtedly been made more difficult by the disputes generated by monotheistic faiths that hold that there can be only one true god and therefore one true religion. Other faiths are thereby disqualified – either they are 'just' ritual, or, more often, they are false, evil, the work of the devil or whatever. That move of disqualification was at the heart of the dispute that sprang up not between Chinese and Westerners, but between different Western sects, in the so-called Rites controversy in the sixteenth and seventeenth centuries. The first missionaries to engage in a systematic project to convert the Chinese to Christianity were Jesuits, foremost among them Matteo Ricci, who took great care to familiarise himself with Chinese ways, to learn Chinese and even to write tracts in that language.[43] His view was that it was perfectly

---

[41] See Lloyd 1996: ch. 2; Lloyd and Sivin 2002: 27–41, 82–103.   [42] Pace Reding 1985.
[43] See Gernet 1985.

possible for Chinese Christian converts to continue with their traditional customs, including the worship of their ancestors. They did not constitute an alternative religion but could be thought of as ritual behaviour, little more significant from a religious point of view than styles of dress.

But back in Rome in the seventeenth century that policy of tolerance was vehemently opposed by the Dominicans especially, who insisted that Chinese customary ritual ancestor worship was incompatible with Christianity. Various edicts were issued forbidding Chinese converts to continue with their traditional customs – with, of course, disastrous consequences for the Jesuit mission. The Kangxi emperor had been very sympathetic to the Jesuits, finding their astronomical learning and their technological gadgetry very useful. But he soon came to find Christian intolerance intolerable and reacted by first limiting the missionaries' activities and then banning them altogether.

I recount this well-known episode since it illustrates the confusion that may arise over the very definition of religion. To clear a way ahead let me use my usual tactic of thinking about the component elements of what may be considered religious. At one level it is easy enough to find points in common between the ways in which people pray or hold certain objects or places or occasions in special veneration. Who they pray to, who they worship indeed, exhibits great variety, but at the most basic level it is generally possible to register some contrast between the sacred and the profane in any society. When it comes to our comparative study of ancient civilisations, the first thing to say is – as before – that to attempt to generalise about *the* Greco-Roman or *the* Chinese religious experience is ridiculous, given the variety of observances and beliefs found in both societies (cf. Lewis 2007: ch. 8, Sterckx 2010 and Michael Puett's chapter below).

At the level of the household, in both, as already noted, certain particular rituals were observed, including when a child was born, when it was inducted into the family, and on the death of a family member. On the far grander scale of the town or city there were imposing temples to city gods or those of the nation as a whole. In China the Emperor had the privilege and the duty to carry out the most sacred rituals of all, such as the *feng* and *shan* sacrifices on Mount Tai inaugurated by Qin Shi Huang Di.[44] But in both pagan Greco-Roman antiquity, and in China both before and after the unification, notions of the exclusive right of one set of practices and beliefs to be accepted got little traction. Particular groups of believers

---

[44] See Sterckx 2010 and Barrett 2010.

no doubt saw themselves as special, but even in the early centuries CE, no one was in any position in the Greco-Roman world to ban other faiths – not until some time after Christianity became, with Constantine, the official religion of the Roman Empire. A similar situation obtained also in China, even with the rise of Buddhism, whose fluctuating fortunes at court from the third century CE onwards reflected the personal choices and allegiances of members of the imperial family.

So what can we learn from this aspect of the comparative study of ancient civilisations, over and above the point already made about pluralism and diversity? The actual practices of prayer and worship, whether domestic or at the state level, continued more or less uninfluenced by the debates that were held, in both ancient societies, by members of the literate elite. Their discussions of the problems of theology, of the relationship between belief in the gods, piety, and morality, were largely intellectual exercises of speculative argument. The chief point at which belief could make a considerable difference in practice in real life is the one we mentioned in the previous section on medicine.

I have discussed all too briefly a number of topics where the comparison between the Greco-Roman world and China can suggest some similarities and more especially differences that we might otherwise miss if we concentrated on just one of these ancient civilisations. A great many other subjects might similarly be passed under review. They include such social institutions as the rise of 'bureaucracy',[45] an interest in economic factors, including supply and demand, taxation, the monetary system and trade, next techniques of predicting the future, then many aspects of technology including in relation to warfare, and attitudes to war itself, to death, to sexual relations, as well as many areas where understanding was attempted, of the motions of the stars and planets, for instance, or the behaviour of animals or the properties of plants, or of the phenomena we associate with reflection and refraction. Some of these will be discussed in the chapters that follow. Walter Scheidel mentions demographic factors, for example. Lisa Raphals investigates notions of the boundaries between humans and animals. Vivienne Lo and Eleanor Re'em have a lot to say about aphrodisiacs, and Zhou Yiqun about images of dangerous women. But of course no claim can be made to an exhaustive coverage here. However, let me end these introductory notes with some brief comments on two other areas where issues surface not just in relation to Greco-Roman and Chinese comparisons, but also and more

---

[45] See Lloyd and Sivin 2002: 34.

particularly to do with the existence or absence of cross-cultural universals. I refer to 'music' and 'art'.

The part played by music in education and in culture more generally in both the Greco-Roman world and China is well documented. 'Music' for the Greeks included poetry and other activities under the auspices of the Muses. Music was indeed part of the basic education of the sons of citizens. One of the things they were taught was to play a musical instrument, though while some were approved (the lyre), others (the *aulos* or clarinet) were frowned on. The Greeks distinguished between a large number of different 'modes', defined by the scales and attunements used, and each was associated with a particular character. There were modes that stimulated manliness or courage, but others that were considered depraved, and teachers such as Plato made clear the importance of such distinctions. There were also complex Greek analyses of harmonies and competing views as to how the harmonious is to be explained. Some based their theories on the numerical relations that (as all agreed) were exhibited by the octave (2:1), fifth (3:2) and fourth (4:3). But others treated musical sound as a continuum that could be treated on the analogy of a geometrical line.[46]

With the exception of the epistemological debate represented in that last example, these features are also present in China, to the extent that there too music was a key element in culture and certainly part of a gentleman's education. As for the moral and aesthetic implications of different styles of music, Confucius is said not to have tasted meat for several days after hearing the uplifting sounds of one style of music, while he was emphatic about the lasciviousness induced by the music of Zheng.[47]

But what we cannot do is to assess quite why certain types of music were prized, others not. There have been valiant attempts, on the basis of meagre evidence, to reconstruct what ancient Greek and Chinese music sounded like and some ancient Chinese musical instruments, bell chimes and drums, are extant. But though we can react to such reconstructions, that tells us nothing about how the Greeks and Chinese themselves reacted, nor the extent to which those reactions were culturally induced. The question of whether there are inherently pleasing sounds to which humans everywhere will react similarly is an open one on which ethnomusicologists have barely begun to make much progress.[48] It is an issue to bear in mind as we

---

[46] The classic discussion is Barker 1989.   [47] *Lunyu* 15/11. On which see Kern 2010.
[48] Blacking 1987 is something of an exception.

consider the variety of musical experiences for which we have evidence from our ancient societies.

An analogous problem arises in an even more severe form in the case of the category of 'art'. How do we or can we recognise works of art produced by other cultures? It is all too easy to assume that our reactions to the aesthetic qualities of a piece of carving, or weaving, or painting, are shared by the people who made them. But the grounds they may give for their appreciation may refer not at all to beauty, but rather to (say) efficacy, the power of the objects in question to induce an effect on those who see them.[49] Greco-Roman and Chinese representations of human figures share certain general characteristics, as Jeremy Tanner's discussion shows in the case of the depiction of heroic persons. We can, to some extent, follow the critical or appreciative comments we find in Greco-Roman and Chinese writers themselves. Aristotle, for instance, notes that we can enjoy looking at a representation of an object where the object itself is repulsive.[50] But all too obviously we are often at a loss to account for ancient tastes. This provides us with a second example where the question of cross-cultural universals is at stake. If we have to doubt their existence, how nevertheless do we account for the diversity we find? Here the category of 'art' itself may be an impediment to understanding.

It is appropriate to draw these introductory comments to an end on a distinctly aporetic note. At the same time there are positive conclusions we can draw from our comparative studies, always assuming that we are successful in avoiding the two main pitfalls, of anachronism and of the application of inappropriate conceptual categories. Three great advantages accrue from the successful critical application of the comparative method. First my principal theme has been that it enables us to register points that we might miss if we stay with the study of just a single society, and we can then ponder the factors in play in each case even while admitting that these are often difficult to pin down. Secondly, we may be led, as I have been in the last two sections, to raise the thorny question of the possibility of cross-cultural universals: what is it that we can expect all humans to share and how do ancient cultures testify to this, if and when they do? Finally, the comparative analysis of ancient societies serves important functions when it stimulates us to question the viability of our own categories. Thus probing the differences in the 'philosophy' or 'mathematics' practised in the Greco-Roman world and China can

---

[49] The classic study is Gell 1998.   [50] Aristotle, *On the Parts of Animals* 1.5.

help us to expand our understanding of what those categories may include and how they may include them.

Cross-cultural investigations of the type we practise here are still in their infancy and much work lies ahead. The problems, the risks and the rewards vary according to the subject matter that our different contributors tackle. But we are united in the hope that these pioneering studies will inspire others to take up the challenge to open up new lines of inquiry to advance our understanding of different aspects of ancient societies by means of sustained, critical comparisons between them.

References

Atack, C. (2014) 'The discourse of kingship in classical Athenian thought', *Histos* 8: 329–62.
Barker, A. D. (1989) *Greek Musical Writings*, vol. II: *Harmonic and Acoustic Theory*. Cambridge.
Barrett, T. H. (2010) 'Religious change under Eastern Han and its successors', in Nylan and Loewe: 430–48.
Behr, C. A. (1968) *Aelius Aristides and the Sacred Tales*. Amsterdam.
Blacking, J. (1987) *A Commonsense View of All Music*. Cambridge.
Boltz, W. G. (1993) 'Lao Tzu Tao te ching', in *Early Chinese Texts: A Bibliographical Guide*, ed. M. Loewe. Berkeley: 269–92.
Carsten, J. and Hugh-Jones, S. (eds.) (1995) *About the House*. Cambridge.
Chemla, K. (ed.) (2012) *The History of Mathematical Proof in Ancient Traditions*. Cambridge.
Cheng, A. (ed.) (2005) 'Y a-t-il une philosophie chinoise? Un état de la question', *Extrême-Orient, Extrême-Occident* 27.
Dean-Jones, L. A. (1994) *Women's Bodies in Classical Greek Science*. Oxford.
Deleuze, G. and Guattari, F. (1994) *What Is Philosophy?* (trans. H. Tomlinson and G. Burchill of *Qu'est-ce que la philosophie?*, Paris, 1991). London.
Edelstein, E. J. and Edelstein, L. (1945) *Asclepius*, 2 vols. Baltimore.
Finley, M. I. (1965) 'Technical innovation and economic progress in the Ancient World', *Economic History Review* 2nd ser. 18: 29–45.
  (1983) *Politics in the Ancient World*. Cambridge.
Garnsey, P. (1998) *Cities, Peasants and Food in Classical Antiquity* (ed. with addenda by W. Scheidel). Cambridge.
Gell, A. (1998) *Art and Agency: An Anthropological Theory*. Oxford.
Gernet, J. (1985) *China and the Christian Impact* (trans. J. Lloyd of *Chine et christianisme*, Paris, 1982). Cambridge.
Goody, J. (1977) *The Domestication of the Savage Mind*. Cambridge.
  (1986) *The Logic of Writing and the Organization of Society*. Cambridge.
  (1987) *The Interface between the Written and the Oral*. Cambridge.

Harper, D. (1998) *Early Chinese Medical Literature: The Mawangdui Medical Manuscripts*. London.
Huangdi neijing suwen 黃帝內經素問 (1986) Ren Yingqiu 任應秋 ed. Beijing.
Huffman, C. (ed.) (2014) *A History of Pythagoreanism*. Cambridge.
Hulsewé, A. F. P. (1955) *Remnants of Han Law*. Leiden.
Humphrey, C. (1974) 'Inside a Mongolian tent', *New Society* 30: 273–5.
  (1988) 'No place like home in anthropology: the neglect of architecture', *Anthropology Today* 4: 16–18.
Kern, M. (2010) 'Tropes of music and poetry from Wudi (r. 141–87 BCE) to ca. 100 CE', in Nylan and Loewe: 480–91.
King, H. (1998) *Hippocrates' Woman: Reading the Female Body in Ancient Greece*. London.
Laks, A. and Louguet, C. (eds.) (2002) *Qu'est-ce que la philosophie présocratique?* Lille.
Lang, M. L. (1990) *The Athenian Agora*, vol. XXV: *Ostraka* (American School of Classical Studies at Athens). Princeton.
Lévêque, P. and Vidal-Naquet, P. (1964) *Clisthène l'Athénien* (Annales Littéraires de l'Université de Besançon). Paris.
Lévi-Strauss, C. (1962/1966) *The Savage Mind* (trans. of *La Pensée sauvage*, Paris, 1962). London.
Lewis, M. E. (2007) *The Early Chinese Empires*. Cambridge, MA.
Lloyd, G. E. R. (1979) *Magic, Reason and Experience*. Cambridge.
  (1990) *Demystifying Mentalities*. Cambridge.
  (1996) *Adversaries and Authorities*. Cambridge.
  (2002) *The Ambitions of Curiosity*. Cambridge.
  (2003) *In the Grip of Disease*. Oxford.
Lloyd, G. E. R. and Sivin, N. (2002) *The Way and the Word*. New Haven.
Lo, V. and Li Jianmin (2010) 'Manuscripts, received texts and the healing arts', in Nylan and Loewe: 367–97.
Loewe, M. (1967) *Records of Han Administration*, 2 vols. Cambridge.
  (2004) *The Men Who Governed Han China*. Leiden.
  (2010a) 'Imperial tombs', in Nylan and Loewe: 228–31.
  (2010b) 'The laws of 186 BCE', in Nylan and Loewe: 253–65.
Ma Jixing (ed.) (1995) *Shen-nong bencao jing ji zhu*. Beijing.
Nylan, M. (2001) *The Five 'Confucian' Classics*. New Haven.
Nylan, M. and Loewe, M. (eds.) (2010) *China's Early Empires: A Re-appraisal*. Cambridge.
Olson, D. R. (1994) *The World on Paper*. Cambridge.
Olson, D. R. and Torrance, N. (eds.) (1991) *Literacy and Orality*. Cambridge.
Pleket, H. W. (1973) 'Technology in the Greco-Roman world: a general report', *Talanta* (Proceedings of the Dutch Archaeological and Historical Society) 5: 6–47.
Pokora, T. (1975) *Hsin-lun (New Treatise) and Other Writings by Huan T'an (43 B.C. – 28 A.D.)*. Ann Arbor, MI.
Reding, J.-P. (1985) *Les Fondements philosophiques de la rhétorique chez les sophistes grecs et chez les sophistes chinois*. Berne.

Sakamoto, T. and Makito, L. (1973) 'Japan', in *Comparative Reading: Cross-National Studies of Behavior and Processes in Reading and Writing*, ed. J. Downing. New York: 440–65.

Scheidel, W. (ed.) (2009) *Rome and China: Comparative Perspectives on Ancient World Empires*. New York.

Sivin, N. (1987) *Traditional Medicine in Contemporary China*. Ann Arbor, MI.
  (1995a) *Science in Ancient China: Researches and Reflections*, vol. I. Aldershot.
  (1995b) *Medicine, Philosophy and Religion in Ancient China: Researches and Reflections*, vol. II. Aldershot.

Sterckx, R. (2010) 'Religious practices in Qin and Han', in Nylan and Loewe: 415–29.
  (2011) *Food, Sacrifice and Sagehood*. Cambridge.

Tambiah, S. J. (1969) 'Animals are good to think and good to prohibit', *Ethnology* 8: 423–59.

Thomas, R. (1989) *Oral Tradition and Written Record in Classical Athens*. Cambridge.

Vanderpool, E. (1973) *Ostracism at Athens*. Cincinnati, OH.

Vernant, J. P. (1965/1983) *Myth and Thought among the Greeks* (trans. J. Lloyd and J. Fort of *Mythe et pensée chez les Grecs*, Paris, 1965). London.

Zysk, K. G. (1991) *Asceticism and Healing in Ancient India*. Oxford.

PART I

Methodological Issues and Goals

1 | Why Some Comparisons Make More Difference than Others

NATHAN SIVIN

If you set out to compare an apple and an orange, you may have to decide whether to perform this operation upon an Egremont russet apple with a small brown wormhole in its side, and a slightly under-ripe Valencia orange, both bought in the Cambridge market square and now sitting on your kitchen table. On the other hand, what you have in mind may equally well be two fictitious essences that represent all the varieties of oranges and apples at all times and in all places. Once you have made this fateful decision, it is highly likely (no matter which your choice turned out to be) that your two will turn out to be similar in some respects and different in others. If you chose the fruit you can smell and taste – and have to pay for – you will not be able to claim you have discovered something about all apples or oranges. So it goes.

You may prefer to compare the *pneuma* as Stoic philosophers described it and *qi* 氣 in the various Chinese syntheses of cosmos, state and body in the last three centuries BCE. That may seem to you a more becoming project for a humanistic scholar. It is less confining than stacking up the *pneuma* of Zeno of Citium against the King of Huainan's *qi*, and less airy than comparing all the conceptions of *pneuma* in all the Greek, and *qi* in all the Chinese, classics. When you have itemised what was like and what was unlike, you may conclude that the ideas have too much in common to be explained by mere coincidence. That might tempt you to speculate that they must be related in some way. Possibly there was influence one way or the other. If that is too unlikely, you might come to believe they are simply local varieties of reasoning of a kind that might emerge in any culture of some category that includes China and Greece.

You may or may not ask yourself what effect your conclusions will have on the sum total of useful human knowledge. If this question doesn't occur to you, it may occur to the panelists of the research foundation that you hope will support your investigation. That is only one of several reasons that it ought to occur to you.

It is not given to many scholars, no matter what they study, for the outcomes of their research to affect the thinking of everyone, or at least of all educated and open-minded people. Fellowship panels are not at all likely to demand it. But they (or you, if you are realistic) may very well ask whether a year's work is worth being memorable to the dozen people in the world who actively care about whether *pneuma* and *qi* are more like than unlike. You might, on the other hand, hope that your comparison will complicate all classicists', or all Sinologists', convictions about the physical, political and moral worlds. I say 'complicate' because one more claim about those worlds that simply confirms or adds one small qualification to the conventional wisdom isn't likely to result in noticeably richer understanding.

Complicating humanists' convictions does not come easily or quickly. Comparison has yielded some genuinely useful results. For instance, as a result of years of labour, and considerable patience, much of the learned world now admits that any treatise called *A History of Science* needs to pay attention to cultures outside of Western Europe. Scholars are gradually recognising that the goals of alchemy in Alexandria, in Europe, and in East Asia had to do with attaining spiritual perfection rather than with increasing chemical knowledge. Despite rich evidence, many have not yet noticed that the diseases recognised by modern physicians are ethnocentric, and that any ancient nosology is likely to repay understanding if we analyse it. These examples suggest that comparison can significantly increase understanding.

Comparanda

I'm always happy to learn from any comparison between cultures, no matter how narrow or unlikely. Scope is not the only way that comparisons vary. Another is that the comparisons that many scholars write about, rather than leading me to think in a new way, turn out to be quite forgettable.

That usually has to do with whether their choice of what to compare is productive. Let me explore this question with a cross-cultural comparison between diseases. The term *re* 熱, as any Chinese–English dictionary will tell you, means 'fever'. But if you are reading medical books written before modern times, you quickly learn that it's not so simple. It quickly becomes obvious that as a symptom *re* is the opposite of *han* 寒, 'chills'. Context will tell you that *both* are likely to describe a body temperature higher than normal, but that's not the point for early doctors. They were not signs that the doctor read on the outside of the patient's body, but abnormal hot or cold feelings inside – symptoms that the doctor could not observe, but learned about only if the patient described them.[1] They figure as symptoms in an immense number of disease entities.

In addition to *re* as a symptom, there is also *rebing* 熱病, 'hot disease'. *On the Origins and Symptoms of Diseases*, a handbook written by a court physician in 610 or 611 CE and authoritative for five centuries, lists twenty-eight varieties. Some of these by modern standards are syndromes, and some are diseases (that is, in addition to a regular combination of symptoms they have a regular course). As the handbook asserts, 'hot diseases belong to the class of Cold Damage Disorders', of which it describes sixty-seven types. There are also thirty-four Warm Disorders and a mere seven Cold-hot Disorders, in which chills and hot sensations alternate.[2]

Let me remind you that identifying ancient diseases using biomedical terminology is actually a project in comparison, and not at all a trivial one. Now that we have an idea of how multifarious the concept of *re* is, we might expect a modern physician who has studied all 136 varieties of its diseases to conclude that early Chinese were all too successful at hopelessly complicating simple entities. In other words, that kind of comparison tends to end in exasperation rather than illumination.

That often happens when people compare things that have much less in common than they think they do. Comparing ancient medical entities with modern ones is apt to yield useless results. Medicine anywhere before the nineteenth century had no reliable way to connect the signs and symptoms of disease with what was going on in the living body, and no way to be certain what the result of therapy on body processes was. Therapists' ability to relieve suffering or make it less serious relied on great ingenuity in getting round these obstacles.

If we want the work of comparison to be fruitful, in other words, we have to pick carefully what we compare, and in what times and places. In this example, the ideal comparandum would be seventh-century European nosology. But that would not be a practical choice. It is no longer judicious to refer to, say, the seventh century in Germany as part of the Dark Ages, but medical knowledge then and there was undeniably dim. Some of it survived from antiquity in Latin texts, but it is very hard to say how many healers could read such books, or even lay hands on them, then or for some centuries afterward.

---

[1] When early physicians referred to fevers, in the pre-modern sense of abnormally high body heat, which the doctor read directly by touch, they normally used the compound *fare* 發熱.
[2] On *rebing*, see *Zhu bing yuan hou lun* 諸病源候論 9: 57a–60a; Cold Damage (*shanghan* 傷寒) occupies the whole of *juan* 7 and 8; Warm Disorders (*wenbing* 瘟病) 10: 61–4; and Cold-hot Disorders (*lengrebing* 冷熱病) 12: 72–4.

From the twelfth century on, as educating physicians became a main role of European universities, therapeutic literature gradually became elaborate. Eventually we can find handbooks that define and classify diseases. That of William Cullen (1769) was arguably as authoritative as the earlier Chinese treatise, although not for as long. Even as late as the mid-nineteenth century it is easy to find practical handbooks that itemise a very large number of diseases they call 'fevers'.[3] I leave it to you to carry out a comparison of this kind, but it is likely to be fruitful. After you have done work of this sort, modern biomedical knowledge can play a productive part in forming conclusions. When adduced too early in the project it is more likely to be a distraction.

Just as we can compare something in two places at the same time, we can also compare a thing in the same place at different times. In that sense all history is comparative, but that does not mean all historians want to draw explicit comparisons. Still, it's not hard to find comparisons that uncover interesting historical questions. I find fascinating, for example, the ancient Chinese usage that forbade an official to serve two successive dynasties *(buerchen* 不貳臣*)*. The force of this taboo fluctuates oddly. If we examine instances where one would expect it to hold, sometimes it does and sometimes it doesn't. Let's look at two transitions from a Han government to an alien one. When the Mongols vanquished north China in the 1240s, they had no difficulty recruiting the experts they needed to plan and carry out a more or less Chinese-style administration (not to mention a conquest of the south). Liu Bingzhong 劉秉忠 (1216–74) eagerly went to work for Khubilai, and recruited many leading administrators, philosophers, astronomers and others.[4]

But in the transition from the Ming dynasty to the Qing (after 1644), many exceptionally able people refused civil service appointments under the Manchus, even those who had never been Ming officials. Instead a few of them became private teachers of astronomy and mathematics, and physicians. Mei Wending 梅文鼎 (1633–1721), Wang Xishan 王錫闡 (1628–82) and Xue Fengzuo 薛鳳祚 (c. 1620–80), the best astronomers of their time, are examples.[5] Fu Shan 傅山 (1607–84), an outstanding medical practitioner and author, equally celebrated as a calligrapher and painter, was ready to die rather than to accept an appointment that the Qing court pressed upon him.[6]

Here is an explicitly comparative problem. How can we attack it? The difference could be due to a change in political thought, in dominant

---

[3] E.g., I have found useful Barclay 1857. [4] Sivin 2009: 153–6.
[5] Sivin 1995: ch. 5, and ch. 7: 63–4. [6] Bai 2003: 215–18.

ideology, in government policy, in prevalent religious or philosophical convictions, even in economics. How do we decide, keeping in mind that each one of these calls for a different historical specialist to do the work? And what if a satisfactory understanding is too complicated for any one of these specialisations? It was questions of this kind that led Geoffrey Lloyd and myself to recommend attention to what we called in *The Way and the Word* "cultural manifolds".

Dimensions of Comparison

The point of cultural manifolds is that history unfolds in one big thing, the past. On the other hand, academia is a confederation of specialties, organised into departments, centres, research institutes, and so on. Despite much change, it has not yet found a replacement for this model, invented in the German research universities of the early nineteenth century. The historical profession is an alliance of sub-specialties, which from time to time step on each other's toes, but tend to be hesitant and apologetic about doing so. If it happens too often, the result is likely to be, in the old German mode, a new interdisciplinary department with a new title, meant to maintain a defensible turf.

City governments in the nineteenth-century German-speaking cultural sphere paid for the faculty of the first research universities. Those who passed the budgets were persuaded that, as scientific specialists generated rigorous, confirmable results, higher levels of scholars would weave from them a richly patterned, seamless fabric of knowledge. They expected that the humanities would follow the same pattern, evolving into humanistic sciences.

There were two long-term problems. One was that the humanities never became sciences. Most specialists did not find that goal attractive. The few that found ways to quantify or use experimentation relabelled themselves as social scientists, although the success of their predictions has been poor by the standards of physics or chemistry. The other difficulty was that hyper-specialisation was such a success that ambitious scholars lost interest in becoming generalists. That became the pursuit of a quirky few professors, and a certain number of popular authors, many of whom relied on research assistants to read the technical papers. The specialist rank and file tended to concentrate on what their own technical tools could yield with more or less confidence. The rest became mere context, which one could speculate about with serene freedom.

According to that model, putting whatever one studies in context is a perfectly good thing if one happens to have a taste for such undemanding pursuits. But in comparative studies the outcome is often unconvincing or forgettable, because what they compare doesn't fit neatly into a specialism, and offhand speculations about context don't put the emphasis where it needs to be.

What Geoffrey Lloyd and I did was to try doing away with the conventional division between foreground and context. The idea is to begin by examining all the dimensions of a complex phenomenon, and also the interactions that make all of these aspects into a single whole – a specimen of the past. To explain a given phenomenon we decided to consider how people make a living, their relation to structures of authority, what bonds connect those who do the same work, how they communicate to each other and to outsiders what they have understood, and what concepts and assumptions they rely on. We didn't assume that social factors determine thought, or that ideas determine social change. This turned out to let us comprehend the interactions within each manifold as thinkers respond to, but at the same time influence, institutions and prevalent values.

In other words, when we decided to compare the beginnings of science in China and Greece, Geoffrey and I surveyed all the possible dimensions that occurred to us, found most of them pertinent, and investigated the roles of all of them as well as their interactions, from income through politics to theoretical assumptions. We began with some doubts that there would be adequate sources for some of these, but discovered, once we began looking, that there were usually more than we expected. One outcome that helped us keep going over the dozen years of this project was that, comparisons aside, we found ourselves gradually looking at China in my case, and Greece in Geoffrey's case, in ways we had not anticipated.

As for wider outcomes, of the twenty or so reviews of *The Way and the Word* published in Europe and America, only two even noticed that a new methodology was one of its important features. One of those two reviewers made it clear that in history she considers methodology distasteful. Since then, perhaps a dozen studies have used cultural manifolds in the USA, none in Europe, and a number of them in China. Some of these have led to breakthroughs of one sort or another, but change on a larger scale will be neither quick nor easy.

To tell the truth, like most methodologies, cultural manifolds is not entirely new. It is in essence a way to remind oneself that one can always step outside the limits of specialism and be guided by what the problem demands. One's willingness to do that, I submit, is why some comparisons make more difference than others.

Bibliography

Bai, Q. (2003) *Fu Shan's World: The Transformation of Chinese Calligraphy in the Seventeenth Century.* Cambridge, MA.
Barclay, A. W. (1857) *A Manual of Medical Diagnosis: Being an Analysis of the Signs and Symptoms of Disease.* London.
Chao Yuanfang 巢元方 (610) *Zhu bing yuan hou lun* 諸病源候論 (*Origins and Symptoms of Medical Disorders*). Reprint, Beijing, 1955.
Cullen, W. (1769) *Synopsis nosologiæ methodicæ.* Edinburgh.
Lloyd, G. E. R. and Sivin, N. (2002) *The Way and the Word: Science and Medicine in Early China and Greece.* New Haven.
Sivin, N. (1995) *Science in Ancient China: Researches and Reflections.* Aldershot. Chapters separately paginated.
(2009) *Granting the Seasons: The Chinese Astronomical Reform of 1280, With a Study of its Many Dimensions and a Translation of its Records.* Secaucus, NJ.

2 | Comparing Comparisons

WALTER SCHEIDEL

In the study of History, comparative analysis remains rare. Explicit reflection on the uses, methodology and problems of historical comparison is rarer still. In this respect, the divide between History as an academic discipline that has at least occasionally been counted among the Social Sciences and fields such as Economics, Political Science and Sociology is as wide as it can be.[1] I have decided to focus on the 'how' and 'why' of comparative history rather than present a specific case study. This decision is in part motivated by what have turned into years of lingering anxiety about the 'proper way' to conduct comparative history, a concern that I suspect may well be shared by many others. In my case, these doubts have been heightened by my own efforts to encourage comparative interests in others – a case of the one-eyed leading the blind? I am above all keen to learn what others think about these issues, and hope that these cursory remarks will stimulate fruitful reflection and discussion. In my experience there is always a temptation to 'get on with it' – plunge into a discussion of specific case studies – and I want to encourage some soul-searching on why we think a comparative perspective is worth adopting, and more importantly on how to go about applying it in practice and developing it to greater maturity.

The key questions are, what is comparative history good for; how should it be done; and how has it been done (or not) so far? First of all, is it worth it? Comparison combats hyper-specialisation, the great bane of modern professional scholarship. Neither Classics nor East Asian Studies have displayed much resistance to this particular affliction. Phiroze Vasunia notes that comparisons 'generate inferences ... that speak to the concerns of other times and places'[2] – surely a welcome bonus feature for historians of early periods who may sometimes find themselves at the margins of their discipline. Comparison defamiliarises the deceptively familiar. By observing alternatives, the characteristics of one's 'own' case

---

[1] For relevant reflections in the latter fields, see esp. Bonnell 1980; Skocpol and Somers 1980; Tilly 1984; Ragin 1987; Mahoney and Rueschemeyer 2003a. For History, Haupt and Kocka 1996a and Lange 2013 are central.
[2] Vasunia 2011: 224.

become less self-evident, and appreciation of what is possible increases accordingly. Geoffrey Lloyd and Nathan Sivin even regard this as the principal benefit: 'The chief prize is a way out of parochialism.' Comparison improves our understanding of X as it took different forms in different societies, whereas 'Scholars whose work is confined within a single cultural area easily suppose that its ways are natural and inevitable.'[3] Could it be that this is more of a problem in intellectual history – whether there is only one 'philosophy', 'science', 'medicine' – than in other areas of History? Or should we take this observation to mean that any complacency about the 'natural and inevitable' interferes with, or seemingly obviates the need for, explanation of observed traits?

This brings us to the statement of purpose for the conference on which this volume is largely based. Qiaosheng Dong and Jenny Zhao observe that only through a comparative approach 'can the distinctive features and commonalities between these two civilizations [i.e., Greece and China] be identified'. Once this has been accomplished, the task at hand is to explain observed differences – in philosophy, science, medicine, historiography, etc. (To which one might add that observed trans-cultural commonalities, as long as they are non-trivial, are likewise in need of explication, as they cannot readily be taken for granted.) Yet I wonder if the purpose of comparative history is to explain difference (why A is not like B): at a more basic level, it may turn out to be the best means of explaining the properties of each case (why A is like A). The underlying objective is causal explanation of features and developments of any one case, which may be more difficult or perhaps even impossible in the absence of a comparative approach.

Comparative history contributes to the understanding of any given case. This is true in a fundamental way: how can we move from description to explanation except by contrast? When Weber asked why capitalism arose in Europe, the question was also, Why did it not arise elsewhere? I am delighted by Jeremy Tanner's opening shot against classicists' wariness of comparison due to the perceived incomparability of 'the Classical'[4] – for how can anything be established as 'classical' if not by comparison?

In the worst case, 'single-case historians' resemble the drunk who looks for his lost keys under a street light – not because that's where he lost them but because that's where he can see. Put more academically,

Analyses that are confined to single cases ... cannot deal effectively with factors that are largely or completely held constant within the boundaries of the case (or

---

[3] Lloyd and Sivin 2002: 8.   [4] Tanner 2009: 89.

are simply less visible in that structural or cultural context). This is the reason why going beyond the boundaries of a single case can put into question seemingly well-established causal accounts and generate new problems and insights.[5]

More specifically, 'single-case' studies may be misled by the nature of the sources (and/or established scholarship, hardly an independent variable): if the authorities (of either kind) emphasise A, it is difficult to realise that B, which is given short shrift, might have been critical in producing observed outcomes. Comparison offers a way out of this common trap. (For A, read 'Confucianism' or 'Mediterranean', depending on your field.)

Heuristically, comparative history helps us identify problems and questions that would not be clear without comparison. When Bloch sought to explain similar agrarian developments in England and France he looked for French equivalents of English enclosure, something 'French-only' historians would not have done. Descriptively, it allows us to identify particular cases as unusual (e.g., the Greek polis). But the greatest gain lies in the ability to explain. 'Comparative historical inquiry is fundamentally concerned with explanation and the identification of causal configurations that produce major outcomes of interest.'[6] Causal argument is central to this type of analysis, which must focus on processes over time.

Analytically, comparison allows us to delineate chains of development and in the process to critique established 'local' explanations (which may turn out to be pseudo-explanations). For example, consideration of shared input that is correlated with common outcomes in different places helps us supersede strictly local narratives of causation. (On the grandest scale, climate change or pandemics are suitable candidates: see below.) Comparative analysis may also be employed to contest or reject generalising (pseudo-)explanations, such as expectations or 'norms' derived from too few cases (A always leads to B), which may turn out not to be true.

This latter issue may strike us as a less than pressing concern, given that the identification of normative causal relationships is not normally regarded as a principal task of the historian. This is why I will stop here, well short of the ambitions of the Social Sciences: to use comparative historical analysis to test a theory, or to create typologies. I have summarised elsewhere historical sociologists' methodological discussions of 'parallel demonstration of theory', where comparison is meant to verify theory, and macro-causal analysis that seeks to generate new theory (and is therefore the more reliable the

---

[5] Rueschemeyer 2003: 332.   [6] Mahoney and Rueschemeyer 2003a: 11.

more different cases are involved).[7] There is no need to reiterate this here as it would lead us beyond what historians usually seek to do.

It is however worth noting that this is precisely the area that has attracted the most explicit engagement with procedural and epistemological questions. The more modest applications of comparative analysis favoured by historians have suffered from neglect. There is no manual on how to do comparative history. As an approach, it is not well conceptualised, formalised, let alone theorised. I have not even been able to find a general introduction to Comparative History.[8] Where social scientists are eager to fret, historians generally tend not to. This deficit of self-examination need not be an insuperable hurdle to the success of comparative history, but it can hardly be considered helpful. At the very least it poses the risk of having to reinvent the wheel every single time we get down to business.

Comparison is perhaps best defined as a perspective or an approach rather than a formal method. Two basic principles merit attention.[9] First, comparison is about similarities and differences, not about connections per se (although they may of course affect observed outcomes). This is important because it shows how a comparative approach has the potential to liberate us from conventional constraints of time (as in the timeless question routinely asked of historians, 'What is your period?') and space. Comparanda do not have to be spatially adjacent or contemporaneous. In a sense, the less close and connected they are, the better. Distance suppresses interaction effects, thereby simplifying causal analysis. (Do 'Silk Road Studies' qualify as comparative history?) Comparison between 'East' and 'West' is inter-cultural rather than intra-cultural. In many contexts – say, for Europeanists – it is often hard to distinguish between these categories, but this is a very straightforward matter for students of the ancient Mediterranean and early China. In practice, inter-cultural comparison tends to be limited to a few, often just two, sharply profiled cases.[10] Transcultural comparison, by contrast, tends to focus on a potentially universal repertoire of possible forms of features and processes (power, production, socialisation, cultural symbolism, etc.). Historians are more likely to privilege the former approach, historically minded social scientists the latter.

Second, comparison cannot be an end in itself but has to be a means to an end. This may seem trivial but undoubtedly bears emphasising, especially in

---

[7] Bonnell 1980; Skocpol and Somers 1980; cf. Scheidel 2009b: 5–6.
[8] Contrast Crossley 2008: *What Is Global History?* Lange 2013 comes closest to providing an introduction for historians.
[9] Haupt and Kocka 1996b.   [10] Osterhammel 1996.

view of the limitations of some of the work that has been attempted so far (see below). The two basic types of comparative reasoning – contrast and generalisation – go back at least as far as John Stuart Mill's 'method of difference' and 'method of agreement', which have repeatedly been taken up by modern comparativists (e.g., Theda Skocpol and Charles Tilly's distinction between 'contrasting' and 'universalising' types of comparison). The Millian methods serve to eliminate potential necessary and sufficient causes, thereby narrowing our choice of putatively significant causal factors.[11] The method of agreement focuses on equivalent outcomes in different cases: if some cause is only present in some of these cases, it cannot be necessary to produce this particular outcome. According to the method of difference, if outcomes differ in different cases, shared causes cannot be deemed sufficient to produce equivalent outcomes. Basic as this may seem, this logic provides a good way to judge and set aside rival explanatory hypotheses. In practical terms, the underlying rules may have to be relaxed in a probabilistic fashion 'to permit causes that are "usually" or "almost always" necessary or sufficient'.[12] This takes account of the messiness of history, specifically of measurement problems and related issues that make patterns of association difficult to identify in the record.[13]

The search for causation favours analysis structured around discrete variables. This is a common approach in the Social Sciences but less so among historians. More generally, History and the Social Sciences have differed in terms of practitioners' expectations regarding the nature of comparison. Three characteristics of comparative work are specific to historical scholarship.[14] (1) The Enlightenment notion that historical research ought to be close to the sources in order to count as professional and authentic has imposed disciplinary standards that encourage scepticism against generalisations and are strictly applicable only to certain kinds of endeavours, most notably specialised studies – but less so, if at all, to larger syntheses. For comparative analysis to become feasible, such standards must not be over-prioritised at the expense of alternatives that allow an appreciation of broader patterns. Concerns over disciplinary standards are closely linked to questions of expertise, which I discuss below. (2) Historians are by definition interested in change over time; the entire field is characterised by a special relationship with the dimension of time. Analysis progresses from older to newer without severing connections over time. History is not seen as a sum of cases from which general principles

---

[11] Mahoney 2003a. [12] Mahoney 2003a: 334.
[13] Mahoney 2003a: 334–7. See 348–53 for a response to criticisms of Millian methods.
[14] Haupt and Kocka 1996b.

can be abstracted; instead, individualistic models (about A or A versus B) dominate. (3) Historical processes are seen as deeply embedded: any element of the historical experience is considered hard (if not impossible) to understand outside the context provided by other elements. The underlying expectation is that it is necessary to understand the whole in order to understand elements thereof. In as much as this principle prevails, and history is viewed as deriving meaning from synchronic and diachronic contextualisation, a focus on discrete variables might seem constricting, unprofessional, or worse. Moreover, the *ceteris paribus* condition implicit in variable-centred approaches is in practice rarely met.

All three of these premises create tensions with the principles of comparative analysis. The more cases are involved, the less proximity to the sources can be attained (due to language problems and greater reliance on secondary scholarship); yet multi-case studies may produce more robust findings. Cases have to be defined and hence to some extent isolated in order to be subjected to comparison, and to be related to each other as individual cases. This process breaks continuities: the focus shifts from change over time to similarities and differences. Most importantly, comparison is predicated on selectivity: cases tend to be decontextualised and stripped down, especially in multi-case comparisons.

Various strategies are available to cope with historians' reservations arising from these tensions. (1) Comparison may be limited to a few, ideally just two, cases, in order to reduce the need for simplification and second-hand scholarship. (2) Abstraction is limited by retaining as much context as possible. Emphasis is placed on contrast rather than generalisation of commonalities. (3) A focus on processes helps preserve the link to change over time. Much of the work being done on ancient East/West comparisons is fairly representative of this approach. Yet it is important to realise that there is no silver bullet. Emphasis on richly textured narratives that strive to preserve as much nuance as possible is a problematic solution: the more of the original context of each case is retained, the less systematically comparative the resulting study will be. Inevitable trade-offs appear built into the comparativist venture, regardless of individual idiosyncrasies of perspective and approach. Moreover, the palliative strategies outlined here in turn raise new problems. Historians would do well to engage more with social scientists' concerns about what is known as the 'small-N problem' that threatens to undermine comparisons between only two (or few) cases: 'the combination of many factors assumed to be causally relevant with evidence from only a small number of comparable cases', which may leave us with 'too few cases chasing too many causal factors'.[15] Although worries about the formal (statistical) significance of putatively necessary or sufficient conditions in small-N studies may seem of little relevance to qualitatively oriented historians, the underlying problem is the same:[16] how can we be confident that the factors that are thought to account for meaningful differences between two cases (say, ancient Greece and early China) are in fact critical to these observed outcomes if our analysis is confined to just those two cases?

On a more positive note, we must remember that issues of selectivity, perspective and construction are inherent in any kind of historical study. Comparative history is special only in so far as it renders them particularly conspicuous. This should be considered a gain, as it compels historians to acknowledge more explicitly what it is they are trying to accomplish, and how. Comparative history is intellectually demanding because it requires continuous reflection. What are the appropriate units of comparison? There is no single answer: our choice depends entirely on the questions we wish to ask. What is to be compared with what? Once again, this is determined by our questions: apples and oranges make for fine comparanda if we are interested in fruit.

This leaves us with one of the biggest elephants in the room, the problem of professional expertise. Tanner may miss an important factor when he muses that classicists' wariness of comparison might be linked to ideological reasons and concerns about its usefulness: insularity can also be engendered by self-imposed disciplinary standards that severely constrain scholars' ability to move beyond their own field of specialisation. Virtually every time I disclose my own comparative interests and projects to classicists, the first question is, 'So are you learning Chinese?' If Classics is seen as predicated on the mastery of classical philology, 'Comparative Classics' logically ought to entail mastery of two separate philologies. Strictly applied, this premise would either exclude most ordinary mortals from comparative endeavours or latently discredit comparative work undertaken by such lesser beings. Neither one of these reactions can reasonably be expected to sustain a viable programme of inter-cultural comparative research. Just as the perfect is the enemy of the good, insistence of conventional disciplinary standards is hard to reconcile with the demands of comparative history, especially once it transcends one-on-one comparisons and covers multiple cases. From a traditionalist's standpoint, 'serious' comparative history might well be impossible.

---

[15] Rueschemeyer 2003: 305, 325. [16] Mahoney 2003a: 350.

What are the solutions? Subject matter is relevant. Research questions that require close engagement with textual sources would seem impossible to pursue without appropriate linguistic skills. Different agenda might accommodate a relaxation of this premise: the nature of the questions we are asking is vital in determining the means necessary to address them. Although Classics and Sinology/East Asian Studies may count as especially text-centred fields, the challenge of inter-cultural expertise is well recognised by comparative historians of other periods. Social scientists tend to side-step the problem by focusing more on 'big' questions, where reliance on secondary scholarship is both acceptable and inevitable.

Not coincidentally, similar problems apply to the field of Comparative Literature: the need to privilege theoretical sophistication over language competence, and concurrent charges of dilettantism. In my very limited understanding, Comparative Literature has moved from something like comparative history – comparing discrete cases, often in the context of nation states – to something more akin (in terms of outlook though not method) to Social Science, transcending traditional divisions and approaching world literature as a quarry to explore specific questions. No comparable Comparative History has yet developed.

Even so, avoidance strategies that prevent comparative historians from engaging with the full range of the evidence (and often language-specific secondary scholarship) can only lead to a very impoverished research agenda. Collaboration may be the only feasible solution.[17] If one scholar cannot master all the required skills, two or more of them need to pool their complementary resources. This conflicts with the largely solitary character of much Humanities scholarship, the result of tradition, personal inclination and entrenched academic incentive structures. Participation in conventional edited volumes or big editions cannot count as valid exceptions to this principle. Thanks to its overlap with the sciences, archaeology offers a more promising paradigm of collaboration (not only among specialists in different areas but also transnationally) – yet historical research resolutely remains more individualistically organised.

Given the considerable hurdles of moving between Greco-Roman and early Chinese sources and scholarship, the near-absence of genuine inter-area collaboration is indeed striking. Tanner's marvellous bibliography of Sino-Hellenic Studies reveals hardly anything at all.[18] The only exceptions

---

[17] E.g., Meier 1996: 266. [18] Tanner 2009: 106–9.

are Lloyd and Sivin's 2002 book, plus Steven Shankman and Stephen Durrant's 2000 monograph and 2002 edited volume.[19] Who has been behind these rare collaborations? The balance of the Shankman and Durrant collaboration is already signalled by the reversal of the authors'/editors' surnames. In her review of their 2000 book, Yiqun Zhou notes that 'it is evident that the book is to a much greater extent informed of the personal mission of Shankman the classicist than that of Durrant the sinologist'.[20]

This meshes well with my own experience in running Stanford's 'Ancient Chinese and Mediterranean Empires Comparative History Project'.[21] I suspect that the relative heft and maturity of the two fields account for this imbalance. 'Classics' has produced around one million publications since 1900 and is relatively well represented in academia as a legacy function of its privileged position in the age of global European hegemony. Several thousand scholars attend the annual meetings of the North American Classics association; over 500 Greco-Roman historians hold faculty positions at Anglophone universities.[22] Whatever the corresponding numbers for early China studies (in the West), they are bound to be much smaller. In some ways, early China scholars operate in a context that is reminiscent of Classics a century or more ago – with fundamental texts being edited for the first time, much of the existing sources unavailable in translation, and archaeology rapidly expanding the body of knowledge. All this may concentrate minds on the more essential tasks at hand. But this is merely a conjecture: I would greatly welcome feedback from China scholars on their field's incentives and disincentives to inter-cultural collaborative research. Scholars of the Greco-Roman world, it must be said, in any case lack any pragmatic excuses for their failure to instigate more comparative work.

What has in fact been done? The trend is upward, even as the overall volume of relevant work remains deplorably minuscule.

Tanner's pioneering survey of 2009 dealt with the liveliest area, that of comparative intellectual history – 'history of science and medicine ... literature and historiography, philosophy, religion, law, cultural history', which coincides with the principal interests of the contributors to this volume. This relieves me of the obligation to cover familiar ground. Tanner also very

---

[19] Lloyd and Sivin 2002; Shankman and Durrant 2000a, 2002b. Hall and Ames – 1995, 1998 – are both China scholars, which does not count for my present purposes.
[20] Zhou 2000: 175.
[21] ACME 2005–. 'The Stanford ancient Chinese and Mediterranean empires comparative history project (ACME).' www.stanford.edu/~scheidel/acme.htm (accessed 22 June 2015).
[22] Scheidel 1997, 1999.

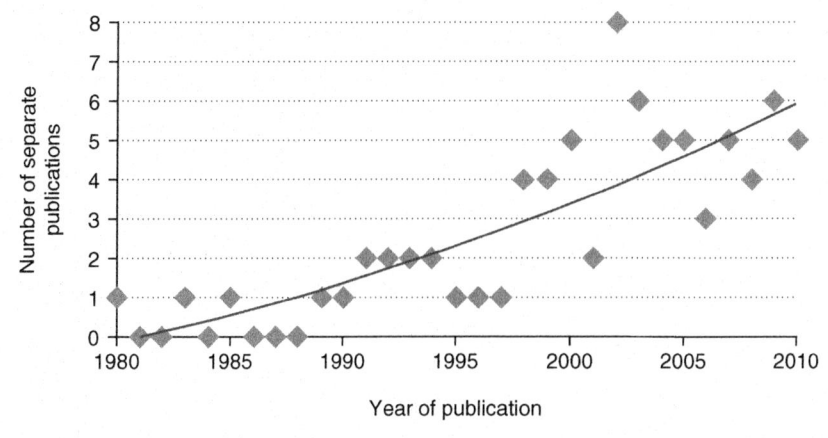

Figure 2.1 Comparative ancient East/West publications (counting edited volumes as single items).

helpfully furnishes me with a template for comparing comparisons: how does existing work in comparative intellectual history compare to that in other areas?

Tanner[23] describes Lloyd's method as contextualising knowledge production in socio-political conditions, such as civic institutions that favoured persuasion and use of evidence in Greece and monarchical arrangements in China. Lloyd's rejection of holistic generalisation (Greece here, China there) is consistent with an interest in factors that can be causally linked to observed outcomes. This places his approach in proximity to the variable-based and causation-driven comparisons favoured by social-science-friendly historians. 'Explanations of cultural difference' are a key objective.

Fritz-Heiner Mutschler has followed a similar approach in his writings on historiography, contextualising and explaining divergent traits with reference to the social circumstances of text production.[24] Hyun Jin Kim, in a comparative study of representations of ethnicity, contrasts the Greeks – on the margins of a larger civilisation/empire – with the more centrally situated Chinese.[25] His goal is 'to determine the historical, political and cultural factors that determined the Greek and also Chinese perception of foreigners'. His main concern is 'causal factors' that account for specific outcomes. Differences are traced back to specific contexts: while the polarising Greek–barbarian divide is interpreted as the result of conflict with Persia that prompted anxious Greeks to play up their martial and phenotypical superiority, the early imperial Chinese tradition stresses

---

[23] Tanner 2009: 90, focusing on Lloyd 1994, 1996.   [24] Tanner 2009: 103.   [25] Kim 2009.

differences in material culture. Imperial inclusiveness emerges as a significant variable: from a metropolitan vantage point, Sima Qian portrays nomads as radically different but is prepared to incorporate other (assimilable) sedentary cultures as (faux-)Chinese, whereas Herodotus more flexibly switches between Greek/barbarian and civilised/uncivilised dichotomies as his perspective warrants. All this comes across as a fairly straightforward variable-centred approach: specific differences in context are held responsible for observed differences in outcome. The question remains, however, to what extent inter-cultural comparison is required to establish these connections.

Zhou finds that social solidarity was pursued within different institutions – festivals, symposia or gymnasia in Greece; ancestral sacrifice, family banquets or communal drinking parties in China – highlighting a contrast between peer-group- and kinship-centred activities.[26] While the Greek tradition emphasises extrafamilial homosocial bonds, the Chinese tradition revolves around patrilineal family and kinship. This contrast is complemented by differences in the portrayed nature of mother–son bonds and female homosocial ties. Causation is traced back to the dynamic but divisive environment fostered by the principles of equality and competition in Greece and the perceived centrality of hierarchy (instead of gender) in early China. This amounts to a causal model of differences in traits that stem from differences in socio-political context and structure, similar to Lloyd's approach.

Students of comparative institutional history are likely to be comfortable with this line of reasoning. They share both a preoccupation with causation – the question of how and why divergent forms emerge – and an interest in how they are maintained or modified over time. For instance, my own work on ancient Mediterranean and East Asian coinage employs the same procedure.[27] In this case, a clearly defined phenomenon – the creation of coined metal money – independently occurred only twice in world history. Discrete factors are identified to account for differences in outcomes: resource endowments (sustaining large-scale precious-metal coinage in western Eurasia); political ecology (heavily fragmented polities in the Aegean that relied on full-bodied issues and larger imperial formations in China that were able to accommodate a greater degree of nominalism and rely on base-metal issues for fiscal circulation); military ecology (the uneven demand for military pay especially in the Hellenistic and Warring States contexts); and the long-term consequences of path-dependence, as traditions crystallised over time (with later Chinese regimes reverting to the

---

[26] Zhou 2010. [27] Scheidel 2009a.

original norms even as contextual conditions changed). The focus is on variable-based causal explanation from an extended developmental perspective.

The single largest effort in the area of East/West comparison concerns what has become known as the 'Great Divergence',[28] the divergent economic development of 'the West' and China since around 1800. The literature is enormous and cannot be referenced here. One-on-one comparisons between the relevant parts of Europe and China suffer from a particularly extreme version of the 'small-N problem': a whole array of possible causes has been proposed to explain divergent outcomes in no more than two cases. On one end of the spectrum, geographical-ecological factors almost obviate the need for specific inter-cultural analysis: if Europe enjoyed geographical advantages (Jared Diamond) or was closer to the New World (Ian Morris) or farther from the Eurasian steppe (Peter Turchin), its eventual ascendancy might be considered a long-term lock-in.[29] If we assign greater significance to institutions, as most historians would do, the picture becomes more complex and ancient historians potentially have a more important role to play. For example, if persistent political polycentrism is regarded as critical to particular 'Western' outcomes, the post-Roman non-reconstitution of universal empire in Europe takes centre stage. Once again, a number of highly diverse variables may account for long-term differences in European and East Asian state formation, from steppe exposure and sheer spatial spread to the configuration of the main sources of social power, fiscal regimes, religion and so on.[30] Once more, the small-N problem causes observed outcomes to be heavily overdetermined (as multiple causes may all contribute to the same difference in outcomes). Multi-case comparison, pitting one case against many, that allows more systematic discrimination between variables may be the only way out of this conundrum, as one-on-one comparisons on that scale may simply not be capable of identifying the principal causal associations. In other words, more comparison may be the best remedy for overly narrow comparative history.

Another option is exemplified by Victoria Tin-bor Hui's 2005 study of why the Warring States environment resulted in universal empire in China whereas intense inter-state competition in early modern Europe failed to do so. Applying the 'uncommon foundations' method advocated by Doug McAdam, Sidney Tarrow and Charles Tilly, Hui tracks different combinations of often-shared causal mechanisms with varying initial and environmental

---

[28] After Pomeranz 2000.   [29] Diamond 1999; Morris 2010; Turchin 2009.
[30] Turchin 2009 (steppe); Hui 2005 (space); Zhao 2015 (social power); Wickham 1994; Scheidel 2011 (fiscal regimes).

conditions that generated different outcomes.³¹ It is telling that this pioneering study across periods was produced by a political scientist, not a historian; that historians' reactions have prioritised points of historical detail instead of engaging with the merits of the overall thesis or approach; and that historians have more generally shied away from this kind of problem-centred comparative analysis that transcends conventional periodisation.

It is only in certain cases that synchronicity is a crucial element of historical comparison. World-systems approaches come to mind, not so much in the radical version that seeks to identify effects of supposedly interactive world systems thousands of years ago but in the appreciation of exogenous inputs such as climatic variation that may be causally linked to equivalent outcomes in otherwise separated societies.³² Frederick Teggart's notorious 1939 study of interaction effects between eastern and western Eurasia was an early, if inept, example of this approach. Conversely, asynchronous comparison challenges the intellectually lazy notion that absolute chronology is the most obvious way of structuring comparative analysis.³³ To name just one example, the study of economic efflorescences in imperial contexts invites comparison between Rome and Song China, which as Morris suggests had reached comparable levels of social development a millennium apart.³⁴

For now, however, we have to make do with what is available. Several more conventional comparative studies have made significant contributions to our understanding of case-specific outcomes. Hsing I-tien's Hawai'i dissertation, which has unfortunately remained unpublished and therefore completely ignored, analyses the role of the army in imperial succession in the Roman Principate and the Western Han period.³⁵ He identifies three key differences: a well-established principle of closed dynastic succession in China, very much unlike in Rome; close contact between rulers and the military in Rome but not in China; and the structure of the armed forces, which were better able to develop corporate interests in the Roman context. Hsing I-tien carefully distinguishes between factors that merely provided opportunities for military intervention in the political process (the first two) and the one factor that crucially accounted for different incentives for it (the third one). This raises a new question, why

---

[31] McAdam, Tarrow and Tilly 2001: 81–4; Hui 2005: 8.
[32] See Frank and Gills 1993; Frank and Thompson 2005, 2006 for the former approach, and e.g., Chase-Dunn, Hall and Turchin 2007 for the latter.
[33] Whereas it requires at the very least explicit justification: e.g., Scheidel 2009b.
[34] Morris 2010.   [35] Hsing I-tien 1980.

the two empires ended up with different types of army. This anticipated Lloyd's call for 'deparochialisation' and demonstrates very clearly how a variable-centred approach not only can improve historical explanations for individual cases but also helps identify the most important questions.

Margot Custers' thesis is in its entirety focused on variables and their configuration in addressing problems of long-term imperial stability in Rome and China.[36] Nathan Rosenstein links divergent trends in state formation in the Roman Republic and Warring States China to the nature of competition: as Rome experienced a relaxation of foreign threats (compared to China), it embarked on an alternative trajectory.[37] As noted by Vasunia, this entails an implicitly counterfactual claim of anticipated commonality had contextual circumstances been more similar.[38] However, James Tan arrives at congruent conclusions by explaining the absence of coercion-extraction cycles in Republican Rome that were typical of early and mature modern European states under military pressure.[39]

At the same time, a number of existing works fall short of the demands of comparative historical analysis. For instance, Ryoji Motomura assumes that comparanda need to be very similar for comparisons to be feasible.[40] Christian Gizewski is primarily concerned with identifying parallel processes in ancient eastern and western Eurasia without addressing the question of their causal underpinnings.[41] Samuel Adshead, in a series of admirably lucid comparative observations,[42] is content with producing what are essentially laundry-lists of observed differences between the Roman Empire and Han or Tang China: the ultimate purpose of this exercise remains unclear. A step forward in a similar vein is Morris' long-term comparative appraisal of East and West through the lens of a 'social development index' based on the four variables of energy capture, urbanism as a proxy of organisational capacity, information processing and war-making capabilities.[43] The end result is a kind of score card on who was 'on top' at any given time.

Fritz-Heiner Mutschler and Achim Mittag (2008), in a well-attended project, favour a somewhat idiosyncratic form of hands-off comparison, whereby 'the comparative aspect ... [is] addressed, if only indirectly, in the pairing of papers for each topic, thus freeing contributors from drawing explicit comparisons, and hence from forays into unfamiliar fields of

[36] Custers 2008. [37] Rosenstein 2009: esp. 49–50. [38] Vasunia 2011: 227. [39] Tan 2011.
[40] Motomura 1991. [41] Gizewski 1994; cf. Scheidel 2009b: 13–14.
[42] Adshead 2000: ch. 1; 2004: 20–9. [43] Morris 2010: 148–9.

specialised knowledge'.[44] It is perhaps not entirely obvious why, if experts for particular topics had already been found and paired, they could not be encouraged to collaborate – perhaps even co-author – in the service of sustained comparative analysis. It is also unclear why the reader is supposed to do all the hard work ('Readers themselves must ... have noticed many parallels and differences'). And in any case, comparative history is not primarily a matter of 'noticing parallels and differences' but of trying to explain and understand commonalities and differences. Their 'Epilogue' addresses this deficit only in part by belatedly pulling some loose ends together.[45]

Parallel exposition likewise dominates the chapter on 'Imperial rule in Rome and China' in Jane Burbank and Frederick Cooper's world history of empires.[46] The ostensible question of what made both polities successful is not well served by the avoidance of any causal comparative analysis. Only the question of post-ancient divergence prompts brief comparative considerations, but just a single variable – direct versus indirect managerial strategies in Qin/Han China and Rome, respectively – is proffered without exploring alternative explanations.

Finally, I am left wondering about the insights meant to emerge from Corey Brennan and Hsing I-tien's erudite and entertaining speculation about the fictional experiences of travellers to ancient Chang'an and Rome.[47] The only causal observation I was able to discover refers to the impact of the republican regime on Rome's cityscape. This is unfortunate, as urbanism invites and indeed richly rewards more systematic comparison. In two separate contributions to my latest edited volume on China and Rome, Mark Lewis and Carlos Noreña contextualise differences in Roman and Han urban features much more fully and explicitly.[48] Lewis focuses on the public sphere and its public spaces, contrasting the 'city of the Romans' with its deep historical texture and the multiple capitals of Chinese dynasties that manifested a de-historicised and well-ordered environment (that among other things eschewed military monuments, thereby decentring the military) in which the absence of public spaces served to equate the public sphere with the state. The regional cities of the Roman world were run by locally autonomous elites whereas the Chinese district centres sought to replicate the principal metropolis and its state apparatus on a smaller scale, as loci of government presence and control. Noreña likewise causally associates differences in cityscapes with differences in state formation: whereas Han

---

[44] Mutschler and Mittag 2008: 421; also XVI.   [45] Mutschler and Mittag 2008: 421–47.
[46] Burbank and Cooper 2010: 23–59.   [47] Brennan and Hsing I-tien 2010.
[48] Lewis 2015; Noreña 2015.

cities served as instruments of social control, Roman civic autonomy rested on independent bases of localised social power. Noreña tentatively recasts what Roman historians are parochially used to seeing as the success of Roman-style city-based governance as a sign of state weakness, in contrast to Han arrangements, and considers the consequences for later imperial reconstitution.

It is comforting to be able to end this very brief and superficial survey on an optimistic note. Yet its very brevity, and the noted widespread absence of explicit engagement with problems of approach and process (to avoid the lofty term 'method'), are cause for serious concern. By any standard, the comparative history of the ancient world is still a very immature area of scholarly activity. It is too promising to be left to 'outsiders' (although their potential contribution should by no means be underrated).[49] Yet unless professional historians on both sides embrace comparative perspectives and its vital corollary, collaboration, little will change. I am offering these pages in the hope they will provoke debate and dissent,[50] and encourage us to reflect more deeply on our shared interest in historical comparison.

References

Adshead, S. A. M. (2000) *China in World History* (3rd edn). New York.
  (2004) *T'ang China: The Rise of the East in World History*. Basingstoke.
Bonnell, V. E. (1980) 'The uses of theory, concepts and comparison in historical sociology', *Comparative Studies in Society and History* 22: 156–73.
Brennan, T. C. and Hsing I-tien (2010) 'The eternal city and the city of eternal peace', in *China's Early Empires: A Re-appraisal*, eds. M. Nylan and M. Loewe. Cambridge: 186–212.
Burbank, J. and Cooper, F. (2010) *Empires in World History: Geographies of Power, Politics of Difference*. Princeton.
Chase-Dunn, C., Hall, T. D. and Turchin, P. (2007) 'World-systems in the biogeosphere: urbanization, state formation and climate change since the Iron Age', in *The World System and the Earth System: Global Socioenvironmental Change and Sustainability since the Neolithic*, eds. A. Hornberg and C. Crumley. Walnut Creek: 132–48.
Crossley, P. K. (2008) *What Is Global History?* Cambridge.

---

[49] A very substantial comparative history of the Roman period and early China was rejected by several university presses primarily because the author, a very well-read senior academic at an elite US institution and native Mandarin speaker, was not a professional historian. A massive causal analysis of Chinese state formation by a respected historical sociologist only narrowly eluded the same fate, having been considered not historical enough by historians and too historical by social scientists. The list will no doubt keep growing.

[50] I expect that my unfashionable preoccupation with causal explanation will raise some hackles.

Custers, M. (2008) 'Balancing acts: comparing political and cultural unification and persistence in the Roman Empire during the Principate and the Western Han empire', unpublished MA thesis, Utrecht.

Dettenhofer, M. H. (2006) 'Das römische Imperium und das China der Han-Zeit: Ansätze zu einer historischen Komparatistik', *Latomus* 65: 880–97.

Diamond, J. (1999) *Guns, Germs, and Steel: The Fates of Human Societies*. New York.

Edwards, R. A. (2009) 'Federalism and the balance of power: China's Han and Tang dynasties and the Roman Empire', *Pacific Economic Review* 14: 1–21.

Frank, A. G. and Gills, B. K. (eds.) (1993) *The World System: Five Hundred Years or Five Thousand?* London.

Frank, A. G. and Thompson, W. R. (2005) 'Afro-Eurasian Bronze Age economic expansion and contraction revisited', *Journal of World History* 16: 115–72.

  (2006) 'Early Iron Age economic expansion and contraction revisited', in *Globalization and Global History*, eds. B. K. Gills and W. R. Thompson. London: 139–62.

Gizewski, C. (1994) 'Römische und alte chinesische Geschichte im Vergleich: Zur Möglichkeit eines gemeinsamen Altertumsbegriffs', *Klio* 76: 271–302.

Hall, D. L. and Ames, R. T. (1995) *Anticipating China: Thinking through the Narratives of Chinese and Western Culture*. Albany.

  (1998) *Thinking from the Han: Self, Truth, and Transcendence in Chinese and Western Culture*. Albany.

Haupt, H.-G. and Kocka, J. (eds.) (1996a) *Geschichte und Vergleich: Ansätze und Ergebnisse international vergleichender Geschichtsschreibung*. Frankfurt.

  (1996b) 'Historischer Vergleich: Methoden, Aufgaben, Probleme. Eine Einleitung', in Haupt and Kocka 1996a: 9–45.

Hsing I-tien (1980) 'Rome and China: the role of the armies in the imperial succession: a comparative study', unpublished PhD thesis, Manoa.

Hui, V. T. (2005) *War and State Formation in Ancient China and Early Modern Europe*. Cambridge.

Kim, H. J. (2009) *Ethnicity and Foreigners in Ancient Greece and China*. London.

Lange, M. (2013) *Comparative-Historical Methods*. Los Angeles.

Lewis, M. E. (2015) 'Public spaces in cities in the Roman and Han empires', in Scheidel 2015a: 204–29.

Lloyd, G. E. R. (1994) 'Methodological issues in the comparison of East and West', in *Is It Possible to Compare East and West?*, eds. H. Numata and S. Kawada. Tokyo: 23–36.

  (1996) *Adversaries and Authorities: Investigations into Ancient Greek and Chinese Science*. Cambridge.

Lloyd, G. E. R. and Sivin, N. (2002) *The Way and the Word: Science and Medicine in Early China and Greece*. New Haven.

Mahoney, J. (2003) 'Strategies of causal assessment in comparative historical analysis', in Mahoney and Rueschemeyer 2003b: 337–72.
Mahoney, J. and Rueschemeyer, D. (2003a) 'Comparative historical analysis: achievements and agendas', in Mahoney and Rueschemeyer 2003b: 3–38.
  (eds.) (2003b) *Comparative Historical Analysis in the Social Sciences*. Cambridge.
McAdam, D., Tarrow, S. and Tilly, C. (2001) *Dynamics of Contention*. Cambridge.
Meier, C. (1996) 'Aktueller Bedarf an historischen Vergleichen: Überlegungen aus dem Fach der Alten Geschichte', in Haupt and Kocka 1996a: 239–70.
Morris, I. (2010) *Why the West Rules – For Now*. New York.
Motomura, R. (1991) 'An approach towards a comparative study of the Roman empire and the Ch'in and Han empires', *Kodai* 2: 61–9.
Mutschler, F.-H. and Mittag, A. (eds.) (2008) *Conceiving the Empire: Rome and China Compared*. Oxford.
Noreña, C. F. (2015) 'Urban systems in the Han and Roman empires: state power and social control', in Scheidel 2015b: 181–203.
Osterhammel, J. (1996) 'Transkulturell vergleichende Geschichtswissenschaft', in Haupt and Kocka 1996a: 271–314.
Pomeranz, K. (2000) *The Great Divergence: China, Europe, and the Making of the Modern World Economy*. Princeton.
Ragin, C. C. (1987) *The Comparative Method: Beyond Qualitative and Quantitative Strategies*. Berkeley.
Rosenstein, N. (2009) 'War, state formation, and the evolution of military institutions in ancient China and Rome', in Scheidel 2009b: 24–51.
Rueschemeyer, D. (2003) 'Can one or a few cases yield theoretical gains?', in Mahoney and Rueschemeyer 2003b: 305–36.
Scheidel, W. (1997) 'Continuity and change in classical scholarship: a quantitative survey, 1924 to 1992', *Ancient Society* 28: 265–89.
  (1999) 'Professional historians of classical antiquity in the English-speaking world: a quantitative survey', *Ancient History Bulletin* 13: 151–6.
  (2009a) 'The monetary systems of the Han and Roman empires', in Scheidel 2009b: 137–207.
  (ed.) (2009b) *Rome and China: Comparative Perspectives on Ancient World Empires*. New York.
  (2011) 'Fiscal regimes and the "First Great Divergence" between eastern and western Eurasia', in *Tributary Empires in Global History*, eds. P. F. Bang and C. Bayly. Basingstoke: 193–204.
  (ed.) (2015) *State Power in Ancient China and Rome*. New York.
Shankman, S. and Durrant, S. W. (2000a) *The Siren and the Sage: Knowledge and Wisdom in Ancient Greece and China*. Albany.
  (eds.) (2002b) *Early China/Ancient Greece: Thinking through Comparisons*. Albany.
Skocpol, T. and Somers, M. (1980) 'The uses of comparative history in macrosocial inquiry', *Comparative Studies in Society and History* 22: 174–97.

Tan, J. (2011) 'Competition between public and private revenues in Roman social and political history (200–49 B.C.)', unpublished PhD thesis, Columbia University.

Tanner, J. (2009) 'Ancient Greece, early China: Sino-Hellenic studies and comparative approaches to the classical world. A review article', *Journal of Hellenic Studies* 129: 89–109.

Teggart, F. (1939) *Rome and China: A Study of Correlations in Historical Events*. Berkeley.

Tilly, C. (1984) *Big Structures, Large Processes, Huge Comparisons*. New York.

Turchin, P. (2009) 'A theory for formation of large empires', *Journal of Global History* 4: 191–217.

Vasunia, P. (2011) 'The comparative study of empires', *Journal of Roman Studies* 101: 222–37.

Wickham, C. (1994) *Land and Power: Studies in Italian and European Social History, 400–1200*. London.

Zhao, D. (2015) *The Confucian-Legalist State: A New Theory of Chinese History*. New York.

Zhou, Y. (2000) Review of Shankman and Durrant (2000), *Chinese Literature: Essays, Articles, Reviews* 22: 175–7.

  (2010) *Festivals, Feasts, and Gender Relations in Ancient China and Greece*. Cambridge.

3 | On the Very Idea of (Philosophical?) Translation

ROBERT WARDY

You would be hard-pressed to rustle up a philosopher likely to utter the dismissive phrase, 'but that's just semantics!' 'Semantics' means the theory of meaning; and an impressive quantity of philosophical work of impressive quality has been devoted to semantics during the twentieth and twenty-first centuries. Works of philosophical semantics which deservedly enjoy the status of classics explore such questions as: Whence does linguistic meaning originate? How do meanings change? How do sub-sentential items combine syntactically to yield assertions, or ask questions, or issue commands? What role might a theory of truth play in the theory of meaning? What grasp must a person have on the semantics of some given language, in order to count as a competent speaker of it? The questions are of formidable complexity; their inter-relations are intricate and often quite opaque. The best answers on offer are brilliant, but, almost without exception, rather contentious. However, despite the remarkable creativity and intensity of the philosophy of language, philosophers more or less entirely neglect the topic of translation. One might object that *The Dictionary of Untranslatables: A Philosophical Lexicon*, just published in English translation and weighing in at a massive 1,344 pages, gives the lie to my accusation. In due course I shall return to this doorstop.

That neglect is *prima facie* surprising. One of the things I should like to establish is that the surprise should not subside: philosophical neglect of translation is an abiding enigma. Here is the game plan: there are going to be four bits. In the first bit, I shall sketch out how it is that plenty of non-philosophical folk – that is, just about everybody – are, on occasion, exercised by translational phenomena, whether rightly or wrongly. In the second bit, I shall contrast that non-philosophical attitude with the exiguous attention philosophy pays translation. In the third bit, I shall speculate about what some distinctively *philosophical* problems of translation might be. At last, in the fourth bit, I shall get down to business by exemplifying my hunches with some ancient Chinese and ancient Greek documents.

Here is the first bit: how it is that non-philosophical folk are exercised by translational phenomena. Monty Python have a sketch dating back to 1970 wherein the villain of the piece is a tourists' phrasebook which rather unhelpfully renders the Hungarian original of 'please direct me to the railway station' as 'please fondle my buttocks'. Is the sketch funny? Sophomores consider it hilarious. I don't know about that; but the sketch is rather poignant, at a subterranean level. How so? Lots of people think that much that is valuable is lost in translation; I am robustly sceptical. Just think about the translation of poetry: should this not be (virtually) impossible? But, as any modal logician will verify, actuality implies possibility. In fact, most Western poetry is 'translational'; to pick on only the most overwhelming, magisterial instances, the inter-lingual, inter-cultural, synthetic transpositions of Milton, Dante and Virgil. Homer alone is a radical beginning – and perhaps even that impression is the mere artefact of our ignorance of his forebears in the tradition of oral epic. However that might be, 'please direct me to the railway station' is dead easy: why, a machine could re-language the likes of that. The outrageous sketch confounds the expectation that *some* exercises in translation are a no-brainer.

And now for something not completely different. Regard the quixotic Italians. To this day it is very difficult indeed to catch an undubbed foreign film on an Italian screen. I vividly recollect an exultant celebration at a Mondadori bookshop to mark the publication of the first, partial translation of *Finnegans Wake* into Italian. As it happens, there is a lovely book, *Impossible Joyce: Finnegans Wakes*, about rendering Joyce's putatively untranslatable work into all manner of languages: so put this example alongside poetry for demonstration of the marvellously unproblematic potentialities of translation. One might still be left wondering whether it wouldn't be easier for those Dutch, Japanese and Korean Joyceans to learn English so as to revel in the *Wake* – if, that is, the *Wake* is written in English. Compare Jonathan Barnes' estimable 'translation' of Aristotle's *Posterior Analytics* (I refer to the brutal, unrevised edition): easy enough to read, so long as one is relying on the ancient Greek original.

In Hungary, too, there are few undubbed films. The countries where they never dub films tend to be those with the better quality of English: not just the Scandies and the Netherlands, but also Croatia and Slovenia. Linguistic/Hollywood imperialism? This question will come back later, in philosophical guise. At this juncture I should like to remark that it ain't necessarily so. *Pace* our memories of Laurence Olivier speechifying in a posh language which must be Ciceronian, the Roman Empire was polyglot; and, in the East, Greek was always dominant. Likewise, China under the Qing was a regime afloat on negotiations carried on in many languages (this was also the case under the sway of some earlier dynasties). These are not imperial rarities: compare and contrast the use of French at the court of Catherine the Great. As the saying goes, 'a language is a dialect with an army'. *Je suis né à Montréal, et je me souviens des guerres linguistiques.* Dialects, and languages of the subjugated, stubbornly survive.

Back to *The Dictionary of Untranslatables: A Philosophical Lexicon*, which I left heavily hanging. To quote from the blurb: 'this is an encyclopedic dictionary of close to 400 important philosophical, literary, and political terms and concepts that defy easy – or any – translation from one language and culture to another'. As I said, this is a recent English translation of the French original, *Vocabulaire européen des philosophies: dictionnaire des intraduisibles*, and 188 pages even bigger than its Anglophone descendant. The dictionary entries, which trumpet the difficulty, and indeed even the impossibility, of philosophical translation, have themselves been seamlessly translated from French into English. No one at Princeton University Press seems to have noticed that there is a paradox lurking in this *tour de force*. Despite the independent merits of individual entries, the dictionary hangs on an unreal and grossly naive idea of what translation really is.

From the unproblematically poetic to the prosaically problematic. An explanation – if not the only one – of my abject failure to make heads or tails of IKEA instructions would point the finger at their corporate translators. Automotive nomenclature is far less amusing than in the old days: who can forget the Daihatsu Charade? Nowadays car manufacturers employ software designed to OK candidate names in all languages spoken where the car is to be marketed: evidently the memo failed to reach Skoda, proud maker of the Yeti.

And from the prosaically problematic to a very strange idiom relevant to our modest theme of inarticulacy and our grand theme of ineffability: my last example of non-philosophical linguistic turbulence. Above the sinks of the gents' toilet in the Classics Faculty of the University of Cambridge one reads this scolding order: 'in the interests of health and safety, wash <u>your</u> hands thoroughly'. I trust that any native speaker of English can figure out what is more than faintly surrealistic about the emphatic underscoring of the word 'your'. I could unpack this (presumably unintentional) piece of bizarre humour: but its analytical translation would kill the joke.

Here is my second bit: a contrast between where we have just been and the exiguous attention philosophy does pay translation. Let us begin with a boring, but possibly significant reason for its near-invisibility: English imperialism of the linguistic variety. For example, the influential Finnish philosopher Edward Westermarck, von Wright's teacher, published almost exclusively in English; but von Wright himself, professor at Cambridge, was a Swedish-speaking Finn who disseminated his work multilingually (not to speak of his voluminous countryman Jaakko Hintikka): so one must generalise with considerable caution. It remains the case that anecdotal evidence for the emigration of non-Anglophone analytic philosophers into English is plausible enough; and analytical conversations are largely conducted in English. Things don't improve as one moves back in time: the ancient Greek for 'translation' is ἑρμηνεία, a fairly esoteric word with which philosophers do not conjure (the alternative μεταφράζω fares no better). Mention of translation in ancient Greek philosophy is a conspicuous rarity.

Now for the most prominent instance of modern philosophical translation: *the sentence 'snow is white' is true if, and only if, snow is white*. Non-semanticists may well rub their eyes: where's the translation? This is what one calls 'homophonic translation into a metalanguage'. Ordinary appearances to the contrary, more than one language is in play: the language for whose sentences we are attempting to define truth locally, and a 'richer' language in which we construct that definition; this latter has names for all the former's sentences, certain logical expressions, and a critical mass of set theory. Why bother with the recondite technicalities of such translation? There is a cluster of excellent reasons. A negative one is that if a language contains names for its own expressions as well as semantic terms, then it is vulnerable to the Liar paradox, because one might formulate sentences within it true only if false. Since Alfred Tarski presumed that the paradox is unacceptable and that we should hang onto 'the ordinary laws of logic', he introduced a schema for translation from object- into metalanguage to serve as a prophylactic against the Liar paradox and its vicious cousins (he had not anticipated paraconsistent logic, which has no truck with the ordinary, and is easily tolerant of paradox).[1] Although he was a genius, Tarski's way with the Liar wasn't his best idea. The totally *ad hoc* stratagem is to ensure that only the metalanguage has terms like 'true' and the ability to refer to sentences: that is what it means to say that the object-language is 'poorer'. There is a special case: the metalanguage itself contains the object-language, yielding homophonic translation. Tarski's solution to the Liar and the homophonic treatment are distinct themes; however, Donald Davidson's adaptation of Tarski brings homophony into the limelight.

Tarski was a fabulous philosopher of world-historical importance. Still and all, if the formulae *'snow is white' is true if, and only if, snow is white*

---

[1] Graham Priest is the doyen of paraconsistency.

and its ilk dominate the translational agenda of philosophical semanticists, one easily sees why they don't scratch where non-philosophers itch. At least partially to alleviate that isolation, let us make a brief foray into speculative history of logic. English-speakers that most of us are, some of us can quote the chapter and verse of Tarski's English article, 'The semantic conception of truth' (published 1944). But that most famous article has a more rigorous ancestor: 'Der Wahrheitsbegriff in den formalisierten Sprachen' (published in German, in 1935). And that is the offspring of a Polish original (published in 1933). The illustrations change. Here is the German: '*Es schneit*' *ist eine wahre Aussage dann und nur dann, wenn es schneit.* And here is the core of the Polish: 'pada śnieg'.[2] The Polish 'pada śnieg', 'snow is falling', is a subject-predicate proposition, as is the English 'snow is white'; however, the German 'es schneit', like its English counterpart 'it's snowing', is an impersonal construction, wherein 'es' and 'it' feature as *ersatz* subjects, dummy place-holders (the linguist's term for the 'it' here is 'expletive'). From the grammatico-logical point of view, there just is no subject whatsoever, expressed, tacit, repressed, whatever; and, in some quarters, the question of how to represent such expressions formally has proved to be something of a puzzler. So I am wondering whether the move from a subject-predicate proposition to an impersonal construction then back to a subject-predicate proposition is a mere coincidence.

Avoidance of impersonals is venerable – if hardly due to logical unease. The ancient Greek ὕει is to be classed with its English translation 'it's raining', the German 'es regnet' and so forth as another impersonal construction: and the ancient ὕει stands alone as perfectly grammatical. However, already in Homer we read ὗε δ' ἄρα Ζεὺς συνεχές, 'Zeus rained continuously' (*Iliad* 12.25–6), and other examples from different periods of Greek literature are abundant, including one from Aristotle (ὕει ὁ Ζεύς, *Physics* 198b18), who for sure did not think that it's Zeus who is really raining. So far as I am aware, the earliest recognition of these as a group, where one is to 'understand' Zeus as subject, as traditional grammarians say, is in Apollonius the Grumpy, who is dated to the second century CE (*On Pronouns* 24). This phenomenon is not a localised eccentricity of ancient Greek: it is a curious fact about most early Indo-European languages that they tend to transfer some range of impersonal into personal constructions.[3] I do not know why, and nor, I think, does anyone else: thus e.g. Ζεὺς ὕει. And there is plentiful evidence for the thesis that 'Zeus'

---

[2] To my delight, I find that 'Pada Snieg' is the *musical* translation of 'Jinglebells' into Polish.
[3] Cf. the Sanskrit *Várshati* ('it/Indra rains').

originally referred to the sky-god – which is to say, to the sky itself. Therefore Ζεύς ὕει is not to be construed as '[personified] Zeus rains', but rather 'the sky is raining' – much more in keeping with my down-to-earth sensibilities.[4]

However, if not a parochial oddity of ancient Greek, personalisation of the impersonal is nevertheless a peculiarity of Indo-European: the Chinese for 'it's raining' is *yü* 雨, full-stop. From talk of the weather to existential quantification. Ancient Chinese has a pair of impersonal existential verbs, *you* 有 and *wu* 無 ('there are . . .' and 'there are not . . .' respectively: the 'there' here is an 'expletive'). They are subjectless; and Chinese, in marked contrast to Indo-European, displays no tendency to personalise. Hence the irony of this nonsense on stilts emanating from Angus Graham:

> the existence of a thing is affirmed by saying that the cosmos has it as itself it has shape, colour, sound. Since in verbal sentences the nominalisation of a verb generally shifts the reference from action to agent, nominalised *yu* 'having' and *wu* 'not-having' become 'that which has (shape, colour and other characteristics)' and 'that which does not have', which however logically implies also being had by the cosmos or not being had.[5]

Wheeling in the cosmos itself to 'possess' whatever exists is on all fours with treating 'nothing' as a funny name for something with all the being knocked out of it, to paraphrase Gwil Owen.[6] You might protest: '*there is* (excuse the joke) a reasonably natural paraphrase (translation?) from Graham's version of ancient Chinese into English, as when we might say "this room has five hundred chairs in it;" and then expand outwards, until we reach "the universe has many galaxies in it; so the universe has all existing things in it!"' Is this a form of possession, in some abstract sense – as one might, for example, possess a shape? But this is a dead end; for the 'has . . . in it' construction does not *really* mean possession: you can *have* things without *possessing* them, and the Chinese 有 (*you*) does not really mean possession, either. All grist to my mill. Pseudo-ontology recapitulates blundering philology. Angus Graham was the most eminent philosophical champion of pre-Han thought as a wonderful complement to Western

---

[4] 'Kurt utters the words "es regnet" and under the right conditions we know that he has said that it is raining' (Davidson 1984a: 125).

[5] Graham 1989: 411. The irony is compounded by the fact that he does handle the meteorological case correctly (394).

[6] 'As impersonal existential verbs, *you* 有 and *wu* 無 have no subjects but there is often a noun or noun phrase in front providing a kind of pseudo-subject. In one common type, which is paralleled in Modern Chinese, it is a locative phrase that fulfills this role' (Pulleyblank 1996: 30). Maybe this grammatical possibility is related to Graham's fantasy.

philosophy, or sometimes a corrective for its distortions or even an antidote to its corruption; but in this instance he himself succumbed to the frankly weird Indo-European urge to personalise the impersonal. I freely concede that I am dirtying my philosophical hands with 'natural' languages ('natural' here is an unnatural coinage of the philosophers); but when doing semantics, that grubbiness comes with the territory.

Aficionados of so-called 'analytical' philosophy – or, to express myself non-tautologously, of philosophy – will have caught the allusion in my title. It refers, of course, to a justly celebrated paper by Donald Davidson. I should like to believe that Davidsonian semantics sort-of works, on little firmer ground than the approach's sheer elegance. To paraphrase Keats, there should be no dividing elegance and truth; but I fear the ugly truth is they can all too readily come apart. Be that as it may, the Quine-Davidson legacy of radical translation or interpretation supplies us with a third, rather paradoxical, potential reason for philosophical neglect of translation. Viewed – or better, heard – from the Davidsonian perspective, every last one of us is willy nilly a radical interpreter, modest or heroic, intrepid or reckless, talented or clumsy beyond all saying.[7] And I am talking about us deploying interpretative heuristics so as to cook up *homophonic* interpretations! Dragging in other languages would only muddy the water and blur the picture. So here is another paradox. Barbara Cassin & co. – 'continental' philosophers – are obsessed with the (imaginary) impossibility of translation. But, as I argued, they do not even address real translation. On the other side of the ideological fence, Quine's indeterminacy thesis inaugurated a most fruitful discussion of the meaning of meaning: but what is translation but semantic identity or at least close similarity in meaning? Thus a sharp philosophical concentration on meaning goes along with neglect of (real questions about) translation: odd.

Fourth potential reason why translation makes so fleeting an appearance in philosophy. Consider this bold generalisation:

when people talk, they lay lines on each other, do a lot of role-playing, sidestep, shilly-shally, and engage in other forms of vagueness and innuendo. We all do this, and we expect others to do it, yet at the same time we profess to long for plain speaking, for people to get to the point and say what they mean, simple as that. *Such hypocrisy is a human universal.* Even in the bluntest societies, people don't just

---

[7] 'The problem of interpretation is domestic as well as foreign: it surfaces for speakers of the same language in the form of the question, how can it be determined that the language is the same? ... All understanding of the speech of another involves radical interpretation' (Davidson 1984a: 125).

blurt out what they mean but cloak their intentions in various forms of politeness, evasion, and euphemism.[8]

This is what philosophers call 'bullshit'.[9] Here, *pace* Pinker, are some games people actually play, or abstain from: 'might you please be so kind as to pass me the grape shears?' (an utterance on my college's high table); 'que no dejéis de escribirnos, ¿eh?' (an utterance in my family circle); 'les patates, petit con!' (another utterance in my family circle). Shudder wholesomely at the perils of detecting linguistic universals – that is, at the superficial, cultural level, so far below Quine's radar trained on the thought-experiment of radical translation, bang-on in Davidson's sights targeting the real life of radical interpretation. You'll end up with egg on your face. Philosophers are a vain bunch, so they keep punctiliously clean.

Fifth and final potential reason, in the form of a presumptive diagnosis of philosophical purblindness to the intrinsic fascination of translation, red in tooth and claw: the tedious, and tediously fashionable, affectation of 'translation' from 'natural' languages into formalese, so as to regiment and assess arguments – or such is the pretence. Let us separate the talking sheep from the goats. Those of us philosophers with a persistent interest in translation, ranging from the moderate to the radical, have the gift of tongues, as do specialists in definite descriptions; things are not so rosy, when one passes to ultra-formalists pretending to rank-order 'natural' languages in terms of the degree of logicality domestic to them. In the past I have inveighed against the benighted notion that there might be 'logically deficient' natural languages. To recur very briefly to this theme.[10] There is always more than one way to skin a philosophical cat. In some 'natural' languages – sorry, 'languages' – one takes rather the long way round, but still gets there in the end. And what about quixotically cumbersome writing systems? Think on Chinese graphs. There is the repulsively 'mystical' vapouring of such as Ezra Pound, say. Then again, there is the relative potency of Chinese calligraphy (as opposed to its puny Western shadow) as a resource of cultural memory – if now a sadly fragmented one. No comparative advantages or disadvantages stand forth.

Here is the third bit: disjointed speculation about the identity of some distinctively *philosophical* problems of translation. What manner of 'translation'

---

[8] Pinker 2007: 374, emphasis added.
[9] Against which Frankfurt 2005 is the ferociously amusing safeguard.
[10] I ventilate my dissatisfaction with the conceit that formalistic regimentation might qualify as 'translation' in anything more than the thinnest sense of the term in the first part of Wardy 2000.

is the 'translation' of words into action? Sometimes I scramble to make sense of – or should that be 'translate'? – the semiotics of my baby: what might eventually compel him to speak? Mimetic deixis leads to articulate speech (wherein we cease to be 'infants', in the strict sense of the word), which trails off into various kinds of ineffability. Let us add Austinian performatives to the mix. Interestingly – to my mind, at least – doing things with some words, sometimes, can or must involve the performance of accompanying gestures, themselves freighted with significance. Consider a monarch's utterance of 'I dub thee . . .', as she simultaneously smashes the champagne bottle against the ship's hull; or a priest's utterance of 'I now pronounce you . . .', as she makes signs of benediction over the couple she is uniting. In this latter kind of case, as often as not the hieratic sign is itself a manner of enacted religious symbol; so I wonder whether, in this instance, embedded within the ritual context, articulate speech and symbolic action somehow combine semantically. At least some such semantic units are, I suppose, untranslatable – at any rate without viable recreation of a ceremonial contributor to replicate the meaningful but non-linguistic share of the original hybrid performative.

Another route to ineffability: I think I could instruct a real country bumpkin in the art of urban pedestrian traffic-dodging. I don't know whether I *could* articulate the instructions; I do know I wouldn't bother, and that anything articulate beyond the level of 'hey, watch out!' would most likely prove counterproductive. There's what you teach me through good talk, where there is no alternative to speech; an intermediate case is cooking recipes, as likely to inhibit as to assist; then there are a whole bunch of aptitudes one schools into skills without any rules at all. And I might well aspire to point at things whereof I cannot speak, or anyway point in their general direction, for all the world like some latter day Cratylus.[11]

Here is the fourth bit, consideration of some ancient Chinese and ancient Greek documents. In the European artistic tradition, pendant portraits of 'weeping' Heraclitus and 'laughing' Democritus had a lengthy vogue during which many sets were painted for the delectation of learned viewers. Why the epithets? As those in the know would appreciate, the misanthropic Heraclitus weeping in his lamentation over wretched human folly is

---

[11] I enthusiastically recommend the work of Adrian Moore in this area. Cratylus was an extremist disciple of Heraclitus who seems to have felt obliged to refrain from unconstrained speech, confining himself to what his finger might indicate. That the reasons for Cratylus' retreat into silent deixis in response to what he seems to have perceived as the (near) ineffability of things are cryptic is a fine irony.

counterpoised by Democritus' scornful reaction to human idiocy, perhaps arising from the association of the early Atomists with Pyrrhonian seekers after detached tranquillity on Timon's sardonic pattern.[12] Democritus has had a good innings;[13] but let us substitute a mysteriously smiling Daoist for the Western mocker, in order to tease out some implications of what these rearranged pendants do not, and perhaps cannot, say outright on behalf of their respective philosophical visions.

Why do I imagine that focusing our gaze on this particular pair of philosophers might be a profitable endeavour? I know where *not* to look, I think. Many times I have been solemnly assured by so-called, *soi-disant* 'comparativists' that Mencius and Aristotle were contemporaries – and then left to my own baffled devices to extract some edification from this synchronicity. It so happens that the pop singer Madonna and I are not merely rough contemporaries, but very nearly of the same age; yet one should not doubt that to compare Robert Wardy to Madonna would be a pretty pointless exercise. That is more or less how I feel, most of the time, about the presumption that Aristotle and Mencius might figure as valid philosophical comparanda – that is, such is my recalcitrant feeling, when the bald fact of synchronicity is meant to underpin the comparison on its own. Very occasionally I am softened by the thought that there might possibly be something to Karl Jaspers' axial age hypothesis, according to which the evolution of what its proponents regard as similar intellectual trends in China and the Mediterranean West, among other places, is no coincidence (although not the consequence of anything like bread-and-butter intercommunication). That axial enthusiasts of great scholarly calibre are especially keen on juxtaposing the intellectual ferment of ancient Greece (pre-Macedonian Empire) and Warring States China (pre-Qin Empire) gives me pause. But then I tend to harden up once more, as the unreconstituted Logical Positivist in me comes back to the surface: I remain unconvinced that the axial age hypothesis is either verifiable or falsifiable, and so dismiss the pious collocation of 'axial' luminaries as vacuous suggestiveness.

That is intended as a salutary lesson delivering the moral that, for all we are customarily told, there is no salient justification for Aristotle's and

---

[12] Timon was an acolyte of Pyrrho, the enigmatic fountainhead of what would become Pyrrhonian Scepticism. There are indubitable but murky connections between Atomists and proto-Sceptics in the early phases of their history, and Timon is notorious for the bitter satire of his *Silloi*; the tonality of these poems is reminiscent of Democritean laughter.

[13] An illustrious impersonation: in his *The Anatomy of Melancholy* Robert Burton tellingly denominates himself 'Democritus Junior' to signal to the reader his ambition of puncturing contemporary pretensions.

Mencius' occupying the same frame; so on what grounds more capable of withstanding inspection might we advantageously gather up Zhuangzi with Heraclitus? Both these daunting philosophers are associated with ineffability, in that they are said either to have doctrines of the ineffable, or to have ideas which in some strong sense of 'cannot' cannot be articulated, or both.[14] In confronting these iconoclasts, we rightly find ourselves receptive to the widespread collective impression that what, at the limit, we should take away from their supremely challenging assaults on commonplace ways of going on certainly cannot be enunciated or, perhaps, even so much as verbalised, on penalty of debasing or subverting their unutterable truths. Here, then, are our concluding questions: does ineffability come in something like different cultural flavours and, if so, to what effect? Are the rationales for obligatory silence we apprehend in Heraclitus and Zhuangzi altogether disjoint, or might we discern some overlapping reasons for their recourse to gesturing at the inexpressible?

In the cultivated popular imagination, Zhuangzi does much better out of unsayability than Heraclitus; for it is his fiercest critics who convict the Greek of embracing contradiction long before Graham Priest was a paraconsistent twinkle in anyone's eye, so that Heraclitus' driving language to or beyond the breaking-point is deemed the crippling effect of loony illogicality, as all signification is voided from his fake discourse. Some of Zhuangzi's fans, on the other hand, are besotted with what, in their bleary eyes, is the *mystical* ineffability of Daoism.[15] Now if there is a single thing one should like even less than common or garden-variety bullshit, it is the insidious higher waffle, anathema to any decent thinker. So if bound to choose, we might well plump for being kicked with Heraclitus over being stroked with Zhuangzi; or instead opt out to follow a much superior course, and delicately uncover terms adequate for the delineation of profound wordlessness.[16]

With dreary regularity students see fit to inform the supervisors of their essays that 'Heraclitus is a Presocratic philosopher, extant only in fragments.' Yes and no. Yes, Heraclitus survives only in scattered scraps. No,

---

[14] Within the scope of this chaper I can do no more than acknowledge, without coming to grips with, Chad Hansen's controversial, heterodox reading, on which Zhuangzi's Dao is *not* ineffable.

[15] Kukla 2004 canvasses the prospects for a logically reputable path from 'mystical' insight to ineffability; his level-headed conclusion is that they are not very bright.

[16] We should take to heart the parting words of '*Philologos*': 'to label something ineffable in an unqualified way is to shirk the job of making explicit the ways in which it *can* be talked about ... There may be something in the world which can't be talked about in any way, but if so we can only signalise the fact by leaving it unrecorded' (Alston 1956: 522).

there's no missing bit where Heraclitus expatiated on what he was meaning us to infer from such aphorisms as 'asses prefer garbage to gold' (fr.9) or 'the way up and down is one and the same' (fr.60) – or so I strongly maintain. Plainly enough, Heraclitus goes to some pains to indicate that he *explains* exactly nothing: 'nature loves to hide' (fr.123); 'the unclear attunement is superior to the clear one' (fr.54); and, magnificently, 'the lord whose oracle is in Delphi neither speaks out nor conceals, but gives a sign' (fr.93).[17] Nietzsche is an epigone floundering in his wake. Heraclitean philosophy comes in nothing but aphorisms; if the dots are assuredly to be connected, they won't be by Heraclitus: 'I went in search of myself' (fr.101).

Zhuangzi also does aphorism with a memorable vengeance, but in the *Inner Chapters* and elsewhere, more relaxed modes of exposition have pride of place: if the stories are gracefully lacunose, they do not frequently rise to Heraclitus' pitch of blatantly aggressive ellipticality.[18] His noetic texture is loose-weave, compared to the man with tears in his eyes; but again, it is into the Daoist's intentional gaps that we should be looking. 'A way (道) that illuminates does not guide (道), speech that argues does not have reach.'[19] Heraclitus and Zhuangzi are alike systematic in one respect: the deliberate courting of destabilising paradox. That the bright road where our footing is sure only leads us astray seems to suggest that we should throw ourselves into darkness – but how then not to stumble? That argumentative speech is ineffectual seems to suggest that the effort to reason things through is a waste of time – but how then to escape collapse into meaninglessness? If the *bian* (辯) which is argument is the (futile) apogee of distinction-marking pure and simple,[20] then the Daoist would seem to advocate a scrupulously carefree blank refusal to discriminate. How to sum up in words that advocacy of disengagement? 'Therefore division entails that there is what is undivided, argument, that there is what is unargued. "How so?" one asks. The sage cherishes it in his breast, while the vulgar argue over it for the sake of mutual display.

---

[17] ὁ ἄναξ οὗ τὸ μαντεῖόν ἐστι τὸ ἐν Δελφοῖς οὔτε λέγει οὔτε κρύπτει ἀλλὰ σημαίνει.

[18] E.g. the riposte to Hui Shi at the end of 'Going rambling without a destination' and the eloquent apologies for crooked timber in the second series of 'Worldly business among men' have the form of extensive parables; and Wang Ni's reply to Gaptooth amounts to a detailed relativistic catalogue ('The sorting which evens things out' 11). (Section numbers in the *Zhuangzi* and the *Daodejing* are given in accordance with J. Legge 1891.)

[19] 道昭而不道，言辯而不及 ('The sorting which evens things out' 10). All translations are my own, unless otherwise indicated.

[20] The graph for 辯 (*bian*) 'to argue' is cognate with that for the homophonous 辨 (*bian*) 'to discriminate'; the former is a specification of the latter, since to argue through or out is to distinguish between what is right/true and what is wrong/false.

Therefore it is said: "argument entails a failure to see".'[21] The progression of thought is very obscure. Does the first sentence say that division-*cum*-argument inevitably leaves behind an untreated remainder? If so, why should the rationalist enterprise be stymied: might the idea be that it nourishes illusory dreams of impossible finality? And how in any case does that sentence anchor the moralistic repudiation of vainglorious chatter? What is the *it* sages hug to themselves? 'The great argument is not expressed'[22] – which would disconcertingly seem to imply that, after all, there is some manner of *bian* (辯) accessible to the best of us which bypasses stultifying discrimination. How? Or is that a question unanswerable (in words)?

'Now what if there were to be speech about something, in ignorance of whether it is of a given kind or not? If what is of a kind and what is not are considered to be of a kind, then there is no means for distinguishing an other.'[23] One should be forgiven the initial suspicion that, absent basic knowledge of what we purport to be discussing, for all one can know at best we are at cross-purposes, at the likely worst, we are talking about nothing at all; unremarked referential slippage would frustrate speech even at its most simple. Accordingly, one might have thought that a disastrous confusion of sameness and difference of topic is surely the springing of a *reductio*.

But nothing of the kind:

(1) Speaking is not blowing breath: (2) but although in the speaker there is speech, what is said is never determined. (3) Is there really speech – or has there never been any? (4) If one regards speech as different from fledgelings' chirping, is there an argument for this view, or is there not? (5) By what is the Way obscured, giving rise to the authentic and the counterfeit? By what is speech obscured, giving rise to affirmation and denial? Wherever one goes, will the Way not be there? Wherever one is, will speech not be licit? (6) The Way is obscured by trivial completion, speech is obscured by florid splendour.[24]

---

[21] 故分也者，有不分也；辯也者，有不辯也。曰：何也？聖人懷之，眾人辯之以相示也。故曰：辯也者，有不見也。('The sorting which evens things out' 10).

[22] 大辯不言 ('The sorting which evens things out' 10). Ziporyn has 'great demonstration uses no words' (Ziporyn 2009: 16). Cf. this neat inversion: 'the knower does not speak, the speaker does not know' (知者不言，言者不知。) (*Daodejing* 56).

[23] 今且有言於此，不知其與是類乎？其與是不類乎？類與不類，相與為類，則與彼無以異矣。('The sorting which evens things out' 8).

[24] 夫言非吹也。言者有言，其所言者特未定也。果有言邪？其未嘗有言邪？其以為異於鷇音，亦有辯乎，其無辯乎？道惡乎隱而有真偽？言惡乎隱而有是非？道惡乎往而不存？言惡乎存而不可？道隱於小成，言隱於榮華。('The sorting which evens things out' 4).

This is one of the hardest passages of an inscrutable text: what could be the import of this vertiginous flight back and forth? (1) blandly reassures us that language is more than unmeaning sound; but (2) denies that its meaning is to be sought in fixity, of which there is none to be had. (3) is an interrogative pretence; for once we take Zhuangzi seriously as a questioner, it matters not how we answer, since our formulation, whether affirmative or negative, is itself already speech – whatever that might be worth. (4), however, teasingly undercuts any such assurance: for if the birds are speechless, that is not to say that their twittering conveys nothing, they do not blow their breath idly ('the sun rises', 'my nest is here') – only avian messages are innocent of pretentious aspirations to the would-be conclusive vindication of a *bian* (辯) busy with discriminations. Then (5) promises that, despite the prevalence of obfuscating appearances, the conditions for legitimate talk of what is real cannot *not* obtain; the sting in the tail is (6)'s warning that hyperbolic indulgence in rationalistic rhetoric clouds what should be our untroubled awareness that nothing can impede untrammelled expression of what could be worth saying – or, by the same token, retaining in one's breast.

A provocative companion piece:

Hui Shi asked Zhuangzi: 'can human beings really lack an essence?' Zhuangzi replied: 'yes'. Hui Shi: 'if they lack an essence, how are they to be called human beings?' Zhuangzi: 'since the Way has conferred the appearance and Heaven has conferred the shape, how should they not be designated human beings?' Hui Shi: 'but given that they are designated human beings, how might they lack an essence?' Zhuangzi: 'affirmation and denial are what I designate the human essence; what I mean by lacking it is that they do not inwardly injure their persons through liking and aversion, that they remain constant in spontaneity and do not add to life'.[25]

This might well be the pivotal episode, with regard to our project. Why does the proposition that we might countenance the existence of *x*'s bereft of their essence (*qing* 情)[26] not disintegrate into an incomprehensible contradiction in terms? Hui Shi, despite his standing as the paradox-monger par excellence, is stunned by Zhuangzi's rejection of *qing*. But it

---

[25] 惠子謂莊子曰：「人故無情乎？」莊子曰：「然。」惠子曰：「人而無情，何以謂之人？」莊子曰：「道與之貌，天與之形，惡得不謂之人？」惠子曰：「既謂之人，惡得無情？」莊子曰：「是非吾所謂情也。吾所謂無情者，言人之不以好惡內傷其身，常因自然而不益生也。」('The signs of fullness of power' 6).

[26] That otherwise, as in Xunzi and his followers, *qing* might be narrowly specified as the unschooled passions is no more than a red herring, since that association is itself premissed on identification of 'raw' human nature as essential. Therefore Watson's 'feelings' (Watson 2013: 40) is no good; Ziporyn's 'characteristic human inclinations' (Ziporyn 2009: 38) is better, but still wrongly underplays Zhuangzi's extremism.

is not tantamount to nihilism: or so Zhuangzi would seem to be hinting, with his proposal that the look of humanity suffices for being so designated. Needless to say, it is designed to exasperate: the expansion of Hui Shi's plaintive question is 'but how might their *mere* external appearance go proxy for whatever the *x*'s really are?' From where the Daoist sits, such doubts, in their assumption that one risks ignorantly mistaking the external and accidental for the internal and essential, could not be more badly misguided. And Zhuangzi's response could not be more richly ironic, although yet again it is extremely hard to decipher. My hesitant gloss: 'the *x*'s in question are *our* kind, which obstinately persists in hankering after illumination of depths when all the while they are already on a Way which cannot be lost. Were there an essential humanity to be found, it would reside in the footling, laborious scrabbling after such redundant "essences": human "kind" unnaturally sickens for natural kinds! The "inward" health worth nurture is to be found in shucking off deluded commitment to affirmation and denial which strive to delve down.'

Confucius advises Yan Hui: 'moreover, do you know that what squanders power is the very thing which produces knowledge? Power is squandered by reputation, knowledge is produced by competition. As for reputation, it is mutual conflict; as for knowledge, it is a competitive instrument. The pair are cruel instruments, and should not be employed in the perfection of conduct.'[27] Vigorously indignant anti-intellectualism in full flow from the Confucian sage pressed into the Daoist (non-)cause; the typical trickiness to give us pause lies in the seemingly casual 'do you *know* …': if I heed the worthy injunction and keep my hands off the instruments of cruelty, whence will spring my knowing confidence that by shunning knowledge I shall preserve power? Perhaps this simile gestures at the answer: 'the ultimate man's employment of the heart is like a mirror, neither leading nor escorting, responsive but not receptive, and therefore able to overcome things without suffering injury'.[28] Since the ultimate mind registers the analogue of mirrored images, it is not dully impervious; but the neutrality of reflection circumvents any calamitous temptation to divide and be conquered. The mind secure in its abandonment of knowledge is oblivious, perhaps first and foremost, of itself: 'to

---

[27] 且若亦知夫德之所蕩，而知之所為出乎哉？德蕩乎名，知出乎爭。名也者，相軋也；知也者，爭之器也。二者凶器，非所以盡行也。('Worldly business among men' 1).
[28] 至人之用心若鏡，不將不迎，應而不藏，故能勝物而不傷。('Responding to the emperors and kings' 6). Legge has 'thus he is able to deal successfully with all things, and injures none', but construing *shang* 傷 passively, with Watson, Graham and Ziporyn, is much more satisfactory.

match from the outset and never fail is the matching forgetful of itself'.[29] To dilate on such spectacular competence would bring no gain in understanding, and swiftly degenerate into empty mouthing.

Now look at the Greek pendant. At first blush, one might be disposed to fear that let alone furnishing us with a stock of suggestive material linked to ineffability, Heraclitus is quite the wrong choice: his pronounced stress on the omnipresence[30] and unity[31] of *logos*, from which the tenet that it is universally shared follows,[32] must militate forcibly against his exploitation as a source for comparison with Zhuangzi on what cannot be said – how should *logos* not always speak to us all? True, the *logos* is a communication vehicle than which no grander can be imagined: but the devil is that 'people are deceived in their recognition of obvious appearances',[33] their truth is (in)accessible. As will emerge, what is required for dissolution of that primal deception might well prove ineffable. Heraclitus is invested with the ruling tension of a saying (*logos*) which eludes saying (*legein*).[34]

'According to Heraclitus, the Sibyl in her utterance with maddened mouth of things mirthless, unadorned and unperfumed, reaches with her voice through a thousand years because of the god' (fr.92).[35] As in its relative fr.93, here too Heraclitus unmistakably appropriates Delphic prestige for the *logos*: but when we map his revolutionary philosophy onto the traditional religious configuration, where are we to locate Heraclitus himself? If the sign-giver is lord Apollo, the Sibyl functions as his intimidating, rebarbative mouthpiece, a channel, not an origin; and the implied imperative 'listening not to me, but to the *logos*' (fr.50) aligns the philosopher squarely with the mantic conduit, not the god. The speech of the prophetess is unperfumed, that is, not enveloped in the soothing myrrh of routine observance; and it is also soberly unprettified, cleansed of any semblance of the 'florid splendour' Zhuangzi decries. This much of the characterisation migrates smoothly enough from Sibyl to Heraclitus; but what are we to make of her insanity? The shock should not be dissipated with the thought that her verbiage's subrational wildness is camouflage for a super-rational

---

[29] 始乎適而未嘗不適者，忘適之適也。('Fathoming life' 13). [30] E.g. frs.1 and 50.
[31] E.g. frs.2, 89, 114 and 50. [32] E.g. frs.2, 89 and 114 again.
[33] ἐξηπάτηνται οἱ ἄνθρωποι πρὸς τὴν γνῶσιν τῶν φανερῶν (fr.56). [34] Fr.93 again.
[35] Σίβυλλα δὲ μαινομένῳ στόματι καθ' Ἡράκλειτον ἀγέλαστα καὶ ἀκαλλώπιστα καὶ ἀμύριστα φθεγγομένη χιλίων ἐτῶν ἐξικνεῖται τῇ φωνῇ διὰ τὸν θεόν. The extent of verbatim Heraclitus within this citation from Plutarch is contested. The majority of editors attribute only the words 'Σίβυλλα δὲ μαινομένῳ στόματι' and 'ἀγέλαστα' to Heraclitus; I think that the entire phrase 'ἀγέλαστα καὶ ἀκαλλώπιστα καὶ ἀμύριστα' is an original unit, and that the *implication* that Apollo communicates through his prophetess must have been present, regardless of the wording. Consult Kahn's discussion *ad loc*.

lulcidity, that it serves only as the debased medium for an exalted message temporarily infected with random noise we shall come to filter out. Her words are plumb crazy – as are (some of) Heraclitus'. Language behaving normally would be inadequate to their hermeneutic tasks.[36]

'As Heraclitus says, for god all things are fair, good and just; but men have presumed that some are just, others, unjust' (fr.102).[37] One complains: 'it is all very well for Heraclitus to (pretend to) say such things; yet if I cannot come to sit whence god sees, then, with the best will in the world, while I might biddably parrot "all things are <compatibly incompatible>", where "*compatibly incompatible*" is a placeholder for "just"–"unjust", etc., I shall simply have descended into crazy babble. Whatever some insouciant Daoist might allege, the matrix of human discourse is discrimination; and whatever Heraclitus might allege the *logos* capaciously embraces, *our logos* is generated by the choice of one opposite at the expense of another. Let there be divine discourse: the brute fact for us is that its inapprehensible meaning is, and must remain, indistinguishable from cacophony.'[38] Heraclitus remonstrates: 'one must know that war is common, justice, strife, and that all things occur in accordance with strife' (fr.80).[39] That harsh saying must be taken together with 'all things occur in accordance with this *logos*' (fr.1),[40] a conjunction which reveals the identity of *logos* with conflict. If *logos* necessarily has – or even *is* – structure, how might its constitutive organisation coexist with disruptive struggle? A model which has conflicting forces constrained within a pacifying container falls short of Heraclitus' maximalist anarchy; he posits a fundamental discord which penetrates all the way down. If there is no undisturbed residue, can the *logos* all the same transcend meaningless chaos? 'The push apart gathers together, and from things at variance comes the fairest harmony, and all things

---

[36] Hence I dissent from Kahn's preferred, deflationary reading: 'the contrast between the Sibyl's madness and her social prestige as spokesman for Apollo may have been part of Heraclitus' critique of current religious practices ... if one reflects upon the fact that people accept wisdom from raving lips, one is likely to judge them as mad as the Sibyl herself' (Kahn 1979: 126).

[37] ἅπερ καὶ Ἡράκλειτος λέγει, ὡς τῷ μὲν θεῷ καλὰ πάντα καὶ ἀγαθὰ καὶ δίκαια, ἄνθρωποι δὲ ἃ μὲν ἄδικα ὑπειλήφασιν ἃ δὲ δίκαια. Flat paraphrase, and so a good way to approach ineffability.

[38] Kahn tries to palliate the discomfort: 'it is not that the human distinctions cease to have validity – for the only validity they ever had was validity *for men*' (Kahn 1979: 184); and 'notice that there is still some *meaning* attached to the term "unjust" at the level of cosmic order, although here the term has no true application' (*ibid.*). This is unconvincing, since he has no substantive account of how cosmically inapplicable terms might at a lower 'level' gain parochial semantic purchase.

[39] εἰδέναι χρὴ τὸν πόλεμον ἐόντα ξυνὸν καὶ δίκην ἔριν καὶ γινόμενα πάντα κατ' ἔριν ...

[40] γινομένων γὰρ πάντων κατὰ τὸν λόγον τόνδε.

occur in accordance with strife' (fr.8).[41] Violent division – not to be assimilated to the discriminations we conceptualise, or which create our limited representations of the *logos* – effects combination. Or perhaps to divide *is* to combine: an article of faith beyond our comprehension? 'Graspings: wholes and not wholes, borne together and apart, consonant dissonant, from all things one and from one all things' (fr.10).[42] What might be snatched from this ringing summation whose disparate elements defy combination? If the saying which pointedly unsays itself cannot be grasped, then our concurrence, if forthcoming, will not take the form of expressed agreement.

Finally, look at the diptych's components together. 'The Way has never had boundaries, speech has never had norms – making an affirmation produces borders.'[43] In their primary, concrete significations, the graphs 封 (*feng*) and 畛 (*zhen*), which I have translated as 'boundaries' and 'borders', can mean 'dike' and 'path intersecting fields' (that is, flooded rice paddies). Therefore one might hazard the guess that this praise of infinity – the Way's untouchable and inviolate, speech's susceptible to betrayal through reductive exclusion – evokes the image of a continuous watery expanse unsullied by intrusive earthworks. In Chinese mythology, the legendary emperor Yu was responsible for the introduction of flood control, thereby creating the settled conditions permitting the inauguration of the Xia. So we might further guess that by painting this picture of primordial water, Zhuangzi is perhaps also summoning a prelapsarian vision (for him, equivalent to 'predivisarian') combining pre-dynastic political liberty with linguistic liberation from the tyranny of deadly knowledge given over to discriminations never amounting to authoritative norms. 'One who does not expect the unexpected will not find it out, since it is unsearchable and impassable' (fr.18).[44] Heraclitus is recommending a precariously balanced state of anticipation, trickily poised between opposed cognitive outlooks. His perplexing recommendation is motivated by the conviction that what we are after can indeed be got at, despite its impermeability to the analytical intelligence: it is accessibly '*aporon*', 'impassable', like the Homeric Ocean, like Zhuangzi's aqueous Way. But, on the other hand: 'one travelling every road could not go to find

---

[41] τὸ ἀντίξουν συμφέρον καὶ ἐκ τῶν διαφερόντων καλλίστην ἁρμονίαν καὶ πάντα κατ' ἔριν γίνεσθαι: an admixture of quotation (τὸ ἀντίξουν συμφέρον?) with paraphrase.

[42] συλλάψιες· ὅλα καὶ οὐχ ὅλα, συμφερόμενον διαφερόμενον, συνᾷδον διᾷδον, ἐκ πάντων ἓν καὶ ἐξ ἑνὸς πάντα.

[43] 夫道未始有封， 言未始有常， 為是而有畛也。 ('The sorting which evens things out' 10).

[44] ἐὰν μὴ ἔλπηται ἀνέλπιστον οὐκ ἐξευρήσει, ἀνεξερεύνητον ἐὸν καὶ ἄπορον.

out the soul's limits: so deep is the *logos* it has' (fr.45).⁴⁵ To the infinite world corresponds an inexhaustible self; or maybe they coincide in the *logos*. This powerful psychological turn is Heraclitus' alone.⁴⁶

'Without an other there is no self, without self there is no choosing.'⁴⁷ What is Zhuangzi economically *not* saying in this exemplary recapitulation of his withdrawal from distinctions? He skews the symmetry by replacing *wo* 我 ('self') with *qu* 取 ('choosing'). Erase the self – the sense of self – and, ultimately, no tenable ground for discrimination is to be discovered. Said unsupportable picking and choosing includes what is requisite for linguistic articulation saddled with the delusional burden of 'knowledge', so goodbye to wrongheaded speech itself. And what remains to say after that definitive dismissal? 'The god: day night winter summer war peace satiety hunger. But it alters, as when mixed with spices, it is named in accordance with idiosyncratic scent' (fr.67).⁴⁸ Heraclitus is a linguistic spendthrift, compared to Zhuangzi. We read two sentences. The first consists of a syntactic minimum, approximating to the default Chinese abstention from morphology: but of course in the ancient Greek, walking away from morphological resources is an ostentatious surrender of linguistic articulation. How to *say* that 'opposites are one', the motto emblazoned on Heraclitus' banner, and divinise this ineffable unity to boot? In his second sentence, the weeper cracks up, as he bursts into a flamboyantly conditionalised simile, calling on the full armoury of what can be explicitly said in ancient Greek, or 'named in accordance with' its inflectional syntax⁴⁹ – but no more than implying that you should not be fooled by the aftershave.⁵⁰ There is a full counterpoint with fr.92. The perfumed spices bathing god oppose the unperfumed ravings of the Sibyl; and since the Greek I have rendered 'in accordance with idiosyncratic scent' is an untranslatable pun also meaning 'in accordance with the pleasure of each', the opposition with her 'mirthless' pronouncements is reinforced.

---

⁴⁵ I accept Betegh's persuasive reconstruction: ψυχῆς πείρατα ἰὼν οὐκ ἂν ἐξεύροι ὁ πᾶσαν ἐπιπορευόμενος ὁδόν· οὕτω βαθὺν λόγον ἔχει.

⁴⁶ 'I believe that Diels was right in locating the central insight of Heraclitus in this identity of structure between the inner, personal world of the psyche and the larger natural order of the universe' (Kahn 1979: 21).

⁴⁷ 非彼無我，非我無所取。('The sorting which evens things out' 3).

⁴⁸ ὁ θεὸς ἡμέρη εὐφρόνη, χειμὼν θέρος, πόλεμος εἰρήνη, κόρος λιμός. ἀλλοιοῦται δὲ ὅκωσπερ ὁκόταν συμμιγῇ θυώμασιν ὀνομάζεται καθ' ἡδονὴν ἑκάστου.

⁴⁹ 'There is thus a sharp formal contrast between the two sentences: the first consists of nine nouns in the nominative, with no syntax, simply a list of names; the second sentence is all syntax, with three finite verb clauses but no subject noun' (Kahn 1979: 277).

⁵⁰ 'If all things were to become smoke, our nostrils could distinguish them' (fr.7: εἰ πάντα τὰ ὄντα καπνὸς γένοιτο, ῥῖνες ἂν διαγνοῖεν). But as it is, odours deceptively mask what they imbue.

Introduce the august Heraclitean god to Zhuangzi's risible, chaotic victim:

The Emperor of the South Sea was Fast, the Emperor of the North Sea was Furious, the Emperor of the centre was Hun-tun. Fast and Furious met from time to time in the land of Hun-tun, who treated them very generously. Fast and Furious were discussing how to repay Hun-tun's bounty. 'All men have seven holes through which they look, listen, eat, breathe; he alone doesn't have any. Let's try boring them.' Every day they bored one hole, and on the seventh day Hun-tun died.[51]

Did Hun-tun once blissfully repose in homogeneous, sweet oblivion, solipsistically unaware of all it incorporated? Its perforation enables both perception and understanding, but only at the cost of subjecting Hun-tun to the mortality of human (*ren* 人) input-output. How should we gauge the tone of this parable's oblique narration of the decline from undifferentiated inexpressivity: ruefully bleak? But also laughing: if Heraclitus' relatively dignified sense modality is olfactory, samplings of spice consumed in a ritual flame, Zhuangzi offers a dumpling to scoff.[52]

'Beginningless said: "the Way cannot be heard: whatever is heard, that is not the Way; the Way cannot be seen: whatever is seen, that is not the Way; the Way cannot be expressed: whatever is expressed, that is not the Way. Do we know that the shaper of shapes is unshaped? The Way does not fit a name".'[53] Perhaps reliant on the principle that properly originative causes themselves bear no trace of their effects, Zhuangzi intransigently insists that the Way as ground for names must evade linguistic capture.[54] Is that the last word? 'The wise is one alone, unwilling and willing to be spoken of

---

[51] 'Responding to the emperors and kings' 7, in Graham's frisky translation (Graham 1981: 98). Legge, Watson and Ziporyn all have 'Chaos' for 'Hun-tun'; I suppose Graham transliterates the name because 'Hun-tun is the primal blob which first divided into Heaven and Earth and then differentiated as the myriad things. In Chinese cosmology the primordial is not a chaos reduced to order by imposed law, it is a blend of everything rolled up together' (98–9). This is to take an overly specific view of the semantics of 'chaos'.

[52] 'Hun-tun' = 'wun-tun'. Of course I do not ascribe an archaic pedigree to the dumpling, but beg your indulgence of a helpfully amusing anachronism.

[53] 無始曰：「道不可聞，聞而非也；道不可見，見而非也；道不可言，言而非也。知形形之不形乎？道不當名。」('Knowledge roams north' 7).

[54] 'We cannot name the undifferentiated, since names all serve to distinguish, and even to call it "Way" reduces it to the path which it reveals to us. However, since that path is what one seeks in it, the "Way" is the most apposite makeshift term for it' (Graham 1981: 21). One conjectures that here might be an opportunity for the substitution of Heraclitus by Parmenides as Zhuangzi's Greek pendant; for if the Eleatics' global embarrassment is how to square a discursive, structured presentation with their allegiance to unqualified unity, Parmenides nevertheless chastises the original sin of *naming* two cosmic forms in binary opposition, when to designate even one would already have been a fatal error (Parmenides, fr.8 lines 53–4: see Coxon's commentary on these much-disputed lines).

by the name of Zeus' (fr.32).[55] If Zhuangzi, at least in some moods, adamantly prohibits speech of the Way, Heraclitus is tolerant of a murky accommodation with language – but one which flaunts its wayward fragility with contradictory flourishes. 'Everyone knows the use in the useful, but no one knows the use in the useless.'[56] Might the Heraclitean asses in their preference for trash over gold know that? For both Zhuangzi and Heraclitus, our sovereign, self-imposed challenge is the difficulty of recovering the easily apparent – not fabricated, misleading appearances, but rather what is staring us in the stupidly knowing, unseeing face.[57] Some large measure of the overweening intellectual arrogance polluting our minds stems precisely from the over-readiness first to brush aside the apparent as superficial, and then to condemn it as specious. Language released to hunt wisdom is the self-defeating tool or weapon inimical to our recuperation. Casting off any vestige of recognisable linguistic discipline or propriety, Heraclitus and Zhuangzi, in their expressive resourcefulness and occasional savagery, courageously venture to repair the damage by vandalising language. That will have to do as a final reflection – not the last word.[58]

Bibliography

Alston, W. P. (1956) 'Ineffability', *Philosophical Review* 65: 506–22.
Barnes, J. (ed. and trans.) (1976 – unrevised 1st edn) *Aristotle: Posterior Analytics.* Oxford.
Betegh, G. (2009) 'The limits of the soul: Heraclitus B45 DK. Its text and interpretation', in *Nuevos Ensayos sobre Heráclito*, ed. E. Hülsz. Mexico City: 391–414.
Burton, R. (ed. H. Jackson) (1932) *The Anatomy of Melancholy: What It Is, with All the Kinds, Causes, Symptomes, Prognostickes & Severall Cures of It.* New York.
Cassin, B. (ed.) (2004) *Vocabulaire européen des philosophies: dictionnaire des intraduisibles.* Paris. English trans. eds. E. Apter, J. Lezra and M. Wood) (2014) *The Dictionary of Untranslatables: A Philosophical Lexicon.* Princeton.
Coxon, A. H. (1986) *The Fragments of Parmenides.* Assen.

---

[55] ἓν τὸ σοφὸν μοῦνον λέγεσθαι οὐκ ἐθέλει καὶ ἐθέλει Ζηνὸς ὄνομα.
[56] 人皆知有用之用，而莫知無用之用也。('Worldly business among men' 9).
[57] Cf. 'what I say is very easy to comprehend and to put into practice; but no one in the world is able to do either'. 吾言甚易知，甚易行。天下莫能知，莫能行。(*Daodejing* 70).
[58] With my warm thanks to James Clackson, Nick Denyer and especially Tim Crane for their kind assistance with this tantalising material. Previous versions of this chapter were delivered at the Central European University, Budapest, and as the inaugural Berg Gruen lecture for the philosophy department at UCLA: I also thank these generous audiences for their reactions.

Davidson, D. (1984a) 'Radical interpretation', in *Inquiries into Truth & Interpretation*. Oxford.
  (1984b) 'On the very idea of a conceptual scheme', in *Inquiries into Truth & Interpretation*. Oxford.
Frankfurt, H. G. (2005) *On Bullshit*. Princeton.
Graham, A. C. (1981) *Chuang-tzu: The Inner Chapters*. London; reprint Indianapolis (2001).
  (1989) *Disputers of the Tao*. La Salle, IL.
Hansen, C. (1992) *A Daoist Theory of Chinese Thought: A Philosophical Interpretation*. Oxford.
Kahn, C. H. (1979) *The Art and Thought of Heraclitus: An Edition of the Fragments with Translation and Commentary*. Cambridge.
Kukla, A. (2004) *Ineffability and Philosophy*. Oxford.
Legge, J. (1891) *The Sacred Books of the East*, vol. XXXIX. Oxford.
Moore, A. W. (1997) *Points of View*. Oxford.
O'Neill, P. (2013) *Impossible Joyce: Finnegans Wakes*. Toronto.
Pinker, S. (2007) *The Stuff of Thought: Language as a Window into Human Nature*. New York.
Priest, G. (1995) *Beyond the Limits of Thought*. Cambridge.
Pulleyblank, E. G. (1996) *Outline of Classical Chinese Grammar*. Vancouver.
Tarski, A. (1933) 'Pojęcie prawdy w językach nauk dedukcyjnych', Towarzystwo Naukowe Warszawskie.
  (1935) 'Der Wahrheitsbegriff in den formalisierten Sprachen', *Studia Philosophica* 1: 261–405.
  (1944) 'The semantic conception of truth', *Philosophy and Phenomenological Research* 4: 341–76.
Wardy, R. (2000) *Aristotle in China: Language, Categories and Translation*. Cambridge.
Watson, B. (2013) *The Complete Works of Zhuangzi*. New York.
Ziporyn, B. (2009) *Zhuangzi: The Essential Writings, with Selections from Traditional Commentaries*. Indianapolis.

PART II

Philosophy and Religion

4 | Freedom in Parts of the *Zhuangzi* and Epictetus

R. A. H. KING

Preliminaries

The *Zhuangzi* is widely associated with freedom; and the Stoics, or at least some of them, were responsible for connecting freedom with the will. The core of the present comparison lies in the idea that the Stoics require obedience to Nature, Zeus, God or Law, and the *Zhuangzi* to Tian or Dao. The question then arises: what freedom is left in such a context? The answer to be argued for here is: living without impediment. This formulation would fit the picture of Cook Ding (*Yangshengzhu* 2), and would fit the vocabulary used of freedom by Epictetus. In Stoicism, this lack of impediment is associated with reason, in the *Zhuangzi* with practices which align one with Tian or Dao. Thus freedom here, I will argue, is a freedom for something, namely, what cannot be avoided. Yet this, despite being unavoidable, allows human life to flourish.

Coin common to Greco-Roman thinkers and the early Chinese might include a cosmos full of powers that can enslave or subordinate you, and social systems which take hierarchy as the norm, indeed the standard of order. Where there is political freedom, it contrasts with slavery, and so is hierarchical. The world is full of powers (*daimones, theoi, shen, gui*), good and bad, which can influence you, and even command you to do things. Now, here is not the place to compare the spirits of East and West,[1] but this is relevant to the question of freedom, insofar as freedom is conceived of as something you are granted or earn within a hierarchy of powers. The problem of freedom, generally speaking, is not the straitjacket of determinism of the materialists, but of the elbow room[2] humans have in the cosmic pecking order. The Stoic view that man is constructed free stands out in that Zeus uses his wisdom to allow someone naturally subordinate

---

My thanks are due to the organisers of the meeting where this paper was presented, Zhao Jingyi and Dong Qiaosheng, and above all to Geoffrey Lloyd for inspiration and support in the comparative entreprise over the years. An earlier version of this chapter was presented at the Forum für Asiatische Philosophie, Vienna. David Machek also commented on an earlier version.

[1] For China, see Sterckx 2002, for the Greeks Burkert 1987, for the Romans Rüpke 2007.
[2] Cf. the title of Dennett 1984. He is of course concerned exclusively with the problems of determinism.

responsibility for how he lives. In part this answers the Greek fear that we humans, after all, are nothing at all.[3] In the *Zhuangzi* the destruction of self enables one to live with a degree of freedom, despite the despotic nature of princes and of 'the maker of things' (*zaowuzhe*, we return to this notion below – not to be confused with a creator God or even a divine Demiurge). The contrast is between the rationality which Stoics thought makes one free, and spontaneity, which means following the course of events. In both cases, I hope to show that the upshot is an unhindered life.

There are of course reasons for resisting such a comparison. It is perhaps bold to compare any Greco-Roman authors on freedom with Chinese material. For one may argue that the Chinese have neither the political framework (assemblies, a sharp distinction between slave and free) nor the conceptual framework (causality).[4] However, debate did happen in early China, even without assemblies; and there is a keen perception that different ways of living constrain one in different ways. And being constrained can be felt to be bad, even without the thought that causes constrain. More specific to the present project is the objection that the Stoics are dogmatists, whereas the *Zhuangzi* is a sceptical text, especially the second chapter, *Qiwulun*.[5] This may seem to be a convenient way of placing the *Zhuangzi* in the context of Hellenistic philosophy; but it is not without problems, above all because it is not to be expected that the *Zhuangzi* follows a sceptical line rigorously. This lack of rigour may of course be due to the composite nature of the *Zhuangzi*. Another important problem concerns rationalism: the Stoics think that we are our reason or thought; and it is arguable that the *Zhuangzi* does not mention reason at all; how *bian*, debate, and *lun*, ordering, relate to views of rationality would have to be decided. The *Zhuangzi* is, of course, critical of *bian*, debating, but has a more positive view of *lun* (the second chapter, already mentioned, is entitled 'the ordering, *lun*, which levels things out', *Qiwulun*; *lun* may also mean 'discourse'). When we turn to the Stoics, much work has gone into a generalised picture of what 'the Stoics' thought. But Stoicism has a lively history, some five hundred years of debate both within the school and outside it. The plurality of traditions is something Geoffrey Lloyd has laid great emphasis on.[6] Hence the decision to pick on one Stoic author. Michael Frede argues in his posthumously published Sather lectures[7] that Epictetus was responsible for the introduction of the concept of a free will. That is one reason for picking Epictetus, even while withholding assent to Frede's major claim. The *Zhuangzi*

---

[3] Cf. Plotinus 6.8.1.26–7.
[4] See Raaflaub 1996; Hankinson 2001 on these aspects of Greco-Roman thought.
[5] Cf. the essays collected in Kjellberg and Ivanhoe 1996.
[6] For example in Lloyd 2005: ch. 1, 'The plurality of philosophical traditions'. [7] Frede 2011.

itself presents a wide variety of approaches, and I have restricted myself largely to the *Inner Chapters*, in fact mainly to a single story.

Modern concerns with freedom are based on the unforsakeable[8] value of responsibility, freedom within the causal ordering of the world, political freedom, the value of the autonomous development of personality, the value of artistic expression. One line of inquiry concerns the role of freedom vis-à-vis the causal ordering of the world. At least the first three of these topics have their root in the ancient Greco-Roman debate. We will not be concerned with the question of freedom and causality, despite its prevalence in the Stoics, since there is little concern for causality in the *Zhuangzi*. The modern debate about the Stoics has indeed tended to concentrate on causality.[9] To look for similarities with Chinese thought it is perhaps more useful to consider the shape of a life as a whole,[10] and what determines this shape. Here one would think of *zhi* 志, 'will', 'aspiration' and *prohairesis* 'choice'. Michael Frede himself gives, not a justification of the concept of the 'will', as he translates *prohairesis*, and hence of the actions motivated by it, but an explanation in terms of the Stoic concept of god in his chapter 'The emergence of a notion of free will in Stoicism'.[11]

The freedom of the will is construed by analogy with the political concept of freedom.[12] But how separate are these conceptions? Are there really two independent ideas of freedom? If we are not, as a matter of fact, free, then political freedom threatens to be an empty shell. One Stoic paradox is that 'Only the wise man is free, everyone else is a slave.' Michael Frede says that, obviously, they do not mean that we are all slaves in the legal or political sense, just as they do not mean that only the wise person is king in the political sense, when they say that only the wise person is a ruler.[13] But we see in Epictetus that political and ethical freedom are closely linked: just that political freedom is not really freedom.

The *Zhuangzi*

There is no word in the *Zhuangzi* which is usually translated 'free'; even if there were, it would require interpretation. As things are, there is, on the one

---

[8] The term is David Wiggins' (in his lectures on ethics, 2006).   [9] See above all Bobzien 1998.
[10] Cf. Annas 1993: 28–9 for a take on Greco-Roman ethics as individuals reflecting on the whole of a life.
[11] Frede 2011: ch. 5. This is relevant to the question of naturalism in ancient ethics: what is the role of nature in ethical talk? Not of giving immediate justification to actions, but of providing background that deepens understanding. See Gill 2005; he is close to Annas 1993 on this question.
[12] Frede 2011: 9.   [13] Frede 2011: 66.

hand, a series of words which have to do with unhindered movement or action. And on the other hand there is the binding of duty. While the *Zhuangzi* on several occasions opposes Zhong Ni ('Confucius'),[14] this does not mean that all forms of obligation are void. Some readers assume that because the *Zhuangzi* is critical of the 'morality' of the Ru, that is the experts on rites, the lineage which Confucius aligned himself with, and which gave his followers their name, it is not concerned with the norms that should govern life.[15] But this is a very narrow view of what falls under morality; much of the *Zhuangzi* discusses how to organise our lives and how to regulate the polity.[16] The *Zhuangzi* competes with the Ru, so they are playing the same game. What is at issue is the nature and source of the obligations we are under.

Many readers of the *Zhuangzi* see freedom as central to the work. For example, the translator Burton Watson writes, 'The central theme of the *Chuang Tz'u* [*Zhuangzi*] may be summed up in a single word: freedom.'[17] Watson's basic idea seems to be that one is free, in a negative sense, namely from conventions, and then from all ills, by a change in attitude towards them: they are ills, only because one recognises them as such. Apparently, this is an achievement in cognition, a change in the way one sees things. The historian of Chinese philosophy Fung Yu-lan, in Dirk Bodde's translation, talks about 'absolute freedom'.[18] Referring to the story about Liezi in the *Xiaoyaoyou* chapter, 'Wandering without a destination' which we will come to in a moment, Fung contrasts the dependency of Liezi with an absolute freedom which does not consist in depending on something: this seems to be a negative sense of freedom, namely as freedom from dependence. And finally, the most influential reader of *Zhuangzi* in recent times, Angus Graham, devoted a section of his Introduction to his translation of the Inner Chapters to 'Spontaneity'.[19] Here are six points he makes there:

1. As a common insight to 'Daoists': 'while all other things move spontaneously on the course proper to them, man has stunted and maimed his spontaneous aptitude by the habit of distinguishing alternatives, the right and the wrong, benefit and harm, self and others, and reasoning in order to judge between them'.

---

[14] According to *Shi ji* (47, p. 1905) this is his style (*zi*); his name (*ming*) is Qiu, because his mother prayed to the Mountain Qiu. *Fu zi*, 'this man', is a stronger form of *zi* (in *Lun Yu* only Confucius is called this, in the *Zuo Zhuan* and *Mengzi* others are also so designated). In the present story, Confucius is called 'Fuzi' by Yan Hui, as his pupil, whereas the narrator uses 'Zhong Ni'.
[15] E.g., Kupperman 1999: 83; Moeller (who regards Zhuangzi as a 'Daoist') 2004: 116.
[16] See for example the 'constitution' at the start of the *Tianxia* chapter, also the chapters *Tiandi*, *Tiandao* and *Tianyun*.
[17] Watson 1968: 3–4.   [18] Fung 1952: 243.
[19] Graham 1981: 6–8. I have converted Graham's Romanisation to pinyin.

2. The knack stories show craftsmen spreading 'attention over the whole situation, let its focus roam freely, forget themselves in their total absorption in the object, and then the trained hand reacts spontaneously with a confidence and precision impossible to anyone who is applying rules and thinking out moves'.

3. 'In responding immediately and with unsullied clarity of vision one hits in any particular situation on that single course which fits no rules but is the inevitable one' (bu de yi 不得已). This course is the Way (dao 道).

4. The spontaneous aptitude Graham identifies with *de* 德, a 'Power', or 'Virtue' as in 'the virtue of cyanide is to poison', rather than in 'Virtue is its own reward.' Like the Way this belongs to all things, and includes not only the full potentialities of the sage.

5. *De* is trained by 'cultivating the spontaneous energies', which are conceived of physiologically: everything is activated by *qi* 'breath', 'energy', 'a fluid, in its pure state is the breath which vitalises us'. The only technique for this 'education' named in the *Zhuangzi*, and that casually, is 'controlled breathing'.

6. Our 'responses then spring directly from the energies inside us. For Zhuangzi this is an immense liberation, a launching out of the confines of self into a realm without limits. A word which regularly quickens the rhythm of his writing is *yu*, [*you*] roam, travel.'

There are many questions the philosophical reader can pose at this point: How important is explanation in this view of the *Zhuangzi*? Does spontaneity require or preclude causal explanation? What kind of inevitability is at stake? There is a tension about the 'liberation' Graham speaks of; on the one hand, our actions come from within us; on the other, we are freed from the confines of self.[20]

Graham cites two texts in which *you*, which he translates 'roam, travel' is crucial: the opening story of *Xiaoyaoyou*, already referred to above as cited by Fung Yu-lan, which ends with the man who 'rides a true course between heaven and earth, with the six energies as his chariot to travel into the infinite, is there anything he depends on?'[21]

Secondly,[22] there is a story of a diplomat being sent on a mission, and it is this text I wish to examine in detail. In fact the first story is also to be placed in the context of service. For the 'traveller to the infinite' is contrasted with

---

[20] Cf. Graham 1983/2003: 171.

[21] Graham 44. The *Zhuangzi* is cited by reference to Guo Qingfan's edition (1961), and Graham's translation (1981), the latter for comparison with the versions I offer here.

[22] Machek 2015: ch. 2. Freedom as doing necessary things, interprets the notion of freedom using above all the story of Cook Ding (*Yangshengzhu* 2), comparing this with the three most important imperial Roman Stoics.

officials who do well in office and run their district to the satisfaction of their prince. This earns them the contempt of Song Xing, but he was unable to escape *shi* (世 generations, glossed as *shi* 事 affairs), and Liezi, another second-rate worthy, travelled on the wind, but depended on (*dai*) the wind. The traveller into the infinite (*wuqiong*), on the other hand, has three negative attributes: 'The utmost man is selfless, the daemonic man takes no credit for his deeds, the sage is nameless.'[23]

'Spontaneity' translates no one term in the *Zhuangzi*. If a single word here is relevant it is *you* 遊 'wander, travel'. Of course, spontaneity is not simply freedom: there is blue water between the two notions which has to be bridged. If one looks at Graham's other writings on the *Zhuangzi*, light is thrown on his view of spontaneity; however, this light makes it more problematic to link freedom and spontaneity.[24] For what Graham means by spontaneity is not the activity of a libertarian agent, who moves without being externally moved, but reactive spontaneity, as one could call it: the reactions one has immediately, without the mediation of reflection, to a whole situation or the decisive parts of it. The reason that this makes a connection between freedom and spontaneity problematic is that such a reaction may be thought to be caused by the givens. Thus we are being moved by the situation; and it is not up to us (*eph' hēmin*, to use an Aristotelian and Stoic term) to act thus or otherwise.[25] The way we act may well be determined by what we are, or the kind of human we are: 'a spontaneous reaction has a merely causal connection with the perception which it follows'.[26] Graham explicitly uses, without further explanation, the language of causation in his exposition of the spontaneity in the *Zhuangzi*. What he does not do is discuss the kinds of causes and how they relate to inevitability or 'necessity'. This is a large topic, which I can do no more than gesture towards here. Above all, one would need to discuss the way causes make things necessary, and how, if at all, the good (ends, purposes) makes things inevitable.

However, one way freedom and spontaneity can be connected is precisely through reason. Graham denies that this is possible, since all that he sees in reason is 'refining and systematising imperatives and deducing them from one another'.[27] Spontaneity is taken to be a mark of reason, by Kant for example. This is fundamentally because reason is active, whereas perception is receptive. Yet clearly it is risky to apply this notion to the *Zhuangzi*, insofar as the *Zhuangzi* does not have a

---

[23] Graham 44–5; Guo 17. For use of Graham's views on freedom, see Kupperman 1999: 84.
[24] Graham 1985, and the summary version of this in Graham 1983/2003. [25] See Frede 2007.
[26] Graham 1983/2003: 166. [27] Graham 1983/2003: 174.

concept of reason, and does not think that spontaneity attaches to thought and hence to action, but to humans following the Way.

If we stay at a fairly loose level of interpretation, 'freedom' is a common theme in the work. There are other stories, for example, which have 'release' (解 *jie*) (*Dazongshi* 5) as a major motif, the story of five men who become friends since they all recognise that life and death, persisting and ceasing to exist are one body. One of the men, Zi Yu, falls ill, but he is quite content with his lot. He notes that the 'maker of things' has made him into the disfigured human he now is: 'be content with the time and settled on the course, and sadness and joy cannot find a way in. This is what was of old called "being loosed from the bonds"; and whoever cannot loose himself, other things bind still tighter. And it is no new thing after all that creatures do not prevail against Heaven. What would be the point of hating it?' (trans. Graham). Another of the friends then falls ill, Zi Lai. He compares the process of disintegration to a sword-smith making swords: the metal does not complain whatever it is made into, and so he will not object whatever he is made into. This story speaks of 'a maker of things' (*zaowuzhe*). While the identity of the maker is difficult to establish (a thing, a person, a process), it seems to be responsible for the changes, including living and dying, that things undergo. And at least in this story, there are commands making things do as they should (*wei ming zhi cong* 唯命之從).

Let us now turn to the main story I wish to focus on: *Renjianshi* 'Service among humans' 1. Yan Hui asks Zhong Ni leave to travel to the state of Wei (衛) to improve the circumstances which have been created by the Lord there. So many humans have been killed by him that the whole country is full of corpses. Angus Graham's take on the whole is as follows:

For Yan Hui to go to the King full of good intentions and well-thought-out plans will do harm instead of good. He must first train the motions in himself which can spontaneously move another in the direction of the Way. He must trust to the *qi* (translated 'energies'), the breath and other energising fluids which alternate between activity as the Yang and passivity as the Yin (as in breathing out and in), training them with the meditative technique including controlled breathing which is mentioned elsewhere ... When the purified fluid has become perfectly tenuous the heart will be emptied of conceptual knowledge, the channels of the senses will be cleared and he will simply perceive and respond. Then the self dissolves, energies strange to him and higher than his own (the 'daemonic') enter from outside, the agent of the actions is no longer the man but heaven working through him, yet paradoxically (and it is in hitting on this paradox that Hui convinces Confucius that he understands) in discovering a deeper self he becomes for the first time truly the agent. He no longer has deliberate goals, the 'about to be' at the centre of him belongs to the transforming processes of heaven and earth.[28]

This is a more explicit account of what is necessary for Yan Hui to be able to take on the task of minister or adviser. The point is the effect of his involvement, and how this will be best achieved: Graham's formulation is remarkable – 'spontaneously move another in the Direction of the Way' – for it poses the question of the nature of the connection between Yan Hui's service and the *resulting* order. For action to be effective, one might think that the actions must have effects. And the result is not spontaneous, strictly speaking, but a response to the action. Yet this is to conceive of Yan Hui's service as a course of action, comprising cause and effect.

Zhong Ni listens to various suggestions as to how Yan Hui hopes to achieve his purpose, forms of behaviour that are ritually secured and sanctioned, and dismisses them all: either Yan Hui will be killed or he will not change (*hua*) the Lord.

Text 1
The Way does not desire variety: if there is variety, then there is plurality, if there is plurality, there is annoyance, if there is annoyance there is worry, if there is worry there is no deliverance. The perfect humans of old first of all established themselves, and then established others. If the establishment in yourself is not yet fixed, what leisure have you for the conduct of tyrants? And do you know that what disperses *de* is what brings forth knowledge? *De* is dispersed by fame, knowledge issues from competition. The famous conflict with one another. Those with knowledge are the instruments of competition. How can inauspicious tools be the means of perfecting conduct? (Guo 135, Graham 66)

There is much to unpack here. For present purposes, the following points are relevant. *Dao* and *de* are the key norms which determine, in the one case, I take it, unity, and in the other the rejection of knowledge. Knowledge here, far from being an umbrella term for human cognition, relates rather to competitions between those who know:[29] they compete for a good name, and this disperses *de*. I think that what this means is that, because of the conflict between the masters of truth, the degree they can put one under obligation is reduced.[30] If there is only one person with a claim to knowledge, then you have to listen to that person. If there are several, who is one to listen to? A common picture of what 'those with knowledge' do in late Western Zhou is to

---
[28] Graham 1981: 69.
[29] Cf. 'Masters of truth', a term Geoffrey Lloyd (1996: 129) has adopted in the context of comparative thought.
[30] On *de* 德 and obligation see Gassmann 2011.

attempt to produce peace. That is not the analysis of the *Zhuangzi*,[31] of course, the competition here is to start with between those who know. But part of Zhong Ni's point is that you cannot produce concord in a state if you are a competitor.

The second line of thought which is important here is the idea, widespread in late Zhou thought,[32] and here referred to as 'the perfect humans of old', that one first has to achieve oneself a form of perfection before being able to improve rulers. This is important because part of what Zhong Ni will go on to advise Yan Hui is to change his own heart by fasting. What is at issue here is *xing* 行 conduct. One question that we have to ask is whether individual actions are meant, or the conduct of a whole life. For example at the start of the story, the Prince of Wei is said to have conduct which is 'selfish' (*qi xing du* 其行獨) (Guo 130). Clearly, this means an established pattern of conduct, not an individual piece of behaviour.

In part, Zhong Ni's criticism is that Yan Hui's procedure is to 'take the heart as commander' (*shi xin* 師心). This procedure is too simple, or rather it cuts off the chain of authority too early. For 'simplicity' does not befit the clear sky or heavens (*hao tian* 皞天). *Tian* is the final instance against which the servant's disposition has to be measured. He then suggests fasting of the heart (*xinzhai* 心齋) as a *fang*, a technique, which is distinguished from abstention from meat and wine as a result of poverty, and which is also associated with ritual. Yan Hui asks for clarification:

Text 2
Zhong Ni said: unify your will. Do not listen with your ears, but with the heart, do not listen with the heart, listen with *qi*. Hearing stops with the ear, the heart stops at the tally, *qi* however, is empty and waits on things. Only the Way collects emptiness. Emptiness is the fasting of the heart. (Guo 147, Graham 68)

The first injunction that Confucius gives concerns the 'will', *zhi* 志. Translating *zhi* with 'direction of the heart' is perhaps helpful elsewhere,[33] but there is reason to reject that reading here. For Confucius rejects the idea that the heart is the highest commander. So let us take it that *zhi* is a striving that structures a life largely, and in all areas of endeavour. One question is just how a striving is distinguished from cognition, if at all. But there is also the question of unity: is this unity consistency? And, supposing unity to be

---
[31] This passage bears comparison with the *Tianxia* 'The empire' chapter (*Zhuangzi* 33) on the feuding of those who know.
[32] The *locus classicus* is *Daxue* 'The Great Learning' 2.
[33] See Shun 1997: 66 on the *Mencius*, although in some of that text the heart too is subject to authority.

consistency for a moment, what is the value of consistency? Is it simply a good thing to be rational? Or is it simply impossible to follow different masters, at least consistently? The way the text continues suggests that what is at stake is finding the highest authority under which all else falls. Perhaps the point is that Yan Hui should integrate what he wants with the highest authority.

Three levels of listening *ting* 聽 are distinguished here, with ears, heart and *qi* 氣 'breath' (translated 'energies' by Graham). I take it that *ting* is being used to mean both listening *and obeying*. These levels are ranked; clearly, the listening gets better, or the obedience is better (more imperative) because the commands come from a higher authority. And what one is hearing are commands; this is at least suggested by the tally, which is where the heart stops. The *fu* 符 'tally' is a mark of office, more generally, of a contractual obligation, and hence a sign of authority.[34] The officer is given half, the prince retains the other half. And listening with the ears? Well, you hear what your superior who is there tells you to do. A *fu* or tally is only needed when you are away from your sovereign to perform your office.

So if the second kind of hearing consists in following one's (absent) sovereign, what about the third? *Qi* would seem here to be something not, unlike the heart, restricted to oneself, but relating to all things: it is 'empty' and 'waits on things'.[35] This emptiness (*xu* 虛) is a form of receptivity.[36] Presumably what is taken in is a normative order of things, i.e. the way things are to be or to be changed, and this is collected (unified?) in the Way. So the heart, which obeys the commands implicit in a *fu*, a tally, is to fast. 'Fasting' (*zhai* 齋) has strong ritual connotations; but the fasting of the heart here trumps ritual fasting. The result is that one can wait (*dai* 待) on things.[37] If the context is one in which one receives commands, then the idea is that through the fasting of the heart one will receive, and obey, the correct injunctions. Thus one is here free *for* something. Thus where Watson sees freedom as purely negative, we have to complete this with a positive aspect, what one is free for.

Where does the determination of the *zhi*, 'will' come from? If the will is directed purely by the things on which it waits, then the *qi* does not determine itself. This is suggested by its being 'empty'. Now, interpreters seem to think that 'waiting on things' (*daiwu*) means adapting to a changing situation. This

---

[34] It appears elsewhere in the Inner Chapters of the *Zhuangzi* only in the chapter title *Dechongfu* 'The complete tally of power'. The source of these chapter titles is unclear.
[35] Cf. also *Mencius* 2a2 *hao ran zhi qi* 'flood-like qi'.
[36] Legge translates: 'free from preoccupation'.
[37] Here 待 *dai* is waiting on things, that is to say, so that one can act. In *Xiaoyaoyou* 1, *dai* denotes a dependence which is to be avoided.

would seem, unless this is qualified in some way, to mean that in a situation of deciding what to do, one has no resources from oneself: the things tell you what to do. Clearly, the interpretation of the situation and the weighing of different courses of action have to be considered, insofar as courses of action are the way in which things are to be changed from disorder to order. No doubt, part of the point is that one should not be determined by *qing*, the inclinations we start with, made up of a tendency to make judgements about what is right and wrong.[38]

Yan Hui's reply confirms that, at least in his view, we are concerned with obeying instructions, and that, once the instructions have been received, then Hui (or any servant?) has no control over the actuality. Before he receives his instructions, Hui does control the actuality:

Text 3
Yan Hui said: If Hui has not begun to fulfil the instructions, then the actuality comes from Hui. Once the instruction has been fulfilled, then there is no beginning for Hui. May that be called emptiness? (Guo 148, Graham 68-9[39])

The first question is who is giving instructions (*shi* 使). Since Hui has not yet taken up office, it would appear to be whatever the emptiness in Yan is open to: the Way, or his duties. The emptiness is collected in guidance by the Way, and comes about by fasting. Just what is going on here is pretty obscure; but this is the most we learn about fasting the heart. Zhong Ni clearly thinks that Yan Hui understands what fasting the heart is, and he needs nothing more to be able to practise this *fang*, 'art'. The simple answer shows that Hui is already in possession of the *fang*; the conversation suffices to give him an indication. The heart is the origin of the *shi* 實 actuality, until it has been fasted.

Graham's translation makes explicit the claim that Hui is here an agent: the point is then the actions derived from Hui's heart. But perhaps it is more than just actions, the whole constellation with the ruler may be meant. What Hui has to mould at court is not just action, but a situation where the country is not filled with corpses.

---

[38] See Chan 2015.
[39] Contrast the following translations: 'When Hui has never yet succeeded in being the agent, a deed derives from Hui. When he does succeed in being its agent, there has never begun to be a Hui. Would that be what you call attenuating?' (Graham 1981: 68-9). 'Before I was able to put this into practice I was full of thoughts of myself. But now that I am capable of putting it into practice, [I realize] that my self has never existed. Can this be called tenuousness?' (Slingerland 2003: 183). Slingerland thinks that 'emptiness' denotes a lack of self-awareness (2003: 33), hence his translation of *shi zi Hui ye* 實自回也. No reason is given for understanding emptiness like this, rather than, say, as the emptiness that follows on fasting.

It is tempting to connect this denial of action with forgetting, or losing, (*wu sang wo* 吾喪我, 2.1) the self.[40] One important text for this is the story at *Dazongshi* 9 about Yan Hui's progress: he is able to 'sit and forget': 'limbs and organs fall away, he dispels clear hearing and sight, leaves his shape, dismisses knowledge, joins with the Great Passage: this is called sitting and forgetting'. Zhong Ni then becomes Yan Hui's pupil in stark contrast to the present story. This raises questions about how one should approach the coherence of the narratives in the *Inner Chapters*. The coherence is not that of a narrative with continuous persons, at any rate.

The idea in the present story is that the desires or motions of the heart hinder receptivity for the proper commands. Graham speaks of a 'deeper self', and calls this a paradox. But is there still a self at all? Indeed, the previous existence of Hui seems to be cancelled retrospectively (*weishi you Hui ye* 未始有回也 'there is not yet a Hui'). The desideratum is an effective and living minister, and the method (*fang*) is to fast the heart, so that the correct orders are followed by Hui. He has then left all the manners behind which he thought would be so useful, and indeed lost his self.

Text 4
The Master said: Perfect! I tell you, you can enter his cage, and wander (*you*) there, but do not respond to his name (or: fame). When you enter, sing, when you do not enter, stand still. If there are no entrances and no exits,[41] then all habitations are one, and you find your resting place in what cannot be hindered (*bu de yi*). Then you are close. (Guo 148, Graham 69)

This is the text where freedom is most evident in this story: not only is a cage mentioned, but Yan Hui is meant to wander (*you*) in it. 'His cage': I take it, the cage of the ruler. It is conceivable that it also applies to the human condition generally. *You* 遊 'wander, travel for pleasure' is important in the *Zhuangzi*, as has been pointed out already. For example in *Yangshengzhu* 2 Cook Ding's knife moves with ease in a narrow gap.[42] Or in the story in *Renjianshi* immediately after the one we are considering:[43]

---

[40] See the collection of texts in Fung 1952: 243, and cf. Slingerland 2003: 33.
[41] For the emendation here, see Graham 1982/2003: 21.
[42] See Vervoorn forthcoming on cognition in the knack stories. Machek 2015: ch. 1 discusses this story in detail and argues that virtuosity, i.e. great skill and freedom, go together. This may chime well with the story discussed here, if fasting the heart, which is called here a *fang*, a method, can be assimilated to the arts of the butcher and the wheel-maker. At first blush, it appears very different.
[43] Cf. also Guo 307; Graham 98, the penultimate story from *Yingdiwang* 'Responding to emperors and kings'.

Text 5

Ride things, so the heart wanders. Trust what cannot be altered to nourish the middle: that is the highest. What can [Qi] do as a reparation? Nothing exceeds performing orders. That is the hardest thing. (Guo 160, Graham 71)

'Wandering' is perhaps a misleading translation, in that it suggests a lack of purpose, but the word should suggest ease of movement, unhindered movement.

Commentators[44] suggest that the cage is the fasting of the heart, and the fame is that of those using it. The wandering, *you*, accompanies this fasting – freedom goes along with discipline. But perhaps the cage is the cage of the Prince of Wei, and the 'singing' is the advice Yan Hui will give. When Yan Hui is at court, the emptiness of his heart allows him to advise; and otherwise not. But in both cases, fame is not to be responded to: this was one of the constraints Zhong Ni warns Yan Hui against at the outset of the story.

This wandering is not something that any but the complete man can do: only the wise are free. This is the central point where *Zhuangzi* and Stoics meet. A question to be raised but not answered here is the extent to which the conceptions of wisdom diverge and coincide. Nor does it appear in this context that this wandering is something one can do anywhere: the service of the prince is necessary. In this text at least, engagement in government is a standard to be fulfilled. Again, this is something many Stoics would concur in. Yan Hui quotes a saying of Zhong Ni's to this effect[45] when motivating his desire to go to Wei.

There would appear to be no exits from this cage, thus leaving the wanderer Hui only there for a habitation: it is 'what cannot be avoided'. Does this mean, once at court, you cannot escape? That is not a problem, as long as the state is well ordered. However, when there is no order, then there is danger, and no way out, and Hui has to accommodate himself to 'what cannot be avoided' (*bu de yi*). This can reasonably only be seen as freedom in his flourishing or success under these conditions.

If this applies to the advice to the Prince, then it would appear that Yan Hui is to advise him under the constraints of what is bound to happen. Yet this is not something that comes from Yan Hui. What is his contribution to the decisions to be made? As little as possible. His contribution is the ability to take things in, and so live well with them.

---

[44] Wang Shumin 1988: I, 133.   [45] Cf. *Lunyu* 8.13.

Text 6

If ear and eye inside are open, and the heart's knowledge is outside, then ghost and spirits come to dwell nearby – and how much more humans! This is the transformation of the ten thousand things. This is where the knot for Shun and Yu is, where Fu Xi and Ji Qu finished their journey, and how much more commoners. (Guo 150, Graham 69)

In the preceding lines Confucius has said that Yan Hui does not know about using ignorance to know, indeed, galloping while sitting: the consequences of this is that inside and outside are reversed – ear and eye work inwards, and the heart is outward: that ghosts, spirits and humans draw near, I take it in obedience, as the people flock to a good ruler. The model rulers Shun and Yu are mentioned here. But it is not just humans, also the spirit world will collect itself around someone with this knowledge: things are transformed by the good ruler. This change is the change of the 'ten thousand things', that is living things, their flourishing. The fasting of the heart makes a difference to the way in which the situation at court develops. But it has repercussions far beyond the court.

Some Stoics, especially Epictetus

Freedom belongs to the fundamental concepts of Stoic political theory from the outset.[46] Zeno discussed it in his *Republic*; Cleanthes wrote a book on it. Of Chrysippus we have nothing explicitly attributed to him; we shall turn to a definition which may go back to him in a moment. Stoic ethics defends a series of paradoxes, that is opinions which conflict with our normal opinions. One of these is that only the wise are free.[47] The wise have a set of entirely consistent opinions, which form a *technē*. This could well be compared with the *fang* we have seen in Zhuangzi; and there are various non-intellectual aspects which are also crucial to Stoicism, for example *askēsis*.[48] This raises interesting questions as to the relation between exercise and opinion, especially if, as the Stoics think, desire or impulse is a species of opinion.[49]

---

[46] Diogenes Laertius (henceforth abbreviated to D.L.) 7.32-3, on Cleanthes 7.175. Plutarch, *On Listening to Poetry*. Long and Sedley 1985 (henceforth abbreviated LS) 670. For a sceptical view of the use of politics for Stoics, see Sedley 1997.

[47] D.L. 7.32-3; Cicero, *Academica* 2.136, *Stoic Paradoxes* 5.

[48] E.g. Herillus of Carthage wrote on *askēsis*, as did Dionysius of Heraclea (D.L. 7.165-6); it is responsible for the powers of the soul, Stobaeus 2.62.15, von Arnim *Stoicorum Veterum Fragmenta* III 278.

[49] Plutarch, *On Stoic Self-contradictions* 1037F (LS 53R), *On Moral Virtue* 446F-447A (LS 65G).

The Stoic cosmos is ordered by reason, aka Nature, God, Zeus, Law. This conception of order in the cosmos leads to another key doctrine of Stoicism: determinism. Since the universe is wholly material and therefore governed by physical laws, and there is also a rational ordering force who contributes to the order of events, there is no room for arbitrary free will. The good life is the one lived 'according to nature'. This formulation, as the followers of Zeno discovered, was in need of clarification. Stoic cosmology provided some grounds upon which such clarification could be made. To act in accordance with nature is first of all to act in accordance with your own nature as a human being. For man, this means to act rationally, since his nature, which distinguishes him from other living things bar gods, is to be rational. This constraint is even stronger because nature itself is rational, being ordered by a rational mind. The problem with this view is that it is not clear what it means to live according to nature.

There is a definition of freedom which may go back to Chrysippus, reported by Diogenes Laertius,[50] namely, *autopragias exousia*, 'the authority to act on one's own initiative'. Only the wise are free, everyone else is a slave: fools take things to be good and bad which are not such. This develops inappropriate attachments, which are enslaving since they prevent fools from doing what one should do for one's own good. The objects of fears and appetites determine the life of the fool, rather than their reason. To be free is to act on one's own initiative, that is, *autopragia*. *Exousia* is the kind of authority which comes with office, or is fixed by law.[51] In the case of *autopragias exousia*, the law is divine law: if you do not enslave yourself, you have the authority to act on your own. That is the way God has arranged things. This is a privilege of humans. The god of Stoicism is a workman god, a demiurge, who makes things, in fact everything. We have seen that there is a pendant to this conception in the *Zhuangzi*, even if one where there seems to be no suggestion that *everything* is to be put down to him. For living things, the Stoic cosmos is so arranged that they can maintain themselves. Humans can do more: they can understand what is good for them, and be motivated by this understanding. They can do of their own accord what needs to be done,[52] in Frede's formulation. So, good humans contribute to the good order of the world. Like goodness, freedom does not admit of degrees: either you have it or you don't. A single wrong attachment, a single false belief enslaves

---

[50] D.L. 7.121; LS 67M, cf. Plutarch, *On Stoic Self-contradictions* 1034B.
[51] Origen, *Commentary on the Gospel of St John* 1.4, 2.16.
[52] Cicero, *On Ends* 3.17.22 (LS 59D); Epictetus 1.6.12–22, LS 63E. The following interpretation is influenced by Frede 2011: 67ff.

you. Clearly, a special sense of what needs to be done is in play here; for it is what is good.

How does freedom relate to responsibility? In some interpreters' views, to begin with responsibility and freedom are not connected. Chrysippus thinks you are responsible for an action because you assent to an appearance or impression.[53] The choice reflects on, expresses your character, as the individual human you are. Alternatives are possible, if the nature of the thing allows it to have the predicate in question, and the circumstances are no hindrance.[54] So it is possible to give assent or not to give assent; the situation does not control this. The fool is forced to assent, the free human not. The free human is motivated by insight.

Cicero defines freedom in the *Stoic Paradoxes* as the power to live as you will (§[34] *quid est enim libertas? potestas vivendi, ut velis*).[55] The crucial question is one of control, 'as you will'. But it is assumed that what you will is living rightly, and enjoying duties (*quis igitur vivit, ut volt, nisi qui recte vivit, qui gaudet officio, cui vivendi via considerata atque provisa est?*). Lurking in Cicero's use of this old formula is thus a very strong account of what *voluntas*, will, is. Crucially, the agents themselves are the origin of all that they do and think, and they are responsible for it (*cuius omnia consilia resque omnes, quas gerit, ab ipso proficiscuntur eodemque referuntur*). This may make one think that the subject is free in the sense of being autonomous, but really the self here is merely the internalised divine law,[56] which no human has any say in formulating. The idea is that the free human has subjected himself completely to the divine law. The will is responsible for the act of assent constituting every action. It is of course crucial to the idea of an action in Stoicism that the assent is the action. But in Cicero it is not the will that is free, but the human. The motivation for obeying the laws (here, immediately, the laws of the republic) lies in judgement that obeying them is the most beneficial thing to do. The deciding factor in the free man is his *voluntas atque iudicium*, his will and judgement.

---

[53] Cicero, *On Fate* 39–43; LS 62CD; Gellius, *Attic Nights* 7.2.6–13.   [54] Bobzien 1998: 112–16.

[55] Also Cicero, *On Duties* 1.20.70. See Plato, *Laws* 701A, *Republic* 557B. In Aristotle, *Politics* 6.1310a27, this is one of the marks of a *bad* definition of freedom. Newman comments (1902: IV, 411, *ad loc.*) 'The passage before us makes it probable that Aristotle would define freedom as obedience to rightly constituted law.' Contrast the Senecan *deo parere libertas est*, 'Freedom is obeying God' (*On the Happy Life* 15.7), cf. Cicero, *Tusculan Disputations* 2.48; Plutarch, *On Listening to Lectures* 37d. *Libertas* and cognates are by no means the only way Cicero has to speak about being one's own master – *On Duties* 1.4.13 gives as the *propria* of humans the investigation of the truth alongside *adpetitio principatus*, 'hunger for supremacy', which he understands as being subject to no one else's commands.

[56] Cf. Cooper 2004 on *Oration* 8 of Dio Chrysostom on freedom.

There is no sense of a problem with determinism in *Stoic Paradoxes* in general. And, conversely, freedom plays a minor role in *On Fate*;[57] on the one hand this might confirm the view that the discussion of moral responsibility and determinism was conducted without systematically connecting it to questions of freedom.[58] On the other hand, there *is* some connection between freedom and responsibility in Cicero, in his accounts of both the Stoics and Epicurus.

The one mention of fate in Paradox 5 (§34) connects it, not with the intricacies of Stoic doctrine on causality, but with an unnamed poet: *Fortuna ipsa cedit, ut sapiens poeta dixit, suis ea cuique fingitur moribus.* 'Fate yields, if, as the wise poet puts it: "Fate is formed by the mores of each man."' Cicero in fact is going too far, in his interpretation both of Stoic doctrine and of the poet: for fate is made up *inter alia* of the character of the actors. The character is not independent of fate, so that fate can yield to them. There is room for thinking, however, that responsibility is being invoked here: as in the Chrysippan image of the rolling cylinders and the rolling cones, the way they roll is due to their own nature.[59] Go with the flow you must, but the way you go is up to the kind of human you are. In the case of humans, this is, as we have seen Cicero saying, due to the will (*voluntas*) or judgement. The wise man is free of two main kinds of slavery – to pleasure, for example in costly works of art (§§37–8), and the dangers of the desire for office (§40) and from fear. Here too we are close to Yan Hui.

Only the wise are free: just as with Yan Hui's wandering depending on his fasting his heart, so too the freedom of the Ciceronian Stoic sage depends on themselves. This freedom is one that imposes a certain form of living on the sage, acting according to insight, if Stoic, or waiting on things in the *Zhuangzi*. In both cases, holding office is a danger, whether because of the things it allows one to do or because of the inherent dangers from the powerful. Although the *Zhuangzi* nowhere mentions

---

[57] §20: Those who introduce a chain of causes, i.e. the Stoics with their conception of Fate, deprive the human mind of free will [sic!], and bind it to the necessity of fate. Cf. §38 (of Chrysippus' position): reason forces us to say that things are true from eternity, and not bound in a series of causes *and* free of the necessity of fate; (cf. §39 *motus animi liberatos necessitate fati*). §23 Epicurus introduced the theory of the swerve of the atoms because he was concerned to preserve freedom for us.

[58] As is the contention of Bobzien 1998. She relies heavily on the Stoic division of teaching into logic, ethics and physics being absolutely rigorous, rather than, say, an interpenetration of the disciplines. In this way she claims that the early Stoics isolated political talk of freedom from moral responsibility. The price one has to pay is to admit a lack of systematising on the part of the early Stoics.

[59] Cicero, *On Fate* 41–5; Gellius, *Attic Nights* 7.2.

fear, it would appear also to be something banished by the fasting of the heart.

Frede sees talk of freedom and talk of responsibility coming together in Epictetus' *Discourses*.[60] Epictetus devotes the longest of his *Discourses* (*diatribai*) to freedom, *eleutheria* (4.1), as well as another to what is up to us and what is not up to us (1.1). Arrian is responsible for the two styles Epictetus is presented to us in, the pithy apothegms of the *Manual*, and the discursive, sometimes argumentative form of the *Discourses*.[61] They are conversations written in *koinē*, that is, not in the polished Attic of Arrian's other works. Stoic dialectic, by question and answer, was already practised by Zeno.[62]

The first step towards a conception of freedom is responsibility (*to eph' hēmin* – the subject of 1.1). The body is not free and unhindered, for it is not something that belongs to one, merely artfully moulded clay. Zeus cannot give this to humans; instead he has given 'a part' (*meros*) of himself to humans, 'the power of impulse and aversion, of striving and avoidance, in short, the power of using impressions' (1.1.12). The power of using impressions (*phantasiai*) correctly (1.1.7[63]) is the power of impulse and repulsion, and is identified with reason (1.1.4–5). Hence there is great emphasis on the testing of impressions (e.g. 2.18.24). Here, this power is not identified with reason; but that is what it is (see 1.1.12, where it is also said to be a part of God). Stoics think that humans, as rational animals, are 'offshoots' of Zeus. Self-respect is enjoined on us by God (2.8.23): he entrusts us to ourselves. Reason is identified with each human's *daimōn*, or guardian spirit in more traditional Greek thought,[64] which Zeus gives to each of us (1.14.11). Counting intellects is notoriously difficult;[65] perhaps the Stoics are in a better position here, if one allows them the identification between intellect and bodies. Further, this seems to imply for Stoics that we have no difficulty in understanding the mind of Zeus; we just have to understand our own mind. In fact, they see no great distinction in quality between the wise man and Zeus. These points are very relevant to the question of freedom; for one is left asking to what extent I am free, and to

---

[60] Bobzien 1998 argues that, at least on a textual level, responsibility and freedom are not connected before Epictetus. Above all, this requires a careful reading of Cleanthes.

[61] Arrian's role is controversial; for discussion, see Dobbin 1999. On the various titles in the ms. tradition, see Souilhé's edition. All references of the form 4.1.1 without further attribution are to the *Discourses*.

[62] D.L. 7.18.   [63] Cf. D.L. 7.49.

[64] E.g. Homer, *Odyssey* 12.296, 14.488; cf. Plato, *Timaeus* 90A.

[65] For an early use of the plural, see Aristotle Fr. 471; it is commoner in later philosophy, e.g. Plotinus 6.7.17.26.

what extent do I simply submit to the overwhelming rationality running the cosmos. This is the Stoic take on the Platonic and Aristotelian idea that one is duty bound to assimilate oneself to God.[66]

How should one distinguish between submission to and assent to rationality? Is *submission on the basis of reasons* equivalent to *assent to*? Or is assent the simpler concept? Obedience plays a major role in Epictetus: to God, above all, and then myself (4.12.11). A common way of talking is to say that there is concordance (*homologia*) between a *daimōn* and the will of the governor of the cosmos: this is virtue. But there is no doubt about the direction of fit in this concordance: what I want and think is to fit Zeus, not the other way around. This is quite clear from the toil necessary to make one's *prohairesis* harmonious with nature (1.4.18). Not everyone has free will, only those who have, with much work, mastered Stoic philosophy (4.1.128–31). There is of course a weaker sense in which all humans are such, as humans, as to be able to have free will. Nonetheless, Epictetus says that he has been 'emancipated by God, I know his orders, no one can enslave me anymore, I have the liberator I needed, the judges that are necessary' (4.7.17).

Our value lies in our reason: this is what we should attribute value to, not the body. We should be guided by our conception (*hupolambanein*) of things, and our lack of humility (*tapeinoi*) about ourselves is based on the view that one is, as a child of Zeus, born for 'trust, shame, and the secure use of impressions' (1.3.4). Long sees this as 'complete autonomy'.[67] Clearly, we need a distinction between arbitrary power and justified power, which Epictetus does not give us, because he assumes that the world is rationally run in the best way possible. But even with that, there is an assumption about it being *my* reason; and perhaps also, more controversially, that the deliverances of reason, anyone's reason, necessarily converge.

Part of the great interest of ancient ethics, both Greco-Roman and Chinese, lies in pondering just how accessible it is to us, and a title such as 'Autonomy and integrity'[68] suggests great proximity to contemporary concerns. Crucial to Long's idea of 'autonomy' is *prohairesis*. This is, as Long puts it, 'Epictetus' favourite name for the purposive and

---

[66] See 2.14.13. Plato, *Theaetetus* 176A2–C2; Aristotle, *Nicomachean Ethics* 1177b33. See Sedley 2004: ch. 3.4.
[67] Long 2002: 156.
[68] Long 2002 devotes a whole chapter to 'Autonomy and integrity'; the latter is his rendition of *aidōs*, more traditionally rendered as 'shame'. Long follows Kamtekar 1998. For the close connection between shame and external signs, see 3.7.27. Blushing mentioned here is related to shame, surely, not integrity.

self-conscious centre of a person',[69] which he translates 'volition', Frede 'will'.[70] This term is Peripatetic in origin, but takes on a new dignity in Epictetus, above all because of the way it is connected to rationality.[71] There are both political and ethical aspects to *prohairesis*. Epictetus considers the man threatened by the tyrant (1.19.9): if he values his *prohairesis*, then he will say to the tyrant: God made me free. In the *Discourse* on *ataraxia*, the tranquillity of the wise, the natural (i.e. best) condition of your *prohairesis* is arrived at by being satisfied with the things that are 'completely at one's disposal (*autexousia*) and naturally free' (2.1.1–2). Here, as elsewhere, the crucial thing is that no one, not even Zeus, can constrain or compel (*kōleuesthai, anagkazesthai*) this power. Naturally, *prohairesis* is unimpeded and unconstrained (1.17.21): no one can prevent me from assenting to a truth. This of course depends on a view of the relation between truths and assent.

The political aspects of *prohairesis* compare well with the fasting of the heart in the *Zhuangzi*. For the prince of Wei cannot threaten Yan Hui if he has fasted his heart.

The goodness of humans is a quality of their *prohairesis* (1.29.1). This is crucial for Frede's claims about the emergence of 'will': for this we need a dispositional sense of *prohairesis*, so that it is not the actual choices, but the ability to choose. As we will see, this is not what the text actually gives us. The will accords with nature: the will is made by Zeus to be free (1.4.18), that is, not prevented from making the choices it regards as right, such that it cannot be forced to make a choice it does not want (1.12.9, 1.14.18, 3.5.7). One question here is what makes the choice? It might be the *hēgēmonikon* (the controlling factor in a living thing in Stoicism), a human, or *prohairesis*.[72] In

---

[69] Long, 2002: 207, ch. 8.   [70] Long 2002: 214; Frede 2011: ch. 5.

[71] See Aristotle, *Nicomachean Ethics* 1139b4 for a view of *prohairesis* which already defines it as being closely linked to reason, namely as desiring intellect, or intellectual desire. The question arises of whether Epictetus in fact does represent something new, if one takes *prohairesis* in Aristotle as a standing disposition to choose, regulated by intellect (deliberation). As Long 2002: 214 notes, in both authors *prohairesis* relates to what is up to us, and is a determinant of our character. He also says that practical reason is present in both authors. I am not convinced about practical reason in Stoicism. The main point of contact between the Stoic and (some) modern thought, which Aristotle does not have, is the identification of the person with reason or *prohairesis*. Cf. Frede 2011: ch. 3. Graver 2003 provides evidence that this use of *prohairesis* goes back to the early Stoa.

[72] If it is *prohairesis*, we would have in English the strange 'the will chooses'. See Frede's formulation, 2011: 80: 'let us return to free action. This is accounted for in terms of a free choice of the will.'

contrast to fools, constrained by false opinions, the good do what god plans, because it is the best thing to be done in those circumstances.

After this brief survey of some of the aspects of *prohairesis*, let us turn to freedom. *Discourses* 4.1 kicks off with a definition of the free man, which fits well with Cicero (see above note 55) to start with, but adds a dose of characteristic rigour:

Text 7
He is free who lives as he will, whom it is not possible to constrain or hinder or force, whose impulses are unhindered, whose strivings are successful, and whose aversions not prevented.

Why is it not possible to constrain or hinder or force the free human? The answer emerges that it is not a human as such but only the wise man who cannot be treated in this way, even by Zeus (1.1.23). 'Constrained' here translates *anagkazesthai*, a kind of necessitation, as one might say, by Fate. Thus the explanation for freedom lies in the actualised capacity for reason in humans. The background is of course the Stoic theory of action: action is assent to an impression. Here we have something much more special, as we have seen; not just anyone's assent is unconstrained, only that of the wise man. Thus it is not the nature of assent *tout court* that it cannot be constrained.[73] It must be completely rational assent. Epictetus gives examples of philosophers who were free: Diogenes the Cynic, the 'grandfather of Stoicism', (4.1.151–8) and Socrates (4.1.159–69). It would appear that we have here two sides to freedom: you cannot be forced or constrained to something, or prevented from something. Neither of these can be constrained or necessitated by Fate. This two-sidedness of freedom is confirmed by those passages where Epictetus links negative and positive impulses,[74] the two species of impulse (*hormē*). Remarkable in this passage is the idea that one's impulses should be successful: that sounds as though Epictetus is not buying into the Stoic story that the value of action lies purely in the assent to the right impressions; what actually happens is irrelevant. But in fact he is very strict in his restriction of freedom to the use of impressions (1.1.7): only that is up to us, and hence only there can we be free. It is this which is the function of reason. Here we have unhindered motions that characterise a free life.

Prohairesis is not used here, and indeed very sparingly in this *Discourse* on freedom.[75] This suggests that actually it is not the 'will'

---

[73] Contrast Bobzien 1998: 335.
[74] This does imply that freedom for Epictetus is linked to alternatives, *pace* Bobzien 1998: 334.
[75] This omission is notable, in the face of Frede's claims for Epictetus' use of *prohairesis*.

that is free, but the human. After all, the free human is his starting point in this text. It is true that the term *prohairesis* enjoys a great expansion in Epictetus as a whole, from its Peripatetic use. Where I have spoken of reason in the last paragraph, Epictetus would no doubt be happy to speak of *prohairesis*, for this in fact expanded to refer to the human psyche.[76]

What Epictetus is doing is transforming talk of freedom in terms of slave and master into talk about choice, relating not to social arrangements but to the structure of the soul. The internalisation of social structure, based on the parallel structures of soul and city is familiar at least from Plato's *Republic* on. In these terms, even a freeman or woman, in the social sense, is not free (§§8–10). There is much play with the 'freedom', or wide scope for action, that supposedly, in view of Epictetus' dialogue partner, is granted by social status and being 'friends' of the emperor. None of this is relevant to the speaker.[77] There is tension here with the Stoic emphasis on each of us being a part of the whole. The bonds between the status of humans and their rationality is very close: we are citizens of the cosmos, unlike animals, because we understand the divine administration and the reasoning that follows from it (2.10.3).

The grounds for this freedom Epictetus thinks lie in *hē epistēmē tou bioun* ἡ ἐπιστήμη τοῦ βιοῦν (64), 'the science of living', just as in other areas one's unimpeded action lies in knowledge of what to do, so too in life as a whole. Notably, it is a science (*epistēmē*) here, not a *technē*. This anyway is not so much a problem in that the Stoic conception of a *technē* was so generous as to lose the sharp contours it has in Aristotle, for example.[78] The crucial point both in leading your life and in the areas covered by the other sciences is that one is unhindered. The second step (65–7) is to ask about what is up to you: external things, health, beauty and suchlike are not up to you. So what is under your authority (*autexousion*) (68)? The only thing that Epictetus finds is assenting or not to the false. The crucial point in his view is that no one can force you to do this; and this activity is thus unimpeded (69–70). This emerges again when he summarises the status of the free man as having his assent to what appears to him being beyond constraint or prevention by anyone, just like Zeus (90).

---

[76] The good is: proper *prohairesis* and use of impressions, *Discourses* 1.30.4; cf. 1.8.6, 2.22.29, 3.22.103; Dobbin 1999: 76–7 on 1.1.23.

[77] §§8–10. There is a tension here between individuality and social roles, which elsewhere are heavily emphasised in Epictetus, as in 2.5.24–6 – a human is part of a community just as a foot is part of a living thing. On social roles and autarchy in Roman Stoicism, see Reydams-Schils 2005.

[78] On this loose use, see Annas 1993.

We have noted that the term *prohairesis* is used very sparingly in the *Discourse* on freedom. In fact, it is not the *prohairesis* that Epictetus says is given to us, but the *prohairetika*, the things to be chosen. God orders things, we are told, and the questioner asks:

Text 8
(99) How do you mean ordered? – Such that what He wants, you want too, and what He does not want, (100) you do not want yourself. – How can that happen? – How indeed except by examining God's impulses and his administration. What has he granted me, as mine to dispose of (*autexousion*)? – What is left up to him? He granted me things to be chosen (*prohairetika*), he made them to be up to me, unimpeded, unhindered.

It seems remarkably easy for the Stoic to read the mind of God: look at the administration, and you will understand the governor. But the really tricky point is that the governor grants us things; and one may well wonder how much of a gift this is, since things are so ordered that, if we are wise, we wish for the same things as God. One might argue that the reason these things are given to me is that I have *prohairesis*, and this is free. But Epictetus does not express it like that. He concentrates here on the individual actions that are to be chosen, and that are up to me. It is not the freedom of the will that is mine, but the things to be chosen, the actuality, not the faculty.

The doctrine of the will, and our freedom demand a rigid distinction between intellect and body.[79] And along with the body, all goods around me, including family and friends are to be excluded from consideration.

To round this discussion off, Epictetus gives a useful summary, in the guise of points where agreement has been reached:

Text 9
(128) So let us repeat what we have agreed on. The unhindered human is free, for whom matters are to hand as he wishes them. The slave is he who can be prevented or constrained or impeded, or thrown into something unwillingly. Who is not prevented? He who desires nothing alien. What are alien things? Whatever is not up to us to have or not to have, or to have such qualities or in a certain state.

So the body and all that goes with it fall under alien things.

---

[79] It is controversial to what extent there is a break in the causal nexus due to Epictetus' concept of the will. Dobbin 1991 argues for there being such a break. Long 2002 is unconvinced. I agree with Long.

Freedom: The Unhindered Life

If we try to collect together correspondences between the *Zhuangzi* and some Stoics, the first thing to be emphasised is that only the wise are free. Only they 'wander'. A useful formula which bears interpretations of both groups of thinkers is 'the unhindered life'. And the political context for people who are often professional advisers of despots is revealingly similar. Yet this unhindered life in fact consists in fulfilling certain obligations or norms. For the Stoics, these norms are those of reason. But what is rationality?[80]

Reason (*logos*) is the 'matter' of the philosopher, says Epictetus, not his coat. He goes on to quote Zeno, as saying that it is the elements of reason, what each is, how they fit together, and all that follows on them (4.8.12). Clearly, no formal account of reason will be enough – after all, the primary fire, one of the guises of Zeus, the ordering principle of the cosmos, contains the *logoi* possessing the causes of all events.[81] The Stoics are much praised for their systematic thought. One might think that it is in fact a straitjacket forcing them to absurd conclusions. This is the way Cicero presents them in the *Pro Mureno*, arguing against the younger Cato, whom he is so polite about in the *Stoic Paradoxes*; and also in *On Ends*. But in fact it is a very flexible system. Interpreters emphasise the impossibility of deducing ethical judgements from ultimate principles in Stoic ethics.[82]

The very idea of looking for reason, let alone will, in the *Zhuangzi* may take many readers aback. Yet in that text clearly there is an ordering, on the one hand, of the context of human action, and of this action itself, and there is a direction of human movement, dependent on being able to be receptive to the most authoritative injunctions. One may object that what the *Zhuangzi* advocates is to externalise the source of human movement: it is not Yan Hui who acts, rather an external divine power. But in the Stoic case also one may ask who is doing the acting, at least, whose reason it is controlling the action. In the *Hymn to Zeus*[83] Cleanthes prays that Zeus will guide him, and at a fundamental level there are issues about the identity of my intellect, and how it relates to Zeus. So there is room for doubting if the contrast between the *Zhuangzi* and the Stoics is as stark as might appear. Where the Stoics say: action must issue from me,[84] they mean: from my reason, and as long as this relation between this reason and

---

[80] Cf. Frede and Striker 1996. [81] Eusebius, *Evangelical Preparation* 15.14.2; LS 45G.
[82] E.g. Frede 2011; Annas 1993; Striker 1991. [83] LS 54I. [84] Cf. Cicero, *Stoic Paradoxes* 34.

that governing the cosmos is unclear, it remains unclear just what is happening. For of course, supposing for a moment we understand what determinism is, as the Stoics did suppose, then Nature, God and reason will determine what I do; all I can do is try to latch onto this – the strivings of God, and his administration.

The assumptions that Michael Frede finds used by the conception of the free will in Epictetus are about ourselves, mainly in the notion of a will, an ability to make choices, but also that the world is planned down to the smallest detail by a provident god. These are not assumptions that everyone in Greco-Roman antiquity share, let alone in China. There are two ideas here, however, which Frede thinks we should not discard without further consideration, and they provide a useful touchstone for our comparison:

1. Humans are sensitive to the truth, and this guides them in what they do.
2. There is no closed set of rules which you could use, if you knew them, to deduce what to do in any circumstances.

The first of these ideas appears to be a basic assumption of much Greek philosophy, and is not prominent in Chinese thought. One question is whether there is a more important analogue, for example in our ability, actualised in the wise, to follow the Way. Angus Graham's insistence on 'responding with awareness' in the *Zhuangzi* must, despite his use of the notion of 'objectivity', relate to the Way of Heaven. Frede's second idea is much closer to the *Zhuangzi*. But the pitch is a different one, since the tradition of the *Zhuangzi* texts attacks such lists of rules, especially in *Tianxia*, 'The empire', whereas some Stoics, and opportunist Stoics such as Cicero, have a great appetite for rules, even if they do not think they can enumerate all of them. Freedom, supposing it to exist, is a good however one conceives of the order within which one is free. In both the *Zhuangzi* and the Stoics it imposes discipline, a regulation of behaviour.[85]

References

Annas, J. (1993) *The Morality of Happiness*. New York.
Arnim, H. von (1903–1905) *Stoicorum Veterum Fragmenta*, 3 vols., vol. IV Index by Max Adler. Stuttgart.

---

[85] This could form an argument against the division of freedom into positive and negative freedom, in the style of Berlin 2002: freedom from restraint is one aspect of freedom, and freedom to follow norms another.

Berlin, I. (2002) 'Two concepts of liberty', in I. Berlin, *Liberty: Incorporating Four Essays on Liberty*. Oxford: 166–217.
Bobzien, S. (1998) *Determinism and Freedom in Stoic Philosophy*. Oxford.
Boter, G. (2007) *Epictetus, Encheiridion*. Berlin.
Burkert, W. (1987) *Greek Religion*. Oxford.
Chan, A. K. L. (forthcoming) 'Two ethical perspectives on the emotions in the *Zhuang zi*', in King and Schilling.
Cooper, J. M. (2004) 'Stoic autonomy', in *Knowledge, Nature and the Good: Essays on Ancient Philosophy*, ed. J. Cooper. Princeton: 204–44.
Dennett, D. (1984) *Elbow Room: The Varieties of Free Will Worth Wanting*. Cambridge, MA.
Dobbin, R. (1991) '*Prohairesis* in Epictetus', *Ancient Philosophy* 11: 111–35.
  (1999) *Epictetus: Discourses*, Book 1 (Clarendon Later Ancient Philosophers). New York.
Frede, M. (2007) 'The *eph'hemin* in ancient philosophy', Φιλοσοφια 37: 110–23.
  (2011) *A Free Will: Origins of the Notion in Ancient Thought. Sather Classical Lectures 68*, ed. A. A. Long. Berkeley.
Frede, M. and Striker, G. (eds.) (1996) *Rationality in Greek Thought*. Oxford.
Fung, Yu-lan 馮友蘭 (1952) *A History of Chinese Philosophy*, 1st edn in English, 2 vols., trans. D. Bodde. London.
Gassmann, R. H. (2011) 'Coming to terms with *dé* 德: the deconstruction of "virtue" and an exercise in scientific morality', in King and Schilling: 92–125.
Gill, C. (2005) 'Are ancient ethical norms universal?', in *Virtue, Norms and Objectivity*, ed. C. Gill. Oxford: 15–40.
Graham, A. C. (1981) *Chuang-tzu: The Inner Chapters*. London; reprint Indianapolis (2001).
  (1982) 'Chuang Tzu. Textual notes to a partial translation'. London; reprinted in *A Companion to Angus C. Graham's Chuang Tzu*, ed. H. D. Roth, Hawai'i, 2003 (pages are cited from the reprint).
  (1983) 'Taoist spontaneity and the dichotomy between "is" and "ought"', in *Experimental Essays on Chuang Tzu*, ed. V. Mair. Hawai'i: 3–23; reprinted in *A Companion to Angus C. Graham's Chuang Tzu*, ed. H. D. Roth, Hawai'i, 2003 (pages are cited from the reprint).
  (1985) *Reason and Spontaneity*. London.
Graver, M. (2003) 'Not even Zeus: a discussion of A. A. Long, *Epictetus: A Stoic and Socratic Guide to Life*', *Oxford Studies in Ancient Philosophy* 24: 343–59.
Hankinson, R. J. (2001) *Cause and Explanation in Ancient Greek Thought*. New York.
Inwood, B. (2005) *Reading Seneca: Stoic Philosophy at Rome*. Oxford.
Kamtekar, R. (1998) 'Αἰδώς in Epictetus', *Classical Philology* 93: 136–60.
King, R. A. H. and Schilling, D. (eds.) (2011) *How Should One Live? Comparing Ethics in Ancient China and Greco-Roman Antiquity*. Berlin.
  (eds.) (forthcoming) *The Ethics of Ease: Zhuangzi on the Norms of Life*. Wiesbaden.

Kjellberg, P. and Ivanhoe, P. J. (eds.) (1996) *Essays on Skepticism, Relativism, and Ethics in the Zhuangzi*. Albany.
Kupperman, J. (1999) *Learning from Asian Philosophy*. New York.
Legge, J. (1891) 'The works of Chuang Tzǔ', in *Sacred Books of the East*, vols. XXXIX–XL. Oxford.
Lloyd, G. E. R. (1996) *Adversaries and Authorities: Investigations into Ancient Greek and Chinese Science*. Cambridge.
  (2005) *The Delusions of Invulnerability*. London.
Long, A. (2002) *Epictetus: A Stoic and Socratic Guide to Life*. Oxford.
Long, A. and Sedley, D. (1987) *The Hellenistic Philosophers*. Cambridge.
Machek, D. (2015) 'Virtuosos of the ordinary: comparative interpretations of Daoist and Stoic Thought', PhD thesis, University of Toronto.
Moeller, H.-G. (2004) *Daoism Explained: From the Dream of the Butterfly to the Fishnet Allegory*. Chicago.
Muller, R. (2006) *Les Stoïciens: la liberté et l'ordre du monde*. Paris.
Newman, W. L. (ed., trans. and comm.) (1887–1902) *The Politics of Aristotle*, 4 vols. Oxford.
Pohlenz, M. (1955) *Griechische Freiheit: Wesen und Werden eines Lebensideals*. Heidelberg.
Raaflaub, K. (1996) *Die Entdeckung der Freiheit: Zur historischen Semantik und Gesellschaftsgeschichte eines politischen Grundbegriffes der Griechen*. Munich.
Reydams-Schils, G. (2005) *The Roman Stoics: Self, Responsibility, and Affection*. Chicago.
Rüpke, J. (ed.) (2007) *A Companion to Roman Religion*. Oxford.
Schenkl, H. (ed.) (1916) *Epicteti Dissertationes ab Arriano Digestae* (Greek text 2nd edn). Leipzig.
Sedley, D. (1997) 'The ethics of Brutus and Cassius', *Journal of Roman Studies* 87: 41–53.
  (2004) *The Midwife of Platonism: Text and Subtext in Plato's Theaetetus*. Oxford.
Shun, K. (1997) *Mencius and Early Chinese Thought*. Stanford.
Slingerland, E. (2003) *Effortless Action: Wu-wei as Conceptual Metaphor and Spiritual Ideal in Early China*. New York.
Souilhé, J. (trans.) (1948–65) *Epictète: Entretiens*, 4 vols. Paris.
Sterckx, R. (2002) *The Animal and the Daemon in Early China*, Albany.
Striker, G. (1991) 'Following nature: a study in Stoic ethics', *Oxford Studies in Ancient Philosophy* 9: 1–73.
Vervoorn, A. (forthcoming) 'Dead ashes encounter the great clod: correct knowledge and correct action in *Zhuang zi*', in King and Schilling.
Wang Shumin 王叔岷 (1988) *Zhuangzi jiao quan* 莊子校詮. Taibei.
Watson, B. (1968) *The Complete Works of Chuang Tzu*. New York.
Wiggins, D. (2006) *Ethics: Twelve Lectures on the Philosophy of Morality*. Harmondsworth.

5 | Shame and Moral Education in Aristotle and Xunzi

JINGYI JENNY ZHAO

Introduction

Not infrequently have Aristotle and Xunzi been viewed as each other's counterparts on the basis of an apparent similarity in the written form of their texts and in some of their ideas.[1] K. J. Spalding goes so far as to call Xunzi 'a Chinese Aristotle',[2] a general remark that is not conducive to a proper understanding of the two philosophers.[3] Indeed, much can be achieved by going beyond the superficial comparisons and undertaking a detailed analysis so as to account for their points of similarity and difference.

Taking shame-related concepts as a way into examining ideals of moral education and the good life in Aristotle and Xunzi,[4] this study explores the values that are present in the ancient philosophers and in the societies to which they belonged. Further investigation of the major differences in the societies of Aristotle and Xunzi cannot be undertaken here: I just note that Aristotle presupposes a body of citizens who all participate to a greater or less degree in the political process, while the kingdoms of Warring States China with which Xunzi was familiar all had rulers who were the ultimate decision-takers and who were therefore the target of ambitious persuaders.

Aristotle's and Xunzi's discussions of shame-related ideas can be seen as reflections on moral development, on inter-personal relationships and on the individual's place within society – all of which play an important part in the two philosophers' ethical and political frameworks and which give

---

[1] Xunzi, in contrast to his predecessors, is one of the first to have written in an essay style rather than in aphorisms or dialogue form, which allows for extended arguments. Yet such assimilation overlooks fundamental *differences* in the written form of their texts and problems of genre.

[2] Spalding 1937. Examples where Xunzi and Aristotle are compared in passing include, among others, Homer Dubs 1927: xix, 50, 150, 157; Spalding 1947: 168; Fung, Yu-lan 1952 (1): 106; and Knoblock 1994: III, Preface.

[3] This has also been recognised in Eric Hutton 2002.

[4] For ease of reference, I sometimes use locutions such as 'Xunzi says' or 'Xunzi believes' to refer to ideas in the text, but without implying that Xunzi the historical figure composed the passages in question.

them sufficient commonality for comparisons to be made. Aristotle incorporates examinations of *aidōs* and *aischunē* into his ethics and the *Rhetoric*, where ideas about shame and disgrace are discussed in different contexts, while the *Politics* provides a window for us to see the impact of moral education on society. As for the *Xunzi*, the chapter *Of Honour and Disgrace* contains extensive discussion of the topic under investigation, and discourses on shame and related ideas and moral education more generally can also be found in other chapters of the text.

Antonio Cua's article 'The ethical significance of shame: insights of Aristotle and Xunzi' is the major scholarly discussion that compares the two on this topic. Cua aims to use Aristotle's conception of shame 'as a sort of catalyst, an opening for appreciating Xunzi's complementary insights',[5] and he helpfully locates Xunzi within the 'Confucian' tradition by including Confucius and Mencius in the discussion. Relevant terms in the *Xunzi* are clearly identified (*xiu* 羞, *chi* 恥, *ru* 辱), yet Cua uses the English word 'shame' for discussions on Aristotle, only adding a brief note on *aidōs* and *aischunē* in the notes section. It is stated towards the beginning of the article that 'for both Aristotle and Xunzi, shame is not a moral virtue'.[6] This kind of statement is fraught with problems, for Cua does not explain either what, precisely, 'shame' entails for both thinkers, or what he means by 'moral virtue', especially as there simply is not an equivalent idea in the Chinese materials.[7] Despite the advances that Cua has made on this topic, then, he has failed to acknowledge the problems involved in comparing concepts across cultures and to offer solutions for these challenges.

Shame-related vocabulary, such as *aidōs* and *aischunē* on the Greek side, and *xiu, chi, ru* and their binomes on the Chinese side, all have their own semantic fields and connotations, which suggests differences in how shame-related ideas are conceptualised. In making cross-cultural comparisons on 'shame', and indeed on any such concept, evidently one needs to engage with *clusters* of concepts for the study to be methodologically viable, for related concepts are quite often entangled in a way that makes

---

[5] Cua 2003: 147. [6] Cua 2003: 147.

[7] *De* 德 has been conventionally yet inadequately translated as 'virtue', yet that is a term which has wide connotations and cannot be said to be equivalent to the Greek *aretē*, nor the English 'virtue'. For complexities surrounding this term, see Robert Gassmann 2011, who interprets it in terms of 'obligation', and Anne Cheng, who discusses *de* in terms of 'kingly virtue', mediated as a form of power that is able to move other things without resorting to a form of external coercion (2012: 135–6). We cannot therefore responsibly say that anything in the *Xunzi* is a 'virtue' in the Aristotelian sense of *aretē*, and not in the least discuss these two philosophers as if they had the same conceptions of 'moral virtue', as Cua does in his article. For a discussion of 'virtue' in a cross-cultural context, cf. King 2011: 9–13. See also King 2012 which discusses the problems in categorising *ren* as 'virtue' in the *Analects*.

separation impossible and undesirable. The fact that vocabularies across cultures do not map onto one another exactly presents no insurmountable obstacle to the comparative enterprise, but serves as a window through which we might see how ideas about honour, shame and disgrace, etc. are construed in different authors and operate within a complex network of ideas. Since such ideas are concerned with the notion of moral responsibility, a focus of this paper lies in discussing the ways that Aristotle and Xunzi conceive of the internalisation of values. 'Shame' in this study, then, is used as a placeholder term which is liable to being problematised and reinterpreted as one engages deeper with the ancient materials.

Having discussed 'shame' in a cross-cultural context, now what does 'moral education' signify for the ancient philosophers? The phrase 'moral cultivation', which pervades much contemporary scholarship on Confucian ethics, helpfully draws attention to the idea that education is not a simple matter of the reception of an outside influence, but must also involve the active will and effort of the individual who accepts what is taught, gradually forms an understanding of why he should be taught that way, and himself tries to contribute to the success of that education by monitoring his own words and actions. In this way, education is not a one-way process of the moulding of an individual by the educator, but involves recognition on behalf of the individual that he has the capacity to be cultivated and that it is a worthwhile activity to better himself through the cultivation process. For Aristotle, moral education involves possessing intellectual as well as moral virtues so that one is habituated into performing the right kinds of actions, doing them for the sake of the fine (*to kalon*) itself and leading a life of eudaimonia, which is the activity of the rational part of the soul in accordance with the virtues.[8] As for Xunzi, moral education is important in terms of transforming what one is born with so that through learning (*xue* 學) and cultivating oneself (*xiushen* 修身), one acts in accordance with rituals and a sense of propriety (*liyi* 禮義). We should not expect to find a single word or phrase in the Greek and Chinese to correspond to the 'moral education' that is in question. *Paideia* is an obvious choice for 'education' in the Greek society; its meaning is broad and spans from the acquisition of skills to that of notions of the fine and the disgraceful, both aspects of which are relevant

---

[8] Aristotle's conception of eudaimonia is associated with political activity in the earlier books and contemplation in Book 10 of the *EN* and there have been extended debates concerning how to reconcile the contemplative and the practical life. Given the limitations of space, I will not discuss in detail the problems here, but one may consult, for example, J. L Ackrill 1980 and John Cooper 1999 on this topic.

to what we mean by 'education' in English (which is also a broad term). For Xunzi, *jiaohua* 教化 is commonly used to indicate personal transformation (usually in moral behaviour) from teaching, and learning (*xue* 學) is an important idea that pervades the corpus of the work. Although Aristotle's and Xunzi's conceptual frameworks of 'moral education' differ, for both it is important to meet the goal or the ideal which is seen as the best state for a human being, thereby fulfilling humans' unique capabilities. As I shall show, ideas of honour and shame are important elements in an individual's moral development and in the achievement of the ideal.

Shame and the Pursuit of Goods

For Aristotle and Xunzi, certain negative notions are established as opposites of the fine and the honourable, and for that reason they have significant educative value for the correct judgement of the place of the various goods in life such as pleasure, reputation and profit. Such notions encourage one to pursue certain actions that are regarded as worthwhile by society and/or by the individual, and to avoid others. This section examines in turn the ways that Aristotle and Xunzi portray a priority of goods in life through shame-related discourse.

Aristotle, both in the *Nicomachean Ethics* and in the *Rhetoric*, particularly stresses the importance of *aidōs* to the young who are on their path to excellence and speaks of the different ways through which the young may be prone to experiencing that affection, suitably so because of the nature of *aidōs* in monitoring actions.

Firstly, it seems that Aristotle attributes the appropriateness for the young to have *aidōs* to their living by affections and making many mistakes:

But the affection in this case is not fitting for every time of life, only for youth; for we think that young people should have a sense of shame (*aidēmonas einai*) because they live by affection and so get many things wrong, but are held back by a sense of shame (*hupo tēs aidous de kōluesthai*); and we praise those of the young who have it, whereas no one would praise an older person for being prone to feeling shame (*aischuntēlos*), since we think it necessary that he does nothing from which hangs shame (*aischunē*).[9] (*EN* 1128b15–21)

---

[9] Unless otherwise stated, my translations are based on the following, with modifications: for Aristotle, I use the Jonathan Barnes edition (1984) as set out in the Notes on Editions, except the *Nicomachean Ethics*, for which I use Sarah Broadie and Christopher Rowe (2002). For translations of the *Xunzi*, I generally cite John Knoblock (1988–94), though with moderate

This statement, however, does not reveal much as to how living by affections might lead to inappropriate behaviour. To answer that question, we ought to look to other parts of the *EN* where Aristotle discusses the particular characteristics of the young, and also to *Rhetoric* 2.12 which features the various types of human character in relation to affections, states of character, ages and fortunes, and starts with the youthful type of character. Firstly, it is said that the young are *epithumētikoi*, and changeable and fickle with regard to desires. They act by gratifying their desires, especially with regard to bodily ones. Furthermore, the young live by affection, and more than anything pursue what is pleasant for them and what is immediately before them (*EN* 1156a32–3). Such qualities render them lacking in self-control (*akrateis, Rhet.* 1389a5), which, as we learn from Book 3 of the *EN*, means that actions are committed from appetitive desire (*epithumia*) but not purposive choice (*prohairesis*) (*EN* 1111b13–14). Purposive choice is deliberate desire (*orexis bouleutikē*), and good purposive choice (*prohairesis spoudaia*) requires the reasoning to be true and the desire to be right (*EN* 1139a23–5), so that the two parts of the soul, the rational and the non-rational, are in harmony with each other. It appears, then, that young people are prone to making mistakes because, in taking action, they are propelled by desire and have a tendency to pursue the pleasant at the expense of over-riding rational judgement. That may explain also why their mistakes are in the direction of doing things excessively and vehemently (*Rhet.* 1389b2–3) and why their actions fail to arrive at the mean.

Secondly, apart from being prone to be swayed by affections and desires, young people are said to have a love of honour (*philotimia*) and cannot bear being slighted (*Rhet.* 1389a10–11). They are prone to shame (*aischuntēloi*) and accept the rules of society in which they have been trained, not yet believing in any other standard of honour (*Rhet.* 1389a28–9). Those who experience shame, then, are aware of a social standard against which their actions and thoughts will be judged, and of the fact that they are members of a community with certain shared notions of right and wrong. We might imagine that a child who is indifferent to notions of the 'fine' and the 'shameful' that are prescribed by society will live a lawless life resembling that of the Cyclopes who do not participate in community life but only care

---

modifications where appropriate and with reference to Hutton's (2014) recent translation. I abbreviate the works of Aristotle as follows: *Nicomachean Ethics* – *EN*, *Politics* – *Pol.*, *Rhetoric* – *Rhet.*, *De Anima* – *DA*.

for themselves.[10] However, that idea is almost inconceivable since for us, as well as for Aristotle, human beings live in societies (though of course the society that Aristotle envisages as a norm would be a polis) and are to a great extent dependent upon their communities for resources, interaction and personal development. Therefore a sense of shame appears to be a prerequisite step for a young person to be integrated into the operations of the society in which he lives and not to be ruled as an outcast. Young people's honour-loving character may again be traced to their *epithumētikoi* nature, since for Aristotle *epithumiai* are not limited to bodily desires, but on occasion also extend to desire for wealth, victory and honour (*EN* 1148a25–6, *Rhet.* 1369a12–13, 1370b32–4).[11] *Aidōs* is defined as a fear of loss of reputation in the *EN*, while *aischunē* is defined in the *Rhetoric* as 'a kind of pain or disturbance in respect of bad things, past, present, or future, which seem to tend to lead to dishonour (*adoxia*)'. Because of their love of honour, then, the young strive towards anything that may gain them honour and shun anything that may bring disgrace; in this way, their love of honour acts as a motivation for them to seek the honourable and reject the shameful.

Friendship plays an important role in young people's pursuit of excellence by helping them avoid mistakes (*EN* 1155a12–13), and it can be said to be the third defining feature of young people's lives that might encourage them to pursue honour and avoid shame. In the *Rhetoric*, we are told that 'people compete with their equals for honour' (*Rhet.* 1384a31), that we find it shameful (*aischron*) if we are 'lacking a share in the honourable things shared by everyone else, or by all or nearly all who are like ourselves' (*Rhet.* 1384a11–12), and that 'we feel most shame (*aischunontai*) before those who will always be with us and those who notice what we do, since in both cases eyes are upon us' (*Rhet.* 1384a34–b1). Because young people spend much time in the company of friends whose judgements they greatly esteem and because their love of honour disallows them from not sharing in the honourable things with friends, we might say that, for Aristotle, friends inadvertently act as monitors for one another so that they might perform honourable actions and seek to rival their friends in terms of gaining

---

[10] In *Odyssey* 9.106–15, words such as *athemistōn* and *oute themistes* are used to describe the Cyclopes, indicating that, unlike humans, they are not community-oriented. Aristotle uses *sporades* to describe the Cyclopes who live in scattered households (*Pol.* 1252b22–3).

[11] For a detailed examination of *epithumia* and a scope of its objects, see Giles Pearson 2012: 91–110, who argues that the notion of *epithumia* 'is one which retains the link to pleasure, but extends the notion of pleasure in play to include other kinds of bodily pleasures and also non-bodily pleasures, such as pleasures of learning or victory. Aristotle thus appears to employ two different notions of *epithumia*, one narrow, one broad' (at 110). It could be said that Aristotle does not have two different notions of *epithumia* but two ranges of application.

honours. Friendships can be, of course, for interest, for pleasure or for the good, according to Aristotle. Good friendships, then, exert a positive kind of peer pressure to help one avoid mistakes and to steer one onto the right path.[12]

In order to understand well Aristotle's disinclination to attribute *aidōs* as a positive feeling to an older and decent person, we ought to look to *EN* 3.7–8 for discussions of various types of courage and an assessment of the different kinds of motivations behind them. Firstly, let us establish what it is that the truly courageous man and the civically courageous endure dangers for. The distinctions are drawn very clearly: the courageous man acts for the sake of the fine (*EN* 1115b23–4), while the civically courageous acts on account of the penalties imposed by the laws and the reproaches he would otherwise incur, and on account of the honours that he could gain with such actions (*EN* 1116a18–19). It is clear, then, that the civically courageous man undertakes courageous actions not for the sake of 'the fine' *qua* fine, but in order to gain personal honour, which should only come as a consequence or 'by-product' of fine actions and not as that on account of which fine actions should be performed. Though the truly courageous and the civically courageous may both undertake the same dangerous tasks in battle and gain honour for themselves, there is an essential difference in the motivations of their actions which distinguishes the two. In their definitions both *aidōs* and *aischunē* are concerned with *adoxia* – 'disrepute' – which is very much consequent upon external judgements of what is improper and wrong; we might say that one who acts out of *aidōs* or *aischunē* is concerned with conforming to social standards of what is noble. Often enough, of course, what is prescribed by society and followed by the civically courageous man may just be what the truly virtuous man himself would choose to do. However, as I hope to have illustrated, the goals of their pursuits are different, one for *to kalon* and the other for *timē*, two very different concepts that reflect the different stages of a person's moral development.

In the existing literature there are disagreements as to what the difference between the civically courageous man and the truly courageous man amounts to. Myles Burnyeat 1980 sees a close association between shame and pleasure, noting that shame, as a 'semi-virtue of the learner', allows the learner to find pleasure in noble things. Martha Jimenez 2011, too, believes that shame makes the acquisition of full-virtue possible, though, in a different approach from Burnyeat's, she stresses that it is an 'integration of the rational and orectic tendencies that provide learners with the ability to identify noble

---

[12] For the idea that friends can help those in their prime towards fine action, see *EN* 1155a12–15.

actions and objects as noble and place considerations about nobility and shamefulness at the center of their reasons for action' (175). More recently, Zena Hitz 2012 has argued for a very different take on the role of shame in the acquisition of virtue. She believes that the one who acts for the sake of the fine and the one who acts out of a sense of shame do not reflect different *stages* in moral education, but different kinds of education altogether which has led them to become habituated to having different kinds of motivations. I am sympathetic to Hitz's views to a certain extent, particularly to the idea that a method of education that relies too heavily on external incentives could be harmful to a person's moral development. Nonetheless, I am inclined to view the honour-driven young man and the morally mature man as belonging to different *stages* of moral development since Aristotle recognises that *aidōs* is fitting for people of a particular age: he believes it to be a praiseworthy quality in youth, though not in an older man who is expected not to rely on a fear of disrepute to check his actions. This appears to be evidence that Aristotle expects an older man to reach a different stage in moral development whereby he chooses actions for the sake of the fine itself.

Yet it would appear that sometimes actions done out of a sense of honour or shame are closely assimilated to ideas of the fine itself. For example, in Aristotle's discussions of the magnanimous man (*megalopsuchos*), it is said that 'sometimes we praise the honour-loving one as manly and loving what is fine' (*EN* 1125b11–12) and that 'honour is a prize of excellence and is meted out to the good' (*EN* 1123b35–1124a1). Book 10 of the *EN* provides further evidence that having a sense of *aidōs* is to be praised. There, Aristotle distinguishes between those who by nature obey a sense of shame and the many who obey only fear. He then distinguishes between two groups of people: those who abstain from bad acts because of their baseness and those who do so through fear of punishment (*EN* 1179b11–13). Though there is no explicit link between the two statements, in making logical sense of the phrasing, it appears that Aristotle associates those who obey a sense of shame with abstaining from bad actions on account of their baseness, and he associates those who obey fear with abstaining from bad actions through fear of punishment. This passage, then, complicates the idea that *aidōs* is very much concerned with conforming to social standards of what is noble, for shunning bad actions because of their baseness suggests taking actions that could go beyond concerns for external judgement.[13] So then we might say

---

[13] Jimenez 2011, as mentioned above, believes this to be the essential role of *aidōs* in Aristotle. Cf. also Cairns, who argues for the positive role of shame in moral development on the basis that it can 'give one a genuine desire to do what is *kalon* and avoid what is *aischron*' and enable one to

that Aristotle attributes an ambivalent place to actions done out of *aidōs*, sometimes in praise of them yet at other times disapproving of their motives. Indeed, the ambivalence surrounding the idea points to the fact that individual morality is tied to social values in such a way that often they cannot be easily separated.

When we turn to the *Xunzi*, we notice that discussions of the role of shame in moral education are not centred on the youth who according to Aristotle live by affection and have particular tendencies to satisfy their strong and fickle desires. Instead, Xunzi emphasises the idea that learning is a lifetime pursuit,[14] as is evident from the first chapter *An Exhortation to Learning*: 'learning ought not to stop' (1/1/1) and 'learning continues until death and only then does it stop' (2/1/27). He describes desires (*yu* 欲) as common to each and every person, and, unlike Aristotle, does not portray the young as a group particularly prone to gratifying their desires.[15] Because human nature is bad in Xunzi's view and everyone is born a petty person, moral education plays a particularly significant role in transforming one into a gentleman who is capable of moderating his desires and performing actions that are in accordance with ritual and a sense of propriety. In such a way, one is able to avoid detestable consequences and attain a life of true honour.

In *An Exhortation to Learning*, it is said that there must be a beginning for every type of phenomenon that occurs, and that honour and disgrace are necessarily reflections of (one's) *de* (1/1/13). Honour (*rong* 榮) in the *Xunzi* is spoken of together with things that are valued in a good life and promote survival, such as success (*tong* 通), peace/security (*an* 安), and profit/benefit (*li* 利)[16], while disgrace (*ru*), on the other hand, is

---

act, in some sense, 'for the sake of the noble' (1993: 425). Yet we should remember that Aristotle's definition of *aidōs* is a fear of disrepute, which may or may not be a genuine desire to avoid what is *aischron*; the emphasis, rather, is on the fear of dishonour.

[14] Cf. Van Norden 2000: 132n49: 'One of the major differences between Xunzi and Aristotle on self-cultivation is that Aristotle thinks one must have gone through the first stage by the onset of middle age, whereas Xunzi, in common with other Confucians, sees self-cultivation as a more long-term process.' Here I might add that even though Aristotle explicitly expresses in *EN* 4.9 that *aidōs* is only suitable to the young, assuming that the older man will no longer commit actions of which he would be ashamed, in Book 10 of the *EN* he clearly portrays *aidōs* as a positive quality without specifying a particular age group for whom it would be appropriate.

[15] The morally immature person, of course, *is* particularly prone to indulging in unseemly pleasures due to a lack of cultivation.

[16] *Li* 利 in the *Xunzi* is ambiguous and can be positive or negative. It may be translated as profit or benefit, and corresponds to that which brings advantage to the individual. For example, when *li* is spoken of as the counterpart of harm (*hai* 害), it is positive; yet when it acts as the counterpart of propriety (*yi* 義), it is almost always negative. For more discussions on occurrences of the term *li* in the *Xunzi*, see Defoort 2008: 158, 160, 165n37, 177–8, 180.

associated with all the things that endanger life, such as poverty (*qiong* 窮), danger/crisis (*wei* 危) and harm (*hai* 害). The following passage makes clear distinctions between *rong* and *ru*:

> The great distinctions between honour and disgrace and the invariable conditions of security and danger and of profit and harm are thus: those who put a sense of propriety before profit are honourable; those who place profit before a sense of propriety are disgraceful. Those who are honourable always gain success; those who are disgraceful are always reduced to poverty. The successful always exercise control over others; the poor are always controlled by others. Such is the great distinction between honour and disgrace. (9/4/22–3)

From this passage, it can be established that the distinction between honour and disgrace ultimately depends upon how one chooses between profit and propriety. Those who put a sense of propriety before profit are honourable, often meet with success and have the ability to exercise control over others; by contrast, those who place profit before a sense of propriety are disgraceful and find themselves in a state of poverty and being controlled by others. Honour and the good things that are associated with it are not bound in a one-way causal relationship in the sense that honour causes success, or success honour. Rather, honour belongs to a class of good things which are the results of praiseworthy action – that of prioritising a sense of propriety over profit; the opposite can be said for disgrace and all the deplorable states associated with it. In other words, 'honour' in the *Xunzi* acts rather like *to kalon* in Aristotle which stands for 'the good', while 'disgrace' resembles the role that *to aischron* plays in Greek, meaning that which is bad. In speaking of honour and disgrace, Xunzi is ultimately concerned with the ethical choices that one makes in life, detailing the good and bad things that follow upon those choices, hence prescribing correct behaviour rather than singling out the importance of obtaining honour and shunning disgrace for themselves.[17] Likewise, when Xunzi says that the gentleman is 'apprehensive about avoiding disgrace' (6/2/45), we may understand that the gentleman is not simply afraid of the loss of reputation itself, but he is all the more afraid of allowing himself to commit unworthy actions that he deems despicable.

---

[17] I am therefore in agreement with Cua on this point, who concludes in his study that 'the emphasis in both Aristotle and Xunzi on the condition of moral agents paves the way toward a better appreciation of ethical shame, for what matters ultimately is not the feeling of pain or uneasiness, which is bound to be episodic anyway, but on the enduring state of moral character that is marked by the concern with intrinsic rather than extrinsic honor' (2003: 180).

Even though it is said that one should prioritise a sense of propriety over profit, Xunzi paradoxically implies that the gentleman will come to have profit, while the petty man will only obtain harm. *Li* (profit/benefit), then, is no longer opposed to *yi* (propriety), but assumes the role of the antonym of *hai* (harm). In other words, *li* becomes a good in life that only the gentleman is able to obtain, paradoxically and precisely because he is able to put *yi* above it, despite his love for *li* which is dictated by his nature:

> In physical substance,[18] nature, awareness and capability, the gentleman and the petty man are one and the same. Liking honour and detesting disgrace, liking profit and detesting harm, the gentleman and the petty man are the same. They differ, however, in the ways by which they seek these. (10/4/32–3)

The passage cited above suggests that obtaining personal profit need not necessarily be associated with disgraceful behaviour. The *way* through which one seeks profit is of crucial importance, so that the gentleman, by positing a sense of propriety before profit, gains honour and other goods, while the petty man, by indulging in the desire for personal profit, faces disgrace and other unwelcome consequences. In other words, whether honour or disgrace befalls depends crucially upon how one values profit and a sense of propriety and prioritises one over the other. In such a way, Xunzi successfully links together private (*si* 私) and public (*gong* 公) interests and illustrates that they are far from being mutually exclusive.

Pleasure, Desire and the Internalisation of Values

I shall now investigate how the idea of shame is associated with the 'internalisation' of values, an important aspect of moral education according to Aristotle and Xunzi, and an idea that I shall expound in more detail. 'Guilt' has often been associated with the internalisation of values whereby the agent experiences remorse and a realisation of the badness of his conduct, while 'shame' has been associated with an overwhelming concern for the opinions of others and therefore sensitivity to external judgement. This dichotomy is often oversimplified, as Bernard Williams and Douglas Cairns have rightly shown, for 'shame' could certainly involve reflections upon one's behaviour that is not dependent on disapproval from others. In the ancient Greek and early Chinese sources that we are dealing with, the 'guilt' versus 'shame' conceptual cluster is absent, and the distinctions between a

---

[18] Knoblock's 'natural talent' is an over-translation for *cai* 材, and hence should be rejected.

genuine concern for one's moral integrity and a desire for mere social recognition are demarcated in their own distinctive ways. I address this question by analysing Aristotle's and Xunzi's discourses on pleasure and desire. Despite their differences in postulating how an agent might eventually come to act upon the right desires, I will come to show that Aristotle's and Xunzi's discussions of desire share a commonality in attributing an importance to the internalisation of values, which is an indication of a morally mature individual. For both philosophers, good actions are not simply conducted on the grounds of securing honour, but are internally approved by the agent for being good in themselves, thereby reflecting the right kinds of motivations for taking action.

Desire (*orexis*) is an important concept in Aristotle's ethics because it is concerned with the pursuit of goods that are deemed worthy by the agent, which in turn serves as a reflection of the stage of his moral development. Pearson rightly notes that 'desire seems either central or at least relevant to understanding his [Aristotle's] accounts of, for example, virtue, *akrasia*, choice (*prohairesis*), deliberation, voluntary action, moral education, and animal locomotion'.[19] As mentioned above, Aristotle makes a direct link between appetitive desire (*epithumiai*) and the concept of shame by attributing young people's sense of shame to their being driven by desires (*epithumiai*) and hence making many mistakes. It is said in *EN* 4.9 that, for a morally mature person who is older, *aidōs* would not be relevant because there would not be anything he does (thoughts and actions included) that would be deemed shame-inducing. This could be understood to mean that it is by virtue of not making mistakes through excessive *epithumiai* that the morally mature person finds it unnecessary to check himself through experiencing *aidōs*, and he does not need the fear of disrepute to act as a motivating factor in his decision-making process. According to the *De Anima*, when the object is pleasant or painful, the soul makes a sort of affirmation (*kataphasa*) or negation (*apophasa*), and pursues or avoids the object (*DA* 431a9–10). In Book 2 of the *EN* it is said that:

excellence of character has to do with pleasures and pains: it is because of pleasure that we do bad things, and because of pain that we hold back from doing fine things. This is why we must have been brought up in a certain way from childhood

---

[19] Pearson 2012: 2. The various accounts of desire in Aristotle's works certainly deserve book-length studies themselves, as for example Pearson's work serves to show. However, the scope of the current study does not allow for a close examination of all the roles of desire (including *epithumia, thumos, boulēsis*; rational and non-rational) in Aristotle's ethical and psychological works as a whole.

onwards, as Plato says, so as to delight in and be distressed by the things we should. This is what the correct education is. (*EN* 1104b8–13)

Aristotle further justifies the claim by saying that 'if the excellences have to do with actions and affections, and every affection and every action is accompanied by pleasure and pain, this will be another reason for thinking that excellence has to do with pleasures and pains' (*EN* 1104b13–16). Although desiring something cannot be equated to taking pleasure in it on the grounds that the desire may only imply the *prospect* of taking pleasure,[20] it is clear that desires often anticipate pleasures which may or may not include those associated with excellence.

We might recall that *aidōs* and *aischunē* are defined as a fear of disrepute or a kind of pain in respect of bad things that tend to lead to disrepute. The fact that young people have a particular tendency to pursue what is pleasant (*EN* 1156a31–3) and that they are honour driven suggests that the pain associated with shame acts as a motivating factor for them to avoid shameful behaviour. Notably Aristotle makes distinctions between different types of pleasures so that it is important to educate people to consider pleasant what is truly pleasant and not merely what is apparently pleasant. By following his sense of shame, a young person learns not to pursue what is immediately in front of him, which may be the apparently pleasant but not the truly pleasant. At an early stage in the education process, then, it may be understood that young people are to be habituated to pursuing honourable actions by associating them with pleasure, and to avoiding disgraceful ones by associating them with pain (cf. *EN* 1179b23–6, 1179b29–31). It is then assumed that after acquiring the correct habits ('the that'), young people would gradually come to understand the true reasons for taking such kinds of actions ('the because').[21]

The avoidance of shameful behaviour for the sake of avoiding disrepute can be contrasted with the actions of the morally mature man whose rational judgement and desire are in harmony and who acts in accordance with values of which he himself approves. Aristotle's discussions of the 'incontinent' man (*akratēs*) and the 'continent' man (*enkratēs*) are particularly enlightening as to what it means when desires conflict with rational thought. The incontinent man is said to act in accordance with his desires (*epithumōn*) but not purposive choice (*EN* 1111b13–14), thus giving in to temptation despite

---

[20] For a fuller discussion on the relation between desire and pleasure, see Pearson against Charles 2012: 205.
[21] This reading is proposed by Burnyeat 1980. It is, however, not uncontested (cf. Jimenez 2011; Curzer 2002; Hitz 2012), as there remains the question of how young people may come to understand the reasons behind virtuous actions merely by practising them.

knowing it to be a vice, while the continent man does carry out the correct actions, but does so with restraint and unwillingly because his desires encourage him to act otherwise. Neither is an ideal situation, and they form a contrast with the morally mature person who arrives at good purposive choice through true reasoning and correct desire (*EN* 1139a22–6). Much of Aristotle's ethics has to do with having the appropriate affections for actions, for example feeling generous in bestowing gifts, which suggests internal approval for such actions. Thereby it may be said that while young people act by way of following a social standard so as to achieve the pleasant (honour) and avoid pain (loss of reputation) and we see a sense of shame which is mostly concerned with social approval or disapproval, the morally mature man acts out of an individual standard of the fine and the shameful because his desire is in harmony with true reasoning that allows him to carry out fine actions, and he exhibits the affections appropriate to the given situation. This is perhaps the reason that Aristotle is prepared to grant conditional shame to the morally mature man, in the sense that if he were to do something bad, he would feel ashamed, because he would know that it does not match his own criteria for fine action.

As for Xunzi, the moderation of desires is a central concept which involves the harmonisation of nature and conscious exertion (*xing wei he* 性偽合), thereby bringing about order in society and fulfilment for the individual.

The relationship between desire (*yu* 欲), nature (*xing* 性) and feelings (*qing* 情)[22] can be difficult to gauge, especially as *yu* is sometimes said to be the response to *qing* and yet sometimes included in a list of examples of *qing*. The following passage illustrates the relationship between these concepts, though as it is beset with textual problems, it cannot be fully relied upon:[23]

Nature is the consequence of heaven. *Qing* is the substance of nature. Desire is the response to *qing*. (85/22/63)

The basic picture that emerges is that desires exist because of the make-up of human nature, and that they are a necessary part of human life. Human beings are said to have certain desires when born, including the desire for food when hungry, for warmth when cold, for rest when tired, and to be fond

---

[22] *Qing* can be understood as manifestations of *xing* and it is not to be limited to mere feelings. Because of its multiplicity of meanings, I have generally left the term transliterated. For a range of essays that discuss the range of meanings of *qing*, see Eifring 2004.
[23] See Knoblock 1994: III, 344n101.

of what is beneficial and to hate what is harmful (10/4/42–4, 13/5/24–5). These features are all part of the human condition and are aspects of human nature; for such a reason, they are neither good nor bad in themselves. Hence Xunzi does not argue for the eradication of desires or even the limitation of the number of desires, and he criticises those who advocate such views (85/22/55–7). So then, it is not the number of desires but the *regulation* of desires (*jieyu* 節欲) that plays a crucial role in determining the correctness of conduct. Xunzi attributes the important task to the heart-mind (*xin* 心), which 'chooses' the desires that are to be fulfilled:

Qing being so, the heart-mind's choosing between them is called 'deliberation' (*lü* 慮). Taking action upon the heart-mind's deliberation is called conscious exertion. (83/22/3–4)

Therefore when the desires are excessive, action may not follow upon them because the heart-mind stops the desires [from being fulfilled]. If the dictates of the heart-mind are in accordance with the correct principles (*li* 理), then even if the desires are many, what harm do they do to order? When desires are deficient and yet action follows upon them, that is because the heart-mind directs them. If the dictates of the heart-mind are not in accordance with the correct principles, then even if the desires are few, the results could be far worse than disorder. Therefore order and disorder depend upon the dictates of the heart-mind, not upon the desires of *qing*. (85/22/60–2)

I agree with Winnie Sung's claim that 'any attempt to address the issue of moral action in Xunzi should begin with *xin*',[24] which plays a prominent role in human agency and is said to be 'the lord of the body and master of spiritual intelligence. It issues commands but does not receive commands' (80/21/44–5). An essential aspect of moral cultivation, then, lies in training *xin* so that it knows the Way (*zhidao* 知道) and then supervenes upon the desires so as to choose the right courses of action. So then, 'although desires cannot be got rid of, one seeks to moderate them' (85/22/65). There are two kinds of desires involved – the first being those unmoderated desires which all men have by birth, and the second being desires that have been approved by *xin*. In his analysis of *xin*, Cua contrasts 'natural' and 'reflective' desires, the former being 'a mere biological drive'.[25] In a similar vein, Kurtis Hagen chooses to speak of 'basic desires' and 'specific desires', the former being those kinds of desires that cannot be altered, and the latter those desires which we come to have once *xin* has deliberated and moderated the initial desires.[26] In other words, the correct functioning of *xin*

---

[24] Sung 2012: 380. [25] Cua 2005: 49–50n28. [26] Hagen 2011: 62.

allows the agent to act upon a certain degree of self-reflection and rational calculation rather than the primal responses that humans have by birth.

Rather similar to Aristotle, Xunzi is suggesting that the morally mature person gradually learns to have reflective desires that overcome his biological drive for immediate pleasures that might be inappropriate:

> The gentleman knows that which lacks completeness and purity does not deserve to be called fine. Therefore he recites and enumerates his studies in order that he might perpetuate it, ponders in order that he will fully understand it, acts so as to be a person in such a disposition to deal with it, and eliminates what is harmful within him in order that he will nurture it. Thereby he causes his eye to be unwilling to see what is contrary to it, his ear unwilling to hear what is contrary to it, his mouth unwilling to speak anything contrary to it, and his heart-mind unwilling to contemplate anything contrary to it. (3/1/46–8)

In the passage above, it is not specified what it is that the *junzi* recites, enumerates and ponders, etc., and what he causes his eyes to be unwilling to see, ears to be unwilling to hear, mouth unwilling to speak and heart-mind unwilling to contemplate. Xunzi may be referring to the studies, so that only by perfecting them would the gentleman reach completeness and purity; or perhaps he means to suggest the broader concept of *dao*, which, to put it simply, would be the universal principle that governs all affairs. These two interpretations are compatible, and it may be understood that the gentleman is forever seeking to better himself, knowing well that learning must never stop. There is a strong emphasis on the importance of the accumulation of learning and the repetition of good practices so that whether one becomes Yao or Shun, Jie or Zhi,[27] workman or artisan, peasant or merchant, depends entirely on the accumulated effect of circumstances, on how one concentrates on laying plans, and on the influence of habits and customs (10/4/45–6). Through the accumulation of good practices, one gradually forms an understanding and comes to desire nothing that is contrary to *dao*. In such a way, even though the teaching that one receives is external, one ultimately learns to internalise the things taught. In other words, once the agent has acquired the appropriate knowledge from teachings and models (*shifa* 師法), he is capable of becoming master of his own learning process. By practising self-reflection (*xing* 省 or *zixing* 自省, e.g. 1/1/2–3, 3/2/1–2), he no longer requires an external voice to dictate to him what to do and makes improvements on his conduct.

---

[27] Yao and Shun are legendary sage kings; Jie is a tyrant, and Zhi an infamous robber.

The gentleman, then, tries to improve his own ethical conduct, taking as a source of shame moral failings that fall within one's own responsibilities, not those that lie outside of one's powers:

> Because the gentleman reveres what lies within his power and does not long for what lies with heaven, he progresses day by day. Because the petty man lays aside what lies within his power and longs for what lies with heaven, he day by day retrogresses. (63/17/27–8)

> Thus the gentleman is ashamed of not practising self-cultivation but not ashamed of being vilified; he is ashamed of not being trustworthy but not ashamed of not being trusted; ashamed of not being an able person but not ashamed of being unrecognised. (17/6/40–1)

The structure of the sentence in the latter example allows the object towards whom shame (*chi* 恥) is directed to be open-ended – it could be the gentleman himself and/or someone else whose behaviour to him constitutes a source of shame. In either case, the point is that the gentleman is capable of distinguishing between actions that are apparently shameful and those that are truly shameful, and it is not the consequences that determine the correctness of actions but motivations. Unlike Aristotle's idea of the older man who should not feel shame at all because the feeling is understood to be consequent upon bad thoughts or actions, Xunzi's gentleman is forever examining himself to identify positive traits that ought to be preserved and negative traits that should be got rid of.

Further to the passages cited above, there is other strong evidence to suggest that Xunzi goes to great lengths to distinguish between superficial and true honour, and superficial disgrace and true disgrace (69/18/104–8). There is disgrace that derives from force of circumstance (*shiru* 勢辱), e.g. corporeal punishments, which is not necessarily a reflection of one's moral character or consequent upon morally bad action, and true disgrace that derives from bad actions (*yiru* 義辱).[28] Xunzi makes a clear case that not all outward manifestations of honour are indications of good moral disposition, nor are all outward manifestations of disgrace indications of bad moral character. Rather, one must be able to distinguish between ideas of true

---

[28] For detailed discussions of these distinctions see Cua 2003, who translates these terms as 'intrinsic shame' and 'extrinsic shame', and Van Norden 2002, who translates these as 'conventional shame' and 'ethical shame'. Hutton 2014 chooses to leave *yi* untranslated and offers 'honor in terms of *yi*' and 'honor in terms of one's circumstances'. My translation is based on that of Knoblock, though I modify it to 'honour/disgrace that derives from inner disposition' and 'honour/disgrace that derives from force of circumstance' to emphasise the differences in the causes of one's *rong* and *ru*.

and false moral goodness and recognise that not all instances of disgrace are to be condemned. Xunzi therefore places the moral disposition of the individual far above his social status, which is often reflected in public honours and punishments. Rather than extolling privileged social positions for their own sake and the benefits that come with them, Xunzi praises those whose honour is a result of their moral cultivation (69/18/105).

Conclusion

Through discourses on shame-related ideas, Aristotle and Xunzi make certain distinctions and establish models of behaviour that are to be followed, for a sense of shame calls for the overcoming of a 'falling short of something' and makes moral progress possible. In other words, notions of honour, shame and disgrace intricately revolve around one's sense of self-worth and give one guidance as to which actions to adopt and which goods are to be prioritised over others. While Xunzi's discussions of honour and shame are framed by the correct ranking of a sense of propriety over personal profit, Aristotle frequently compares actions guided by a sense of shame (*aidōs*) to those guided by other motivations, so that actions done out of a fear of punishment or out of the gaining of honour *per se* are less noble, while only those done for the sake of the fine itself are unqualifiedly good. Actions and thoughts are to be judged not solely through external factors, we learn from Aristotle and Xunzi, but more importantly through moral disposition, which indicates that motivation is an important criterion for judging actions.

Both philosophers recognise the fact that human beings in their natural state (that is, prior to receiving the kinds of moral education that Aristotle and Xunzi recommend) seek after what is most pleasurable to them and avoid pain. We could say that their desires are for external goods that tend to generate immediate (and often physical) pleasure. Such reactions are rather more 'instinctive' than 'reflective' since these people are not yet capable of evaluating the moral weight of thoughts and actions. These kinds of pleasures or desires can, indeed, lead to bad consequences. However, for Aristotle and Xunzi, the morally mature person is capable of exercising his unique human characteristics – the Aristotelian *phronimos* exercises purposive choice which involves the combination of rational calculation with the right kind of desire, while Xunzi's *junzi* has a heart-mind that is so cultivated that it is able to 'choose' the right kinds of desires that are to be fulfilled, thereby taking actions based on reflection. Both philosophers, then, share the view that on the path to moral goodness, human beings must transcend their basic desires and learn to take action with a view to what constitutes the good. The morally mature person not only conducts himself in the right way, but also desires to behave in such a way because he understands the goodness of his behaviour.

In this study, shame-related ideas have been taken as the starting point for comparison; the aim was to go beyond philological analysis and to use such ideas to gain valuable insight into Aristotle's and Xunzi's ethical frameworks as a whole. Reading the relevant passages in parallel has brought about certain advantages: we see that behind these ideas lie two complex systems whereby the notion of the good life is defined and that there are fundamental differences in how Aristotle and Xunzi choose to project their views. At the same time, through observing those differences closely, we are able to formulate a correct understanding of the level on which Aristotle and Xunzi might be said to hold common ground. What has become evident is that, in the texts studied, both Aristotle and Xunzi are concerned with making distinctions between motivations for actions – those that are a result of internal reflections and those that are based on concerns for external judgements. They share some remarkable similarities in their expectations of the exemplary person who goes beyond mere public opinions and makes decisions based on his cultivated understanding of what is to be pursued. By discussing the different ways through which Greek and Chinese philosophers use shame-related ideas to illustrate the position of the various goods in life and place an unmissable emphasis on the moral cultivation of the individual, this study has shown alternative ways of conceptualising the 'internal' versus 'external' without being confined to the vocabulary of 'shame' and 'guilt'.

Bibliography

Ackrill, J. L. (1980) 'Aristotle on *eudaimonia*', in *Essays on Aristotle's Ethics*, ed. A. O. Rorty. Berkeley: 15–33.

Broadie, S. and Rowe, C. (2002) *Aristotle: Nicomachean Ethics. Translation, Introduction and Commentary*. Oxford and New York.

Burnyeat, M. F. (1980) 'Aristotle on learning to be good', in *Essays on Aristotle's Ethics*, ed. A. O. Rorty. Berkeley: 69–92.

Cairns, D. L. (1993) *Aidos: The Psychology and Ethics of Honour and Shame in Ancient Greek Literature*. Oxford.

Cheng, A. (2012) 'Virtue and politics: some conceptions of sovereignty in ancient China', *Journal of Chinese Philosophy* 38: 133–45.

Cooper, J. M. (1999) *Reason and Emotion: Essays on Ancient Moral Psychology and Ethical Theory*. Princeton.

Cua, A. S. (2003) 'The ethical significance of shame: insights of Aristotle and Xunzi', *Philosophy East & West* 53.2: 147–202.

(2005) *Human Nature, Ritual, and History: Studies in Xunzi and Chinese Philosophy*. Washington, DC.

Curzer, H. J. (2002) 'Aristotle's painful path to virtue', *Journal of the History of Philosophy* 40.2: 141–62.

Defoort, C. (2008) 'The profit that does not profit: paradoxes with *li* in early Chinese texts', *Asia Major* 21.1: 153–81.

Dubs, H. (1927) *Hsüntze, the Moulder of Ancient Confucianism*. London.

(1928) *The Works of Hsüntze*. Translated from the Chinese, with Notes. London.

Eifring, H. (ed.) (2004) *Love and Emotions in Traditional Chinese Literature*. Leiden and Boston.

Fung, Y. (1952) *A History of Chinese Philosophy*, 2nd edn in English, trans. D. Bodde, 2 vols. London.

Gassmann, R. H. (2011) 'Coming to terms with *dé*: the deconstruction of "virtue" and an exercise in scientific morality', in King and Schilling: 92–125.

Hagen, K. (2011) 'Xunzi and the prudence of Dao: desire as the motive to become good', *Dao: A Journal of Comparative Philosophy* 10.1: 53–70.

Hitz, Z. (2012) 'Aristotle on law and moral education', *Oxford Studies in Ancient Philosophy* 42: 263–306.

Hutton, E. (2002) 'Moral reasoning in Aristotle and Xunzi', *Journal of Chinese Philosophy* 29.3: 355–84.

(2014) *Xunzi: The Complete Text*. Princeton.

Jaeger, W. (1939) *Paideia: The Ideals of Greek Culture*, trans. G. Highet, 2 vols. Oxford.

Jimenez, M. (2011) 'The virtues of shame: Aristotle on the positive role of shame in moral development', PhD thesis, University of Toronto.

King, R. A. H. (2011) 'Rudimentary remarks on comparing ancient Chinese and Graeco-Roman ethics', in King and Schilling: 3–17.

(2012) '*Ren* in the *Analects*: skeptical prolegomena', *Journal of Chinese Philosophy* 39.1: 89–105.

King, R. A. H. and Schilling, D. (eds.) (2011) *How Should One Live? Comparing Ethics in Ancient China and Greco-Roman Antiquity*. Berlin.

Knoblock, J. (1988, 1990, 1994) *Xunzi: A Translation and Study of the Complete Works*, 3 vols. Stanford.

Lloyd, G. E. R. (2007) *Cognitive Variations: Reflections on the Unity and Diversity of the Human Mind*. Oxford.

Pearson, G. (2012) *Aristotle on Desire*. Cambridge.

Spalding, K. J. (1937) 'A Chinese Aristotle', in *The Individual in East and West*, ed. E. R. Hughes. London: 58–86.

(1947) *Three Chinese Thinkers*. Nanking.

Sung, W. (2012) '*Yu* in the *Xunzi*: can desire by itself motivate action?', *Dao: A Journal of Comparative Philosophy* 11.3: 369–88.

Van Norden, B. W. (2000) 'Mengzi and Xunzi: two views of human agency', in *Virtue, Nature, and Moral Agency in the* Xunzi, eds. T. C. Kline III and P. J. Ivanhoe. Indianapolis: 103–34.

 (2002) 'The emotion of shame and the virtue of righteousness in Mencius', *Dao: A Journal of Comparative Philosophy* 2.1: 45–77.

Wang Kai 王楷 (2011) *Tian ran yu xiu wei: Xunzi dao de zhe xue de jing shen* 天然與修為：荀子道德哲學的精神. Beijing.

Williams, B. (1993) *Shame and Necessity*. Berkeley.

6 | Human and Animal in Early China and Greece

LISA RAPHALS

Some forty years ago, Jean-Pierre Vernant argued that the ancient Greeks defined the human condition as one element of a triadic relationship between animals and gods, and recent research by Geoffrey Lloyd has expanded this area of inquiry.[1] This chapter contributes to a comparative discussion on what it is to be human by juxtaposing Chinese and Greek accounts of humans as part of a continuum of living things.[2] I also examine Chinese and Greek accounts of boundaries between humans and animals, accounts of the transformation (or 'evolution') of humans from animals (or vice versa) and explicit scales of nature and taxonomies. Important Warring States and Han texts include the *Zhuangzi, Xunzi, Liezi* and *Huainanzi*. Greek texts of particular interest include the works or fragments of Hesiod, Anaximander, Xenophanes, Empedocles, Plato and Aristotle. On the surface, Chinese accounts of the continuity of natural species seem to contrast with Greek accounts – Aristotle especially – of species distinction. But in both cultures, there is considerable diversity of viewpoint, and substantial disagreement and debate about the relation between humans and animals.

Humanity–Animal Continuity

I first turn to two Chinese and several Greek accounts of human–animal continuity. Some also suggest continuities between humans, animals and gods.

Human and Animal *Ming* and Intelligence

An unusual discourse on destiny in the *Zhuangzi* describes 'destiny' (*ming* 命) in the biological senses of lifespan (*sheng ming* 生命), allotments (*fen* 分) and 'years allotted by heaven' (*tian nian* 天年). What is striking is the

---

[1] Vernant 1980 [1972]; Lloyd 2011, 2012.
[2] Unless otherwise specified: translations of Aristotle are taken from Barnes' edition of 1991, with slight modifications; other translations are my own.

insistence that *ming* in this sense is not limited to humans. This account of *ming* suggests an appreciation of what in modern terms we would call a shared biological heritage between humans and animals.

The *Zhuangzi* uses the terms *ming* and *fen* to name an allotment that governs or commands the lifespans of all living things. Life and death are *ming*; that there are regularities of night and day is Heaven. Everything in which people cannot intervene is the inherent nature of living things (6: 241). In another account of the origin of the world, the One arose from nothing and had no form; when it had allotments (*fen*) it was called *ming*.[3] The *Zhuangzi* also links *ming* with the theme of uselessness, arguing that plants whose wood is useful to humans are cut down and cut off from living their full lifespans. The gnarled tree, by contrast, is able to live out its allotted years.

Uselessness may characterise an entire species. For example, the *chu* 樗 (ailanthus) is big but useless to the carpenter (1: 39). Sometimes uselessness is particular: an ancient tree, too gnarled for the carpenter, is left to live out its allotted lifespan (4: 176, 20: 667). Cultivated trees are stripped as soon as their fruits are ripe: 'therefore they do not live out their Heaven[-allotted] years, but die prematurely, mid-life, by the axe, and bring on themselves the destruction of the world's customs. *There is no living thing for which it is not like this*' (emphasis added).[4] All living things have a lifespan allotted by Heaven (*tian nian*), but human activity causes many to die prematurely.

The *Zhuangzi* also suggests that some humans, 'spirit-people' (*shen ren* 神人), have a distinctive ability to enhance or prolong their lives by 'realizing their *ming* and exhausting their essential nature (*qing* 情)' (12: 443). These passages attribute *ming* as lifespan or destiny to humans, plants and animals. The *Zhuangzi* does not attribute *ming* to gods and spirits (*shen* 神, as opposed to *spirit-people*, *shen ren*) or to conscious dead ancestors. *Ming* is thus constrained to mortals; spirits are not mortal and ancestors no longer are. Mortality, however, is shared by humans, animals and plants.

These passages also treat lifespan as an upper limit rather than a predetermined quantity. If lifespan were predetermined, there would be no use in uselessness; the trees that die mid-life and do not live out their Heaven-allotted years would simply be fulfilling their *ming*. Instead, the *Zhuangzi* laments the utility that kills them before the upper limit of time allotted to them.

---

[3] *Zhuangzi* 12: 424, cf. Graham 1981: 156.
[4] *Zhuangzi* 4: 172, cf. Graham 1981: 73; cf. *Zhuangzi* 4: 177, Graham 1981: 74.

Understanding *ming* as lifespan nuances a continuum between human and animal in the *Zhuangzi*. By juxtaposing the allotments of *ming* and the 'natural' lifespans allotted by Heaven (*tian nian*), we see a continuum in the 'fates' in living things. This locates our human decisions within a natural continuum of living things, mirroring the *Zhuangzi*'s attitudes towards humans as part of the cosmos and subject to the same processes as other living things.

On this account, natural lifespans are determined by several factors. The first is the norm for a species. The morning mushroom lives a day, the long-lived trees of southern Chu for centuries (1: 39). But each individual also has a *ming*, an individual lifespan, which is subject to circumstance. Animals also have allotted lifespans, but presumably lack the human ability to enhance their *ming* by deliberate self-cultivation. Humans differ from animals and plants in that human lifespans are determined, not by class membership, but by individual circumstances and choices. Only humans make deliberate choices that optimise their *ming*, and only spirit-people get it right.

A very different account of human–animal continuity appears in the *Liezi*, which describes birds and beasts as similar in intelligence to humans, and claims that originally they lived together with humans. Long ago, they were frightened away, but in the country of Jie 介 in the east, the speech of domestic animals is still understood: 'The divine sages of remotest antiquity knew the habits of all the myriad things, interpreted the cries of all the different species. They called them together for meetings and gave them instructions in the same way as human beings.' Therefore, the passage concludes: 'there are no great differences in the mind and intelligence of the kinds made of blood and *qi*' (e.g. living things).[5] This portrayal of a continuum among living things puts the *Zhuangzi* and *Liezi* at odds with the implicit or explicit hierarchies of living things in most Warring States texts.

Zoogonies and Anthropogonies

Early Greek accounts of zoogony, anthropogony, transformation and evolution vary considerably. The group that Aristotle calls the theologians (*theologoi*) were primarily concerned with the generation and generations of gods. In particular, Hesiod's *Theogony* is an account of the birth of the gods, but in the process it describes the emergence of order from chaos. But

---

[5] 血氣之類心智不殊遠也. *Liezi* 2: 85 (*Huang di*), trans. after Graham 1960: 55.

Aristotle also names Hesiod as the first to inquire into the efficient cause, since Hesiod speaks of Eros along with Earth and Chaos at the beginning of the generation of the cosmos.[6] Here two points are of particular interest. First, in the perspective of the *Theogony* and other texts, order is closely linked to the kingship and the reign of Zeus. Second, the gods whose birth Hesiod describes are both anthropomorphic and theriomorphic; in this sense, they blur the line between animal and human in a very different way than do accounts of animal–human transformation.

Anaximander describes the cosmos coming to be out of the boundless (*to apeiron*), including the emergence of the earth and stars and the generation of life. He describes the origins of humans as the transformation of another species, probably some kind of fish: 'Anaximander of Miletus conceived that there arose from heated water and earth either fish or creatures very like fish: in these humans grew, in the form of embryos retained within until puberty; then at last the fish-like creatures burst and men and women who were already able to nourish themselves stepped forth.'[7] This is an account of gestation, rather than evolution, since the fish are the parents, rather than ancestors, of humans, who are capable of nourishment at birth. Anaximander also introduces what became the widely held view that life was generated from the action of heat on water and earth.

A number of early Greek zoogonies describe animal life arising from the interaction of earth and water, and some emphasise continuities between humans and animals. Xenophanes held that life arose through interactions of earth and water (21B29 and 33 DK); the evidence of fossils (21A33 DK) suggested that these interactions occurred repeatedly over a long period of time.[8] According to Anaxagoras, animals initially arose from moisture, but later from one another (59A42 DK).

Empedocles describes the creation of animals and humans from random limbs produced by the earth, under the influences of Love and Strife (31B57–62 DK). In his version of natural selection, the earth produces 'shoots' of men and women; these 'whole-nature forms' (*oulophueis*) lacked limbs and language (31B62 DK).[9] There were also human–animal amalgams at other points in the cosmic cycle, including 'human-faced ox-progeny' and

---

[6] *Metaph.* 1.984b23–9, cf. Hes., *Th.* 116–17, 20.
[7] 12A30 DK, trans. after Kirk, Raven and Schofield 1983: 141.
[8] Translations of Presocratic texts are numbered according to Diels and Kranz 1952 (DK). Most of these texts come from secondary sources, and our understanding of them is complicated by the biases of the ancient secondary sources, Aristotle especially.
[9] Similarly, Diodorus Siculus (1.7) held that life begins through fermentation from wet clay heated by the sun.

ox-headed humans (31B61 DK). Here, the same forces produce animals and humans. Empedocles makes no strong distinction between zoogony and anthropogony: humans and animals not only have the same origins, but continue to be fundamentally similar. It is also important to recognise that Empedocles' agenda was not naturalistic explanation. Although several passages seem to criticise the views of predecessors such as Homer and possibly Heraclitus and Parmenides, Empedocles retains a religious agenda, and there is debate about to what extent his system was naturalistic.[10] Nonetheless, this account of the production of humans and animals adds two new elements: that creatures and their parts arose in a random way, and that their transformation into species occurred through the extinction of non-viable creatures.

In the zoogony of Empedocles, the interactions of Love and Strife cause the generation of animals and humans (31B57–62 DK). But insofar as Love and Strife create their component limbs at random, Empedocles positions chance and necessity as the driving forces behind zoogony. Combinations of features arose by chance; necessity determined which became extinct, and which well-adapted combinations were well enough adapted to their environment to survive.[11]

Archelaus of Athens also merges zoogony with anthropogony. In his view, as the lower parts of the earth warmed:

many animals began to appear, including humans, all with the same manner of life and all deriving their nourishment from the slime. These were short-lived; but later they began to be born from one another. Humans were distinguished from animals, and established rulers, laws, crafts, cities and so on. Mind, he says, is inborn in all animals alike; for each of the animals, as well as humans, makes use of Mind, though some more rapidly than others.[12]

Even though he distinguishes human mastery of technology and its products from the activities of other animals, he insists that mind is common to all zoogony.

Despite this insistence that mind is common to humans and animals, Archelaus distinguishes humans for their creation of culture in the form of cities, technology and laws. All these accounts are non-teleological, in contrast to the zoogonies of Plato and Aristotle, which break from them in several important ways. In Plato's *Timaeus* humans are created before animals, who emerge through an evolutionary process of mutation from one species to another. Plato, like Archelaus, strongly differentiates

[10] For discussion of some of these issues see Sedley 2007: 60–6.
[11] For this point see Lloyd 2006: 7.   [12] 60A4.5–6 DK, trans. after Kirk et al. 1983: 387.

anthropogony from zoogony.[13] There is no account of either spontaneous generation of life from the earth or of any extinction. Aristotle rejects Empedocles' zoogony specifically because it is non- and even anti-teleological. It cannot be a coincidence that front and back teeth, for example, fit the purpose of tearing or grinding food:

Wherever then all the parts came about just what they would have been if they had come to be for an end, such things survived, being organized spontaneously in a fitting way; whereas those which grew otherwise perished and continue to perish, as Empedocles says his 'man-faced oxprogeny' did.[14]

This passage is complex but the chief point on which Aristotle agrees with Empedocles is that organisms that are well organised survive. However, he disagrees with Empedocles' view that the characteristics of animals are due to chance (*PA* 640a19). Aristotle, by contrast, is firmly committed to teleology.

Simplicius comments that in Empedocles' version of events, the rule of Love created parts of animals and then combined them at random. The combinations that were viable became animals and survived, and those that did not cohere died.[15] Empedocles' zoogony thus relies on a combination of chance and necessity. These accounts are not evolutionary because these adaptations take place only at the origin of animal life, not as an ongoing process of adaptation and extinction.[16]

As Campbell has argued, Plato appropriates and subverts Presocratic ideas on evolution.[17] In particular, intra-species evolution is standard in ancient Greek scientific thinking; inter-species evolution only appears in the *Timaeus*. There, demiurges and lesser gods create living things (41d–43a) out of the four Empedoclean elements into four kinds: stars (39e, subsuming astronomy under zoogony), birds, water animals and land animals (39e, 41b). Humans are land animals, but humans are formed first (42a), and other animals are formed by inter-species (reverse) evolution from one to the other (42bff) until the world is populated by all animal species in an original world of which ours is a copy (91a–d. This passage implicitly commits Plato to the immutability of species). Inter-species evolution is caused by changes in behaviour, which in turn result in physical change (42c). Women are formed in a second generation (42aff), though it is not clear whether this is considered a form of

---

[13] For Plato on evolution of species see Sedley 2007: 127–32.
[14] *Ph.* 198b16–32, cf. 31B61 DK.   [15] Simplicius, *in Ph.* 371.33–372.14.
[16] Campbell 2000: 151–2.
[17] Campbell 2000, to which this discussion of the *Timaeus* is indebted.

intra-species evolution. This schema abandons earlier themes of spontaneous generation from earth and water and extinction of maladapted species.

These Greek accounts show oppositions on two questions: first, between teleological and non- or anti-teleological zoogonies; and second, on whether anthropogony was fundamentally different from zoogony.

Early accounts of human–animal continuity are given a very different form in Aristotle's account of the faculties of the soul.[18] He describes the soul as: the first principle of all animal life (*archē tōn zōōn*, *de An.* 402a6–7) and 'the first actuality of a natural body that potentially has life' (412a27). It is inseparable from the body (413a5); and is the cause and principle of the living body (415b10). Several things are striking about these passages. First, Aristotle defines the soul as a set of faculties possessed by all living things, albeit to varying extents. Second, he makes the original and important move of hypothesising living things (including humans) as complex composites of body and soul. He also applies the form/matter distinction to living things: with body supplying matter or potentiality and soul supplying form or actuality. For example, if an axe were alive, its soul would be what defines it as an axe: the ability to hew, chop, etc., and its body would be metal (*de An.* 412b11–16).[19]

De Anima describes six faculties of the soul that are, to varying degrees, common to all living things: nutrition (and reproduction, *threptikon*), desire (*orektikon*), sensation (*aisthētikon*), locomotion (*kinētikon kata topon*), imagination (*phantasia*) and reason (*nous*). Plants have only the faculty of nutrition (*de An.* 414a29–414b1). All animals with sensation also have desire, but imagination (*phantasia*) is more obscure. Some kinds of animals have the faculty of locomotion, and others – humans and possibly another order like or superior to humans – the faculty of reason (*to dianoētikon te kai nous*) (*de An.* 414b15–19).

In this continuum, animals are distinguished from plants by the faculties of locomotion, sensation and desire; and from humans by imagination and reason. There are also cases of 'fuzzy natures': cases of ontological indeterminacy where Aristotle hesitates to establish a clean boundary between plants and animals.[20] The first instance is in Book 8 of *History of Animals*: 'Nature proceeds little by little from things lifeless to animal life in such a way that it is impossible to determine the exact line of demarcation, nor on which side thereof an intermediate form should lie . . . there is observed in

---

[18] Plato anticipates but does not pursue the idea that living things are composites of bodies and souls (*Phd.* 79a, *Ti.* 42e–44d). However, Plato's view of the soul is very different from Aristotle's.
[19] On these points see Lloyd 1983 and 1996; French 1994.   [20] Lloyd 1996.

plants a continuous scale of ascent towards the animal' (*HA* 588b4–589a2). Examples include the ascidians (sea-squirts), almost plants but more animal than sponges (*PA* 681a10–15). The interest of these passages for the present discussion is their emphasis on the continuity of living things, despite Aristotle's commitments elsewhere to both human uniqueness and to the fixity of species.[21]

Several of these accounts of human–animal continuity are based on the claim of similar constitution: of blood and *qi* 氣 (breath/energy) in the Chinese case and of the four roots in the case of Empedocles. The *Zhuangzi* is singular in its suggestion that all living things have a destiny (as distinct from an ultimate purpose or *telos*). Both the *Zhuangzi* and the *Liezi* seem to be serious in their account of human–animal continuity, as are two other passages from these texts on the transformation of humans from other forms of life (discussed below). Archelaus and Aristotle, by contrast, introduce the theme of continuity as a prelude to accounts of human uniqueness.

Theories of Transformation

Theories of transformation or evolution describe the transformation of populations through time, and how existing species have changed (not necessarily for the better) from their biological ancestors.[22] Evolution can refer either to inter-species evolution, the creation of new species through the accumulation of changes over time (the Darwinian account), or to intra-specific evolution: variation within a species that does not result in the development of a new species.[23] Evolution in the strict sense requires both descent with modification and natural selection.

Transformation of *Qi* in the *Zhuangzi* and *Liezi*

Almost a century ago, Hu Shi made the important point that theories of *qi* introduce issues of potentiality and actuality. The idea that all actualisations are contained within the potential of *qi* introduces the possibility of theories of biological evolution. If all organisms arise from some kind of

---

[21] Human uniqueness: Lloyd 1983: 26–35 esp. 30. Fixity of species is discussed below.
[22] For important caveats about the retroactive application of terms such as 'evolution' and 'biology' to texts written before about 1800, see Cunningham 1988 and Cunningham and Williams 1993.
[23] On this point see Campbell 2000: 146.

elemental and generative *qi*, it must contain the potential for all later forms. Further, Hu argued that Warring States thinkers recognised organic continuity throughout the gradations of the animate world, beginning with undifferentiated *qi* and culminating in humanity. (This view of *qi* also makes comprehensible several of the paradoxes of the last chapter of the *Zhuangzi*.)[24]

This view of *qi* also offers a perspective on several Warring States and Han accounts of the evolution of living things in two specific senses of the term: (1) that one kind of living thing is descended from another and (2) that living things change by adapting to their environment.[25] In particular, several passages in the *Zhuangzi* describe some kind of evolution that involves the *ming* of living things: 'We may discuss the principle of the myriad creatures. The life of living things is like the galloping of a horse, changing at every moment and moving at every moment. What do they do; what do they not do? They transform themselves.'[26]

Hu Shi interprets this to mean that all things are species which develop into one another through the process of variation in forms, but the passage is brief and this view may be open to question. 'Ultimate Felicity' (*Zhuangzi* 18) ends with a more elaborate account of how species transform into one another under the influences of different environments:

Species [*zhong* 種] have minute beginnings [*ji* 幾]. When they reach water they become minute organisms [*kui* 蠿, lit. filaments]. When they reach the border of water and land they become algae [lit. the clothing of frogs and oysters]. When they germinate in elevated places they become *lingxi* 陵舄. When the *lingxi* reaches fertilized soil it becomes crowsfoot [*wuzu* 烏足]. The crowsfoot's roots become *qicao* 蠐螬 grubs; its leaves become butterflies. The butterflies suddenly transform into insects that live under the kitchen stove. They have the appearance of new-grown skin and are called *qutuo* 鴝掇. After a thousand days the *qutuo* become birds called *ganyugu* 乾餘骨, whose saliva becomes the *simi* 斯彌 insect. The *simi* becomes a *shixi* 食醯 wine fly, which gives birth to the *yilu* 頤輅. *Huangguang* 黃軦 are produced from the *jiuyou* 九猷; *mounei* 瞀芮 gnats are born from putrid *huan* 腐蠸 bugs. The *yangxi* 羊奚 plant couples with bamboo that has not shooted for a long time, the bamboo produces the green *ning* 青寧 plant. The green *ning* plant produces panthers; panthers produce horses; horses produce humans. Humans return to minute beginnings. All living things come from minute beginnings and return to minute beginnings.[27]

---

[24] Hu Shi 1922: 121–2, cf. Hu Shi 1917. Needham and Leslie 1955 quote Hu Shi's translation.
[25] The latter is not natural selection, which is necessary for evolution in the Darwinian sense.
[26] *Zhuangzi* 17: 585, cf. Hu Shi 1922: 135.
[27] *Zhuangzi* 18: 624–5, cf. Graham 1960: 21–2; Hu Shi 1922: 135–6; Sterckx 2002: 168.

A variant of this passage also occurs in the *Liezi*.[28] Both passages are extremely obscure, which is why translations of some of the creatures in question are not attempted.

Nonetheless, in both versions, humans arise from and return to minute beginnings (*ji*). As such, these passages describe repeating cycles of transformation, rather than evolution. Nonetheless, they include two very interesting points. First, they depict living things evolving from minute creatures, to plants, insects, birds, animals and humans. Second, these transformations occur not spontaneously but in response to different physical environments: water, the boundary of water and land, higher places on land, fertilised soil, etc. Third, they occur over time, though this point is not very clear.

The *Liezi* contains another possible account of evolution that is not in the *Zhuangzi*. It begins by distinguishing things that do and do not reproduce and do and do not change: 'That which does not reproduce can produce that which does. That which does not change can transform that which does. That which reproduces cannot not reproduce; that which changes cannot not change. Therefore they constantly reproduce and constantly change.'[29] These processes of change and reproduction are ongoing and never stop, and include *yin* and *yang* and the four seasons: 'What does not reproduce is fixed and unitary; what does not change comes and goes. As for what comes and goes, its limits are endless; what is fixed and unitary, its Way (*dao* 道) is boundless.'[30]

The contrast between reproduction and change and their causes continues in distinctions of form, colour, sound, taste and what causes them. What is reproduced may die, but not what causes reproduction. Form, sound, colour and taste may be perceived, but their causes are never perceptible.[31] The passage goes on to identify this primal material with the action of *wuwei* 無為 and with a series of apparent opposites (soft and hard, long and short, life and death, etc.). It concludes: 'It is without knowledge and without capability, yet there is nothing it does not know or cannot do.'[32] Importantly, the *Liezi* passage identifies the generative

---

[28] *Liezi* 1: 12–18 (*Tian rui*).
[29] *Liezi* 1: 2–3 (*Tian rui*). For dating issues concerning the *Liezi* see Loewe 1993. For additional discussion of theories of evolution in the *Zhuangzi* see Hu Shi 1922: 134–9.
[30] *Liezi* 1: 2–3 (*Tian rui*). I read 疑獨 as *ning du*, after Hu Shi 1922: 132 n. 2 and *Grand Ricci* (*ning* 疑).
[31] *Liezi* 1: 9–10 (*Tian rui*), trans. Hu Shi 1922: 133.
[32] *Liezi* 1: 10 (*Tian rui*). *Wuwei* refers to the notion that the most effective action occurs by not acting. It is a key concept in the *Daodijing* and *Zhuangzi* and appears across a range of Warring States texts.

force with *dao* and the action of *wuwei*. It describes a generative force that does not change or reproduce, but generates what does change and reproduce.

Comparing these debates highlights three important points. First, it is noteworthy that most zoogonies – Chinese and Greek – describe processes of transformation rather than evolution. Even the zoogonies that strongly distinguish anthropogony from zoogony describe species transformation as a one-time event, for example Anaximander's transformation of humans from fish. The notable exception is the *Timaeus*, which gives a devolutionary account of the generation of animals from morally inadequate humans. Second, most Greek accounts, notably including Plato and Aristotle, describe intra-species transformation within a fixed number of existing species.

By contrast, the *Zhuangzi* and the *Liezi* give an explicit account of inter-species transformation over time. While the return to minute beginnings tends to undermine the evolutionary force of these accounts, they nonetheless portray animals adapting and changing in response to different environments, in particular the transition from water to land. These passages stress the mutability of living things, changing spontaneously 'like the galloping of a horse' (17: 585). There is no pre-existing model to constrain the number of species; the *Liezi* describes both what reproduces and what does not reproduce as boundless and without limit (1: 2–3). Further, all the Greek accounts describe the emergence of order out of chaos in positive terms, associating order with the gods (Hesiod) and the divine craftsman (Plato and Aristotle). The *Zhuangzi* and the *Liezi*, by contrast, valorise original chaos, which they associate with *wuwei*.

A second point is the tension in both traditions between purely materialistic accounts of species change and teleological accounts that variously feature gods, designers or first causes.

A third contrast emerges if we ask what broader cosmological role zoogony and anthropogony fulfil in these texts. In both Chinese and Greek contexts, zoogony and anthropogony are part of a larger account of the nature of the cosmos and specifically the balance and interaction of complementary forces. In a Chinese context, these are *yin-yang* and *qi*. In a Greek context, they are the Empedoclean four elements. These cosmic forces account for the generation of the actual from the potential, and distinguish between what comes to be and what is unchanging.

Here, the *Liezi* provides an important counter-argument to a stereotypical contrast between Chinese models of constant change and Greek fundamental distinctions between being and becoming. The *Liezi*'s *dao* is itself immovable.

Scales of Nature

Charles Darwin described evolution as a scale of nature, but the two notions are distinct:

> The inhabitants of each successive period in the world's history have beaten their predecessors in the race for life, and are, in so far, higher in the scale of nature; and this may account for that vague yet ill-defined sentiment, felt by many palaeontologists, that organisation on the whole has progressed.[33]

A scale of nature is an explicit series of steps from lowest to highest, inevitably ending with humans, spirit-people or gods. Chinese scales of nature seem to organise around two distinct principles: ethical and technological distinctions between humans and animals. Greek scales of nature are linked with the teleologies of Plato and Aristotle especially.

The *Xunzi* and *Huainanzi* on Human Uniqueness

Warring States Chinese texts differ considerably on whether there is an ascending order of living things. Those that assert a scale of nature all put humans at its apex, but for different reasons. The *Xunzi* describes an ascending scale of specifically ethical faculties:

> Water and fire have *qi* but no procreation. Grasses and trees have procreation but no capacity to know. Birds and beasts have the capacity to know but not the capacity to behave correctly [*yi* 義]. Humans have *qi*, procreation, the capacity to know and also the capacity to behave correctly; therefore they most of all are the honored of the empire. (*Xunzi* 9: 164)

This scale of living things makes a set of distinctions between: (1) non-living things, which possess *qi*; (2) plants, which have life without awareness; (3) animals, which have awareness without morality; and (4) humans, who have morality. The *Zhuangzi* contrasts to the *Xunzi* in important ways. First, it is not teleological (as Xunzi is in a hierarchical sense, discussed below). The *Zhuangzi* recommends animals as models because of their freedom from destructive emotions. Animals do not fret over changes in their environment, and are not upset by the illusory shifts of human emotions (21: 714, discussed

[33] Darwin 1859: 345.

above). But second, it does grant that humans have power to determine their destiny that animals do not; only we can optimise our *ming* in order to live out our full lifespan.

Warring States and Han texts include other more general accounts of human superiority over animals. Humans and animals are both composed of blood and *qi*, but the fine *qi* (*jing qi* 精氣) of humans is distinguished from the coarse *qi* (*cu qi* 麤氣) of animals.[34]

But the claim that, among animals, humans are at the apex of an ascending scale is not uncontroversial, as the Chinese evidence shows. In addition to the general accounts of human–animal continuity discussed above, at least one text – the *Liezi* – specifically argues that humans and animals are equal. At a sacrificial feast by Duke Tian of Qi 齊田氏, the host asserts that Heaven has provided the five grains, and that fish and birds exist for use by humans. A young boy disagrees:

The myriad living things of Heaven and Earth are born equally with us in kind. These kinds do not have noble and base, it is only that they overpower each other by greater and lesser intelligence and strength. They eat each other by turns, but it is not the case that one is born for the use of another. We humans seize what we can eat and eat them, but how can we say that Heaven originally gave birth to them for our sakes? Besides, mosquitoes and gnats bite our skin, and tigers and wolves eat our flesh, but did Heaven originally produce humans for the sake of mosquitoes and gnats, or our flesh for the sake of tigers and wolves?[35]

The *Huainanzi* takes an opposite view. It argues that animals belong to separate categories or species (*lei* 類) and that humans are superior to animals. The separate species argument is explicit, and is not linked to claims for human superiority: 'That birds and beasts do not gather in the same place is because they belong to different species. That tigers and deer do not travel together is because their strength is unequal.'[36] Some *Huainanzi* accounts of species and categories reflect blood and *qi* taxonomies in which species differentiate as a result of the differentiation of *qi* in the world of the myriad things (*wan wu* 萬物); others account for species differences by *yin-yang* and the five phases (*wuxing* 五行) taxonomies.[37]

---

[34] E.g. *Huainanzi* 7: 218 and *Wenzi* 1.14b.
[35] *Liezi* 8: 269–70 (*Tian rui*), trans. after Graham 1960: 79. An interesting Greek example that shows an opposite idea is Aristotle's claim that plants exist for the sake of animals (as food) and animals exist for the sake of humans (*Pol.* 1256B15–21). The boy's questions are rhetorical, whereas Aristotle seems to be dead serious.
[36] *Huainanzi* 9: 286, trans. Major et al. 2010: 310.
[37] Blood and *qi*: *Huainanzi* 7: 218 and 221 and 19: 645, cf. Sterckx 2002: 74–6. *Yinyang wuxing*: *Huainanzi* 3: 81–2; 4: 142–55; 16: 529, cf. Sterckx 2002: 82–5.

Yet others seem to suggest scales of nature in which species differentiate through differing capabilities:

The myriad [living] creatures all are born as different kinds. Silkworms eat but do not drink. Cicadas drink but do not eat. Mayflies neither eat nor drink. Armored and scaly creatures eat during the summer but hibernate in the winter.[38]

As John Major points out, the passage moves from so-called 'lower animals' through oviparous animals and mammals, suggesting but not emphasising a hierarchical taxonomy.[39] But as the scale moves from animal to human, human nature specifically includes the intelligence and artifice that allow humans to control animals for human purposes:

What Heaven creates includes birds, beasts, plants and trees. What humankind creates includes rites, ceremonies, regulations and measures.[40] Thus that the ox treads on cloven hooves and grows horns, and that the horse has a mane and square hooves, this is Heavenly (i.e., natural). Yet to put a bit in a horse's mouth and to put a ring through an ox's nose, this is human.[41]

Here the crucial ability that distinguishes humans from animals is language:

Though their claws and teeth are sharp, though their muscles and bones are strong, they cannot avoid being controlled by people, [because] they cannot communicate their intelligence to one another, and their abilities and strength cannot be made to act as one.[42]

Tigers and leopards have better speed, black bears and brown bears have more strength, yet people eat their meat and make mats of their hides, because [animals] are not able to communicate their knowledge and unite their strength.[43]

These passages emphasise not technological skill but the use of language. This argument is distinct from other claims of the *Homo faber* type, that technology is what separates humans from animals, for example in the *Mozi* and in accounts of the civilising activity of the sages as inventing the technologies that separated humans from animals.[44]

Contrasting the taxonomy of the *Zhuangzi* to later accounts of transforming *qi* and the differences between humans and animals in the *Xunzi*

---

[38] *Huainanzi* 4: 144, trans. Major et al. 2010: 162–3. For this argument see Major 2008.
[39] Major 2008: 141. [40] *Huainanzi* 20: 691, trans. Major et al. 2010: 830–1.
[41] *Huainanzi* 1: 20, trans. Major et al. 2010: 58.
[42] *Huainanzi* 19: 645, trans. Major et al. 2010: 777.
[43] *Huainanzi* 15: 507, trans. Major et al. 2010: 601, cf. Major 2008: 142–3.
[44] For the *Mozi* see *Mozi jiaozhu* 2: 109–210; 3: 116; 6: 255; 8: 382. For building dwellings see *Zhuangzi* 29: 994–5 and *Hanfeizi jishi* 19: 1040. For discussion see Sterckx 2002: 94–5.

and *Huainanzi* adds to our understanding of the *Zhuangzi*'s account of responses to *ming*. The account of *ming* as lifespan for a continuum of living things allows the *Zhuangzi to* suggest a taxonomy of animals, humans and gods that differs in important ways from the later taxonomies of the *Xunzi* or *Huainanzi*. Humans are not distinctive because of their moral sense (as for Xunzi) or because of the intelligence and mastery of language that allows them to control animals (as in the *Huainanzi*), or for their mastery of technology *per se*. The key difference is agency: the ability to make individual choices that allow us to live out our allotted lifespans. Yet on the *Zhuangzi*'s account, we should use our unique human faculties, but not at the cost of forgetting our continuities with other living things. The *Zhuangzi* seems to want to retain more of our animal nature, which, because it *is* natural, provides an antidote to false desires and attachments that obscure *dao* and interfere with individual autonomy. The *Zhuangzi* would have us use reason but, at a certain point, put it aside.

Aristotle's Scale of Nature

Aristotle also states that the faculties of the soul form a series in which each earlier step is a precondition for later steps: without the nutritive soul the sensitive soul does not exist, and so on, culminating in the highest faculty of all, reason:

Finally and most rare are reason and thought (*logismon kai dianoian*), for those perishable beings [mortals] who have reason and thought also have all the other faculties of the soul, but not all that have each of the others [faculties] have reason. Some do not have imagination, and others live solely by imagination. (*de An.* 415a7–11)

In Book 3, Aristotle argues that all animals perceive, but very few imagine. (Non-human) animals may have imagination, but none has reason (*de An.* 428a23–4); some animals have the ability to form mental images, but lack understanding (*de An.* 433a9–12). Imagination may be based on sensation (animals) or on reason (human, *de An.* 433b27–30).[45]

From these passages we see that Aristotle saw animals as part of a hierarchy of existence or scale of nature with human beings at the top, and this is another major difference between his views and the account of humans and animals in the *Zhuangzi* and several other Chinese taxonomies and biological hierarchies considered above. First, Chinese

---
[45] For Aristotle's views on the intelligence of animals see Lloyd 2013.

taxonomies followed several schemata, but they did not represent humans as biologically superior to animals. On the contrary, some of the *Huainanzi* accounts discussed above emphasise human biological inferiority. Humans do come out at the top of the scale, but because of moral capability, language or technical mastery. Similarly, while Aristotle concedes that humans are inferior to animals, for example in the sense of smell, he is clear that humans are in general superior. Animals lack speech and so cannot form societies. For Aristotle humans are the teleological purpose of the scale of nature.

Several striking similarities between the scales of nature of Xunzi and Aristotle serve to contrast both with the *Zhuangzi*. For Aristotle only humans possess all six faculties of the soul, and humans are the apex of the ascending scale. Aristotle's scale of faculties resembles Xunzi's hierarchy in several ways: (1) Non-living things possess *qi* (Xunzi) but no soul (Aristotle). (2) Living things have souls, and grow and reproduce (Aristotle); plants have life without awareness (Xunzi). (3) Animals have awareness, desires and locomotion (Aristotle), or awareness without morality (Xunzi). Finally, the apex of the scale is (4) humans. Humans have reason and full imagination (Aristotle) or morality (Xunzi). Both accounts are teleological in biological (Aristotle) or ethical (Aristotle, Xunzi) senses.

The *Zhuangzi* contrasts to both Aristotle and Xunzi in important ways. Both the *Zhuangzi* and the *De Anima* class humans as animals, and attribute important mental abilities to both. Both also distinguish human reason from the agency of animals, but in very different ways and for very different reasons. First, the *Zhuangzi* recommends animals as models because of their freedom from destructive emotions: animals do not fret over changes in their environment; they are not upset by the illusory shifts of human emotions (21.714). Even if animals are used for rhetorical purposes, the *Zhuangzi* seems to side more with the attitude of the *Liezi* – and early 'Daoist' texts in general – in stressing the equality and continuity of animals and humans, and eschewing hierarchical accounts. Nonetheless, the *Zhuangzi* does ascribe to humans a power that animals lack: the potential to optimise our *ming* in order to live out our full lifespan. The *Zhuangzi* also introduces the category of spirit-people (*shen ren*); they are not gods, but they present a higher state than normal humanity, and a prospect of reaching a higher level, through self-cultivation techniques. Here again, the *Zhuangzi* differs from Aristotle and much of Greek religion, where the boundary of mortality separates humans from gods.

Taxonomies

A taxonomy is an arrangement of living things into named groups on the basis of shared characteristics, regardless of how they got that way. Although there were considerable debates about taxonomy in both early China and Greece, humans inevitably come out on top, in contrast to our present-day taxonomies.

Chinese Taxonomies of Blood and *Qi*

The *Zhuangzi* account of human *ming* along a continuum of living things corresponds to several Warring States and Han accounts of biological continuity of species in de facto classifications.

The *Zhouli* distinguishes between plants (stable things, *zhi wu* 植物), moving things (*dong wu* 動物) and people (*min* 民).[46] Early dictionaries distinguish birds – feathered bipeds – (*qin* 禽, *niao* 鳥) from beasts (*shou* 獸) – hairy quadrupeds.[47] Both are distinguished from the six kinds of domestic animal (*liu chu* 六畜): horses, oxen, sheep, pigs, dogs and chickens, a group that includes both birds and beasts.[48] The *Zhouli* also refers to six kinds of sacrificial animal (*liu sheng* 六牲).[49] The *Erya* dictionary mentions five types of animal: insects and invertebrates (*chong* 蟲), fish (*yu* 魚), birds (*niao*), beasts (*shou*) and domesticated animals (*chu*).[50] Finally, the *Huainanzi* (discussed in detail below) refers to five kinds of animal: scaly (*lin* 鱗), armoured (*jie* 介), hairy (*mao* 毛), feathered (*yu* 羽) and naked (*luo* 裸/臝).[51]

Other expressions for living things include: beasts and birds (*shou niao* 獸鳥) and birds, beasts, grasses and trees (*niao shou cao mu* 鳥獸草木).[52] Finally, in 'Seven Standards', the *Guanzi* describes 'models' (則 *ze*) and categorises both kinds (*lei*) and comparability (比 *bi*) as physical qualities (*xiang*): 'What takes its roots in the *qi* of Heaven and Earth, the harmony of cold and heat, the inherent properties of water

---

[46] *Zhouli zhushu* 10.3b–4a, cf. Zou 1982 and Gou 1989: 95. The following discussion is indebted to Sterckx 2002: 15–21.
[47] *Shuowen jiezi zhu* 14B.18b–19a; *Erya zhushu* 10.11a.
[48] Domesticated animals: Kong Yingda commentary to *Shangshu zhengyi* 11.18b (Wu cheng) and *Chunqiu Zuozhuan zhengyi* 51.10a–b; *Erya zhushu* 10.25b. Six kinds of domestic animal: *Zuozhuan*, 1457 (Zhao 25); *Shuihudi Qin mu zhujian* 192, 194, 195, 212, 213, 233, 237.
[49] *Zhouli zhushu* 4.6b, 13.1a, cf. *Zuozhuan* 116 (Huan 6).   [50] *Erya zhushu* 13–19.
[51] *Huainanzi* 4: 371–2.
[52] *Lunyu zhushu* 17.5a; *Chunqiu fanlu jinzhu jinyi* 5.140 (*Zhong zheng* 重政), repeated in *Da Dai Liji* 5.8a (*Zhong zheng*).

and earth, the life of humans, birds, animals, grasses and trees, and, which, in spite of the great variety of things, is inherent in all of them and never changes or transforms is called models.'[53]

As Roel Sterckx has pointed out, Chinese taxonomies consistently emphasised the continuity of natural species based on blood and qi.[54] The major source for early Chinese animal taxonomies is Book 4 of the *Huainanzi*. It describes the differentiation of *yin* and *yang qi* as living things of different species or kinds (*lei*) as an aspect of the manifestation of *dao* from a prior state of undifferentiated *qi* into the phenomenal world of the myriad things. One passage states that: 'Various sorts of earth gave birth (to living creatures), each according to its own kind.'[55] Every thing has its own inherent nature (*xing* 性), which is expressed in its kind; as a result, animal species are fixed, based on their nature, characteristics and habits:

> They emerged together from unity, in such a way that each was distinctive: there were birds, there were fish, there were beasts; this is called the differentiation of living things. Regions are distinguished by means of their categories; living things are differentiated according to their groupings. Their natures and destinies are not the same; each took its form in the context of its existence. Separate and not connected, they are differentiated as the myriad things, and none can return to its ancestor.[56]

Another de facto classification appears in a passage describing how spring winds and rain enliven and nurture the different kinds of living thing, each adapted to its proper environment. Grasses and trees grow leaves and flowers in spring and die back to their roots in fall; birds build nests and hatch eggs in spring and pursue prey in fall. Furred animals gestate and give birth; insects hibernate; fish and turtles seek the deep sea: 'Each produces what it urgently needs in order to adapt to aridity or dampness. Each accords with where it lives in order to protect against cold and heat. All things attain what is suitable to them; things accord with their niches.'[57]

---

[53] *Guanzi* 6: 101 or 2.6 (*Qi fa*), 23.12.2b11, 22.12.1b7, Rickett 1985–98: I, 128.

[54] Sterckx 2002: 69–92 and 2005 argues for three kinds of taxonomy in early China, based on: blood and *qi* (*xue qi* 血氣), *yin-yang* and *wuxing*, and normative distinctions between humans and animals. Blood–*qi* continuities provide links between humans and animals in the *Huainanzi* and *Lunheng* especially. See *Huainanzi* 7: 221–2; 8: 250; 15: 489; *Lunheng* 15: 161 (*Qi guai*); 48: 719 (*Zao hu*); 49: 716 (*Shang chong*), and 68: 976 (*Si hui*).

[55] *Huainanzi* 4: 338, trans. Major 1993: 167.

[56] *Huainanzi* 14: 991, trans. cf. Major et al. 2010: 536–7, from which this is quite different. It is worth noting that classical Chinese has no one generic category word for 'animal'.

[57] *Huainanzi* 1: 19, trans. Major et al. 2010: 56.

The result is not the explicitly systematic taxonomy of Aristotle; a logic of differentiation by *yin-yang* and *wuxing* informs the *Huainanzi* account of species. Animals are classified by *yin-yang* characteristics, often correlated with *wuxing*. But, as John Major emphasises, the *Huainanzi* taxonomy is based primarily on close observation, albeit modified by a *yin-yang* conceptual framework.[58] It classifies a number of features according to several *yin-yang* characteristics (in that order): mode of birth (oviparous, viviparous, by night or by day), locomotion (flying, swimming, walking, running), nutrition (non-masticating, masticating), patterns of activity (migrating, hibernating, continuously active), physical structure (eight or nine orifices; wings, fins, forelegs or arms) and bodily covering (shells, scales, feathers, hair or hairless).

Sub-categories of animals (mammals) are based on the presence or absence of horns, fat, upper incisor teeth, and incisor versus molar teeth.[59] The taxonomy does not make explicit its classes of animals, but they clearly appear in a later section that describes the progenitors of five kinds of animal: naked or scanty-haired (human), feathered (birds), hairy (beasts), scaly (fish) and armoured or shelled (turtles).[60] The *Huainanzi* makes binary distinctions elsewhere, but unlike the Greek dualists whom Aristotle criticises, most of its binary pairs are not contraries, for example producers of eggs and foetuses, swimming and flying animals, and animals with eight or nine bodily orifices. Others are binary oppositions based on the presence or absence of: horns, fat, incisor (front) teeth, molar (back) teeth, and chewing food before swallowing. Different animals also have different periods of gestation, and different legendary or mythological progenitors.[61]

Humans and animals are also unified by shared emotional makeup, although humans are distinguished by the refinement of their *qi* and emotions.[62] At least some of what Sterckx describes as a third category of taxonomy – distinctions based on moral criteria – might be better described as scales of nature that purport to demonstrate the moral or technological superiority of humans, and differentiate at least humans from other animal species.

Aristotelian Taxonomy

While several pre-Aristotelian works group animals into dichotomous divisions of various kinds (e.g. land and sea, tame and wild, etc.), the first

---

[58] Major 1993: 179–81.   [59] *Huainanzi* 4: 347–8, cf. Major 1993: 180–1.
[60] Five classes of animals: *Huainanzi* 4: 371–2, cf. Major 1993: 208–12 and Lloyd 1996: 107.
[61] *Huainanzi* 4: 370–2, cf. Major 2008: 140–1.   [62] See Sterckx 2002: 76 and nn. 26–7.

substantial and explicit Greek taxonomy was that of Aristotle. Even this claim is controversial, as contemporary scholars debate whether or to what extent taxonomy was Aristotle's concern.[63] The relation of the philosophy of zoology presented in the first chapter of *Parts of Animals* to the method of inquiry presented in the *Prior* and *Posterior Analytics* remains an object of disagreement.[64] I concentrate on two issues: Aristotle's criteria and reasons for classifying animals and his view of the fixity of species.

In the *Posterior Analytics* (89b23–5, 29–31, 34–5), Aristotle argues that systematic inquiry should address four questions: the fact, the reason why, if it is and what it is. Further, when we know the fact we can ask about the reason why. And knowing that something is so, we can ask what it is. *On the Parts of Animals* (639a12–15) begins by locating its purpose within the inquiry about nature (*tēs peri phusin historias*) to establish the principles on which demonstrations may be based. In particular, Aristotle is interested in the causes of zoological phenomena: explanations of attributes common to many animals, rather than independent descriptions of particular ones. *Parts of Animals* and *Generation of Animals* attempt causal explanations of facts established in the *History of Animals* according to the methods developed in the *Analytics*. *Parts of Animals* and *Generation of Animals* in particular are concerned to explain the differentiation of animal species.[65]

Parts of Animals explicitly asks which attributes of animals should be the criteria for differentiation. Aristotle rejects the 'dichotomist method of obtaining the species by dividing the genus into two differentiae.[66] The method he criticises consists of two moves: dichotomy and division by nonessentials. Dichotomy is the splitting of a higher differentiae by the presence or privation of a particular characteristic (feathers, feet, etc.):

So, on their view, it is necessary to divide by privation and that is what the dichotomists do to divide. But there is no differentia of a privation qua privation; for there cannot be a species of what is not, for example, of footlessness or the featherless, as there are of featheredness and of feet. (*PA* 642b21–2)

Aristotle here criticises division by non-essentials, for example after dividing animals into winged and wingless, subdividing winged into tame and wild, or dark and pale. The second distinction is incidental to the first. The

---

[63] For Aristotle's biology and philosophy of biology see Balme 1975 [1961]; Grene 1972; Pellegrin 1986 [1982]; Lloyd 1983, 1991, 1996; French 1994; Lennox 2011.
[64] Charles 2000; Leunisson 2010; Lennox 2011.
[65] Lennox 2011: 10–13. For zoological classification see Lloyd 2004: 105.
[66] *Diairoumenoi to genos eis duo diaphoras, PA* 642b5.

result is that essentially different things are grouped together and essentially similar things are grouped apart.[67] Nor were they capable of expressing an animal's essence – the issue of primary interest to Aristotle – or of explaining how a given animal achieved its final cause, the best way of life for the adult of the species. Finally, Aristotle considered some animals to 'dualise' (*epamphoterizein*).[68] They did not fit clearly into rubrics of classification because they shared some features of one group and others of another: for example, animals such as seals, which are partly terrestrial and partly aquatic; and bats, which are anomalous whether judged as winged or as quadruped.[69]

In establishing differentiae for animal species, Aristotle clearly rejects as insufficient the mere combination of a genus and a single differentia; one of his major criticisms of dichotomy and division is that they do not reflect essentially significant distinctions. Instead, he requires that each species be described by a unique set of differentiae, but what it might consist of is not explicitly stated.[70] These differentiae are not arbitrary or merely descriptive; they must reveal the nature of their object. First, Aristotle distinguishes between the nature of the genus and differentia by specifying that genus refers to substance and differentiae to what kind of thing (*poion ti*) it is (*Top.* 122a3ff, 122b15). Second, he insists on successive differentiation, where each differentia is determined by its predecessor. Third, he insists on dividing the genus by multiple differentiae.[71]

Aristotle's differentiae come under four headings: bodily parts (including their composition and position); habits or life histories; actions; and character or mode of subsistence, including their social character.[72] The *History of Animals* groups them under ten 'major genera': (1) humans, (2) viviparous quadrupeds, (3) oviparous quadrupeds, (4) birds, (5) fish, (6) cetaceans, (7) molluscs (i.e. cephalopods), (8) crustaceans, (9) testaceans and (10) insects.[73] Aristotle also refers to animals by many other differentiae. Meyer's still influential account of these differentiae focuses on two faculties of the soul (discussed above):

---

[67] *PA* 643b22–5. For a very clear account of these passages see Lennox 2011: 15–16.
[68] *PA* 697b2. For discussion see Peck 1965. For dualising animals see Lloyd 1983: 44–53.
[69] *PA* 697b5–10, cf. French 1994: 46–8.
[70] See Balme 1975 [1961], 1987a, 1987b; Lloyd 1983: 18–19.
[71] For these points see Balme 1975: 184–5.
[72] *HA* 486b22–487a14. Parts are discussed in Books 1–4, modes of activity and character in Books 5–9.
[73] *HA* 490a26–b3 (cf. *PA* 678a26–31), 505b25–32, 523b3–21, 534b14–15, 539a8–15.

modes of locomotion and reproduction, and the anatomical structures that make them possible.[74]

For present purposes, three questions are of interest: Aristotle's reasons for classifying animals (however he did so), the broad kinds of differentiae he sought to establish, and the balance between theoretical and empirical considerations.

Several passages in the *Metaphysics*, *On the Generation of Animals*, *De Anima* and *On Generation and Corruption* suggest that Aristotle thought that species are fixed.[75] Lennox argues that these passages support the view that there is an eternal generation of organisms of one form and therefore that kinds (including species) are eternal.

> Aristotle, then, has a carefully developed theory to the effect that organisms of various kinds, though incapable of individual immortality, are eternal in form. To support this theory he argued that the process of coming to be of an organism of a specific kind and then its eventual passing away was to be viewed as one 'cycle' in an everlasting, continuous preservation of the form of that kind.[76]

The arguments surrounding these passages are complex, but for purposes of the present discussion, two points are especially important. First, individuals are mortal but kinds are eternal. Aristotle gives an account of this difference in *On the Generation of Animals*, where he argues that the soul (which is better than the body and the soulless) causes the form (*eidos*) and life (which is better than not being alive) of living things:

> This is the cause of the generation of animals. Since the nature of a class [*genos*] of this sort [individual living things] cannot be eternal, that which comes into being is eternal in the manner that is open to it. Now it is impossible for it to be so numerically … it is however open to it to be so by species [*eidei*]. That is why there is always a class [*genos*] of humans, animals and plants.[77]

This point is repeated in Book 2 of *On Generation and Corruption* (338b1–19), where Aristotle addresses the question of why some things come to be cyclically (*kuklōi ginomena*), while some recur numerically

---

[74] Meyer 1855 lists the most important differentiae as: blooded and bloodless; terrestrial, aquatic, flying and stationary; viviparous, ovo-viviparous, oviparous, larviparous and spontaneously generated; multiparous, pauciparous and uniparous; solid-hooved, cloven-hooved and fissiped (animals with toes separated at the base); footless, biped, quadruped and polypod; fish-scaled, horny-scaled, feathered and hairy; social, solitary, wild and tame. See Balme 1975: 186. For problems with this list see Lloyd 1991: 5.

[75] *Metaph.* 1033b11–19, 1034b7–19, 1039b20–1040a8, 1043b14–21; *GA* 731b21–4; *de An.* 415a22–b8; *GC* 338b1–19. For particular discussion see Lennox 1987, as well as Grene 1963: 136–7; Lloyd 1968: 88–90; Sorabji 1980: 145–6. For a contrasting view of evolution see O'Rourke 2004.

[76] Lennox 1985: 79.   [77] *GA* 731b24–732a1, trans. modified from Peck 1965 and Balme 1972.

(*arithmoi*) and others only by species (*eidei*). He argues that things whose substance is imperishable are numerically the same, but things which are perishable must recur by species, not numerically.

Second, immortality through reproduction is the most natural activity for living things. In *De Anima* II Aristotle argues that the nutritive and reproductive soul (*threptikē psuchē*) is the most basic faculty, which is possessed by everything that has life. He describes it as the most natural (*phusikōtaton*) activity for a normal living thing to create another such as itself, in order to share in the eternal and the divine, and repeats the point that what persists is not one in number but one in form (*de An.* 415a22–b8) so that each instance of reproduction preserves the form of the parents beyond their individual lives.

Other evidence suggests that Aristotle may not have been totally committed to the fixity of species.[78] As Balme points out, Aristotle's views do not preclude the evolution of species, for example the evolution of new species from fertile hybrids (*GA* 746a30). Nor was there any clear need for him to address the question, since he neither possessed any evidence of evolution nor had occasion to debate evolutionary theories by predecessors.

Aristotle differs in important ways from these Chinese taxonomies. The taxonomies of both Aristotle and the *Huainanzi* are informed by a broader cosmological agenda, but their concerns are very different. Aristotle's classification of animals is part and parcel of a comprehensive philosophy of science and an over-arching concept of nature (*phusis*). The Chinese accounts of species transformation and metamorphosis describe processes that are part of the action of *dao*, specifically its differentiation into *yin* and *yang* and subsequent return to the original undifferentiated state.[79] The *Huainanzi* taxonomy is part of a comprehensive *yin-yang* cosmology. Both Aristotle and the *Huainanzi* share the problem of balancing between the larger problem that informs their inquiry and the demands of accurate empirical observation.

Second, as has been remarked by Needham, Lloyd and others, most Chinese accounts of animal transformation emphasised the continuity of natural species and all living things, rather than species distinction, and these stand in strong contrast to Aristotle's ideas on fixity of species.[80] The *Huainanzi* stresses, not only continua between different kinds of animals,

---

[78] See Balme 1972: 97–8 and Lennox 1985: 90–1.
[79] E.g. *Liezi* 1 (9–10, discussed above) identifies the generative source of form, transformation and reproduction with *wuwei*.
[80] Needham 2004: 157.

but also the continuum between ordinary animals and divine or mythical creatures; thus the *Huainanzi*'s interest in metamorphosis and transformation presents an even greater contrast to Aristotle's notion of (at least relatively) fixed species and fixed natures.

Third, Aristotle contrasts the cyclical movements of the sun and seasons with the coming to be and passing away of humans and animals, who individually are born and die, but whose numbers (species) are constant (*GC* 338b6–12). By contrast, in the *Zhuangzi* and *Liezi* passages, living things return to the original germ, and thus participate in, rather than contrast with, other cycles of nature.

Finally, the taxonomies of both Aristotle and the *Huainanzi* differ from current taxonomies in one very important respect. The Chinese and Greek taxonomies are hierarchical, and non-evolutionary. Humans always come out on top – albeit for different reasons – but they are not claimed to do so as the result of a process of historical evolution. The evidence of modern genetics has made possible taxonomies based on shared DNA in complex structures of clades and subclades. In this sense modern taxonomies are non-hierarchical and evolutionary.[81]

Conclusion

We are now in a position to reassess early Chinese and Greek accounts of humans between animals and gods. Several areas of broad consensus bear remark. In both traditions we find a view that humans emerged from animals. This view is perhaps surprisingly widespread, despite many disagreements about its details. Also perhaps surprising is the prevalence of the idea that living things changed in response to environments, and that maladapted species died out.

Second, we find a widespread view that humans share a common nature and common faculties with other animals, including intelligence. Among this list, the *Zhuangzi* account of *ming* is distinctive because its criterion for having a *ming* is mortality. It articulates a different conceptual relation to animals than do other 'continuum' theories because

---

[81] Pre-Darwinian Linnaean taxonomy was based on morphological similarity, including misleading similarities due to convergent evolution. Darwin's theory of evolution provided a theoretical basis for a 'natural system' of taxonomy in which groups represent branches on the evolutionary tree of life, and contemporary taxonomy reflects evolution. The biological taxonomy of phylogenetic systematics, better known as cladistics (from Greek κλάδος, 'branch') groups items on the basis of shared unique characteristics derived from the group's last common ancestor. See Hennig 1966, 1975; Dupuis 1984.

the possibility that animals have *ming* suggests that animals have some kind of agency. But for all its egalitarianism the *Zhuangzi* restricts the possibility of optimising *ming* to humans; the tree cannot transform its wood or the animal its nature. This account of *ming* is also consistent with the rejection of scales of nature based on human morality or technical mastery.

Nonetheless, most of the texts surveyed here consider humans to be in some sense distinct from and superior to other animals, for a wide variety of reasons. Finally, accounts of humans and animals, including taxonomies, are pervasively informed by cosmological theories, including Greek four elements and Chinese *yin-yang* and *qi*.

Equally noteworthy is the extent of disagreement within each tradition on the particulars of this broad picture. In a Greek context there is especially a strong line of division between teleologists and their opponents. In a Chinese context, there is a broad polarisation between two viewpoints. Some theories championed continuous transformation, and the continuity, similarity and even equality of humans and animals. Others, which are not restricted to those traditionally identified as 'Confucian', were primarily concerned with social and political order and ethics. Of texts surveyed here these include the *Lunyu, Mozi, Guanzi, Xunzi, Wenzi, Zhouli, Zuozhuan, Chunqiu fanlu* and *Huainanzi*. We find a corresponding distinction between Chinese 'egalitarian' taxonomies of blood and *qi* and taxonomic scales of nature, which were based on human–animal distinctions understood in terms of technological superiority (*Mozi, Huainanzi*) or morality (*Xunzi*).

Bibliography

Balme, D. M. (1972) *Aristotle's De Partibus Animalium I and De Generatione Animalium I*, ed. A. Gotthelf (2nd edn). Oxford.
  (1975) *Articles on Aristotle*, vol. I, eds. J. Barnes, M. Schofield and R. Sorabji. London and Swansea: 183–93. Original publication 1961: 'Aristotle's use of differentiae in zoology', in *Aristote et les problèmes de méthode*, ed. S. Mansion. Louvain: 195–212.
Campbell, G. (2000) 'Zoogony and evolution in Plato's *Timaeus*: the Presocratics, Lucretius and Darwin', in *Reason and Necessity: Essays on Plato's Timaeus*, ed. M. R. Wright. London and Swansea: 145–80.
Charles, D. (2000) *Aristotle on Meaning and Essence*. Oxford.

Chunqiu fanlu jinzhu jinyi 春秋繁露今註今譯 (*Luxuriant Dew of the Spring and Autumn*), att. Dong Zhongshu 董仲舒 (second century BCE), ed. Lai Yanyuan 賴炎元. Taipei, 1984.

Chunqiu Zuozhuan zhengyi 春秋左傳正義 (*Standard Edition of the Spring and Autumn Annals and Zuo Transmissions*), ann. Du Yu 杜預 (222–84). *Shisanjing zhushu* edn, vol. 6.

[*Chunqiu*] *Zuozhuan zhu* 春秋左傳注 (*Commentary on the Spring and Autumn Annals and Zuo Transmissions*), ed. Yang Bojun 楊伯峻. Gaoxiong, 1991.

Cunningham, A. (1988) 'Getting the game right: some plain words on the identity and invention of science', *Studies in History and Philosophy of Science* 19.3: 365–89.

Cunningham, A. and Williams, P. (1993) 'De-centring the big picture: the origins of modern science and the modern origins of science', *British Journal for the History of Science* 26.4: 407–32.

Da Dai Liji 大戴禮記 (*Elder Dai's Record of Rites*), att. Dai De 戴德 (fl. c. 72 BCE), in *Han Wei congshu*. Shanghai, 1925, vol. 1.

Darwin, C. (1859) *On the Origin of Species by Means of Natural Selection, or, the Preservation of Favoured Races in the Struggle for Life*. London. Accessed online at http://darwin-online.org.uk/converted/pdf/1859_Origin_F373.pdf.

Dupuis, C. (1984) 'Willi Hennig's impact on taxonomic thought', *Annual Review of Ecology and Systematics* 15: 1–24.

Erya zhushu 爾雅注疏 (*Commentary and Subcommentary on the Erya*), ann. Xing Bing 邢昺 (932–1010). *Shisanjing zhushu* edn, vol. 7.

French, R. (1994) *Ancient Natural History: Histories of Nature*. London.

Gotthelf, A. (ed.) (1985) *Aristotle on Nature and Living Things*. Pittsburgh.

Gotthelf, A. and Lennox, J. G. (eds.) (1987) *Philosophical Issues in Aristotle's Biology*. Cambridge.

Gou Cuihua 荀萃華 (1989) *Zhongguo gudai shengwuxue shi* 中國古代生物學史 (*History of Ancient Chinese Theories of Living Things*). Beijing.

Graham, A. C. (1960) *The Book of Lieh-Tzu*. London; reprint New York, 1990.

 (1981) *Chuang tzu: The Inner Chapters*. London.

Grene, M. (1963) *A Portrait of Aristotle*. London.

 (1972) 'Aristotle and modern biology', *Journal of the History of Ideas* 33.3: 395–424.

Guanzi 管子. Ed. Liu Xiang 劉向 (c. 126 BCE). Sibu beiyao edn.

Hanfeizi jishi 韓非子集釋 (*Collected Explanations of the Hanfeizi*), by Han Fei 韓非 (d. 233 BCE), ed. Chen Qiyou 陳奇猷. Beijing, 1958.

Hennig, W. (1966) *Phylogenetic Systematics*, trans. D. D. Davis and R. Zangerl. Urbana; reprint 1999.

 (1975) 'Cladistic analysis or cladistic classification? A reply to Ernst Mayr', *Systematic Zoology* 24.2: 244–56.

Hu Shi 胡適 (1917) 'Xian Qin zhuzi jinhualun' 先秦諸子進化論 ('Theories of evolution in the philosophers before the Qin period'), *Kao xue* 考學 3.1: 19–41.
  (1922) 'The development of the logical method in Ancient China', PhD thesis, Columbia University. Shanghai.
Huainanzi 淮南子 (*Huainan Annals*) by Liu An 劉安 (d. 122 BCE), in *Huainanzi jishi* 淮南集釋. Xinbian zhuzi jicheng edn, ed. He Ning 何寧. Beijing, 1998.
Kirk, G. S., Raven, J. E. and Schofield, M. (1983) *The Presocratic Philosophers*. Cambridge.
Le grand dictionnaire Ricci de la langue chinoise (Le Grand Ricci), ed. Institut Ricci, Paris and Taipei and Desclée de Brouwer. Paris, 2001.
Lennox, J. G. (1985) 'Are Aristotle's species eternal?', in Gotthelf: 67–94.
  (1987) 'Divide and explain: the *Posterior Analytics* in practice', in Gotthelf and Lennox: 90–119.
  (2011) 'Aristotle's biology', in *Stanford Encyclopedia of Philosophy*, ed. E. N. Zalta. http://plato.stanford.edu/archives/fall2011/entries/aristotle-biology/.
Leunissen, M. (2010) *Explanation and Teleology in Aristotle's Science of Nature*. Cambridge.
Liezi jijie 列子集解 (*Collected commentaries on the Liezi*), fourth century BCE, ed. Yang Bojun 楊伯峻, Xinbian Zhuzi jicheng edn. Beijing, 1979.
Lloyd, G. E. R. (1968) *Aristotle: The Growth and Structure of his Thought*. Cambridge.
  (1983) 'The development of zoological taxonomy', in *Science, Folklore and Ideology: Studies in the Life Sciences in Ancient Greece*. Cambridge: 7–57.
  (1991) 'The development of Aristotle's theory of the classification of animals', in *Methods and Problems in Greek Science*. Cambridge: 1–26.
  (1996) *Aristotelian Explorations*. Cambridge.
  (2004) *Ancient Worlds, Modern Reflections: Philosophical Perspectives on Greek and Chinese Science and Culture*. Oxford.
  (2006) 'The evolution of evolution: Greco-Roman antiquity and the origin of species', in *Principles and Practices in Ancient Greek and Chinese Science*. Aldershot, ch. XI: 1–15.
  (2011) 'Humanity between gods and beasts? Ontologies in question', *Journal of the Royal Anthropological Institute* 17.4: 829–45.
  (2012) *Being, Humanity, and Understanding*. Oxford.
  (2013) 'Aristotle on the natural sociability, skills and intelligence of animals', in *Politeia in Greek and Roman Philosophy: A Festschrift for Malcolm Schofield*, eds. V. Harte and M. Lane. Cambridge: 277–93.
Loewe, M. (ed.) (1993) *Early Chinese Texts: A Bibliographical Guide*. Berkeley and Los Angeles.
Lunyu zhushu 論語注疏, ann. Xing Bing 邢昺 (932–1010). *Shisanjing zhushu* edn, vol. 7.

Major, J. S. (1993) *Heaven and Earth in Early Han Thought: Chapters Three, Four, and Five of the Huainanzi*. Albany.
  (2008) 'Animals and animal metaphors in *Huainanzi*', *Asia Major* 21:1: 133–51.
Major, J. S. et al. (trans.) (2010) *The Huainanzi: A Guide to the Theory and Practice of Government in Early Han China*. New York.
Meyer, J. B. (1855) *Aristoteles Thierkunde, ein Beitrag zur Geschichte der Zoologie, Physiologie, und alten Philosophie*. Berlin.
Mozi jiaozhu 墨子校註 (*Collected Commentaries on the Mozi*), att. Mo Di 墨翟 (c. 479-381 BCE), eds. Wu Yujiang 吳毓江 and Sun Qizhi 孫啓治. Beijing, 1993.
Needham, J. (2004) *Science and Civilisation in China*, vol. VII: *The Social Background*, part 2, *General Conclusions and Reflections*. Cambridge.
Needham, J. and Leslie, D. (1955) 'Ancient and mediaeval Chinese thought on evolution', *Bulletin of the National Institute of Science of India* 7: 1–18.
O'Rourke, F. (2004) 'Aristotle and the metaphysics of evolution', *Review of Metaphysics* 58.1: 3–59.
Peck, A. L. (1965) *Aristotle, Historia Animalium, Books IV-VI*. London and Cambridge, MA.
Pellegrin, P. (1985) 'Aristotle: a zoology without species', in Gotthelf: 95–115.
  (1986) [1982] *Aristotle's Classification of Animals: Biology and the Conceptual Unity of the Aristotelian Corpus*, trans. A. Preus. Berkeley.
  (1987) 'Logical difference and biological difference: the unity of Aristotle's thought', in Gotthelf and Lennox: 313–38.
Rickett, W. A. (1985–98) *Guanzi: Political, Economic and Philosophical Essays from Early China*, 2 vols. Princeton.
Sedley, D. (2007) *Creationism and its Critics in Antiquity*. Sather Classical Lectures 66. Berkeley.
Shangshu zhengyi 尚書正義 (*Standard Edition of the Venerated Documents*), ann. Kong Yingda 孔穎達 (574–648) et al. *Shisanjing zhushu* edn, vol. 1.
Shisanjing zhushu 十三經注疏 (*Commentary and Subcommentary to the Thirteen Classics*), comp. Ruan Yuan 阮元 (1764–1849), 1815; facsimile reprint Taipei, 1980.
Shuihudi Qin mu zhujian 睡虎地秦墓竹簡 (*The Inscribed Books from the Qin Tombs at Shuihudi*). Beijing, 1990.
Shuowen jiezi zhu 說文解字疏 (*Commentary to the Shuowen jiezi*), ann. Duan Yucai 段玉裁 (1735–1815). Taipei, 1965.
Sorabji, R. (1980) *Necessity, Cause, and Blame: Perspectives on Aristotle's Theory*. Swansea and London.
Sterckx, R. (2002) *The Animal and the Daemon in Early China*. Albany.
  (2005) 'Animal classification in ancient China', *East Asian Science, Technology and Medicine* 23: 26–53.
Vernant, J.-P. (1980) 'Between the beasts and the gods', in *Myth and Society in Ancient Greece*, trans. J. Lloyd. Hassocks: 130–67.
Wenzi 文子. Att. Yin Wen 尹文 (c. 359–270 BCE). Sibu beiyao edn.

Xunzi jijie 荀子集解 (*Collected Commentaries on the Xunzi*), ed. Wang Xianqian 王先謙. Beijing, 1988.

Zhouli zhushu 周禮注疏 (*Commentary and Subcommentary to the Rites of Zhou*), ann. Jia Gongyan 賈公彥 (fl. 650 CE). *Shisanjing zhushu* edn, vol. 3.

Zou Shuwen 鄒樹文 (1982) 'Zhongguo gudai de dongwu fenlei xue' 中國古代的動物分類學 ('A study of ancient Chinese theories of the taxonomy of living things'), in *Explorations in the History of Science and Technology in China*, eds. Li Guohao, Zhang Mengwen and Cao Tianjin. Shanghai: 511–24.

7 | Genealogies of Gods, Ghosts and Humans: The Capriciousness of the Divine in Early Greece and Early China

MICHAEL PUETT

Divine powers in ancient Greece and early China could hardly appear more different. Most obviously, the divine powers in Greece have, well, personalities. The stories of a Zeus, an Aphrodite, a Poseidon have been repeated for millennia precisely because the divinities in question are such complicated figures. Complicated figures, with complex motivations, relating to each other and to humans through emotions of pride, jealousy, at times even contempt.

At first glance, the divine figures from China may seem to offer a radical contrast. We know almost nothing about Heaven, the highest god. In early texts, Heaven is often presented as primarily a force for good, handing a mandate to rule to moral kings, and withdrawing the same mandate from kings if they behave improperly. Later, Heaven is often described as simply a cosmic force, with, again, no emotional qualities at all. And that's just Heaven. Where is the rest of the pantheon? Where is the equivalent of a Hera, an Apollo, an Athena? In contrast to early Greece, early China may appear to be lacking in a pantheon of gods and goddesses with personalities. The divine in China, at this first glance, seems to be defined more as sets of forces – moral, cosmic, or both – rather than as individual agents. And, as such, humans in early China also appear to relate to the divine radically differently than they did in ancient Greece. If in Greece the gods and goddesses had complex personalities, humans would frequently find themselves trapped in the conflicts that would accordingly ensue. The gods and goddesses were capricious, and humans were often caught in the crossfire.

Here as well, China would appear to offer a contrast. If the divine powers have no personality, and are instead simply instantiations of cosmic and moral forces, then presumably they are not capricious either. Working with the divine would be, from this perspective, simply a question of according with the larger cosmic and moral order, rather than one of dealing with complex and contradictory personalities. If we seem to be missing in China the complex personalities that dominate the Greek pantheon, we also seem to be missing the stories of the humans who would have to interact with these prideful and jealous gods and goddesses.

Where is the equivalent of a Prometheus, an Achilles, or a Heracles? As David Keightley once famously remarked, in China one finds 'no tension between the counterclaims of god and man, between a Zeus and a Prometheus'.[1]

In short, a radical contrast is often drawn between the visions of the divine found in ancient Greece and early China. Divine powers in Greece are often portrayed as a pantheon of individual gods and goddesses (Zeus, Aphrodite, etc.), each with a highly distinctive personality, and each with highly antagonistic relationships with humans. In contrast, divine powers in early China are often portrayed as lacking in the distinctive personalities that are seen to characterise the gods and goddesses of ancient Greece.

How do we account for the difference?

How to Compare

As G. E. R. Lloyd has argued, one of the common mistakes in comparative analyses involves pulling materials from different genres in two or more cultures and then presenting these as examples of contrasting mentalities.[2] This danger is particularly evident with the material at hand. Stories from, for example, Greek tragedy are placed in contrast to statements in Chinese political theory concerning the importance of rulers following the moral dictates of Heaven. The contrast says a great deal about the different genres, but very little about the larger comparative questions at hand. But if, as Lloyd has argued, we alter the questions we are asking, and take seriously the different genres of texts we are using when we draw these contrasts, we may find more productive ways of developing comparisons between these two cultures than can be achieved through the frameworks discussed above.

I have argued elsewhere that one of the recurrent problems in dealing with early Chinese material is the tendency to take statements – made either in ritual contexts or in philosophical literature – as assumptions. A statement to the effect that the cosmos is moral and harmonious is taken as an assumption – namely, that early Chinese assume the cosmos to be moral and harmonious. Such an approach is a problem in any case. But it is a particular problem in the case of early China, where statements concerning harmony have played such a crucial role in our interpretative frameworks.

---

[1] Keightley 1990: 32.
[2] The argument was developed fully in Lloyd 1990. See also his more recent Lloyd 2014.

The result has been a recurrent use of comparative frameworks in which Greece and China are contrasted for having 'tragic' and 'harmonious' cosmologies respectively.[3]

As a first step in making the comparison, therefore, let us begin by lining up the comparative project in terms of genre. When we do so, we will certainly see many differences, but they will be ones that we will hopefully be able to deal with more productively.

Ritual Spaces in the Bronze Age

I will begin my discussion in a seemingly bizarre place – one that may at first glance appear to exemplify many of the stereotypes that this chapter is intended to question. The text is an inscription on a Western Zhou bronze vessel entitled *He zun* (JC: 6014; Sh 48.1:171). The *He zun* is a sacrificial vessel from the fifth year of King Cheng, one of the first rulers of the Western Zhou. It would therefore date to roughly the eleventh century BCE:

It was the time when the king (Cheng) first moved and settled at Chengzhou. He once again received[4]

King Wu's abundant blessings from Heaven. It was the fourth month, bingxu (day 23).

The king made a statement to the young men of the lineage in the great hall, saying: 'Earlier

your father, the duke of the clan, was able to accompany King Wen. And then King Wen

received this (great mandate). It was when King Wu had conquered the great city Shang that he then, in court, announced to Heaven, saying: "I will settle this central territory, and from it rule the people." Wu

hu! You are only young princes without knowledge. Look up to your elders, who have merit in Heaven. Carry out my commands and respectfully make offerings. Help the king uphold his virtue, and hope that Heaven will accord with our lack

of diligence.' The king completed the announcement. He 何 [the maker of the vessel] was awarded thirty strands of cowries that he used to make

for Duke X this treasured sacrificial vessel. It was the king's fifth ritual cycle.

At first glance, the inscription appears to fit into the general picture outlined above. The primary divine figure is Heaven, which certainly has

---

[3] Puett 2002. For a fuller critique of Keightley's argument on the lack of a Zeus and Prometheus in China, see in particular 73–6.
[4] Following Tang Lan's reading of the graph (1976: 60).

no personality. Heaven is simply portrayed as offering a mandate to rule and as continuing to support the worthy thereafter. The ancestors are equally without personality. They are simply, well, good ancestors. King Wu resides in Heaven, and gives benefits to his son. And the descendants are called upon to be good descendants, to continue the work of their ancestors, and to continue making offerings to the ancestors. Everyone is defined by his role (benevolent deity, supportive ancestor, obedient descendant), and everyone performs his role properly. There are no personalities here, no conflicting emotions, and no complexity of relationships defined by these conflicting emotions. Where, indeed, are the Zeus and the Prometheus?

Of course, this is an inscription from the Bronze Age. One might wonder if this is simply a product of a Bronze Age society, where social roles were tightly defined, and where the divine world was accordingly thought of in a similar way. Surely, one might think, as society changed dramatically over the course of the next several centuries, so too would notions of the divine.

As we will see, some of this (the changes, anyway) was the case. But, intriguingly, many of the characteristics that we are seeing in these Bronze Age rituals of ancestral worship were to be developed and appropriated later.

But then does this not seem to lend support to the religious contrasts mentioned above?

Not really. The inscription is a ritual text. It is inscribed in a ritual vessel to be used in making sacrifices to the ancestors of the makers of the vessel. The reason it is inscribed inside presumably means that at least one of the intended audiences is the ancestors themselves. So what we are seeing here represents not an assumption of what the ancestors and Heaven are like. These are ritual statements, performing a vision within the ritual space of what the world should be like. It is not that Heaven or the ancestors were assumed to be supportive figures, properly playing their role, with no personality. And it certainly is not the case that the descendants were simply following their roles and living out the plans of their ancestors.

So what existed outside the ritual space? A very different world. Here's a poem about Heaven from a different context:

> Heaven, vast and great,
> Does not hurry its virtue.
> It sends down death and starvation,
> It cuts down and destroys the states of the four quarters.
> Great Heaven is sickeningly awesome

> It exercises no discretion, no forethought.
> It abandons those with fault:
> They have already suffered their hardships;
> But even those without fault,
> Are ruined all the same.[5]

Heaven throws down death and famine indiscriminately.

So if this is Heaven outside of the ritual, let us return to the ritual, and more specifically to the inscription above.

A little background will help.

King Cheng was the reigning king at the time when the inscription was composed. The inscription concerns his attempt to gain the support of the lineages that had aided his father, King Wu, at the time of the conquest. It was, as we know from other sources, a period of great instability. King Cheng assumed the throne at a very young age, and his support was weak. Indeed, he would soon face a major revolt from his own uncles (the brothers of King Wu). King Cheng's rule would be saved by another uncle, the Duke of Zhou, who may well have been attempting to usurp the throne himself.[6]

One of King Cheng's (or the Duke of Zhou's – exactly who was really in power at this stage is unclear) moves to consolidate power was to establish a new capital at Chengzhou. The capital would be more in the centre of the new Zhou kingdom, and would hopefully allow the king to be more directly in control of the set of uncles ruling the eastern part of the kingdom. As we know from what would come later, this did not succeed.

And, of course, where Heaven and the ancestors of the various figures vying for power stood in all this is very unclear.

What is clear, however, is the ritual claim within the inscription. It is Heaven that gave the mandate to King Wen. His son, King Wu, followed his deceased father's plan by conquering the Shang and starting the Zhou dynasty. King Wu was aided in the conquest by the other lineages, the next generation of which is being addressed by King Cheng, the son of King Wu. According to this vision, Heaven and the ancestors are the driving forces behind the conquest, and the living are being called upon to continue the path laid out by these divine figures and ancestors.

Given the context, such ritual claims should be read not as an assumption concerning the nature of the relationship between humans, ancestors and Heaven but rather as a performative act – i.e., a statement that changes the reality of the situation. In the case at hand, the participants in the ritual

---

[5] Mao #194. [6] Shaughnessy 1993: 41–72.

are being called upon to take on these relationships. King Cheng, in his address, is claiming that Heaven supported the founding of the Zhou and that the father of the young men being addressed was a supporter of the Zhou founders. The claim is further that Cheng's founding of the new capital is simply a continuation of the actions begun by Wen and Wu, and that similarly the young men of the lineage, if they are to continue their ancestors' work, should support Cheng as well.

One of these young men was He. The king awarded He thirty cowries of shells that he took to the royal foundry to have the vessel, with this inscription, cast. The ritual vessel would then be used to sacrifice to He's ancestors. Within the ritual, therefore, the call would be for the deceased to be proper ancestors and the living to be proper descendants, each playing their proper role in supporting King Cheng.

In short, the inscription is not a statement of a belief. It is a ritual text, not aimed at making statements about the world as it is believed to be but rather making ritual claims exhorting the entities in question to be transformed into supportive beings.

Gods, Ghosts and Spirits

Why would a Bronze Age ritual vessel be helpful for explicating classical understandings of gods and humans? Particularly considering the tremendous social changes that occurred over the subsequent few centuries as the great aristocratic families were destroyed?

Let's turn to some of these social changes, some of the religious worlds these changes spawned, and some of the ritual responses.[7]

Over the course of the fifth to second centuries BCE – a period roughly corresponding to the period we have come to call 'classical Greece' – much of the aristocratic world of the Bronze Age was destroyed. Centralised states emerged that took as one of their primary goals the breaking down of aristocratic control. These efforts involved developing bureaucracies that would be as independent as possible from the aristocracies, creating legal systems that would hold aristocrats and commoners equal before the law, and building mass infantry armies to replace the aristocratically dominated chariot warfare of previous centuries. One of the keys for accomplishing the latter goal was to take direct control over all resources and populations within a

---

[7] For an excellent discussion, see Falkenhausen 2006.

given territory such that they could be exploited for war. This involved, among other things, taking full censuses of the entire population. And this in turn involved ensuring that the entire population be placed within lineages.

How far down the social ranks the ancestor rituals we have been discussing were performed is impossible to say. But certainly the elite families – whether the elite status came from aristocratic birth or bureaucratic position – practised them. So much so that restricting how far up the ancestral line sacrifices could be given became a recurrent concern of the emerging states. (As we shall see, how high up the ancestral sacrifices could go was significant, as it allowed one to move to higher levels of spirits above.)[8]

And comparable rituals were performed to other entities than just the deceased members of one's family.

One of the many things we have learned from the explosion of new discoveries from early China is the ubiquity of sacrifices and offerings to spirits and ghosts.[9] We have also learned that the spirits and ghosts were seen as extremely difficult to deal with, albeit in different ways.

Many of the ghosts were of recently deceased humans.[10] There were also other ghosts whose provenance was unknown. They may or may not have once been human. (The term used here, *gui*, could also be translated as 'demon'.) All tended to be highly dangerous.

As I have argued elsewhere, the recurrent concern throughout this period was to transform potentially antagonistic gods and ghosts into an orderly and controllable pantheon.[11] The ghosts of those one was related to would hopefully be turned into ancestors, while other ghosts would be transformed into gods. The result of all this was not a weakening of the sacrificial system that we have seen from the Bronze Age but rather a generalisation of it.

Humans, Ghosts and Personalities

And all of this is very telling for the nature of the personalities – or lack thereof – of the resulting pantheon.

But let us begin with living humans.

---

[8] For a helpful summary of the evolving kinship system, see Lewis 2010: 155–77. For one of the many attempts to give a normative system for how high up the ancestral line each social rank should be allowed to sacrifice, see the *Liji*, 'Ji fa', ICS, 122.24.5 (discussed in Puett 2005b: 77–8).
[9] Sterckx 2011.   [10] On ghosts, see Poo 2003 and 2004.   [11] Puett 2002.

A common understanding of the self by the Warring States period was that humans consist of a mess of dispositions, energies, souls, faculties and spirits. What one becomes over time then depends on how these various aspects are (or are not) trained, developed and domesticated.

But, at death, the training process would end, and the various energies that were held within the body would be released.[12] Once unmoored from their bodily container, the spirits would float upward into the heavens, where other spirits reside. The sense was that over time the spirit would continue to move upward into the heavens, becoming more and more removed from the human realm. Increasingly, it would become more like the other spirits – largely indifferent to the concerns of humans.

But if the concern was that the spirits would ultimately become indifferent, the period right after death contained far greater dangers. The energies and souls associated with what we would call emotions would also become unmoored. And potentially very dangerous. Death could unleash extraordinary levels of anger and resentment aimed at the living, whom the deceased would see moving on with their lives. And such energies of anger and resentment, if they were connected with the spirit before it became too distant, would be directed at the living with incredible degrees of power.[13]

This was what would be called a ghost.

Thus, one of the goals of the ritual work with the deceased was to disconnect these energies and souls from the spirit. The energies would be sealed in a tomb with the body. Inside the tomb would be placed things that the person enjoyed in life – hopefully therefore helping to keep the souls in the tomb, and hopefully also helping to keep them domesticated. And then the souls would be called upon to stay in the tomb and not leave.

If this was successful, the souls and energies – all of what we would call the personality – would thus be separated from the spirit. Over time, the souls would either dissipate or move off into various afterlives – paradises or hells.[14]

---

[12] On notions of death in early China, see Guo 2011; Cook 2006; Seidel 1987; Yu 1987; Brashier 1996, Puett 2011.

[13] This is a problem that we can trace to our earliest writings from China. In the Shang oracle inscriptions, one of the key questions for divination when one became dangerously sick was to see if the illness was the result of a curse by one of the recently deceased. Those who had died long before were more powerful, but were also relatively indifferent to the living. So, if one of the living became sick, it was the recently deceased who were the likely culprits. For a careful reconstruction, see Keightley 2000.

[14] We do not yet have a full study of all of the various conceptions of possible paradises and hells – largely because new evidence keeps coming in through new excavations. For an excellent study of the excavated evidence from the state of Chu, see Lai 2015.

But, either way, the hope was that they would stay away and not haunt the living.

The spirit, on the contrary, is the part one would try to make into an ancestor. That is the piece of a former human that would be above ground (and ever more so over time), that one would call down to participate in rituals in a temple, and that one would call upon to be a supportive ancestor. To the degree to which the ritual was successful, the spirit would become an ancestor and would work on behalf of the living.

But the rituals rarely worked fully. The souls would not stay in the tombs, and the spirits of the recently deceased would not remain supportive ancestors. They would on the contrary become dangerous ghosts that would haunt the living, and the rituals would have to be performed again and again.

Over time, the spirits would continue to float further into the heavens. As they did so, they would become increasingly distant, increasingly removed from the concerns of humans, and increasingly indifferent. This is another reason that so much ritual activity was focused upon the recently deceased. Not only were the recently deceased far more dangerous, they were also far more pliable by human sacrifices.

And then, of course, there were also the spirits already far above in the heavens. The most extreme was Heaven itself. Heaven does not appear ever to have been a human. Heaven was rather a distant spirit. And, like other spirits, Heaven was capricious and indifferent to the concerns of humans. Or perhaps one should say: at best indifferent to the concerns of humans. Sometimes, as we shall see, Heaven seemed to act directly contrary to human attempts to create a better world.

Given Heaven's distance, it was often relatively unresponsive to human attempts to control it through ritual activity. Accordingly, one of the goals was to work more with the recently deceased figures, call on them to behave as ancestors, and call on these ancestors in turn to move up the pantheon to ever more distant spirits. Ultimately, the hope was to influence Heaven. This is why the rulers would try to restrict how many ancestors non-royal lineages would offer sacrifice to: the hope was to restrict access to the more distant spirits, and particularly to Heaven.

And what about the ghosts that were not made into ancestors? Those of uncertain origin, or those that did not have descendants to make them into ancestors? Those are the ones that would be made into gods and goddesses. There would be no tomb for the souls and energies, however, so the goal would be to take those elements of the ghost/demon and attempt to transform them into a god or goddess who would be helpful to humans.

But here too, the rituals were often inadequate, so gods and goddesses frequently too would become either dangerous (reverting to their ghostly sides) or indifferent (floating up into the heavens and becoming unconcerned with the needs of living humans).

As much as possible, the hope was to create a divine world of supportive ancestors and gods, shorn of their capriciousness. And, yes, shorn of their personality. Indeed, one of the precise *goals* of the ritual work was to remove the personality from the ancestral spirit or god.

The Creation of the Gods

We have already seen this at work with ancestors and with Heaven. Some examples of attempts to make demonic figures into gods will be helpful.

Gaozu, the first ruler of the Han empire, initiated sacrifices to Chi You as a god of war.[15] Chi You is otherwise known as a vicious warrior. An entire cycle of stories surrounds the figure.[16] According to numerous stories in the cycle, Chi You, prior to his death, was a rebel who attacked Huangdi (the Yellow Emperor), the figure often credited with beginning the first state in China. Elsewhere, he is presented as a monster.

One example among many of the story cycles concerning Chi You is the 'Da huang jing' section of the *Shanhaijing*:

Chi You created weapons and attacked Huangdi. Huangdi thereupon ordered Ying Long to subdue him in the fields of Jizhou. Ying Long held back the waters, and so Chi You asked Fengbo and Yushi to let loose great winds and rain. Huangdi then sent down the Heavenly female called Ba, and the rain stopped. He thereupon killed Chi You.[17]

If Chi You was a rebel, a creator of weapons and a vicious warrior, the goal was to domesticate these traits posthumously. The point of the sacrificial acts was to preserve Chi You's skill in warfare, while also hopefully domesticating Chi You's dangerous sides and gaining Chi You's support.

Of course, sometimes the aspect that was worth keeping was not so dangerous. Huangdi himself became a major object of sacrifice by rulers during the early Han.[18]

---

[15] *Shiji* 28.1378–80.   [16] Puett 2001: 92–140.
[17] *Shanhaijing jianshu*, 'Da huang bei jing', SBBY, 17.5a–5b.   [18] *Shiji*, 28.1386.

And many of the stories told about the gods equally emphasise that the divinisation is based upon good things that the human did while alive. As the *Huainanzi* puts it:

Yandi created fire; when he died, he was made into the God of the Stove. Yu labored under Heaven; when he died, he was made into the God of the Soil. Houji created sowing and reaping; when he died, he was made into the God of the Grains. Yi rid all under Heaven from harm; when he died, he was made into the God of the Ancestral Temple. This is the means by which ghosts and gods were established.[19]

The sense here is that the actions the person took in life define the type of god that the person would be made into posthumously.

The same logic is at work in the placement of nature spirits into the sacrificial canon. The *Book of Rites* describes the work of deciding which natural powers would be made into objects of sacrifice:

When it came to the sun, moon, stars, and constellations, they were what the people looked up to; as for the mountains, forests, rivers, valleys, and hills, these were the places from which the people took their resources to use. If they were not of this type, they were not entered into the sacrificial canon.[20]

Those that were made into objects of sacrifice were defined as spirits:

The mountains, forests, rivers, valleys, and hills that could send out clouds, make wind and rain, and cause to appear strange phenomena – all were named 'spirits'.[21]

Even a specific ritual such as the *she* is defined as one of making the earth into a spirit: 'The *she* is that by which one makes into a spirit the way of the earth.'[22]

The entire pantheon, in short, is a product of ritual domestication. A product of taking various powerful forces and forming them into ancestors and spirits.

Indeed, the very act of placing a name on a spirit was part of this practice of domestication. As the *Huainanzi* states, the creation of writing was a key part of the human project of domesticating the ghosts and divinities:

In ancient times, when Cang Jie created writing, Heaven rained grain and the ghosts cried all night.[23]

Writing was one of the creations that allowed humans to gain some degree of control over the divine powers and the ghosts.

---

[19] *Huainanzi*, 'Fanlun', ICS, 13/131/9–13.   [20] *Liji*, 'Ji fa', ICS, 123/24/9.
[21] *Liji*, 'Ji fa', ICS, 122/24/3.   [22] *Liji*, 'Jiao te sheng', ICS, 70/11.17/14.
[23] *Huainanzi*, 'Benjing', ICS, 8/62/27–8.

But the ghosts needn't have cried too much. Yes, within the ritual space, Heaven would be called upon to be a perfectly moral agent, the gods and goddesses to be fully reliable, and the ancestors to be fully supportive. But, despite these calls, the spirits would often return to being dangerous and capricious outside the ritual space. The human domestication of the divine was all too limited. The ghosts and spirits were more powerful than the rituals, more powerful than human attempts to domesticate them.

Undomesticated Divinities

If these rituals of domestication were among the dominant religious practices of the time, many movements arose in opposition to such practices. The views of the gods that appear in such movements are extremely telling.

One of the more influential such movements centred around the teachings of Confucius and Mencius. The claim here was that ritual did matter, but that the importance of ritual lay not in transforming divine powers but rather in transforming the human participants.

But the result of this latter approach was that divine powers were seen as not subject to human domestication. One of the key teachings was thus that the world was inherently capricious, and that ethics in part consisted of trying to domesticate human emotions while accepting that the divine world could not be counted on to support human endeavours.

The capriciousness of Heaven, indeed, became a crucial part of such ethics. The goal was to cultivate oneself to become a better human being, working to create situations in which others could flourish. And only if one knew one would not necessarily be rewarded for doing this would one do it fully.

Thus, the texts in this tradition strongly emphasise that Heaven is at best indifferent to the concerns of humans. And at times Heaven seems to act directly against the work of humans to construct a better world.

When Confucius' best disciple died young, Confucius is presented as looking to the skies, calling out: 'Heaven is destroying me!'[24]

And such a vision pervades the view of history seen in the *Mencius*.

In distant antiquity, according to the stories told in the *Mencius*, sages governed the world. And, since sages act to create environments in which humans can flourish, having sages on the throne ensured that other sages

[24] *Lunyu*, 11/9.

would be emerging as well. Thus, when the ruler was aging, he would look around and choose the most sagely in the population to succeed him. The sage Yao was accordingly succeeded by the sage Shun, who in turn was followed by the sage Yu.

But then the pattern was broken. Instead of handing the throne to the most sagely in the realm, Yu gave it to his son. And thus began hereditary monarchy. This ensured that sages would rarely if ever be on the throne, since the principle of succession was based on heredity rather than sagacity. Moreover, since sages were not on the throne creating environments in which other sages might emerge, sages became extremely rare. Not only were they not on the throne, there were almost no sages around anyway. And it was Heaven that created this change:

All of this was due to Heaven. It is not something that man could have done. If no one does it, and yet it is done, then it is Heaven. If no one brings something about, and yet it is brought about, it is mandated.[25]

Fortunately, according to Mencius, a sage has nonetheless tended to emerge every five hundred years or so. Since sages are no longer rulers, sages who do emerge are forced to go to those who have the political position to put the teachings into practice. When this happens, a new dynasty can be formed.

If one is a sage, then, the most one can hope for in terms of political position is to become a sage minister.

Towards the end of his life, Mencius decided that the time was ripe for the creation of a new order. He began travelling from state to state, speaking to the rulers who would be in positions of power to begin a new dynasty. When these efforts ended in failure, the text narrates a scene of Mencius returning home:

When Mencius left Qi, Chong Yu asked him on the way, 'Master, you seem to look displeased. A few days ago I heard you say that "a gentleman does not resent Heaven nor bears a grudge against men."' Mencius responded, 'That was one time, this is another time. Every five hundred years, it must be the case that a king will arise. In the interval there must arise one from which an age takes its name. From the Zhou until now, it has been more than seven hundred years. The mark has passed, and the time, if one examines it, is proper. Yet Heaven does not yet wish to bring order to all under Heaven. If Heaven wished to bring order to all under Heaven, who in the present generation is there other than me? How could I be displeased?'[26]

---

[25] *Mengzi*, 5A/6.   [26] *Mengzi*, 2B/13. See Yearley 1975; Puett 2005a: 49–69.

Heaven, in other words, was actively working to block the creation of order. And humans must learn to live in such a capricious world.

Thus, texts in this tradition emphasise the powers of an implacable Heaven that bizarrely kills Confucius' best disciple, that inexplicably creates hereditary monarchy and thus brings to an end a period when the most virtuous would always rule, that prevents a proper order from being created even when the time is ripe. If human rituals cannot domesticate Heaven, then one must strive to live properly in an inherently capricious world.

A Moral Cosmos

A very different approach can be seen in an early religious movement started by a charismatic figure named Mozi, who argued that, contrary to much of the religious practice of the day, Heaven was in fact a good deity. And Heaven presided over a pantheon of ghosts who were themselves fully moral and completely reliable. The ghosts would always reward the good and punish the bad, and the key was for all humans to believe in the reliability of these ghosts. The stories the Mohists tell about Heaven and ghosts, therefore, are precisely the ones that in other texts would appear only in ritual contexts. The move here was essentially one of taking these ritual statements and calling on people to believe them as being true outside the ritual space as well.

Moreover, there are ways that I (Mozi) know Heaven loves the people deeply. It shaped and made the sun, moon, stars, and constellations so as to illuminate and guide them (i.e., the people). It formed and made the four seasons, spring, autumn, winter, and summer, so as to weave them into order. It sent down thunder, snow, frost, rain, and dew so as to make the five grains, hemp, and silk grow and prosper, and sent the people to obtain materials and benefit from them. It arranged and made mountains, streams, gorges, and valleys, and distributed and bestowed the hundred affairs so as to oversee and supervise the goodness and badness of the people. It made kings, dukes, and lords and charged them with, first, rewarding the worthy and punishing the wicked, and, second, plundering the metals, wood, birds, and beasts and working the five grains, hemp, and silk so as to make the materials for people's clothing and food.[27]

---

[27] *Mozi*, 'Tianzhi, zhong', SBBY, 7.6b–7a.

Far from trying to domesticate a capricious deity and dangerous ghosts into a (hopefully) supportive pantheon, the goal was rather simply to follow and accord with the proper order of Heaven and the ghosts:

> Therefore, in ancient times the sage kings made manifest and understood what Heaven and the ghosts bless and avoided what Heaven and the ghosts detest so as to increase the benefits of all under Heaven and eradicate the harms of all under Heaven. This is why Heaven made coldness and heat, placed the four seasons in rhythm, and modulated the yin and yang, the rain and dew. At the proper time the five grains ripened and the six animals prospered. Diseases, disasters, sorrows, plagues, inauspiciousness, and hunger did not arrive.[28]

The cosmos is already moral, and the spirits and ghosts are not capricious at all.

Similar reactions to the dominant religious practices of the day would continue to populate the religious landscape in early China. Several centuries later, in 142 CE, Zhang Daoling would receive revelations from a high deity Laozi. Laozi was a good deity who, like Heaven for the Mohists, created proper guidelines for humans to follow. The followers of these teachings formed an autonomous community called the Celestial Masters, who created a meritocratic society based upon the degrees to which the followers put into practice the revelations of Laozi.

But unlike the Mohists, the Celestial Masters were taught that ghosts were not moral beings but rather highly dangerous creatures. And the goal was not to sacrifice to them: according to the Celestial Masters, sacrifice only empowers the ghosts. The practitioners were told on the contrary to reject sacrifice altogether and instead simply to believe in the revelations of Laozi.[29]

Similar claims would reappear throughout subsequent millenarian movements in China. But the power of such movements can only be understood when they are seen as a rejection of the dominant practices of the time.

Stories of the Living, Stories of the Dead

Having explored these sacrificial practices as well as attempts to deny their efficacy or reject them entirely, let us return to the earlier point about the supposed lack of stories concerning the personalities of the gods in China.

---

[28] *Mozi*, 'Tianzhi, zhong', 7.6a–6b.   [29] Puett 2004.

As we explore these religious practices and the responses to them, it becomes clear that we have simply been looking in the wrong places.

In early China, there was no lack of concern with the capricious and dangerous qualities of divine powers. Hence the endless concern with domesticating and humanising them. And this is how one must understand the stories that are told about them.

Given the nature of these ritual practices in early China, the stories about the personalities of divine figures are to be found in the story cycles concerning what humans did before they died and were made into gods and goddesses. A Chi You before he becomes a god of war, for example. Or, posthumously, those figures who were not made into ancestors or gods. Hence the endless obsession with ghost stories in China.

And one finds as well an endless obsession with the capriciousness of the spirits. A capriciousness that manifests itself when, for example, Heaven throws ruin upon the innocent despite ritual entreaties. Or when Heaven acts to disrupt human attempts to build a better world.

In contrast to such stories, the ritual texts – like the bronze inscription mentioned above – present the gods and ancestors as perfectly moral and supportive figures playing out their roles flawlessly. Heaven is simply a moral force, rewarding the good and punishing the bad; ancestors are simply benevolent figures, acting to support their descendants. But that is because they are ritual texts, making ritual claims. They are not statements of belief. Or, when one finds such calls to believe that both Heaven and the ghosts are inherently good and supportive – as in the recurrent appeals of the Mohists – these are calls for a belief very much at odds with the practices of the day.

Ritual and Non-Ritual Worlds

As we have explored the nature of these materials, early Chinese notions of the divine no longer seem so different from those found in early Greece. Indeed, what is striking on the contrary is how similar the two cultures now appear.

In both societies, one of the dominant religious concerns was to work with a series of divine figures that were often seen as either highly capricious in their dealings with humans or overly indifferent to the concerns of humans. In both cases, ritual, and particularly sacrifice, was one of the key ways of trying to work with and hopefully gain the support of these capricious powers. In short, instead of a broad contrast between two radically different cosmologies, we see on the contrary a surprising set of similarities.

But if the basic problem – dealing with capricious and potentially dangerous divinities – was extremely similar, the responses went in different directions.

And this is where things get interesting.

The differences between Greece and China lie not in contrasting overall conceptions of the nature of the cosmos, or, more immediately, contrasting overall conceptions of the divine. Certainly, as we have seen, the divine figures in China were in no manner, shape or form more harmonious or inherently predisposed towards the living than those in Greece.

But what if we think in terms of problems, rather than assumptions? If we focus on the problems that figures in the two cultures were facing, then the comparatively interesting questions emerge in the differing ways that the problems were wrestled with.

Ritual, Belief and the Imagination

Often with comparisons between Greece and China, the comparison begins with categories taken either implicitly or explicitly from the Greek side. So let's try going the other way.

In the ritual theory that develops in the Warring States period of China, one of the points that becomes emphasised is the notion of as-if worlds being created in a ritual space.[30] The idea is that the participants enter a ritual space where they are transformed by acting in different roles. The living act as if they are filial descendants and devoted worshippers, making offerings to supportive ancestors or divinities (rather than dangerous ghosts and capricious spirits), within a harmonious and coherent cosmos.

Hopefully, the dangerous ghosts and capricious spirits will in fact enter the ritual space and be transformed. But, regardless, one sacrifices to them as if this is the case. As Confucius is quoted as saying in the *Analects*: sacrifice to the spirits 'as if they are present'.[31] Although this has often been read in twentieth-century Western scholarship as a statement of agnosticism about whether spirits really exist or not, it in fact is a statement concerning the as-if nature of ritual action.

---

[30] Seligman, Weller, Puett and Simon 2008: 17–42, 179–82. For an analysis of 'as-if' from a larger philosophical perspective, see Vaihinger 1911.
[31] *Lunyu*, 3/12.

An entire body of ritual theory developed in the Warring States and early Han devoted to such theories of ritual. During the early Han, this was consolidated into the *Book of Rites*. In the thirties BCE, the *Book of Rites* became defined as one of the five classics, and much of state ritual practice became modelled upon the ritual vision found therein.

One of the key arguments in the chapters on sacrifice in the *Book of Rites* is that, within the ritual space, the entire cosmos is like a single family. Each lineage has a defined number of ancestors it is allowed to make offerings to, all of the lineages in turn are called upon to think of the ruler as their father and mother, and the ruler is called upon to be the Son of Heaven. Thus, within the ritual space, everything is connected through genealogical lines, with the ruler serving as the fulcrum connecting the entire populace with Heaven.[32]

Except, of course, this isn't true outside the ritual space. Heaven is not seen as having actually given birth to the ruler; the ruler certainly is not the parent of the population, and even the descendants rarely think of deceased ghosts as inherently supportive ancestors outside of ritual contexts. The ritual serves as an as-if space, in which participants are called upon to become something different than they were before they walked into the ritual space. To the degree to which it works, the living will act as filial descendants to the deceased; the ghosts of the deceased will behave as supportive ancestors to their descendants; the people will follow the ruler as if he were their parent; the ruler will treat the population as his own children; and Heaven will support the ruler as his own son. But, over time, the transformative effects of the ritual will weaken. The deceased will return to being ghosts; Heaven will become indifferent. And thus the rituals will be performed again.

This is, needless to say, a ritual theory that is built upon the practices that we have traced back to the Bronze Age, now being self-consciously appropriated and theorised.

What if we use this model for our comparative endeavour? If we think of ritual not as socialising participants into a belief system but rather as creating imaginary as-if possibilities – trying to create a world that is perceived as not yet existing – then the comparatively interesting questions turn to issues like: What are the as-if worlds being created in the ritual space? And what are such as-if worlds being posited in opposition to?

So let us now return to our comparison, bringing the discussion of the Chinese material into conversation with the Greek material and looking in

---

[32] Puett 2005b, 2008, 2014.

more detail at what the rituals entail and how the imaginary space of the rituals operated.

Genealogies of Descent, Genealogies in Reverse

In both Greece and China, we are dealing with cultures in which divine powers were seen as highly capricious. Ritual in general, and sacrifice in particular, was a crucial way to try to gain the cooperation of the divine figures, and perhaps even control them. Depending on the context, therefore, Zeus could be treated as a great and good divine ruler as well as a highly capricious divinity. And the same was true of Heaven.

Given this similarity, the interesting comparative issues thus come down to the permutations that play off these similarities. What is the nature of the capricious spirits with whom one is struggling, and what is the nature of the world one is trying – even if only for brief moments – to create within the ritual space?

A standard sacrifice in ancient Greece would consist of the slaughter of an animal. The carcass would then be divided, with the meat being eaten by the humans and the bones being offered to the gods. In short, the sacrificial structure consisted of division, with a clear demarcation of the places of humans and gods.[33]

Perhaps the most famous elaboration of this sacrificial practice of division is that of Hesiod. In his *Works and Days*, Hesiod portrays the division as a result of Prometheus' theft of fire – a transgression that won for humanity autonomy from the gods, but at the cost of a life of toil and, ultimately, death. The sacrificial division was a part of this same ambivalence. Hesiod presents the division as a ruse: Prometheus surrounded the bones with fat, hoping thereby to fool Zeus into believing he had been given the better portion, while Prometheus kept for himself the meat. But underlying the ruse was the reality of the relationship: humanity needed food in order to survive, while Zeus, an immortal, did not.[34]

The deeper and fuller narrative elaboration of the division, however, is to be found in the *Theogony*. Hesiod reconstructs the genealogy of the gods

---

[33] Perhaps the most influential studies of sacrifice in Greece are those undertaken by Jean-Pierre Vernant and Marcel Detienne. See the collection Detienne and Vernant 1989. More recently, these interpretations have been deepened through a closer attention to the implicit theology of the sacrificial acts. See in particular Naiden 2015, as well as the edited collections by Faraone and Naiden 2012, and Hitch and Rutherford 2017.

[34] See the excellent study by Vernant 1989.

that led ultimately to the world of the present. This is the world of genealogically related immortals that the all-too-mortal humans are now both autonomous from yet dependent upon.

Different figures would, of course, develop the genealogy differently. In various contexts, the ancestry of a given god or goddess would be traced one way rather than another. But the permutations reveal the implicit logic. The imaginary of the world of Greek divinities was one of an inter-related group of immortals, all connected through complex and interweaving descent lines.

For humans, the goal was to break from this world and win for humanity a life of autonomy – even if that also meant a life of want, deprivation and ultimately death. The consequent need for food and help thus meant that humans continued to be dependent on the gods, while still maintaining, as much as possible, distinction.

The ritual as-if, in short, was one of trying to gain the support of the gods while also demarcating the line between the gods and the human supplicants. The sacrifice thus consisted of both supplication and division, both submitting to the will of the divine while at the same time defining for each its proper place.

In early China, the divine powers were seen as equally capricious – perhaps even more than in Greece. But the goal in the ritual space was one of connecting – ideally into familial relationships. Even actual ancestral offerings in early China, as we have seen, were based on constructing ancestors – transforming dangerous ghosts of the recently deceased into ancestors who would be called upon to act on behalf of humanity. The movement, in other words, went from the living upwards to the deceased, as the living formed the deceased into (hopefully) supportive ancestors. When done fully, the world within the ritual space would be a single patrilineal lineage, with the king serving as the Son of Heaven and the father and mother of the people, pulling together all of the disparate and capricious energies of the cosmos into a harmonious family.

This was not a question of descendants winning their autonomy from the ancestors; the goal of sacrificial practice in early China was not to create discontinuity. It was rather a never-ending attempt to create continuity. The problem was not to break from a genealogically related set of immortals; the problem was rather to bring disparate beings together into a ritually constructed lineage.

In Greece, the 'Son of Zeus' was, well, the son of Zeus, in a genealogical sense – Heracles, Dionysus, Apollo. The 'Son of Heaven' in China, on the contrary, was a ritual claim. The ruler was not seen as having actually descended from Heaven, and the ruler was never called upon to in some sense succeed in gaining his autonomy from such an ancestral figure. The problem was rather the opposite: the divine powers were discontinuous from humans, and the goal was to create linkages.

The sacrificial as-if, in other words, goes in opposing directions in the two cultures. Greek sacrificial practice involved (hopefully) gaining the support of the gods while also creating a ritual distinction from them – the sacrifice thus recapitulating the dependence of humans on the gods along with the (ultimately doomed) attempt to gain autonomy from them. In contrast, the ritual as-if in early China was predicated upon a claim of connecting and domesticating, of endlessly trying to create (also ultimately doomed) continuity where none before was seen as existing.

In short, by focusing on competing cosmologies – with early China being portrayed as 'harmonious', and early Greece as 'tragic', we have missed what is most interesting in these relations between humans and divinities in the two cultures. The problematic – dealing with highly capricious divine powers – is actually quite similar. But the ways of working with this comparable problem have taken very different forms. In early Greece, the imaginary was one of presenting the world of capricious spirits as an inter-related world of immortals who had to be supplicated while also being kept at a distance. In early China, the imaginary was of domesticating the divine powers into a humanly constructed lineage.

Both cultures, then, are fully 'tragic'. In both cultures the endless problem was one of working with highly capricious divinities through a set of ritual constructions. And these ritual constructions were doomed to failure: the divine powers were incomparably more powerful than the human rituals designed to control them.

Divine Personalities, Divine Forces

So, finally, let us return to personalities. There is another similarity between these two cultures. Families are messy. And, yes, they often involve complex emotional responses – jealousies, resentments, anger. Some of this we might call ingredients of a personality, but that actually is not the term used in either culture at the time. If our tendency is to fall into complex emotional responses with the ones with whom we are close, what is intriguing from a comparative perspective is where these jealousies, resentments and angers are located in the divine.

In the imaginary of early Greece, such emotional responses are pervasive among the gods and goddesses, all of whom are inter-related. And they are pervasive in the stories (outside the ritual space, of course) of gods and goddesses as they relate to humans as well. Hence the need to divorce such emotions from the ritual space.

In early China, such emotional responses are pervasive among humans, but they are seen as growing less and less significant the longer one is dead. Eventually, one simply becomes like the spirits above – powerful, no longer driven by deep-seated angers and resentments, but also indifferent to the needs of humans. That, of course, is a huge problem for humans. But, before that, the problem is how to deal with these angers, jealousies and resentments before they dissipate – the angers, jealousies and resentments of the recently deceased, of the ghosts. And that is one of the crucial goals of ritual work: to construct a world that as much as possible would function like a harmonious family. And the nature of the family was clear from the claims within the ritual space. The family would be one in which each figure would play his role perfectly; one, in other words, where the angers, jealousies and resentments would be driven out.

Hence the ramifications we see playing out in our sources: cycles of stories in early Greece playing upon the angers and jealousies of the gods and goddesses, cycles of stories in early China playing upon the angers and jealousies of ghosts and the capriciousness of the higher spirits. And, in both cases, a ritual world of perfect relationships.

Conclusions

As we have seen, the contrast so often drawn between ancient Greece and China concerning the purported antagonistic relationship between humans and gods in Greece versus the purported harmonious relationship in early China is based upon taking statements out of radically different contexts and then reading such statements as assumptions of the culture in question. But, once we focus on the contexts in which such statements were made, and the problems such statements were trying to solve, a different set of issues emerges. What is striking on the contrary is the tremendous similarity in concerns with dealing with divine powers. In both cases, the hope was to bring the divine powers into the ritual space. Sometimes the divine powers would come, and sometimes they would not. When they would come, the divine powers would be treated within the ritual space as if they were supportive beings, and the relationship between humans and gods would be presented as if it were harmonious.

Outside the ritual space, however, narratives and protests would circulate about the capriciousness of the spirits. And entire movements would develop based upon reacting against the capriciousness of the spirits and the seeming inadequacy of human efforts to control them through sacrifice.

In China, the capricious and dangerous divine powers were seen as being either ghosts (remnants of deceased humans filled with anger and resentment) or indifferent spirits. And the solution was one of trying, to whatever extent possible, to transform these ghosts and spirits into a pantheon of supportive ancestors, gods and goddesses. This attempt to domesticate the world of the divine was seen as never-ending, since the ghosts and spirits are always more powerful than human attempts to control them. But, to whatever extent it succeeded, the result would be a world in which these dangerous beings would on the contrary become a genealogically linked set of supportive ancestors and divinities.

In Greece, the imaginary worked the other way. The capricious gods and goddesses were represented as genealogically linked, and the problem for humans was to win a level of autonomy from them, even though this break also meant that humans would be mortal and dependent upon the more powerful gods. The goal of the sacrificial act was thus not to transform the divine into (ritually speaking) genealogically related ancestors; the goal on the contrary was to break from them and define the respective spheres of humans and gods, while also requesting their support.[35] If the goal of the sacrificial act in China was to create continuity, the goal of the sacrificial act in Greece was to create discontinuity.

These differences help to illuminate the types of stories concerning divinities found in the two cultures. In both cases, the imaginary focuses on what sacrifice is being called upon to change – in other words, what exists outside or prior to sacrifice.

The imaginary that develops out of sacrifice in Greece inspires a constant concern with the interconnected world of divine beings – a world that sacrifice helps to win autonomy from, even while that world is also hopefully being transformed into a more supportive one through the sacrificial act. In contrast, the imaginary that develops out of sacrifice in China is focused on the lives of humans before they died, including the personality

---

[35] This was, of course, for ordinary mortals. Heroes, on the contrary, were humans who would be divinised after death and sacrificed to as such. Instead of marking a distinction between humans and gods, sacrifices to heroes involved the role of heroes as a mediating force.

traits that sacrifice domesticates by either expunging or transforming; the angers and resentments of the ghosts; the indifference and capriciousness of the spirits and natural powers.

In short, if sacrifice – like ritual in general – operates in an as-if world, the imaginary world of the stories often plays on what the sacrificial action is working upon.

The seeming lack of a Zeus or a Prometheus in early Chinese ritual constructions is not due to a lack of capricious deities or a lack of human attempts to respond to such capriciousness. On the contrary. This is precisely the sort of all-pervasive relationship the rituals in early China were trying to expunge.

Bibliography

References to the early Chinese primary texts are to the Ancient Chinese Text Concordance Series, Institute of Chinese Studies, Chinese University of Hong Kong (cited as ICS) and the Sibu beiyao editions (cited as SBBY).

Brashier, K. E. (1996) 'Han thanatology and the division of "souls"', *Early China* 21: 125–58.

Cook, C. A. (2006) *Death in Ancient China: The Tale of One Man's Journey*. Leiden.

Detienne, M. (1981) 'Between beasts and gods', in *Myth, Religion and Society: Structuralist Essays*, eds. M. Detienne, L. Gernet, J.-P. Vernant and P. Vidal-Naquet, and trans. R. L. Gordon. Cambridge: 215–28.

  (1989) 'Culinary practices and the spirit of sacrifice', in *The Cuisine of Sacrifice among the Greeks*, eds. M. Detienne and J.-P. Vernant, trans. P. Wissing. Chicago: 1–20.

Detienne, M. and Vernant, J.-P. (1979) *La cuisine du sacrifice en pays grec*. Paris.

Falkenhausen, L. von (2004) 'Mortuary behavior in pre-imperial Qin: a religious interpretation', in *Chinese Religion and Society*, vol. I, ed. J. Lagerwey. Hong Kong: 109–72.

  (2006) *Chinese Society in the Age of Confucius (1000–250 BC): The Archaeological Evidence*. Los Angeles.

Faraone, C. A. and Naiden, F. S. (eds.) (2012) *Greek and Roman Animal Sacrifice: Ancient Victims, Modern Observers*. Cambridge.

Guo, J. (2011) 'Concepts of death and the afterlife reflected in newly discovered tomb objects and texts from Han China', in *Mortality in Traditional Chinese Thought*, eds. A. Olberding and P. J. Ivanhoe. Albany: 85–115.

Hitch, S. and Rutherford, I. (eds.) (2017) *Animal Sacrifice in the Ancient Greek World*. Cambridge.

Keightley, D. (1990) 'Early civilization in China: reflections on how it became Chinese', in *Heritage of China: Contemporary Perspectives on Chinese Civilization*, ed. P. S. Ropp. Berkeley: 15–54.
  (2000) *The Ancestral Landscape: Time, Space, and Community in Late Shang China, ca. 1200–1045 B.C.* Berkeley.
Lai, G. (2015) *Excavating the Afterlife: The Archaeology of Early Chinese Religion.* Seattle.
Lewis, M. (2010) *The Early Chinese Empires: Qin and Han.* Cambridge.
Lloyd, G. E. R. (1990) *Demystifying Mentalities.* Cambridge.
  (2014) *Being, Humanity, and Understanding.* Oxford.
Naiden, F. S. (2015) *Smoke Signals for the Gods: Ancient Greek Sacrifice from the Archaic through Roman Periods.* Oxford.
Perkins, F. (2014) *Heaven and Earth Are Not Humane: The Problem of Evil in Classical Chinese Philosophy.* Bloomington.
Poo, M. (2003) 'Imperial order and local variation: the culture of ghost in early imperial China', *Acta Orientalia* 56: 295–308.
  (2004) 'The concept of ghost in ancient Chinese religion', in *Religion and Chinese Society*, ed. J. Lagerwey. Hong Kong: 173–91.
Puett, M. (2001) *The Ambivalence of Creation: Debates Concerning Innovation and Artifice in Early China.* Stanford.
  (2002) *To Become a God: Cosmology, Sacrifice, and Self-Divinization in Early China.* Cambridge.
  (2004) 'Forming spirits for the Way: the cosmology of the Xiang'er commentary to the *Laozi*', *Journal of Chinese Religions* 32: 1–27.
  (2005a) 'Following the commands of Heaven: the notion of Ming in early China', in *The Magnitude of Ming: Command, Allotment, and Fate in Chinese Culture*, ed. C. Lupke. Honolulu: 49–69.
  (2005b) 'The offering of food and the creation of order: the practice of sacrifice in early China', in *Of Tripod and Palate: Food, Politics, and Religion in Traditional China*, ed. R. Sterckx. New York: 75–95.
  (2008) 'Human and divine kingship in early China: comparative reflections', in *Religion and Power: Divine Kingship in the Ancient World and Beyond*, ed. N. Brisch. Chicago: 199–212.
  (2011) 'Sages, the past, and the dead: death in the *Huainanzi*', in *Mortality in Traditional Chinese Thought*, eds. A. Olberding and P. J. Ivanhoe. Albany: 225–48.
  (2014) 'Ritual disjunctions: ghosts, philosophy, and anthropology', in *The Ground Between: Anthropologists Engage Philosophy*, eds. V. Das, M. Jackson, A. Kleinman and B. Singh. Durham, NC: 218–33.
  (2015) 'Ghosts, gods, and the coming apocalypse: empire and religion in early China and ancient Rome', in *State Power in Ancient China and Rome*, ed. W. Scheidel. Oxford: 230–59.

Seidel, A. (1987) 'Traces of Han religion in funeral texts found in tombs', in *Dôkyô to shûkyô bunka*, ed. Akitsuki Kan'ei. Tokyo: 21–57.

Seligman, A., Weller, R., Puett, M. and Simon, B. (2008) *Ritual and its Consequences: An Essay on the Limits of Sincerity*. Oxford.

Shaughnessy, E. L. (1993) 'The Duke of Zhou's retirement in the east and the beginnings of the ministerial–monarch debate in Chinese political philosophy', *Early China* 18: 41–72.

Sterckx, R. (2011) *Food, Sacrifice, and Sagehood in Early China*. Cambridge.

Tang Lan 唐蘭 (1976) 'He zun mingwen jieshi' 何尊銘文解釋, *Wenwu* 1: 60–3.

Vaihinger, H. (1911) *Die Philosophie des Als Ob: System der theoretischen, praktischen und religiösen Fiktionen der Menschheit auf Grund eines idealistischen Positivismus*, trans. C. K. Ogden (1935) *The Philosophy of 'As if': A System of the Theoretical, Practical and Religious Fictions of Mankind* (2nd edn). New York.

Vernant, J.-P. (1989) 'At man's table: Hesiod's foundation myth of sacrifice', in *The Cuisine of Sacrifice among the Greeks*, eds. M. Detienne and J.-P. Vernant, trans. by P. Wissing. Chicago: 21–86.

Yearley, L. (1975) 'Toward a typology of religious thought: a Chinese example', *Journal of Religion* 55.4: 426–43.

Yu Y.-S. (1987) '"O soul, come back!" A study in the changing conceptions of the soul and afterlife in pre-Buddhist China', *Harvard Journal of Asiatic Studies* 47.2: 363–95.

PART III

Art and Literature

8 | Visual Art and Historical Representation in Ancient Greece and China

JEREMY TANNER

Comparisons between Greek and Chinese history writing have a long genealogy. Their visual counterparts do not, although they include canonical works of early Greek and Chinese art, from the Tyrannicides of early fifth-century Athens (Figure 8.1) to the Wu Liang Shrine in Han China (Figure 8.2). Drawing on recent approaches to 'regimes of historicity', this chapter explores how the past is brought into play and 'set on stage' in the present in the visual art of ancient Greece and China.[1] It focuses on the social agents who put history on stage, the institutional contexts of presentations of the past and their consumption, the distinctive cultural and material strategies that inform such stagings, and the capacity of such representations of the past to shape the larger social worlds within which they circulate. Taking a long-term perspective, I argue that, notwithstanding differences in scale, social structure and political organisation between late Bronze Age Chinese states and their archaic Greek counterparts, there are significant parallels in the ways visual art was used to materialise the past in the present. By means of 'ancestralising strategies' elite kin groups sought privileged positions within weakly integrated states, using visual (and textual) media to link themselves to heroic and even divine forebears whose charisma they appropriated. Exploring the development of visual depictions of history in early imperial China and classical Athens, I analyse the role played by an increasingly differentiated state in creating pictures of historical events as a new medium of collective memory. The use and character of such depictions were shaped by the differing balance of power amongst key constituencies controlling the cultural apparatus of the state and the broader public sphere: the imperial bureaucracy and the *shi* (literati) in China, the *dēmos* and the political elite, the orators and generals, of classical Athens.

Staging History through Visual Art

Significant differences between Greek and Chinese history writing have been explained in terms of the specific literary models which informed

[1] Hartog 2000, 2003; Detienne 2007: 53.

Figure 8.1 Tyrannicides: Harmodius and Aristogeiton. Roman marble copy of bronze statues by Kritios and Nesiotes, 476 BCE.

their beginnings and cut across the broadly parallel development of self-conscious historical awareness in the two traditions. Herodotus' account of the Persian Wars and Thucydides' history of the Peloponnesian War are characterised by their focus on war, a unified structure and continuous narrative, all features attributed to the model of epic poetry. Sima Qian's

Figure 8.2 Wu Liang Shrine, West Wall. Second century CE. Rubbing after the original stone engravings.

Records (*Shiji*), by contrast, is divided into sections which correspond to categories of social hierarchy: the annals of the ruling dynasty, histories of the noble houses, and collections of biographies of famous men of lower social status, paralleling early Chinese lyric, in particular the *Classic of Poetry*, an anthology of poems concerning the lives of ordinary people (Book 1), the noble houses (Books 2–3), and the state rites of the ruling dynasty (Book 4). This background is held to inform the affective orientation of history writers to their past: the broadly objective, radically secular and scientific history of Thucydides is contrasted with the 'participationist' orientation of Sima Qian's history, where both author and reader are empathetically involved with the events narrated, in the context of a broader vision of man's place within the patterns of a dynamically transforming cosmos.[2]

Art historians' accounts of the picturing of history in early Greece and China apparently confirm this impression of distinctive cultural mentalities fully articulated in historical texts and reflected in the corresponding visual art. Wu Hung has demonstrated how the Wu Liang Shrine is organised in terms of the same social and cultural categories as the *Shiji*,[3] even appropriating captions for the pictures from the *Shiji*.[4] Hölscher has drawn similar parallels between history writing and history painting in classical Greece: both manifested processes of cultural secularisation and the establishment of critical reflective distance from the horizons of archaic thought, elements of the transformation from a life lived in tradition to one lived in history.[5]

Approaching pictorial representations of history in terms of their parallels with textual counterparts, however, naturalises the category of 'history' in ways increasingly seen as problematic. Modern disciplinary concepts of 'history', formulated in the nineteenth century, cannot be straightforwardly applied to the investigations of Herodotus' *historia* ('inquiry'), or to the activities of Sima Qian in compiling his 'records'.[6] The category of 'history painting' is not an ancient one in either Greece or China, but the formulation of the Renaissance art theorist Alberti, describing narrative representations in general, and later codified as a category of Academic painting theory.[7] Recent work has relativised the modern disciplinary concept of history, seeing it as merely one orientation to the past amongst others.[8] Whilst some kind of orientation towards the past is an anthropological universal, the character of such orientations is diverse in terms of the material modes and cultural forms in which the past can be accessed, encoded, and re-presented in relation to contemporary events and social purposes.[9] Different 'memory strategies' realised through different media may vary widely in the ways in which they transform experiences into accounts of the past which in turn can have variably binding effects on futures.[10] The concept of 'memory strategies' implies agents who pursue those strategies, constructing representations of the past which are perspectival, shaped by 'an interest structure

---

[2] Prusek 1970; Mutschler 1997; Shankman and Durrant 2000: 90–120.   [3] Wu 1989.
[4] While the inscriptions are the most likely elements of the shrine to have been recarved in more recent times (Liu, Nylan and Barbieri-Low 2005), arguments that the shrines are eighteenth-century forgeries are not persuasive. The closely related Songshan shrines, for example, come from a reliable archaeological context: Bai 2008; Akiro 2010.
[5] Hölscher 1973: 201–6; 1988: 115.   [6] Lloyd 2011; 2002: 2–12.   [7] Goldstein 1996: 40–1.
[8] Rusen 1996.   [9] Hirsch and Stewart 2005.   [10] Assmann 2011: 50–60.

that is dependent on specific life situations' in the present.[11] Within any society, a variety of competing historicities may be at play, linked to differing institutional contexts, to distinctive media and traditions of representation, and to specific social groups who are the bearers of such traditions.

Emphasis on comparative study of 'historicities' underlines the variety of representations of the past at play at any one time, rather than assuming a uniform Greek or Chinese 'historical consciousness'. It brackets the debate over whether the works of Herodotus and Sima Qian, or of the artists of the Stoa Poikile and the Wu Liang Shrine, are 'true history' or not. Instead, it sees the status of 'true history' as one of the stakes at play within cultures of historical representation themselves: different modes of historical representation are constituted through different kinds of performance, using 'framing devices' which make varying rhetorical claims about the truth value of the representations in question.[12] Paradoxically, it is the attack on unreliable popular accounts of the past, in both textual and visual narratives, which allows us to recognise the existence in classical Greece and Han China of some concept of works of visual art as vehicles for history, not mere myth or fancy, bearing a family resemblance, if a rather distant one, to their more recent Western counterparts. The stories concerning the Tyrannicides, the founding fathers of Athenian democracy, as narrated in works like the famous statue group, are attacked by Thucydides for their largely fictional character, contrasting with the accuracy (*akribeia*) of his own history.[13] Similarly, the Han essayist Wang Chong attacks paintings retailing popular accounts of Wu Zixu, 'seeming to be true, but in fact unreal': the surviving consciousness of this loyal minister of the fifth century, boiled alive in a cauldron and then dumped into a river, was manifested, it was held, by the stormy waves he stirred up on the river to revenge himself upon an ungrateful world.[14]

Pre-History: Visual Art and Ancestral Memories in Archaic Greece and Late Bronze Age China

Bronze Age China of the Western Zhou (1045–771 BCE) has been characterised as a 'delegatory kin-ordered settlement state':[15] city-states were ruled by local dynasties whose position depended on their seniority within a hierarchy of patrilineal corporate groups, leading up to the Zhou king, the

---

[11] Frisby 1992: 9.   [12] Alonso 1988: 35.   [13] Thucydides 6.53–9.
[14] *Lunheng* 4.1, trans. Forke II, 247–51; Wang 1994.   [15] Li 2008: 23.

head of the most senior lineage, from whom the authority of settlement lineages was in theory delegated, notwithstanding their considerable practical autonomy.[16] The paramount prestige symbols of this political order were bronzes, used in the context of ancestral cults. The right and possibly the material to make such vessels were awarded to their owners by the Zhou king at court ceremonials, when members of the aristocracy were honoured for their services and appointed to, or confirmed in, titles and positions within the court hierarchy.[17]

The vessels, and their inscriptions, were major vehicles of historical memory. They recorded events of investiture which thereby entered the historical memory of lineages and could be reproduced in subsequent generations during ancestral sacrifices at lineage temples. They reached back in time, recording a history of merit (*gong* 功) and service to the Zhou state by ancestors of the honorand, as exemplified by an eleventh-century *zun* (Figure 8.3) recording the honouring of one He by Cheng Wang:

It was at the time when the king began the building of the Cheng Zhou, and offered a Fu sacrifice in the Hall of Heaven to [his father] Wu Wang. In the fourth month, on the day *bing xu*, the king was in the Jing Hall and exhorted me saying: 'In days past, your late ancestor Gong Shi was able to serve Wen Wang. Wen Wang accepted the great command, and Wu Wang carried out the conquest of the Great City of Shang, announcing it to Heaven with the words: "I must dwell in the center, and from there rule the people". Now take heed! You must cherish the memory of the services that Gong Shi rendered to Heaven. Sacrifice to him with reverence!' Our king has indeed a virtuous character, compliant with Heaven, an inspiring example to my own feebleness. When the king had concluded, I, He, was given thirty strings of cowries, which I have used to make this vessel for sacrifices to Gong Shi. This happened in the king's fifth year.[18]

The Shi Qiang Pan (Figure 8.4), a large water vessel, exemplifies the historical character of such bronzes. The elaborate inscription presents a eulogy of seven generations of Zhou kings, before celebrating the services to the Zhou of the ancestors and immediate ascendants of Scribe Qiang: he dedicates the vessel for use in the ancestral cult, hoping that the 'vibrant freshness, fortunate peace and blessed wealth' afforded by these satisfied ancestors will enable him to continue to 'be worthy to preserve his ruler' during the course of a 'prolonged life'.[19] These inscribed histories are designed for their ritual context. Formulated for investiture ceremonies,

---

[16] Keightley 1990: 46–7; Falkenhausen 2005: 240; Li 2008.   [17] Bagley 1980a; Kern 2009: 163.
[18] Bagley 1980a: 198, 203–4.
[19] Bagley 1980a: 198; Shaughnessy 1991: 1–4, 183–92; 1999: 242–4.

Figure 8.3(a) *He zun*, eleventh century BCE.

and intended to procure the satisfaction and support of ancestors, they present the achievements of both the Zhou and lineage ancestors in a favourable light. The Shi Qiang Pan celebrates King Zhao's subjugation of the Chu and the Jing in the south, but fails to mention that both the king and his army were annihilated during the campaign.[20] The ancestral lines recorded on bronzes could be manipulated, and even partially invented, to include an ancestor among the founders of the Zhou royal house, and to realise an ideal coordination with the Zhou royal succession, thus demonstrating generations of loyalty on the part of the lineage to the Zhou,[21] ancestralising practices with close parallels among the aristocracies of archaic Greece.

Bronzes' efficacy as media for historical memory depended on their role in sacrifices made to ancestors in lineage temples. Accumulating over time, vessel collections materially embodied lineage history. The distinction of that history could be seen at a glance: the Shi Qiang Pan is one vessel from a hoard of 103 bronzes, 74 of them marked with the same clan name, and

---

[20] Kern 2009: 152–3. [21] Falkenhausen 2005: 248–9, 267–75.

Figure 8.3(b) Rubbing of the inscription from the interior of the *He zun*.

Figure 8.4 Shi Qiang bronze *pan* vessel, tenth century BCE. Zhuangbai, Fufeng, Shaanxi Province.

spanning the entire history of the Western Zhou.[22] Within such massive assemblages, the design of bronzes as sets facilitated the identification of vessels associated with specific ancestors, and hence the appropriate performance of sacrifices.[23] The ritual actions involved in the performance of ancestral sacrifice were mediated by the material affordances of the bronzes – shape, weight and design encoding appropriate bodily movements.[24] Ritual performance permitted the spirits of the ancestors to mingle with those of the living: life-giving sacrifice flowed in one direction, ancestral blessings returned.[25] Read aloud, or simply viewed, the primary recipients of inscriptions, alongside the living lineage community, were the ancestors. The inscriptions are often placed in inaccessible recesses within vessels, or at the bottom of the interior (as on the *He zun*), largely covered by food or drink offerings during the ceremonies.[26] Bronzes, in this ritual context, were both index of and medium for the accumulation of *de* (德), the 'virtuous force' which sustained the life-forces and power of the lineage,[27] guaranteeing history future through history past, joined in the historic present of commemorative ritual. Successfully performing the sacrifice, and hosting the banquet, the sacrificier demonstrated his piety, and transformed himself into an ideal successor to the ancestor commemorated, to be venerated himself for generations to come.[28] This orientation to a historical future was marked in the conventional closing formula of ritual bronze inscriptions: 'may sons of sons, grandsons of grandsons forever treasure and use [this sacrificial vessel]'.[29]

In the Eastern Zhou, bronzes became increasingly popular, as cities and states repudiated Zhou hegemony and local rulers sought to institute their own local systems of lineage hierarchy and exchange of ritual bronzes as prestige goods.[30] But they also lost some of their ritual character, as the 'old economy of gift exchange in ritually prescribed events' was displaced by the monetary economy and rationalising polities of the Warring States.[31] Long inscriptions disappeared, replaced by embellishments such as inlays and engraved pictures, on smaller, lighter bronzes, luxury objects for personal use, eschewing the monumental character of traditional bronzes, whose scale and decoration were determined by their ritual function.[32] By the Han, most bronze vessels were little more than 'cook pots and canisters';[33] other objects had become the focus of ritual investment.

---

[22] Bagley 1980b: 241; Shaughnessy 1999: 236–47: collection from ancestral temple, buried during Quan Rong invasion.
[23] Rawson 1999: 113–19.   [24] Rawson 1999: 117.   [25] Kern 2009: 153.   [26] Cook 2005: 11.
[27] Cook 2005:14; Kern 2009: 151–2.   [28] Kern 2009: 180–1.   [29] Kern 2009: 154.
[30] So 1980a.   [31] Cook 2005: 10.   [32] So 1980b: 308–9.   [33] Cook 2005: 9–10.

The art and the societies of archaic Greece and late Bronze Age China might seem too dissimilar for fruitful comparison. Zhou China manifests continuities with the Shang, in terms of scale, social complexity and artistic technologies. Iron Age Greece develops from a drastically restricted base – demographically, sociologically and artistically – following the collapse of the Bronze Age Mycenaean civilisation.[34] There is no real parallel in the Greek case for the unilineal descent groups 'linked by kinship and bound by common property and religious cult' found in Zhou, and later, China:[35] the civic community of the polis with its public assembly seems always to have transcended the family as the paramount social organisation, visible already as early as the Homeric poems.[36] There are nevertheless significant parallels with the Chinese case in the ways works of art were used as anchors for historical memory in archaic Greece. As in China,[37] gift giving and ritualised exchange inform memory practices which underwrite the authority of aristocratic elites. Although there is no cult of ancestors as such, or at least nothing of the formality, scale and sociological presence of ancestor worship in Zhou China, ancestralising strategies certainly informed the memory practices of elite families in archaic Greece.

In archaic Greece, the closest counterparts to Chinese bronzes as material anchors of historical memory, and as objects to be treasured (*bao* 寶), were *agalmata*, objects in which their owners might take delight (*agallein*). Whilst such objects have nothing material in common with Chinese ritual bronzes – and little material unity amongst themselves – they manifest a common logic in their operation as embodiments of value and objects of memory. Like ritual bronzes, they are acquired through forms of exchange that promote the personal merit of both giver and recipient, and which stand in strong contrast to commercial relationships.[38] They are often made of some intrinsically valuable and enduring material, such that they can be transmitted down the generations, acquiring social value by virtue of their pedigree and the historical memories with which they are associated. Ritualised feasting amongst aristocratic guest friends offers one of the primary occasions for realising the historical memories embodied in such objects and for their exchange.[39] Some objects are transmitted straightforwardly down a family line, embodying its history, and legitimating its authority, analogously to the bronzes of China: the sceptre of Agamemnon, for example, was made by the god Hephaistos, and given by Hermes to Zeus, the king of the gods, who presented it to Pelops, from

[34] Osborne 1996: 18–50; Whitley 2001: 77–101. [35] Zhou 2010: 12.
[36] Osborne 1996: 147–60; Raaflaub 1997. [37] Cook 2005: 10.
[38] Gernet 1981; Csapo and Miller 1998: 99. [39] Grethlein 2008.

whom it passed down the family line, Atreus, Thyestes and Agamemnon.[40] Other objects accumulate pedigree by means of more entangled histories of transmission, like the boars-tusk helmet of Meriones: stolen from Amyntor, the grandfather of Odysseus, presented as a *xenia* gift to Amphidamas, and then Polos, inherited by his son Meriones, who in turn gives it to Odysseus, so the object returns to its family.[41] Like Chinese bronzes, such *agalmata* are paramount prestige symbols, objects in which extraordinary, even divine, artistic and technical skill had been invested, which would preserve the memory of their former owners when used by their successors.[42] Of course, there are differences in both the memory practices and the objects which mediate them: the exchanges in the Greek case are as likely to be lateral (between guest friends), as vertical (between generations of a family), and are not capped by any paramount ruler corresponding to the Zhou king. Further, the pattern of exchange and the typology of objects exchanged are less codified, less institutionally crystallised. But these differences represent variations in practices which have at least a family resemblance, variations which correspond to the limited development of state structures in the early Iron Age Greek world, and the smaller scale of social and political organisation, compared with Western Zhou China.

The concept of *agalma*, and ancestralising practices oriented to forebears as far back as the Bronze Age, remained important to the aristocratic elites of the Greek world throughout the archaic period, although the character of these practices changed over time in the context of ongoing struggles between elitist aristocrats, emulative of the hierarchical regimes of the Near East and Egypt, and other social groups favouring a more egalitarian civic culture.[43] In the eighth century BCE, tomb cults were established in Mycenaean *tholoi* and rock-cut tombs in some regions of mainland Greece, notably Attica and Argos, as means to establish 'ancestral' land rights.[44] Some, like the Menidhi *tholos* in Attica, become the focus in the seventh century of dedications of special categories of pottery (ritual vessels, decorated in an orientalising style), deposited in offering trenches distinct from the burials themselves, indicative of something other than simple grave goods.[45]

Without texts, we cannot be specific about the kinds of ancestral memory that such practices sustained, but sixth-century evidence permits sharper resolution. A new type of statue, the *kouros* (youth), based on

---

[40] *Iliad* 2.100–9. [41] *Iliad* 10.261–90. [42] Grethlein 2008: 37–40; *Odyssey* 15.54–5, 8.431–2.
[43] Morris 2000. [44] Langdon 1987: 15; Antonaccio 1994. [45] Whitley 1994: 217–18.

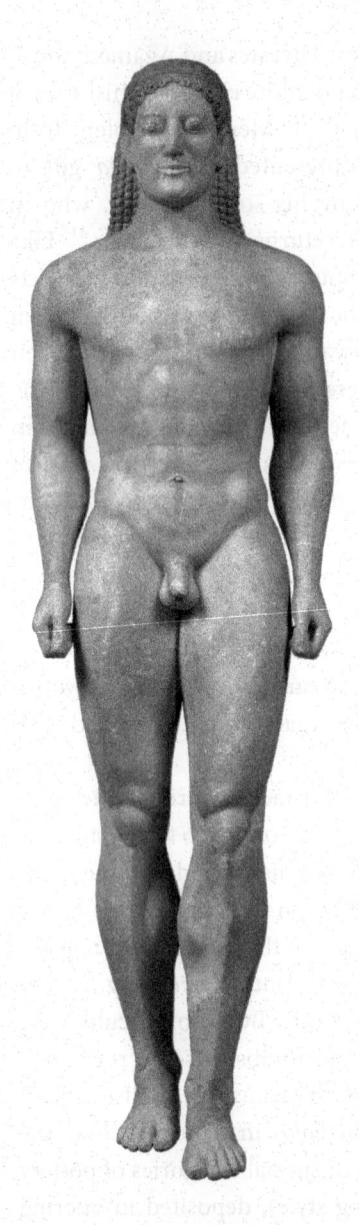

Figure 8.5 Croesus, Anavyssos *kouros* (NM Inv. 3851), c. 540 BCE. National Archaeological Museum Athens.

Egyptian models, became popular for representations of men, as votives in sanctuaries and funerary statues in cemeteries. Its popularity derived from the elitist iconography of an image equally appropriate for a man or a god, flattering the pretensions of an aristocracy whose prestige was partly based on privileged control over cults and claims of special propinquity to the gods.[46] Like the memory objects of the Homeric poems, *kouroi* can be described as *agalmata*.[47] An inscription on the base associated with one (Figure 8.5) reads: 'Halt and show pity beside the marker of dead Croesus, whom raging Ares once destroyed in the front rank of battle.'[48] Association with a group of similar statues, and grave tumuli which had been the site of elaborate tomb cult since the seventh century, suggest a long-standing family cemetery, probably of the Alcmaeonid clan. The name of the deceased – Croesus – is not Greek but Lydian, and points back to Alcmaeon, perhaps the grandfather of the deceased, who had been enriched by a relationship of guest friendship with Croesus, king of Lydia.[49] The content and vocabulary of the epigram, with their heroic allusions, echo odes by poets like Pindar, celebrating the victories of aristocratic athletes in the festival games of the Greek world.[50] Although an epigram offers little scope for elaborating ancestry, the name Croesus evokes distinguished genealogy and illustrious relations of inherited guest-friendship. Pindar's odes describe genealogies to a depth comparable with Zhou bronze inscriptions. The sixth Nemean ode celebrates Alcidamas of Aegina, winner of the boys' wrestling, as heir to a succession of athletic victors stretching back five generations (all individually named), the glory of the Bassidai clan, descendants of Heracles. Statues of ancestors, almost certainly *kouroi* given the date,[51] could be the focal objects of ritual performance of such odes in their honorand's home town: the fifth Nemean celebrates the 'inherited destiny' (*potmos syggenes*), which brings Pythias to embellish (*agallei*) the lustre inherited from his ancestors, his uncle Euthymenes, also a Nemean victor, and his grandfather Themistios whose statue (*agalma*) in the sanctuary of the hero Aeacus is crowned with garlands and the victor's fillets as the closing gesture of the chorus performing the ode in celebration of Pythias' victory.[52]

In most victory odes the glory of athletic victory accrues also to the polis as a whole, but this does not indicate a radical opposition between the principles which informed the social construction of memory in archaic Greece and Zhou China: the inscriptions of Zhou bronzes show a similar

---

[46] Stewart 1986. Aristocratic cult dominance: Parker 1996: 56–66 Athens; Tanner 2006: 57; Fearn 2010: 176 Aegina, 192 Thebes.
[47] Karusos 1961; 1972: 93–102.
[48] Hansen, *Carmina epigraphica graeca saeculorum* 27, trans. after Day 1989: 19.
[49] Herodotus 6.125; Whitley 1994: 229; Neer 2011: 22–30.   [50] Day 1989: 19.
[51] Pausanias 8.40: *kouros* as athlete portrait.
[52] Pindar, *Nemean Ode* 5.40. Mullen 1982: 143–64; Steiner 2001: 259–64.

tendency in their expression of allegiance to the Zhou king, notwithstanding the disintegration of practical Zhou hegemony. The material forms in which the ancestralising memory practices of archaic Greek and Western Zhou aristocrats were realised have almost nothing in common, indebted rather to the specific histories of the two civilisations, based on continuities with Shang traditions in the Western Zhou, on cultural discontinuity and on renewed contacts with the civilisations and artistic traditions of the Eastern Mediterranean in the case of archaic Greece. Differences in social and political structure inflect these practices, performed in distinctive institutional settings: ancestral cults in temples open only to lineage members in China,[53] linked to the larger Zhou polity by the rituals of investiture which bronzes also memorialised; the dedication of statues in cemeteries and sanctuaries, and their ritual appropriation as focus or frame for funerals and choric performances in the archaic Greek world, more open to the broader civic environment with which the elites of the small-scale city-states were required to engage. Notwithstanding these differences, the two cases are interestingly comparable in so far as the historical memory articulated in the verbal and visual arts of both archaic Greece and Western Zhou China was dominated by the ancestralising strategies of aristocratic elites, and had a strongly ritual and performative character, focused on prestige objects, rather than involving the picturing of history which developed later.

Picturing History in Classical Athens

The Persian Wars are often considered a turning point in historical self-consciousness amongst the Greeks, particularly the Athenians who played a leading role in defeating the Persians at the battles of Marathon and Salamis. Two memorials of the wars indicate the changing role of visual art in the construction of historical memory, marking the transition from aristocratic traditions of the archaic period to a practice of picturing history informed by a more strongly civic and democratic ethos: the Marathon Monument at Delphi and the painting of the battle of Marathon in the Stoa Poikile in Athens.

Pausanias describes a statue group at Delphi celebrating Athenian victory at the battle of Marathon.[54] It was erected in the 460s BCE, instigated by the Athenian general Kimon, at the height of his influence in Athens

[53] Wu 1996: 8–10.   [54] Pausanias 10.10.1.

Figure 8.6 Stoa Poikile, Athens, c. 460 BCE. Restored perspective by W. B. Dinsmoor.

after victory over the Persians at the battle of Eurymedon.[55] It showed Miltiades, Kimon's father, flanked by Apollo and Athena, and accompanied by a group of ten Attic heroes, some of them eponymous heroes of the Attic tribes, but with three substitutes – Kodros, Theseus and probably Philaios. The monument has been considered 'an expression of filial piety' on the part of Kimon, and is shaped by the same kind of ancestralising strategies as characterised archaic art and Pindar's poetry.[56] It claims for Miltiades alone the victory at Marathon – he was in fact just one of the board of ten generals, and technically the command was that of the polemarch Callimachus – elevating him, a mortal, into the company of gods and heroes. The choice of Philaios amongst the substitute heroes alludes to Kimon's genealogy, as a member of the Philaid clan, descended from Zeus via the hero Ajax and his son Philaios.[57]

The paintings of the Stoa Poikile were also indebted to the initiative of Kimon and his family (Figure 8.6). The Stoa was originally known as the Peisianakteion, named after Peisianax, the brother-in-law of Kimon, who presumably provided some of the funds for its construction, in the late 460s.[58] But stories concerning the development of the iconography, the labelling and the composition of the painting all indicate the increasingly tight democratic control of civic art characteristic of classical Athens.[59]

[55] Harrison 1996: 23–8. [56] Castriota 1992: 81. [57] Connor 1970: 164.
[58] Stansbury O'Donnell 2005: 81. [59] Rouveret 1987/9: 103.

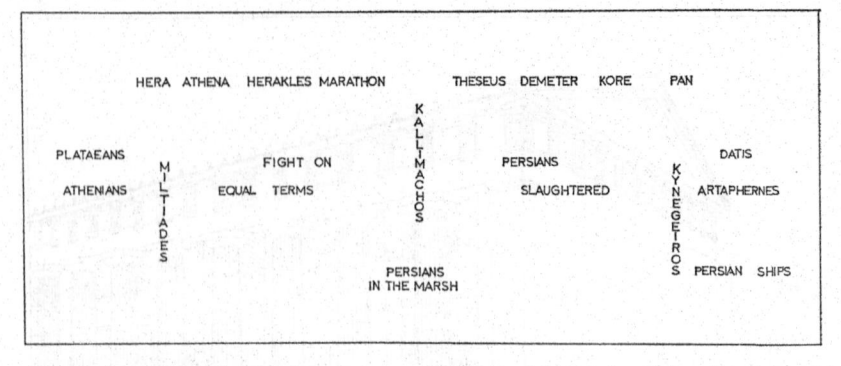

Figure 8.7 Reconstruction of compositional scheme of the Battle of Marathon Painting in the Stoa Poikile.

Correspondingly, the character of the paintings is sometimes held to be a democratic response to the elitist and ancestralising claims of the Delphi statue group, shaped by the radical democratic reforms of Ephialtes which marked the eclipse of Kimon's influence.[60] A request that Miltiades, alone amongst the protagonists, be identified by an inscription stating that he had led the Athenians to victory was refused – the victory was of all Athenians, not of one man alone – although it was granted that Miltiades be shown in the forefront, urging on the soldiers.[61] An experimental perspective effect by Mikon, showing some Greeks in the background smaller than Persians in the foreground – and misread as a demeaning representation, since lower-status figures were conventionally represented smaller than higher-status figures – earned the painter a fine of thirty minas.[62]

Although the painting no longer survives, we can reconstruct some key features from ancient descriptions (Figure 8.7).[63] At the left, the painting showed the Athenians and Plataeans, drawn up in battle line on the slopes above the plain: Miltiades gives the signal committing them to battle. Immediately to the right were the forces of the two armies meeting on the plain, broken up into individual duels, and culminating in the heroic death of the polemarch Callimachus at the centre of the painting. This represents the turning point of the battle: the Persians are driven back to the marshes at the edge of the plain, and then in headlong flight towards their ships. Here, at the extreme right, the last iconic scene of the battle was depicted: Kynegeiros grasps the bowsprit of one of the Persian ships,

---

[60] Harrison 1996: 26. [61] Aeschines 3.186. [62] Reinach 1921, no. 141.
[63] Pausanias 1.15; Harrison 1972; Hölscher 1973: 50–84; Stansbury O'Donnell 2005.

attempting to prevent the flight of the Persian commanders Datis and Artaphernes, only to fall to the blow of a Persian axe which lops off his arm. The top register of the painting included representations of deities and heroes – Athena, Theseus, Heracles – who were held to have been present, and supportive, at the battle, though they were not depicted as actually taking part in it. Two smaller paintings, pendants to the Marathon painting, showed the Sack of Troy and an Amazonomachy.

Contemporary vase-painting, and later relief sculpture, allow us to visualise aspects of the Marathon painting. Depictions of Greeks fighting Persians in vase-paintings, and especially the increasingly realistic and detailed representation of their weapons, reflect the historical turn in contemporary painting, contrasting with the epic-mythological character of warfare in earlier black-figure vases.[64] Persians are sometimes depicted already on the run, as they turn to face their Greek pursuers, emphasising the effeminate propensity to flight of the Persians, described in contemporary texts and encoded in the structure of the Marathon narrative (Figure 8.8).[65] Harrison argues that the south frieze of the temple of Athena Nike represents the battle of Marathon and is modelled on the Poikile paintings. One section (Figure 8.9) shows a Greek warrior delivering the coup de grâce to a Persian. The Greek is naked, *himation* falling around his knees (a conventional heroic motif), his right arm raised up to deliver the mortal blow to his Persian adversary. His left arm swings away from his body, leaving him vulnerable, echoing in detail the posture of Harmodios from the Tyrannicide group (Figure 8.1). This was a deliberate choice, informed by the same account of the battle of Marathon as that of Herodotus. At the end of a debate between the Athenian generals whether to attack the Persians immediately, before their army is fully disembarked, or to wait for assistance from the Spartans, Miltiades, advocating immediate attack, addresses Callimachus, the polemarch with whom the final decision lies: 'Callimachus. It is up to you either to enslave Athens or to make her free and leave for yourself a memory such as neither Harmodios nor Aristogeiton left.'[66] The tyrannicide-like figure on the frieze is Callimachus, at the moment of his *aristeia*, as depicted at the centre of the painting of the battle of Marathon in the Stoa Poikile.[67] The Persians are fully clothed, in tunic and trousers, a touch on the corpulent side, and sluggish in their movement.[68] The Athenians, contrastingly, manifest an ideal and elevating nudity. Their muscled bodies and striking postures

---

[64] Csapo and Miller 1998: 116–17.   [65] Castriota 1992: 83–4.   [66] Herodotus 6.109.
[67] Harrison 1972: 355.   [68] Stewart 1985: 62.

Figure 8.8 Greek battles fleeing Persian. Attic red-figure Nolan amphora. New York, Metropolitan Museum of Art.

embody an ethos which was held to be characteristic of the men of Marathon, and their descendants, ready 'to use their bodies as if they were those of other men, when it is in the service of their city ... to accomplish anything on her behalf'.[69] The figure of Callimachus evokes the concept of the beautiful death, informed by a positive decision to sacrifice one's own life on behalf of the polis.[70]

The juxtaposition of mythical and contemporary events, and the elaboration of the meaning of the latter through analogies with the former, were a convention of epinician poetry like that of Pindar, celebrating individual athletic victors. Extended to civic history in Simonides' poem on the battle of Plataea, it also characterises inscribed herms celebrating the victory of Kimon and the Athenians at Eion.[71] Framing the Marathon painting with an Amazonomachy and Ilioupersis, and presenting it in

[69] Thucydides 1.70.   [70] Loraux 1986: 98–118.   [71] Boedecker 1998: 190; Aeschines 3.183.

Figure 8.9 South frieze from the Temple of Athena Nike, Athens. Slab G, British Museum.

terms of value-laden iconographic codes, gave specific ideological inflection to the depiction of history. The battle was given a pedigree in deep time, similar to that in Herodotus who attributes the origins of the enmity between the Greeks and the Persians to the rape of Helen and the sack of Troy.[72] The Amazonomachy paralleled the defensive character of the Athenians' struggle against the Persians, since Theseus' heroic battle against the Amazons had taken place in Athens itself, in the immediate environs of the Acropolis, where the sites of the Amazon encampments could still be pointed out.[73] Most importantly, as the Tyrannicide imagery implied, the battle of Marathon was fought for freedom.[74] Further resonance derived from the contemporary use of Tyrannicide iconography for representations of Theseus, mythical founder of Athenian democracy, punishing violators of moral order in his cycle of deeds.[75] The courage of the Athenians in the protection of freedom at Marathon thus appears as the expression of an intrinsic virtue, rooted in time immemorial.

This artistic programme was elaborated during the following half-century to provide a strongly affirmative, but increasingly tendentious and ideological, account of the history of Athens, not only in the Persian Wars, but also in those of the later fifth century. Another painting was added to the Stoa Poikile, showing a battle at Oinoe, between the Athenians and the Spartans, at the beginning of the Peloponnesian War.[76] In 425 BCE, the Stoa was decorated with shields captured from the Spartans at Sphacteria. Painting and shields alike added a new layer of meaning to the existing programme, legitimating the wars against Sparta and her allies as a continuation of, and congruent in their character with, the great struggles of earlier, historical and mythical, eras.[77] The late fifth-century wars, however, were fought not against Persians, but against other Greeks, in

[72] Herodotus 1.3–4. [73] Connor 1970: 157; Plutarch, *Theseus* 27.
[74] Harrison 1972: 362; Castriota 1992: 79–80. [75] Henle 1973: 80–2. [76] Taylor 1998.
[77] Stansbury-O'Donnell 2005: 80.

defence less of Greek liberty than Athens' freedom to control and exploit the dependent cities of an empire which she had established following the Persian Wars.

The increasingly ideological character of Athenian historical representation is highlighted by the Temple of Athena Nike. This temple was likely built with the fruits of Athenian victories in the first phase of the Peloponnesian War, and possibly also with allied tribute money. It was constructed in the mid-420s BCE, and a priestess installed in 423, shortly after the annual payments of Athens' allies had been reassessed to include symbolic tribute of arms and cattle to be presented to Athena at the annual Panathenaic festival. This was part of the muscular imperialism associated with the leadership of Cleon. It is no coincidence that the bastion on which the temple stood was decorated with shields captured by Cleon in his great triumph over the Spartans at Pylos and Sphacteria.[78] The south frieze, depicting Marathon, was juxtaposed with two further scenes of warfare. The west frieze is thought to represent a contemporary battle, perhaps Sphacteria or an Athenian victory in north-western Greece during the first phase of the Peloponnesian War.[79] The north frieze depicts the slaying of Eurystheus. After the death of Heracles, his children fled the Peloponnese for Athens, pursued by their father's persecutor King Eurystheus, who sought to enslave them. They begged sanctuary with the Athenians, who refused to give them up to Eurystheus, who had invaded Attica in their pursuit, with an army from the Peloponnese.[80] Athenian support for the Heracleidai had been invoked as early as the battle of Plataea (479 BCE), as one of the grounds for the Athenian claim to a privileged position in the Greek battle line against the Persians: it revealed the exceptional piety and compassion of the Athenians – they alone amongst the Greeks had offered the Heracleidai sanctuary – as well as their unrivalled virtue as defenders of freedom and punishers of hubris.[81] The message of the programme of the temple of Athena Nike is clear: all Athens' wars, even those against other Greeks, are defensive wars; she intervenes only in order to punish the lawless, to protect the weak and liberate the enslaved, all in a spirit of compassion and self-sacrifice.[82]

Combining myth with history to celebrate the *aretē* of Athens, the programmes of the Stoa Poikile and the Temple of Athena Nike parallel the *topoi* of the Funeral Orations, delivered annually at the burial of the Athenian war dead. Here too the Amazonomachy and the rescue of the

---

[78] Lippmann, Scahill and Schultz 2006: 559.   [79] Stewart 1985; Schultz 2009: 130, 150.
[80] Schultz 2009: 142–6.   [81] Loraux 1986: 67.   [82] Stewart 1985; Schultz 2009.

Heracleidai are invoked as paradigms of Athenian virtue, and the loss of the war dead redeemed for posterity as 'beautiful deaths', willing sacrifices on behalf of the city.[83] This rhetorical tradition indicates the cultural and institutional horizons in terms of which these picturings of history were appropriated by Athenian viewers. In Plato's *Menexenus*, Socrates describes the effect that hearing the funeral oration has on him: he feels himself 'mightily ennobled', and imagines himself to have become 'at once taller, nobler and more handsome', as he seems also in the eyes of foreign friends who accompany him, a feeling which lasts for several days.[84] Describing the 'bewitching' effect (*goēteia*) of the funeral oration, Socrates insists on the visual as the medium in which the glorious deeds of the Athenians and their ancestors are best grasped.[85] Considering the *aretē* of the generation of Marathon, 'it is necessary to visualise it (*idein*), if we are to praise it fitly, placing ourselves in thought in that very time, when the whole of Asia was already in bondage to the third of the Persian kings'.[86] In evoking the achievements of that epoch, and their inspirational character, Socrates seems to describe a visual experience, like looking at a painting of the battle of Marathon (which, like other monuments, might be described as an *ergon*): 'I affirm that those men were the begetters not only of our bodies, but also of our freedom; for it was with their eyes fixed (*apoblepsantes*) on this great work (*ergon*) that the Greeks dared to risk the battles joined in later times for their salvation, learning the lessons of the men of Marathon.'[87]

Athenian rhetoric transforms myth and history into visual, even visionary, experience, appropriated as an ethical model to shape the actions of a citizen audience. The fourth-century orator Lycurgus praises the dramatist Euripides for staging the story of the Attic king Erechtheus and his family, saving the city from a Thracian invasion, in one of his plays, 'considering that the finest example (*paradeigma*) to offer the citizens is the heroic acts of former times: they have only to look at (*apoblepontas*) them, and contemplate (*theōrountas*) them to cultivate love of country in their hearts'.[88] In other speeches the Marathon paintings themselves are invoked for jurors to envision them in their mind's eye (*dianoia*), as the source of exemplars against which to judge the character and contributions of later benefactors of the city.[89] As described in the *Menexenus*, these visions are 'theoric': the viewer is presented with a vision which is the object of wonder

---

[83] Loraux 1986. [84] 235e; Porter 2011: 66.
[85] *Goēteia* is used by Gorgias and Plato to describe the powers of painting and rhetoric alike.
[86] *Menexenus* 239d, trans. Loeb. [87] *Menexenus* 240e.
[88] Lycurgus, *Leocrates* 100; Loraux 1986: 136. [89] Aeschines 3.187; Demosthenes 59.94.

and reverence, a religious spectacle of transcendent beauty. Similarly, Thucydides has Pericles, in the first funeral oration of the Peloponnesian War, instruct his audience 'to gaze (*theōmenous*) on the power of the city day after day, becoming her lovers'.[90] Just such an enduring vision of Athens' power was offered both in the Marathon programme of the Stoa Poikile and in the depictions of history on the temple of Athena Nike, raised high on its bastion, glistening with shields of Athens' defeated opponents (Figure 8.10a–b).[91] Pictured history was a vehicle for affective identification with the manifest destiny of Athens: it recompensed the dead, comforted the bereaved and encouraged the living, 'appealing to their children and their brothers to imitate the *aretē* of these men'.[92]

Picturing History in Early Imperial China

There is sufficient interest in the pictorialisation of history in early China to refute any claims of an essential difference between the two traditions, as opposed to the differential elaboration of shared cultural possibilities. Contributions to the military successes of the Zhou are amongst the achievements commemorated and rewarded in the ritual bronzes of the Western Zhou, and warfare is a central theme of the pictorial bronzes of the Warring States (So 1980a). Furthermore, there are depictions of battles between Han Chinese and foreign (nomadic) barbarians in Han funerary art, mostly of a rather generic character. One which may be intended to depict a particular historical event is that on the Xiaotangshan shrine, where – amidst scenes of battle, and decapitation of prisoners – one of the figures is specifically named as 'Hu Wang', the King of the Hu (barbarians). This is by some margin the largest surviving Han shrine, and such an unusual example that it has been suggested that it was dedicated to a prince of the ruling dynasty, perhaps the brother of Emperor He, rather than a member of the *shi*.[93]

Depictions of specific historical battles, however, seem very unusual in Han art. A story in the History of the Former Han tells of a Chinese commander commissioning paintings of a campaign in Central Asia, including the siege of a fortified city of the Xiongnu. On his return to the capital, the victories were reported to the High Gods and the Imperial Ancestors, before the paintings were ultimately displayed at a celebratory

---

[90] Thucydides 2.43; Stewart 1997: 83 (trans). [91] Nightingale 2001. [92] *Menexenus* 236e.
[93] Soper 1974; James 1988/9.

Figure 8.10 (a) Temple of Athena Nike, Athens, c. 425 BCE.

banquet in the imperial palace. Three comments are worth making. First, the paintings seem to have had a rather exceptional motivation: the commander in question had forged an imperial edict in order to mobilise the troops necessary for the expedition, and the paintings seem to have functioned as part of a publicity campaign to save his neck. Second, the incentive for the emperor to translate such paintings into some kind of monumental memorial was rather limited, since, unlike his Roman counterparts, for example, he played no personal role in military campaigns.

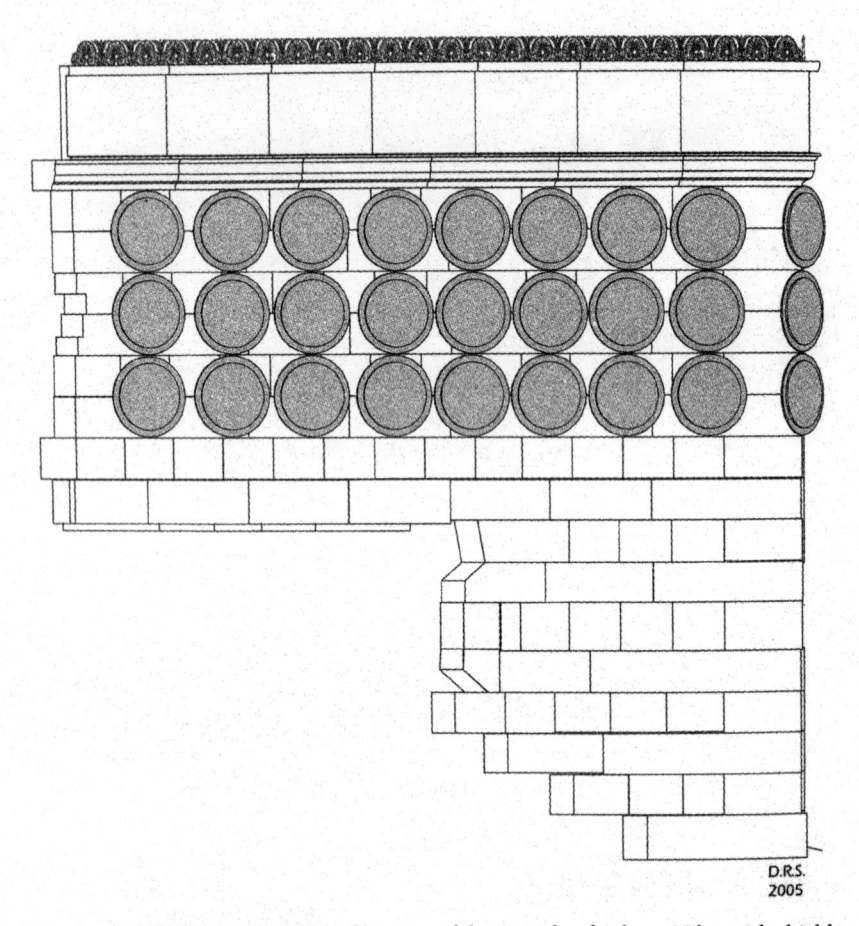

Figure 8.10 (b) Reconstruction of bastion of the Temple of Athena Nike, with shields attached. Drawing: David Scahill.

Third, it is symptomatic of the status of such paintings that an important part of their interest for the historian Ban Gu was that the scenes of women warriors in Central Asia were so striking that the paintings were even circulated amongst the ladies of the imperial harem, for their amusement.[94] This is not to say that there was no monumental art of a historical character oriented to the celebration of military victory in Han China, only that it was not as institutionally central as in classical Greece or ancient Rome.[95]

[94] Duyvendak 1939/40; Barbieri-Low 2007: 173–7. Such paintings are so unusual in their character that Duyvendak attributes them to the influence of Roman soldiers and artisans who may have been present in the Xiongnu city.
[95] The tomb of the great general Huo Qubing (d. 117 BCE), constructed within the imperial funerary park on the instructions of Han Wudi, included a tumulus modelled on a mountain

The picturing of history in early imperial China developed in a different direction. A prose poem by Wang Wenkao (second century CE) describes the decoration of the 'Hall of Numinous Brilliance', built by the Han King, Liu Yu, King Gong of Lu in the mid-second century BCE. Amongst elaborate carvings of prowling tigers and leaping dragons, enriching the columns and rafters of the hall, the poet describes a programme of wall-paintings, recording the history of the world from its beginnings – 'Above they record the Opening of Chaos,/The beginnings of remote antiquity' – through the (mythological) Nine Sovereigns, to stories of more recent times: 'Last come the Three Sovereigns,/Depraved consorts, misguided rulers,/Loyal statesmen, filial sons,/virtuous *shi*, chaste women,/Worthies and fools, the failed and accomplished,/None have gone unattested./The wicked are warnings to the world,/The good are examples for posterity.'[96] Wang Wenkao's vocabulary echoes that of history writing, indicating that he viewed the paintings as pictorial records of the past parallel to those transmitted in texts by royal scribes and annalists. Representing the story of the world as a unified whole from the remote past of legendary rulers like the Yellow Emperor, through the rulers of the Xia, Shang and Zhou dynasties, to loyal ministers, and then stories of ordinary men and women, memorable for their filial piety or virtue, these paintings remarkably anticipate both Sima Qian's *Shiji*, written at least a generation later and structured along similar lines, and the most famous and systematic pictorialisation of history in early China, the engravings of the Wu Liang Shrine (mid-second century CE).

Like the Numinous Hall, the pictures of the Wu Liang Shrine present a universal history embedded within a cosmic frame.[97] The frame is provided by depictions of omens on the ceiling, and of the deities the Queen Mother of the West and the King Father of the East and their realms in the gables of the west and east walls.[98] The remainder of the three walls of the shrine reads, like a Chinese text, from right to left and from top to bottom (Figure 8.2). It starts on the upper row with Fuxi and Nuwa, the creators of mankind, followed by the Nine Sovereigns, and Jie, the last king of the Xia (2000–1600 BCE), whose shortcomings led to the fall of the dynasty, and its replacement by the Shang (1600–1400 BCE). There follows – upper row, back and left walls – a series of representations of famous women of the Eastern Zhou (771–256 BCE). The second register has depictions of

---

that had been the site of one of Huo's victories, as well as an expansive programme of sculpture: horses trampling barbarians, and various animals and monsters – Paludan 1991: 17–27.
[96] 160–8; Knechtges 1987: 275.   [97] Croissant 1964; James 1988/9; Wu 1989.
[98] Wu 1989: 73–141.

stories from the lives of famous men, mainly filial sons, but also exemplary brothers and friends, starting with figures from the Zhou, and culminating with a filial son of the Eastern Han (25–220 CE), who had died not long before the construction of the shrine. The directional sequence of the figures – all facing right – emphasises movement in historical time.[99] The central panel of the lower half of the walls shows a large columned pavilion, in which homage is being paid to the deceased. This is flanked by stories of notables of Eastern Zhou history: six assassin retainers, including Jing Ke's attempted assassination of the King of Qin, later the First Emperor; distinguished ministers, Lin Xiangru and Fan Sui; and Zhongli Chun, an ugly woman nevertheless valued as an adviser by King Xuan of Qi. The larger theme informing the whole programme, Wu Hung argues, is the patterning of history, shaped by the Three Bonds of Confucian morality – the ruler–subject relationship, parent–son, husband–wife – within the context of a correlative cosmology in which Heaven-sent omens respond to the moral status of the empire.[100] This concept of history is informed by Sima Qian's *Shiji*, and, like Sima Qian, Wu Liang depicts himself at the end of the history, as its recorder, in the final scene of the shrine, at the bottom left-hand extreme of the east wall.[101] This systematic appropriation of history constitutes the shrine as a well-ordered universe for the *hun*-soul of the deceased, and offers a vision of righteousness and faithfulness to his descendants.

The Wu Liang Shrine is, however, not fully representative of the general character of the pictorialisation of history in Han art. Far more common are much smaller shrines, with no more than a couple of historical pictures, lacking the systematic programme which allows Wu Hung to trace the Wu Liang carvings to the same horizon of historical consciousness as that of the *Shiji*. One of the Song Shan shrines, for example, has just two historical pictures – Two Peaches and Three Warriors, and Ji Zha dedicating his sword at the tomb of the Lord of Xu (Figure 8.11a–b) – amongst a series of engravings dominated by standard elements drawn from the broader repertoire of funerary iconography (chariot procession, Queen Mother of the West, King Father of the East, the standard 'homage scene', and a kitchen scene).[102] Even the largest surviving shrine, the Xiaotangshan Shrine, includes only a small selection of historical scenes – King Cheng and the Duke of Zhou, the First Emperor and the Loss of the Zhou Tripods,

---

[99] Wu 1989: 143–4.   [100] Wu 1989: 218–30.   [101] Wu 1989: 213–17.
[102] Ruitenbeek 2002: 40–5.

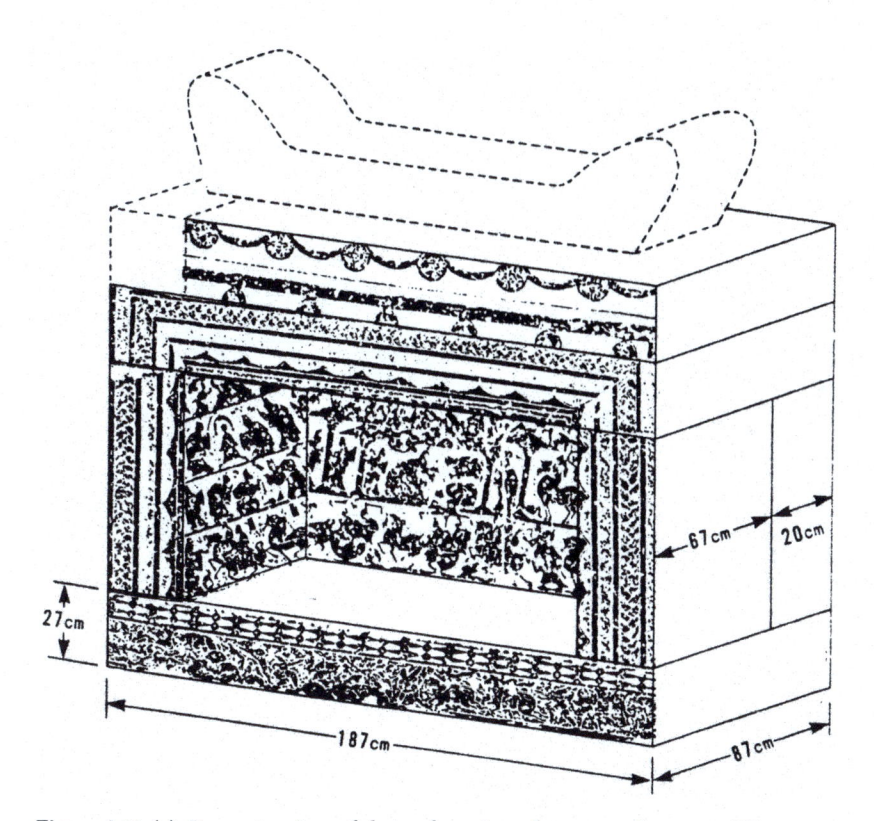

Figure 8.11 (a) Reconstruction of shrine from Songshan, second century CE.

and a battle with the Hu barbarians – amongst the more generic repertoire. The picture is complicated by the fact that many of the depictions from tombs and shrines survive only as isolated slabs, sometimes recycled in later tombs, and do not lend themselves to reconstruction as integrated monuments so easily as the Songshan shrines.

The impression emerges that individual tomb-designers selected, from a larger repertoire, a handful of sometimes rather disparate narratives that somehow resonated with the specific concerns of the sponsor of the tomb or shrine in question. It is this broader practice of the pictorialisation of history which is my focus. Rather than looking at specific programmes in individual tombs or shrines, it may be fruitful to examine some of the historical scenes which prove particularly popular, recurring frequently in the corpus of funerary art, especially of the Eastern Han, from which the bulk of the evidence dates: the story of Jing Ke's attempted assassination of the King of Qin (Figure 8.12), King Cheng and the Duke of Zhou (Figure 8.13), Two Peaches and Three Warriors (Figure 8.11b), and the

Figure 8.11 (b) West wall of shrine from Songshan, second century CE. Rubbing after engraved stones in Shandong Provincial Museum. Top: Queen Mother of the West. Second register: Ji Zha dedicates his sword to the Lord of Xu. Third register: Two Peaches and Three Warriors. Fourth register: Departure of chariot procession.

First Emperor and the Loss of the Tripods of Zhou (Figure 8.14). How can we understand the process by which these scenes were selected, and the special resonance that these particular historical events seem to have had for the producers and viewers of funerary engravings in the Eastern Han?

Wu Hung's study of the Wu Liang Shrine offers some initial clues. The shrine's programme was indebted to traditions of textual production characteristic of the *shi*, the literate elite from whose ranks the officials of the imperial bureaucracy were drawn, and who were the primary sponsors of the tombs and shrines decorated with these historical pictures.[103]

---

[103] Status of tomb patrons: Thompson 1998: 105–37, esp. 128–37; 1999: 6–9.

Figure 8.12 Jing Ke and the King of Qin (top register). Rubbing after engravings on the south wall of Shrine 1, Wu Family Cemetery. Second century CE.

Although Sima Qian's *Shiji* provided the 'organizational principles' for the Wu Liang Shrine,[104] a number of other texts, and authors, seem also to have been important to its design, most notably Liu Xiang (79–78 BCE), a Counsellor of the Palace in the Western Han, and a major figure in the collation and editing of inherited classical texts.[105] Liu Xiang was responsible for the compilation of the 'Stratagems of the Warring States', a collection of anecdotes about the intrigues which had informed the relations between the Warring States. Although today an important source for Warring States history, it is not so much a history or chronicle as a manual of examples, for practical and rhetorical use.[106] Liu Xiang also assembled more focused compilations, including the *Shuoyuan* (*Garden of Discourse*). This collects stories in twenty chapters, some of which are miscellanies (*za*), while others have a specific political focus,[107] and even touch on some of the same stories as recur in funerary art. The chapter 'The Way of the Minister' includes the story of Lin Xiangru and the precious jade, one of the more popular themes in Han funerary art, demonstrating the moral integrity, the ingenuity and the readiness for self-sacrifice of the ideal

[104] Wu 1989: 150–4. [105] Loewe 1993: 178, 246; Schaberg 2011:402.
[106] Schaberg 2011: 402. [107] Schaberg 2011: 402.

Figure 8.13 Rubbing after engraving from Eastern Han shrine, Songshan, Shandong Province. Top register: Queen Mother of the West. Second register: King Cheng and the Duke of Zhou. Third register: Liji and the death of Shen Sheng. Fourth register: Chariot procession and reception.

minister.[108] 'Commissions' (*fengshi*) includes a series of assassin-retainers, like Jing Ke, exemplifying relations of righteousness and faithfulness between a ruler and a subject whom the ruler is able to persuade to undertake the commission.[109] Some of Liu Xiang's compilations had very specific scope, occasioned by particular circumstances at court. The *Lienü Zhuan* (*Arrayed Biographies of Women*) was designed to enhance

[108] Wu 1989: 188–90, 305–8; Thompson 1999: 17; Finsterbusch I.319, 3.A83, A84.
[109] Wu 1989: 188–91.

Figure 8.14 The First Emperor fails to recover the Zhou Tripods. Rubbing after engravings on the East Wall, Chamber 2, Wu Family Cemetery, Shandong.

standards of moral conduct at the court, in the wake of Emperor Cheng's infatuation with and indulgence of the Zhao sisters,[110] and a broadly similar purpose must have informed the 'Arrayed Biographies of Filial Sons'. The specific selections of images of virtuous women and filial sons on the Wu Liang Shrine seem to imply dependence on Liu Xiang's compilations as a source of inspiration.[111]

Liu Xiang's writings represent one important instance of a much broader phenomenon of the textualisation of authority, well under way in Warring States China, and institutionalised in early imperial China.[112] The *shi* emerged out of the conflicts of the Warring States, in which the autonomous city-states of the Western Zhou were gradually incorporated into larger states. Descendants of displaced and junior lineages took up service in the courts of more powerful states, offering specialist knowledge of texts and rituals.[113] In early imperial China, the *shi* occupied a strategic position. The Han practice of government developed a strongly textual character, requiring a high level of literary competence on the part of the governing elite in practices such as record keeping, the writing of memorials, the transmission of orders and much else besides.[114] This acquired an institutional basis with the creation of an imperial academy, where

---

[110] Wu 1989: 170–1; Barbieri-Low 2007: 163. [111] Wu 1989: 170–86. [112] Connery 1998.
[113] Cheng 2001: 105–7; Barbieri-Low 2007: 37. [114] Connery 1998: 7–10; Cheng 2001: 105–6.

candidates for government office were trained in mastery of canonical texts of the Confucian tradition, and in the commentaries which elucidated them and were a major category of *shi* textual production. Chinese 'literature' developed out of, and in relation to, the wide range of textual practices which the *shi* engaged in as part of their official duties.[115]

This textualisation of culture extended to visual art and informed the pictorialisation of history. Liu Xiang's *Lienü Zhuan* was translated into pictorial formats – screens and handscrolls – more or less contemporaneously with the production of the text, and under Liu Xiang's own direction.[116] In the Eastern Han, the Emperor Ming instructed the historian Ban Gu (32–92) and Jia Kui (30–102), a well-known classical scholar, to make selections from classics and histories of stories which could be depicted by the painters of the Imperial Manufactory, in order to decorate the palace, probably as wall- or screen-paintings. Ban Gu and Jia Kui also provided the evaluative captions (*zan*) which anchored viewing of the images in the appropriate, textually prescribed, moral codes.[117]

We need not assume that the historical images we find in funerary contexts were based on models created at the imperial court – although in some cases ('Jing Ke', 'Two Peaches') the iconography is so consistent that a single prototype seems likely – or trace specific instances to specific texts, in order to see a parallel between the practices which informed the pictorialisation of history at the court and their counterparts in the funerary repertoire. The excerpting and juxtaposition of specific visual narratives parallel the textual practices of the *shi* less as historians than as compilers of 'treasuries of anecdotes' which could be drawn upon as rhetorical exempla ideally adjusted to a range of specific purposes.[118] The contextually appropriate selection and application of anecdotes from such compilations were amongst the group-defining cultural practices of the *shi*. The historical narratives chosen for funerary contexts affirmed – alongside the innumerable pictures of the pupils of Confucius, and stories of filial piety – the commitment of the deceased to the core values which informed

---

[115] Connery 1998: 141–6; Lewis 2007: 222–6.
[116] *Hanshu* 30.1727; Wu 1989: 170–1; Barbieri-Low 2007: 163.
[117] Zhang Yanyuan, *Lidai Minghua Ji* in Yu Anlan ed., *Huashi Congshu* 1963, *juan* 3: 56. Barbieri-Low 2007: 196; Murray 2007: 33: the pictures may have been scrolls rather than screen- or wall-paintings. Possibly the paintings referred to by Zhang Yanyuan are versions on scrolls which may have served as models for palace decorations such as screens. Wu 1989: 193, parallel with Liu Xiang's selections of 'exemplary historical figures and events for the *Shuo Yuan*'.
[118] Schaberg 2011: 389. Wu 1989: 173–9: Wu Liang's selection from *Lienü Zhuan*, focused on widows' preservation of chastity and responsibility towards the sons of their husbands, aimed at his widow.

the imperial system of government and of which the *shi* were the social embodiment.[119] Furthermore, they had a specifically political charge, whereby moral critique was clothed within manifest commitment to the ruling dynasty.

The later Eastern Han was an exceptionally problematic period for relations between the imperial court and the *shi*, who found themselves faced with conflicting pressures. Consort families were particularly powerful when the emperor was a minor, and they sought to arrogate the reins of government to themselves. Eunuchs, as personal servants in the inner court, were able to establish intimate relationships with the emperor and marginalise the *shi* officials of the outer court in the conduct of government, even placing their own favourites in posts.[120] These abuses were the subject of protests and critical memorials by officials, but outspoken criticism of the court was sometimes met with reprisals, including dismissal and disqualification from office.[121] Historical exempla informed the terms in which these political conflicts were fought out. Displaying the tribute that vice pays to virtue, the Empress Dowager Liang – having installed two child emperors in succession – announced her retirement from the role of regent with a quotation of the words attributed to the Duke of Zhou. In fact, control over the young Emperor Huan simply passed to the Dowager's brother, Liang Ji, until, some years later in 159 CE, Huan was able to assert his autonomy of Ji and his clan with the assistance of a eunuch coup.[122]

The use of historical images in tombs and especially funerary shrines (which could continue to be viewed even after the funeral and the closure of the tomb) should be seen against this background of political tensions and conflict.[123] Funerals of scholars and officials were a major focus for the articulation of *shi* identity. Colleagues, friends and former fellow-students of the deceased travelled long distances to participate in memorial celebrations, and contributed to the erection of memorial tablets.[124] More specifically, the *la* sacrifice – at which the deceased's ancestors were invoked and his own *hun*-soul was the recipient of offerings welcoming it to the shrine as its new abode[125] – was specifically intended to 'rectify the relation between rulers and ministers', as well as establishing harmony in family relations and serving to 'adjust the relations between high and low'.[126]

---

[119] Wu 1989: 180–5.   [120] Powers 1991: 207–8.   [121] Powers 1991: 261–3, 345–52.
[122] Powers 1991: 209–10.   [123] Powers 1991; Thompson 1999; Lewis 2007: 200.
[124] Powers 1984: 142–4; 1991: 97–103.
[125] Hence the popularity of scenes of kitchens and feasting on shrines.
[126] James 1996: 106–7, quoting *Li Ji* – Legge 1885: 27.369–72.

The Duke of Zhou had long been seen as a model minister and official by the *shi*. On the death of King Wu, the conqueror of the Shang and founder of the Zhou dynasty, the Duke of Zhou took on the role of regent for Wu's young son, King Cheng. An engraving from one of the Songshan shrines (Figure 8.13) depicts the scene with the child-king Cheng placed in the centre, standing on a podium, facing forward with a crown on his head. To either side he is flanked by officials, all leaning forward at their waists in a posture strongly coded as an expression of respect, holding their tablets of office. To the king's right, one official holds a protective parasol over his head, whilst, on his left, the Duke of Zhou kneels, with covered hands, to make report to the king concerning his conduct of official business, treating him with exactly the same ritual respect and propriety as would be appropriate to an adult emperor.[127] Such images had an immediate relevance to the circumstances of the Eastern Han court, with a series of child emperors controlled by the consort family. Indeed, the use of the image of the Duke of Zhou for admonitory purpose already had excellent precedents. In his history of the Western Han, Ban Gu relates that the Emperor Wu, nearing death, presented a painting of King Cheng and the Duke of Zhou to his minister Huo Guang (131–68 BCE), as an intimation that he was to act in a similar way on behalf of the emperor's eight-year-old son, Liu Fuling, whom he was designating as successor.[128]

'Two Peaches and Three Warriors' (Figure 8.11b) is an interestingly ambivalent story, and one of the most popular in Han tomb art.[129] Set in the Spring and Autumn period, the story is one of the three brave warriors from the state of Qi. The diminutive prime minister Yanzi, whether personally slighted by the warriors or deeming their power a threat to himself or the state, persuaded the Duke of Qi to present the warriors with two peaches, to be distributed among them according to their merits. Two of the warriors boast of their prowess in warfare, and claim their peaches, the moment shown in the engraving; the third then trumps them with his account of a triumph over a monstrous river turtle. The first two return their peaches and, humiliated, commit suicide, as does the third, filled with remorse at being the unwitting cause of the death of his two friends. The

---

[127] Powers 1984: 153: 'the Duke attempts to compress his physical bulk into a space commensurate with the inferior status he assumes ... Although the young king stands on a platform, in a space set apart by a parasol, and wears a three point crown, the highest point of his crown still falls short of the Duke's hat as he kneels before his lord.' Barbieri-Low 2007: 168: identification of the figure on the left holding the parasol as the Duke of Zhou in condensed versions of the scene.

[128] *Hanshu* 68.2932; Barbieri-Low 2007: 167; James 1996: 95–6; Powers 1991: 209–10.

[129] Eleven examples in Finsterbusch: Henan, Shandong, including Yinan and Wu family shrines.

story could be interpreted in two ways, emphasising the loyalty of the minister to his lord, and his strategic intelligence, or the tragedy of the three warriors, undone by the low cunning of a devious courtier monopolising the ear of the ruler. The latter interpretation has obvious resonances with the fate of the *danggu* (黨錮), the *shi* critics of eunuch corruption at the court, who had been hounded out of office, harassed and persecuted even to the extreme of death by the eunuchs and their party.[130] This is certainly the point of view of a Han poem on the subject, 'The Song of Mount Liangfu'. Departing from the capital of Qi, the poet stops and mourns at the warriors' three tombs: 'Their strength was such that they could move the Southern Mountain;/ Their wisdom exhausted the principles of the earth./But one morning they were slandered,/And two peaches killed the three heroes./Who could have made such a plot?/The Prime Minister Yanzi of Qi.'[131]

Two stories from more recent history are particularly popular in the repertoire of Eastern Han funerary art, both concerning the First Emperor, Qin Shihuangdi: Jing Ke's attempted assassination of the King of Qin (Figure 8.12); and the First Emperor's failure to recover the Zhou Tripods (Figure 8.14). Fearful of Qin expansion, Prince Dan of Yan sought to attract resourceful advisers and retainers to his court, amongst them Jing Ke. Together they plotted an attempt to assassinate the King of Qin (later First Emperor). This involved Jing Ke winning the king's confidence by presenting him with the head of Fan Yuqi, a former Qin general now fugitive at the Yan court, and a map of some Yan territories as a token of submission. Inside the map-roll was concealed a dagger, which Jing Ke was to use to assassinate the king. The plot went awry. Jing Ke failed to take the king sufficiently by surprise, and, as Sima Qian tells the story, the two men end up pursuing each other around a column in the audience chamber, until the king is finally able to draw his sword. He wounds Jing Ke, who is then subdued by the guards, not before a final desperate effort to kill the king, hurling the dagger which pierces the central column in the hall – the moment shown in the picture.[132] This scene is one of the most frequently recurring in Han funerary art, and found in many different regions in China.[133] Pictures of the story of the First Emperor's loss of the Zhou Tripods are similarly popular and widespread in their

---

[130] Thompson 1999: 13.
[131] Chaves 1968: 10 (trans.); Thompson 1999: 16–17 Yinan; Ruitenbeek 2002: 41–2 Songshan.
[132] *Shiji* 86.
[133] Finsterbusch I.71, 85, 324, 463; III.A84, A252, E400, I17, O22, IV.B122; not including the three examples on the Wu family shrines, a second example from the Mahao tombs in Sichuan (Rudolph and Yu 1951: 19; Tang 1997), or the scene on the Gao Yi Que in Sichuan (Paludan 1991: 36).

distribution.[134] According to legend, the Nine Tripods had originally been cast by the Xia, the founding dynasty of China, out of bronze submitted by the nine regions as tribute.[135] Amongst other miraculous powers, these precious treasures embodied imperial legitimacy. Shining brightly or fading as the mandate of a dynasty waxed and waned, they had in turn been transmitted from the Xia to the Shang and the Shang to the Zhou, only to be lost in the River Si with the final collapse of the Zhou in 327 BCE. After reunifying China, the First Emperor sent an expedition to the River Si, to recover the tripods which had reportedly surfaced. The pictures show imperial officials assembled around some kind of gantry, equipped with pulleys and ropes, whereby they seek to raise one of the tripods. They are thwarted by a dragon, which bites through the rope, leaving the officials to fall over on each other, as the tension in the rope disappears.[136]

Both of these pictures could be seen as manifestations of loyalty to the Han, whose legitimacy partly rested on the claim that the First Emperor was a tyrant who had lost – if he ever held – the mandate to rule. But they also had a critical edge. Part of their appeal – to a *shi* audience – seems to have been the way in which they bring the emperor down to the same level as the *shi*, 'who considered themselves "teachers and friends" of the rulers, rather than mere subjects'.[137] In both cases the scene is given a distinctly comic treatment, hardly conformable with imperial dignity. It is a rather galumphing emperor who rushes around the column, in flight from Jing Ke; and the officials, falling back on their bottoms as the rope snaps, bitten through by the dragon, stand in striking contrast to their more conventional representation as embodiments of corporeal propriety, respectfully bowing to their superiors, as in the scenes of the Duke of Zhou and King Cheng. It was a *topos* of Han historical thought that the 'Yin [Shang] could have used the Xia as a mirror, and the Zhou could have used the Yin as a mirror.'[138] So too, the unworthiness of the autocratic First Emperor, manifested by his harsh treatment of scholars, might be a mirror for the emperors of the late Han. More significantly, the scene of the loss of the tripods signalled not only that the mandate of Heaven was changeable, but even that 'the age of ritual art' had ended,[139]

---

[134] Finsterbusch I.169, 193, 261k, 368; III.A134, E871, E872, O44, O50c, O148, O155, O158, O187, O191, O287, O357; IV.A358.
[135] Wu 1989: 92–6; Marsili 2005.
[136] James 1985: 287–9; Wu 1989: 92–6; James 1996: 54–5, 120–3 disregarding the story of the dragon biting through the rope as specifically associated with Qin Shihuangdi in later texts – Wu 1989: 96.
[137] Pines 2008: 24. [138] *Han shi wai zhuan* 19, trans. Hightower 1952: 178–9.
[139] Wu 1996: 11.

and that forms of legitimacy dependent on a purely ritual aura, transmitted within the ancestral line and the ancestral temples of the ruling family, were increasingly displaced by a more publicly accountable moral authority, which the *shi* were the best placed to judge, and which pictorial histories explored.

All these images offer material for political reflection, corresponding to the admonitory role attributed by Wang Wenkao to the paintings of the Numinous Hall. This understanding of the role of pictures of historical events was part of the broader concept of history as 'mirror'. This *topos* of *shi* thought was already an old one by the Han: the text from Master Han's 'Outer Commentary to the Book of Poetry' quoted above was commenting two lines of a poem in the *Classic of Poetry* and spelling out their implications. The *topos* obviously informed the beginnings of what we tend to classify as history writing proper in the *Shiji* of Sima Qian. But it is clear that the concept was also extended to pictures of history in the Han. A passage in the *Kongzi Jiayu*, a late Han compilation of stories about the life of Confucius, describes Confucius visiting the Ming-Tang (Bright Hall):

He saw on the four gates and walls the countenances of Yao and Shun, and images of Jie and Zhou, showing the good and bad characters of each and giving warning by their success or failure. There was also [a picture of] the Duke of Zhou acting as minister to King Cheng, holding him in his arms with his back to the hatchet-screen, and with his face towards the south to receive in audience the feudal lords. Confucius walked to and fro looking at them, and said to his followers: 'This is why the House of Zhou has prospered. A bright mirror is the means by which one examines the face's form, the past is the means by which one knows the present.'[140]

A comment attributed to Cao Zhi (192–232 CE) praises the moral efficacy of visual depictions of history: 'There is none who seeing a picture of usurping ministers stealing a throne would not grind his teeth ... Who at the sight of loyal vassals dying for their principles would not harden his own resolve; and who would not sigh at beholding banished ministers and persecuted sons ... From this we may know that paintings are the means by which mirrors and admonitions are preserved.'[141] The character translated 'mirror' in both the *Han shi wai zhuan* passage and the comment attributed to Cao Zhi requires discussion. *Jian* 鑑 as a noun means 'mirror', as a verb 'to scrutinise'. The base of 鑑 is the metal radical; on top of it is the homophone 監, indicating a man lying down and looking into a sacrificial vessel, probably filled with water, and entailing self-scrutiny of a divinatory

---

[140] *Kongzi jiayu*, pt 3, page 2; Drake 1943: 287.
[141] Acker I.74–5; translation modified, cf. Wang 1994: 517.

character – as it appears in the Shang oracle bones.[142] Consequently, the concept of the painting as 'mirror' in this cultural context has none of the disparaging connotations that the comparison of painting with a mirror has in some strands of Greek thought, notably that of Plato.[143] On the contrary, the vocabulary implies a close and critical scrutiny, a deep divinatory viewing of the patterns of the past in order to construe the events of the future, ideally anticipating and averting disaster by applying the lessons of the past in the present, specifically through moral rectification of oneself and moral admonition of one's colleagues and superiors.[144]

This implies a very different kind of spectatorship than the affirmative 'theoric' viewing afforded by classical Greek history paintings. Greek historical pictures operated above all through beautiful surfaces, iconographic parallels like the Tyrannicide imagery in the Marathon frieze, which created superficial, highly ideological parallels between myth, history and present action.[145] Congruent with the divinatory, critical, style of viewing, the monumentality of Chinese pictorialisation of history is a rather intimate monumentality, by comparison with the imposing stoas and temples which were the architectural support for historical pictures in classical Athens. Even in the case of the largest surviving Han funerary shrine, the Xiaotangshan, the viewer needs to kneel to view the pictures. It is hard to imagine more than one viewer at a time looking at smaller shrines, like those from Songshan. The viewer, kneeling in front of the shrine, making offerings to the deceased (and thus echoing the homage scene which commonly decorated the back wall of shrines), would read the imagery, simply by turning his head from right to left, or vice versa, and up and down, like studying a written text, as Wu Hung has suggested. This is radically different from the very public and collective viewing context for the Marathon painting in the Stoa Poikile, and even more so for the battle friezes on the temple of Athena Nike, looked up to from a distance by the

---

[142] Huang 1995: 76. The links between mirroring, history and divinatory prognostication are also apparent in a saying of Mozi, quoted in the *Shiji* 79/47: 'I have said that he who looks into water will see the form of his face, but he who looks at men will know fortune (*ji* 吉) and misfortune (*xiong* 凶)', invoking the terminology of divination (Watson 1958: 136): the character for 'fortune' shows words from the mouth of a *shi*/scholar.

[143] *Republic* 596de.

[144] The divinatory affordances of mirrors, and their moral potential as media of self-scrutiny, are similarly developed in Greco-Roman culture, along with plays on the notion of painting as a moralising mirror, particularly in Roman art (Taylor 2008); in classical Athens, however, they do not seem to have been linked to history painting in the way they were in China.

[145] Which led to disaster, as Thucydides (6.53–9) seeks to show in his deconstruction of the Tyrannicide myth against the background of the Athenian expedition to Sicily, which ultimately lost Athens the Peloponnesian War.

viewer, as he approaches the entrance to the Akropolis, processing up the sacred way, the route for the Panathenaic procession. Of course, there is a danger of being misled by the character of the very partial surviving material evidence, the funerary shrines of the *shi*. The depictions of history as wall-paintings in palaces may have had a more monumental character. But it is worth bearing in mind that the texts discussing the production and viewing of such paintings within the context of the palace more often refer to more personal objects, screens and even handscrolls, than wall-paintings, and even if some of those paintings were more monumental, it should not distract us from identifying the specific character of the elaboration of the practice of picturing history in late Han China, evidenced by funerary art. As in late fifth-century Athens, so also in second-century CE China, and in particular in the Shandong region, we encounter an intensified interest in the pictorialisation of history, but informed by rather different interests on the part of its primary sponsors, the *shi*, and correspondingly having rather different purposes: namely formulating and encouraging a broadly critical orientation towards the state and state power – or at least its abuse – in contrast to the ideological idealisation of imperialism in the art of the Athenian state.

Conclusion

Long-term comparative social history of art *as an institution* avoids either essentialising contrasts between the two traditions or a reductive assimilation of them in terms of a handful of minimal common denominators. Focusing on strategies for 'staging' history, and the agents who manage such stagings, demonstrates how the broadly comparable strategies of historical representation in early Greece and China are given a specific shape by the distinctive character of their respective sponsoring elites, as actors in the complex configurations which constituted the states in each case. The 'memory objects' of Zhou China and archaic Greece have little that is formal in common, but they both operate in the context of ancestralising strategies which bear at least a family resemblance to each other. To be sure, those ancestralising strategies are significantly different, but we can explain those differences in terms of differences in political and social structure: aristocratic lineages securely established as the rulers of autonomous city-states and competing for office and status within the broader field of the loosely integrated Zhou kingdom in Bronze Age China, as opposed to aristocratic lineages struggling for dominance primarily within the emergent *poleis* of archaic Greece, against the background of pan-Hellenic relations of guest-friendship and of competition, in festival and games, within a loose civilisational framework that lacked the higher-level political organisation characteristic of the Zhou kingdom.

Traditions of picturing history in classical Greece and early imperial China developed out of this broadly comparable background. This took place in a comparable political context, namely the emergence of more differentiated state structures, entailing new forms of specifically political solidarity transcending kinship, and also a much extended dependence for state administration on elites with a high level of textual competence, the *shi* of China and the *rhētores* and *stratēgoi* of classical Athens. The role and significance of the pictorialisation of history were refracted through the different structures of the two states, and the positions of the cultural elites within them. Depictions of military victory, celebrating the state through the Athenian people, were the focus of Athenian picturing of history, shaped by the interests of the *dēmos*, who were the primary patrons of state art, and their rather direct control, through the institutions of the democratic assembly, over the political and cultural elites who were responsible for realising projects like the paintings of the Stoa Poikile or the sculptures of the Temple of Athena Nike. In China, by contrast, the state apparatus was much more complex, and power balanced uneasily between the *shi* and the bureaucracy of the outer court, and the eunuchs and the consort families of the inner court, all competing for the ear of the emperor. Athenian historical representation was directed primarily towards relations outside the state, with the Persians and with other Greeks. Chinese picturing of history was directed towards the inner workings of the state, in particular to exploring and regulating the relationship between the *shi* and other holders of state power, including the emperor. It defined that relationship in ways which questioned uses of state power which might seem arbitrary from a *shi* point of view, and supported the moral authority of the *shi* as the paramount cultural elite.

References

Acker, W. R. B. (1954–74) *Some T'ang and Pre-T'ang Texts on Chinese Painting*, 3 vols. Leiden.

Akiro, K. (2010) 'Are the Wu Liang Shrine pictorial stones forgeries? Examining the Han era evidence', *Asia Major* 23.2: 129–51.

Alonso, A. M. (1988) 'The effects of truth: representations of the past and the imagining of community', *Journal of Historical Sociology* 1.1: 33–57.

Antonaccio, C. (1994) 'Contesting the past: hero cult, tomb cult and epic in early Greece', *American Journal of Archaeology* 98.3: 389–410.
Assmann, J. (2011) *Cultural Memory and Early Civilization: Writing, Remembrance and Political Imagination.* Cambridge.
Bagley, R. W. (1980a) 'The rise of the Western Zhou dynasty', in *The Great Bronze Age of China*, ed. W. Fong. New York: 193–213.
  (1980b) 'Transformation of the bronze art in later Western Zhou', in *The Great Bronze Age of China*, ed. W. Fong. New York: 241–8.
Bai Qianshen (2008) 'The intellectual legacy of Huang Yi and his friends: reflections on some issues raised by *Recarving China's Past*', in *Rethinking Recarving: Ideals, Practices and Problems of the 'Wu Family Shrines' and Han China*, ed. C. Liu. New Haven: 286–337.
Barbieri-Low, A. J. (2007) *Artisans in Early Imperial China.* Seattle and London.
Boedeker, D. (1998) 'Presenting the past in fifth century Athens', in *Democracy, Empire and the Arts in Fifth Century Athens*, eds. D. Boedeker and K. Raaflaub. Cambridge, MA: 185–202.
Castriota, D. (1992) *Myth, Ethos and Actuality: Official Art in Fifth Century BC Athens.* Madison.
Chaves, J. (1968) 'A Han painted tomb at Loyang', *Artibus Asiae* 30: 5–27.
Cheng, A. (2001) 'What did it mean to be a Ru in Han times?', *Asia Major* 14.2: 101–18.
Connery, C. L. (1998) *The Empire of the Text: Writing and Authority in Early Imperial China.* Oxford.
Connor, W. R. (1970) 'Theseus in Classical Athens', in *The Quest for Theseus*, ed. A. Ward. New York: 143–74.
Cook, C. (2005) 'Moonshine and millet: feasting and purification rituals in ancient China', in *Of Tripod and Palate: Food, Politics and Religion in Traditional China*, ed. R. Sterckx. London: 9–33.
Croissant, D. (1964) 'Funktion und Wanddekor der Opferschreine von Wu Liang Tz'u: typologische und ikonographische Untersuchungen', *Monumenta Serica* 23: 88–162.
Csapo, E. and Miller, M. (1998) 'Democracy, empire and art: towards a politics of time and narrative', in *Democracy, Empire and the Arts in Fifth Century Athens*, eds. D. Boedeker and K. Raaflaub. Cambridge, MA: 87–125.
Day, J. W. (1989) 'Rituals in stone: early Greek grave epigrams and monuments', *Journal of Hellenic Studies* 109: 16–28.
Detienne, M. (2007) *The Greeks and Us: A Comparative Anthropology of Ancient Greece.* Cambridge.
Drake, F. S. (1943) 'Sculptured stones of the Han dynasty', *Monumenta Serica* 8: 280–318.
Duyvandak, J. J. L. (1939–40) 'An illustrated battle account of the Former Han Dynasty', *T'oung Pao* 34: 249–64; 35: 211–15.
Falkenhausen, L. von. (2005) 'The inscribed bronzes from Yangjiacun: new evidence on social structure and historical consciousness in Late Western Zhou China (ca. 800 BC)', *Proceedings of the British Academy* 139: 239–95.

Fearn, D. (2010) 'Aeginetan epinician culture: naming, ritual and politics', in *Aegina: Contexts for Lyric Poetry: Myth, History and Identity in the Fifth Century BC*, ed. David Fearn. Oxford: 175–226.

Finsterbusch, K. (1966–2004) *Verzeichnis und Motivindex der Han-Darstellungen*, 4 vols. Wiesbaden.

Forke, A. (1907) *Lun-Heng: Philosophical Essays of Wang Ch'ung*, 2 vols. London.

Frisby, D. (1992) *The Alienated Mind: The Sociology of Knowledge in Germany, 1918–1933*. London.

Gernet, L. (1981) 'The mythical idea of value in Greece', in *The Anthropology of Ancient Greece*. London: 73–111.

Goldstein, C. (1996) *Teaching Art: Academies and Schools from Vasari to Albers*. Cambridge.

Grethlein, J. (2008) 'Memory and material objects in the *Iliad* and the *Odyssey*', *Journal of Hellenic Studies* 128: 27–51.

Hansen, P. A. (1983) *Carmina epigraphica graeca saeculorum VII-V a. Chr. n., Texte und Kommentare XII*. Berlin and New York.

Harrison, E. (1972) 'The south frieze of the Nike Temple and the Marathon Painting in the Painted Stoa', *American Journal of Archaeology* 76: 353–78.

  (1996) 'Pheidias', in *Personal Styles in Greek Sculpture*, eds. O. Palagia and J. J. Pollitt. Cambridge: 16–65.

Hartog, F. (2000) 'The invention of history: the prehistory of a concept from Homer to Herodotus', *History and Theory* 39.3: 384–95.

  (2003) 'Ordres du temps et régimes de historicité', *Divinatio* 17: 71–90.

Henle, J. (1973) *Greek Myths: A Vase-Painter's Notebook*. London.

Hightower, J. R. (1952) *Han shi wai zhuan: Han Ying's Illustrations of the Didactic Application of the Classic of Songs*. Cambridge, MA.

Hirsch, E. and Stewart, C. (2005) 'Introduction: ethnographies of historicity', *History and Anthropology* 16.3: 261–74.

Hölscher, T. (1973) *Griechische Historienbilder des 5. und 4. Jahrhunderts v. Chr.* Würzburg.

  (1988) 'Tradition und Geschichte: Zwei Typen der Vergangenheit am Beispiel der griechischen Kunst', in *Das kulturelle Gedächtnis: Schrift, Erinnerung und politische Identität in frühen Hochkulturen*, eds. J. Assmann and T. Hölscher. Munich: 115–49.

Huang Chun-chieh (1995) 'Historical thinking in classical Confucianism: historical argumentation from the Three Dynasties', in *Time and Space in Chinese Culture*, eds. C. Huang and E. Zürcher. Leiden: 72–85.

James, J. M. (1985) 'Interpreting Han funerary art: the importance of context', *Oriental Art* 31.3: 283–92.

  (1988/9) 'The iconographic programme of the Wu family offering shrines', *Artibus Asiae* 49.1/2: 39–72.

  (1996) *A Guide to the Tomb and Shrine Art of the Han Dynasty 206 BC – AD 220*. Lampeter.

Karusos, C. (1961) *Aristodikos: zur Geschichte der spätarchaisch-attischen Plastik und der Grabstatue*. Stuttgart.

(1972, o.v. 1941) 'ΠΕΡΙΚΑΛΛΕΣ ΑΓΑΛΜΑ –ΕΧΕΠΟΙΗΣ' ΟΥΚ ΑΔΑΗΣ: Empfindungen und Gedanken der archaischen Griechen um die Kunst', in *Inschriften der Griechen*, ed. G. Pfohl. Darmstadt: 85–152.
Keightley, D. N. (1990) 'Early civilization in China: reflections on how it became Chinese', in *Heritage of China: Contemporary Perspectives on Chinese Civilization*, ed. P. Ropp. Berkeley: 15–54.
Kern, M. (2009) 'Bronze inscriptions, the *Shijing* and the *Shangshu*: the evolution of the ancestral sacrifice during the Western Zhou', in *Early Chinese Religion, Part One: Shang through Han (1250 BC – 220 AD)*, eds. J. Lagerwey and M. Kalinowski. Leiden: 143–200.
Knechtges, D. R. (trans.) (1987) *Xiao Tong: Wen Xuan or Selections of Refined Literature, vol. II: Rhapsodies on Sacrificing, Hunting, Travel, Sightseeing, Palaces and Halls, Rivers and Seas*. Princeton.
Langdon, S. (1987) 'Gift exchange in the Geometric sanctuaries', in *Gifts to the Gods*, eds. T. Linders and G. Nordquist. Uppsala: 107–13.
Legge, J. (trans.) (1885) *Li Ki*, in *Sacred Books of the East*, ed. F. M. Muller, vols. XXVII–XXVIII. Oxford.
Lewis, M. E. (2006) *The Construction of Space in Early China*. New York.
  (2007) *The Early Chinese Empires: Qin and Han*. Cambridge, MA.
Li Feng (2008) *Bureacracy and the State in Early China*. Cambridge.
Lippmann, M., Scahill, D. and Schultz, P. (2006) 'Knights 843–59, the Nike Temple Bastion, and Cleon's shields from Pylos', *American Journal of Archaeology* 110.4: 551–63.
Liu, C., Nylan, M. and Barbieri-Low, A. (2005) *Recarving China's Past: Art, Archaeology and Architecture of the 'Wu Family Shrines'*. New Haven.
Lloyd, G. E. R. (2002) *The Ambitions of Curiosity: Understanding the World in Ancient Greece and China*. Cambridge.
  (2011) 'Epilogue', in *The Oxford History of Historical Writing, vol. I: Beginnings to AD 600*, eds. A. Feldherr and G. Hardy. Oxford: 601–19.
Loewe, M. (ed.) (1993) *Early Chinese Texts: A Bibliographic Guide*. Berkeley.
Loraux, N. (1986) *The Invention of Athens: The Funerary Oration in the Classical City*. Cambridge, MA.
Marsili, F. (2005) 'Tripod vessel (*ding*)', in *Recarving China's Past: Art, Archaeology and Architecure of the 'Wu Family Shrines'*, eds. C. Liu, M. Nylan and A. Barbieri-Low. Princeton: 315–21.
Morris, I. (2000) *Archaeology as Cultural History: Words and Things in Iron Age Greece*. Cambridge.
Mullen, W. (1982) *Choreia: Pindar and Dance*. Princeton.
Murray, J. K. (2007) *Mirror of Morality: Chinese Narrative Illustration and Confucian Ideology*. Honolulu.
Mutschler, F.-H. (1997) 'Vergleichende Beobachtungen zur griechisch-roemischen und altchinesischen Geschichtsschreibung', *Saeculum* 48: 213–53.
Neer, R. (2011) *The Emergence of the Classical Style in Greek Sculpture*. Chicago.

Nightingale, A. (2001) 'On wandering and wondering: theoria in Greek philosophy and culture', *Arion* 9.2: 23–58.
  (2004) *Spectacles of Truth in Classical Greek Philosophy: Theoria in its Cultural Context*. Cambridge.
Osborne, R. (1996) *Greece in the Making, 1200–479 BC*. London.
Paludan, A. (1991) *The Chinese Spirit Road: The Classical Tradition of Stone Tomb Statuary*. New Haven.
Parker, R. (1996) *Athenian Religion: A History*. Oxford.
Pines, Y. (2008) 'A hero terrorist: adoration of Jing Ke revisited', *Asia Major* 21.1: 1–34.
Porter, J. I. (2011) *The Origins of Aesthetic Thought in Ancient Greece: Matter, Sensation and Experience*. Cambridge.
Powers, M. (1984) 'Pictorial art and its public in early imperial China', *Art History* 7.2: 135–63.
  (1991) *Art and Political Expression in Early China*. New Haven.
Prusek, J. (1970) 'History and epics in China and in the West: a study of differences in conception of the human story', in *Chinese History and Literature: Collection of Studies*. Dordrecht: 17–34.
Raaflaub, K. (1997) 'Homeric society', in *A New Companion to Homer*, eds. I. Morris and B. Powell. Leiden: 624–58.
Rawson, J. (1999) 'Chinese burial patterns: sources of information on thought and belief', in *Cognition and Material Culture: The Archaeology of Symbolic Storage*, eds. C. Renfrew and C. Scarre. Cambridge: 107–33.
Reinach, A. (1921) *Textes grecs et latins relatifs à l'histoire de la peinture ancienne*. Paris.
Rouveret, A. (1987/9) 'Les lieux de la mémoire publique: quelques remarques sur la fonction des tableaux dans la cité', *Opus* 6/7: 101–24.
Rudolph, R. C. and Wen Yu (1951) *Han Tomb Art of West China: A Collection of First- and Second-Century Reliefs*. Berkeley.
Ruitenbeek, K. (2002) *Chinese Shadows: Stone Reliefs, Rubbings and Related Works of Art from the Han Dynasty (206 BC – AD 220) in the Royal Ontario Museum*. Ontario.
Rusen, J. (1996) 'Some theoretical approaches to intercultural comparative historiography', *History and Theory* 35.4: 5–22.
Schaberg, D. (2011) 'Chinese history and philosophy', in *The Oxford History of Historical Writing, vol. I: Beginnings to AD 600*, eds. A. Feldherr and G. Hardy. Oxford: 394–414.
Shankman, S. and Durrant, S. (2000) *The Siren and the Sage: Knowledge and Wisdom in Ancient Greece and China*. London.
Shaughnessy, E. L. (1991) *Sources of Western Zhou History: Inscribed Bronze Vessels*. Berkeley.
  (1999) 'Bronzes from Hoard 1, at Zhuangbai, Fufeng, Shaanxi Province', in *The Golden Age of Chinese Archaeology*, ed. Yang Xiaoneng. New Haven: 236–47.
Schultz, P. (2009) 'The north frieze of the temple of Athena Nike', in *Art in Athens during the Peloponnesian War*, ed. O. Palagia. Cambridge: 128–67.

So, J. (1980a) 'New departures in Eastern Zhou bronze designs: the Spring and Autumn period', in *The Great Bronze Age of China*, ed. W. Fong. New York: 250–69.

(1980b) 'The inlaid bronzes of the Warring States period', in *The Great Bronze Age of China*, ed. W. Fong. New York: 304–20.

Soper, A. C. (1974) 'The purpose and date of the Hsiao-tang Shan offering shrine: a modest proposal', *Artibus Asiae* 36: 249–65.

Stansbury-O'Donnell, M. D. (2005) 'The painting programme in the Stoa Poikile', in *Periklean Athens and its Legacy*, eds. J. Barringer and J. Hurwit. New Haven: 73–87.

Steiner, D. T. (2001) *Images in Mind: Statues in Archaic and Classical Greek Literature*. Princeton.

Stewart, A. (1985) 'History, myth and allegory in the program of the temple of Athena Nike, Athens', in *Pictorial Narrative in Antiquity and the Middle Ages*, eds. H. L. Kessler and M. S. Simpson. Washington, DC: 53–73.

(1986) 'When is a kouros not an Apollo? The Tenea "Apollo" revisited', in *Corinthiaca: Studies in Honour of Darrell A. Amyx*, ed. M. del Chiaro. Columbia, MO: 54–70.

(1997) *Art, Desire and the Body in Ancient Greece*. Cambridge.

Tang Changshou (1997) 'Shiziwan Cliff Tomb, no. 1', *Orientations* 28.8: 72–7.

Tanner, J. (2006) *The Invention of Art History in Ancient Greece: Religion, Society and Artistic Rationalisation*. Cambridge.

Taylor, J. G. (1998) 'Oinoe and the Painted Stoa: ancient and modern misunderstandings', *American Journal of Philology* 119.2: 223–43.

Taylor, R. (2008) *The Moral Mirror of Roman Art*. Cambridge.

Thompson, L. (1998) '*The Yi'nan Tomb: narrative and ritual in pictorial art of the Eastern Han (25–220 CE)*', PhD dissertation, New York University.

(1999) 'Confucian paragon or popular deity? Legendary heroes in a late Eastern Han tomb', *Asia Major* 12.2: 1–38.

Wang, E. (1994) 'Mirror, death and rhetoric: reading later Han Chinese bronze artefacts', *Art Bulletin* 84.3: 511–34.

Watson, B. (1958) *Ssu-ma Ch'ien: Grand Historian of China*. New York.

Whitley, J. (1994) 'The monuments that stood before Marathon: tomb cult and hero cult in archaic Attica', *American Journal of Archaeology* 98.2: 213–30.

(2001) *The Archaeology of Greece*. Cambridge.

Wu Hung (1989) *The Wu Liang Shrine: The Ideology of Early Chinese Pictorial Art*. Stanford.

(1996) *Monumentality in Early Chinese Art and Architecture*. Stanford.

Yang Xiaoneng (ed.) (1999) *The Golden Age of Chinese Archaeology*. New Haven.

Zhou Yiqun (2010) *Festivals, Feasts and Gender Relations in Ancient China and Greece*. Cambridge.

9 | Helen and Chinese Femmes Fatales

YIQUN ZHOU

Helen, the Spartan queen whose abduction by Paris the prince of Troy ignited the Trojan War, may be regarded as the femme fatale par excellence. As such, Helen is the subject of numerous representations in the Greek tradition, from the Homeric epics to archaic lyric to classical drama, orations and historical writings, and the prominence of her images is as notable as their complexity and ambiguity. Alongside commonplace condemnations of Helen as the cause of a devastating war, there are enduring efforts to exonerate, to redeem, and even to exalt her act. The coexistence of variegated and oftentimes conflicting views of Helen and the literary ingenuity exerted to paint her in many different shades account for the mystery shrouding her and make her arguably the most intriguing figure in the Greek tradition.

Ancient China had its own lore of femmes fatales. The fall of each of the three earliest Chinese dynasties is blamed on a woman, the evil consort of the last monarch: Mo Xi, consort to King Jie of Xia; Da Ji, consort to King Zhou of Shang; and Bao Si, consort to King You of Western Zhou. The judgement passed on the three women in the sources is invariably negative. Their stories are invoked as cautionary lessons for rulers and noble houses, and the disastrous consequences of failures to heed such lessons, in turn, confirm the historical wisdom of such tales and yield further theories on the potential dangers of female beauty. Whereas the indeterminacy of Helen's images perpetuates over time and becomes ever more elusive with the proliferation of representations, the portrayals of the three classical Chinese femmes fatales conform to one broad pattern that is only clarified and reinforced with the multiplication of texts.

In this chapter I shall illustrate the contrast just laid out and also attempt to explain why the two ancient societies engaged their common suspicion, anxiety and fear about iconically beautiful and attractive women in strikingly different ways. The reader will notice that the Chinese material primarily comprises historical writings (or texts that purport to be historical), whereas the sources on Helen consist of a wider range of texts, including epic, lyric, drama, oratory and history. At the end of the chapter I shall argue that the two distinct patterns emerging from our comparison are not the skewed result of generic disparity but point to many real social and conceptual differences between ancient China and Greece, regarding such things as the views of female beauty and conduct, the functions of literature and history, and the degrees of cultural diversity.

Helen

The *Iliad*

The *Iliad*, which provides the earliest and most canonical portrayal of Helen, presents a highly ambivalent view of her. The epic evades the question of whether Helen came to Troy willingly or by force, thus appearing to vacillate on the pivotal issue of what her role was in causing the war, and it depicts Helen in a sympathetic light even as it shows her to be an object of general opprobrium in Troy.

Helen is portrayed as being constantly tortured by a guilty conscience. In one of her bitterest moments, she curses herself as 'bitch' and wishes that she had died before embarking on her fateful trip to Troy (*Il.* 6.344–53). The remorseful stance of Helen sets her apart from Paris, who not only is a coward on the battlefield but never even shows any burden of conscience in the fury of a war set off by him. At least, Helen understands moral responsibility and is alive to the terrible impact of her act on others. This difference explains why Hector, the bulwark of the Trojans and an exemplar of loyalty and honorability, treats Paris with scorn but is kind and protective towards Helen, and Hector's attitude cannot but influence how the reader views Helen, despite the otherwise intense animosity that she feels in Troy.[1]

While the bard draws sympathy for Helen by showing her sensitive, contrite and helpless side, he does not portray her as a passive figure who is only in a position to endure what others have to say about or to do to her. Instead, Helen is depicted as being highly conscious of how events and experiences are shaped into historical memory and also seeking to play a part in that transformation and transmission. In her very first appearance in the *Iliad* (3.125–8), Helen is shown at the loom, weaving a large web on which she embroiders the struggles that the Trojans and the Greeks are

---

[1] According to Helen, Hector has never uttered one word of insult or unkindness to her and also would stop others from doing so (*Il.* 24.768–72). She also says that King Priam is kind to her as though he were her own father (*Il.* 24.770). Blondell 2010a argues that Helen's self-blame is a strategy that serves to disarm and win sympathy from the men whose protection is essential to her survival in a hostile environment.

engaged in for her sake. As has been argued, Helen has undertaken this activity of weaving with a view to offering her own version of the story about the war.[2]

The alternative story that Helen would have wished to be heard, I suggest, is along the lines of the complex, ambivalent and sympathetic representation that she receives in the *Iliad*. The attitudes of Hector and King Priam are indices of the success that the alternative storytelling has achieved with the audience whom Helen would have attempted to influence. Helen's greatest sympathiser, however, is the bard himself. In what may seem a curious move, Homer makes Helen the singer of the last and climactic dirge at Hector's funeral (following his wife and mother) towards the end of the epic. In her song, Helen remembers how Hector showed her unfailing kindness and protected her from others' hostility, and laments that with his death she is left to face the curse of a whole nation (*Il.* 24.762–75). In reserving for Helen the final tribute to Hector the fierce patriot and warrior, Homer endeavours to stake out a place for the transcending spirit of compassion and generosity in the understanding of the colossal tragedy of the Trojan War.[3] The best evidence of the bard's striving is the image of Helen herself. A femme fatale who at once arouses hatred, sympathy and awe (the best example of this being the Trojan elders' stupefied reaction to her stunning beauty when she joins Priam on the city wall in Book 3), her complexity and ambiguity exemplify the very condition of the conflicting desires and emotions in which she and her Greek and Trojan contenders are engulfed.

Post-Homeric Helens

Helen was to have numerous defenders after Homer. One of them is Sappho (*fl.* 600),[4] who will recuperate Helen as a lover in fr. 16. After declaring in the first stanza that the most beautiful thing in the world is 'whatsoever a person loves', the speaker of the poem continues:

> It is perfectly easy to make this understood
> by everyone: for she who far surpassed
> mankind in beauty, Helen,

---

[2] On Helen's weaving and its association with poetic composition, see Austin 1994: 37–8 and Suzuki 1989: 40–1.

[3] Roisman 2006 argues that Helen's participation in the funeral lamentations not only elevates the dignity and authority of this complex and suffering woman but also finally joins her in the community of the war's female victims.

[4] All dates are BCE unless otherwise indicated.

> left her most noble husband
> and went sailing off to Troy
> with no thought at all for her child or dear parents,
> but (love) led her astray.

Sappho takes no issue with the received opinion that the adulterous Spartan queen brought huge losses and profound agony to numerous families in two lands, including her own. Rather, Sappho accepts all those consequences as being real and dire, and yet she not only refuses to condemn Helen but even holds her up as an exemplar for the passionate pursuit of love, which equals 'the most beautiful thing on the black earth' in the Sapphic scheme of things. Besides the war's terrible impact on others, Helen may have also made an unfortunate choice for herself in trading a 'most noble husband' for what turns out to be an unworthy lover, and yet the irrationality of Helen's choice bears the best testimony to the power of love. In allowing herself to be thus 'led astray' onto a journey that would change the fate of so many, Helen is the most radical and most persuasive votary of love. In that capacity, Helen's culpability for the Trojan War becomes an irrelevant issue, because, in Norman Austin's words, 'Eros is a force so powerful that it writes its own laws.'[5] In making Helen's active pursuit of love, not its consequences or outcome, the absolute focus, Sappho brackets moral judgement and allows Helen the symbol of beauty to shine and inspire as a paragon of love.[6]

In his *Encomium of Helen*, the sophist Gorgias (c. 485–c. 380) sets out to refute the unanimous yet crooked view of Helen (who has now become 'a byword for calamities') that has been perpetuated by 'those who are called poets'. Once again, Homer's authority is under attack, and Gorgias vows to clear Helen of her ill repute by relying on reason and speaking straight. The orator then proceeds to demonstrate that the gods rather than Helen, a woman, and the barbarian abductors rather than their abductee, are to be held responsible, and that in submitting to the potent power of persuasive speech and love, Helen is an unfortunate victim but does no wrong. In short, Helen should be pitied rather than reviled, and Gorgias declares that his speech has successfully put an end to the injustice and ignorance that have plagued Helen's reputation throughout the ages.

In line with Gorgias' confession at the end of his speech that he composed the piece as a game/diversion (*paignion*), the *Encomium of Helen* has much more often been analysed as a rhetorical feat than as a good-faith

---

[5] Austin 1994: 65.
[6] As Blondell 2010b: 383 and DuBois 1996: 87 point out, Sappho does not judge Helen.

apology for Helen. In this speech Gorgias may be simply engaged in the rhetorical exercise of 'arguing both sides of the case' regardless of one's true position. I suggest, however, that such practice, while being morally dubious, is conducive to the engagement with perspectives and values that differ from what is accepted as authority or common sense, a benefit that is particularly important in the case of a notorious woman like Helen.[7] Even if the orator does not believe in any of the things that he has said in Helen's defence, the fact that such apology can be openly and legitimately made shows that considerable space existed in classical Greece for questioning the conventional label on her, and rhetoric may well have played a special role in creating such space.

In 412, three years after the staging of *The Trojan Women*, in which Helen appears as a stock villain whose only concern is to save her own skin after the fall of Troy and who spins dazzling sophistic arguments on the stage for that purpose,[8] Euripides offered a fantastic revision of the story of Helen in another play. In *Helen*, we learn that the real Helen never ran away with Paris; Hera, enraged by the slight that she had suffered in the Judgement of Paris, deprived him of his prize by transporting Helen to Egypt and depositing a phantom of hers in Troy. The Greeks and the Trojans turn out to have fought a long war without knowing that Helen was leading a chaste life in Egypt and yearning for reunion with Menelaus all this time. When Menelaus' ship is wrecked in a storm and washed ashore in Egypt during his homecoming journey after the war, the couple meet by accident, clear up the misunderstanding, and successfully engineer a plan to return to Sparta together.

The Helen of Euripides' eponymous play is a complete reversal of the femme fatale figure that he portrays in *The Trojan Women* and a brand-new remake on the model of Penelope. The two plays demonstrate Euripides' awareness of the intrinsic complexity of Helen and represent his conscious attempt to use her to explore such issues as the limits of moral judgement and the relationship between perception and reality.[9] The sorrow of the heroine in *Helen* is that she has been universally reviled for a wrong she has not done, and she understands the cause of her misfortune thus: it is 'partly because of Hera, but in part my beauty is to blame. If only I could have been erased, like a picture, and then have taken a meaner form

---

[7] On classical suspicions about the immorality of rhetoric, most famously articulated by Plato, see Garver 1995: ch. 7 and de Romilly 1975.

[8] Worman 1997: 189 compares Helen's speech with Gorgias' piece.

[9] For readings that relate this play to contemporary philosophical debates, see Burnett 1960 and Segal 1971.

in place of this beautiful one' (*Helen* 261-3). Helen is destined to take on numerous different images, because physical beauty, the basis of Helen's iconic status, is mere appearance and the only certain knowledge about her. Anyone aiming to portray Helen is engaged in an effort to uncover the 'essence' beneath that beautiful appearance, and what is 'uncovered' will only be ever multiplying perceptions. The eternal alienation between her image and her real self is the price that Helen pays for her beauty. Euripides creates his Penelopean Helen to convey this lesson in a radical way, not to declare that he has finally discovered the 'truth' about Helen and would like to come clean with it by renouncing his previous misunderstanding.

Euripides did not invent the idea that Helen had not gone to Troy. Before him, there were at least Stesichorus (*fl.* 600) the lyric poet and Herodotus the historian (c. 484–425). Only a fragment remains of Stesichorus' poem:

> The story is not true.
> You [Helen] did not board the well-benched ships,
> You did not reach the towers of Troy.

Stesichorus is said to have composed this poem to retract the blasphemy he had committed in an earlier ode. The 'blasphemy' apparently consisted in Stesichorus' calling Helen and Clytemnestra bigamists, trigamists and deserters of husbands, in line with the two sisters' reputation in the Homeric tradition, and as a punishment for his slanderous speech Stesichorus was allegedly struck blind. As soon as he had composed the palinode, however, his sight was restored (Plato, *Phaedrus* 243a; Isocrates, *Helen* 64).

A common explanation for Stesichorus' act of recantation is that the poet, who was a native of Sicily, where Helen was the object of a cult due to Spartan influences, was bowing to the local tradition in rejecting the more influential Homeric version.[10] Another interpretation understands the recantation in terms of the spirit of rationalism that had arisen in archaic Greece, which questioned traditional ways of making sense of history, morality and the natural world (the authority of epic poetry being a primary target).[11] Either way, it is notable that Stesichorus' poem makes a straightforward and unprecedented repudiation ('The story is not true') of the most canonical tradition about Helen's role in the Trojan War (Sappho accepts the Homeric account but gives positive value to Helen's action).

---

[10] On the cult of Helen in Sparta, see Pomeroy 2002: 114–18.   [11] Austin 1994: 111–13.

The impact of local traditions and rationalistic inquiry in the development of Helen's images can be more clearly seen in Herodotus. A central concern of the *Histories* being to investigate the origins and events of the Persian Wars (492–49), Herodotus begins his work by tracing the conflict between the Greeks and the barbarians all the way back to the Trojan War and beyond (*Histories* 1.1.1–4.1). Allegedly based on his travels and interviews in Egypt, Herodotus' account about Helen and Paris is as follows: when Paris sails home after having abducted Helen, a wind blows his journey off course to the shores of Egypt. There, Paris' servants run away to inform on their master, who has just perpetrated a great injustice against his Greek host, and the Egyptian king Proteus, angered, sends Paris packing and promises Helen protection until she is reclaimed by her lawful husband. Without knowing about the Egyptian episode, the Greeks besiege Troy to demand the return of Helen and would not believe the Trojans' answer that she is being kept in Egypt. Thus is the war carried on until the Greeks capture Troy and discover no trace of Helen therein. It is only then that Menelaus sails to Egypt and there he finds his wife in safe custody (*Histories* 2.112–120.5).

In providing the above account, Herodotus explicitly dismisses Homer's version as being more suited to poetry and myth and asserts his intention to 'show my own opinion' on the basis of empirical investigation. He claims to have gathered his information from a conversation with some Egyptian priests and also from his visit to a sanctuary dedicated to an 'Aphrodite the Foreigner (or the Guest)', whom he infers to be none other than Helen. To Herodotus, the Homeric account befits the mythical and poetical (read 'untrue') because it defies common sense: how could one believe that the Trojans would choose to fight a ten-year war and eventually suffer the destruction of their city for an unfaithful Greek wife? The Egyptian version, by contrast, offers a reasonable explanation for an apparently senseless war: it is the horrible consequence of a grave and perhaps inevitable misunderstanding (the Greeks refuse to believe the Trojans' reply that Helen is in safekeeping in a faraway land, taking it as deliberate mockery). The Egyptians, whom Herodotus esteems as superb historians (*Histories* 2.77.1), get the story right, and the existence of a cult of Aphrodite/Helen the Foreigner/Guest in Egypt bears testimony to the hospitality that was generously extended to the drifting Spartan queen.

It is unclear whether the reported conversation between Herodotus and the Egyptian priests actually took place. The liberty that Herodotus apparently took in identifying the Egyptian cultic object as Helen when it might well have been Astarte, the originally Phoenician goddess of fertility and sexuality accepted as a 'foreign' Aphrodite in Egypt, casts doubt on the credibility of the historian's claim about his interview with the priests.[12] It is possible that Herodotus invented the conversations and knowingly misidentified the Egyptian goddess for the purpose of repudiating Homer's account. Be that as it may, of the greatest interest for us is Herodotus' conscious desire to distinguish his own trade from Homer's and to prove the superiority of historical inquiry, in both methodology and the value of the knowledge thereby acquired, to poetry and myth. It would of course be ironical if Herodotus had indeed resorted to fabrication and misinformation in order to best Homer,[13] but pending judgement on this issue, let us conclude with two observations about Herodotus' treatment of Helen.

First, Herodotus' approach shows where different sources of authority could be found to challenge that which had enjoyed long-standing authority in Greek culture. To counter the most authoritative version of Helen's story in the Greek world, one could turn to the Egyptians, a people who were known for their wisdom and knowledge derived from their long history and their respect for tradition. To discredit the hearsay filtered through the epic poems down the centuries, one could cite evidence from what one claims to have seen with one's own eyes and heard with one's own ears.

Second, aiming to find out what happened and what could have reasonably happened before, during and after the Trojan War, Herodotus is not much interested in judging the morals of Helen. He treats her abduction and the historical role of that incident in the same vein as the other instances of kidnappings of women that had taken place between Asia and Europe and perpetuated the tensions between the two. He may not have a high opinion of Helen (hence his disbelief at the duration and cost of the war allegedly fought for her sake), but in that regard she is treated the same as all the other famous women who have been trafficked between Asia and Europe (Io, Europa and Medea) and have played a role in shaping the relationship between the two civilisations. Focusing on the actions of the men (Greek, Trojan and Egyptian) in the events surrounding the Trojan War, Herodotus provides no information that can lead to a judgement on Helen's own conduct and mentality in the course of those events.[14]

---

[12] On the identification of Astarte, see How and Wells' 1957 commentary *ad loc.*

[13] Calame 2009: 174, stating that 'For Herodotus, what counts above all is to draw the correct lesson from the most likely version', regards the Father of History as 'a craftsman of story-telling and a direct successor to the Homeric bards, if not the melic poets'.

[14] Austin 1994: 125 argues that Herodotus' motive in reporting the Egyptian version is 'suspiciously Greek', that is, to rehabilitate Helen's reputation by denying that she went to Troy.

Chinese Femmes Fatales

The Genealogy of the Classic Trio

To my knowledge, the *Discourses of the States* (*Guoyu*), dated to the fourth century, is the first text that clearly lays out a genealogy of the three femmes fatales who brought down China's first three dynasties. The context is a conversation that reportedly took place between Scribe Su and several ministers in the state of Jin after Duke Xian of Jin (676–651) had conquered a barbarian state and made Li Ji, the daughter of the barbarian leader, his favourite consort. Scribe Su tells his colleagues that he has an ominous feeling about their ruler's action: 'Female warfare (*nürong*) is bound to follow upon male warfare (*nanrong*). If Jin has defeated the barbarians through male warfare, the barbarians will certainly defeat Jin through female warfare.' Scribe Su goes on to say the following about 'female warfare':

> In the past, when King Jie of Xia attacked the state of You Shi, You Shi married Mo Xi to Jie; after she had won the king's favor, Mo Xi collaborated with Yi Yin to destroy Xia. When King Zhou of Shang attacked the state of You Su, You Su married Da Ji to Zhou; after she had won the king's favor, Da Ji collaborated with Jiao Ge to destroy Shang. When King You of Zhou attacked You Bao, Bao married Bao Si to the king; after she had won the king's favor and given birth to Bofu, Bao Si, in collaboration with Guo Shifu, expelled the Crown Prince Yijiu and installed Bofu in his position. The Crown Prince took refuge in the state of Shen, and the people of Shen and Zeng called upon Western Rong to attack Zhou, thus causing the destruction of Zhou. Now the ruler of Jin, while deficient in virtue, is at ease with a captive woman and showers favor upon her. Isn't it appropriate to compare him to the last rulers of the three dynasties? (*Guoyu*, Jin 1, 90–1)

In tracing a genealogy of femmes fatales, Scribe Su aims at establishing full historical repeatability. He adopts the same sentence pattern in depicting the three women's involvement in the destruction of Xia, Shang and Western Zhou, only going into slightly more detail in the last segment of the narrative, presumably because it happened in a period very close to the present and therefore was deemed to be of greater cautionary significance. The identical sentence pattern is meant to highlight the identical nature of the historical roles played by the three women, from how they got to be in a position to do what they were to do, to what they did, to the consequences of what they had done. In Scribe Su's streamlined narrative, the lives of Mo

---

However, keeping Helen in Egypt would hardly accomplish that purpose; she should not have left Sparta to begin with.

Xi, Da Ji and Bao Si all serve to illustrate the same lesson for rulers – to let a woman from a conquered state into your bed is to ensure the demise of your rule – and none of the three has any distinguishing feature of her own. The uniformity of the three women's life stories is precisely Scribe Su's point: Duke Xian of Jin's infatuation with Li Ji will bring down the same disaster upon his state.

In his speech on the three classic femmes fatales Scribe Su performs the typical role of the court scribe frequently encountered in pre-imperial Chinese texts: a figure of wisdom who is able to draw on the past to interpret the present and predict the future. However, the value of the historical wisdom distilled by Scribe Su is not dependent upon factual veracity; rather, he seems to have manipulated or even fabricated the facts about the three women in order to come up with a uniform pattern that serves his didactic purpose. No other source corroborates Scribe Su's claim that Mo Xi and Da Ji entered King Jie's and King Zhou's harems as gifts from conquered states, and another record in *Discourses of the States* about Bao Si's origins (discussed below) directly contradicts Scribe Su's account of how she became King You's consort. The strikingly neat parallels in the trajectories of the three women's lives seem to have been manufactured to fit the present circumstances of Scribe Su's discourse. What can more effectively demonstrate the perils faced by Duke Xian than the 'fact' that every last ruler of the three dynasties lost his kingdom by throwing himself at the feet of an attractive but treacherous war trophy?

In summary, Scribe Su's genealogy of femmes fatales has three main features. First, the three women are treated as one homogeneous unit, exemplifying a single, replicable pattern of behaviour. Second, the destructiveness of the three women is highlighted by the military context that frames their stories and the memorable dictum 'female warfare is bound to follow upon male warfare' (a war fought between two armies propels a femme fatale onto the historical stage, and she leaves the world in the ruins of another war). Finally and most importantly, the conception of the genealogy is guided by an over-riding didactic purpose, and it is less important to ask whether all three dynasties actually fell because of an evil woman and whether each woman had exactly the same career than to understand the moral point of the stories. That is, it is dangerous for rulers to allow themselves to be controlled by their consorts, especially women whose main recommendation is their beauty (as tends to be true of war trophies), and if historical precedents would help prove this point, then it falls upon a scribe, or anyone who has access to knowledge of the past, to identify, clarify and even manipulate such precedents.

If Scribe Su may be accused of manipulating historical precedents in constructing his genealogy of femmes fatales, he is vindicated by his correct prediction about Li Ji. Li Ji's subsequent attempts to estrange Duke Xian from his sons borne by other consorts resulted in the suicide of the Crown Prince, the exile of two other princes, and the designation of the son that she bore for the duke as the heir. In the record following the one under discussion, Scribe Su delivers another speech regarding Li Ji, which ends with the reiteration of his point that 'chaos necessarily originates in female warfare; that was what happened in the Three Dynasties' (*Guoyu*, Jin 1, 93). This speech is then followed by the narrator's statement, 'Li Ji indeed turned out to stir up troubles, causing the death of the Crown Prince and exiling two other princes. The Gentleman observes, "[Scribe Su] understood the origins of disaster"' (*Guoyu*, Jin 1, 93). In this historical vision, it is irrelevant to examine the reliability of Scribe Su's knowledge about the three femmes fatales independently of how he uses that knowledge to diagnose a current situation and foretell how it will evolve, and it is the successful 'application' that certifies him as someone who truly understands historical precedents. In other words, the factual truth about the three women is no longer important; they function as a unitary sign with predetermined meaning, ready to be invoked whenever the threat of a femme fatale arises in new circumstances, and the deeds of the new femme fatale serve to confirm what is known about the classic trio, without raising questions about what they were really like.

Mo Xi and Da Ji

Both women are shadowy figures in pre-imperial sources. Mo Xi appears in texts such as *Master Lü's Spring and Autumn Annals* (*Lüshi chunqiu*) and the *Bamboo Annals* (*Zhushu jinian*), but none provides clear evidence about her misdeeds. Nor does Sima Qian's (c. 145–c. 87) *Records of the Archivist* (*Shiji*) provide any further information. At the beginning of his chapter on the maternal and affinal relatives of the Han emperors, Sima Qian invokes both good and bad examples from the Three Dynasties to illustrate the important influence of wives and mothers on rulers, and Mo Xi is included among the femmes fatales, along with Da Ji and Bao Si. 'Jie was expelled because of Mo Xi'; thus observes Sima Qian (*Shiji* 49.1967), but nowhere in his work does he furnish any evidence to back up that claim.[15]

---

[15] According to Sima Qian, King Jie lost his kingdom because he neglected the cultivation of virtue and indulged in military operations, but without mentioning whether Mo Xi had anything to do with Jie's misconduct (*Shiji* 2.49–50).

The first fantastic details about Mo Xi's misconduct will be found in her biography in Liu Xiang's (79–78) *Biographies of Women* (*Lienü zhuan*, here abbreviated to *LNZ*). Described as a woman who is 'beautiful in looks but lacking in virtue', Mo Xi not only fully participates in Jie's licentious activities but instigates him to take them to higher levels of absurdity. They drink and watch lewd performances day and night. He places her in his lap and obeys whatever she says, and the two indulge in the most arrogant and abandoned behaviours together. One thing he has done is to dig a wine pool that is big enough to sail boats, gather three thousand people for a binge, and force some of them to drink by submerging their heads into the pool, while she derives great pleasure from laughing at those who get drowned. Outrageous acts such as these eventually lead to Jie's downfall, and Mo Xi as his accomplice is exiled together with him (*LNZ* 7.1b–2a).

The images of Da Ji underwent a similar evolution in the early sources. According to the 'Oath of Mu' chapter in the *Book of Documents* (*Shangshu*), which records the charges that King Wu of Zhou laid against King Zhou of Shang before their armies met for the battle that would end the latter's rule, the last Shang king was guilty of 'letting a woman dictate his affairs' (*Shangshu* 11.183), but it does not actually identify Da Ji as that woman.[16]

Sima Qian is the first author to explicitly give Da Ji the role of accomplice and abettor in King Zhou's misconduct (*Shiji* 3.105). Sima Qian's account begins thus: '[King Zhou] indulged in wine and licentious pleasures, and had female favorites. He loved Da Ji and obeyed everything she said. Therefore …' What follows is an enumeration of the projects that the king undertook, presumably at the behest of Da Ji (as suggested by the preceding 'therefore') to gratify their sensual enjoyments together. These include: enacting soft new songs and dance; raising taxes to fund their pleasure facilities; filling the palaces with collections of exotic dogs and horses; and expanding the parks and placing in them beasts and birds. Completing the list is the report that they hosted grand gatherings where the guests engaged in all-night drinking orgies and watched naked men and women chasing each other by a pool filled with wine and in a forest of hanging meat.

Liu Xiang's biography of Da Ji elaborates on Sima Qian's version and significantly enhances her culpability (*LNZ* 7.2a–3a). Where Sima Qian's

[16] Texts such as the *Analects*, *Han Feizi* and *Master Lü's Spring and Autumn Annals* condemn King Zhou for numerous flagrant behaviours (Gu Jiegang 1982), but none of them suggests that a woman named Da Ji had a part in those behaviours.

account only lists the extravagant pleasurable activities in which Da Ji participated along with King Zhou, Liu Xiang summarises the list with the statement that 'Da Ji liked it.' Where Sima Qian leaves Da Ji out in relating the terrible punishments that King Zhou used against his enemies and critics, Liu Xiang portrays her as an interested observer and pernicious instigator. Watching those subjected to brutal tortures, 'Da Ji laughed'; when a nobleman's remonstration angered King Zhou, it was Da Ji's claim about sages' hearts having seven apertures that prompted the king's order to open up the remonstrator's chest. Where Sima Qian simply reports the punishments that King Wu meted out to King Zhou and Da Ji after the military conquest, leaving it to the reader to infer the victor's view of her culpability, Liu Xiang spells out the significance of the act and also supplies a detail that is not in Sima Qian's version: 'King Wu . . . had Da Ji's head cut off and hung from a small white flagstaff, because he regarded her as the woman who caused the fall of King Zhou.'[17]

Bao Si

A verse in the *Book of Poetry* (*Shijing*) flatly blames Bao Si for the fall of the Western Zhou: 'Splendid was the ancestral capital of the Zhou, but Bao Si brought it down' ('Zheng yue', *Shijing* 12.1.443). A passage in *Discourses of the States*, which reports a conversation between Duke Huan of Zheng (r. 806–771) and Scribe Bo in the court of King You of Zhou (r. 782–771), purports to explain Bao Si's role in the fall of the Western Zhou (*Guoyu*, Zheng, 187). While Scribe Bo does name other elements that exerted bad influences on King You (sycophants and evil ministers), he assigns major blame to Bao Si, who had a legendary origin that predestined her to be a bane for the Zhou dynasty. According to the legend cited by Scribe Bo, Bao Si was the reincarnation of the patron deities of an ancient people called Bao. At the end of the Xia dynasty, these deities transformed themselves into two dragons and vanished, but their saliva was collected in a box and preserved intact by the kings down through the ages until the end of the reign of King Li of Zhou (r. 857–842), when he opened the box to look at the contents. Once opened, the overflowing saliva turned into a black reptile, which had an encounter with a girl-servant in the royal court and impregnated her. After years of pregnancy, during the reign of King Xuan of Zhou (r. 827–782), the servant gave birth to a baby girl but abandoned it because she was still an unmarried woman. The baby was found by a couple

---

[17] All the points in this paragraph except the last have been made in Liu Yongcong 1998: 95.

who sold bows of wild mulberry and quivers of beanstalk and were fleeing for their lives because there was at that time a children's song that predicted the fall of the Zhou caused by the bow of wild mulberry and quiver of beanstalk and King Xuan had ordered the arrest and execution of anyone selling these items. The couple fled to Bao with the foundling, who grew up to be a beauty and became a favourite consort of King You when a man of Bao presented her to the king as a gift.

This beauty, of course, was Bao Si, and Scribe Bo marvels at how Heaven's command could not be averted and how strong a poison must be that took ages in the making. Scribe Bo goes on to predict that Bao Si would cause destruction to the Zhou shortly. King You's infatuation with Bao Si has led him to incline towards naming her son as his heir instead of the current Crown Prince borne by the queen, but making this move is to court trouble, because the queen's natal state and its allies can be expected to side with the Crown Prince and a war will break out if the king tries to enforce his will. As it turned out, a war induced by the succession crisis, as foreseen by the scribe, was to result in King You's death and the end of the Western Zhou.

In Scribe Bo's account, Bao Si inspires dread and revulsion almost entirely in light of the uncanny prehistory provided for her birth, and not in the person of the beautiful consort who is said to have ruined King You. Nothing is said about how Bao Si managed to lead the king to ill-fated decisions, and the reader is left to imagine her manners and deeds both before and during the succession crisis that directly brought down the dynasty. It sounds as if Scribe Bo lacked information about the historical Bao Si's alleged misconduct and had to invoke a bizarre legend to convince his audience of the woman's extremely poisonous nature. Scribe Bo may have achieved his intended effect, although it is hard to avoid the impression that his account fails to show how Bao Si's actions bear out the inordinate evilness foretold by her legendary birth.

Sima Qian and Liu Xiang attempted to fill in what Bao Si did to cause the fall of the Western Zhou. Both essentially copied Scribe Su's account of Bao Si's birth but elaborated on her conduct as King You's consort. Sima Qian's narrative focuses on one peculiar habit of Bao Si's that allegedly directly caused the ultimate disaster:

Bao Si did not like to smile. King You tried ten thousand ways to make her smile, but she still would not smile. King You had beacons and giant drums built, and would light the beacons when an enemy arrived. The vassal lords all came in response to a lit beacon fire but no enemy was present when they arrived. Bao Si burst into laughter at this. King You was pleased with it, and repeatedly lit the beacons for her. Thereafter, he lost the trust of the vassal lords, and by and by they stopped responding to the beacon fires ... (King You's trust of the evil minister Guo Shifu created widespread discontent among his people, and his demotion of the Queen and the Crown Prince invited the military attack by the queen's natal state and its allies.) King You lit the beacons to summon the troops, but no troops came. Consequently, the attackers killed King You at the foot of Mount Li, captured Bao Si, and looted the entire treasures of the Zhou before leaving. (*Shiji* 4.148–9)

In this account, Bao Si is guilty of making light of a very grave matter and allowing the king to act recklessly just to see her smile, but arguably this is a passive fault on her part: she is not said to have wished him to do what he did (even though it can be inferred that she was delighted with his efforts to please her), nor do we hear about her having any other vices. Although it is tempting to follow the narrative's lead to hold Bao Si directly responsible for the demise of King You and the Western Zhou (witness the expression 'consequently ...'), one is given pause by the lack of more substantial charges against Bao Si and also by the report that King You's use of a vicious minister caused general disaffection among his people. In short, Sima Qian's account is open to the suspicion that Bao Si and her alleged perversity merely serve as a convenient pretext for the real political problems that brought down the Western Zhou.[18]

Liu Xiang would vigorously address the 'deficiency' of Sima Qian's account in his biography of Bao Si, significantly multiplying the number of her vices and extending her bad influences to the political realm (*LNZ* 7.3a–3b). We are told that King You neglected state affairs and went riding and hunting at irregular times, all 'in order to gratify Bao Si's wishes'. The two also indulge in drinking and entertainment by actors day and night. The account of the beacon-fire hoax is almost taken verbatim from Sima Qian, but with a notable alteration. While Sima Qian states that 'King You was pleased with it (*Youwang yuezhi* 幽王說之), and repeatedly lit the beacon fires for her', Liu Xiang writes 'King You wanted to please her (*Youwang yu yuezhi* 幽王欲悅之), and repeatedly lit the beacon fires for her.' The two versions may not be that different, but Sima Qian's gives the king greater subjectivity (he takes pleasure in seeing Bao Si smile and the purpose of his subsequent actions is to repeat such pleasure), whereas Liu Xiang's highlights the power that Bao Si exerts over the king (her pleasure

---

[18] Li 2006: 194–203 examines the development of the stories about Bao Si in terms of how they demonise and make a scapegoat of her in order to explain the fall of the idealised Western Zhou dynasty. He does not discuss Liu Xiang's version, to which we turn now.

dictates his actions) and thus heightens her responsibility for his flagrant abuse of the vassal lords' allegiance. The same goal to hold Bao Si accountable also led Liu Xiang to diverge dramatically from Sima Qian in the following narrative:

[King You] killed those who were loyal and remonstrated with him, and only listened to Bao Si. Superiors and subordinates [in the government] flattered each other, and the people turned against them. Therefore, the Duke of Shen [the deposed Queen's home state] allied with Zeng, the Western Yi, and Quan Rong and launched an attack on King You. King You summoned troops by lighting the beacons, but no troops came. Consequently, the attackers killed King You at the foot of Mount Li, captured Bao Si, and looted the entire treasures of the Zhou before leaving. (*LNZ* 7.3b)

This passage radically rearranges the logic of the factors that Sima Qian invoked to explain the fall of the Western Zhou. In Sima Qian, King You's complete dependence on a minister who was unrighteous, obsequious and greedy had alienated his people, his demotion of the Queen and the Crown Prince then invited a military attack by an allied army (no word on whatever active role Bao Si might have played in the displacement of the Queen and the Crown Prince), and it is at this juncture that the beacon-fire hoax proved the undoing of King You. Presented in this way, Bao Si still has to shoulder considerable responsibility for the final disaster, but she can hardly be regarded as the fundamental cause of King You's downfall. Liu Xiang's version, by contrast, portrays Bao Si as the culprit of everything. King You brutally repressed criticism and rejected good advice because he only heeded Bao Si's words, and the breakdown of the relationships both within the government and between the government and the people followed as a result of the misconduct at the highest level. Most strikingly, Liu Xiang disregards the consensus in all previous accounts of the cause of the allied military attack on King You, namely, that it happened because of one of the allies' vested interest in maintaining the status of the Queen and the Crown Prince. Instead, Liu Xiang presents the attack as being prompted by the rampant breakdown of the Zhou political order, which is, of course, ultimately blamable on Bao Si. If the previous accounts, Sima Qian's included, mainly invoke the mysterious and the strange in portraying Bao Si as a femme fatale and are short on the specifics of her culpability, the narrative rewoven by Liu Xiang locates her firmly in the moral sphere and endows her with deeds and wishes that would demolish any doubt about her evil nature.

Discussion

The most striking contrast that emerges from the preceding pages is between the diversity and complexity of Helen's images in the Greek sources and the uniformity and one-sidedness of the images of the three Chinese femmes fatales. Before assessing whether this difference is due to the fact that the Greek texts are predominantly either literary or rhetorical whereas the Chinese texts are mainly historical or purport to be,[19] I propose four reasons to explain the complexity of Helen's images.

First, it has to do with the prominent celebration of beauty in the Greek tradition. As one critic puts it, 'Greek society was grounded in the praise of what is beautiful (*kala*) and the blame of what is ugly (*aischra*). How can one, then, reproach the most beautiful of all? ... The very qualities and deeds for which [Helen] is to blame are inseparable from her infinitely desirable beauty.'[20] Sappho esteems Helen's action and invokes her as a paragon, because the emblem of beauty must be the authority in judging what is beautiful and worth pursuing in life. In a speech that we have not discussed, Isocrates (436–338) explicitly claims that Helen not only is beyond criticism but deserves the highest praises inasmuch as she is the most beautiful (Isocrates, *Helen*). Apart from these two extreme cases, in the other authors, the mix of admiration and anxiety at Helen's unsurpassable beauty and its impact to a great extent accounts for the nuances and tensions in her images. Helen, who flaunts a split between the good and the beautiful, illustrates how some of the most distinguished Greek authors could allow their adoration of beauty to erode their commitment to virtue.

Second, to Greek authors, their mission was to educate, but also to entertain and to investigate. The didactic urge was constantly undercut by the desire to amuse, to surprise, and to inquire into the nature, causes and consequences of historical events. The endeavour to outdo each other in the task to 'delight, provoke, inquire' facilitated the exploration of complex human character and the discovery of new historical knowledge. The post-Homeric texts of various genres all aim to contest in some way the authority of the first portrait of Helen, even ironically as they generally prove true to its spirit in perpetuating the complexity of her character and expanding the context against which to understand the significance of the events in which she is a main actor.

---

[19] Raphals 1998: 24–5 discusses the use of historical sources in Liu Xiang's work and its status as 'putative biographies'.
[20] Blondell 2010b: 386.

Another factor that may have contributed to the complexity of Helen's images is the Greek penchant for adversarial processes, which was taken to a new height in the political and legal realms in the classical age and deeply influenced the rhetorical and literary practices of the time. Helen may be a villain according to conventional moral standards, but she will be granted a chance to defend herself on the public stage, and teachers and students of rhetoric also vie to demonstrate their brilliance by presenting bold and innovative ways to exculpate and eulogise her. Moral standards may have suffered because of these practices, but Helen has emerged as a beneficiary.

Regional diversity may also have been a factor. Stesichorus' palinode was likely a nod to the cult of Helen as a goddess in areas under Spartan influences, and the alleged Egyptian lore provided Herodotus with arsenal to attack Homer's authority. The tradition that had a pan-Hellenic status transcended and enjoyed greater influences than the local traditions but without completely suppressing them. The constant exchange with other cultures in the Mediterranean and the special place of Egypt in the Greek imagination fostered the awareness that different versions of reality existed elsewhere and that they might have a point.

In short, the above four factors served to slacken the hold of conventional morality and generate diversity and complexity in Greek perceptions of Helen. Now we come to the uniform and unidimensional character of the images of Chinese femmes fatales.

Whereas the portrayals of Helen show that many Greeks could idolise beauty to the extent of being willing to compromise their pursuit of the good, no matter how uncomfortable they might feel in doing so, our Chinese authors seem to have been guided by the conception that female beauty is inherently dangerous and subversive. This mentality of dread and high alert is epitomised by a remark that Shuxiang's mother, a sixth-century aristocratic matron, made in her comments on the notorious femmes fatales in history (including the classic trio): 'Extreme beauty must have in it extreme evil' (*Zuozhuan*, Zhao 28, 4:1492; *LNZ* 3.7a). Such conviction, of course, forestalls sympathetic views of the women accused of being femmes fatales. Whereas the many facets of Helen exemplify the working of a large spectrum of human emotions that are set off by her presence as the embodiment of Beauty, the beauty of the Chinese femme fatale is portrayed entirely in a sinister light, with the intention to arouse repugnance and fear, feelings that will only be confirmed by everything she is shown saying and doing.

Moreover, there was no practical motivation to seek alternative views of the three femmes fatales. In undertaking defence and praise of Helen, the

Greek authors were expressing their local allegiances or finding an opportunity to impress their audiences with their pure oratorical genius. Scholars have posited that there must have existed long, complex narratives of the heroic past of various regions in ancient China and that such narratives were completely suppressed in early imperial times for fear of fostering parochial sympathies and heterodox beliefs.[21] No matter how attractive this hypothesis is, the fact that we have no sample left of the allegedly suppressed narratives makes it pointless to speculate what diverse and unorthodox accounts might have existed about ancient personalities, our three classic 'evil women' included. Moreover, the philosophical masters of various persuasions displayed their rhetorical skills in disputing with each other and in attempting to sell their ideas to rulers and patrons, but 'arguing both sides of the case' style of argument does not seem to have been a regular part of their rhetorical exercises, and the danger of female beauty was a common thesis in the repertoire of the would-be political counsellors in the few centuries before the Qin unification.[22]

Most of the extant descriptions of the three femmes fatales are from texts that share a broadly conventional morality. For these authors, 'the fundamental realities of the universe were moral realities, and so wise men turned to history not to relive the heroic achievements of their ancestors (or to learn about the causes of wars and revolutions), but to discover the moral pattern woven into its very fabric'.[23] From Scribe Su to Shuxiang's mother to Sima Qian to Liu Xiang, their understandings of the three femmes fatales' historical roles were guided by the mission to identify and interpret useful moral patterns, and the early development of the stories of the three women is a process in which these patterns become increasingly clear and more forcefully articulated. The moralistic side of Herodotus may account for the presence of some thematic patterns and symbolic events in his work that are reminiscent of the historiographic techniques familiar in early Chinese texts, but his self-professed task was first and foremost to inquire, not to educate. The early Chinese authors' approach to history writing adopts a different priority: they do investigate, but more importantly, they aim to instruct.[24]

---

[21] Johnson 1981: 270–1.
[22] Han Feizi's (c. 280–233) 'Bei nei' chapter is an example of the cautionary discourses about female beauty. Lloyd 1996 compares the different institutional contexts, goals and styles of Greek and Chinese persuasive speech.
[23] Johnson 1981: 270.
[24] On the deployment of patterns and symbols in Herodotus, see Lateiner 1989: ch. 9. On the principles of early Chinese historiography, see Li 2008; Pines 2002; Schaberg 2001. Lloyd 2002: ch. 1 compares the self-images of Greek and Chinese historians.

Now we can address the objection that the lack of literary representations of the three femmes fatales in early China might have skewed the comparison. First, it is anachronistic and misleading to draw a hard and fast line between ancient historical and fictive discourse. As an illustration, the reception of Homer in antiquity testifies to a perpetual and irresolvable tension between his status as a poet and as a historian, and the *Book of Poetry* played a critical role in imparting historical knowledge and creating historical consciousness throughout early China.[25] Moreover, even if we operate with the modern conceptual vocabulary of historicity and fictionality, I venture that, given the exalted epistemological and moral status of knowledge about the past in early China and given the deeply prejudiced view of beautiful women attached to men of power, any literary accounts that might have existed about personages in the calibre of the three femmes fatales were also likely to fall victim to the didactic urge.[26] This speculation may be corroborated by the fact that the early portrayals, especially those in Sima Qian and Liu Xiang, would set the paradigm for later Chinese literary representations of the three femmes fatales. If anything, the tales and novels that deal with the Three Dynasties would only exceed the early texts in depicting the three women as licentious, pernicious and cruel.[27] To my knowledge, in no genre or historical period do the images of the three classical femmes fatales see any significant departure from the early versions, let alone take on the complexity that characterises the portrayals of Helen in Greek texts. For all their imagination and creativity, Chinese poets, storytellers or playwrights produced no admirers and defenders of Mo Xi, Da Ji and Bao Si.

Let me conclude my sweeping and adventurous remarks on 'paradigm' and 'literature versus history' with a brief observation on the extraordinarily multifaceted portrayal of Cleopatra (69–30) in Plutarch's (c. 45–120 CE) *Lives*, a collection of biographies that has been valued for its historical as well as its literary significance. On the one hand, Plutarch leaves no doubt that he holds the seductive and wily Egyptian queen accountable for the fall of her lover Mark Antony. On the other hand, Plutarch demonstrates profound appreciation for Cleopatra's long list of fine qualities, among which her physical beauty is not on the top. She is intelligent, witty, conversant in languages and sophisticated in taste; she is a

---

[25] Kim 2010; Kern 2010.
[26] On the moral status of history writing in early China, see Li 2008; Pines 2002; Schaberg 2001.
[27] For example, in *The Investiture of the Gods* (*Fengshen yanyi*, dated to the sixteenth century CE), Da Ji becomes the inventor of all the cruel punishments implemented by King Zhou. Peng Lizhi 2005 examines the images of Mo Xi in late imperial Chinese fiction.

skilful, considerate and dignified ruler; as Antony's lover, she appears genuinely devoted and eager to please, even as she is capable of mocking him openly and mercilessly when he behaves ludicrously. She is a femme fatale endowed with grace, dignity, and motives that are understandable and vary with circumstances. Whether we take the Plutarchean Cleopatra as a 'historical' or 'literary' character, her complexity harkens back to the Helens in the earlier sources, and stands far apart from the Chinese femmes fatales, who function as interchangeable symbols of evil, do not have a single redeeming attribute, and never receive a chance to speak for themselves. In short, our comparison has demonstrated two ancient societies' distinct ways of engaging with the anxieties and fears caused by beautiful and attractive women, and I hope that I have provided some useful perspectives, at both social and conceptual levels, for understanding the different patterns.

References

Greek primary sources (Loeb Classical Library unless indicated otherwise)

Euripides (2007) *Helen*. Trans. Peter Burian. Oxford.
  (1999) *Trojan Women*. Trans. David Kovacs.
Herodotus (1920–1) *Histories*. Trans. A. D. Godley.
Homer (1925) *Iliad*. Trans. A. T. Murray.
Isocrates (1945) *Helen*. Trans. La Rue van Hook.
Plutarch (1920) *Lives*, vol. 9 (Life of Antony). Trans. Bernadotte Perrin.
Sappho (1994) In *Greek Lyric*, vol. 1. Trans. David A. Campbell.
Stesichorus (1991) In *Greek Lyric*, vol. 3. Trans. David A. Campbell.

Chinese primary works other than those in the general bibliography (my own translations)

Guoyu 國語 (1988). Shanghai.
Shangshu 尚書 (1980) Shisanjing zhushu edn. Beijing.
Shijing 詩經 (1980) Shisanjing zhushu edn. Beijing.

Secondary works

Austin, N. (1994) *Helen of Troy and Her Shameless Phantom*. Ithaca.
Blondell, R. (2010a) '"Bitch that I am": self-blame and self-assertion in the *Iliad*', *Transactions of the American Philological Association* 140: 1–32.
  (2010b) 'Refractions of Homer's Helen in archaic lyric', *American Journal of Philology* 131.3: 349–91.

Burnett, A. P. (1960) 'Euripides' *Helen*: a comedy of ideas', *Classical Philology* 55: 151–63.
Calame, C. (2009) *Greek Mythology: Poetics, Pragmatics, and Fiction*. Cambridge.
de Romilly, J. (1975) *Magic and Rhetoric in Ancient Greece*. Cambridge, MA.
DuBois, P. (1996) 'Sappho and Helen', in *Reading Sappho: Contemporary Approaches*, ed. E. Greene. Berkeley: 79–88.
Garver, E. (1995) *Aristotle's Rhetoric: An Art of Character*. Chicago.
Gu Jiegang 顧頡剛 (1982) 'Zhou e qishishi de fasheng cidi' 紂惡七十事的發生次第, in *Gushi bian* 古史辨, vol. II. Hong Kong: 82–93.
How, W. W. and Wells, J. (1957) *A Commentary on Herodotus*. Oxford.
Johnson, D. (1981) 'Epic and history in early China: the matter of Wu Tzu-hsü', *Journal of Asian Studies* 49.2: 255–71.
Kern, M. (2010) 'Early Chinese literature, beginning through Western Han', in *The Cambridge History of Chinese Literature*, vol. I: *To 1375*, eds. Kang-I Sun Chang and S. Owen. Cambridge: 1–115.
Kim, L. (2010) *Homer between History and Fiction in Imperial Greek Literature*. Cambridge.
Lateiner, D. (1989) *The Historical Method of Herodotus*. Toronto.
Li, F. (2006) *Landscape and Power in Early China: The Crisis and Fall of the Western Zhou, 1045–771 BC*. Cambridge.
Li, W. (2008) *The Readability of the Past in Early Chinese Historiography*. Cambridge, MA.
Liu Yongcong 劉詠聰 (1998) *De cai se quan: lun Zhongguo gudai nüxing* 德才色權: 論中國古代女性. Taipei.
Lloyd, G. E. R. (1996) *Adversaries and Authorities: Investigations into Ancient Greek and Chinese Science*. Cambridge.
  (2002) *The Ambitions of Curiosity: Understanding the World in Ancient Greece and China*. Cambridge.
Peng, Lizhi 彭利芝 (2005) 'Mo Xi xingxiang kaolun: jianlun Ming Qing lishi xiaoshuo zhong de nühuo xianxiang' 妹喜形象考論: 兼論明清歷史小說中的女禍現象, *Ming Qing xiaoshuo yanjiu* 明清小說研究 2: 146–57, 234.
Pines, Y. (2002) *Foundations of Confucian Thought: Intellectual Life in the Chunqiu Period, 722–453 B.C.E.* Honolulu.
Raphals, L. (1998) *Sharing the Light: Representations of Women and Virtue in Early China*. Albany.
Roisman, H. (2006) 'Helen in the *Iliad*; causa belli and victim of war: from silent weaver to public speaker', *American Journal of Philology* 127: 1–36.
Schaberg, D. (2001) *A Patterned Past: Form and Thought in Early Chinese Historiography*. Cambridge, MA.
Segal, C. (1971) 'The two worlds of Euripides' *Helen*', *Transactions of the American Philological Association* 102: 553–614.
Suzuki, M. (1989) *Metamorphoses of Helen: Authority, Difference, and the Epic*. Ithaca.
Worman, N. (1997) 'The body as argument: Helen in four Greek texts', *Classical Antiquity* 16: 151–203.

PART IV

Mathematics and Life Sciences

10 | Divisions, Big and Small: Comparing Archimedes and Liu Hui

REVIEL NETZ

The Box-Lid – the figure produced by the intersection of two cylinders circumscribed within the same cube[1] – was studied in both China and Greece, in a very similar context. Both Archimedes and Liu Hui (or his later reader, Zu Gengzhi) employ a method of indivisibles similar to that of Cavalieri.[2] Such curious specimens – two cultures, converging – present a challenge to the historian.

In the first section I shall present the discussions of the Box-Lid in Archimedes and in Liu Hui/Zu Gengzhi. The second section presents the differences. I will point out that Archimedes is not necessarily more scientific or even comes closest to anticipating modern science. And ultimately I will emphasise the importance of fine-grained, mathematical detail. What sets apart Archimedes as more sophisticated than Liu Hui or Zu Gengzhi is not at the level of broad cultural contrasts: rather, specific differences, having to do with the specific mathematical objects studied, change the contours of the mathematical study itself.

The Two Box-Lids in Context

Archimedes and the *Method*

When Heiberg announced the discovery of the Archimedes Palimpsest he included a transcription of the *Method*,[3] the Palimpsest's greatest treasure.

---

[1] The term 'Box-Lid' is a common translation of the Chinese term found in Liu Hui, *Mou He Fang Gai* 牟合方蓋. (Other translations are possible: I find 'Double Umbrella' to be the most suggestive to a modern reader, as it vividly brings to mind the articulation of the umbrella into its segments; but I did not study ancient Chinese umbrellas.) For more on this question of translation, see Wagner [1978] http://donwagner.dk/SPHERE/SPHERE.html n.10, accessed on 18 April 2016. Notice that the same object is not named at all by Archimedes but is simply referred to through a long description specifying its construction.

[2] In what follows I refer interchangeably, and anachronistically, to 'Cavalieri's principle' or to 'the method of indivisibles', referring to a technique where an $n + 1$ dimensional object is composed of parallel slices of n-dimensional objects. In the West, this procedure was first explicitly discussed in Cavalieri 1647/1980 (see Andersen 1985).

[3] Heiberg 1907: revised in Heiberg's second edition of Archimedes' *Opera*, 1913.

(a)   (b)

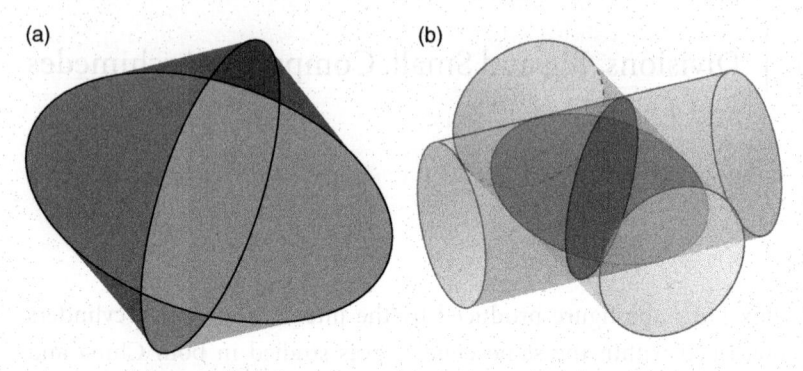

Figure 10.1 The 'Box-Lid'.

To discover the *Method* in the Palimpsest was to unlock a secret, and this sense of a secret revealed was reinforced by Archimedes' own words, at the introduction to the treatise, where Archimedes stated that, in this treatise, he sets out a procedure with the aid of which he was able to make new discoveries.

What is this procedure? In propositions 1–13 Archimedes relies on a dual combination. First, an object is sliced into infinitely many slices of a lower dimensionality (a solid, divided into infinitely many plane areas; or a plane, divided into infinitely many line segments). Second, those slices are considered as mechanical objects, manipulated through their centres of gravity.

This series of propositions mostly proves – with the aid of this new combination – results already published. Right at the beginning of the treatise, however, Archimedes announces that he has found two *new* measurements, which he considers remarkable regardless of any methodological considerations. These are of the following objects:

1. The cylindrical cut produced by an oblique plane passing through the diameter of the base of the cylinder, and the edge of a prism circumscribing that cylinder.
2. The cut produced by the cylinders cutting each other (the bicylinder mentioned above, that is the Box-Lid).[4]

Propositions 12–16 derive the new results.

What has been labelled by Heiberg, and by translators following him, as propositions 12–13, is in fact a single, complex argument deriving the measurement of the slanted cylindrical cut, based on the new procedure.

---

[4] As mentioned above, Archimedes does not name his new objects but simply describes their manner of construction. To make comparisons easier to follow, from now on I shall usually refer to the objects as 'slanted cylindrical cut' and 'bicylinder'.

This is followed by another, much simpler though still extremely elegant argument deriving once again the measurement of the slanted cylindrical cut. Our reading of this proposition 14 has been significantly improved with the new transcription of the Palimpsest[5] and we now recognise in it a daring application of a theorem on the summation of proportions (*Conoids and Spheroids* I), to an infinitary case; remarkably, Archimedes needs, as part of his argument, to refer to the number of terms in what we would call infinitely large sets. At any rate, and crucially, here is a case applying indivisibles – without mechanics.[6]

Here we begin to enter the territory directly comparable to the Chinese evidence and so we should elaborate a more developed sense of the mathematical operation.

The slanted cylindrical cut is considered in half, that is the figure inscribed within half a prism. The cutting plane defines a triangular prism, half of the half-cube, as well as the slanted cylindrical cut itself.[7]

Consider now an arbitrary plane passing inside the half-cube, orthogonally to the diameter through which the slanted plane was drawn. This arbitrary plane produced the following:

1. Within the triangular prism, it cuts off a triangle NMF. We shall call this the prismatic triangle or pr.tr.
2. Within the slanted cylindrical cut, it also cuts off a triangle NΣQ. We shall call this the cylindrical triangle or cyl.tr.
3. Within the base plane of the half-cube – a base plane which is a rectangle – it cuts off a line NM. We call this the rectangle line or rect.l.
4. Within the base plane of the cylinder itself – a base plane which is a semicircle – it cuts off another line NΣ. We call it the circle line or cir.l. (Even though we call it 'circle', this is a straight line.)

We add as follows. In the same base plane of the half-cube and the cylinder we draw a parabola, passing through the points of the diagram EZΛH. This parabola determines a parabolic segment whose base is the original diameter EH through which the slanted plane was drawn. Now, the same arbitrary plane producing 1–4 above can be seen to produce also:

---

[5] See Netz, Saito and Tchernetska 2001–2.

[6] The special role of this proposition within the scheme of the *Method* was barely touched upon by the literature preceding Netz et al. 2001–2, but an important exception is Knorr 1996, who argued that such propositions should show how, at least in some contexts, the application of indivisibles could be considered by the Greeks as rigorous.

[7] The following argument refers to Figure 10.2. In this figure the original diagram for Archimedes 14 (which represents only the two-dimensional base) is supplemented by a three-dimensional extension above the base. To clarify this, I follow Archimedes' Greek labelling for the base but label the additional, elevated points with Latin characters. Otherwise the figure is adapted from Hayashi and Saito 2009.

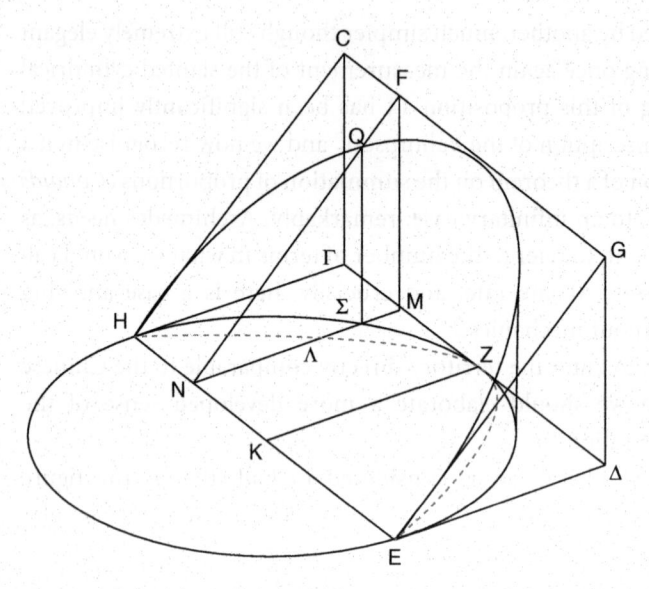

![Figure 10.2]

Figure 10.2 Archimedes' *Method* 14 supplemented by a three-dimensional extension above the base.

5. A line cut off from the parabolic segment NΛ. We shall call this the parabola line or para.l. (and once again, even though we call it 'parabola', this is a straight line).

It is readily apparent that the two triangles – the prismatic and the cylindrical – are similar to each other. Therefore, they are to each other as the squares on any of their sides or specifically:

$$(\text{pr.tr.}) : (\text{cyl} : \text{tr.}) :: (\text{rect.l})^2 : (\text{cir.l})^2$$
or in the diagram terms : NMF : NΣQ :: NM^2: NΣ^2

We now note an interesting geometrical fact:

$$(\text{rect.l.})^2 : (\text{cir} : \text{l.})^2 :: (\text{rect.l}) : (\text{para.l.})$$
or in the diagram terms : NM^2: NΣ^2:: NM : NΛ

An aside that will become interesting in what follows. Archimedes merely asserts the above fact – which is in fact typical of this proof where hardly any deductive work takes place. Archimedes, in this passage, constructs and claims, but hardly ever proves.

Now, Saito suggests we may prove the above as following.[8] In the given construction where the parabola passes through the points HΛZE, the parameter of the parabola has to be equal to the radius of the circle (this is

---

[8] This derivation is contained in Netz et al. 2001–2: 111–12 n. 6.

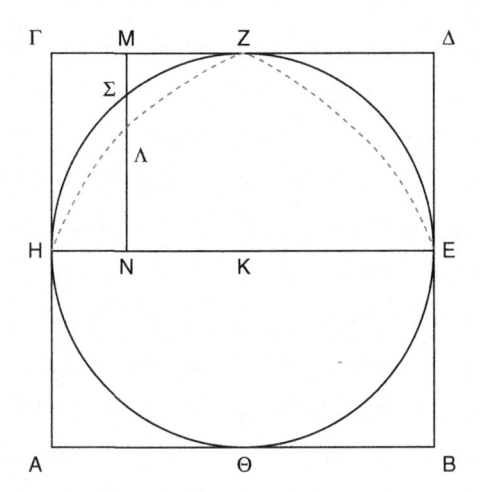

Figure 10.3 Proof of properties in Figure 10.2.

obvious, since the square on the ordinate HK is to be equal to the rectangle contained by: the segment of the parabola's diameter KZ, and the parameter). We know (Pythagoras' theorem and obvious equalities) that

1. $MN^2 = KZ^2 = K\Sigma^2 = \Sigma N^2 + KN^2$

    But we have (through the property of the parabola)

2. $KN^2 = $ rect. $(MN, M\Lambda)$

    (If the above is not evident, remember that MN = parameter of the parabola; and that KN is equal to the ordinate of the parabola drawn, parallel to KN, from the point Λ).
    Take 1 and 2 together and we have

3. $MN^2 = \Sigma N^2 + $ rect. $(MN, M\Lambda)$.

    And since

4. $MN^2 = $ rect. $(MN, M\Lambda) + $ rect. $(MN, \Lambda N)$ (because $M\Lambda + \Lambda N = MN$)

    We find, taking 3 and 4 together, that

5. $\Sigma N^2 = $ rect. $(MN, \Lambda N)$

This is equivalent to the statement that ΣN is the mean proportion between ΛN, MN, or to the proportion

$$MN : \Sigma N :: \Sigma N : \Lambda N$$

Or indeed to the proportion:

$$(\text{rect.l.})^2 : (\text{cir : l.})^2 :: (\text{rect.l.}) : (\text{para.l.})$$
$$\text{or in the diagram terms}: NM^2 : N\Sigma^2 :: NM : N\Lambda$$

As noted above, this is taken together with

$$(\text{pt.tr.}) : (\text{cyl} : \text{tr.}) :: (\text{rect.l.})^2 : (\text{cir.l.})^2$$
or in the diagram terms : $\text{NMF} : \text{N}\Sigma\text{Q} :: \text{NM}^2 : \text{N}\Sigma^2$

The result is that:

$$(\text{pt.tr.}) : (\text{cyl} : \text{tr.}) :: (\text{rect.l.}) : (\text{para.l.})$$
or in the diagram terms : $\text{NMF} : \text{N}\Sigma\text{Q} :: \text{NM} : \text{N}\Lambda$

The same plane cuts off two pairs in the same ratio: a pair of triangles – prismatic and cylindrical – and a pair of lines – rectangle and parabola.

Archimedes then implicitly recalls a result in the summation of proportions, *Conoids and Spheroids* I. When we have a set of ratios of the form A:B::C:D, where:

1. The antecedents such as A are of the same number as the antecedents such as C
2. Within the sets A and C we find what we may call, anachronistically, isomorphism under ratio (we can find an arrangement where for any couple of As A_i, A_j, there's a couple of Cs C_i, C_j, such that $A_i:A_j :: C_i:C_j$), and
3. The sets B and D are constructed by a similar type of isomorphism from their respective origins in A, C, so that if we have $A_i:B_i$ in a given ratio, we also have $C_i:D_i$ in the same ratio,

Then we may sum up all the As, Bs, Cs and Ds in four large sums, so that

$$\Sigma A : \Sigma C :: \Sigma B : \Sigma D$$

Archimedes merely alludes to this result (by pointing out the relevant equalities of multitude which – remarkably – are equalities between infinite sets). It applies here to the extent that the prismatic triangles (the As) and the rectangle lines (the Cs) are indeed isomorphic under ratio, trivially – they are all equal to each other; while indeed each cylindrical triangle (each of the Bs) is produced out of prismatic triangle (an A) by the same ratio in which a parabola line (a D) is produced out of a rectangle line (a C). (The rub is that the result was proved in *Conoids and Spheroids* I for a finite case, a complication we put aside for this exposition.) If indeed we apply this result, then, we get

$$\Sigma A : \Sigma C :: \Sigma B : \Sigma D$$

Which in this case means that the prism is to the cylindrical cut as the rectangle is to the parabolic segment. We know that the parabolic segment is two-thirds the rectangle (this, indeed, we proved in the first proposition of the *Method*, but is a result proved not once but twice in published form, before, in a treatise called *Quadrature of the Parabola*). Hence, the cylindrical cut is two thirds the triangular prism or one sixth the circumscribing cube.

It appears likely that proposition 14 is considered still as a non-rigorous proof. This is because it is followed by proposition 15, essentially identical to it, and now argued for, in full, rigorous detail. This proposition is now in fragmentary form (and Heiberg could read no more than a fraction of this fragment). From what survives, it is clear that Archimedes produced an argument deriving the same proportion as in proposition 14, but instead of considering planes on top of lines, he considered thin prismatic slices on top of thin rectangles. The proposition is developed in considerable detail, developing the precise manner in which the result for the composite objects made of prisms can serve to yield the result for the curvilinear object, based on the method of exhaustion familiar from elsewhere in Archimedes. We thus obtain a geometrically rigorous proof of the measurement of the slanted cylindrical cut.

Proposition 15 is fragmentary in the palimpsest and, in particular, its end is lost. In fact, it is here that our evidence is cut off for the treatise as a whole, so that we do not have the final proposition. However, the codicology of the original Archimedes manuscript has been reconstructed in sufficient detail[9] to allow us to calculate with some certainty the remaining length of the treatise.[10] It appears that there were between five and six columns of text available for this last proposition. Now, as noted above, Archimedes states in the introduction that he would provide, at the end, 'geometrical' proofs for both new results, and proposition 15 discharges this duty for the slanted cylindrical cut. Hence those five to six columns should accommodate at the very least some suggestion of a rigorous proof for the measurement of the bicylinder. It can definitely be ruled out by considerations of space that Archimedes produced a proof exactly analogous to 14–15 (providing first an argument based on indivisibles, then a rigorously modified version). It would also be nearly impossible to fit in merely a rigorous proof in the manner of proposition 15 – however lightly sketched – into the space allowed. There are thus two possibilities. One is that we should somehow qualify our understanding of Archimedes' introduction, and assume that he did not in fact explicitly produce a rigorous proof for the measurement of the bicylinder – perhaps instead offering a non-rigorous argument merely hinting at

---

[9] Originally by Hope Mayo, producing the catalogue for Christie's sale of the Palimpsest (Christie's 1998), confirmed by later studies by Abigail Quandt that are summed up in Netz et al. 2011: I, 41.

[10] This calculation was produced independently in Netz et al. 2011: I, 317 n. 86, and in Saito and Napolitani 2014: 222. (It is my understanding that the key results of Saito and Napolitani 2014 were already published in Japanese by Hayashi and Saito 2009.)

266   REVIEL NETZ

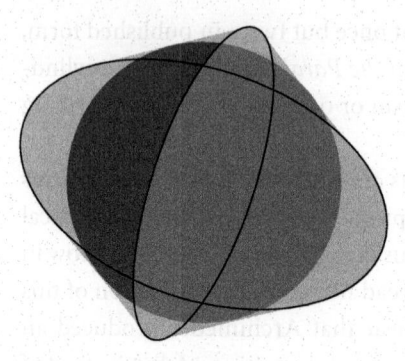

Figure 10.4 Bicylinder and circumscribed sphere.

the rigorous version as an open task[11]. Or he could have provided another rigorous, geometrical argument altogether. The second alternative is the more attractive, as it would add to the sense of geometrical variety, otherwise so evident in this treatise, and in particular in the treatment of the slanted cylindrical cut, approached in no less than three distinct ways, each having a very different character – the abstruse mechanical approach of 12–13, the light and elegant argument with indivisibles in 14, the heavy geometrical apparatus of 15. To have 16, following that, nearly aping 14, would be something of an anticlimax.

Let us make the alternatives more concrete. First, let us consider a measurement of the bicylinder based on parallel slicing.

There are several ways of slicing the bicylinder, and Sato 1986 and 1987 proposed a slicing principle that directly continues that of proposition 14. For reasons which will become apparent in what follows, I will briefly outline another slicing principle. In Figure 10.4, we have the bicylinder and, for good measure, we also add in the sphere circumscribed in the same cube.

We now slice this three-dimensional figure with an arbitrary plane passing parallel to the base of the cube. In the plane figure we find the

---

[11] In what follows I will consider the option that such a non-rigorous argument could be based on indivisibles (analogously, that is, to proposition 14), and not mechanical (analogously, that is, to proposition 12–13: though as a matter of practice it would have been related to Archimedes' result concerning the sphere and would have been easier). This is slightly more likely, as such an argument is, I think, somewhat briefer and also because it is indeed a straightforward task to transform an argument based on indivisibles to a rigorous method of exhaustion. To take a mechanical proof and turn it into a rigorous version is a much more difficult task and this would seem to run directly counter to Archimedes' promise, at the introduction, rigorously ('geometrically') to prove both new measurements. (Though this does remain a possibility: it is, after all, quite in the manner of Archimedes to mislead us!) Rufini 1926 produces explicitly such a mechanical argument.

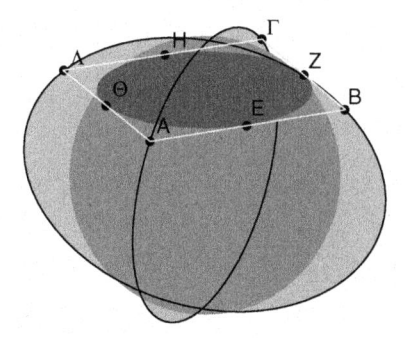

Figure 10.5 Figure 10.4 with added plane parallel to the base of the cube.

square ΑΒΓΔ, which is the cut taken off from the bicylinder; and the circle ΕΖΗΘ, which is the cut taken off from the sphere (Figure 10.5).

By a reasoning comparable to that of proposition 14 (though in an important sense simpler: more on this below) we find that the bicylinder is to the sphere as a square is to the circle it circumscribes or, to extend into the third dimension (I will discuss such extensions below), as the cube is to the cylinder it circumscribes. We have:

> bicylinder : sphere :: cube : cylinder   that is
> bicylinder : cube :: sphere : cylinder

But we know already from *Sphere and Cylinder* I – a result proved again in the second proposition of the *Method* – that the cylinder in question is 1.5 times the sphere; the cube is therefore 1.5 times the bicylinder.

This would be a nice proposition which, with some effort, could fit into the remaining space.[12] If indeed the treatise concluded on such a note, however, this would give rise to serious problems of interpretation – are we to take such a method of indivisibles as directly rigorous? Or are we to finish the treatise on a note of a task assigned to the reader? To be clear, these are genuine possibilities, but I think Saito and Napolitani are right to prefer an alternative.

Their alternative is to emphasise a relationship between the slanted cylindrical cut and the bicylinder. Namely, it is possible to decompose the bicylinder into eight slanted cylindrical cuts, as in Figure 10.6. We can measure each of these eight slanted cylindrical cuts as a fraction of its cube,

---

[12] All Archimedes would have to do is to set out the construction (which is indeed difficult). Unlike proposition 14, one does not need to develop any geometrical ratios for this proof, merely to identify the square and the circle as the ensuing slices; nor is it necessary to recall again the machinery of *Conoids and Spheroids* I (which, having evoked it once, Archimedes could simply take for granted at this point).

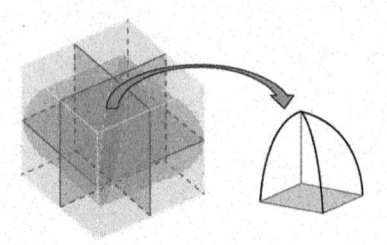

Figure 10.6 Box-Lid decomposed.

from which we can easily calculate the bicylinder as a fraction of its own cube. This argument is developed in Saito and Napolitani 2011: 207–8, and they point out that this very simple claim, too, can take an extensive argument as, after all, the references of the solid terms involved would be very abstruse. (As they point out, the mere construction of the bicylinder took, in the introduction, no less than 16 lines! – Here it becomes important that Archimedes never *names* the new figures.[13])

I think that Saito and Napolitani's reconstruction is far from certain; but that it remains the likeliest. This brief argument of decomposition is clearly distinct from the preceding ones, and so it leaves less sense of 'more of the same'. Instead, we get, at the end, an unsuspected surprise. Cutting a cylinder by a plane and cutting it by another cylinder are almost the same thing, even though the cylinder is everywhere curved. And we then have the final proposition 16 neatly following from the preceding results, putting a finishing touch to a series of suggestions that marks the treatise as a whole, where each proposition suggests and leads to the following propositions (for this, see Netz et al. 2011: I, 309–10).[14] Above all, Saito and Napolitani are right, I believe, in their emphasis of the difficulty of the terms to be discussed in this proposition. A more detailed proof could be squeezed in – but with difficulty. The mere statement of decomposition fits the space better.

In what follows, I will assume that such was the conclusion of the *Method*, making the obvious caveats where needed. We see Archimedes proposing, as two separate projects, the study of the slanted cylindrical cut

---

[13] A good comparison is *Elements* 12.7, the proposition decomposing the prism into three pyramids. This in fact takes some geometrical work, as one needs to *show* that the various sections are in fact equal.

[14] To be fair, there is a stylistic advantage to the indivisibles argument mentioned above, as well. For a final proposition based on the indivisibles argument above would entail that the final proposition is related to the *second* proposition of the *Method* (the volume of the sphere) in exactly the same way that the preceding propositions 14–15 are related to the *first* proposition of the *Method* (the area of the parabolic segment). Archimedes' choice of examples of his method, from among published results, would then be rather elegantly motivated.

and the bicylinder; providing three different proofs for the slanted cylindrical cut; finally, in a brief addendum, pointing out that the bicylinder follows directly from the slanted cylindrical cut. Of the three different proofs, one relies on a combination of indivisibles and mechanics and one on indivisibles alone. Both rely, specifically, on the summation of infinitely many proportions, whether through a mechanical principle (12–13) or through a principle from proportion theory itself (14). Apparently, both summations of infinitely many proportions are considered to be non-rigorous.

Zu Gengzhi, Liu Hui and the *Nine Chapters*

Let me admit: my knowledge of Chinese mathematics is as thin as the slices of the sphere above. In what follows, I rely entirely on secondary literature, as I cannot even read the Chinese (translation of which I take, instead, from Wagner 1978[15] and Dauben 2007).

The *Nine Chapters* were the central mathematical canon in China. As a consequence, they accumulated from early on a body of commentary, in which the work transmitted under the name of Liu Hui occupies a central position.[16]

The end of the fourth of the *Nine Chapters* states a couple of problem-and-solution pairs of finding the diameter of a sphere whose volume is given, the simpler of which is (Wagner 1978: 6.1; Qian Baocong 1963: 154.18):

Consider a volume of 4500 *chi*. If it is a sphere, what is the diameter?
  Answer: 20 *chi*.

This is followed by a general method statement[17] (Wagner 1978 6.2):

Lay out the number of [cubic] *chi* in the volume; multiply by 16; divide by 9; extract the cube root of the result; this is the diameter of the sphere.

That is, a sphere is taken to be 9/16th of its circumscribing cube.

---

[15] Wagner 1978 is best accessible online as http://donwagner.dk/SPHERE/SPHERE.html. I will therefore refer below to this work based on its sections, not its page numbers.
[16] Questions of authorship in the Chinese canon-and-commentary tradition are extremely vexing and of course beyond my competence: for a preliminary discussion, see Chemla 2013. In what follows, I will use 'Liu Hui' and 'Zu Gengzhi' as stylised references to two steps in the commentary discussion, most of which is known, in fact, through the work of the later seventh-century author Li Chunfeng.
[17] This order – problem, solution, method – is universal in the *Nine Chapters*; I return to this point below.

Liu Hui in his commentary takes it for granted that the *Nine Chapters* assume here a value of π = 3, and does not dispute this value (indeed, this being an approximation, it is no problem of principle to take a rough one). He does dispute the implied geometrical claim, that the ratio of the sphere to the cube is $(\pi{:}4)^2$. It is obvious, he agrees, that the cylinder is to the cube in the ratio π:4 (in Liu Hui's terms, 'the proportion of a square'). But the implication – that the cylinder is to the sphere also in the ratio π:4 – is, Lui Hui explains, wrong.

Since the *Nine Chapters* implies the thought that the sphere is somehow like the cylinder squared, the cylinder applied upon itself, it is very natural indeed to consider at this point the bicylinder. Liu Hui constructs it and circumscribes it around the sphere. He then observes that the bicylinder, in fact, stands in the ratio π:4 to the sphere. The argument must be that of the indivisibles argument delineated above, that Archimedes *could* have produced in his *Method* proposition 16 (but probably didn't), that each of the squares in the bicylinder circumscribes a circle in the sphere. As it is, Liu Hui merely asserts this relation.

The bicylinder is in the ratio π:4 to the sphere. A negative result follows: the cylinder – obviously distinct from the bicylinder – can *not* be in the ratio π:4 to the sphere.

It is obvious that a measurement of the bicylinder in terms of either the cylinder or the cube would have provided Liu Hui with a formula superior to the one of the *Nine Chapters*. He did not offer such a measurement and instead concluded with the observation that the measurement of the *Nine Chapters* remains, after all, a good enough numerical solution – adding in a brief piece of poetry lamenting the difficulties of bringing together the square and the circle. So much for Liu Hui; before concluding our discussion of his contribution, we should mention that he produced a visual indication of the nature of the bicylinder (or, as he named it, the Box-Lid), by considering its decomposition into eight equal segments (see Figure 10.6).

Those were produced in the 'natural' way, by bisections of three faces of the cube circumscribing the bicylinder, so that each eighth section contained a kind of puffed-up, curved pyramid-like object. Liu Hui directly connected this object to the pyramid, and it should be mentioned that earlier on in his commentary he did produce a measurement of the pyramid, so that this visual exposition added a sense of continuity to his work.

This comparison to the pyramid forms the basis of Zu Gengzhi's own contribution (fifth–sixth century) that went beyond Liu Hui's negative comments to produce a correct derivation of the volume of the sphere. It is now lost, but we have an extant commentary to the *Nine Chapters*, by Li Chunfeng, from the seventh century, that is written with a close attention to issues of authorship (perhaps, an attention unprecedented in this canon-and-commentary tradition[18]). Li preserves a report which (given this attention to authorship) we tend to take as an accurate representation of Zu Gengzhi's approach.

Recall that Liu Hui, perhaps for the purposes of visualisation, considered the Box-Lid as composed of eight segments, each a curved, pyramid-like object. Zu Gengzhi proceeded to measure this object directly, based on an explicit statement of a Cavalieri-type principle, as well as an elegantly indirect subtractive approach.

First, to the explicit statement of the Cavalieri principle. This goes as follows (Wagner 1978: 6.5.1; Qian Baocong 1963: 158.5):

> If blocks are piled up to form volumes,
> And corresponding areas are equal,
> Then the volumes cannot be unequal.

'Blocks' clearly mean in context plane areas. Patriotic Chinese mathematicians who wish to emphasise that Cavalieri's principle (Figure 10.7) was first stated in China are perfectly justified in doing so,[19] and it is indeed very striking that nothing analogous is to be found in Archimedes – so much so that it was never clear, to his ancient readers, that indivisibles (and not mechanical principles) were even crucial to his operation. I shall return to this point below.

Second, to the indirect subtractive approach (as Fu 1991 points out, this is Zu Gengzhi's main original departure as a mathematician).

In the curved pyramid-like object, consider an arbitrary plane drawn parallel to the base. This plane cuts off, from the cube enclosing the curved pyramid-like object, a square QDEF; it also cuts off, from the curved pyramid-like object itself, another, smaller square QABC. And it also determines the *complement* to that square, a gnomon (ABCFED in the figure: Zu Gengzhi does not conceptualise this directly as a gnomon but rather as a combination of two rectangles and a square, a detail which need not detain us).

What is the area of this gnomon? Clearly, this area is the difference between the area of the big square QDEF and the small square QABC. So now let us consider another, three-dimensional figure, where we also take into consideration the height at which the cutting plane passes. We note

---

[18] See note 16 above.   [19] See for instance He 2004.

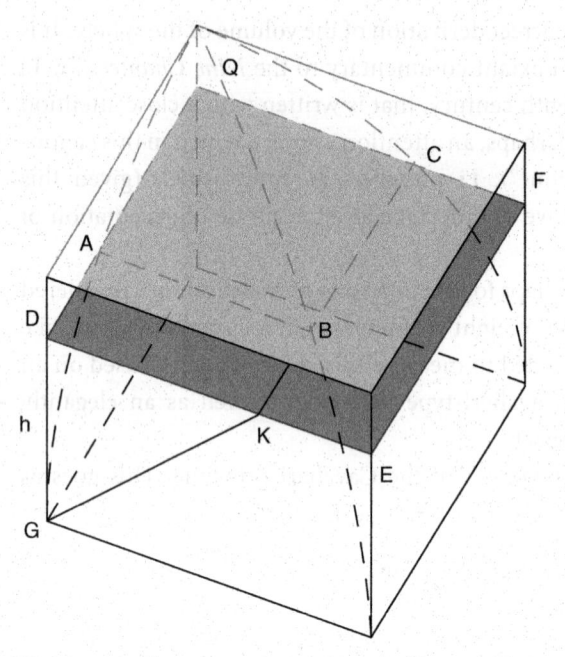

Figure 10.7 Illustration of use of Cavalieri's principle.

immediately a Pythagoras theorem arrangement: in the triangle DGK, the hypotenuse GK is equal to the side of the cube DE (because it is also the radius of the circle arising from the cylinder). Thus the difference between the areas of the big square QDEF and the small square QABC is the difference between the squares, on an hypotenuse, and on a side, in a right-angled triangle (squares on GK, DK in the triangle DGK in Figure 10.7). This is the square on the remaining side DG, which is the same as the height.

The surprising result is that the area of the gnomon, at each height selected for the cutting plane, is equal to the square on that height. This is the key geometrical operation of this proof by Zu Gengzhi. I propose that it is not fanciful to compare this operation to the operation with which Archimedes could have derived the main proportion of proposition 14, cited above, where we find that the circle line is the mean proportional between the rectangle line and the parabola line. Recall that in both cases we have a circle boxed in a square, of which we consider a quadrant; and an arbitrary line passing through that quadrant. Both Archimedes (according to Saito's reconstruction) and Zu Gengzhi rely on the resulting equality between the side of the square and the hypotenuse of the resulting right-angled triangle. At this point, the routes diverge: Zu Gengzhi relates the configuration to a three-dimensional embedding which brings in another, related square; Archimedes relates it to a parabola embedded in the two-dimensional figure itself (this parabola, though, is essentially a two-dimensional shortcut representation of what is, once again, a three-dimensional configuration involving related squares). This then allows to subtract squares from squares and to obtain the desired geometrical relation. The point of this comparison is to bring out the very close level of geometrical sophistication – and to emphasise that the difference, in this case, is once again, surprisingly, that Archimedes is *less* explicit about his argumentation!

Otherwise the denouement is close at hand. Since the gnomon, at any arbitrary plane, is equal to the square on the height of that plane, we can associate 'block by block' the gnomons to the squares on the heights. The sequence of squares on the height is clearly the same as the pyramid contained within the small cube. Also, the sequence of gnomons is clearly the complement volume, remaining when we subtract the curved pyramid-like object from the same cube. The pyramid is one-third the cube, a result due to Liu Hui itself; so that the curved pyramid-like object is two thirds the cube. We conclude that the Box-Lid as a whole (composed as it is of eight curved pyramid-like objects, each enclosed within a small cube, an eighth of the big cube) is two thirds its enclosing cube.

What's more, we have already from Liu Hui himself that the sphere is to the Box-Lid as 'the ratio of the circle', or π:4. This is taken here to be 3:4. Now, if the cube is to the Box-Lid as 3 to 2, while the Box-Lid is to the sphere as 4 to 3, we may eliminate the Box-Lid and retain the ratio of the cube to the sphere which is 2:1. Quite fittingly, Zu Gengzhi ends on a song of joy (Qian Baocong 1953: 158.8), responding to Liu Hui's song of lament. The circle and the square are now married.

This amazingly simple calculation is of course partly a construct of the value chosen for π, but this choice does not reflect a crude level of the calculation of that number – in fact, we know that in other contexts Zu Gengzhi did have available longer approximations of π – but rather is justified by considerations of continuity within the canon and commentary tradition. In the *Nine Chapters*, 3:4 is in fact 'the ratio of the circle' and while improvements on such numbers could be justified, in other contexts, there is also an advantage in solving a problem within the terms of the *Nine Chapters* itself. Thus, as a matter of commentary, Zu Gengzhi is entirely precise in asserting that the ratio of the volumes of the cube and the sphere should be seen as 2:1, and that, no less, Liu Hui should have been able to notice that.

We may conclude by noting, then, that both measurements, by Archimedes and by Liu Hui / Zu Gengzhi, are triumphantly successful.

Divisions and Indivisions

A Similar Trajectory

First of all, we should note that the underlying route leading from curvilinear solids to indivisibles is indeed directly comparable in our two cases.

Zu Gengzhi formalises his own procedure based on Liu Hui's model, most directly in the treatment of the ratio between the bicylinder and the sphere. This last ratio was transformed by Liu Hui into the sum of infinitely many ratios between plane areas, one of which is in 'the proportion of a square', the other being in 'the proportion of a circle'. The conclusion is then that the solids as a whole are in the same proportions, respectively. Now, notice this repeated tool of the two proportions of 'square' and 'circle'. This is in fact one of the key assumptions of the operation in question, already from the *Nine Chapters* itself: namely, that cubes and cylinders are to each other as squares and circles. We note an innocuous assumption, one that in and of itself does not seem to involve infinitary considerations. It may be phrased, for instance, as the claim that solids set up perpendicularly to the same height from their respective bases stand to each other as the ratio of their bases. From this follows, in China, very directly, the ratio of the cube to the cylinder which, we now see, is a very direct inspiration for a Cavalieri-like principle.

Now, moving into Greece, we note first of all that the same assumption is used of course in the lower-dimensional case where the ratio of rectangles under the same height is taken to be the same as the ratio of their bases. This is very fundamental for Euclid, proved in *Elements* 6.1, and so it is not surprising that the three-dimensional related result is proved, for parallelepipeds, in *Elements* 11.32. The last is proved right at the end of Book 11 (and so does not play precisely the same foundational role), but its position is nevertheless fitting, forming a bridge to the next book. This Book 12 is all about extensions of such ratios to the case of curved objects. Specifically, this book – famously credited, on the authority of Archimedes himself, to Eudoxus[20] – finds the ratio of a cylinder and a cone, and obtains this by connecting the ratios of solids to the ratios of their bases, specifically

---

[20] Archimedes asserts this not once but twice: Heiberg 1910: 4.5; 1913: 430.2 (now revised: Netz et al. 2011: 297).

reducing the volumes of cones and pyramids to the volumes of circles and polygons. (All of this has other parallels elsewhere in Liu Hui, who found the volumes of both the pyramid – a key step of *Elements* 12 – as well as the cone itself.) When Archimedes evokes Eudoxus as a model, he probably has in mind not only the result but also the specific technique developed by Eudoxus in Book 12, often referred to as the 'method of exhaustion', which is the finitary, rigorous version of what we find in Archimedes' *Method* (i.e., it is the technique in evidence in *Method* proposition 15). It is based on taking small, finite slices (instead of infinitesimal slices). This finite approach clearly served as the model for Archimedes' infinitary technique in the *Method*.

The precise route leading Zu Gengzhi and Archimedes to their experiment with a Cavalieri principle is therefore closely related:

- An interest in measurement becomes an interest in measuring curved objects, and then
- The complexity of measuring curved solids makes it natural to consider them as extensions of their bases. Specifically:
- This is channelled through the cylinder, which is obviously 'as the circle', thus reducing the problem of measuring this three-dimensional, curved object, into the problem of measuring the circle.
- Once this technique has become standardised, it becomes possible to suggest that one conceives of three-dimensional, curved objects, in general, as infinitary summations of lower-dimensional objects.

In both cultures, infinitary summations emerge as a response to the measurement of solid, curvilinear objects; and in both cultures, they do so gradually, as a response to accumulated layers of such measurements. So far, the overall similarity is indeed quite real. Let us move on to note some differences.

Differences: A Matter of Method

I start from a matter of mathematical detail. In Liu Hui, the circle is related to the square circumscribing it; in Eudoxus, the circle is related to the polygon it circumscribes. This immediately suggests a different manner of division of an object into its constituents: in Liu Hui, the clear example is that of a parallel slicing, because this is the manner in which cube and cylinder are like square and circle: as the piling up of squares and circles. In Eudoxus, on the other hand, the relation between the circle and the polygon is more complicated and suggests a variety of other cutting devices. This, indeed, will provide inspiration for Archimedes who, in *Sphere and Cylinder* I, divides the sphere into a series of cone-based objects (rather than a series of parallel circles), while in *On Spirals* he will divide the spiral area into a series of sectors (rather than a series of lines passing parallel to the diameter). We may praise Archimedes for his greater versatility,[21] or we may praise Liu Hui and Zu Gengzhi for their clear focus on parallel slices which, in fact, lead more directly to a Cavalieri-like approach.

But here we get to the key point: Archimedes does *not* develop, in fact, a Cavalieri-like principle. As a matter of fact, all the divisions discussed in the *Method* are parallel. However, this parallelism is never explicitly addressed as such, for the good reason that it is contingent to Archimedes' actual methods. For his actual measurements, Archimedes relies not on parallelism, but on two other principles, each distinct. In propositions 1–13, what matters is that in all infinitely many pairs of objects, the centre of gravity be the same; in proposition 14, what matters is that the conditions of *Conoids and Spheroids* I be obtained. That the slicing involved is parallel is of course mentioned, but is never made into a cornerstone of the operation, the objects in question referred to, for instance, as 'the lines' rather than as 'the parallel lines'. If Archimedes is aware of the significance of parallelism as a constitutive principle to his techniques, he does not present this awareness at all.

Does Archimedes even *have a method*? There is in fact nothing remotely resembling an algorithm, a method of discovery. There is no particular rule from which we can infer when arrangements of infinitely many plane areas will all have the same centre of gravity, and the terms of *Conoids and Spheroids* I are very abstract and difficult to ascertain in advance.

The centrality of methods in Chinese mathematics is well known and has been most precisely observed by Chemla.[22] As noted above, the *Nine Chapters* is organised in a rigid pattern of particular problems stated, followed by particular solutions, and then summarised as the statement of a general method, introduced as a purely numerical algorithm. Liu Hui's general strategy as a commentator – which is typical in the commentary tradition – is to take such method statements and verify them, sometimes

---

[21] Saito and Napolitani 2014 indeed emphasise Archimedes' interest in varied divisions, and not merely parallel division, as a key to his non-modern character (since parallel division is already suggestive of the modern approach to integration). Indeed, as they point out, the more integration-like divisions of *Conoids and Spheroids* are due to the specific form of construction of those objects, in terms of rotations that give rise to parallel circles: no interest in parallel division *as such*, then!

[22] See especially Chemla 2005; a concise statement of the position can be found in Cullen 2002.

(as in this case) with a certain modification. Chemla's central contribution is to note the extent of demonstrative, deductive work implicit in such verifications of methods, thus exploding the lazy narrative as if mathematical proof was alien to Chinese mathematics.

Indeed, the passages we have followed from Liu Hui and Zu Gengzhi are among the clearest examples of Chinese geometrical proofs. But notice what is proven: a *method*. What in the Greek context is understood as a theorem – say, the finding of the volume of the sphere in terms of its diameter or vice versa – is understood in the Chinese case as a *method*, a series of operations with which one transforms a volume statement to a diameter statement. Chinese mathematics is dedicated to proofs of the validity of methods.

A variation on what modern scholars sometimes refer to, colloquially, as a cut-and-paste proof technique in geometry, typical of such situations as *Elements* Book 2 and much of Babylonian geometry, is explicitly recognised as a method in Chinese mathematics, the 'In Out' principle (the objects 'out' are superposed on the objects 'in'). When, in his commentary on chapter 5 of the *Nine Chapters*, Liu Hui measures various volumes, the most central being the pyramid, he explicitly sets out a similar cut-and-paste method (which however does not obtain a stylised name) based on the conceptualisation of the solid in terms of the dissection and superposition of component cubes. Now, it is in this context that we need to understand Liu Hui's presentation of the Box-Lid as the combination of eight figures (curved pyramid-like objects) dissected from smaller cubes. This made the treatment of the Box-Lid, hence of the sphere, fit within a more general method. Zu Gengzhi, as we recall, took this as his starting point and measured not the Box-Lid as a whole, but rather the curved pyramid-like object. These he dissected not into constituent solids, but into constituent planes, which he must have understood as an explicit extension of Liu Hui's methods. In short, we see Cavalieri's principle emerging in China as the result of a continuous tradition of the explicit discussion and extension of methods:

In/Out (traditional, stylised cut and paste technique) → Liu Hui's dissection of volumes in terms of cubes → Zu Gengzhi's dissection of volumes in terms of planes.

There is no comparable route leading on to Archimedes' *Method*. The introduction to this treatise is often read as if Archimedes was defensive about applying mechanics into geometry, but in fact he is defensive about the very act of talking *about* mathematical procedures, as opposed to talking about the discoveries themselves, obtained through such procedures. And thus it is not just the accident, of Archimedes' open-ness to various non-parallel divisions, that stopped him from making explicit a Cavalieri-style principle. More simply, *he did not promulgate principles*. Such was not the done thing, in Greece; to have a Cavalieri, Western mathematics had to shed something of its Greek character and to become a little more like China.

But, it would be urged, it would still be Western: Cavalieri, after all, provides proofs! And proof is Greek, not Chinese!

Or is this so simple in this case? Before I let go of the issue of method, I wish to add a word about proofs in Archimedes and in Zu Gengzhi. I have already hinted at the trend of modern scholarship – led by Chemla – to explode that lazy notion of a proof-less Chinese mathematics. But in this case one does not require Chemla's subtle arguments. It is enough to note that, at some key stages of the argument in front of us, it is Archimedes who is elusive and opaque, Zu Gengzhi who is explicitly demonstrative. Both main derivations – Archimedes' measurement of the slanted cylindrical cut and Zu Gengzhi's measurement of the bicylinder – rely on a combination of general infinitary arguments, as well as a specific, elegant geometrical claim. The general infinitary argument, in Archimedes, is *Conoids and Spheroids* I; in Zu Gengzhi, it is Cavalieri's principle. The specific geometrical claim in Archimedes is that the circle line is the mean proportional between the rectangle line and the parabola line; in Zu Gengzhi, it is that the gnomon, at a given height, is equal to the square on that height.

Archimedes does not make explicit his reliance upon *Conoids and Spheroids* I. It is not only that he does not cite the result. He does not even make any effort to make his statement correspond to the terms of *Conoids and Spheroids* I, merely asserting that certain terms are equal 'in multitude' to others, which is no more than a single condition among several mentioned in *Conoids and Spheroids* I (that the other conditions apply, and that it is even *Conoids and Spheroids* I that we are trying to apply, is left as an exercise to the reader!). Zu Gengzhi, on the other hand, makes his Cavalieri's principle explicit.

Archimedes does not argue at all for the specific geometrical claim. Instead, he merely asserts it (the argument provided above is a reconstruction offered by Saito). Zu Gengzhi, on the other hand, explicitly explains how Gou Gu considerations ('Pythagoras theorem', conceived as a method!) derive the equality of the gnomon and the square involved.

It is not just that Zu Gengzhi is more explicit: in both cases, with Cavalieri's principle as well as with the specific geometrical result, he is explicit about *methods*. He introduces a new method, an extension of Liu Hui's, that of the Cavalieri-like principle; and he applies a very old method, that of Gou Gu. And in both cases, he takes care to specify the methods employed. We see here an example of general import. It is not the case that Greek mathematics is more explicitly demonstrative, Chinese mathematics less explicitly demonstrative. Rather, Greek and Chinese mathematicians are explicit about different things. Greek mathematicians are (sometimes, though not in this case) explicit about the detail of first order demonstrations; Chinese mathematicians are more explicit about the place of demonstrations within overall methods. At some level, what we have in front of us is a contrast not between the explicit and the implicit: but between first order, and second order explicitness.

Now, when Archimedes is explicit, he *is* explicit. It remains true that proposition 15 is like nothing we ever find in the Chinese evidence. Thus for instance (Arch28 v col. 2 lines 9–27):

[it is required] to prove that the circumscribed figure exceeds the inscribed <by a difference smaller> than any given solid magnitude. For since the smaller of the prisms in the circumscribed figure, that on the parallelogram ΘΟ, is equal to the smaller prism in the inscribed <figure>, the one on the parallelogram ΠΟ – for they have a base equal to the same, and an equal height – and similarly, the second prism among those in the inscribed figure is equal to the second prism among those in the circumscribed figure <composed> prisms, being on the same <base> ...[23]

This is the heart of the sense of the claim that the Greeks, more than the Chinese, have 'proofs': they have those stretches of text that are written like nothing else. In the Chinese texts, nothing departs significantly from the language elsewhere in canons and commentaries and it is indeed significant that the key contribution by Zu Gengzhi – the explicit statement of Cavalieri's principle – is set out precisely in that most widespread elite form of Chinese writing, the five-syllable verse of parallelism (Qian Baocong 1963: 158.5):

> If blocks are piled up to form volumes,
> And corresponding areas are equal,
> Then the volumes cannot be unequal.
> 夫疊棋成立積，緣冪勢既同，則積不容異.

Two contrasts, then: a difference of subject matter (Chinese tend to be explicit about the second order, Greeks about the first order) and of genre (Chinese use a less distinctive genre in their mathematical writings, compared to Greeks). The two are obviously connected, as the second order is more general in its scope, hence it is natural to present it in a language

---

[23] And so it goes on for several more lines and the page breaks off before the sentence does.

whose scope, too, is more general. Indeed, it has been observed that Chinese second order reflections on mathematics are related to wider metaphysical reflections and that when Liu Hui reflects on his methods he clearly has in mind the metaphysical as well as epistemological questions of infinity (so, for instance, Horng 1995[24]).

Differences: Archimedes' Sophistication, Archimedes' Autonomy

Some of my readers might be outraged by the above. Am I engaging in a contrarian, somewhat relativist exercise, elevating Chinese mathematics, removing Archimedes from his pedestal? Is it not just obvious that Archimedes is the greater mathematician?

Indeed he is and I believe our comparison will not be complete until we recognise just where Archimedes' greater sophistication resides. This, I will argue, is *not* primarily a matter of broad methodological contrasts, of Archimedes' deeper attention to meta-mathematical concerns: to the contrary. Archimedes' sophistication is to be found in the fine grain of mathematical detail. This, however, is of great moment.

There are two main contrasts we may draw between Archimedes and Liu Hui / Zu Gengzhi at the level of the fine grain of mathematical sophistication. The first has to do with the nature of the summed proportions; the second has to do with the nature of the objects whose proportions are studied.

First, to the proportions. To recall, Liu Hui's key Cavalieri-like intuition was that the bicylinder was to the sphere as a square to the circle, since each parallel slicing gave rise to 'this same ratio'. Archimedes might have used the very same argument in his now lost proposition 16 (though more likely he did not), but certainly he did rely, in proposition 14, on a somewhat comparable claim: that the triangular prism was to the slanted cylindrical cut as the rectangle to the parabolic segment, since each parallel slicing

---

[24] The evidence is found in Wagner 1979, once again best accessed online as http://donwagner.dk/Pyramid/Pyramid-5.html (Qian Baocong 1963: 168.2–3).

Liu Hui's words run as follows: 'The smaller they are halved, the finer [*xi* 細] are the remaining [dimensions]. The extreme of fineness is called "subtle" [*wei* 微]. That which is subtle is without form [*xing* 形]. When it is explained in this way, why concern oneself with the remainder?', and, as Wagner comments: 'The terms used in this statement, *xi* ("fine"), *wei* ("minute," with overtones of "subtle, mysterious"), and *xing* ("form"), demand further study ... are important concepts in ancient Chinese metaphysics.' The fundamental point is that Liu Hui produces a sufficiently general, second order statement, for it to create the thickness of intertextual relations with other, philosophical discourses that allow us to position Liu Hui within contemporary Chinese metaphysics – all absent in the case of Greek mathematics.

came out as a proportion involving terms from the slices of those four objects.

The contrast immediately stands out. In the case of Liu Hui, I could simply refer to each parallel slicing giving rise to 'this same ratio' (that of 4:π), but I could no longer do that in describing Archimedes' claim. This is because *Method* proposition 14 relies not on a fixed, but on a varied proportion.

Let us make this a bit more precise, with the aid of Archimedes' tool, *Conoids and Spheroids* I. For the application of *Conoids and Spheroids* I, we require – putting aside the issue of cardinality – that:

1. The two sets of antecedents, As and Cs, be isomorphic under ratio (for any couple of As A_i, A_j, there's a couple of Cs C_i, C_j, such that $A_i:A_j::C_i:C_j$), and that
2. The two sets of consequents B and D are constructed by a similar isomorphism (if we have $A_i:B_i$ in a given ratio, we also have $C_i:D_i$ in the same ratio).

As noted above, the antecedents' isomorphism is trivial in *Method* proposition 14: these are the triangles in the prism, and the lines in the rectangle, all equal to each other. However, the second condition is difficult: in fact, in a given quadrant of the base circle of the cylinder, we have the same ratio exactly once. The closer the parabola comes to the middle of the rectangle, the closer the ratio of prismatic triangle to cylindrical triangle comes to 1, and so does the ratio of the rectangle line to the parabola line; the closer the parabola comes to the side of the rectangle, the closer the ratio of the prismatic triangle to cylindrical comes to infinity, and so does the ratio of the rectangle line to the parabola line. Archimedes sums up not merely infinitely many ratios, but infinitely many *different* ratios. The converse holds for Liu Hui's summation of proportions. Here, the antecedents are structured in a more interesting way (it is in fact true that the squares in the bicylinder, as well as the circles in the sphere, are each, as a set, internally unequal, and yet isomorphic under ratio). But it is the ratio of the antecedents to the consequents that is trivially isomorphic: all of them are the *same* ratio. As such, it becomes extravagant to consider here anything as sophisticated as *Conoids and Spheroids* I. The summation here is best seen, instead, within a Greek context, as the extension of a much more basic result, *Elements* 5.12:

If any number of magnitudes are proportional, it will be the case that as one of the antecedents is to one of the consequents so are all the antecedents to all the consequents.

(This of course is proved by Euclid only for the finite case: but the same is true for Archimedes' proof of *Conoids and Spheroids* I as well.)

We find that Archimedes' summation of proportions invokes a problem that Liu Hui never did encounter. Nor did Zu Gengzhi, whose specific geometrical contribution involved not the summation of ratios between areas into the ratio between solids but instead the direct summation of equal areas into equal solids. The study of the curved pyramid-like object does not involve proportions at all and once again the infinitary move – that if all slices are equal pair-wise, so are all taken together – is almost an obvious extension of Euclid's common notions ('if equals are added to equals ...'). Zu Gengzhi makes explicit a Cavalieri-like principle – for a technique that would appear, in the context of Archimedes' *Method*, to be almost trivially evident. In fact it is not the Chinese mathematician's quest for sophistication that drives Zu Gengzhi to make this Cavalieri-like principle explicit; it is the Chinese mathematician's quest for explicit methods.

So much for the proportions. Now, to the objects studied.

Start with Liu Hui. His first observation was that the *Nine Chapters* was wrong in apparently considering the sphere as the outcome of the cylinder, applied twice:

$$\sim(\text{cylinder}^2 \rightarrow \text{sphere})$$

Instead, the sphere can be found through the bicylinder:

$$\text{bicylinder} \rightarrow \text{sphere}$$

Liu Hui himself merely explicated the bicylinder via the curved pyramid or the quasi-pyramid, but certainly his explication clarifies the following structure:

$$\text{quasi-pyramid} \rightarrow \text{bicylinder} \rightarrow \text{sphere}$$

This entire structure was seen by Liu Hui as progress, of sorts – he did find this worthy of being written down, above all because it did show as wrong, in a sense, one of the *Nine Chapters* methods – but he was ultimately frustrated, as we recall, at this stage.

It remained for Zu Gengzhi to show the following derivation

$$\text{pyramid} \rightarrow \text{quasi-pyramid}$$

Which finally completed a satisfying structure:

$$\text{pyramid} \rightarrow \text{quasi-pyramid} \rightarrow \text{bicylinder} \rightarrow \text{sphere}$$

This then is the structure of the Liu Hui / Zu Gengzhi derivation.

Let us now compare this to Archimedes. We are somewhat in the dark, as we have to fill in the details for proposition 16. It is clear that in the main comparable line of derivation Archimedes finds the slanted cylindrical cut via the parabolic segment (propositions 14–15). Now, there are two main options for proposition 16. It could have gone the (reverse) Liu Hui route, from sphere to bicylinder; or it could have derived the bicylinder from the slanted cylindrical cut by way of geometrical decomposition. For the various reasons suggested above, I tend to follow Saito and Napolitani and consider this last option as the more likely, so that overall we have:

parabola → slanted cylindrical cut → bicylinder

This is the structure of the Archimedes derivation.

The two derivations, the Chinese and the Greek, share the bicylinder (which is why we compare them in the first place). Otherwise, they differ significantly.

To begin with, in the Chinese case, the bicylinder is a stepping stone and never was anything else. For Liu Hui, its function is negative, to show the falsity of relating the sphere directly to the cylinder, twiced; he considers his own approach ultimately to be frustrating, inasmuch as it failed to eliminate the bicylinder. In Archimedes, to the contrary, the bicylinder is the goal, proudly announced in the introduction to the *Method* and in some sense forming (together with slanted cylindrical cut) the very excuse for presenting the more meta-mathematical discussion. The method is subordinate to the two new objects, and not vice versa.

We have noted that the Chinese discussion is for the sake of the sphere; we should also note that it is from the pyramid. The significant structure, for Zu Gengzhi, is simply

pyramid → sphere

The stepping-stones along the way are curious and provide for the mathematician's ingenuity, but the achievement consists in reducing the sphere to the pyramid: a remarkable feat indeed.

Archimedes' route ends elsewhere but it also begins elsewhere. His fundamental structure is simply:

parabola →

That is, at some level what he shows us are the things one can do with the aid of the parabola.

Here then is a clear contrast in the fine grain of the mathematical contents. Liu Hui produced a measurement of the pyramid that became paradigmatic. Extensions of Liu Hui naturally took off from that pyramid. Archimedes was heir, instead, to a tradition where conic sections were paradigmatic. *And this explains the contrast with the ratios themselves.* The very complicated structure of ratios we find, summed up in proposition 14, is ultimately due to the structure of the parabola which is significant in Greek geometry precisely as the site for many distinct, and yet correlated, ratios, and as the tool making it possible to treat such systems of multiple ratios.

Now this in and of itself is quite a substantial contrast that sufficiently accounts for our sense of Archimedes' superior sophistication: it is all down to the use of conic sections.

It is all well and fine to describe cuisines in the structural terms such as those of the raw and the cooked, but sometimes important differences are due, simply, to ingredients. There's just so much more you can begin to do with the tomato thrown into your pot, and it would be absurd to account for the historical trajectory of Italian cooking, say, over the last half-millennium, without prominent mention of the possibilities opened up with New World ingredients. Now, historically, tomatoes were specific to the New World. And similarly, historically, conic sections were specific to Greece. The Greek mathematical cuisine, as it were, differs from its Chinese counterpart, not only – perhaps not primarily – in broad structural terms, but simply in this fine-grained level of ingredients.

The irruption of conic sections into Greek mathematics is indeed perhaps, to some extent, a contingent matter, thus no more in need of further historical explanation than the American origin of tomatoes. It is possible however, finally, to step back from the contingent into the structural and to consider the context, at least, within which conic sections became paradigmatic in Greek mathematics.

What are conic sections good for? As I have mentioned above, they provide a site across which multiple ratios are correlated. It is a reasonable hypothesis (proposed by Knorr 1982) that they were first proposed as the curves of constructions, previously considered in terms of a point-wise approximation, that satisfy, specifically, the correlation of three separate ratios so that, ultimately, one produces four lines in continuous proportion (A:B::B:C::C:D) which is equivalent to 'doubling the cube'. However, it is clear that the study of conic sections acquired, perhaps very early on, its own agenda, independent of that of the study of four lines in proportion. We may recall the manner in which the bicylinder, for Chinese mathematicians, was no more than a stepping stone leading from pyramid to sphere.

We could envisage an alternative history for Greek mathematics, where the parabola – or perhaps also the hyperbola – were no more than stepping stones leading from the cone to the duplication of the cube. As a matter of fact, already Euclid, in the end of the fourth century BCE, wrote *Elements of Conics* and it appears that conic sections became at this stage an object of study in their own right. Clearly they present themselves as such in Archimedes' time when, in fact, the greater bulk of his geometry is dedicated to the study of conic sections: in *Quadrature of the Parabola, Conoids and Spheroids*, the *Method* itself, as well as the second (and more important) books of both *Planes in Equilibrium* and *Floating Bodies*.

The structural observation then is very simple. The category of the 'mathematical object of study' is somewhat more fluid in Greece, so that one may sometimes take what originated as a tool, for the sake of mathematical study, and turn it into an object of mathematical study in its own right. Thus, the conic sections, starting as devices for four lines in proportion (but perhaps also: the very problem of finding four lines in proportion, emerging first as a device for the scaling of solids?). The outcome of this process is that one zeroes in on new objects of study, namely those that provide for richer mathematical possibilities. But even at a more basic level, one ends up with a wider repertoire: not just grain, but also tomatoes.

Chinese mathematics is very clearly the mathematics of grain. It is the mathematics of the staple objects, the prism and the sphere, the cone and the pyramid; not the new-fangled conic sections. But more than this: it is the mathematics of grain, in that it is tied down to such terms that have been given by the bureaucratic needs of the state. By this I do not mean simply that the terms of the *Nine Chapters* often suggest the needs of the state (so, for instance, the area measurements of chapter 4 that form the immediate background to the study of the sphere explicitly discuss fields; the preceding chapter 3 is indeed about grain distribution!) but, more fundamentally, that the tradition of canon-and-commentary writing was associated, in China, with the practices of the imperial court.[25] Perhaps early on, such problems were set out explicitly for the sake of examinations, from which follows immediately the emphasis on the study of procedures ('how to solve it!').[26] At any rate, the very text of the *Nine Chapters*,

---

[25] It should be pointed out that while Liu Hui's biography is practically unknown, we do know that Zu Gengzhi was an important official (for an entry point on the complex biography of this mathematician, heir to a mathematical/courtier family, see Martzloff 1997: 80). Both he and Li Chunfeng after him (our main source for Zu Gengzhi's mathematics, for whom see Martzloff 1997: 123) were responsible for reforms in the state calendar.

[26] For Chinese mathematics as a device of state examination, see Volkov 2012.

together with its tradition of commentary, was established as a court practice that valorised it not merely as a starting point but as a canon associated with the imperial Chinese ideals of stability and ancient authority.[27]

Whether as a reference point for court examinations, or as a focal point for imperial ideology, the power of the *Nine Chapters*, the power of court life, was overwhelming. It is thus natural that the terms of reference for Chinese mathematics remained more closely tied to the original, largely pre-theoretical, 'intuitive' shapes such as the sphere. It is also natural that Chinese mathematics remained written largely in the wider language of the canon-and-commentary as a whole, nodding at the elite forms of verse, but never becoming their own distinct genre. Conversely, Greek mathematics became early on a distinct genre, and it developed into a study of largely obscure, unintuitive objects, where mathematicians could pride themselves precisely in the discovery of the new and recherché. In all of this we see a consequence of the relative autonomy of Greek mathematics as a social practice, an observation that is especially valid for the mathematicians of the Hellenistic world, largely self-sufficient within their small networks of communicating elite mathematicians: answering to contemporary court society, if at all, through its special literary idiom of irony and surprise.[28]

Lloyd's insistence on the importance of the comparative study of Greece and China is, of course, the starting point of this study. Above all, he has insisted that we should not limit ourselves to the obvious – and dubious – contrast between 'polemic' Greeks and 'eirenic' Chinese. What about all those Chinese who were, in fact, quarrelsome, all those Greeks who were, in fact, peaceful? At the same time, he taught us not to lose sight of the significance of such broad contrasts – and in particular he led the way, in Lloyd 1990, to a description of the rise of Greek logical practices, in philosophy as well as in mathematics, as the end of a complex process emerging from the Greek emphasis upon persuasion and debate. A specific set of circumstances starts at the polis – and ends with Aristotle and Euclid.

My goal in this chapter has been to elaborate this detailed picture, adding in our more recent insights due to the work of Chemla. The Greeks had no monopoly on proof. True enough, we cannot understand the Greek mathematical genre, with its strong emphasis on making the argument explicit, without due attention to the role of argument in Greek

---

[27] So, Chemla 2013: the text emerges as an act of court canonisation, understood to derive from a lost, imperial antiquity.

[28] For a description of Hellenistic mathematics in the terms of the Alexandrian aesthetic, see Netz 2009.

culture as a whole. But it is the comparative context that brings out clearly just how remarkable it is that the Greeks even develop such a specialised genre of mathematics, and this is best understood not in terms of democracy as such, but rather in terms of autonomy. Even as Greek civilisation became monarchic, it never quite became imperial: court practices with their ideology of stability and unity never quite dislodged the older assumptions of the polis. This greater autonomy of Greek mathematics may account, finally, in no small part, for its achievement.

Bibliography

Andersen, K. (1985) 'Cavalieri's method of indivisibles', *Archive for History of Exact Sciences* 31: 291–367.

Caroli, M. (2007) *Il titolo iniziale nel rotolo librario greco-egizio. Con un catalogo delle testimonianze iconografiche greche e di area vesuviana*. Bari.

Chemla, K. (2005) 'The interplay between proof and algorithm in 3rd century China: the operation as prescription of computation and the operation as argument', in *Visualization, Explanation and Reasoning Styles in Mathematics*, eds. P. Mancosu, K. F. Jørgensen and S. A. Pedersen. Dordrecht: 123–45.

  (2013) 'Ancient writings, modern conceptions of authorship. Reflections on some historical processes that shaped the oldest extant mathematical sources from ancient China', in *Writing Science: Medical and Mathematical Authorship in Ancient Greece*, ed. M. Asper. Berlin: 63–82.

Christie's. (1998) *The Archimedes Palimpsest*. New York.

Clagett, M. (1976) *Archimedes in the Middle Ages*, vol. II: *The Translations from the Greek by William of Moerbeke*. Philadelphia.

Cullen, C. (2002) 'Learning from Liu Hui? A different way to do mathematics', *Notices of the AMS* 49: 783–91.

Dauben, J. W. (2007) 'Chinese mathematics', in *The Mathematics of Egypt, Mesopotamia, China, India and Islam: A Sourcebook*, ed. V. J. Katz. Princeton: 187–384.

Dijksterhuis, E. J. (1987) *Archimedes*. Princeton.

Fu, D. 1991. 'Why did Liu Hui fail to derive the volume of a sphere?', *Historia Mathematica* 18: 212–38.

Hayashi, E. and Saito, K. (2009) *Tenbin no Majutsushi: Arukimedesu no Sugaku (Sorcerer of the Scales: Archimedes' Mathematics)*. Tokyo.

He, J.-H. (2004) 'Zu-Geng's axiom vs Cavalieri's theory', *Applied Mathematics and Computation* 152: 9–15.

Heath, T. L. (1897) *The Works of Archimedes*. London.

  (1912) *The Method of Archimedes Recently Discovered by Heiberg*. Cambridge.

Heiberg, J. L. (1907) 'Eine neue Archimedeshandschrift', *Hermes* 42: 235–303.
  (1910–15) *Archimedes, Opera Omnia*. Leipzig.
Horng, W.-S. (1995) 'How did Liu Hui perceive the concept of infinity: a revisit', *Historia Scientiarum* 4: 207–22.
Knorr, W. R. (1982) 'Observations on the early history of the Conics', *Centaurus* 26: 1–24.
  (1996) 'The method of indivisibles in ancient geometry', in *Vita Mathematica: Historical Research and Integration with Teaching*, ed. R. Calinger. Washington, DC: 67–86.
Lloyd, G. E. R. (1990) *Demystifying Mentalities*. Cambridge.
Martzloff, J. C. (1997) *A History of Chinese Mathematics* (orig. *Histoire des mathématiques chinoises*, Paris 1987). Berlin.
Netz, R. (2004) *The Works of Archimedes*, vol. I: *The Two Books on the Sphere and the Cylinder*. Cambridge.
  (2009) *Ludic Proof: Greek Mathematics and the Alexandrian Aesthetics*. Cambridge.
  (2017) *The Works of Archimedes*, vol. II: *On Spirals*. Cambridge.
Netz, R., Acerbi, F. and Wilson, N. (2004) 'Towards a reconstruction of Archimedes' Stomachion', *SCIAMVS* 5: 67–99.
Netz, R., Noel, W., Tchernetska, N. and Wilson, N. (2011) *The Archimedes Palimpsest*. Cambridge.
Netz, R., Saito, K. and Tchernetska, N. (2001–2) 'A new reading of *Method* proposition 14: preliminary evidence from the Archimedes Palimpsest', *SCIAMVS* 2: 9–29; 3: 109–29.
Qian Baocong 錢寶琮 (ed.) (1963) *Suanjing Shishu* 算經十書. Beijing.
Rufini, E. (1926) *Il 'Metodo' di Archimede e le origini del calcolo infinitesimale nell' Antichità*. Bologna.
Saito, K. and Napolitani, P. D. (2014) 'Reading the lost folia of the Archimedean Palimpsest: the last proposition of the *Method*', in *From Alexandria, through Baghdad: Surveys and Studies in the Ancient Greek and Medieval Islamic Mathematical Sciences, in Honor of J.L. Berggren*, eds. N. Sidoli and G. van Brummelen. Berlin: 199–225.
Sato, T. (1986) 'A reconstruction of "The Method" 17, and the development of Archimedes' thought on quadrature – why did Archimedes not notice the internal connection in the problems dealt with in many of his works?', *Historia Scientiarum* 31: 61–86.
  (1987) 'A reconstruction of "The Method" 17, and the development of Archimedes' thought on quadrature – why did Archimedes not notice the internal connection in the problems dealt with in many of his works?', *Historia Scientiarum* 32: 75–142.
Seffrin-Weis, H. (2010) *Pappus of Alexandria: Book IV of the Collection*. Berlin.
Vardi, I. (1999) 'What is ancient mathematics?', *The Mathematical Intelligencer* 2: 38–47.

Volkov, A. (2012) 'Argumentation for state examinations: demonstration in traditional Chinese and Vietnamese mathematics', in *The History of Mathematical Proof in Ancient Traditions*, ed. K. Chemla. Cambridge: 509–51.

Wagner, D. B. (1978) 'Liu Hui and Tsu Keng-chih on the volume of a sphere', *Chinese Science* 3: 59–79.

(1979) 'An early Chinese derivation of the volume of a pyramid: Liu Hui, third century AD', *Historia Mathematica* 6: 164–88.

Williams, B. J. and Harvey, H. R. (1997) *The Codice de Santa María Asunción: Facsimile and Commentary: Households and Lands in Sixteenth-Century Tepetlaoztoc*. Salt Lake City.

11 | Abstraction as a Value in the Historiography of Mathematics in Ancient Greece and China: A Historical Approach to Comparative History of Mathematics

KARINE CHEMLA

Introduction

Since at least the nineteenth century, comparing has been a major component in the historical studies of sciences in ancient China – in particular mathematics – that developed in Europe. Comparing in this context systematically meant comparing between 'peoples', sometimes focusing on 'their' scientific or technical achievements, sometimes on 'their' styles of scientific practice.[1] Given the scope of the comparison, it happened frequently that observations based on a few ancient books were mixed up with observations carried out by missionaries (notably Jesuits), or other travellers, who had had the opportunity to work with Chinese scholars. Consequently, the views expressed were perceived to hold for the past as much as for the present, some scholars asserting there existed features allowing them to contrast peoples in general.

In these comparisons, abstraction has been a recurring theme. My starting point for this chapter is the remark that in fact, in the nineteenth century, we find distinct views about the use of abstraction in ancient China (and also in China at the time). I will first focus on British missionary Alexander Wylie (1815–87), whose views on that matter are uncommon, but not easy to interpret. They stand in contrast – and in opposition – to views offered by some of his predecessors or contemporaries, for whom clearly Chinese writings and contemporary practices manifested no interest in abstraction. These first remarks lead me to emphasise, next, that, in the same context, the understanding of abstraction, its meaning and its import, was by no means uniform in Europe at the time. This is what, I argue, emerges from Michel Chasles' historiography of geometry. This first part thus establishes how nineteenth-century observers offered diverging evaluations of abstraction in the past and diverging historiographies.

---

[1] By contrast, Lloyd 1997, among other writings, offers refreshing insights into the variety of approaches to which Greek writings testify.

Another factor appears to account for the differences between their views, and I begin my second part with it. Indeed, nineteenth-century observers testify to different ways of reading ancient texts. In this respect, Wylie's mode of approach is specific and calls for interpretation. To interpret his assertions about how ancient Chinese texts expounded mathematical knowledge, and also to examine abstraction as an actors' category, I then turn to the earliest extant evidence, in which Chinese authors explicitly comment on abstraction in mathematical practice.

Direct evidence, I argue, can be found not in canons, but rather in commentaries. The same would hold true, incidentally, if we formed the project of discussing the conception of abstraction in Euclid's *Elements*. Analysing the pieces of evidence available in ancient China suggests an interpretation that shows an unexpected understanding of abstraction, its expression and its function in mathematical practice. This interpretation corresponds to a textual organisation in some canons. If we assume that the understanding and practice of abstraction, at the time when canons were composed, can be grasped from this textual phenomenon, a comparison with the structure of Euclid's *Elements* yields interesting contrasts. I outline this comparison in the conclusion. On the basis of the analysis of Chinese views of abstraction developed in my second part, I also return in the conclusion to nineteenth-century actors' and observers' views of abstraction and how they relate to ancient conceptions.

Abstraction as a Value in Nineteenth-Century Science and its Historiography

Protestant missionary Alexander Wylie (1815–87) arrived in China in 1847, shortly after the first opium war.[2] Several months earlier in London, he had made the acquaintance of missionary James Legge (1815–97), who was looking for someone to take charge of the printing activities of the London Missionary Society based in Shanghai.[3] Wylie, who had already learnt some Chinese by himself, quickly acquired the necessary skills, and the Society hired him.

---

[2] On his life and scientific publications in China, see Cordier 1897; Edkins 1897, Thomas 1897; Han 1998; Xu 2005, on which I rely for the following paragraphs. Han 1998 contains the most extensive view on Wylie's activities in general.

[3] Thomas 1897. With his biography of Legge, Girardot 2002 follows a 'paradigmatic' figure, in a group of scholars which included Wylie, and on which a 'British era of sinological Orientalism during the last part of the nineteenth century' 'depended primarily' (resp. 7, 8).

Five years later, in 1852, the same Society engaged the Chinese scholar Li Shanlan 李善蘭 (1810–82) to come to Shanghai and cooperate with British missionaries, including Wylie, on the Chinese translation of scientific books from the West.[4] Li Shanlan was born into a scholarly family and showed a keen interest in mathematics from an early age. It seems that he sought for, and read, any book on the topic that he could get hold of. Having failed to pass the examinations that could have led him to an official career, he began earning his living as a tutor while continuing his study of mathematics by himself and exchanging with several scholars who shared his passion. The outcome of the opium war reinforced his conviction that the cultivation of mathematics in China was of the utmost importance in developing science and technology.[5] When the London Missionary Society hired him, Li Shanlan had already published several books on the topic. They presented in particular the results of his inquiries into ancient Chinese mathematical books, at a time when important works of the Song and Yuan dynasties, especially from the thirteenth and fourteenth centuries, had just been rediscovered or made more widely available. For instance, in one of his books, titled *Explanations on the Four Unknowns* (*Si yuan jie* 四元解) and published in 1845, Li Shanlan had offered his own reconstruction of the reasonings carried out by Zhu Shijie in his 1303 *Jade Mirror of the Four Unknowns* (*Si yuan yu jian* 四元玉鑒).[6] The latter book, together with the exceptional knowledge of polynomial algebra it contained, had been lost in China since the time of its publication. However, a manuscript of *Jade Mirror of the Four Unknowns* had been rediscovered at the beginning of the nineteenth century, and after years of research in 1834 Luo Shilin 羅士琳 (1783–1853) had been able to publish the text with copious explanations of his own, which suggested interpretations and reconstructions of the missing derivations.[7] In fact, around 1835, Li Shanlan also obtained a copy of the manuscript of Zhu Shijie's *Jade Mirror*, and his 1845 book provided his own independent reconstructions of the reasonings leading to the procedures Zhu Shijie gave after specific mathematical problems (Horng 1991: 65, 115). In the same book Li

---

[4] On Li Shanlan's biography, see Fang 1943; Wang 1990; Horng 1991. The latter publication deals at length with Li's early years and background, especially 58–75.

[5] Wang 1990: 336–7.

[6] On this book, whose title should be literally translated as 'Jade Mirror of the Four Origins', see Hoe 1977, 2007.

[7] Hoe 1977: 19–20. More generally, in his introduction Hoe sketches a history of the knowledge about the book in the East and in the West. On Luo Shilin's biography, see Fang 1943b. Hoe 1977: 6–32 surveys nineteenth- and twentieth-century views on mathematics in ancient China, which complements the present chapter.

Shanlan also offered reconstructions of reasonings for another important Chinese mathematical book of the thirteenth century: Qin Jiushao 秦九韶's *Mathematical Treatise in Nine Sections* (*Shushu jiuzhang* 數書九章), completed in 1247. Likewise, after centuries when the latter book had been hardly available, in 1842 Song Jingchang 宋景昌 published an edition on which Li Shanlan could rely.[8] Qin Jiushao's *Mathematical Treatise in Nine Sections* stated complex algebraic equations to solve some specific mathematical problems, and Li Shanlan suggested how one of these equations had been established. Qin Jiushao's book also offered evidence about how Song-Yuan scholars were determining roots for higher-degree algebraic equations.

Such was the context in which in 1852, at the London Missionary Society, Li Shanlan and Wylie undertook to translate together the nine last books of Euclid's *Elements*, which Matteo Ricci and Xu Guangqi had left untranslated in the first Chinese edition published in 1607. Li and Wylie completed the task within the next four years, with the translation being published in 1857,[9] and they went on with translations of more recent English books. In my view, this context was decisive in shaping Wylie's view on the practice of abstraction in China.

Wylie's View on the Existence of Abstract Science in China

Importantly for our purpose, Wylie had also studied with Li Shanlan's help ancient Chinese books about mathematics, and especially the most recently republished texts documenting Song-Yuan algebra.[10] This is reflected in *Jottings on the Science of the Chinese. Arithmetic* (hereafter abbreviated to *Jottings*), which Wylie published in 1852, only five years after his arrival in China, and which soon became in Europe a key source of information on the history of mathematics in China.[11] Arguably, in China Wylie could read

---

[8] Zhu Yiwen and Zheng Cheng forthcoming analyse the main features of this edition and their impact on the historiography of mathematics.

[9] Han 1998: 61 quotes Li Shanlan's own testimony on the process.   [10] Edkins 1897: 1.

[11] Wylie [1852] 1882 was reprinted as Wylie 1897b, part III: 'Scientific': 159–94. References in this chapter are made to this latter edition. Biernatzki 1856, published shortly thereafter in German, was based on it (see the first footnote of the article), whereas Bertrand 1869 was in turn based on Biernatzki's German publication. Olry Terquem (1782–1862) published a French adaptation of Biernatzki 1856 (Biernatzki 1862, 1863). The first part of Terquem's adaptation appeared in the last issue of the *Bulletin de Bibliographie, d'Histoire et de Biographie Mathématiques,* published at the end of a volume of the *Nouvelles Annales de Mathématiques*. Libbrecht 1973, especially 177–8, 280 n. 67, 310–27, accounts for the impact of Wylie's publication on the historiography of mathematics in Europe. He underlines how Biernatzki's numerous mistakes led to a bias in the image formed in Europe about the history of mathematics in China. A complete study of the

ancient books that had been rediscovered only a couple of decades earlier, and *Jottings* made available in Europe information about their content that had been published in Chinese quite recently. But Wylie also went further.

More precisely, in *Jottings* Wylie outlined the contents of *The Nine Chapters on Mathematical Procedures* (*Jiuzhang suanshu* 九章算術, hereafter abbreviated to *The Nine Chapters*), the oldest mathematical canon (from the first century CE) handed down through the written tradition and whose text, after centuries of oblivion, had been made available again in China around half a century earlier.[12] Immediately after its re-edition, Chinese scholars engaged in reading the canon and interpreting it through many publications. This was the first mathematical book Li Shanlan read, and he later drew inspiration from it, using it to teach mathematics in Beijing from 1869 onwards (Horng 1991: 388–94).

Jottings also presented the procedure for solving algebraic equations used in China as early as the thirteenth century and documented by Qin Jiushao's book; moreover, Wylie identified the procedure as comparable to the method that George Horner had published in the British Isles a few decades earlier, in 1819, and that, Wylie emphasised, Augustus de Morgan had praised (Wylie [1852] 1882: 185). Additionally, Wylie identified knowledge about indeterminate analysis in Qin Jiushao's book and presented Zhu Shijie's practice of polynomials with four indeterminates.[13]

Against this backdrop, it is interesting to examine the few lines Wylie writes as an introduction for *Jottings*. The opening section reads as follows:

There are a few discoveries, such as the magnetic needle and the typographic art, which have been of indisputable service in the advancement of civilization, priority with respect to which, is by universal consent ascribed to the Chinese; a certain *superiority* in some of the arts, *many* will *admit* that *these people possess*; some questions in modern science have received a *practical illustration* in the *ordinary habits of the 'Flowery' race*, and some few have been *constrained to admit*, that they have for time out of mind, possessed a *perfect knowledge of facts*, which have been but *recently arrived* at through the *medium of theory* in the west.[14]

---

transformations each of these translations applied to Wylie's text exceeds the scope of this chapter.

[12] Chu 2010.

[13] Libbrecht 1973: 177–80, 310–27. Libbrecht 1973: 294–309 also evokes early Chinese work on the newly rediscovered indeterminate analysis.

[14] Wylie 1852: 159. My emphasis.

Wylie's formulations can be used as a guide for how he perceives discussions about science and technology in China among Europeans at the time.[15] His observations proceed in four steps that display a subtle gradation. Firstly, some discoveries, he notes, are 'ascribed to the Chinese' without any contention. They are only 'a few', and they are technical. This last point echoes his second observation, that is, the suggestion of granting 'a certain superiority' to 'these people', even if the statement is restricted to superiority in 'some of the arts', already does not meet the same consensus ('many will admit', he writes with care). However, when in the third step Wylie turns to 'questions in modern science', his selection of words testifies to the fact he perceives the issue as sensitive for the majority of his potential interlocutors. He chooses to centre the discussion in this context on the 'knowledge of facts'. In this respect, Wylie emphasises, if a 'perfect knowledge of facts' in China 'for time out of mind' can be established, only a minority will acknowledge it, and, he insists, not willingly ('some few have been *constrained to admit*').[16] In effect, *Jottings* establishes several 'priorities' of that type.

Noteworthy is the fact that, in this third step, Wylie's discussion introduces a new dimension. The technical discoveries and knowledge mentioned earlier were presented as a 'service in the advancement of civilization' without further specification. Interestingly here, 'civilization' was in the singular, and 'the Chinese' were mentioned as a collective to which contributions to civilization could be ascribed. By contrast, when it comes to the knowledge of a given scientific fact, Wylie draws attention to an opposition between *distinct ways* of arriving at this piece of knowledge in China and in the West. Knowledge might have been acquired more recently in the West, he notes. However, it was derived from 'theory'. In the 'habits of the "Flowery" race' (that is, the Chinese), he concedes, the questions were pursued through 'practical illustration'. Now, the Chinese form a race characterised by its way of pursuing knowledge.

Behind the expression 'practical illustration' it is easy to recognise an allusion to the mathematical problems, in the context of which the pieces of knowledge Wylie presents in *Jottings* are dealt with, whether one speaks of *The Nine Chapters, Mathematical Treatise in Nine Sections, Jade Mirror of the Four Unknowns* or other mathematical texts. Wylie thus refers to these problems as 'practical'. Before Wylie published his *Jottings*, this feature of scholarly writings in Chinese had already been

---

[15] *Jottings* occasionally mentions the views that Wylie contradicts (see, e.g., Wylie [1852] 1882: 169).

[16] Han 1998: 63 emphasises the same conclusion on the basis of other passages of Wylie's text.

emphasised more than once – and it is still today often repeated – as evidence for the lack of ability on the part of 'the Chinese' for theory or abstraction. We return to this point below. Interestingly enough, it is precisely on the issue of abstraction that Wylie goes on in the next few lines, in which we read the fourth step of his careful gradation. However, perhaps because he is in conversation with Chinese scholars, or because he has read the newly discovered texts of the Song-Yuan time periods,[17] his conclusion is more nuanced than those drawn by many contemporaries. Indeed, moving one step forward, he suggests:

Beyond this few are disposed to accede to the pretensions of this people, and the suggestion of any degree of eminence in abstract science is by many thought to be unworthy of a moment's consideration. It is possible, however, that a little investigation might establish juster views.[18]

The statement is rich and again shows a careful choice in words. We will comment on it from two different perspectives.

Wylie's Contemporaries' Views about Abstraction in China

Here again, Wylie's formulations appear to echo his own experience of widespread views precisely about 'abstract science' in China, whether he read these judgements in publications or heard them in conversations in which he took part. Indeed, the judgements to which he testifies accord with statements on this issue we encounter in writings published in roughly the same years in Europe. Between 1835 and 1850, for instance, the French sinologist Edouard Biot (1803–50) had extensively published on China, including numerous articles on various facets of the history of science. In fact, before Wylie, he had been the first sinologist in Europe to venture specifically into the history of mathematics in China on the basis of a study of primary sources available to him in Paris – that is, a set of sources much more restricted than what Wylie had access to in Shanghai. If we survey his publications, we find they abound in judgements of the kind Wylie exposes, and they make use of the same terms, though differently.

For Edouard Biot, the Chinese form 'a people utterly *foreign* to any *theoretical* idea'.[19] This is the same opposition we have encountered above, between peoples using, and those not using, theory. Biot's study of a

---

[17] Edkins 1897 put forward the hypothesis that this fact made a difference to the research carried out by the Biots father and son (see below).
[18] Wylie [1852] 1882: 159. My emphasis.
[19] Biot 1839b: 207. On Edouard Biot, see Chemla 2014.

Chinese mathematical book completed in 1592 was published in the same year of 1839,[20] and it contained similar conclusions. There Biot asserts about that book: 'The *Souan-fa-tong-tsong* is a collection of *practical rules of calculation*.' For him, a translation would be of no use since 'it would only present a sequence of applications of rules for the most part elementary'. From this study, Biot draws general conclusions:

In fact, to believe that the Chinese *ever possessed* any real *theory* of the exact sciences, one would have to contradict the repeated assertions of Parennin, Gaubil, Verbiest, and of so many distinguished men who succeeded each other in the 18th century in the China missions ... The Chinese people are *completely practical* and focused on what is *material*.[21]

These judgements echo those against which Wylie argues in the quotation analysed above, and the words employed are similar (most prominently 'practical', but also 'application' instead of 'illustration'). Biot combines the study of an ancient book with recent observations made by European missionaries in China, to draw conclusions about 'the Chinese' as 'a people' and how it deals with knowledge. In Biot's view, their approach to knowledge, characterised by its emphasis on both the practical and the applications of rules, is term by term contrasted to an approach that proceeds through theory and adopts a higher, in fact abstract, viewpoint.

Edouard's father, the scientist Jean-Baptiste Biot (1774–1862), had worked in close connection with his son on these issues and more generally on the history of ancient astronomy. In a review of Sédillot's *Traité des instruments astronomiques des Arabes* Jean-Baptiste published shortly after, in 1841, he derived from the same comparative perspective a more general conclusion, which led him to associate the terms of the contrast with different peoples and assert a hierarchy between these peoples, as follows:

One finds [in this book] renewed evidence for this peculiar *habit of mind*, following which the Arabs, as the Chinese and Hindus, *limited* their scientific writings to the statement of a series of *rules*, which, once given, ought only to be *verified* by their *applications, without* requiring any logical *demonstration* or connections between them: this gives those Oriental nations a remarkable character of *dissimilarity*, I would even add of *intellectual inferiority, comparatively to the Greeks*, with whom

---

[20] Incidentally, that book, *Unifying Basis for Mathematical Methods* 算法統宗, had been one of the first Chinese mathematical writings to which a 1712 edict by Emperor Kangxi (1654–1722) had called attention, when he decided to manifest some interest in the history of mathematics in Chinese (Han 2014: 1224). The emperor's emphasis elicited further interest among scholars, which eventually resulted in the recovery of ancient texts at the end of the eighteenth and the beginning of the nineteenth century.

[21] Biot 1839a: 193, 197, 200, respectively. My emphasis.

any proposition is established by reasoning, and generates logically deduced consequences. This *fixed* writing of scientific methods, in the form of *prescriptions*, must have represented an important *hindrance* for the development of new ideas for peoples for which it was in use, and it is in sharp *contrast* with our *European* motto: *nullius in verba* [*on the word of no one*].[22]

The focal point of Biot's statement lies in drawing a general comparison between the types of intellectual practice of various 'peoples'. To this end, the scientific writings they produced appear to him to yield an adequate approach to these peoples' general mindsets. Here 'contributions' are not as important as ways of approaching knowledge, which constitute the key point of the comparison. One term of the comparison lumps together the 'Oriental nations'. From the choice of presenting scientific knowledge in the form of procedures, which characterises mathematical texts in Chinese, Sanskrit or Arabic, Jean-Baptiste Biot derives the conclusion that *authority* plays a key role in the related practice of knowledge. In other words, Biot views procedures as prescriptions, and peoples using these writings as obeying orders. Moreover, the use of mathematical problems in the same texts apparently suggests to him the idea that instead of 'proving', the authors 'only' checked the rules through their 'applications' – this was precisely the term we saw that Edouard Biot used when referring to mathematical problems. In this context, Jean-Baptiste apparently exposes the lack of generality of the approach, which relates to its use of concrete and unrelated applications. In other words, Jean-Baptiste reads procedures and problems as, respectively, 'prescriptions' and 'applications' – two interpretations still widespread nowadays, and Biot maps onto them a specific attitude towards knowledge and a specific scientific practice. The other term of the comparison brings together the Greeks and modern science – evoked through the motto of the Royal Society. It emphasises proof and freedom of thought, with the rejection of any form of authority. On one side, there is stagnation ('hindrance for the development of new ideas'), whereas on the other, there can be progress. These interpretations led Jean-Baptiste to his conclusion on the dissimilarity of the peoples not only for the present (the superiority of the Europeans), but also for the past (the superiority of the Greeks).

In fact, Wylie was perfectly aware of publications by Edouard and Jean-Baptiste Biot, which he quoted regularly in his writings.[23] Arguably

---

[22] Biot 1841: 674. Except for the Latin quotation, my emphasis. The Latin sentence is the motto of the Royal Society, and can be interpreted as referring to modern science. The first part of this excerpt is quoted in Charette 2012: 274.

[23] Wylie 1897a refers to several French translations of Chinese primary sources by Edouard Biot. Wylie 1867: 102 relies on Jean-Baptiste Biot's publication of *Précis de l'histoire de l'astronomie*

Jean-Baptiste's declaration just quoted fits Wylie's remark that 'the suggestion of any degree of eminence in *abstract* science is by many thought to be unworthy of a moment's consideration' (my emphasis). Further, just as Wylie suggests, the Biots father and son were far from being the only ones holding such views at the time. Commenting in the same years and the same journal (*Journal des Savants*) on the history of chemistry, Eugène Chevreul formulates similar general theses about the Chinese people, past and present. Interestingly, in this quite different context, abstraction still has pride of place, and even more explicitly so. Chevreul's account reads as follows:

> The Chinese people is a nation, remarkable by its Antiquity, its population and the dexterity it has shown in the practice of *useful* arts: what it wanted *formerly*, it still wants it *today*; it is the **application**, it is the **immediate utility of things**. However, neither the chemical arts, nor the mechanical arts, can *achieve the perfection* they have reached in Western Europe, without the study of mathematical, physical and chemical *sciences, cultivated* from the viewpoint of the highest *abstraction* possible, since only this study gives the means of **subduing** the procedures of the arts to the **principles** and **rules** that ensure their execution, and only it presides over the making of any machine and any precision instrument, without which the progress of sciences about the outside world is impossible.
>
> ... The Chinese give the most striking example of what the arts can be in a people for whom the *sciences* have never *guided* or *illuminated* the *practice*, and in whom, moreover, the highest minds show *no tendency* to embrace *abstract* ideas, either in the sciences, or in philosophy.[24]

Comparison between 'peoples' or 'nations' is likewise at the core of Chevreul's article in general, and in this statement in particular. Moreover, abstraction plays a key part in the contrast drawn here. The comparison Chevreul develops between 'technical' knowledge in China and 'Western Europe' aims at accounting for why, despite the ingenuity of the 'Chinese people', 'perfection' in the 'mechanical arts' or in the 'chemical arts' was only achieved in Western Europe. In his view, an exclusive focus, from times immemorial, on 'immediate utility' in the Middle Kingdom has hampered the study of the 'sciences ... from the viewpoint of the highest abstraction possible'. This remark echoes the emphasis we have seen authors placing on the allegedly exclusive focus in China on the practical

---

chinoise (1861), which was based on 1861 publications in the *Journal des Savants*. Wylie 1871 refers to several articles by Jean-Baptiste Biot in the *Journal des Savants*, including 'Recherches sur l'ancienne astronomie chinoise' (1839–40), and, 'Etudes sur l'astronomie indienne' (1859), through its reprint in Biot 1862.

[24] Chevreul 1845: 343–4. When the emphasis is not mine, I add bold characters to it.

in mathematics. The role Chevreul ascribes to abstraction is interesting: abstraction allows the development of a higher kind of knowledge that subordinates the 'procedures of the arts', through highlighting the higher principles that account for their efficiency. Belhoste 2003 has shown how this opposition structured the students' curriculum as well as the institutional system for a school like the Ecole Polytechnique since its establishment in 1794. Interestingly, Chevreul was examiner of chemistry at the school between 1821 and 1851.

Chevreul's argument is completed by a sociological analysis: In China, he argues, the elite was not encouraged to devote its life to such a pursuit, and thus did not value abstraction in any field of knowledge. Consequently, he suggests, the only progress made within the context of each 'art' taken separately was achieved by (specialised) workers practising this art. In the picture Chevreul draws, the advance in abstraction goes hand in hand with the achievement of a generality running across the arts. It is carried out by a social elite and refers to a type of organisation of knowledge, both scientifically and socially.

Chevreul's long discussion on China was repeated *in extenso* a few years later in a mathematical article published in the *Nouvelles Annales de Mathématiques*. The fact illustrates the wider echo Chevreul's analysis of *both* the part abstraction played in science *and* the various attitudes towards it in different social groups, elicited from other scholars in France who were active in mathematics. The context was the French publication of a geometrical proof for a theorem in mechanics, which the editor of the journal, Olry Terquem (1782–1862), a former student in the Ecole Polytechnique, derived from Möbius' *Lehrbuch der Statik* (1837) and published in 1852 under Möbius' name.[25] Terquem took the opportunity of the publication to express general views about the adequate organisation of knowledge, particularly, but not exclusively, with respect to the relationship between statics, dynamics and the study of machines. In his view, as in Chevreul's, abstract knowledge (in the sense used by Chevreul and discussed above) – here, statics and dynamics – had to be taught *together with* knowledge on machines. In formulating this opinion, Terquem explicitly opposed the views of compatriots who, 'owing their living and reputation

---

[25] Möbius (According to) 1852. The attribution to Olry Terquem is made clear in the table of contents of the journal (471 of the same issue). We have seen above that Terquem would publish a few years later a French adaptation of Biernatzki's adaptation of Wylie's *Jottings*. Already in 1816, Terquem had also translated into French documents about Sanskrit mathematics. The description of the impact of the latter translation on Chasles (1863: 242–3) is striking.

to workshops and factories' (284), considered that the study of machines was self-contained. In this case, Terquem associates two opposite attitudes towards abstraction with two different social groups, and he exposes the fallacies of his opponents' views by comparing their antagonism with the contrast Chevreul had developed between diverging attitudes towards knowledge in China and Europe.

In other words, abstraction appears in this context as a key value, whether one considers chemistry or mathematics, and it allows Chevreul, like Terquem, to draw social boundaries, whether they be between distinct peoples or between distinct social groups within France. Abstraction is valued, since it allows practitioners to bring different domains of application into relation to each other through the development of a higher form of knowledge running across them. In the same article, however, Terquem emphasises another facet of Möbius' 1837 book, which points towards another type of abstraction and another historiography. This will eventually bring us back to Wylie's approach to abstraction in China.

Different Views on the Historiography of Abstraction

Terquem's comments on Möbius' book also praised how knowledge was organised in it. Möbius, Terquem emphasised, had derived *all* the propositions of statics from a most simple concept – the couple – and a single *principle* (284). The derivation, logically perfect, thus displayed the fruitfulness of the concept and the principle. Such an ideal for the organisation of knowledge in a domain had been forcefully advocated by Michel Chasles, in particular in his *Aperçu historique sur l'origine et le développement des méthodes en géométrie, particulièrement de celles qui se rapportent à la géométrie moderne*, which Chasles had also published in 1837.[26] Michel Chasles and Terquem knew each other quite well. They had both worked in the new geometry that eventually became projective geometry.[27] Chasles also benefited from Terquem's translations of Sanskrit mathematical texts,

---

[26] Chasles 1837. For the following statements on generality and for the context in which this reflection on generality is developed, see Chemla 2016, which also analyses the historiography of geometry Chasles presents in this book.

[27] Terquem had been one of the correspondents with whom Poncelet had discussed his principle of continuity (Poncelet 1864: 530–52). In the same book, Poncelet (331–2) also alludes to Terquem's publications on Sanskrit mathematics. Terquem is another case of these practitioners of mathematics who were attached to the Ecole Polytechnique and were very interested in the history of ancient mathematics.

which he quotes in his *Aperçu historique* (419). Finally, Chasles prepared a long report on Terquem's 'mathematical works' after the latter's death.[28]

Interestingly for our purpose, the *Aperçu historique* presented a history of geometry from the viewpoint of the value of generality. Through his historical inquiry, Chasles had highlighted a great variety of facets and meanings of generality. One of them was precisely the type of organisation of knowledge Terquem praised in Möbius' *Lehrbuch der Statik*. This practice of generality consisted in identifying a single principle in a domain of knowledge (in Chasles' case, of geometry), whose proof was most simple and from which one could derive the whole domain. Further, the ideal required that derivation of all propositions from the principle could be achieved almost without proof, all propositions becoming 'simple transformations or natural corollaries' of the principle.[29] In Chasles' words,

> To indicate a *means to recognize* . . . whether one has found the true paths of final truth (vraies routes de la vérité définitive), and whether one has *penetrated* up to its *origin*, we believe that we can say that, in each theory, there *must always exist* . . . some *main truth* from which *all* the others are *easily deduced*, as *simple transformations* or *natural corollaries*; and that the fulfillment of this condition will be the only mark of the *genuine perfection* in science.[30]

In this way, Chasles stresses, one brings all propositions in the domain into relation to each other, through showing their direct relation to a single proposition, to which he referred as their 'origin'. The continuity between the promotion of an organisation of knowledge of this type and an emphasis on abstraction such as Chevreul's is manifest. I show below that this conception is the closest we can find to what actors in ancient China refer to as 'abstract'. However, before turning to that point, a few words on Chasles' historiography of abstraction will be useful for my argument in this chapter.

For Chasles, the history of geometry testified to the diversity of meanings generality had taken in this field, and also to the variety of means through which types of generality had been achieved. His *Aperçu historique* provides a historical account of the shaping of these types of generality, some of which, he showed, were essentially attached to the achievement of specific types of abstraction. In fact, as I have done for generality, one could analyse his understanding of various forms of abstraction and the ways in

---

[28] Chasles 1863. Chasles evokes Terquem's activity and their friendship.
[29] Chasles 1837: 114–15 expounds how to practise mathematics to identify such a principle and achieve this ideal in a given scientific domain.
[30] Chasles 1837: 115. My emphasis.

which in his view they had been introduced into geometry. This complete analysis exceeds the scope of this chapter. For the main goal I pursue here, it will suffice to evoke only one of Chasles' main claims in this regard.

Chasles held the view that the fifteenth century marked a watershed in the history of geometry. After having outlined key differences between the approach to geometry before and after the fifteenth century, he concludes:

These considerations, whose upshot is to highlight the difference between the *special* and the *general*, between the *concrete* and the *abstract*, which distinguish between Geometry until the 15th century and later Geometry, lead us to consider this first period as forming the *preliminaries* of science.[31]

To summarise coarsely his point, in the first period, geometry had only addressed 'concrete' questions and 'concrete' figures, whereas, notably from the seventeenth century onwards, geometry had undergone several distinct turns with respect to generality, two of which had 'given to geometry a character of abstraction ... that distinguished it essentially from ancient geometry'.[32] In brief, for Chasles, the figures and questions considered in ancient geometry, that is, in writings by Euclid, Archimedes, Apollonius and Pappus among others, were 'concrete'.[33]

This last remark can be surprising for us, for whom, arguably, Euclid's *Elements* represents a form of abstraction in geometry. It reveals two facts important for us to ponder. First, abstraction has different facets in mathematics, and a historical approach can help us identify several of these facets. Secondly, different actors have accordingly developed different interpretations of abstraction in the past. When additionally, as observers, these actors wrote about the history of mathematics, their views of abstraction conceivably informed how they perceived the conceptions of practitioners from earlier time periods. This is a perspective from which we can interpret the divergence among the views of abstraction mentioned above. In fact, the understanding and practice of abstraction in mathematics underwent key transformations in the nineteenth century. So far, we have no global view on this historical phenomenon. This would, however, provide us with

---

[31] Chasles 1837: 52. Chasles' emphasis.
[32] The first turn, associated with the name of Descartes, is the topic of the statement just quoted (Chasles 1837: 94). The second turn relates to Desargues' and Pascal's approach to geometry, and Chasles makes a similar claim with respect to the achievement of a type of abstraction with respect to it in 1837: 116. For greater detail, see Chemla 2016.
[33] See for instance Chasles 1837: 60, 206. Lloyd 1968: 175–80 makes a comparable observation with respect to Aristotle's dynamics. Chasles' position on abstraction in ancient mathematics is more complex than what I claim here (see, in particular, Chasles 1837: 541–2, 539, 538). I will return to his historical treatment of abstraction elsewhere.

essential information to approach the historical accounts of abstraction in the historiography of mathematics in the nineteenth century. This project also exceeds the scope of this article.

On the basis of these observations, let us return to Wylie's statement. We have touched upon widespread conceptions about the history of science in China, by opposition to which he formulated his judgement. However, when he suggests that 'a *little investigation* might *establish juster* views' on the possible existence of 'abstract science' in China, which idea of abstraction and which type of investigation does he have in view? With respect to the latter question, for sure, he means, at least partly, the investigation whose results he presents in *Jottings*. An item in it is intriguing and deserves some attention. This will be the second perspective from which we will comment on the quotation.

Interpreting Abstraction in the Mathematics of Ancient China in Context

The question of Wylie's view of abstraction in mathematics and its history is all the more interesting in that we know that, soon after having published *Jottings* in 1852, he collaborated with Li Shanlan to translate into Chinese part of Euclid's *Elements* (the translation appeared in 1857) and also Augustus de Morgan's *Elements of Algebra* (1835, the translation appeared in 1859).[34] His views are thus not those of someone who does not know mathematics and its history in Europe. His writings also testify to a broad knowledge of the history of mathematics in India and the Arabic world.[35] His choice of translating de Morgan's book already indicates a mathematical background in which abstraction has taken specific values. A study of Wylie's translations and of the mathematical book he published in Chinese in 1853, *Introduction to Mathematics* (*shuxue qimeng* 數學啟蒙), would allow us to go deeper into this issue.[36] As Han (1998: 601) has already stressed, in Wylie's preface to the latter book, he claimed that the difference between 'Chinese and Western methods' in

---

[34] See, respectively, Xu 2005; Han 1998. Incidentally, *Jottings* several times quotes de Morgan as the highest authority on some mathematical issues (Wylie [1852] 1882: 182–3, 185).

[35] See, for example, Wylie [1852] 1882: 174, 180; 167, 169, respectively.

[36] We can note already that the opposition between the concrete and abstract numbers that Wylie used in *Jottings* (191) is the same as what we find in De Morgan's *Elements of Algebra*. The understanding of abstraction in the context of the so-called 'British algebraic school' and its impact on Wylie await further study.

mathematics was superficial and that 'the principles (*li* 理) were the same'. How could Jean-Baptiste Biot and Wylie come to views diverging to this extent?

Wylie on the Interpretation of Mathematical Books in Chinese

Clarification in this matter will derive from observing how they read ancient texts. I have emphasised above how Biot derived ideas about the nature of science and scientific practice in China from the *form* of Chinese texts. He interpreted texts of algorithms as lists of orders, and problems as applications meant to check *in concreto* the validity of the rules. In fact, a key difference between Wylie and Biot is that Wylie appears to have a different way of reading the sources. He formulates explicitly his awareness that the interpretation of mathematical texts in Chinese cannot be straightforward. As he makes clear in *Jottings*, after he has listed all the books available to document the history of mathematics in China (168):

It is by *no* means an *easy task* to arrive at the *exact meaning* of most of the books here mentioned, for *little assistance* towards their *interpretation* can be gained from the *ordinary* run of *teachers; few general principles* are given, but they are *left* to be *deduced* from a *variety of examples*, and these for the chief part are stated with most *perplexing brevity*, besides being burdened with a number of obsolete terms and antiquated allusions; a separate *rule* is *generally* given for *every problem*, but a *careful analysis* of the various examples will *enable* the student to *gain insight* into the *principles* they *illustrate*.[37]

For Wylie, ancient Chinese mathematical books thus require a specific reading, for which he might have looked for teachers. Accordingly, by contrast to Biot's interpretation, Wylie perceives examples – that is, the mathematical problems – as pointing towards 'general principles'. Moreover, for him, the procedures associated to problems do not constitute an end in themselves – as the thesis of the 'immediate utility' interpreted them – but rather indicate to the reader again, using a specific mode of reading, 'the principles they illustrate'.[38] Wylie thus emphasises a specific way of referring to 'principles'.

Following this argument, Wylie discusses number systems and operations in ancient China, before outlining the main contents of *The Nine*

---

[37] Wylie [1852] 1882: 168. My emphasis.
[38] This seems to be a possible interpretation of Wylie's use of the term 'practical illustration' in the quotation with which we began.

Chapters. Here, once again, he returns to the issue of interpretation with an unexpected declaration about procedures in *The Nine Chapters*. It reads:

> Such is a very superficial outline of this venerable memento of a bygone age. A curious characteristic deserving of notice is the fact that every section and subdivision commences with a stanza of rhyme, embodying in a *general* way the rule in question; the *meaning is not always very apparent* on the surface, but the quaintness of the phraseology is calculated to fix them on the *memory*; and *on a minute inspection* it will be seen that they contain in a concise form the *leading ideas* which they are intended to convey, very accurately expressed.[39]

What does Wylie mean? Could these statements he makes about 'stanzas', placed at the beginning of sections and containing the 'leading ideas', be part of what he means when he claims a 'little investigation' could 'establish juster views' about the cultivation of 'abstract science' in China? To explore these questions, we need to turn to *The Nine Chapters* and observe this phenomenon in its context. Noteworthy is the fact that, as we will now show, Wylie's assertions do echo a phenomenon that is most important in *The Nine Chapters*. Moreover, it is precisely in reference to *this* phenomenon that we find the earliest known reference to abstraction in a mathematical text in Chinese.

To summarise what I have argued so far, I have emphasised how nineteenth- (and twentieth-) century European observers had diverging views on the topic of the history of abstraction in mathematics, depending on their own understanding of that operation. I have also suggested these views were correlated with how they positioned themselves socially in the societies in which they lived. Finally, I have emphasised that different modes of reading sources underlay differences in their historiographies. In these respects, Wylie appeared as a singularity.

I now want to leave the nineteenth century for a while and concentrate on ancient Chinese actors' views on abstraction. Wylie's obscure statement about his perception of the ancient sources singled out *The Nine Chapters* among other documents. Interestingly, it is in this context that we find the earliest extant pieces of evidence for actors' views in this respect. Let us thus turn to their interpretation and what they reveal about ancient Chinese actors' understanding of the expression and value of abstraction in mathematics. We return in conclusion to a confrontation between

---

[39] Wylie [1852] 1882: 174–5. This paragraph has completely disappeared in the French adaptation of Biernatzki's rendering of *Jottings* (Biernatzki 1862, 1863, by Terquem, and Bertrand 1869). The German rendering (Biernatzki 1856: 76–7) emphasises the dimension of memorisation, leaving aside all that refers to the 'leading ideas'.

nineteenth-century observers' views and what we will have gathered of ancient views in China.

Here, a warning is in order. Turning to ancient Chinese actors' categories requires a shift in the mode of argumentation. Indeed, when we deal with ancient history, sources are scarce, and interpreting them demands a minute observation and also a complex argument. The reader might want to skip this and jump to the conclusions, but I cannot state conclusions without displaying the argumentation.

The View on Abstraction in Mathematics Formulated in Commentaries on *The Nine Chapters*

As was explained above, *The Nine Chapters* is the earliest known canon strictly devoted to mathematics that has been handed down in China. The date of its completion is still disputed. I consider that the text of the canon that we read today dates from the first century CE. *The Nine Chapters* is for its most part composed of mathematical problems and procedures solving them. From early on commentaries were composed on this text largely because of its canonical status.

All the extant ancient documents on which the critical editions of *The Nine Chapters* rely contain not only the canon, but two additional layers of commentaries that were handed down with the canon.[40] The oldest extant commentary, completed by Liu Hui in 263, was selected among other commentaries in the context of an editorial project imperially commissioned and placed under the supervision of Li Chunfeng (?602–70). The project aimed at preparing an edition of ten mathematical canons with some relevant ancient commentaries. Under this context, Li Chunfeng and his assistants prepared an edition for *The Nine Chapters* and Liu Hui's commentary. Moreover, they composed a subcommentary on these two earlier writings. The result of this editorial project, the anthology *Ten Canons of Mathematics*, was presented to the throne in 656. Since all extant ancient editions of *The Nine Chapters* contain both Liu Hui's commentary and the subcommentary composed by Li Chunfeng and his assistants, they thus all depend on this seventh-century editorial project.

Commentaries are an essential resource to inquire into topics like abstraction as an actors' category in ancient China. Indeed, exactly like Euclid's *Elements*, writings such as *The Nine Chapters* contain no direct

---

[40] Chemla 2010 outlines the history of the textual transmission of this set of texts. Chemla and Guo 2004 provide a critical edition and a French translation of the canon and its ancient commentaries. All quotations below rely on this publication.

second order remarks on mathematical knowledge or practice. In particular, none of these books states anything revealing their authors' conception or practice of abstraction.[41] In both cases, it is thus *only* from an observer's perspective that we can discuss the views and practices of abstraction to which they testify. We have seen above that different observers had diverging perceptions of the same texts in this respect, whether they deal with Euclid's *Elements* or *The Nine Chapters*.

By contrast to Chinese mathematical canons, commentaries provide proofs of the correctness of procedures contained in the canons, and they regularly formulate reflections on mathematics and its practice. It is in this context that we find pieces of evidence documenting how commentators perceive abstraction in *The Nine Chapters* and the value they attach to it. The key term is *kong* 空, which in my view, in two occurrences at least, must undoubtedly be interpreted as meaning 'abstract'.[42] Noteworthy is the fact that this term, which occurs twice in the same locution 'abstract expressions (*kongyan*)', refers in *both* cases to a type of formulation for procedures by opposition to another type. For instance, commenting on the text of the procedure 'measures in square' (*fangcheng* 方程), which is placed at the beginning of chapter 8 in *The Nine Chapters*, after a problem concerning different types of millet (8.1), the commentary ascribed to Liu Hui states: 'This is a *universal procedure*. It would be difficult to *understand* (the procedure) with *abstract expressions* (*kongyan*), this is why one *deliberately linked* it to (a problem of) millets to eliminate the obstacle' (my emphasis) (此都術也。 以空言難曉， 故特繫之禾以決之。).

Here, the commentator manifests his expectation that the canon may have given an 'abstract' text for the procedure, and he attempts to explain why the authors opted for another formulation. Likewise, the other piece of commentary ascribed to Liu Hui, where the same locution 'abstract expressions' occurs (after problem 8.18), accounts for why the commentator not only gave an abstract formulation for a procedure, but also provided an illustration for it in the framework of an 'example of its use' (施用之例).[43] In effect, the commentator gives there two types of text referring to the same algorithm. In both contexts, the reason the commentary puts forward to explain either that the canon did not give 'abstract expressions' or that he

---

[41] I have nevertheless gathered indirect evidence about practices of abstraction in Chemla 2006. Interestingly, the evidence fits with commentators' remarks on the topic.

[42] Chemla 1997: 95–8 discusses these occurrences and others which are less clear. I will now interpret these expressions slightly differently. More generally, *kong* could also mean 'empty', 'in vain' or 'groundless'.

[43] On the idea that 'the particulars may be richer than the universal abstracted from them', which accounts for this example here, see Lloyd 1997: 144.

gave both a detailed procedure and 'abstract expressions' relates to facilitating 'understanding'.

In the latter case, the commentator refers to a procedure he has himself presented in his commentary. By contrast, the quotation above discusses why in *The Nine Chapters* the authors did not make use of 'abstract expressions'. The commentator manifests his expectation that they could have been used in a specific situation: the procedure given after problem 8.1, he insists, is 'universal'. One could also interpret the expression *dushu* 都術 as designating a procedure presiding over the other procedures, that is, in this case, presiding over all the procedures gathered in the chapter.

The commentary on *The Nine Chapters* ascribed to Liu Hui uses the same expression 'universal procedure *dushu* 都術' in only one other case: that of the procedure *The Nine Chapters* gives to carry out the operation called 'suppose', or, in modern (and weaker) terms, the 'rule of three'. This procedure is likewise placed at the beginning of a chapter, since it is the first procedure in chapter 2. However, in this case, by contrast to the procedure for 'measures in square', its text is given outside the framework of any problem. Moreover, in chapter 2, it is followed by thirty-two problems, each related to a specific procedure for solving it. The key point is that the commentary on each of these procedures shows how its correctness derives from the procedure 'suppose'. In other words, exactly like in the commentary following the problem 8.18, in this chapter 2 texts of procedures are in fact given for each problem, referring to the same operations (simplifications, multiplication and division). One text is common to all problems – it is the procedure for the operation 'suppose' – whereas the other is specific to the problem to which it is attached.

I have argued elsewhere[44] that the commentator uses the term 'abstract expressions' to designate the text of the higher-level procedure, which in this specific *dispositif* is in a relation of abstraction with respect to all the lower-level procedures. By comparison, I have put forward the hypothesis that this is what the commentator would have expected for the first procedure in chapter 8.

Such is, I suggest, the *reference* of the locution 'abstract expressions'. Now, to understand better the *purpose* and the *function* ascribed to abstraction in this context, we need to examine more closely *how* 'abstraction' is actually carried out, and *why* in such cases *The Nine Chapters* gives

---

[44] Chemla submitted. This article also discusses the context from which the locution 'abstract expressions' is borrowed.

```
┌─────────────────┐
│                 │
│  Area    Width  │
│  240 bu  1 bu 1/2│
│                 │
└─────────────────┘
    Length?
```

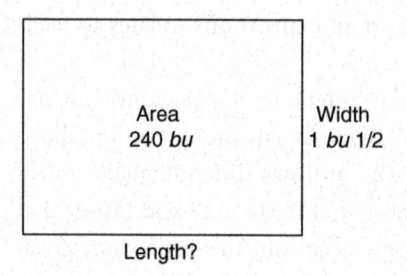

Figure 11.1 The rectangular cropland in the first problem in chapter 4. The question is: what is the length?

two texts for the operations solving each problem. Indeed, I insist that here, the two texts of procedure refer to the same operations. So, why, one wonders, are they both required?

To inquire into these questions, I will focus on a case similar to that of 'suppose' and quite revealing, that of chapter 4 in *The Nine Chapters*, titled 'Reducing the Width'.

The Point of 'Abstract Expressions'

The text of the procedure bearing the same name 'Reducing the Width' is also placed at the beginning of the chapter, outside the framework of any problem, and it is followed by eleven related problems, built on the same model and each associated to a specific procedure.[45] These problems all deal with a rectangular cropland, whose area is 240 *bu* (see Figure 11.1).

The unit *bu* (step) measures lengths and, in ancient China, by extension, it also measured surfaces. As Li Jimin established, a length in *bu* expressed an area by means of a convention: the quantity of area meant is that of a rectangle whose width is 1 *bu* and whose length is precisely this length in *bu*. The area of the cropland for the first problem in chapter 4 can thus be represented as in Figure 11.2.

The length of the rectangle in Figure 11.2 is equal to the product of the length and width of the actual cropland shown in Figure 11.1, which yields the value of 240 *bu*. This might explain why the 240 *bu* is referred to as 'the *bu* of the product' (if one views it from the perspective of the operation yielding the length in Figure 11.2) or 'the *bu* of the area' (from the perspective that it expresses an area).

---

[45] A critical edition, a French translation and explanations of the procedures with a bibliography on this issue are given in Chemla and Guo 2004: 313–22, 342–61. I refer the reader to it for the Chinese text and detailed explanations that I cannot repeat here.

Meaning of the area expressed in units of length (Li Jimin)

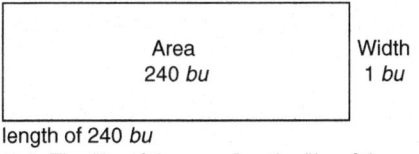

Area 240 bu	Width 1 bu

length of 240 bu
積步 The "*bu* of the area," or the "*bu* of the product" (length of the rectangle times (1+1/2))

Figure 11.2 The representation of a quantity of area of 240 *bu* using measurement units for length.

If the eleven first problems of chapter 4 all deal with a rectangular cropland having the area 240 *bu*, their widths vary. They nevertheless all have the structure of the type:

$$1 + \frac{1}{2} + \frac{1}{3} + \ldots + \frac{1}{n} bu$$

Each problem asks to determine the length. In addition to 1 *bu*, in the first problem, the width only has the first fraction, whereas in the second it has the first two, and so on. Let us illustrate the specific procedure *The Nine Chapters* gives after each problem using the first problem as an example. It corresponds to the following computation:

$$\frac{240 \ bu}{\left(1+\frac{1}{2}\right)bu} = \frac{480 \ bu}{(2+1)bu} \qquad \text{(Eq.1)}$$

The specific procedure reads as follows:[46]

(SINCE) BELOW THERE IS A HALF, THAT IS ONE OF TWO PARTS, ONE TAKES ONE AS TWO, A HALF AS ONE; SUMMING THESE YIELDS THREE, WHICH IS TAKEN AS DIVISOR. ONE PUTS TWO HUNDRED AND FORTY *BU* AND LIKEWISE, TAKING ONE AS TWO, ONE MULTIPLIES IT, WHICH MAKES THE DIVIDEND. DIVIDING THE DIVIDEND BY THE DIVISOR YIELDS THE LENGTH IN *BU*.

With the term 'below', the procedure apparently refers to a layout on the surface on which calculations were executed. In the layout as I suggest restoring it, the area taken as dividend is placed in the middle row, whereas the width, as a divisor, is placed in the lower zone, which is subdivided into sub-rows (see Table 11.1). Under the integral part of the divisor (1),

---

[46] I use capital letters to mark the text of the canon, by contrast to the commentaries, translated in lower-case letters.

Table 11.1 *Initial layout of problem 1*

Components of numbers —>	integer	numerator	denominator
Dividend: the area	240		
Divisor: the integral component	1		
Divisor: a fractional component		1	2

Table 11.2 *The dividend and the divisor transformed (the components of the divisor are shown separately)*

Components of numbers —> (Position for the quotient to come)	integer	numerator	denominator
Dividend: the area	480		
Divisor: the integral component	2		
Divisor: a fractional component	1		

fractions are arranged horizontally, and when there are more than one, in an order of increasing denominators.

The procedure begins with prescribing a change of unit that is determined in relation to the units placed in the lower row. The change entails that values in the lower row all become an integral number of the unit chosen. Here we have below ½ *bu*. ½ is taken as 1, while 1 *bu* becomes accordingly 2. In general, in all the problems, the change of units is carried out using the least common multiple of all the denominators. Once the transformed components in the divisor have been added to make the divisor, the dividend 240 *bu* is transformed to echo the change of unit in the divisor. Taking each of its units as 2 ('likewise', the text says; see Table 11.2), and the division yields the value of the length.

Such are the eleven problems and the specific procedures attached to them. However, as has already been mentioned, another text of procedure referring to the same operations is given before them. Let us follow it sentence by sentence, paraphrasing their meaning and making clear which computations they refer to in the case of the example taken. Along the way, we will point out the differences between this text of procedure and those placed directly in relation to problems, with respect to the computations prescribed and the mode of prescription. We will also occasionally evoke the commentaries on that procedure.

Table 11.3 *Multiplying the integer and the numerators by the lowest denominator (in the example, 2)*

Components of numbers —>	integer	numerator	denominator
Divisor: the integral component	2		
Divisor: a fractional component		2	2

PROCEDURE: ONE PUTS THE INTEGRAL *BU* AS WELL AS DENOMINATORS AND NUMERATORS OF THE PARTS …[47] ONE MULTIPLIES BY THE DENOMINATOR OF THE PARTS THAT IS IN THE LOWEST (POSITION) ALL THE NUMERATORS AS WELL AS THE INTEGRAL *BU*.

The 'integral *bu*' refers to the integer component of the width (here, 1), and the term 'parts' to its fractions (in the example of problem 1, only ½ *bu*). By contrast to the text of procedure examined above, the operands are now referred to by their nature. Given the layout, the lowest denominator is also the greatest one, and the multiplication prescribed yields Table 11.3.

Note that this step does not appear explicitly in the specific procedure attached to the first problem, a point I indicate by adding some grey to Table 11.3. I return to this point. Whereas the text of the procedure prescribes the multiplication of all components of the divisor (that is, the width) using a term designating multiplication, Li Chunfeng makes explicit the 'meaning' of this operation in different ways, depending on its components. His commentary here is essential for my argument. He writes: 'The reason why one multiplies the integral *bu* by the denominators[48] of the parts is to make their parts communicate. The reason why one multiplies the numerators by the denominators is to homogenise the corresponding numerators.'

Li Chunfeng introduces here important technical terms, which we need to explain for our purpose. In this context, '*tong*₁ 通 make their parts communicate' refers to the fact that the units in the integer, being multiplied by the denominator, are cut into as many parts as the denominator, each part having a size measured by the denominator: they are thus 'in communication' with the corresponding numerator, and can be added to it. The term 'make their parts communicate' refers to the 'meaning' or the

---

[47] I thereby indicate where I skip the commentary. In this case, I return to it.
[48] One could choose to interpret that term as a singular or a plural. Given the structure of the procedure, I choose to interpret as plural. As explained below, the procedure contains an iteration. This step will be repeated, and I interpret the commentary as referring to each use of the operation.

'intention' of the multiplication of integers here, thereby accounting for the reason why it is used. It designates a specific meaning in context. However, in other contexts the same term will be used to refer to other operations, which nevertheless share with these operations the 'general' property of similarly bringing entities 'into communication'. I refer to this way of formulating the intention of operations as 'formal' in contrast to the 'material' way, which would emphasise how the operation cuts units into parts.

Li Chunfeng likewise captures the meaning of the multiplication of the numerators by the lowest denominator in a formal way: this operation, he writes, 'homogenises the corresponding numerators'. Introduced in the earlier commentaries, the operation 'homogenising' makes a pair with another operation '$tong_2$ 同 equalising'. Applied to the fractions a/b and c/d, the reduction to a common denominator bd (the 'equalised') transforms the fractions into ad/bd and cb/bd. 'Homogenising' refers to the meaning of the multiplication of a by d and of c by b. We return to the specific meaning of the term in our context below.

The next step of the procedure does not appear in the specific procedures either. It reads:

ONE DIVIDES, RESPECTIVELY, THESE NUMERATORS BY THE CORRESPONDING DENOMINATOR AND ONE PUTS (THE INTEGRAL PART OF THE QUOTIENT) ON THE LEFT HAND SIDE, CALLING THESE THE *PARTS THAT COMMUNICATE*. (My emphasis)

In the context of the first problem, this operation yields Table 11.4.

Given the fact that in the example of the first problem we only have the fraction ½, the operations only involve a single division. The 'respectively' in the text shows that the procedure also covers cases in which there occur several fractions in the successive lines of the lower zone. Each value of a numerator multiplied by the lower denominator would be divided by the denominator to its right, yielding an integer, placed on the left hand side, and a fraction laid out as before and simplified. Probably the lowest denominator just used is erased, and the operation will be reproduced with the next 'DENOMINATOR OF THE PARTS THAT IS IN THE LOWEST (POSITION)'.

Note that the procedure gives a name to the values placed on the left hand side ('the parts that communicate', that is, the components of the quantity forming the divisor that, at this point in the computation, have already been transformed into an integral number of the same smaller unit). 'Naming' *does not correspond to any operation* in the

Table 11.4 *Dividing each numerator (in our example, only one) by the corresponding denominator, to its right; the integral part of the result is placed on the left hand side, while the remaining numerator, if any, replaces the previous numerator in its position.*

	Parts that communicate	numerator	denominator
Divisor: the integral component	2		
Divisor: a fractional component	1		2

specific procedure, nor does it designate any calculation. This implies that the procedure is not purely prescriptive, *pace* Jean-Baptiste Biot and all those for whom a prescription implies a simple-minded practitioner who is content in obeying. But there is more. On the other hand, the name 'THE *PARTS THAT COMMUNICATE*' interestingly involves the term Li Chunfeng's commentary will later use in his analysis of the correctness of the procedure examined above. From the viewpoint of the meaning of the computation, these values are all 'parts' corresponding (in our example) to the denominator 2. If the operation is iterated, they will all be multiplied by the lowest remaining denominator, and hence remain 'in communication'. The name given thus states a property of these values that relates to the meaning of the computations carried out and to the proof of the correctness of the algorithm. The key point is that such terms do not occur in the specific procedures placed directly in relation to problems. Also note that to be able to use the text of the procedure, the practitioner has to understand the meaning of the operations carried out, as Li Chunfeng made explicit.

The following paragraph of the procedure is precisely the one stating the iteration of the operations just executed (Tables 11.3 and 11.4) and formulating the point up to which it must be carried out. It reads:

FURTHER, ONE MULTIPLIES BY THE DENOMINATORS ALL THE NUMERATORS AND THE (VALUES) THAT ALREADY COMMUNICATE. WHEN THE (VALUES) ALL *COMMUNICATE*, THEN ONE HAS *EQUALIZED* THEM AND ONE THUS ADDS THEM TO MAKE THE DIVISOR.

If the first sentence here prescribes the repetition of the above operations, it adds a nuance, which is the main point the text emphasises: together with the numerators, it is no longer the integer (the '1 *bu*' of the beginning), but also the components of the divisor that 'already communicate' (the values on the left) that should be multiplied. Reference to the iteration of the two previous operations is a feature of the text that likewise is *not* explicit in the specific procedures attached to problems. Note that at each repetition of the operations, the reference of the expression 'the (values) that already communicate' changes. Again, the formulation of the text of the procedure betrays the assumption that the practitioner understands the 'meaning' of the operations carried out.

The term 'communicate' is also used in the next sentence to formulate the limit of the iteration: 'when they all communicate', that is, when operations have progressively led to the elimination of all numerators. The 'parts that communicate' are then all attached to a single denominator, whose value occurs at the position where at the beginning of the computation one had placed the '1 *bu*'. This is what the text of the procedure asserts, in a sentence that again corresponds to no computation and has no counterpart in the specific procedures: 'WHEN THE (VALUES) ALL COMMUNICATE, THEN ONE HAS EQUALIZED THEM.' On the other hand, the assertion likewise makes use of terms Li Chunfeng will introduce ('communicate') or evoke ('equalise') in his commentary. I will not analyse further this point.

Incidentally, this common denominator is the least common multiple of all denominators, and the sub-procedure examined gives the means to determine it.[49] The next step of the procedure refers to this denominator as 'accumulated parts (or cutting) of the integral *bu*'. Once more, this expression designates the value by reference to the meaning it acquired through the procedure that yielded it: the least common multiple was obtained through successive cuttings applied to the units of the integral number of *bu* ('1 *bu*') along the iteration. In the specific procedures, only its value is given, without clarification as to how it was obtained. Once the common denominator has been obtained, the final part of the procedure 'Reducing the Width' reads as follows:

ONE PUTS THE QUANTITY OF *BU* ONE SEEKS [THAT IS, 240 *BU*], AND ONE MULTIPLIES IT BY THE ACCUMULATED PARTS (*JIFEN*) OF THE INTEGRAL *BU* TO MAKE THE DIVIDEND ... DIVIDING THE DIVIDEND BY THE DIVISOR YIELDS THE *BU* OF THE LENGTH.

As above, the same operations are prescribed in the procedure attached to the problem, but with different terms. At this point, the procedure

---

[49] This point is of no importance here. For details, see Chemla and Guo 2004.

```
┌─────────────────────┬──────────────┐
│ Area of the         │ Width        │
│   cropland          │ 1 bu 1/2     │
│ ···················│              │
│                     │
│    240 bu           │
│                     │
│    Length?          │
└─────────────────────┘
```

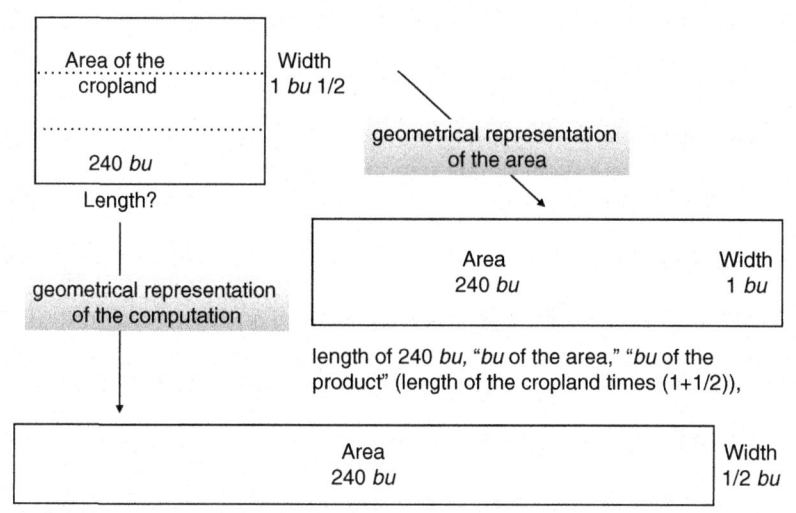

geometrical representation of the area

```
                     ┌──────────────────────────┬──────────┐
                     │         Area             │ Width    │
geometrical          │        240 bu            │ 1 bu     │
representation       └──────────────────────────┴──────────┘
of the computation
                     length of 240 bu, "bu of the area," "bu of the
                     product" (length of the cropland times (1+1/2)),

┌────────────────────────────────────────────────┬──────────┐
│                    Area                        │ Width    │
│                   240 bu                       │ 1/2 bu   │
└────────────────────────────────────────────────┴──────────┘
```

the length of the rectangle representing the area is 480 bu, that is, the bu of the area of the cropland times the "accumulated parts in the integral bu", (in the example 240 bu times 2)

Figure 11.3 Interpreting the expression 'Reducing the Width' using the geometrical representation of the value of areas.

'Reducing the Width' finally yields what was shown in Table 11.2 and corresponds to the result of the specific procedure. In conclusion, the operations prescribed in the 'abstract' procedure can be summarised using the following formulas:

$$\frac{240\ bu}{\left(1+\frac{1}{2}\right)bu} = \frac{240\ bu}{\left(\frac{2}{2}+\frac{1}{2}\right)bu} = \frac{480\ bu}{(2+1)\ bu} \qquad (Eq.2)$$

We return to this summary below. Figure 11.3 suggests an interpretation of the operations in the procedure by reference to the geometrical interpretation of the value of the area. Instead of using 1 bu as a measurement unit for the width of the rectangle representing the area, the computation leads to using a fraction of the bu defined by the accumulation of cuts. Accordingly, the length representing the area of 240 bu is multiplied by the 'accumulated parts' and is the product of the length of the actual cropland by a width that, multiplied by the 'accumulated parts', has been transformed into an integer. Dividing by this integer yields the length sought for. Such an explanation might explain why the overall operation is called 'Reducing the Width'.

We can now return to our main questions about 'abstraction' as a category introduced by Liu Hui. The key point in my interpretation is to consider that a text of procedure like the one just analysed is what Liu Hui would recognise as 'abstract expressions'. Which type of abstraction does it embody, and what is its function? These are the two main questions I will address. To begin with, let me emphasise that what was described above holds true for the relationship between the 'abstract' text and any of the procedures attached to the following eleven problems.

Note that the mention of specific measurement units (*bu*) in the 'abstract' text of procedure would prevent *us* from qualifying it as abstract. This is where these actors' categories differ from our own. On the other hand, this text of procedure presents several key differences from that of specific procedures. These differences, I suggest, characterise formulations in the former that the commentator would recognise as 'abstract expressions'.

Firstly, the text of the upper-level procedure makes use of terms like 'communicate', 'equalised', 'accumulated parts' that do not occur in the texts of these specific procedures. Moreover, these terms relate to the correctness of the procedure, as is made clear by the echoes they present with the commentaries. In fact, these remarks hold true for the text of the procedure given for the operation 'suppose' mentioned above. Similar features also characterise *all* the texts for upper-level procedures. Further, in all the texts of that type recorded in *The Nine Chapters*, the terms refer to the reasons expressed formally. In other words, although these procedures are contained in *The Nine Chapters*, their formulation is related to a statement of correctness: this contradicts the widespread assumption that the canon shows no interest in the correctness of the procedures.

Secondly, by contrast to the text for specific procedures, the text for the abstract procedure requires a 'circulation'. In other words, the user of this text does not pick up sentences linearly, from the first to the last step. Rather, in relation to the iteration described, at each step, depending on the situation created by the computation just carried out, the user knows how to pick up sentences earlier or later in the text to keep computing correctly. The text thus makes sense in a different way, in relation to the fact that the procedure covers all possible cases. Interestingly, the same feature characterises most of the texts for other upper-level procedures. Moreover, exactly the same feature opposes the two procedures described by Liu Hui in his commentary on problem 8.18, the one he refers to as expressed using 'abstract expressions' and the other.

Finally, the text of the procedure for 'Reducing the Width' has an additional feature, which explains why I have chosen it for this discussion. I have emphasised above that it refers to computations that are *not mentioned* in the text of the specific procedures (those displayed in Tables 11.3 and 11.4 – and in the middle formula of (Eq. 2), by contrast to (Eq. 1)). Instead, the specific procedures directly state how one should transform the unit (depending on the case, 'one takes one as two', 'one takes one as six', 'one takes one as twelve', and so on). These additional computations that the 'abstract' text mentions, however, explain the 'origin' of the values chosen to transform the unit in the context of *all* specific procedures.[50] In this other sense, the 'abstract procedure' thus accounts for the correctness and meaning of the lower-level procedures, and it does so in a general way. This meaning is common to all procedures.

Consequently, we can formulate an interpretation of why the same computations solving a problem are described by two distinct texts of procedures. One type of text refers to the operations directly. The other – that is, the 'abstract expressions' – refers to them using terms and adding computations that both relate to the correctness of the procedure. Moreover, that second text relates the specific procedures for the eleven problems to each other by showing how they derive from the same principles.

In my interpretation, these conclusions describe what the locution 'abstract expressions' refers to. It also suggests the function of abstraction: the 'abstract' text designates the operations by terms referring to their 'intention'. It embodies a formulation of reasons for the correctness in the text of *The Nine Chapters* and beyond, but this exceeds the scope of this chapter. Interestingly enough, none of the specific procedures for the eleven problems is followed by a commentary establishing its correctness. It seems that the commentators may have interpreted the first 'abstract' procedure as fulfilling this function. By contrast, in chapter 2, facing exactly the same *dispositif*, the commentators had made explicit how the text of the procedure for 'suppose' underlay all the others, and they accounted for the correctness of the specific procedures, making explicit their relation to the 'abstract expressions'. The commentators thus highlighted the tree-like shape of the set of procedures, their common origin[51] – the most general and

---

[50] I have discussed elsewhere other cases when a procedure accounting for the correctness of another procedure contains additional computations needed not to yield the result, but to explain its meaning from a certain perspective. This is the case of Liu Hui's second proof of the procedure to multiply fractions.

[51] This is the term used by the commentator by reference to the procedure placed at the beginning of chapter 9 and corresponding to 'Pythagorean theorem'. Incidentally, the conclusions presented here suggest that the critical edition of the beginning of chapter 7 should be revised.

abstract procedure – being placed at the beginning of the chapter and formulating the reasons underlying them all in a formal way. Lloyd (1997: 148) discusses several other pieces of evidence in Chinese ancient mathematical sources that point towards the same conclusion from different viewpoints.

Conclusion

It is time to gather all the threads followed in this chapter and conclude.

The Nine Chapters regularly gives for a problem two texts of procedures referring to the same operations. I have argued that the formulation of one of them corresponded to what the commentary ascribed to Liu Hui perceived as 'abstract expressions', while the other, associated to a specific problem, was formulated directly in view of its resolution. This conclusion suggests where, in the commentator's view, abstraction occurs in mathematical practice. It also suggests a function he associates with 'abstract texts': in his view, they somehow state the reasons why operations should be carried out. Moreover, the 'abstract' texts are placed at specific positions in *The Nine Chapters*. For instance, one finds them at the beginning of most chapters in *The Nine Chapters*, where their text relates to many procedures stated after problems contained in this chapter.

These observations strikingly echo the strange statements Wylie made about *The Nine Chapters*, which we attempt to elucidate. Let us quote them again in an abridged form: 'every section and subdivision commences with a stanza of rhyme, embodying in a *general* way the rule in question; the *meaning* is *not always very apparent* on the surface ... and *on a minute inspection* it will be seen that they contain in a concise form the *leading ideas* which they are intended to convey, very accurately expressed'.

The analysis of the text of *The Nine Chapters* developed above immediately suggests an interpretation. The mention of the position of the 'rule' in the book indicates that Wylie refers precisely to the texts formulated 'abstractly' in Liu Hui's sense. Apparently, Wylie was aware of the fact that they are both 'general' and refer to the 'leading ideas' – the term 'leading' interestingly evoking that of '*dushu* procedure commanding (to the others)'. There is more. Elsewhere, still in relation to *The Nine Chapters*, Wylie manifested his awareness that some texts of procedures

---

The formal properties of the main and first procedures (according to some witnesses) are most interesting in this context.

were formulated in such a way that the practitioner understood the point of the operation carried out.[52]

Could this be part of what Wylie had in mind when he argues one could establish 'juster views' about 'abstract science' in China? It is difficult to be categorical without further research. However, if that were the case, Wylie's use of 'abstract' in this context would at least partly fit with Liu Hui's.

This suggestion raises a difficulty, however. Wylie rarely mentions the commentaries as such (Chemla 2010). How would he have gained such an understanding? As was mentioned above, Wylie studied these texts with Li Shanlan.[53] This is reflected in the *facts* Wylie mentions in *Jottings*, with which he claims priorities for Chinese authors (most of the time with respect to British scholars). In effect, Li Shanlan had extensively worked on, and written about, all the mathematical writings from China's past that had resurfaced in the decades before and that Wylie analyses, including *The Nine Chapters* and its commentaries (Horng 1991: 58, 61). Li shaped some terms in modern mathematical terminology on the basis of how Liu Hui used the terms. Further, when from 1869 onwards he taught mathematics at the *Tongwenguan*, Li Shanlan used *The Nine Chapters* as a textbook.

But there is more. Wylie's quotations we tried to interpret deal less with *facts* than with *modes of expression* used in ancient Chinese texts. The key point is that Li Shanlan's interpretation of these ancient texts impresses by the depth of his insights, and, above all, by the mode of reading he brings into play. This was the conclusion I drew from observing how he had interpreted *Measuring the Circle on the Sea-mirror* (*Ceyuan haijing* 測圓海鏡) by Li Ye (1248). This is precisely what is at stake here. Should we conclude that Wylie's assertions on the forms of expression in *The Nine Chapters* derive from his exchanges with Li Shanlan and that Wylie reflects insights Li Shanlan gained in this respect? Recovering Li Shanlan's reading of *The Nine Chapters* goes beyond the scope of this chapter, but deserves further study.

In any event, Wylie's description of those texts of procedures I interpreted as embodying 'abstract expressions' is remarkable for its relevance: they capture the 'leading ideas' which, in my interpretation, derive from

---

[52] He writes about the algorithm for root extraction: 'for the various parts of the process taking their names from the geometrical figure, the *operator* is *enabled* to *see* at every step the particular *object* of what he is performing' (Wylie [1852] 1882: 172, my emphasis).

[53] On difficult issues, Wylie also mentions the views of 'native authors', with whom he discussed. The outlines that *Jottings* gives for *The Nine Chapters* contain weird inaccuracies, which might be explained by the fact that Wylie had partly a second-hand knowledge of the book. Libbrecht 1973: 33 puts forward the same hypothesis for another book.

proofs of the correctness, when they do not purely replace them.[54] This textual organisation opposing the 'abstract' text and the derived procedures is different from what we find in Euclid's *Elements*. I repeat it is impossible in both cases to have access to actors' categories. However, we can compare the structure and organisation of the texts.

At the beginning of the *Elements*, or of certain parts in it, Euclid puts forward common notions and postulates that are common to the propositions and problems. They are 'common' in the sense that they are primitive notions, or authorised (sometimes forbidden) operations. However, the text of the *Elements* does not highlight any *reason* that would be common to different proofs, or anything common at the level of proofs. As observers, we can identify such components. For instance, several proofs are structured following the 'method of exhaustion'. However, revealingly, that 'method' was brought to light, and given a name, only in the seventeenth century. These features are correlated with the fact that, in the interpretation of a geometer like Chasles, Euclid and other Greek geometers were dealing with concrete 'figures' and 'questions'. In Chasles' view, one symptom for that was the fact that the proofs were most particular, most complex, and unrelated to each other. Perhaps, however, had Chasles obtained any insight into the textual organisation of *The Nine Chapters* as emphasised by its commentators, he would have recognised a form of organisation of knowledge closer to what he valued. We remember he suggested that, in each domain of knowledge, one should identify a property from which all the others could be derived most simply and which could itself be proven quite easily. Such an ideal appears closer to what the chapters of *The Nine Chapters* display. In effect, in both contexts, the search for the origin at the level of reasons is an essential endeavour, even if the interpretation of what could constitute an 'origin' may have differed.[*]

---

[54] The commentary on problem 8.18 ascribed to Liu Hui indirectly supports this idea, when Liu Hui quotes together 'accumulated parts' and 'repeated unequal sharing' as 'great achievements' of, respectively, chapters 4 and 6 in *The Nine Chapters*. The former derives from the abstract procedure, the latter from the proof of the first procedures in chapter 6.

[*] The research leading to these results has received funding from the European Research Council under the European Union's Seventh Framework Programme (FP7/2007–2013) / ERC Grant agreement n. 269804. As a token of friendship and a testimony of long-term exchange over decades, which has been most enriching for me, I have chosen to return to a discussion Geoffrey and I began almost twenty years ago in the pages of *Extrême-Orient, Extrême-Occident*, about the use of paradigms and the issue of abstraction (Lloyd 1997, in Chemla 1997.) Geoffrey, Jenny and Qiaosheng have offered important comments on this chapter, and it is my great pleasure to express my warmest thanks to them.

Bibliography

Belhoste, B. (2003) *La Formation d'une technocratie: L'Ecole polytechnique et ses élèves de la Révolution au Second Empire*. Paris.

Bertrand, J. (1869) 'Mathématiques en Chine', *Journal des Savants*: 317–29, 464–77.

Biernatzki, K. L. (1856) 'Die Arithmetik der Chinesen', *Journal für die reine und angewandte Mathematik* 52: 59–94.

(1862) 'Arithmétique et algèbre des Chinois (translated by Olry Terquem)', *Bulletin de Bibliographie, d'Histoire et de Biographie Mathématiques (published with separated page numbers after Nouvelles Annales de Mathématiques: Journal des Candidats aux Ecoles Polytechnique et Normale)* (2nd series) 1: 35–44.

(1863) 'Arithmétique et algèbre des Chinois (fin) (voir Bulletin Mathématique, t. VIII, 1862, p. 35) (translated by Olry Terquem)', *Nouvelles Annales de Mathématiques: Journal des Candidats aux Ecoles Polytechnique et Normale* (2nd series) 2: 529–40.

Biot, E. (1839a) 'Table générale d'un ouvrage chinois intitulé 算法統宗 *Souan-fa-tong-tsong*, ou *Traité complet de l'art de compter* (Fourmont, n° 350), traduite et analysée par M. Ed. BIOT', *Journal Asiatique* 3e série, 7: 193–217.

(1839b) 'Mémoire sur divers minéraux chinois appartenant à la collection du Jardin du Roi, par M. Edouard Biot', *Journal Asiatique* 3e série, 8: 206–30.

Biot, J.-B. (1841) 'Compte-rendu de *Traité des instruments astronomiques des Arabes*, traduit par J. J. Sédillot', *Journal des Savants*: 513–20, 602–10, 659–79.

(1862) *Etudes sur l'astronomie indienne et sur l'astronomie chinoise*. Paris.

Charette, F. (2012) 'The logical Greek versus the imaginative Oriental. On the historiography of "non-western" mathematics during the period 1820–1920', in *The History of Mathematical Proof in Ancient Traditions*, ed. K. Chemla. Cambridge: 274–93.

Chasles, M. (1837) *Aperçu historique sur l'origine et le développement des méthodes en géométrie, particulièrement de celles qui se rapportent à la géométrie moderne, suivi d'un mémoire de géométrie sur deux principes généraux de la science: la dualité et l'homographie*. Brussels.

(1863) 'Rapport sur les travaux mathématiques de M. O. Terquem', *Nouvelles Annales de Mathématiques, Journal des Candidats aux Ecoles Polytechnique et Normale* (2nd series) 2: 241–51.

Chemla, K. (1997) 'Qu'est-ce qu'un problème dans la tradition mathématique de la Chine ancienne? Quelques indices glanés dans les commentaires rédigés entre le IIIe et le VIIe siècles au classique Han *Les neuf chapitres sur les procédures mathématiques*', in *La valeur de l'exemple: perspectives chinoises. Extrême-Orient, Extrême-Occident* ed. K. Chemla. Saint-Denis: 91–126.

(2006) 'Documenting a process of abstraction in the mathematics of ancient China', in *Studies in Chinese Language and Culture: Festschrift in Honor of Christoph Harbsmeier on the Occasion of his 60th Birthday*, eds. C. Anderl and H. Eifring. Oslo: 169–94.

(2010) 'A Chinese canon in mathematics and its two layers of commentaries: reading a collection of texts as shaped by actors', in *Looking at It from Asia: The Processes that Shaped the Sources of History of Science*, ed. F. Bretelle-Establet. Dordrecht: 169–210.

(2014) 'L'histoire des sciences dans la sinologie des débuts du XIXe siècle: les Biot père et fils (preprint handed out for the conference)', in *Jean-Pierre Abel-Rémusat et ses successeurs: deux cents ans de sinologie française en France et en Chine* 雷慕沙及其繼承者：紀念法國漢學兩百週年學術研討會. Paris. https://halshs.archives-ouvertes.fr/halshs-01509318/document.

(2016) 'The value of generality in Michel Chasles's historiography of geometry', in *The Oxford Handbook of Generality in Mathematics and the Sciences*, eds. K. Chemla, R. Chorlay and D. Rabouin. Oxford: 47–89.

(submitted) 'Writing abstractly in mathematical texts from early imperial China', in *Technical Arts and Historical Writing in Early China*, eds. M. Csikszentmihalyi and M. Nylan.

Chemla, K. and Guo Shuchun (2004) *Les neuf chapitres: le classique mathématique de la Chine ancienne et ses commentaires*. Paris.

Chevreul, E. (1845) 'Histoire de la Chimie ... par le Dr Ferd. Hoefer. Troisième article', *Journal des Savants*: 321–37.

Chu Pingyi (祝平一 Zhu Pingyi) (2010) 'Scientific texts in contest, 1600–1800', in *Looking at It from Asia: The Processes that Shaped the Sources of History of Science*, ed. F. Bretelle-Establet. Dordrecht: 141–66.

Cordier, H. (1897) 'Life and labours of Alexander Wylie', in Wylie 1897b: 7–18.

Edkins, J. (1897) 'The value of Mr. Wylie's Chinese researches', in Wylie 1897b: 1–3.

Fang Chao-Ying 房兆楹 (1943a) 'Li Shan-lan', in *Eminent Chinese of the Ch'ing period (1644–1912)*, ed. A. W. Hummel. Washington, DC: I, 479a–80a.

(1943b) 'Lo Shih-Lin', in *Eminent Chinese of the Ch'ing period (1644–1912)*, ed. A. W. Hummel. Washington, DC: I, 538b–40b.

Girardot, N. J. (2002) *The Victorian Translation of China: James Legge's Oriental Pilgrimage*. Berkeley and Los Angeles.

Han Qi 韓琦 (1998) 'Chuanjiaoshi weilieyali zaihua de kexue huodong 傳教士偉烈亞力在華的科學活動 (Alexander Wylie and his scientific activities in China)', *Ziran bianzhengfa tongxun* 自然辯證法通訊 (*Journal of Dialectics of Nature*) 20: 57–70.

(2014) 'Knowledge and power: a social history of the transmission of mathematics between China and Europe during the Kangxi reign (1662–1722)', in *International Congress of Mathematicians*. Seoul: 1217–29.

Hoe, J. (1977) *Les systèmes d'équations polynômes dans le Siyuan yujian (1303)*. Mémoires de l'Institut des Hautes Etudes Chinoises. Paris.

(2007) *The Jade Mirror of the Four Unknowns by Zhū Shìjié: An Early Fourteenth Century Mathematics Manual for Teaching the Derivation of Systems of Polynomial Equations in up to Four Unknowns: A Study*. Christchurch.

Horng Wann-sheng 洪萬生 (1991) 'Li Shanlan: the impact of Western mathematics in China during the late nineteenth century', PhD dissertation, City University of New York.

Libbrecht, U. (1973) *Chinese Mathematics in the Thirteenth Century: The Shu-shu Chiu-Chang of Ch'in Chiu-Shao*. Cambridge, MA.

Lloyd, G. E. R. (1968) *Aristotle: The Growth and Structure of his Thought*. London.

(1997) 'Exempli gratia. To make an example of the Greeks', *Extrême-Orient, Extrême-Occident* 19: 139–51.

Möbius, F. (According to) (1852) 'Démonstration géométrique du parallélogramme des forces et théorèmes sur des forces concourantes', *Nouvelles Annales de Mathématiques* 1st series, 11: 281–6.

Poncelet, J.-V. (1864) *Applications d'analyse et de géométrie qui ont servi de principal fondement au Traité des propriétés projectives des figures. Tome 2*. Paris.

Thomas, J. (1897) 'Biographical sketch of Alexander Wylie', in *Chinese Researches*, ed. A. Wylie. Shanghai: 1–6.

Wang Yusheng 王渝生 (1990) 'Li Shanlan yanjiu 李善蘭研究 (Research on Li Shanlan)', in *Ming Qing shuxueshi lunwenji* 明清數學史論文集 (*Collected Papers on the History of Mathematics during the Ming and Qing Dynasties*), ed. Mei Rongzhao 梅榮照. Nanjing: 334–408.

Wylie, A. ([1852] 1882) 'Jottings on the science of the Chinese (Papers originally published in the *North China Herald*, August–November 1852: 108, 111, 112, 113, 116, 117, 119, 120, 121)', *Copernicus* 2: 169–95 + Plate V. This publication is quoted on the basis of the reprint in Wylie 1897b.

(1867) 'Eclipses recorded in Chinese works', *Journal of the North China Branch of the Royal Asiatic Society* new series, 4: 87–158; reprinted in Wylie 1897b: 29–109.

(1871) 'On the knowledge of a weekly sabbath in China', *Chinese Recorder and Missionary Journal* 4.1: 4–9; 4.2: 40–5; reprinted in Wylie 1897b: 86–101.

(1897a) 'Chinese language and literature', in Wylie 1897b: 195–241.

(1897b) *Chinese Researches*. Shanghai.

Xu Yibao (2005) 'The first Chinese translation of the last nine books of Euclid's *Elements* and its source', *Historia Mathematica* 32: 4–32.

Zhu Yiwen and Zheng Cheng (forthcoming) 'On the first printed edition of *Mathematical Book in Nine Chapters* (1842)', in *Shaping the Sciences of the Ancient World*, eds. A. Keller, K. Chemla and C. Proust.

12 | Recipes for Love in the Ancient World

VIVIENNE LO AND ELEANOR RE'EM

Throughout history, a huge amount of attention has been devoted to *aphrodisia*. Yet, in historical research, they tend to feature only in passing comments in studies of love, sex and the emotions, or of food and medicine. The relative absence of monographs on the subject is, therefore, a significant lacuna.[1] This chapter will argue that it is particularly a lacuna in the history of science, medicine and empiricism.[2] *Aphrodisia*, as a subject involving products and practices that have induced sexual pleasure, allow us to contribute to the 'sensory turn' in history. Calling to mind the aesthetics of an ancient world where the boundaries between what we now think of as the domains of individual senses were less distinct, *aphrodisia* give us privileged access to the gathering of medical knowledge before the observation of the eye took its post-Enlightenment pride of place in the conduct of science.[3] The subject permits an 'inquiry into the conditions under which knowledge, or what passed for it, was produced, and the conditions under which those who claimed to do the producing worked'.[4] It also leads inexorably to an investigation of the history of the 'scientific self' and *self*-experimentation. In what terms did learned people perceive the world in ancient times? These are key issues in comparative histories of knowledge production.

We are deeply indebted to friends who have helped us with this research: Donald Harper, Vivian Nutton, John Wilkins, Penelope Barrett, Andrew Wear and Laurence Totelin. We also thank the editors of the volume for invaluable comments.

[1] Important exceptions include Faraone 1999; Faraone and Obbink 1991; Harper 1998; Umekawa 2005.

[2] In this chapter we use the term 'empiricism' in both its usual senses. The first refers to the practice of medicine where practitioners and communities choose treatments in a logical fashion according to what, in their experience, is deemed to work; and they do not need to know why according to any guiding theoretical framework. The philosophical usage of the term opposes empiricism (anything based on experience) to a priori knowledge arrived at from first principles. Both types of knowledge make claims to universal validity and, notably, a number of philosophers use both. Descartes would provide an example of the latter, though he questioned whether the model of the world derived from first principles was actually so in the experienced world.

[3] Jütte 2005: 25–31. [4] Lloyd 1996: 16.

Figure 12.1 Red-figure *pelike*, attributed to the Hasselmann Painter.

Academic Amnesia

A related case of modern academic amnesia is the erasure of the erect penis from the face of the history of civilisation. In the words of Simon Goldhill, 'the way we differ from the ancient worlds is also profoundly telling about the taboos and anxieties which shadow the modern sense of the self'.[5] He illustrates his argument with the enormous erect phalli that populated the worlds of ancient Greece, in religious statuary and civic ritual, celebrating Dionysus in the world of entertainment, and as smaller day-to-day objects, sometimes winged, candle-holders and door pulls.[6]

The erotic power of phalli was not limited to mundane sexual engagement. A little-known and unique red-figure *pelike* depicts a woman watering erect phalli as if they were plants. There is later European testimony to this harvesting of disembodied penises by women, a subject crying out for gender analysis: perhaps as a joke about male anxiety over the cuckold (it's likely to have been produced by a man), loss of virility, or the sexual power of the

---

[5] Goldhill 2004: 29; see also Keuls 1993: 75–9.   [6] Goldhill 2004: 30–3.

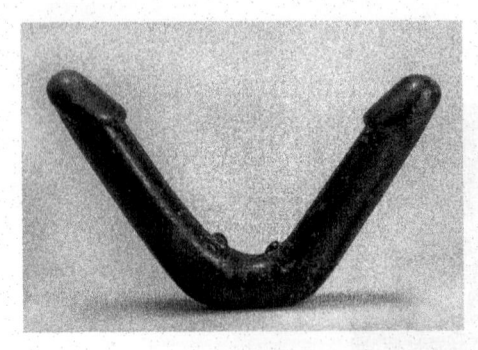

Figure 12.2 Double phalli from Tomb M1 Mancheng, Hebei.

woman in the kitchen (she might cook them), or in connection with mystic ceremonies of Athenian women, such as the Thesmophoria. Some phalli had an apotropaic function to protect the state, community and household, marking the boundaries of the Athenian world. Where erect phalli were part of Greek 'furniture of ancient religion and social life',[7] in China they seem to have been a common feature of funerary furniture. Huge bronze examples, one double shafted, have been found decorating the tombs of wealthy nobles.

In this context they evoke the potency of images of sexual prowess in sustaining the power of the male body, even beyond death. During the twentieth century these phalli were one of the most consistently ignored features of ancient Chinese archaeology.[8] The quantity of aphrodisiac texts from the ancient Chinese world has also gone relatively unacknowledged, and so too virtually has their knowledge in modern Chinese pharmacology.

Twentieth-century censorship of the ancient world's preoccupation with aphrodisiac drugs is also apparent in Sir Arthur Hort's 1961 translation of Theophrastus of Eresos' (c. 370–288/5 BCE) fourth-century BCE *Historia plantarum* (*Enquiry into Plants*), the work that Scarborough claims 'formed the basis for all succeeding studies of plant lore classifications until Linnaeus'.[9] Sir Arthur omitted the section 9.18.3ff about the Orchid (ὄρχις [testicle]) 'on account of the description of the physical effects', testifying to the existential crisis of many historians of the time. The omission elicited the objection: 'Such prudishness in a scientific book is truly shocking.'[10] Fifty years later we can do better. Surely, the nature of these 'physical effects' is of prime importance to a history of self-experimentation and empiricism. Like the erect phallus,

---

[7] Goldhill 2004: 34.   [8] Erickson 2010: 80; Li Ling 2006: plate 8.1–3.
[9] Scarborough 1978; 2010.
[10] As quoted in Gemmill 1973: 127–9; Sarton 1959: I, 555. For a translation of the missing section see Preus 1988: 88–91.

Figure 12.3 A chart of the vulva, Mawangdui tomb 3 (closed 168 BCE)

aphrodisia have also been all-pervasive in the social and religious performance of wealth and power.

Definitions and Sources

The major challenge of comparative history is surely to find commensurate contexts across cultures and time that facilitate matching case with case. *Aphrodisia*, as we understand the Greek term, represent all those techniques to entrap and enhance sensual love, sex and beauty traditionally associated with Aphrodite: cosmetics, binding spells, drugs to enhance performance and attraction. This range of topics is also conveniently germane to related evidence from ancient Chinese literature.

Greek and Roman sources for *aphrodisia* in this broad sense include the writings of the philosophers and naturalists such as Theophrastus, the medical treatises of the Hippocratic writers (fifth to fourth centuries BCE), and Pliny (23–79 CE), as well as Greek and Roman poets and playwrights such as Ovid (43 BCE–17/18 CE), Archestratus (fourth century BCE) and the Attic comedians as cited by Athenaeus (c. second–third centuries CE). Information on ancient Greek products that create sexual pleasure and promote competence is quite common in ancient medical literature. *Materia medica* will mention when a product is aphrodisiac among other indications of its efficacy in treating illnesses and promoting health. Spellbinding texts permit access to the circumstances of everyday love. For love magic, the works of Julius Africanus and the Greek magical papyri (to fifth century CE), including the demotic Egyptian handbooks, provide direct testimony to practices that we know survived from the ancient into the medieval world.[11]

For China, our major focus for *aphrodisia* is also recipe and spellbinding literature from the Western Han tomb at Changsha Mawangdui 馬王堆 (c. 168 BCE), of the old Han kingdom of Chu 楚.[12] Later testimony to the survival of the relevant recipe literature is taken from among the Dunhuang manuscripts (sealed in Cave 17, c. 1035). As in early Greek medical writing, the authors of these recipe texts were anonymous individuals and in the Greek case their work was compiled into large textual corpora. Their findings speak of the collective memory of countless individuals who contributed to establishing and disseminating ancient scientific knowledge across a millennium.

To understand the broader theme of the emotions we also have to scan earlier philosophic literature of the Warring States (475–221 BCE), here texts attributed to Mencius 孟子 (fourth century BCE), and Xunzi 荀子 (c. 313–238 BCE). Our analysis is therefore of the Greco-Roman worlds and China before the first century of the first millennium, with reference to later literature that testifies to the continuity of some traditions. In both Greco-Roman and Chinese worlds this was the period in which one can see major systematisation of medical theory. We could equally be talking of Indian *aphrodisia*, except that the Sanskrit texts that we might consider,

---

[11] Viellefond 1970; Faraone and Obbink 1991.

[12] The Mawangdui burial mound was excavated in the early 1970s. It contains three tombs. Tombs no. 1 and no. 2 belonged to the Marquis of Dai (軑侯), Li Cang 利蒼 (died 186 BCE), and his wife (tomb no. 1). Tomb no. 3, from which the manuscripts were excavated, was occupied by their son, who died in 168 BCE at the age of about 30. For the excavation report see Hunan sheng bowuguan and Zhongguo kexueyuan kaogu yanjiusuo 1973: 39–48.

like *Kāma Sūtra*, are composite texts generally dated to around the third century CE and extant from much later versions. Moreover, in the case of recipes that tie together longevity and sexual prowess – in the process of *vajikarana* – those texts (e.g. *Caraka samhitā* and *Suśruta samhitā*) are notoriously difficult to date and mainly promote milk products for their impact on *ojas* (vital essence) drawing on the association of milk with semen (*sukra*). The Greco-Roman contexts provide a much richer and more coherent comparison.

Love, Sex and Appetites

'Love' is the most difficult of the categories to compare. Different types of passion and affection moved the ancient Greeks: *erōs, storgē, philia* and *agapē*. *Storgē*, understood as the love of a parent for a child and familial bonds of emotion, seems hardly relevant to *aphrodisia*; *agapē*, as the kind of human heartedness that overrides selfishness, *seems* devoid of the kinds of feelings or lust attendant on sensual love. Physico-emotional passions crystallise in the term *erōs*, with potentially unwanted lust, and torture, or in *philia*. The word *philos* was used to describe the family and its close, intimate associates or to describe a philosophical group.[13] *Philia* was a complex emotion: inspired by people with whom one has certain reciprocal commitments, where we also find the encompassing familial feelings of delight and warmth. It was an emotion that might elicit a kiss and embrace or equally hetero or homosexual intercourse with affection.[14]

Modern scholars searching for love in ancient China have also failed to find tidy categories. Attention has centred on the words *ai* 愛 and *qing* 情 (note the modern word for mood or state of emotions, *qingxu* 情緒), and we add here also *qin* 親, which broadly means 'to treat someone as if they were kin'. In the Warring States, *qing* meant something like 'one's natural endowment', and from Han times it was assimilated to an 'array of notions' concerned with passion and emotion.[15] *Ai*, the modern word for 'love' between lovers and family members, as well as for expressing preferences such as an appetite for particular foods, is no less ambiguous. Closely associated in philosophy with 'universal love' or 'love for each and every

---

[13] Humphreys 1983: 67. Humphreys notes that 'the term *philos* overrides the distinctions we make between love, family and friendship'. The conventional translation of *philos* as 'friend' might suit the philosophical context but not the familial.

[14] Faraone 1999: 29-30. For discussions of homosexual, familial and marital love see Humphreys 1983: 17–18, 42–3, 54–7, 66–78.

[15] Andreini 2006; see also Allan 1997: 85.

one' as promoted in the school of Mozi (c. fifth–third centuries BCE), *ai* was a transcendent feeling of benevolence as well as sexual love.

The Sensory Turn

Since the early 1990s there has been increasing research into how the sensory base of emotion operates in different scientific cultures. Rather than cultivating emotional detachment, as was the prescription for objective and unfettered observation among mid-nineteenth-century scientists, early Chinese scholars trained themselves as knowledge gatherers through training their bodily *qi*, a term which came to codify and communicate inner body sensations. This cultivation of learned recorders of the world, their epistemic virtue, meant that the self, the perceiver, embodied what was perceived.[16] Constellations of meaning gathered around the notion of *qi* in the literate communities of ancient China and contributed to a remarkable ability to articulate changes in the inner landscape of the body in their relation to the wider environment. This community attention to the inner world is what might be called an early Chinese 'sixth sense', the cultivation of which enabled the management of digestion, body temperature, emotion, passion and pain, the impact of drugs and breathing. These intimate experiences of the inner body were placed on a synesthetic continuum with experiences of the external world: seasonal affect, the influence of the heavenly bodies, ancestral and other spirits. Initially acting as a social marker that distinguished the self-cultivation of the nobility, a repertoire of *qi* techniques also began to shape the rituals and language of medical practice at the beginning of empire.[17]

Experiments with pleasure found in the earliest extant texts that theorise sexual cultivation were the ground upon which a new medical language of Yin, Yang and *qi* was first constructed – a kind of knowing that informed classical treatises on acupuncture and drugs and that, being mediated through the body, never aspired to levels of pure abstraction.[18] These new techno-physiologies of the body were premised on the authority of pre-existing writings that were more philosophic in tone and sought to restrain the consumption and display of material wealth. Writings attributed to Xunzi recognised delayed gratification and the 'sustaining' or 'connoisseur' pleasures as the mark of the socially stabilising figure of the 'gentleman'.[19] In *Xunzi*, we find reference to a body-centred practice in which calming the

---

[16] Daston and Gallison [2007] 2010: 39–41. [17] Lo 2001: 19–51.
[18] Lo in Bray et al. 2007: 383–423. [19] Nylan 2003: *passim*.

heart and clearing it of anxiety was a key to a deeper and more prolonged appreciation of pleasure – a pleasure that eschewed the loud, brash and gaudy in favour of the refined appreciation of senses honed to simplicity.[20]

The sage ruler was a 'perspicacious' individual who comprehended the deep structures of the universe through a heightened acuity of the senses. Sensory perception 'was valued as a genuine part of moral reasoning in ancient China'.[21] Thus gluttony and the uncivilised pursuit of sexual satiation were contemptible, but the pursuit of culinary finesse and the mastery of sexual *technē* belonged to the highest domain of gentlemanly pursuits. The rationale behind male sexual continence, an anxiety shared across the ancient worlds, was that the more pleasure a woman had, the more benefit there was for the man. Her pleasure was a correlate of the extension of *qi* through her body.[22]

Practical substance in the form of instruction to the man was given to this *technē* of the senses in the literature and culture of self-cultivation.[23] He must learn to recognise, respond to and codify all the stages of female arousal: her aromas, sounds, breathing and movements, the feeling of being inside her. The *qi* (in a sensory experience cognate today with orgasm) emanated from the *zhongji* 中極 Middle Extremity. By the first century CE this term referred to an acupuncture point, but in the second century BCE it had simply been a lyrical anatomical term for the area in the general vicinity of the uterus. At the moment of the woman's orgasm the male partner absorbed the Yin essences of the woman, through the physiological interaction of the essences that occurred with the extension of *qi* in the female body, and the concomitant expression of the emotion of love: If only he can be slow and prolonged, the woman then is greatly pleased. She *qin* 'treats him with the closeness she feels for' her brothers, and *ai* 'loves' him like her father and mother.[24]

At the height of her rapture the woman is apparently overcome with feelings for her sexual partner akin to those she feels for her siblings and parents. As if this isn't uncomfortable enough for a modern reader, the man, reserving his orgasm, is simultaneously deriving an increment to his health and strength from the Yin essences emitted by the woman at the point of orgasm – which resulted in a state of *shenming* 申明, a brilliance of the spirits for him (and possibly for her).

Recording the essential characteristics of female sexual response was a key to this process. They inhabit a larger discourse with a specialist terminology which interlinked restraining pleasure with the generation of the cosmos, so

---

[20] Nylan 2003: 73–124. [21] Sterckx 2003: 72. [22] Pfister 2012: 34–64. MWD 4156.
[23] Lo 2001: in Bray et al 2007. [24] Harper 1998: 438. MWD 4 *He Yinyang* nos. 66–7.

that 'whoever is capable of this way is designated "heaven's gentleman"'.[25] We can already detect that the quality of writing in this technical literature does not reveal the kind of separation between philosophical and technical writing evident in Aristotle's (384–322) hierarchies of knowledge. To Aristotle the *technē* of the physician was inferior to the larger rhetorical skills concerned with philosophy, and it was limited by its utilitarian ambitions.[26] That is not to say that Aristotle eschewed knowledge acquired via the senses. Far from it. The four primary qualities that he espoused were known mainly through touch: hot, cold, dry and wet. But while it was perfectly possible for a philosophically sophisticated doctor to investigate causes and so be 'scientific' according to Artistotle's criteria, the study of medicine alone was insufficient. Only the freedom of leisure and plenitude would create the conditions for pursuing natural philosophy, and the correct synthesis of rational thought and empirical knowledge to understand the body. Rather, the learned physician must enhance the status of his knowledge and practice through an inquiry into first principles, fundamental propositions about the nature of the world, a view echoed later by Galen in his treatise *The Best Physician Is also a Philosopher.*[27]

Famous polarities of opinion, however, provide evidence of the diversity of attitudes towards the knowledge and practice of medicine and healing in the Greco-Roman world, and the figure of the practitioner: famously the Hellenistic medical sect the Empirics valued experience alone, finding an early empiric in Hippocrates.[28] An Hippocratic author of the fifth-century treatise *Ancient Medicine* thought that 'medicine should have its own knowledge independent of philosophy'.[29] For the Empirics, whose work echoed this Hippocratic sensibility, much of the search for first principles and the causes of illness was pointless activity. Valuable knowledge came, for example, from the serendipity of drug discovery, together with the recording and re-recording of drug effects, and trial and error.[30] Already in the sustained attention to this process we can see a trained observer mediating simple collective empiricism with specific ways of framing the medical object, methods which we will see brought to the nature of sexual stimulation in the next section.

Sexual Continence

Early Chinese and Greeks alike left records about the sexual body. For the authors of the Mawangdui aphrodisiac literature, knowledge about the

---

[25] Ibid.   [26] Wear 2013: 63 n.7, n.8.   [27] Wear 2013: 63 n.4 (Kühn 1.53–63).
[28] Lloyd 1987: 158–62.   [29] Quoted in Wear 2013: 63, n. 9.   [30] Nutton 2004: 149–51.

body required a particular kind of preparation, and one in which expertise in the sexual arts provided enhanced insights. The anonymity of the authorial process suggests a collective knowledge, with acquisition of a shared language, resulting from personal experimentation. By suppressing ejaculation, a man strengthened his *qi* and *jing* 精 ('essence') and gained an increment of youth and vitality. This appears to be a rather dispassionate and medical approach to sex, which pursued enhanced health, altered states of spiritual sensibility, power and longevity for the male partner – later texts even claimed that intercourse with multiple female partners would lead to immortality. The following excerpt is the outcome of a technique that includes both breath and sexual cultivation:

Be careful, do not drink wine and eat the five flavours; put the *qi* in order with intent and the eye will be bright, the ear keen, the skin will gleam, the one hundred *mai* will be full and the Yin will rise again. From this you will be able to stand for a long time, go a long way, and live for (ever).[31]

The focus here was not on procreation but on the more esoteric benefits of abstinence from indulgence, strengthening Yin, the word 'Yin' being construed as the penis itself, but also the Yin qualities of the body – its *coolness*, its *moistness*, the health of the *internal* organs and thus the ability to endure both in terms of sexual continence and long life. For men the concern for increasing potency was founded on a fear that, through the loss of the most precious essence and the source of life, ejaculation would deplete their power.

The man who wished to distinguish himself as a learned gentleman had to become a micro-technician of the senses. By the second century BCE practices that trained the appetites involving food, sex and breath cultivation techniques formed the key context within which new physiological ideas emerged. Healing and sustaining a powerful body were thus codified with a new science of the senses. As these anonymous writers began to document an aesthetic experience of how it felt inside to be well and strong, of experiences of desire and pleasure, of digestive satisfaction, of sexual excitement, they created a language of Yin, Yang and *qi* with sufficient semantic traction that it was able to convey the changing states of the inner sensory world.[32]

---

[31] MWD 4 *Shiwen* nos. 40–1. Ma 1992: 914. See also Harper's note on the re-ordering of the bamboo strips by Qiu Xigui. Harper 1998: 396–7 n. 8.

[32] Lo 2000, 2001: 19–51. The faculty of sight was least competent at perceiving any form of internal *qi*. External *qi* was visible as clouds, steam, or the dust and threat of, say, a distant army. Most books on the senses ignore the undifferentiated sea of sensation within the body. See Geurts 2005 for a study of the 'panoply of inner states' described as *seselelame* in West Africa. For the perception of touch see Kuriyama 2002 and Hsu 2010.

Good health was not consistent with male ejaculation, neither in ancient China nor in Greece. Aristotle described the mystical qualities of semen that were related to a divine aether.[33] The Hippocratic treatise *On Generation* notes that a man's seed is drawn from all parts of the body, and particularly its moisture, making it the most powerful part of his make-up, so that 'when we have intercourse we become weak' with the loss of 'the most potent and richest' essence of all the bodily fluids.[34] Sexual stimulation produced a warming of the body followed by agitation. The combined effect was thought to produce fluidity and foaming (*aphrein*), which travelled to the brain and down the spinal marrow to the loins. Sperm was then foaming blood that arose from disturbance (*taraxis*) produced by innate heat.[35] Since it exited the body in a sudden spasm the man's pleasure was brief and his health compromised.

The subjugation of women's health and pleasure to her power of generation is confirmed throughout Greco-Roman medical writing. *On Generation* sets out a rather mundane physiology of sexual processes that stresses reproductive health and the health of progeny. *On the Nature of Women* also recommended having children for general health. Regular sex moistened and plumped up the womb and was a cure for many diseases. Illness came to unmarried women.[36]

Female desire and pleasure were a precondition for conception: 'When women have finished having their periods, they conceive (hold in the belly) especially when they feel desire', a point which rather contrasts accepted notions of the separation of lust and family affection in the concept of *agapē*. A woman disengaged or forced into sex might not conceive for the seed would flow out of her uterus. 'Love (*agapē*: desire and affection conjoined), on the other hand, made the seed fit together and ... intercourse with passion (*erōs*) produces children much faster.'[37] Compared to the sudden male spasm, women's pleasure was protracted. Ideally, to maximise eugenic potential both partners would achieve simultaneous orgasm. A healthy constitution and strong sperm/sperma in both parents together with a coordinated climax would produce a strong child. In a resolutely androcentric approach to female sexuality, however, we learn that the woman stopped enjoying sex once she had captured the sperm. Pleasure was but a necessary side-show, not an end in itself.

In summary, ancient physiologies of sex and reproduction were clearly gendered in the ancient worlds, and delivered alongside prescriptions for

---

[33] Lonie 1981: 100.
[34] Alter 2013: 138. For the Hippocratic work *Generation* 1 see Potter 2012: 1–24.
[35] Lonie 1981: 101. [36] Potter 2012: 194–7. [37] Aetius (16.26) translated in Parker 2012: 116.

avoiding loss of sperm/sperma or the finest *qi* in the Chinese context. In the case of the Hippocratic writings the medical view was trained on the circumstances that would enhance fruitful reproduction rather than the pursuit of pleasure. In the Chinese sources reproduction was only tangential to social, aesthetic and health considerations. In both cases, Greco-Roman and Chinese, the primary sources allow us to consider the epistemic virtues implicated in the cumulative, long-term practices of noting and recording sexual activity.

Love Charms and Binding Spells

The combative nature of sexual engagement, its violent spasms (*tarachē*), the weakening of the body, can be seen in other less noble and gentlemanly domains of Greco-Roman life, and in a very different kind of text that belongs to the realm of cursing. Greek magical papyri describe techniques to entrap the objects (sometimes multiple women) of a man's or woman's desire. Sometimes the spell aimed to work literally through tormenting a woman's body supernaturally with erotic spells so she would feel 'the (?) longing as a she-cat (5) feels for a male cat', 'a yearning, a love, a madness great ... she seeking for him (going) to every place', the fury 'of Yaho, Sabaho, Horyo ... for I cast fury on you': until such time that she succumbed, and thereby released herself.[38]

The Greek magical papyri tend to date from the latter part of our time period until the fifth century CE, but their form, siting and purpose connect them to the *defixiones*, the curse tablets, for which there are examples from as early as the late fifth and fourth centuries BCE.[39] As Faraone points out, the spells aim at controlling the ardent male while arousing the passive female.[40] References to passionate women's spells are also to be found in the *Idylls* of the bucolic poet Theocritus. Here in extracts from *Idylls* 2, the discomfort of sickness and the torment of erotic seizure seem to elide:

I bind you, Theodotis daughter of Eus, by the tail of the snake and by the mouth of the crocodile and by the horns of the ram and by the venom of the asp and by the whiskers of the cat and by the penis of the god, that you may not be able to have

---

[38] Trans. Griffith and Thompson 1921: 185.
[39] 'Nestor's Cup Inscription' is one such inscription. If a man drunk from it he would be seized by a passion for sex. See Faraone 1996: 19.
[40] For Pliny as a later Roman source, see McClure 2002: 236–7. On the gender politics of Greek love charms, see Winkler 1992: 90–1, 95–8.

intercourse ever with another man either frontally or anally, nor to fellate nor to take pleasure with another man except me alone Ammonion Hermitaris.[41]

Some of the speakers are clearly female, aiming to draw and compel the man:

> [1] Where are the bay-leaves, Thestylis, and the charms?
> Fetch all; with fiery wool the caldron crown;
> Let glamour win me back my false lord's heart!
> Twelve days the wretch hath not come nigh to me,
> Nor made enquiry if I die or live,
> Nor clamoured (oh unkindness!) at my door.
> Sure his swift fancy wanders otherwhere,
> The slave of Aphroditè and of Love.
> I'll off to Timagetus' wrestling-school
> At dawn, that I may see him and denounce
> His doings; but I'll charm him now with charms.[42]

Or resolve love-madness:

> [22] First we ignite the grain. Nay, pile it on:
> Where are thy wits flown, timorous Thestylis?
> Shall I be flouted, I, by such as thou?
> Pile, and still say, 'This pile is of his bones.'

The last in this sequence introduces the linking of animals and *aphrodisia*:

> [52] The coltsfoot grows in Arcady, the weed
> That drives the mountain-colts and swift mares wild.
> Like them may Delphis rave: so, maniac-wise,
> Race from his burnished brethren home to me.

There is also evidence that spells were generic forms into which the cursers would insert their own and their would-be-lovers' names, invoking the interventions of common goddesses and animal spirits, spells of fire and the symbolic power of herbs. Binding spells in the ancient Greco-Roman and Chinese worlds shared many features: categories of ingredients such as those belonging to the so-called *Dreckapotheke*, that is the use of human and animal parts such as faeces, nails and hair; incantations; and magical writing. The spells are recorded and inscribed, however, in quite different ritual contexts, in remedy collections, poetry, inscriptions and historical records, as well as in the curse tablets.

---

[41] Winkler 1992: 94; Jordan 1985. [42] Theocritus, *Idylls* II, trans. Calverley 1892.

Allegations of spellbinding and the burying of wooden manikins by palace women to secure the interest of the Han emperors provide well-known stories from the standard histories about early Chinese love magic.[43] The Mawangdui medico-divinatory literature provides further evidence of the use of binding spells, outside and far from the palace.[44] This more direct evidence implies that a third person was responsible for the spells, perhaps a member of the family, but more likely someone charged especially with, and charging for, this kind of ritual service. Here is an excerpt from the Mawangdui text given the modern title of 'Za jinfang' 雜禁方.[45] The art of seduction and binding of lovers seems to be integrated into a category of spells concerned with creating and/or disrupting social harmony: separating, as well as bringing together couples; harmonising mother/daughter-in-law relations; stopping dogs barking.

[1] Where there is a dog that likes to bark in the courtyard and gate, daub mud on the well, in a rectangular band five *chi* long. When the husband ...

[2] ... and wife dislike one another daub mud on the doorway X in a rectangular band five *chi* long. When you wish to seduce a noble person, daub mud

[3] ... on the left and right sides of a gate in a rectangular band five *chi* long. When you have frequent foul dreams, daub mud beneath the bed

[4] ... in a rectangular band seven *chi* long. When the husband's mother and his wife like to fight, daub mud on the doorway in a rectangular band five *chi* long. When an infant

[5] ... likes to cry, daub mud on the window in a rectangular band five *chi* long.

[6] When involved in a suit with another person, write the person's name and set it inside a shoe.

[7] Incinerate and smith the tails of two female doves. Drink it yourself, and seduction will occur.

[8] Take *quantou* that faces east–west. Incinerate and smith. Give it to the husband and wife to drink, and they will be driven apart.

[9] Take four nails from the left claw of a male dove and four nails from the left hand of a young girl. Scorch in a saucepan, combine and smith. Apply it to the person and the person will be obtained.

[11] Put the person's left eyebrow in liquor and drink it. You invariably obtain the person.

This miscellany of spells to bring people together and drive them apart, to resolve household disharmony, and to create it, was buried in a box at

---

[43] Loewe 1974: 42, 81.   [44] See Li Jianmin 1996: 8.   [45] See Liu Lexian 2005, trans. Lo.

Mawangdui tomb 3 together with other literature dedicated to the healing arts and stored separately from works on philosophy, statecraft, astronomy etc. The selection indicates an early form of meta-categorisation concerned with the *technē* of the body and its emotions, in this case directed by the funerary director. The categories also mirror, very closely, the *fangji* 方技 (recipes and techniques) bibliographical category of the Han imperial library (recipe literature, theoretical treatises, the arts of the bedchamber and immortality).[46] This eclectic approach has to be understood as a feature of the systematisation of medicine in Han times, integral to the larger processes of synthesis common to imperial administration.

Spellbinding literature of Chinese origin in a tenth-century Japanese medical compilation and the divinatory and medico-technical writings of the Dunhuang manuscripts suggest the geographic and temporal range of this tradition.[47] Here the first four spells of *Rang nüzi furen shu mifa* 攘女子婦人述秘法 (Detailing the secret art of stealing women) are actually concerned with binding one's own husband:

[103] Whenever you wish to make [your] husband love [you] get the earth from under a red dog's feet and place it below his navel. He will immediately love the wife.

[104] Whenever you wish to attract your husband's love and respect, get his thumb nail and burn it to ashes, mix with wine and take it. Tested.

Chinese and Greek spellbinding involved strategies to resolve the discomforts and desires of passion. It assumed the intervention of spirits, the power of incantation, the resonances between things that are alike, be that the nails of the lover pursued and the claws of a bird, a manikin resembling the object of desire, or the power of rectangular mud symbols when daubed on the walls.

The question of how to evaluate perceptions of the efficacy of spellbinding deserves a sustained analysis which is certainly beyond the scope of this chapter. While there have been many important contributions to this question, notably from medical anthropologists, it is not enough to attribute the impact of ritual techniques to a psychological 'placebo' or an anthropological 'meaning response', solely effective within particular cultural parameters.[48] Modern attempts to explain cause and effect within a discourse of social

---

[46] *Hanshu* 6.1776–80.

[47] *Ishinpō, juan* 26. Cf Qiu Xigui 1992; Li Ling 2001; Li Jianmin 1996. See Pelliot 2661, 2666 and 2610, Bibliothèque nationale de France.

[48] See Moerman 2002 and Geertz 1973.

meanings fail to explore how shared and repeating ritual behaviours gather and preserve knowledge, the efficacy of which is understood differently as time goes by. This is easiest to understand when the ritual involves the sustained ingestion of particular substances. The transition from burning of *Artemisia annua* to determine an environment safe from malevolent disease-causing spirits, to its use in drawing and strengthening *qi* and the treatment of intermittent fever, to its ingestion as modern public health drug of choice in the prevention of malaria is a case in point. The sustained attention to the effect of the plant involves observation and recording within changing, but still linked, ritual, epistemological and institutional domains.

Love charms and binding incantations were often used together with substances considered potent in the arts of love and seduction. The latter may have included tonics put into food or drink or ointments to induce sexual passion in another person.[49] In the next section we turn to the *aphrodisiac* drugs and recipes themselves which reflect a practice of self-medication, the key *technē* upon which the coming argument about empiricism and the senses rests.

The Recipes

> [A]part from powers for health and disease and death, they say that herbs have other powers not only on bodily things but also on those of the soul. I mean by 'bodily' those concerned with generation and infertility. In fact some (plants) do both from the same part, for example the so-called *orchis* [testicle]; for as there are two <roots>, a large and small, the large root, if given in milk of a mountain goat, makes one more functional for intercourse; the small one harms and prevents. This plant has a leaf like the squill but smoother and smaller; the stem is very like that of the euphorbia used in unburnt offerings. (Theophrastus 9.18.3)[50]

Where historical aphrodisiac recipes were placed, how they were categorised and how they circulated reveal a great deal about their role in the ancient world. Just as culinary and medical recipes, they were not merely a guide to practice, they also represent a record of the collective imagination of that practice. In all there are some 1,500 recipes in the Hippocratic Corpus, and most of the aphrodisiac recipes lie in the gynaecological treatises.[51] Totelin emphasises large areas of overlap in antiquity between

---

[49] Dickie 2001: 16–17. The word *philtron* and its calque in Latin – *amatorium* – may have roughly the same range of meanings although the terms are restricted to the procedures of erotic magic.
[50] Tr. Preus 1988: 88.   [51] Totelin, private communication.

cosmetological, gynaecological and sex manuals and all the recipes had procreation as one of their main purposes. This reproductive aim did not, however, preclude sexual pleasure, or the use of ancient cosmetic texts as a kind of pornography. Breath fresheners, face creams, toothpaste, and remedies against freckles, dandruff, alopecia and spots, remedies to whiten scars, hair dyes, depilation creams all point to a lively market for beauty recipes, products and self-improvement in the pursuit of love, sex and marriage. These were Galen's 'vices of embellishment', the concern of all women but not the legitimate cosmetic work of medicine (Galen disingenuously includes his own versions to save women from danger).[52]

What of the remedies designed to enhance sexual performance? Totelin again: 'the Hippocratic compilers of recipes made use of a vast array of ingredients that were sexually connoted', but the gynaecological treatises do not explain efficacy beyond ascribing it to the treatment by opposites, e.g. curing dry vagina with moist figs.[53] Speaking of the Scythians the Hippocratic treatises *Airs, Waters, Places* states that 'people of such a constitution cannot be prolific. The men lack sexual desire because of the moistness of their constitution and the softness and coldness of their bellies, a condition which least inclines men to intercourse.'[54] The remedies to charge up the Scythian constitution, it stands to reason, must be heating food and drugs.

Aphrodisiac efficacy was partly established through what has come to be known, since Paracelsus, as the 'doctrine of signatures', the similarity of plant morphology with parts of the body meant that there would be mutual influence. The orchid bulb, in particular, was well known to enhance male sexual performance since it was reminiscent of testicles. Other plants commonly cited are *Eruca sativa* (rocket, arugula); arugula with honey and spices which might enhance an erection and when laced with *saturia* (aphrodisiac bulbs) would increase both size and pleasure.[55] Theophrastus described a penis cream that could cause 'twelve erections in succession'.[56]

A combination of the exotic, the wild and the rare with the power of the doctrine of signatures in an ingredient was apparently very exciting:

---

[52] Totelin forthcoming.   [53] Totelin 2009: 207.   [54] Trans. Chadwick and Mann 1978: 165.
[55] Faraone 1999: 10 n.93 and 20. The general meaning of *saturia* and the intriguing penis cream alert us to the problem of matching plant and mineral names to modern terminology. We have tackled this problem as best we can. General categories for species such as orchid or the terms for common substances such as 'egg' are undoubtedly correct, but terms we translate as 'mallow' or 'realgar' can only be read with the usual caution. We follow traditional and dictionary conventions that are open to challenge on account of the variations of plant terminology from one place to another and the inevitable distortions of modern categories.
[56] Theophrastus, *Historia plantarum* 9.18.9 (also cited by Pliny, *Natural History* 26.99).

Cyranides, writing on the wild pig (*suagros*) states that 'its testicles, dried and crushed as a drink, incite to the sexual act'. Eggs from the partridge 'incite to the sexual act'.[57] Tail of the lizard or the deer, molar of the skink, brain of the crane, womb of the hare, the *salpe* fish, animals and birds like goats and sparrows noted for their sexual proclivity were all ascribed sexual potency.[58] They could be consumed, worn as a bracelet, carried on the hand or rubbed on the body.[59] Metrodora, the author (some claim) of the oldest medical text written by a woman, writes:

> Recipes that are pleasurable: take the womb of a hare fried in a bronze frying pan, add 3 litrai of rose oil, then mix with sweet perfume, fat (4 drachmai), excrement of crocodile (3 dr.), sap of the plant scorpion, blood-red sumach (2 dr.), honey (4 dr.). Some add also a little fat of sparrow.[60]

There is a small step from observing that two things that have the same physical structure are likely to exert a mutual influence to noticing that activities shared by humans and animals might both be enhanced by the same substance. There are many tales in the ancient world where the substances used to encourage stud animals to mate gain a reputation for stimulating human sexuality. Theophrastus comments, 'in Achea, and especially around Kerynia there is a kind of vine whose wine makes pregnant women abort; if bitches eat the grapes they also abort'.[61] Pliny describes how wines laced with the elusive *saturion* and *hippomanes* were used to stimulate sexual desire in horses.[62] *Yinyang huo* 淫羊藿 (Horny Goat Weed; Epimedium) gets its Chinese name from a story about a Chinese goatherd who discovered its magic after repeatedly observing its effect on his flock.[63] Epimedium contains icariin, a muscle relaxant that exerts a mild biochemical action on the penis similar to Sildenafil, the active ingredient of Viagra.

For the most part the Greek aphrodisiac recipes were simples. Pliny offers many special plants that could increase a man's potency such as terebinth and donax. He also cautions the anti-aphrodisiac effects of herbs such as *Nymphea* which relaxed the phallus, or lettuce, *Agnus castus*, rue or condrille which limited desire in different ways.[64] Valuing the work of

---

[57] *Cyranides* 2.35, 2.47, 3.38.   [58] Faraone 1999: 20 n. 90.   [59] Faraone 1999: 19.
[60] Metrodora 36 ed. Del Guerra 1994: 52–3 trans. courtesy of Laurence Totelin.
[61] Theophrastus, *Historia plantarum* 9.18.3-11, trans. Preus 1988.
[62] For *saturion* see 26.99; *hippomanes* see Pliny, *Natural History* 8.165, 26.181; Faraone 1999: 21.
[63] From *Mingyi bielu* 名醫別錄 (Separate Records of Eminent Physicians) as cited in *Bencao gangmu juan* 12.
[64] Faraone 1999: 19; Lloyd 1983. For terebinth see Pliny, *Natural History* 24.28; donax 24.87; *Nymphea* 25.75; lettuce 19.127; *Agnus castus* 16.26, 110; rue 34.89; condrille 22.91.

those with on-the-ground experience, Theophrastus claimed that his information came from the *pharmakopolai* and the root-cutters. Assertions such as that a drug 'from a man from India' could make a man have tireless sexual energy also suggest hearsay. Multi-substance remedies, as are found in the early Chinese recipe tradition, come some time after with Nicander (fl. second century BCE), Dioscorides (fl. first century BCE) and Galen. Galen's *Simple Remedies*, for example, states that, 'concerning turnip *gongulis*, the seed of turnip leads to sexual desire'.[65] But many of the simples were infused in wine, which was the vehicle for their action – a sure way to achieve part of the desired aphrodisiac effect.

We can see many aphrodisiac substances in ancient China, and especially those that are sexually connoted like asparagus for the shape of its head and the way in which it grows so erect in the ground. They were clearly used for their erotic rather than reproductive value. This was also the domain of longevity practices where new medical ideas were forming. Here is Da Cheng's 大成 (Great Perfection) response to the Yellow Emperor on being asked how to refine one's complexion and delay aging. Da Cheng was an established authority in esoteric teaching.

> When coitus with Yin is expected to be frequent, follow it with flying creatures. The spring dickey bird's round egg arouses that crowing cock. The crowing cock has an essence. If you are truly able to ingest this, the jade whip is reborn. Best is engaging the member. Block that jade hole. When brimming then have intercourse, and bid farewell with round eggs. If the member is not engaged conserve it with roasted-wheat meal. If truly able to ingest this, you can raise the dead.[66]

Here, in what is a set of questions exploring longevity and immortality and its association with sexual competence into old age, the language is replete with euphemisms for the penis (the crowing cock, Yin, jade whip, the member) and the vagina (jade hole). Potency and fertility are represented by the round egg and avian creatures, and simultaneously strengthened by eating eggs and sustained with roasted-wheat meal. When stripped of the literary allusions the methods seem quite ordinary. But here we also find new codes emerging that were ultimately to shape nutritional and medical theory.

The aphrodisiac recipes from the Mawangdui tomb contain all the methods associated with Aphrodite in the Greek tradition. There are recipes for sustained and larger erections, copious semen, and general strength of *qi* for virility, 'contraction' and 'increasing fineness' of the

---

[65] Kühn 11.861.   [66] MWD 4 *Shiwen* nos. 10–14. Harper 1998: 389.

vagina, hair removal after childbirth and for curing genital swellings: asparagus with chicken breast and a whole black rooster to boil the offal of a young black dog, to be taken in the afternoon in whatever quantity required, beef, yam, cinnamon, wild ginger and wormwood combined with oyster and Qin *Zanthoxylum* (a variety of Sichuan pepper) increase strength. Snails charge up the 'horse' (penis). Pork from pigs fed on pine truffles stimulates the woman; cow horn, ginger and cinnamon soaked in vinegar and administered via a vaginal suppository increase her 'craving'.[67]

With food and sex the stuff of everyday life, it is easy to imagine how basic empirical observations about the effects or substances on the body could first be noticed by the authors and compilers of those recipes, and second, feed in to scholarly reflections on the nature of the body and its physiology. Evidence of this process is easily discernible in the body of the aphrodisiac recipes and, in this respect, contrasts with the style of those prescriptions excavated from the same tomb that are aimed at the treatment of other people's diseases. Where the recipes for stimulating one's own sexual appetite and pleasure, and strengthening and conditioning the genitals, are replete with techniques to rid the body of foul *qi*, to fortify, renew and strengthen Yin and *qi*, the collections designed for treating illness (rather than increasing a sense of strength and well-being) have barely any recourse to these terms of the emerging science. Neither can they be read against an esoteric literature framed in its terms. It is therefore to those texts that are concerned with self-experimentation and cultivation that we must turn to trace the history of the interface between the remedies and techniques of the ancient world and the new world that we now associate with the authority of classical medicine.

Measuring and controlling the internal sensory environment of the body are particularly evident in those aphrodisiac recipes that aim to 'cause burning', 'increase craving' and 'cultivate strength'. The fruits of the pagoda tree make the body 'seem[s] to itch but does not itch', a vivid evocation of sexual ardour; various degrees of heat, from subtle to intense, are identified on different surfaces of the skin as the effect, for example, of inserting honey, ginger and cinnamon soaked suppositories and massaging with napkins; wild ginger, curled cinnamon, ginger and monkshood increase *qi* and make a person's face lustrous. Woven cloths soaked in red ants and blister beetles, a universally attested irritant used as an aphrodisiac and known to us as Spanish fly, rubbed on 'the jade whip' startle the horse into action.[68] Dried horsemeat and monkshood soaked in

[67] Ibid.   [68] Harper 2005: 91–100.

alcohol make the 'six extremities strong and increase longevity' while other alcoholic preparations made from fermented millet and herbs 'when ingested for one hundred days, [it] make[s] the eyes bright and ears perceptive; the extremities all become strong'. Interspersed with the aphrodisiac recipes are more general categories which contain prescriptions for strengthening the body, aligning sexual prowess with an overall concern for potency and the general sense that this condition of well-being was consistent with a prospect of prolonging life.[69]

Spellbinding and recipe literature detailing ingredients and practical techniques for entrancing lovers and increasing their sexual desire and performance contrasted with the poetry of the more theoretical literature of the sexual arts with its appeal to new styles of understanding the human body in its relation to the natural, social and cosmological environment. Apart from the more frequent references to Yin, Yang and *qi* the aphrodisiac remedies are structured like the recipes for curing illness, with content lists and category markers, for easy access and retrieval. The aphrodisiac collection, however, ends with a 'discourse' that marks it clearly as a text that stands between the ancient worlds of empirical and ritual healing and the formation of classical medical and nutritional theory. In a brief concluding section that serves to contextualise the remedies, the legendary Yu 禹 is in conversation with his consorts about the perils of excessive sex and the subsequent loss of *qi*. His stated desire is to 'bring together *qi* so that man and woman propagate'. 'Young Beauty' warns against violent engagement and suggests a broth of woolly grass and mugwort to restore him. Thus this endnote suggests that the aphrodisiac literature cannot be read in isolation from the more theoretical treatises on the nature and purpose of sexual union and the techniques themselves. This one reference to 'propagate' is the exception that produces the rule. There is no remedy in this collection that deals directly with reproduction, fertility, or virility in relation to producing children. Most directly address sexual competence, pleasure, generalised strength and longevity.[70]

Does the aphrodisiac record of ancient China mark a transition between passive observation and deliberate research, where the latter involves an active desire to extend knowledge? We have demonstrated a community of

---

[69] Lo forthcoming, 2018.

[70] Regular comments that a recipe has been 'tested' or is 'excellent' suggest there was a hierarchy of good cures established by precedent. Where remedies rely on belief in the direct involvement of the spirit world, the anthropologist's distinction between 'efficacy' and 'felicity', or the 'meaning response' as identified by Moerman, helps gauge the excellence of their contemporary appropriateness, but this hardly explains the full range of connotations. High praise may also simply be a marketing ploy.

researchers engaged in the organisation of data collected through a range of sensory experiences. In what is surely the earliest surviving map of the female genitals appended to one of the aphrodisiac collections we see observation of an idealised anatomy, a line drawing marking pubic hair, locating vaginal aromas *choushu* 臭鼠 (the smelly rat), and the *chizhu* 赤珠 ('red pearl', a euphemism for the clitoris), designed like a control panel in the pursuit of knowledge and power. This is a remarkable diagram, demanding further analysis, but which for our purposes testifies to the range of senses through which information about sexual response was hypothesised and recorded in early China.[71]

While there is both intentionality and theory involved in the matching of animal to human contexts, and traditional knowledge always presupposes an on-going cumulative process of trial and error, in this combined recipe and theoretical literature devoted to the sexual arts we find a specialist literacy and images which demonstrate new and sustained styles of recording observations and sensory perceptions of the body – valuable records of the collective experimentation of a new group of learned self-experimenters. While we cannot locate this project in any particular institution, it is clear that it is part and parcel of a widespread medical culture that was operating through the new networks of knowledge that spanned the Yellow River plains and Yangzi valley in the early centuries of empire.

Conclusion

While disparaging the over-elaborated correlations of turn-of-the-millennium 'proto-science' as 'a low point in the debasement of Chinese thought', Angus Graham made an important point. In China, correlative thinking, exemplified in Yin-Yang and Five Agent cosmology, extended easily in to what, in other contexts, might be thought of as sympathetic magic or *sumpatheia* as often discussed by Greeks and Romans.[72] Thus *yin-yang* divisions of the body, astronomy, astrology and the planetary gods and spirits existed on a continuum, and were embraced within the same natural order.[73] The kinds of observations about resonance and mutual influence between things of the same form and nature are as much at the core of ritual magic and binding spells as they are in translating animal behaviour to the human world. We have provided examples of these records for the ancient worlds of Greece and China.

[71] Ma Jixing 1992: 748. [72] Graham 1989: 349–50. [73] Graham 1989: 382.

Some of the recipes recorded are based on millennia of collective belief and empiricism, anonymous records of the accumulating experience of healers, farmers and root gatherers. Others are the result of a learned community of individuals who contributed their work, still anonymously, to a burgeoning body of technical literature. The Chinese *aphrodisia*, we have argued, stand at the threshold where what one might imagine as the simple empiricism of the former met the learned approaches with which scholars recorded their experience of the body and its care.

The language and structure of key aphrodisiac remedy collections have provided the clearest evidence of the empirical process merging with the new medical theories of Yin, Yang, *qi* and *jing*, for the reason that they reflect the experiences of the body in self-experimentation. This was an intimate process that involved a community of learned practitioners whose aesthetic engagement with their scientific objects (the self, and sexual partners) required comprehensive sensory perception and not just the singular and limiting observations of the eye. This process is *not* evident in the parallel Mawangdui medical recipe texts for treating patients, that is, *other* people, with named illnesses, and therefore indicates that the sexual arts were a key context for medical innovation. To our knowledge, thus far, there is also no reason to believe that in the ancient Greek world aphrodisiacs and the sexual arts formed a special context for the development of medical theory. And this marks a major point of difference.

In this chapter we have surveyed a much-overlooked subject in the history of medicine. We have done so comparatively, demonstrating categories, definitions, concepts and techniques of the sexual arts that were shared in the ancient worlds. Key differences we have discovered include the overarching reproductive aims of Greco-Roman aphrodisiac recipes, and the unique Chinese use of self-experimentation in the sexual arts as a cornerstone of a new medicine. We hope that this small beginning will inspire others to consider serious study of *aphrodisia* as a contribution to the history of the 'scientific self'.

Bibliography

Allan, S. (1997) *The Way of Water and Sprouts of Virtue*. Albany.
Alter, J. S. (2013) 'Sex, *askesis* and the athletic perfection of the soul', in *Subtle Bodies*, eds. G. Samuels and J. Johnson. London: 121–48.
Andreini, A. (2006) 'The meaning of *qing* 情 in texts from Guodian Tomb No. 1', in Santangelo and Guida: 149–65.

Bain, D. (1997) 'Salpe's Παίγνια: Athenaeus 322A and Plin. H.N. 23.38,' *Classical Quarterly* 48: 262–8.

Bjorck, G. and Farrington, B. (1944) 'Apsyrtus, Julius Africanus et l'Hippiatrique grecque (Uppsala Universitets Årsskrift. 1944: 4)', *Journal of Hellenic Studies* 64: 121.

Bray, F., Dorofeeva-Lichtmann, V. and Metailié, G. (eds.) (2007) *Graphic and Text in the Production of Technical Knowledge in China: The Warp and the Weft.* Leiden.

Calverley, C. S. (1869) *Theocritus: Translated into English Verse.* Cambridge.

Chadwick, J. and Mann, W. N. (1950) *The Medical Works of Hippocrates.* Oxford.

Daston, L. and Gallison, P. ([2007] 2010) *Objectivity.* New York.

Del Guerra, G. (1994) *Metrodora, Medicina e cosmesi ad uso delle donne: la antica sapienza femminile e la cura di sé.* Milan.

Dickie, M. (2001) *Magic and Magicians in the Graeco Roman World.* Abingdon.

Erickson, S. N. (2010) 'Han dynasty tomb structures and contents', in Nylan and Loewe: 13–82.

Faraone, C. A. (1996) 'Taking the "Nestor's Cup Inscription" seriously: erotic magic and conditional curses in the earliest inscribed hexameters', *Classical Antiquity* 15: 77–112.

  (1999) *Ancient Greek Love Magic.* Cambridge, MA.

Faraone, C. A. and Obbink, D. (1991) *Magika Hiera: Ancient Greek Magic and Religion.* Oxford.

Fortenbaugh, W. and Sharples, R. W. (1988) *Theophrastean Studies, On Natural Science, Physics and Metaphysics, Ethics, Religion and Rhetoric* (RUSCH III). New Brunswick.

Geertz, C. (1973) *The Interpretation of Cultures: Selected Essays.* New York.

Gemmill, C. L. (1973) 'The missing passage in Hort's translation of Theophrastus', *Bulletin of the New York Academy of Medicine* 49.2: 127–9.

Geurts, K. L. (2005) 'Consciousness as "feeling in the body": a West African theory of embodiment, emotion and the making of mind', in Howes: 164–78.

Goldhill, S. (2004) *Love, Sex and Tragedy: How the Ancient World Shapes Our Lives.* Chicago.

Graham, A. (1989) *Disputers of the Dao: Philosophical Argument in Ancient China.* La Salle, IL.

Griffith, F. L. and Thompson, H. (1921) *Demotic Magical Papyrus of London and Leiden.* Oxford.

Harper, D. (1998) *Early Chinese Medical Literature: The Mawangdui Medical Manuscripts.* London.

  (2005) 'Ancient and medieval Chinese recipes for aphrodisiacs and philters', *Asian Medicine* 1.1: 91–100.

Hebei sheng wenwuju (eds.) (2000) *Hebei wenwu jinghua zhi yi: Mancheng Hanmu.*

Hort, A. (1980) *Theophrastus, Enquiry into Plants: and Minor Works on Odours and Weather Signs.* Cambridge, MA.
Howes, D. (ed.) (2005) *Empire of the Senses: The Sensual Culture Reader.* Oxford.
Hsu, E. (2001) *Innovation in Chinese Medicine.* Cambridge.
  (2010) *Pulse Diagnosis in Early Chinese Medicine: The Telling Touch.* Cambridge.
Humphreys, S. (1983) *The Family, Women and Death.* Ann Arbor, MI.
Hunan sheng bowuguan 湖南省博物館 and Zhongguo kexueyuan kaogu yanjiusuo 中国科学院考古研究所 (eds.) (1973) *Changsha Mawangdui yihao Hanmu* 长沙马王堆一号汉墓. Beijing.
James, S. L. and Dillon, S. (eds.) (2012) *Blackwell Companion to Women in the Ancient World.* Malden, MA.
Jordan, D. (1985) 'A survey of Greek defixiones not included in the special corpora', *Greek, Roman and Byzantine Studies* 26: 151–97.
Jütte, R. (2005) *A History of the Senses: From Antiquity to Cyberspace*, trans. J. Lynn. Oxford.
Keuls, E. C. (1993) *The Reign of the Phallus.* Berkeley.
Kühn, C. G. (1964) *Claudii Galeni Opera omni.* Hildesheim.
Kuriyama, S. (2002) *The Expressiveness of the Body and the Divergence of Greek and Chinese Medicine.* Cambridge, MA.
Lau, D. C. (1970) *Mencius.* London.
Li Jianmin 李建民 (1996) 'Furen meidao kao: chuantong jiating de chongtu yu huajie fangshu' 婦人媚道考: 傳統家庭的衝突與化解方術, *Xin shixue* 7.4: 1–32.
Li Ling 李零 (2001) *Zhongguo fangshu kao* 中國方術考 (Studies of Chinese divinatory and medical arts). Beijing.
  (2006) *Zhongguo fangshu zhengkao* 中國方術正考 (Revised studies of Chinese divinatory and medical arts). Beijing.
Li Shizhen (Ming). (2002) *Bencao gangmu* 本草纲目, Xin jiaozhu ben, ed. Liu Hengru et al., 2 vols. Beijing.
Liu Lexian 刘乐贤 (2005) 'Love charms among the Dunhuang manuscripts', in Lo and Cullen: 165–75.
Lloyd, G. E. R. (1979) *Magic, Reason and Experience.* Cambridge.
  (1983) 'Theophrastus, the Hippocratics and the root cutters: science and the folklore of plants and their use', in *Science Folklore and Ideology: Studies in the Life Sciences in Ancient Greece.* Cambridge: 119–35.
  (1987) *The Revolutions of Wisdom.* Berkeley.
  (1996) *Adversaries and Authorities: Investigations into Ancient Greek and Chinese Science.* Cambridge.
Lo, V. (2000) 'Crossing the "inner pass": an "inner/outer" distinction in early Chinese medicine?', *East Asian Science, Technology and Medicine* 17: 15–65.
  (2001) 'The influence of Western Han nurturing life literature on the development of acumoxa therapy', in Hsu: 19–51.

(2007) 'Imagining practice: sense and sensuality in early Chinese medical illustration', in Bray et al.: 383–423.

(forthcoming 2018) *Potent Substances: On the Boundaries between Food and Medicine*, London.

Lo, V. and Barrett, P. (2012) 'Other pleasures?' in *Sex in Asia, 400–1900*, ed. R. Reyes. London: 25–46.

Lo, V. and Cullen, C. (eds.) (2005) *Medieval Chinese Medicine*. London.

Loewe, M. (1974) *Crisis and Conflict in Han China*, London.

Lonie, I. (1981) *The Hippocratic Treatise, 'On Generation', 'On the Nature of the Child', 'Diseases IV'*. Berlin.

Ma Jixing 馬繼興 (1992) *Mawangdui guyishu kaoshi* 馬王堆古醫書考釋, Hunan.

Mawangdui Hanmu boshu zhengli xiaozu 马王堆汉墓帛书整理小组 (eds.) (1985) *Mawangdui Hanmu boshu* 馬王堆漢墓帛書, vol. 4 (MWD 4). Beijing.

McClure, L. K. (2002) *Sexuality and Gender in the Classical World: Readings and Sources*. Oxford.

Moerman, D. (2002) *Meaning, Medicine and the 'Placebo Effect'*. Cambridge.

Nutton, V. (2004) *Ancient Medicine*. London.

Nylan, M. (2003) 'On the politics of pleasure', *Asia Major* (3rd series) 14.1: 73–124.

Nylan, M. and Loewe, M. (eds.) (2010) *China's Early Empires: A Re-appraisal*. Cambridge.

Ovid (1929) *Art of Love. Cosmetics. Remedies for Love. Ibis. Walnut-tree. Sea Fishing. Consolation*, trans. J. H. Mozley. Cambridge, MA.

Parker, H. N. (1992) 'Love's body anatomized; the ancient erotic handbooks and the rhetoric of sexuality', in Richlin: 90–111.

(2012) 'Women and medicine', in James and Dillon: 107–24.

Pfister, R. (2012) 'Gendering sexual pleasures in early and medieval China', *Asian Medicine* 7.1: 34–64.

Pliny (1940) *Natural History*, vol. III: books 8–11, trans. H. Rackham. Cambridge, MA.

(1950) *Natural History*, vol. V: books 17–19, trans. H. Rackham. Cambridge, MA.

(1951) *Natural History*, vol. VI: books 20–3, trans. W. H. S. Jones. Cambridge, MA.

(1956) *Natural History*, vol. VII: books 24–7, trans. W. H. S. Jones and A. C. Andrews. Cambridge, MA.

Potter, P. (2012) Hippocrates, Volume X. *Generation. Nature of the Child. Diseases 4. Nature of Women and Barrenness*. Cambridge, MA.

Preisendanz, K. and Henrichs, A. (1973–4) *Papyri Graecae Magicae: Die griechischen Zauberpapyri*. Stuttgart.

Preus, A. (1988) 'Theophrastus' phychopharmacology (*Historia plantarum* IX)', in Fortenbaugh and Sharples: 76–99.

Samuel, G. B. and Johnston, J. (2013) *Religion and the Subtle Body in Asia and the West: Between Mind and Body*, vol. VIII. London.

Qiu Xigui 裘錫圭 (1992) 'Mawangdui yishu shidu suoyi' 馬王堆醫書釋讀瑣議, in *Guwenzi lunji* 古文字論集 (A Collection of Essays on Ancient Texts). Beijing: 528–9.

Richlin, A. (ed.) (1992) *Pornography and Representation in Greece and Rome*. Oxford.

Sakade, Y. 坂出祥伸 and Umekawa, S. 梅川純代 (2003) 「気」の思想から見る道教の房中術：いまに生きる古代中国の性愛長寿法 *'Ki' no shiso kara miru dokyo no bochujutsu : ima ni ikiru kodai Chugoku no seiai chojuho*. Tokyo.

Santangelo, P. and Guida, D. (eds.) (2006) *Love, Hatred, and Other Passions: Questions and Themes on Emotions in Chinese Civilization*. Leiden.

Sarton, G. (1959) *A History of Science*. Cambridge, MA.

Scarborough, J. (1978) 'Theophrastus on herbals and herbal remedies', *Journal of the History of Biology* 11: 353–85.

  (2010) *Pharmacy and Drug Lore in Antiquity: Greece, Rome, Byzantium*. London.

Stanton, D. C. (1992) *Discourses of Sexuality: From Aristotle to Aids*. Ann Arbor, MI: 48–77.

Sterckx, R. (2003) 'Le pouvoir des sens: sagesse et perception sensorielle en Chine ancienne', in R. Lanselle (ed.), *Du pouvoir*. Paris: 71–92.

Suzuki, A. and Hisaro, I. (eds.) (2005) 食餌の技法－身体医文化論 4 (Art of Eating – Medical Culture of the Body 4). Tokyo.

Totelin, L. M. V. (2009) *Hippocratic Recipes: Oral and Written Transmission of Pharmacological Knowledge in Fifth- and Fourth-Century Greece*. Leiden.

  (forthcoming) 'From *technē* to *kakotechnia*: use and abuse of ancient cosmetic texts'.

Umekawa, Sumiyo 梅川純代 (2005) '媚薬－中国性技法における食 (The Aphrodisiacs – Diet in Chinese Sexual Art)', in Suzuki and Hisaro: 93–216.

Vieillefond, J. (1970) *Les 'Cestes' de Julius Africanus: étude sur l'ensemble des fragments avec édition, traduction et commentaires*. Florence.

Wear, A. (2013) 'Popular medicine and the new science in England: cross roads or merging lanes?', in *Wissenschaftsgeschichte und Geschichte des Wissens im Dialog*, eds. K. von Greyerz, S. Flubacher and P. Senn. Schauplaetze der Forschung: 61–84.

Winkler, J. (1992) *The Constraints of Desire: The Anthropology of Sex and Gender in Ancient Greece*. New York.

PART V

Agriculture, Planning and Institutions

13 | From the Harvest to the Meal in Prehistoric China and Greece: A Comparative Approach to the Social Context of Food

XINYI LIU, EVI MARGARITIS AND MARTIN JONES

In *Cooking, Cuisine and Class,* Jack Goody (1982) drew attention to some enduring features of culinary practice that exposed resonances between Europe and Asia, but distinguished them from recurrent features of sub-Saharan Africa. In all three continents, the language of food and the performances of food preparation and presentation are intimately entangled with the iteration of social relationships. However, the nature of those languages and performances varies. In Africa, social power is recurrently connected with consumption of quantity. In Europe and Asia, it is recurrently connected with the consumption of a cuisine that was differentiated, both in content and in process.

Goody's observations of *haute cuisine* and other forms of consumption were largely drawn from contemporary and historical examples. They were thematic observations, noting considerable variation between cultures and places. However, as themes they may have some discernible continuity through time. Goody argued for Eurasian resonance in historical times; in this chapter we explore the possibility of an equivalent resonance in prehistory. In comparison with what is available from texts, the archaeological evidence is, in many respects, incomplete and fragmentary. However, the recovery of food remains from archaeological sites has enabled insights, not just into the composition of early foods, but also into the processing and presentational practices of the past. Of particular utility in extending the Eurasian comparison into the first millennium BCE and beyond is the evidence for food processing.

We shall follow the lines of contextual analysis and comparative approach that Jack Goody developed, and consider the periods preceding written texts. Patterns observable in archaeological records from China and Greece will be examined, and the origins of unequal access to food will be explored. We will draw upon Mary Douglas' (1966) ideas about the delineation of insider and outsider. As Douglas (1971: 61) argues, 'The message [of food] is about different degrees of hierarchy, inclusion and exclusion, boundaries and transactions across the boundaries.' Before turning to the archaeological data, we shall first reflect upon some aspects of the social use of food in early Chinese and Greek texts.

The Social Use of Food

Food in the past, as it is in the present, is not merely concerned with production, storage, and conveyance to the kitchens of the people. It is also concerned with who has access to food and who does not. Famines are liable to occur even with good harvests and even in prosperity; in famines recorded in our own era, people die of starvation in front of food-filled shops.

Early treatises on this matter focused largely on issues pertaining to obligatory or prohibited commensalism as a social and psychological bond, uniting or separating social groups, as well as focusing on the totem-taboos that impacted upon the degree of internal social distinctions (Robertson-Smith 1889; Mauss 1925/1954).

Since the 1960s, the analysis of food and food preparation has been associated with the name of Lévi-Strauss (1962/1963), whose work displays a very different focus of interest. As the author himself often emphasised, his approach employs a linguistic model for the analysis of such things as cooking and marriage. Accordingly, food and the meal can profitably be treated as a kind of language, a set of processes permitting the establishment of links, between individuals and groups. Items of food are like words within language systems and women and men within kinship systems.

This theme was further explored by authors such as Marshall Sahlins (1976) and Mary Douglas (1971; 1984). Douglas sees food as a 'code' or a 'symbol' of social relationships; there is 'a correspondence between a given social structure and the structure of symbols by which it is expressed'. She extends the restricted analytic field that Lévi-Strauss adopts on the basis of the linguistic model, and proposes that we place the meal in the context of other meals consumed in the course of the day, of the week and of the year. So 'each meal carries something of the meaning of the other meals; each meal is a structured social event which structures others in its own image' (Douglas 1971: 69).

Placing the process of social exclusion at the heart of his study, Sahlins (1976) argues that human cultures are formulated out of practical activity. Symbolic, meaningful or cultural reason leads to utility, which is its justification. He argues that while hunger was once shared, in modern industrial societies food flows in divergent streams: a trickle of less nourishing foodstuffs to the poor and unprivileged and huge quantities of highly nourishing foodstuffs to the rich. His observations of unequal access to food in societies of our own time echoes those of Jack Goody in relation to the ancient world. In both the ancient Mediterranean and ancient China, cooking was embodied in the written form so as to create a core of practices and recipes that could be subjected to further elaboration in the kitchens and libraries of the rich.

Food and Hierarchy in Written Records

A valuable source on cooking in the Hellenistic period is Athenaeus, a native of the Egyptian town of Naucratis. Around 200 CE, Athenaeus was writing *The Deipnosophists*, 'Connoisseurs in the Art of Dining' or 'Dinner-table Philosophers'. In this work he gathered the manners and the customs of the ancients from 800 different authors. As Goody (1982: 103) observed, much of the treatise has to do with food and its elaboration. At one point the author enumerates seventy-two kinds of bread made in Greece. These variations in the nature of the available foods marked out the social hierarchy, the emphasis being placed on riches, luxury and the geographical distribution of varieties of food. The work is narrated as a conversation at a dinner party given by a rich Roman, reflecting the great interest in gastronomy, in conspicuous consumption, and in servile labour among the upper classes.

> And then two slaves brought in a well-rubb'd table,
> And then another, and another, till
> The room was fill'd, and then the hanging lamps
> Beamed bright and shone upon the festive crowns,
> And herbs, and dishes of rich delicacies.
> And then all arts were put in requisition
> To furnish forth a most luxurious meal.
> Barley-cakes white as snow did fill the baskets,
> And then were served up not coarse vulgar pots,
> But well-shaped dishes, whose well-ordered breadth
> Fill'd the rich board, eels, and the well-stuff'd conger.
> A dish fit for the gods. Then came a platter
> Of equal size, with dainty swordfish fraught,
> And then fat cuttlefish, and the savoury tribes
> Of the long hairy polypus. After this
> Another orb appeared upon the table,
> Rival of that just brought from off the fire,
> Fragrant with spicy odor.
> (Quoted by Goody, 1982: 103–4)

Around 1000 BCE, a similar complexity in the kitchens of the upper-classes Middle Kingdom Egypt is documented in the *Onomasticon of Amenope*, in the list of different categories of baking. Cereals are listed in the catalogue and then related to the different kinds of pastry, bread or cake and beverage made from them. Beer is the first of twenty-three varieties of beverage. The text goes on to enumerate twenty-nine parts of an ox, beginning with the generic term 'meat', then descending to 'head', 'neck', etc. (Goody 1982: 99–100).

Themes of elaborate multi-sensory performance and culinary differentiation can also be discerned in Chinese texts. *Chu Ci* 楚辭, also known as 'Songs of the South', was composed during the Warring States period (481–221 BCE), intermediate in date between the *Onomasticon of Amenope* and *The Deipnosophists*. *Chu Ci* reveals the complexity of meals enjoyed by the upper class of the Chu state, with many dishes elaborately prepared and ranked among the best-treasured enjoyments of life (Chang 1977b). A contemporary poem *Zhao Hun* 招魂 ('The Summons of the Soul') 'summoned the soul' to return home to the good life, a life represented by the following feast. In it, we read:

> O soul, come back! Why should you go far away?
> All your household have come to do you honour; all kinds of good food are ready:
> Rice, broomcorn, early wheat, mixed with yellow millet;
> Bitter, salt, sour, hot and sweet: there are dishes of all flavours.
> Ribs of the fatted ox cooked tender and succulent;
> Sour and bitter blended in the soup of Wu;
> Stewed turtle and roast kid, served up with yam sauce;
> Geese cooked in sour sauce, casseroled duck, fried flesh of the great crane;
> Braised chicken, seethed terrapin, high-seasoned, but not to spoil the taste;
> Fried honey-cakes of rice flour and malt-sugar sweetmeats;
> Jade-like wine, honey-flavoured, fills the winged cups;
> Ice-cooled liquor, strained of impurities, clear wine, cool and refreshing;
> Here are laid out the patterned ladles, and here is sparkling wine.
> (Trans. Hawkes 1985: 227–8)

In yet another poem, *Da Zhao* 大招 ('The Great Summons')

> The five kinds of grain are heaped six ells high, and the corn of zizania set out;
> Cauldrons seethe to their brims, wafting a fragrance of well-blended flavours;
> Plump orioles, pigeons, and geese, flavoured with broth of jackal's meat:
> O soul, come back! Indulge your appetite!

> Fresh turtle, succulent chicken, dressed with the sauce of Chu;
> Pickled pork, dog cooked in bitter herbs, and ginger-flavoured mince,
> And sour Wu salad of Artemisia, not too wet or tasteless.
> O soul, come back! Indulge in your own choice!
> Roast crane next is served up, and steamed duck and boiled quails,
> Fried bream, stewed magpies, and green goose, broiled.
> O soul, come back! Choice things are spread before you.
> Four kinds of wine have been subtly blended, not rasping to the throat:
> Clear, fragrant, ice-cooled liquor, not for base men to drink;
> And white yeast is mixed with must of Wu to make the clear Chu wine
> O soul, come back and do not be afraid!
> (Trans. Hawkes 1985: 234–5)

Another theme arising from both *The Deipnosophists* and *Chu Ci* is the development of *haute cuisine*. In each, a contrast between the local food of peasants and the exotic food of foreigners serves as a basis, for transformation, incorporations and emphasis of difference. In both ancient Greek and Chinese cases, the differentiation in cooking brings the hierarchical together with the geographical; the loftier the hierarchical position, the more expansive the geographical allusion.

Chu Ci probably represents the customs of the south, which differ from those in north China. In some earlier or contemporary records from the North, such as *Shijing* 詩經 (*Classic of Poetry*) and *Liji* 禮記 (*Book of Rites*), we read of similar banquets that emphasise the variation and differentiation of the food that is 'not for the base man'. Between 1000 BCE and 200 CE, a parallel theme runs through the literature from both sides of Eurasia, from Greece to China, that illustrate such rapturous celebration of the rich and rare.

There is no early record to show the number of slaves or servants involved in preparing the great feasts described by Athenaeus and Qu Yuan. In *The Deipnosophists*, we see more and more slaves enter until the room is filled. In *Zhao Hun*, women from Zheng and Wei perform dances while servants from Wu prepare meat. The size of the labour force was specified in some later records. In the Ming court (1368–1644 CE), at different times the kitchen servants/eunuchs numbered between 3,000 and 6,000. From the beginning of the period the eunuch staff were allotted separate spaces for dealing with food and drink; the palace pharmacy, the imperial wine bureau, the flour mill, the vinegar works, the bureau of herds and flocks, and the bureau of vegetable gardening (Goody 1982: 110).

Such an elaborate protocol of food preparation and consumption was not without its critics. Alongside the rapturous celebration of the rich and rare, a parallel theme running through the literature in the ancient world is one of denial, restraint and asceticism. One recurrent complaint is exemplified by Du Fu's (712–70 CE, Tang dynasty) poem: 'while the wine and the meat have spoiled behind the red doors [of rich households], on the road there are skeletons of those who died of exposure' (quoted by Chang 1977a: 15).

Similar contrasts were drawn by Mencius in the fourth century BCE; he was critical of conspicuous consumption, calling on the abnegation of court feasts.

When speaking to men of consequence it is necessary to look upon them with contempt and not be impressed with their lofty position. Their hall is tens of feet high: the capitals are several feet broad. Were I to meet with success, I would not indulge in such things. Their tables, laden with food, measure ten feet across, and their female attendants are counted in the hundreds. Were I to meet with success, I would not indulge in such things ... Why, then, should I cower before them? (Trans. Lau 1970, Book VII, Part B/34)

Such observations find parallels in the Classical West. St Augustine expressed an aversion to 'gluttony' as one of the seven deadly sins. *Gula* had corrupted the world and many theologians attributed Adam's loss of Eden not to pride but to gluttony. As Cosman (1976: 117) quoted by Goody (1982: 139) put it: 'While the Nobleman cultivated tastes and appetites as proof of education, political power, and economic supremacy, the Christian moralists saw in elaborate foods and eating ceremonials a way the devil acquired disciples.'

Archaeological Patterns in China

The above themes relate both to the elaborate performances of food preparation and consumption and the differentiation of those performances, within and between communities. These reveal themselves in a variety of theatrical accounts in the written record. Beyond texts, archaeology can provide additional evidence relating to (i) food processing sequences, (ii) their contexts and (iii) their association with other materials.

In archaeology the 'processing sequence' relies upon the physical structure of the plants and animal species used for food, and the association of different components of the whole plant/animal at different points along a processing pathway. At a butcher's site, hooves and skull bones may be prominent, whereas the refuse from an elite meal may only yield bones closest to the finest meat. Similarly, the threshing floor may retain fragments of straw and chaff, while the kitchen retains ground flour. These general principles allow archaeologists to associate processing stage (e.g. chaff versus grain), context (dispersed farms versus centralised village) and association (coarse pots versus fine tableware) to understand the relationship between the preparation of food and the social relationship of its producers and consumers.

Context can be observed at various scales, from the cooking hearth to the house, to the settlement and beyond to the landscape. In both China and Greece, prehistoric landscapes undergo substantial changes through time that connect with the manner in which food is produced and consumed.

Early Neolithic settlements (c. 8000–5000 BCE) in north China repeatedly reflect a unitary organisation lacking intermediate-level institutions (cf. Peterson and Shelach 2010). This may be inferred from the shared storage facilities and the range of house sizes. Jiahu in Henan and Xinglonggou in Inner Mongolia, for example, are divided into a few residential sectors, each with a number of dwellings ranging from a few to a couple of dozen. Within each sector, dwellings are either arranged around a single larger building as in Jiahu (Henan Institute of Cultural Relics 1999), or arranged in parallel lines as in Xinglonggou (Liu 2004). We may infer that each sector perhaps houses an extended family or lineage group. Storage pits were placed both between and within the dwellings in each sector, so some resources they contained may well have been shared among adjacent households (Liu, Zhao and Liu 2015). These in turn may reflect units of landholding, economic production, redistribution and ceremonial activity.

In north China, the residence patterns of the Early and Middle Neolithic (c. 8000–2500 BCE) were replaced by new forms in the Late Neolithic (c. 2500–2000 BCE) and particularly in the Bronze Age (c. 2000–1000 BCE). The new pattern may resonate with what Stephen Plog (1990) describes as 'restrictive sharing'. At the Bronze Age settlement of Sanzuodian in Inner Mongolia, for example, the stone structures may be interpreted as 'dwellings'. Many of these 'dwellings' have two or three concentric walls. They are sometimes grouped in clusters, each cluster being enclosed within 'yards' by further stone walls. Most of these yards also contained small circular installations built of stone and identified by the excavators as 'granaries'. The 'household units' at Sanzuodian were thus composed of 'dwellings', 'granaries' and 'yards' all enclosed by stone walls. Shelach, Raphael and Jaffe 2011 infer that each unit served as a family household, in which resources are shared among members of that particular household and less between distinct households.

One of the important shifts from the Neolithic to the Bronze Age relates to the preparation of the daily meal (Liu et al. 2015). Two important staple crops for the populations of north China in prehistory were broomcorn and foxtail millet. In the early Neolithic site of Xinglonggou charred millet was confined to a limited number of pit structures (believed to be dwellings) where it is found as dehusked grains. In the absence of chaff we have no evidence of how those grains were processed/dehusked before reaching the domestic fire. By contrast, in the Bronze Age Sanzuodian, charred millet remains were recovered from almost every 'household', from the 'floor' and the 'yard' to the space between the concentric walls. Moreover, the Sanzuodian assemblage features thousands of millet grains in association with fragments of chaff and fragments of broken embryos. Such finds are consistent with the dehusking stage of millet processing.

From these, we may infer that in the Bronze Age site of Sanzuodian the routine processing activities may have taken place inside 'households' where dehusking was carried out in a piecemeal manner. In such a scenario, both the products and the by-products of those activities have a higher probability of reaching household fires and therefore entering archaeological contexts as charred botanical material. This fits well with the more enclosed residence patterns of the Late Neolithic and Bronze Age. By contrast, the evidence from the Early Neolithic site of Xinglonggou indicates a rather different organisation of settlement life involving the participation and cooperation of a larger community: the processing activities had happened somewhere beyond the settlement core.

Turning from food preparation to its consumption, a useful methodology for exploring the consumption of food is stable isotope analysis (Vogel and Van der Merwe 1977; O'Leary 1988). Its application in north China draws primarily upon the prevalent carbon isotopic pattern of the region's vegetation and that of its two major indigenous cereals, broomcorn and foxtail millet. Both crops are C_4 plants, whereas other plants in the region available for human consumption are overwhelmingly C_3. The C_3/C_4 balance can be assessed not just in the plants themselves, but as they pass through the food-chain (Hu et al. 2008; Barton et al. 2009; Liu et al. 2012).

In this way, the stable isotopes from pig bones provide evidence for social containment and commensality or 'eating together'. On the basis of published isotopic data, we can infer that the pigs from the Early Neolithic sites predating 5000 BCE, such as Xinglonggou, Yuezhuang and Dadiwan, consumed a predominantly C_3 diet. After 5000 BCE, the Middle and Late Neolithic and Bronze Age pigs yield much higher carbon isotopic values indicating a C_4 based diet. Given the predominance of C_3 vegetation in this region and archaeobotanical recurrence of millet in those sites, the rise of carbon isotopic values in the pigs from later periods indicates direct or indirect millet consumption, often at a significant scale (Liu and Jones 2014).

The predominantly C_3 diet of the early period is easily explained in terms of feeding pigs in the extant vegetation beyond the settlement area. For the later period, one possible explanation for this pattern is the privatisation of household resources, including animals. Just as the storage pits were internalised within individual households, and daily meals could have been prepared behind the walls of enclosures, so the same could be true of their animals. Their diets would consequently derive from the by-products of human food preparation or human waste. The shift towards the human food chain and the by-products of human food preparation seems clear. However, as we discussed elsewhere, how that greater proximity was enacted, in terms of penning, provision of occasional shelter, provision of food etc. is open to inquiry and needs further investigation.

In summary, since the Middle Neolithic, villages appear to have been characterised by restricted land tenure and growing privatisation and containment of all sorts of food elements and associated activities; what Wills (1992) and Plog (1990) would describe as 'reduced sharing' or 'restricted sharing'. From the Early and Middle Neolithic to the Late Neolithic and Bronze Age, there is a trend of shifting in ownership of risk from the village collective to individual nuclear families (cf. Shelach 2006; Peterson and Shelach 2010; Shelach et al. 2011). In this context, we can imagine an Early Neolithic with widespread pooling and sharing of food. By contrast, Bronze Age societies display a more contained site plan, one which either has widely spaced household units or contained and demarcated eating and storage areas (Liu 2010). Within these contained spaces, in Mary Douglas' (1971: 61) terms, 'each meal carries something of the meaning of the other meals; each meal is a structured social event which structures others in its own image'. The stone walls serve the purpose of highlighting the separation of insiders and outsiders. That may lead on to what Mencius observed, a thousand years later, that a meal was a direct measure of social hierarchy.

Archaeological Patterns in Greece

Far to the west, in northern Greece, the cultural trajectories are in many ways distinct, and yet there are resonances, particularly around the themes of differentiation and hierarchy. There are two predominant settlement types in the Neolithic which co-exist mainly during the Late Neolithic: settlement mounds (tells) and extended sites (Andreou and Kotsakis 1994; Kotsakis 1999). Tells are characterised by a concentration of houses in a well-defined unit (Sherratt 1983), densely occupied and lacking arable or pasture land within their limits (Andreou and Kotsakis 1994). Extended sites on the other hand consist of houses separated by spaces large enough to be used for cultivation or grazing. This arrangement is also observed in other areas of the Balkans (Chapman 1989).

Both types of sites have generated substantial bodies of archaeobotanical evidence for daily meal preparation, refuse disposal and social boundaries. The main crops of the period are wheat, principally glume wheats, such as einkorn and emmer but also free-threshing wheat and barley. There is also a variety of pulses such as pea, lentil, grass pea and bitter vetch, and a variety of fruits and nuts and oil or fibre plants such as flax (Valamoti 2004).

The archaeobotanical record reveals a major difference among the Neolithic sites, which can be distinguished as grain-rich or chaff-rich, according to the products and by-products of glume wheats. In the crop processing sequence, threshing fragments the glume wheat ears into separate spikelets, each containing the grains tightly held within their husks. In order for the grain of glume wheats to be edible, they need to be released from their husks through further processing.

The presence of the chaff of glume wheats along with weeds in some Neolithic sites suggests that the crop processing was undertaken within the settlement limits and in some cases inside different buildings, as chaff was found in pits and ditches, around hearths and ovens and on floors, deposited inside and outside certain buildings, and not restricted to specific areas (Valamoti 2005). This presence of chaff represents everyday refuse, the routine rubbish resulting from cooking, consumption and burning as fuel.

One such site is Makriyalos, a Neolithic settlement in Pieria. The plant remains primarily comprise chaff, widely and fairly evenly distributed throughout the settlement. The almost complete absence of grain and, most importantly, the lack of stored grain indicate an absence of small-scale, household-based storage, and that the presumably communal storage areas were located separately from food preparation areas.

During the Early Neolithic (5500/5400–5000 BCE), at Makriyalos, communal action is also evident in public works such as ditches and collective consumption contexts such as pits (Valamoti 2004). Specific pits yielded animal bones, pottery, shells and ground stone tools in exceptional quantities in comparison with other assemblages of Neolithic Greece. This would suggest a consumption episode on a supra-community scale.

Focusing on the non-plant component of these pits, the fill most likely represents deposition over several months, or at most a year or two. The hundreds of animal bones (pigs, sheep, goat and cattle) would have provided several tons of meat (Pappa et al. 2013). Slaughter on that scale implies consumption of animals by a large social group – maybe the inhabitants of Makriyalos or even a region; however, it is difficult to know who was participating and who was excluded from such feasting episodes.

Communal intention is also evident in the cooking and serving vessels which are highly standardised, signalling an emphasis on solidarity within a larger group, although at the same time cups are highly individualised, which implies also an element of intra-community competition (Halstead 2012), or at least differentiation.

At chaff-rich sites, storage facilities are located outside the households, away from fires and hearths, reducing the risk of fire spreading to them (Valamoti 2004). Storage can be linked to surplus production but also to intensification of production. Storage within households, found in several Neolithic sites, emphasises the household as a unit of production and consumption. The absence of storage facilities from the chaff-rich site of Makriyalos could arise from an emphasis upon pastoralism and small-scale cultivation of crops. On the grain-rich sites, agricultural produce is evident as a stored commodity (Valamoti 2005). The grain-rich assemblages are often associated with tell settlements, suggesting a link between surplus production and continuous, superimposed habitation.

Moving forward to the Late Bronze Age and the second millennium, we observe a different pattern, in which hierarchical differentiation is more evident in both the storage practices and the use of crops. Bronze Age societies were institutionally complex and sometimes characterised by administrative and religious centres, which also sometimes served the role of accumulating and distributing agricultural surplus.

At Assiros Toumba in Thessaloniki, around 1350 BCE, a complex of buildings and rooms devoted to organised storage was destroyed by fire.

Various crops, mainly cereals and pulses, were stored within, whose quantities and pattern of content indicate that they were not controlled by individual families. They are instead compatible with integrated management by the whole community or at least a substantial part of it. This is also consistent with the overall size and capacity of the storerooms. Access to and control of the storerooms must remain a matter for speculation. It is unlikely that they were restricted to individual families but other social mechanisms may have played a part, possibly to ensure the availability of food in times of need, as a communal insurance policy against poor harvests and crop failure. If a redistribution system was in operation, a specific group living within the site would control and distribute accordingly to people living not only within the site but possibly to others, living in other settlements in the vicinity of Assiros. It has been suggested those people might have had access to the crops in return for labour (Jones et al. 1986).

It is also interesting to note that one of the crops stored at Assiros was broomcorn millet, whose distribution was restricted within the complex. Millet is a crop which, although present in the archaeobotanical record of Greece in earlier times, becomes important during the Late Bronze Age. It forms one of the key connections between the two regions under discussion in this paper, China and Greece, as it travelled a great distance to the Aegean from northern China, moving from region to region and community to community (Hunt et al. 2008; Liu, Hun and Jones 2009). The regions from which millet reached Greece are probably the areas of central and eastern Europe. Large concentrations of millet are found during the Late Bronze Age, mainly in northern Greece, found in houses (at Kastanas) or central storerooms (Assiros). If the cultivation of millet was widespread only in the north of Greece, was it practised by specific groups and, if so, who had access to this new crop and how did they come to have it?

Millet is not found in every house at Kastanas, nor is it present in every storeroom in the storeroom complex at Assiros, suggesting that not everybody was cultivating or had access to millet. The presence of millet in the south of Greece is limited; this situation is not a result of climatic or environmental factors, as the environmental conditions are not sufficiently different between south and north, but rather results from a later introduction of millet from the north to the south. Despite the lack of archaeobotanical evidence, isotopic analysis from the south of Greece has shown that millet consumption during the Late Bronze Age is limited to certain individuals who perhaps settled in the south through mating or other networks (Lightfoot, Liu and Jones 2013). Isotopic analysis for the north of Greece indicates that, although millet is regularly found at several sites, it does not seem to be a dietary element at all of them or of all individuals within any given community (Valamoti 2013). Millet cultivation and therefore millet consumption would have varied, and perhaps been limited to people and individuals on the basis of identity, origin and status. As an exogenous crop, millet may have acted as a 'cultural signifier', suggesting a possible origin from millet growing areas in the north or north-east of Europe or could indicate contact with networks with these regions. This kind of connectivity may have entailed brides bringing seeds of millet from their homelands or people trading goods and knowledge, or communities moving towards the south. There is also a possibility that there is a difference in the status and use of millet between north and south Greece, considering the low presence of millet from the archaeobotanical record in the south. Differences in status or origin can be seen during the first millennium in Greece, where various ancient authors describe millet as being cultivated in such areas as Sparta and Thrace but not Athens, or that during the Roman period it was the preferred cereal in the region of the Black Sea (Amoureti 1986).

Broomcorn millet is one of small number of crops, also including foxtail millet and buckwheat, which are of Chinese origin, but had reached Europe by the second millennium BCE (Jones et al. 2011). In a somewhat symmetrical fashion, a series of western crops, most notably wheat and barley, had reached China by that time. The thematic resonances in food practice may be viewed alongside more concrete evidence of the material movement of actual crops.

At the time of this episode of food globalisation, a cemetery excavated at Eulau beside the River Saale in Germany contains a community that died together violently, but whose bodies were laid out with care and respect (Haak et al. 2008). Genetic and isotopic analyses were conducted upon a number of these bodies. A burial group of four, a man of 40–60 years, a woman of 35–50 years and two young boys, was identified, in which the boys shared their maternal DNA with the woman and their paternal DNA with the man. The strontium isotope evidence indicated a geographical match between the three males and the locality of the cemetery, while the woman grew up at some distance, a minimum of a kilometre away. Haak et al. (2008) argued that he had found the earliest direct evidence of a nuclear family.

Whether or not a similarly detailed analysis of earlier sites will confirm the Eulau data, we may have evidence here both of containment and of connectivity in the cross-continental dynamic. Small patrilocal units may seek wives from some considerable distance, bringing food practices and material culture with them, opening up extensive pathways of connectivity. The pottery at Eulau is of ceramic styles that are encountered from the lakes of Switzerland to the Moskva river in western Russia. By the time of the burial, Bell Beaker cultural and Unetice sites within a few hundred kilometres radius contain millet grains, a crop ultimately deriving from north China.

Resonance in Food Patterns, East and West

The prehistoric cultures in the east and west display many differences; the cultural distinction is easy to observe. The same is true of trajectories through time. Yet there are commonalities, without which we would have long since stopped applying such labels as 'Neolithic' and 'Bronze Age' in both places. Some of those commonalities, farming, urbanism, metallurgy and craft development, are well known and recur in each grand narrative of global prehistory. The archaeobotanical evidence reviewed here develops those commonalities in the context of food, and draws a connection with the similarly cross-cultural narrative attempted by Jack Goody in *Cooking, Cuisine and Class*.

In both east and west, the communities gathered within the sizeable settlements of the Neolithic shared many of the practices leading to the consumption of food, and this is evident from the organisation and scale of their crop processing patterns. The recurring theme in both places as we move into the Bronze Age is of containment of these activities within bounded spaces, though not along identical pathways. The actual structures of hierarchy and social organisation are distinctive, and we can infer the same was true of relations of food production and consumption.

By the time food practices had become thus contained within each region, the movement of crops between sites had reached a continental scale, with eastern crops in the west and western crops in the east. This process of food globalisation may by the middle of the second millennium BCE be observed across the Old World, connecting Europe, Africa and Asia. How this local containment and continental connectivity inter-relate is a topic of ongoing debate. Prior to the second millennium BCE, the signs of long-distance interconnection are sporadic, and this applies, for example, to the earliest instances of crop movement. These coincide with big collective Neolithic communities, mainly inward looking, but nonetheless forming a part of networks on a much larger scale. By the middle of the

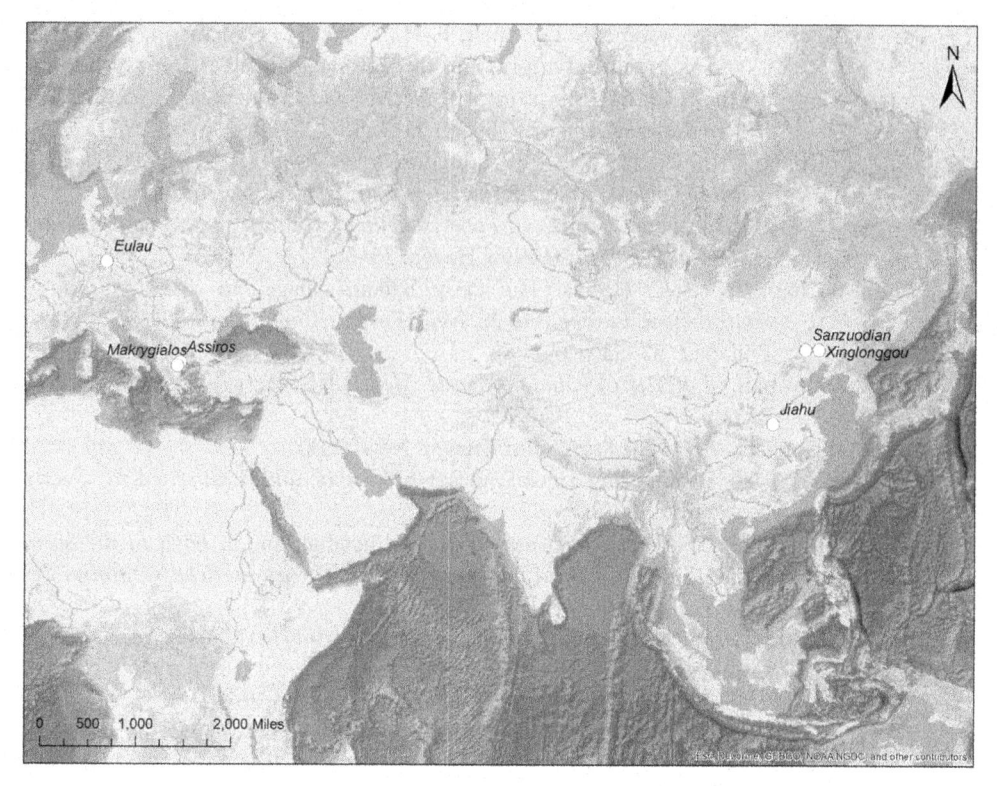

Figure 13.1 Locations of key sites mentioned in the text.

second millennium BCE, Bronze Age communities in different parts of Eurasia are detaching arenas of production and consumption, containing and controlling them on different scales and within different hierarchies. Yet it is between these differentiated hierarchical communities that tangible connections, not just in shared crops, but also in shared animals, wheeled transport and metallurgy, interweave an entire continent.

References

Amouretti, M.-C. (1986) 'Le pain et l'huile dans la Grèce antique: de l'araire au moulin', *Annales Littéraires de l'Université de Besançon* 67: 328. 153–75.

Andreou, S. and Kotsakis, K. (1994) 'Prehistoric rural communities in perspective: the Langadas survey project', in *Structures rurales et sociétés antiques*, eds. P. N. Doukellis and L. G. Mendoni. Paris: 17–25.

Barton, L., Newsome, S. D., Chen, F.-H., Wang, H., Guilderson, T. P., et al. (2009) 'Agricultural origins and the isotopic identity of domestication in northern China', *Proceedings of the National Academy of Sciences of the United States of America* 106.14: 5523–8.

Chang, K. C. (1977a) 'Introduction', in *Food in Chinese Culture: Anthropological and Historical Perspectives*. New Haven: 3–21.

(1977b) 'Ancient China', in *Food in Chinese Culture: Anthropological and Historical Perspectives*. New Haven: 25–52.

Chapman, J. C. (1989) 'The early Balkan village', in *The Neolithic of Southeastern Europe and its Near Eastern Connections*, ed. S. Bökönyi. Budapest: 33–53.

Cosman, M. P. (1976) *Fabulous Feasts. Medieval Cookery and Ceremony*. New York.

Douglas, M. (1966) *Purity and Danger*. New York.

(1971) 'Deciphering a meal', in *Myth, Symbol, and Culture*, ed. C. Geertz. New York: 61–82.

(1984), 'Standard social uses of food: introduction', in *Food in the Social Order: Studies of Food and Festivities in Three American Communities*. New York: 1–39.

Goody, J. (1982) *Cooking, Cuisine and Class: A Study in Comparative Sociology*. Cambridge.

Haak, W., Brandt, G., de Jong, H. N., Meyer, C., Ganslmeier, R., et al. (2008) 'Ancient DNA, strontium isotopes, and osteological analyses shed light on social and kinship organization of the later Stone Age', *Proceedings of National Academy of Science of the United States of America* 105.47: 18, 226–31.

Halstead, P. (2012) 'Feast, food and fodder in Neolithic–Bronze Age Greece: commensality and the construction of value', in *Between Feasts and Daily Meal: Towards an Archaeology of Commensal Spaces. Journal for Ancient Studies, Special Volume* 2: 21–55.

Hawkes, D. (1985) *The Songs of the South*. Harmondsworth.

Henan Institute of Cultural Relics (1999) *Wuyang Jiahu*. Beijing.

Hu, Y., Wang, S. G., Luan, F. S., Wang, C. S. and Richards, M. P. (2008) 'Stable isotope analysis of humans from Xiaojingshan site: implications for understanding the origin of millet agriculture in China', *Journal of Archaeological Science* 35.11: 2960–5.

Hunt, H. V., Linden, M. V., Liu, X., Motuzaite-Matuzeviciute, G., Colledge, S., et al. (2008) 'Millets across Eurasia: chronology and context of early records of the genera *Panicum* and *Setaria* from archaeological sites in the Old World', *Vegetation History and Archaeobotany* 17: 5–18.

Jones, G. E. M., Wardle, K., Halstead, P. and Wardle, D. (1986) 'Crop storage at Assiros', *Scientific American* 254.3: 84–91.

Jones, M. K., Hunt, H. V., Lightfoot, E., Lister, D., Liu, X., et al. (2011) 'Food globalization in prehistory', *World Archaeology* 43.4: 665–75.

Kotsakis, K. (1999) 'What tells can tell: social space and settlement in the Greek Neolithic', in *Neolithic Society in Greece*, ed. P. Halstead. Sheffield: 66–76.

Lau, D. C. (1970) *Mencius*. Harmondworth.
Lévi-Strauss, C. (1962/1963) *Totemism* (trans. R. Needham of *Le totémisme aujourd'hui*, Paris 1962). Boston.
Lightfoot, E., Liu, X. and Jones, M. K. (2013) 'Why move starchy cereals? A review of the isotopic evidence for prehistoric millet consumption across Eurasia', *World Archaeology* 45.4: 574–623.
Liu, L. (2004) *The Chinese Neolithic: Trajectories to Early States*. Cambridge.
Liu, X. (2010) 'Food webs, subsistence and changing culture: the development of early farming communities in the Chifeng region, north China', PhD thesis, University of Cambridge.
Liu, X. and Jones, M. K. (2014) 'Under one roof: people, crops and animals in Neolithic north China', in *Living in the Landscape: Essays in Honour of Graeme Barker*, eds. K. Boyle, R. J. Rabett and C. O. Hunt. Cambridge: 227–34.
Liu, X., Hunt, H. V. and Jones, M. K. (2009) 'River valleys and foothills: changing archaeological perceptions of north China's earliest farms', *Antiquity* 83.319: 82–95.
Liu, X., Jones, M. K., Zhao, Z., Liu, G. and O'Connell, T. C. (2012) 'The earliest evidence of millet as a staple crop: new light on Neolithic foodways in North China', *American Journal of Physical Anthropology* 149.2: 238–90.
Liu, X., Zhao, Z. and Liu, G. (2015) 'Xinglonggou', in *The Cambridge World History*, vol. II: *A World with Agriculture, 12,000 BCE–500 CE*, eds. G. Barker and C. Goucher. Cambridge: 335–52.
Mauss, M. (1925/1954) *The Gift: Forms and Functions of Exchange in Archaic Societies* (trans. I. Cunnison of *Essai sur le don: forme archaïque de l'échange*, Paris 1925). London.
O'Leary, M. H. (1988) 'Carbon isotopes in photosynthesis', *BioScience* 38: 328–36.
Pappa, M., Halstead, P., Kotsakis, K., Bogaard, A., Fraser, R., et al. (2013) 'The Neolithic site of Makriyalos, northern Greece. A reconstruction of the social and economic structure of the settlement through a comparative study of finds', in *Diet, Economy and Society in the Ancient Greek World: Towards a Better Intergration of Archaeology and Science*, eds. S. Voutsaki and S.-M. Valamoti. Leuven: 77–88.
Peterson, C. E. and Shelach, G. (2010) 'The evolution of early Yangshao period village organization in the middle reaches of Northern China's Yellow River Valley', in *Becoming Villagers: Comparing Early Village Societies*, eds. M. Bandy and J. R. Fox. Tucson: 246–75.
Plog, S. (1990) 'Agriculture, sedentism, and environment in the evolution of political systems', in *The Evolution of Political Systems: Sociopolitics in Small-Scale Sedentary Societies*, ed. S. Upham. Cambridge: 177–99.
Robertson-Smith, W. (1889) *The Religion of the Semites*. London.
Sahlins, M. (1976) *Culture and Practical Reason*. Chicago.
Shelach, G. (2006) 'Economic adaptation, community structure, and sharing strategies of households at early sedentary communities in northeast China', *Journal of Anthropological Archaeology* 25.3: 318–45.

Shelach, G., Raphael, K. and Jaffe, Y. (2011) 'Sanzuodian: the structure, function and social significance of the earliest stone fortified sites in China', *Antiquity* 85.327: 11–26.

Sherratt, A. (1983) 'The Eneolithic period in Bulgaria in its European context', in *Ancient Bulgaria: Papers presented to the International Symposium on the Ancient History and Archaeology of Bulgaria*, ed. A. G. Poulter. Nottingham: 188–98.

Valamoti, S. M. (2004) *Plants and People in the Late Neolithic and Early Bronze Age Northern Greece: An Archaeobotanical Investigation*. British Archaeological Reports, International Series 1258. Oxford.

(2005) 'Grain versus chaff: identifying a contrast between grain-rich and chaff-rich sites in the Neolithic of northern Greece', *Vegetation History and Archaeobotany* 14: 259–67.

(2013) 'Millet, the late comer: on the tracks of *Panicum miliaceum* in prehistoric Greece', *Archaeological and Anthropological Sciences*: Published online, DOI 10.1007/s12520-013-0152-5.

Vogel, J. C. and Van der Merwe, N. J. (1977) 'Isotope evidence for early maize cultivation in New York State', *American Antiquity* 42: 238–42.

Wills, W. H. (1992) 'Plant cultivation and the evolution of risk-prone economies in the prehistoric American Southwest', in *Transitions to Agriculture in Prehistory*, eds. A. Gebauer and T. Douglas Price. Madison: 153–76.

14 | On Libraries and Manuscript Culture in Western Han Chang'an and Alexandria

MICHAEL NYLAN

Sir Geoffrey Lloyd, one of the premier historians of science in the world, has won plaudits for taking up the demanding work of comparative history. Inspired by the persistent focus on the institutional logics generated by specific 'cultural manifolds' outlined by Lloyd and his long-time collaborator Nathan Sivin, I take up an institutional subject ripe for comparison: the famous Great Library at Alexandria, probably founded by Ptolemy II (aka Ptolemy Philadelphus, r. 285–246 BCE),[1] and its closest classical-era counterpart, the set of palace libraries assembled, edited and catalogued in the capital of Chang'an under the Western Han emperor Chengdi (r. 33–7 BCE), over a twenty-year period from 26 to 6 BCE.[2] Both of these 'libraries' were destroyed in antiquity.[3] The royal holdings at Alexandria (whose number of manuscripts is debated) were most probably dispersed or destroyed during sieges to the city that took place during the years 269–97 CE, judging from archaeological evidence.[4] The imperial library holdings in the Western Han capital, some 13,269 scrolls altogether,

---

[1] I thank Christian de Pee, Tom Hendrickson, Steven Johnstone, Emily Mackil, Joseph Manning and especially Michael Loewe for offering timely help in formulating this chapter. Ptolemaic Egypt runs from 323 to 30 BCE. Bagnall 2002: 349 notes that the earliest reference to the library is the 'curious' Letter to Philocrates, in the second century BCE, that claims to be a letter by a courtier of Ptolemy II named Aristeas but no such person existed, so far as we know. Joseph Manning says that Ptolemy II gets credit for many things begun by this father (personal communication, 26 August 2014).

[2] In Chang'an the main libraries seem to have been those at Tianlu ge and Shiqu ge. Whereas Eastern Han records credit Liu De 劉德, uncle to Han Wudi (r. 141–87 BCE), with convening classical *scholars* at his court, in later myths these scholars inexplicably turn into classical *manuscripts* held in a library, creating great confusion.

[3] Part of Ptolemy's royal library *may* have been destroyed in 48 BCE, by Julius Caesar, during his siege of the city, but years later the geographer Strabo (fl. 130–87 BCE) reports nothing, so presumably many of the holdings were either left or reconstituted. The library seems to have continued until 269 CE, when Alexandria was besieged, first by Queen Zenobia of Palmyria, and a year later by the forces of Emperor Aurelian (r. 270–5 CE). Under the usurper Domitius Domitianus, Alexandria was also seized in 297 CE. Supposedly Ptolemy VIII, in the year 145/4 BCE, expelled from Alexandria its most impressive intellects; after this time, the scholars associated with the library or Mouseion were of lower calibre. Meanwhile, note the conflation of the Mouseion with the royal library, whose relation has not been established. Fraser 1972: I, 324, surmises that the library probably coincided with the museum itself. However, Johnstone 2014 doubts the significance of this.

[4] See Conqueuegniot 2013a.

may have been scattered by the civil wars following the collapse of Wang Mang's regime in 23 CE, and they were definitely removed, in part or in whole, shortly afterwards, when the Han capital was transferred to Luoyang.[5]

Popular history today touts the purported openness to all comers of the library at Alexandria, despite current scholarly estimates of a small group of clients, roughly thirty to fifty of the 'king's men', enjoying access through royal patronage and wandering into the 'farthest recesses of labyrinthine erudition'.[6] (Libraries as a public amenity seem to be a Roman innovation though they catered mainly for members of the equestrian and Senatorial orders, and the first library conceived of as truly open to all classes of people is Angelo Rocca's Bibliotheca Angelica in the 1600s, even then an exception.[7]) Certainly, in Western Han Chang'an the imperial libraries (not to mention the secret archives) were closed to all but a handful of trusted court officials famed for their learning. The scarcity of contemporary evidence for the hugely famous Great Library at Alexandria is stunning, with most so-called 'evidence' dating to the twelfth century CE or later,[8] whereas multiple sources within a century of their foundation speak in detail of the Chang'an libraries, which experts in EuroAmerica have cheerfully ignored.

As this chapter will show, both Alexandria and Chang'an functioned, for the members of their respective governing elites, as the chief centres for the 'remedying' of books, through collation, translation from one script to another, excision and synthesis, all of which implied a 'decision to elevate precision and rigor over [immediate] moralizing message'.[9] Not coincidentally, this association simultaneously identified the capital as the source of superior knowledge owned, created, and encouraged by the court.[10]

---

[5] It is very unlikely, given the archaeological evidence, that the fire in 23 CE, which ravaged the NW corner of the Chang'an capital, reached the libraries.

[6] See Jacob and Polignac 2000 ('Introduction'), esp. 15–16; Macleod 2002: 3; Bagnall 2002.

[7] Coqueugniot 2013a: 49. In the Roman era, we have several 'public libraries': the Atrium Libertatis library (founded 30s BCE), the Palatine Apollo library (founded 28 BCE) and the Porticus Octaviae library (founded 20s BCE). Public libraries were unknown in China as late as the 1920s, as we know from McDermott 2006.

[8] The roughly contemporary pseudo-Aristeas *Letter to Philocrates* only notes the existence of a royal library. A papyrus list of directors and a few scholars patronised in Ptolemaic Alexandria dates to the second century CE (P.Oxy 10.1241). Strabo the geographer, Pausanias the traveller (fl. 150–75 CE) and Diodorus of Sicily (c. 392) provide some of our literary testimonies about libraries and archives. As Strabo's *Geographia* (13.1.54; 17.1.8) tells it, the Ptolemies sought to recruit talent of every variety, offering everything from tax breaks to entrance to residence halls, dining facilities, and teaching rooms to famous men of learning. Unfortunately Strabo's narrative is wrong on many points, as when he said that Aristotle invented the library and passed the idea onto the kings of Egypt (13.1.54). Tzetzes (twelfth century CE) spoke of 42,800 books in the outer library and 490,000 books in an inner library. Bagnall 2002 rightly scoffs.

[9] McNeeley 2008: 18.   [10] Cf. the Chinese term *zhi shu* 治書.

Meanwhile, these great collections sponsored by emperors and kings in turn asserted the hegemony of new forms of standardised learning over the known world, even as they advertised. The early collections had a function beyond dissemination to readers, insofar as the collectivity asserted a continuous past. Ergo Callimachus' (c. 305–240 BCE) searching for curiosities, rare words, forgotten myths; also Zenodotus' impulse to reduce the plurality of recensions to one great synthetic work, the first Alexandrian edition of Homer, not to mention the wholesale revision of ancient maps at Alexandria.[11] Hence also the nearly three decades long immersion by Yang Xiong 揚雄 (d. 18 CE) in his mammoth philological compilation devoted to dialect words and obsolete expressions, the collation and activist editing of precious manuscripts by a team working under the direction of Liu Xiang 劉向 (79–8 BCE), and the production of the imperial library catalogues by Liu Xiang and Liu Xin 劉歆 (53 BCE–23 CE). In both capitals, then, 'philosophy was transmuted into something more recognizably academic', even if was not divided into the discrete disciplines we use today.[12]

Still, the tendency, East and West, has been to retroject conditions of a millennium or more later onto the Western Han or Ptolemaic Alexandria. Just as the Alexandrian masters could never have predicted the revolutionary changes in the social practices of the text brought on by the codex, none of the classical masters in China could have foreseen the vibrant book culture of the Northern Song periods, if only because neither paper nor woodblock printing existed in their day. Writing paper, invented roughly a century after Western Han, came to rival silk in quality only in the fourth century CE, and woodblock printing of books became common only in the late tenth century, judging from the available evidence.[13] In Western Han, conventions of punctuation, script and size had yet to be regularised, though they were starting to be developed.[14] Reference works in Western

---

[11] Zenodotus, purportedly the first Librarian (i.e., Director of the library or libraries) was true founder of the so-called 'Alexandrian hermeneutics of Homer', insofar as he introduced the systematic use of *recensio* and also the systematic comparison of texts before editing. The editing and exegesis of texts was the centre of Alexandrian activities. See below.

[12] McNeely 2008: 17–18, however, speaks of it being divided into 'discrete disciplines, those of literature, philology, poetry, geography, ethnography, medicine, mathematics, and experimental science' (a clear anachronism).

[13] 'Killing the green' (*shaqing* 殺青), getting rid of the excess moisture in bamboo, was a laborious but necessary process, if the strips were not to split, rot, decay or be eaten by insects. Liu Xiang insisted on this, according to *Taiping yulan* 606/2a; *Hou Hanshu* 60B.1991–2.

[14] Both Roger Chartier and D. F. McKenzie remind us how much the format, size, medium and location of a piece of writing determine its reception and interpretations. In Alexandria, as in the early empires in China, punctuation initially was employed mainly to facilitate oral reading. Even in the pre-Qin era, a few kinds of punctuation marks had appeared, most notably a double parallel line to indicate the need to repeat a single character. But in Qin and Han manuscripts, filled dots

Han were either unknown or in their infancy. True, a few word lists were available to students, but no sophisticated etymological dictionaries or lexicons of regional expressions were known before the last decades BCE, in late Western Han.

Modern scholars would like to pose a series of questions of the two great libraries under examination here, then, whose answers are not at all self-evident:

What was the relationship between fixing knowledge in writing and the recovery of that knowledge through reading?

How was the authority of compilers, editors and authors construed and built during this time?

What do we know about readers in the early empires?

What were their social practices and expectations when reading and reciting?

What changes in reading habits occurred over the long centuries when manuscript culture predominated?

How did the greatest men of learning view actual and potential readers, current and future?

What were the classics and masterworks, and what authority was invested in them?

What did 'the past' represent for the writers and thinkers in the great libraries?

What, if any, were the connections between reading, writing, pleasure and classical learning?

While no essay of appropriate size can provide solid answers for all the foregoing queries, here the aim is to suggest telling similarities in the impact the major manuscript collections exerted upon the literary habits favoured by these two early empires, although each empire operated under different political premises.[15] In laying out its case, the essay will draw from three

---

and empty circles set off divisions in the text (e.g., the end of a sentence, a section or a paragraph); L-shaped marks work like parentheses; black oblongs set off one set of quotations from another; wedge-shaped inserts served as commas in lists; and so on. Conventions were such (as Wang Chong notes) that the more authoritative the contents of the text, the longer the bamboo strips. These technical innovations, because they were relatively new in Han, would have shaped readers' perceptions and affected the readers' appreciation for texts. See Guan Xihua 2002; Giele 2005; cf. Cherniack 1994: 8: 'The use of apparatus changes the reading experience.'

[15] Chengdi's court functioned more as a 'consultative monarchy' than an Oriental Despotism. Manning 2010 argues much the same for Ptolemaic Egypt. However, the economies in the two realms (and hence their funding for armies) were different, as were their management styles and solutions. Meanwhile, scholars ignore at their peril Patricia Crone's 1989 clear-eyed assessment of the long-term viability of autocratic rule in the pre-modern world, given the limitations on transportation and communication.

tried-and-true ways to 'tell the story' about libraries in antiquity: (1) the institutional story, detailing how libraries were founded and funded, and how books were produced, collected, organised and stored; and what sort of access and use scholars had with these collections; (2) the intellectual story surmising the motivations that underlay the decision to write down everything, while basing rhetoric and analysis on a wide familiarity with texts, as well as living experts; and (3) the political story that presumes that libraries attested the cultural capital of those in power, making the patronage of scholars a key part of their claims to authority and legitimacy.[16]

Material Carriers and Constructs

Thinking about libraries and authorial efforts clearly entails examination of the material carriers and constructs.[17] In Alexandria, which used the papyrus roll, an author's collected works did not exist, unless they sat 'in the same bucket'. A book (i.e., one roll) contained between 700 and 2,000 lines of texts; most averaged around 1,000 lines.[18] Only with the spread of the codex after c. 200 CE did it become possible to collect between two covers the contents of as many as ten rolls, or more.[19] Moreover, verbatim transcriptions of any piece of writing were rare, insofar as hand-copying for and within small textual communities encouraged copyists to add to or emend existing texts, oral or written, introducing semantic and graphic variations, interpolations and elisions, in a manner akin to today's note-taking.[20] Turning to Western Han Chang'an, where wooden boards, bamboo bundles and silk scrolls were the norm for the manuscripts worth saving or transmitting, the material carriers were equally bulky and cumbersome to prepare and store, when not prohibitively expensive; there too oral transmission was usual and often preferred.[21] After all, neither the material carriers themselves nor the early formats helped readers to locate the contents and themes of a manuscript once read.[22] 'Roaming through a

---

[16] McNeely 2008: 22–3.
[17] Materiality has been the subject of many recent studies; on the China side, among the best are Giele 2010 and Richter 2012, 2013.
[18] For details on the scroll (column height/width, writing on one/both sides, etc.), see Johnson 1984.
[19] Cameron 1995: 109.
[20] Traditional cultures treat alternative expressions having the same sense as 'the same', in contrast to [modern] literate ones using the stricter criterion of verbatim repetition as 'the same'. See Olson 1994: 87, citing Finnegan 1977. Cf. Cribiore 2001, *passim*; Kaster 1988.
[21] Nylan 2008, 2011.
[22] No one seems to know when the first index for an individual manuscript was produced in China, though Qin and Western Han see the use of postfaces as quasi-table of contents. (Later, in Rome,

manuscript' in the sense of reading at leisure and dipping at will into earlier passages so as to savour them anew was difficult, unless passages had been memorised.[23]

The material carriers of writing inevitably shaped the rhetorical form and content of written compositions no less than the antique habits in manuscript collection and reading. Probably the single greatest difference between antique manuscripts and today's books is the shorter length of most early manuscripts; the much smaller size of the major manuscript collections goes without saying.[24] Other crucial differences relate to notions of authorship: whereas today authors strive, above all, to appear to be 'original', in late Western Han manuscript culture authors strove to demonstrate 'high cultural literacy' via the skilful weaving together of elegant phrases, classical allusions and proverbial bits of wisdom (*zhu wen* 屬文 or *zhui wen* 綴文) by complex prosodic and semantic rules (some barely understood today). Compositions on a given theme were strung together from pre-existing passages (not necessarily on the same topic) that contained the same vocabulary items or, more rarely, the same grammatical patterns, with repetition serving mnemonic functions. Clearly, the typical early composition did not aim at logical consistency. It rather meant to establish the bona fides of the compiler(s) by the *repetition* of tropes and sayings, plus some snippets of authoritative texts, after which the compiler(s) felt free to try to formulate their most persuasive arguments. As with the visual culture of the classical era, the insertion into a piece of literature (oral or transcribed) of what we would castigate as 'extraneous' ornament or even contradictory filler helped the rhetorical piece to exert a most profound impact, in that a liberal dose of formulaic *copia* lent an air of decorum, leisure and erudition to the compilation, its compilers and its performance.[25] After all, to the members of the governing elite in early China – aka the 'worthies' (*xian* 賢) of whom we hear so much – history was born of tradition, and references to a common store of myth and history reified and confirmed the appropriateness of the pre-existing relationships tying listener/reader to the compiler(s),[26] with writing an extension of oral culture.

Pliny's *Natural History* included a table to contents.) For the difficulty of producing tables (increased by the lack of a standardised rendering for reign titles) in antiquity, see Feeney 2007.

[23] Johnson 1984 argues, however, that looking up prior passages in scrolls would not have been as cumbersome as most imagine.

[24] For the second insight, see Bagnall 2002; note 8 above.

[25] Historians of pre-modern Europe have long argued that those with access to power never dreamed it possible for those outside their high-status circle to offer reliable testimony about any aspects of the world, visible or invisible. See, e.g., Shapin and Schaffer 1985.

[26] See Veyne 1988: esp. 7, 10.

Not surprisingly, the idea of 'authorship' in antiquity was far more notional than it is today.[27] No author could possibly hope to earn a living directly from his writing until the printing era or to make his name apart from the court, nearly a millennium after Han, so we cannot rightly speak of 'literati' or 'intellectuals' in the classical era in China, pace Yü Yingshi.[28] Antique authors sought patronage and appointments through their writings instead. Since manuscripts circulated at least as often in the context of gift exchanges as through purchase on the open market,[29] the most an author could reasonably expect was limited circulation for his views among disciples and disciples of disciples,[30] through whom his ideas ideally would be transmitted to future generations who might keep his teachings alive through repeated transcription and circulation.

The deeply pleasurable associations of textual learning derived chiefly from the intensely gratifying relations ideally binding master to pupil, father to child, patron to client, friend to friend, or ruler to subject. Via dictation and recitation students, disciples, officials and clients often transcribed what they had heard from their social or intellectual betters.[31] All this made early manuscripts a visible locus and medium of exchange in the promotion of social solidarity within relatively small communities. This strong correlation between manuscripts and social interchanges made them highly authoritative guides to deliberation and conduct in a culture avidly searching for exemplary models in life or in texts. There was a profound faith in the transformative potential of hand-copying and memorising model manuscripts, so long as the text and its author were thoroughly good. Once the reader-copyist glimpsed and reinscribed the authorial intent behind the texts inviting reflection, he would himself figure as a virtual repository of such authoritative texts. By the same

---

[27] To take one Western example, Alexander Shute in 1888 demonstrated that what we call 'Aristotle' is a collection of writings produced long after the thinker's death. See Montgomery 2000: ch. 1.

[28] In the time period under review, we have no 'intellectuals', only 'advisers' or 'persuaders' (would be and actual). For 'intellectuals' is a relatively modern term that began in the nineteenth century with the meaning of 'socially alienated, theologically literate, anti-establishment lay intelligentsia', see, e.g., McGrath 2004: 53. I worry equally about 'literati' (earliest usage 1620), which refers to a 'class' of people (typically those who can make a living off their literary pursuits in the post-printing era).

[29] There is but one mention, by Wang Chong, c. 95 CE, of book stalls in the Eastern Han capital at Luoyang.

[30] See *Hanshu* 87A.3515; Sima Qian's famous 'Letter to Ren An', the subject of a study by Stephen Durrant et al. 2016

[31] See Yates 2007, on the excavated Liye descriptions of the process of training and hiring of imperial officials at the capital and in the commanderies and counties. As most of the Liye documents remain to be published, Yates is perhaps over-confident.

token, if the manuscript so carefully hand-copied and memorised was inherently misguided, its errors might well colour the learner's experience of the world and thereby skew his judgements. Such dangers notwithstanding, the psychic and cultural benefits endowed via manuscripts, as well as the manuscripts' value as prestige items of great price, made manuscripts a potential source and site of transformative powers.[32]

Archaeological Evidence for Libraries in Alexandria and in Chang'an

Modern academics lament the scant attention paid by early historians and geographers to the built environment that housed the early 'great libraries'.[33] It does not help that the Greek word *bibliothêkê*, the only general term for 'libraries', could refer to (a) a collection of books; (b) the building housing a library, private or public; (c) the bookcases that housed books; (d) the official name for the state archives in Greco-Roman Egypt (as in a papyrus from 145 BCE);[34] or (e) royal or temple archives stored in-house. (This word, attested in only a very few classical Greek texts, e.g., that of Cratinus the Younger (519–422 BCE), appears mostly in the later Roman Empire.) Similarly, in early China, no single word exists for manuscript depositories – only words for the temples, shrines, 'secret chambers' and museums where rare documents tended to be kept. This heightens the suspicion that libraries were hardly 'so central' to literary production as moderns have imagined.[35] The lack of a clear functional distinction between archives and libraries that matches modern expectations probably underlies the multiple designations used for book depositories, as well as the antique view of major book depositories as but one form of treasure house. (In modern parlance, 'archives' contain diverse documents of informative value, mainly practical, with many describing particular transactions, whereas 'libraries' conserve writing of lasting literary value.)[36]

---

[32] Nylan and von Staden have both remarked upon bibliotherapy and the apotropaic powers ascribed to Classics.
[33] There are 182 *testimonia* relating to Greek libraries, according to Platthy 1968. No such figures have been gathered for Roman libraries; see Nicholls' unpublished thesis (2005) on the British Museum website.
[34] Papyrus Strasbourg 624 (Schwartz 1976).
[35] See L. L. Johnson 1984; W. A. Johnson 2013 on this, implicitly contra Jacob 2013. Tutoring in elementary learning (*grammatikē* in Greek; xiao xue 小學 in Chinese) could occur in a very wide range of settings. See Cribiore 2005; Kaster 1988.
[36] Neudecker 2013 explores the consequences.

The archaeological evidence for libraries might resolve many questions, if such could be found. In the Mediterranean world, as of 2013, archaeologists had *tentatively* identified a total of thirty-six sites of archives and libraries, only five of which *reportedly* held libraries (as opposed to archives). A mere two of those libraries – those of Alexandria and Pergamum, neither archaeologically attested – can be confidently assigned to the pre-Roman phase, before Rome's special brand of Hellenism took hold.[37] Of course, archaeologists have worked hard to find the Alexandria site, in the belief that the Great Library of Alexandria was 'one of the most celebrated institutions of knowledge and book preservation in the world'.[38] On the China side, we have names for the major Chang'an palace libraries, but no archaeological excavations in the vicinity,[39] in part because Xi'an archaeologists rest content to accept a Qing scholar's identifications, in part because we have abundant literary evidence from the time (see below) (Figure 14.1). One piece of tenuous archaeological evidence does exist, however: a Han roof-tile end (*wadang* 瓦當) bearing the legends 'Shiqu qianqiu' 石渠千秋, 'Shiqu, Forever' (Figure 14.2).[40] In consequence, we have next to no idea how the libraries at Alexandria and at Chang'an were physically arranged to facilitate editing, writing and reading.[41] What is certain is that the numbers of papyrus rolls is routinely wildly inflated for Alexandria, and more

---

[37] Conqueuegniot 2013a: ix. The precise location of the Pergamum library attested in literary sources is uncertain; the archaeology, first proposed by Alexander Conze in 1884, is likely mistaken; see Coqueugniot 2013b: 110, 123. Johnson 1984: 46–61 and Mielsch 1995: 770–1 point to illogicalities. Inscriptions attest small libraries in gymnasia in Pergamum, Cos, Rhodes and Taormina (all inscriptions dating to the second century BCE). A third(?) royal library at Antioch, under the Seleucids, is not attested before the tenth century CE for the time of Antiochus the Great (r. 224/3–188/7 BCE); see *Suda* s.v. Euphorion (E 3801 Adler). A Roman 'library' in the Villa of the Papyri in Herculaneum represents a unique example of an antique library discovered with books still on the site (but not in their original place, since there was an attempt to save the books from destruction). See Sider 2005: 62–4, plus fig. 64; Hendrickson 2014 explicitly queries this identification, on the basis of recent excavations reported by Guidobaldi and Esposito 2010. See McKenzie 2007: 195–203, for the Serapium in Roman Alexandria.

[38] See Coqueuegniot 2013b.

[39] Zhao Nanfeng, chief archaeologist (personal communication July 2014).

[40] See Fu Jiayi 2002: I, 263, includes an example with the inscription 'Shiqu qianqiu' (Shiqu, Forever), 14.6 cm in diameter; discussed (anonymously) in *Zhongguo dang'an* 1994: 11, 46. Li Yufang 1995, without attribution, cites Chen Zhi 1973 on a 'Tianlu' *wadang* in the collection of a Mr Ke of Huaining 懷寧柯氏所藏拓本, as does an essay by Liu Hong and Li Bilang 2011: 32. Chen Zhi reports a rubbing of it. Unfortunately, I can find no image for the *Tianlu ge wadang*.

[41] The conjectures have libraries stored in niches or in storage boxes, and being read in nearby passages or colonnades. But there is no evidence before the Roman 'public libraries' of any 'reading room' as the defining mark of libraries. See Too 2010.

Figure 14.1 The Tianlu ge library site. The Tianlu ge and Shiqu ge are known to be the two largest libraries in the Chang'an palace complex. This figure and the next show the kind of material evidence for them that we have today.

accurate for late Western Han Chang'an.[42] Ban Si 班嗣, cousin of Ban Gu's father, worked in the Chang'an palace libraries, and Ban Gu reworked in *Hanshu* 30 the inventories earlier compiled by Liu Xiang and his son Liu Xin, whose listing of individual titles with chapter numbers makes inflation difficult.

Several cultural, political and environmental factors that were equally true of the classical Mediterranean and Western Han explain the paucity of

---

[42] As noted before, note 8 above, the pseudo-Aristeas speaks of 90,000 papyrus rolls; Tzetzes, in the twelfth century CE, of nearly 500,000 papyrus rolls at Alexandria. Bagnall 2002: 351–2, scoffs, noting that the Thesaurus Linguae Graecae contains 450 authors or so. The royal quarters could not have held hundreds of thousands of rolls.

Figure 14.2 Han roof-tile end bearing the legends 'Shiqu qianqiu'.

archaeological evidence: (1) the lack of distinctive architectural features, layout or furniture emblematic of libraries alone;[43] (2) the strongly oral character of these early societies;[44] (3) the placement of early libraries within the royal precincts or quarters, which limited access and made them frequent targets during wars; (4) the perishable materials used in transcribing texts (mainly wood, bamboo, silk, papyrus, and parchment), rendering them vulnerable to humidity, fire, insects, theft and careless handling,[45] as are the wooden structures and wooden shelving. These factors mean that nearly all the surviving excavated and 'discovered' (i.e., unprovenanced) texts reportedly have been found in burial contexts in both early China and Ptolemaic Egypt (with some buried with high-status corpses); few of these newly found manuscripts belonged to the large capital collections in pre-Han and Han and pre-Roman eras.[46]

---

[43] This has not prevented 'reconstructions' of libraries from depicting colonnades on a vast peristyle court.
[44] This assertion of oral teaching and transmission of learning is taken for granted for the Mediterranean, but apparently draws fire for pre-Han and Han (e.g., in the work of Edward Shaughnessy), though the evidence seems overwhelming to this author.
[45] Hence the importance of cuneiform clay tablets.
[46] Conqueuegniot 2013a: viii. Jacob 2013: 72, 164, remarks, 'Thus what has survived of the "great library" holdings in the two textual traditions tends to correspond to the "exoteric texts", i.e., texts intended for wider uses beyond the immediate court community, whereas the "esoteric" materials intended for "insiders" have vanished, as no "back-up copies" were thought to be needed.' Excavated manuscripts in China date back to the late fifth century BCE; many scholarly questions remain with regard to unprovenanced manuscripts.

'Libraries' as Empire's Own Project

When it comes to the Mediterranean, the association of great text collections with tyrants and hegemons is usually glossed over, if more acknowledge the tie to the building of empires.[47] At this remove, it seems as if libraries were often the brain-children of overweening ambitions, with libraries within the palace precincts partaking of aspects of the palaces, the museums, and the shrines to the hallowed past.[48] It was not only specific rulers steeped in classical learning who decided to amass huge manuscript collections,[49] for antique libraries were part and parcel of imperial and royal styles of governing through largesse. So long as elites knew of them, they could figure in conspicuous consumption and impressive displays, enlarging the ruler's air of authority in Ptolemaic Egypt and in Western Han, since notions of legitimacy usually involved perceptions about the superiority of a 'mysterious' civilization of great antiquity said to be encapsulated in such innovative collections.[50] In addition, scholars often assume that the two 'great library' projects were originally designed to attract scholars to the capital, assert its supremacy over local centres of learning, and serve an 'intellectual' function, in the nurturing of certain new styles of scholarship or research. One may doubt, however, whether the two manuscript collections under examination were *designed* to serve as 'research centres'.[51] After all, access to both libraries in the early empires was severely limited, and the trusted men assigned to work on manuscripts within the palace precincts combined the tasks of collating, cataloguing and composing with other duties for the court (Figure 14.3).[52]

---

[47] An exception is Conqueuegniot 2013a, b. Note the sparring between Maehler's 2004 characterisation of the 'essentially Greek character' of the Mouseion and Library and El-Abbadi 2004, arguing the Egyptian yet 'universal' character of the same institutions.

[48] The Alexandrian Mouseion was a part of the palace district, as Strabo says. Presumably the Pergamene library was part of the palace, but we lack evidence.

[49] For Chang'an, see Nylan 2011.

[50] For the quotations, see Hirst and Silk 2004: 6. I think here of the multiple stories told by Hecataeus of Abdera, which had Greek poets, philosophers, law-givers and inventors (some of them entirely fictional) travelling to ancient Egypt to be taught 'wisdom' by Egyptian priests; see *Diodorus Siculus* 1.46–9; *FGrH*: IIIA, no. 264, F1–6 (pseudo-Hecataeus). In Western Han, the first classicising movement was probably propelled by the 'discovery' of ancient inscriptions in an illegible script ('seal script' or 'tadpole script') associated with the pre-imperial period (esp. Western Zhou). See Nylan 2011 on this.

[51] The term is often used of Alexandria, with the library and/or the Mouseion, e.g., in El-Abbadi 2004: 167.

[52] Houston 2002. Johnstone 2014 emphasises patronage and royal/imperial euergetism. Erastothenes, for example, was tutor to the king's children, as well as being director of the library. In the case of China, Liu Xiang, Liu Xin and Yang Xiong all had other court duties. Notably, the *taichang* 太常 (Commissioner of Ritual, at ministerial rank) was also bureaucratic head of the imperial libraries and its staff.

Figure 14.3 Western Jin scholars collating texts.

In sum, 'ancient libraries were created by political and military power, and there is no sign that they powered the development of any kind of intellectual activity [wholly] independent of it'.[53]

Histories of libraries invariably note that early rulers and their advisers needed members of their court to consult documents, maps and registers of land and population – the 'charts and registers' (*tuji* 圖籍) or 'charts and writings' (*tushu* 圖書) of the time – given each document's utility to the centralising projects of the various powerful states contending for supreme power.[54] Accordingly, items in archives tend to be pitched when no longer of immediate use to the dynast or the members of his court. Items in full-fledged library collections, by contrast, acquire value in roughly inverse proportion to their practical utility; they concentrate and store time and

---

[53] Woolf 2013: 6. And at p. 5 adding: 'in part because imperial libraries can be seen as part of the wider aristocratic culture of exclusion, wherever they were built'.

[54] Xiao He's (d. 193) possession of 'charts and writings' (*tushu*) supposedly helped Liu Bang to defeat Xiang Yu for possession of the empire. As one persuader put it, 'If you take in hand the charts and registers, in order to command all the empire, none in the empire will dare to disobey you.' See *Zhanguo ce* 44/17/26; cf. SJ 70.2282. From a series of such statements we infer that maps and books on strategy and registers were placed in palace archives long before unification took place in 221 BCE.

space, depth and expanse. Then, too, elegant texts elegantly written functioned as a form of cultural capital for demanding connoisseurs, especially in the classical cultures where texts were prestige items by definition, and added 'worth' could accrue from their age, fragility, relative rarity and place within the entire library collection, as well as the number and range of ritual activities entailed in their textual production and transmission.[55] So it was libraries, and not archives, that sparked passions, even pathologies,[56] being seen as more than the sum of their individual parts. And yet the more expansive the pretensions of the 'great libraries', the greater the likelihood that some part of what local communities once collected would be superseded by or absorbed into those 'great library' institutions that hastened to produce lists of canonical authors and approved recensions of texts, even as they sought and generated newer sorts of materials.[57]

If we ask the two most obvious questions regarding the book collections of Ptolemaic Alexandria and of Western Han Chang'an – 'Why there, and why then?' – we can only speculate: possibly because these were undoubtedly the two richest cities on earth at the time. Surplus wealth has been known to prompt less mundane concerns about reputations in this life and the next. In any event, in both classical-era Mediterranean and in early China, we can discern logically separable stages leading finally to the creation of the self-conscious author in antiquity:

Stage 1: Prior to the political unification under the early empires, there were few if any true 'authors' in the modern sense of the word. If the word 'author' is to have meaning at all nowadays, the word 'authorship' must 'claim that the particular words belong to a specific person and are not merely one possible articulation of a general truth'.[58] Not only the interplay of the spoken and the written but also the fusion of various traditions within each text run counter to the notion of a single identifiable author for the different texts. During the archaic periods, East and West, attribution of a piece or set of writings to a particular figure could be purely conventional; it signified a belief that the writing(s) somehow reflected the teachings or actions associated with a politically prominent person who was nearly always cast as a sage-minister or sage-ruler. (Notably, in Alexandria, as

---

[55] It is these sorts of texts that are used as talismans in the early histories and philosophical works, but our evidence is too limited to know how to interpret this fact.

[56] See Egan 2014, *contra* Owen 1986: 66–79. Seneca says something similar in *Epistles* 88.37.

[57] Fashions in bibliography could also work against collecting certain types of works. See *Tongzhi* 21.1826. It is worth noting here, *contra* the claims of Polastron and Pines, that Qin's destruction of the documents of the conquered Six Kingdoms is dubious history at best, as Derk Bodde and many other Han historians have noted. For a review of the issues, see Nylan 2015.

[58] Owen 1986: 214.

well as in pre-imperial China, we learn that books were important because of the eminence of their authors and not vice-versa.[59]) Very little authority attached to the idea of authorship itself, with rare exceptions. Homer and Kongzi/Confucius, to take two cultural icons, were constructed as transmitters of traditions, rather than as original authors.[60] Moreover, texts were frequently dismissed as the 'mere dregs' of the sage's teachings (recall the sayings ascribed to Plato's Socrates or to Zhuang Zhou), with text-writing a last resort of failed politicians or the next-best alternative, when absent or dead masters made training for brilliant careers in government difficult.[61]

Stage 2: Sometime later one can speak of 'authors emerging'. In this stage, however, most still conceived authorial intent as having less to do with the expression of personal, possibly idiosyncratic feelings cherished by an author than with 'the historically situated, *public* responses' to a specific set of political circumstances by a politically important agent.[62] Not coincidentally, the first compilers of mammoth histories – Sima Qian, Herodotus and Thucydides certainly come to mind – claimed to be motivated by a need to establish the authority of teachings or ways of life tied to their own families or localities.[63] Given the hefty rewards tied to successful oratory,[64] few court advisers turned to writing, unless they were somehow forced out of the political arena.

That said, attributions to single authors gave both readers and empires two immense hermeneutical advantages: readers could logically presume cohesiveness within a body of work ascribed to a single person, no matter

---

[59] On Alexandrian 'authors', see Cameron 1995: ch. 4. In China, the exceptions may include Mozi and Xunzi. According to legend, the first person to put a personal stamp on his compilations was Kongzi (i.e., Confucius), but he, of course, was initially cast not as 'author' but as 'editor' of the *Chunqiu* or *Annals*, also the *Odes* and *Documents*.

[60] Kongzi does not figure as author, so far as we know, before Western Han times.

[61] Significantly, Zhuangzi's famous story about Wheelwright Bian is repeated in *Hanshi waizhuan* 5/6 (Hightower 1952: 167) with no objection registered, suggesting that it is not merely a 'proto-Daoist' story. Kongzi in *Analects* 11/2b spoke of the necessity of reading for edification, rather than for pleasure. For Yang's detailed refutation of the conventional ideas that study and learning are 'useless', unless they lead to an official career, see Nylan 2008.

[62] Vankeerberghen 2010, for China. In China the first identifiable 'author' may be the semi-legendary Qu Yuan (332–295 BCE). In prose the first major author is Sima Qian (145–c. 80 BCE), whose monumental *Archival Records* (*Shiji* 史記) was produced c. 100 BCE, centuries after Qu's 'Li sao'. Possibly poetry was linked to personal authorship long before prose, given the official character of most prose writing at the time. But it is equally possible that Qu Yuan's 'authorship' is itself an artefact of Sima Qian's powerful biography of the southern poet. Early traditions cast Sima Qian as continuing the family business of his ancient forebears and his own father, Sima Tan.

[63] I.e., *cheng yi jia zhi yan* 成一家之言, in *Shiji* 130.3319.

[64] Yang Xiong, for example, was rewarded with ten units of gold after a successful speech against war.

how complex the ascribed personality of the author, and advisers to empires could better hope to gauge the honesty and value of claims made in writing, if a plausible record of that same author's life choices became available. To verify the reliability or judiciousness of a potential adviser was the primary responsibility of all at court, after all, and a nearly continual topic of conversation long before the early empires.[65]

Stage 3: Fully self-conscious authors emerge, with impressive paper-trails in their wake, Callimachus and Apollonius at Alexandria and Yang Xiong, Liu Xiang and Liu Xin at Chang'an being the prime examples of this new phenomenon.[66] Authors prior to Alexandria and late Western Han Chang'an rarely puzzled out the explicit influences on their writing. Self-conscious authorship evidently requires a keen sense on the part of an author that his or her efforts at composition will be situated within the context of all great authors from time immemorial. This mental, if not actual, separation from the more tangible patron–client relations in the flesh meant, in turn, that the new authorial personae could and did position themselves as in opposition to the mainstream culture associated with the chief power-holders at court. Steeped in honoured traditions, self-conscious authors could visualise themselves and appear to others less as clients of rulers than as their potential competitors or even superiors in the cultural sphere (though this was far riskier). Thus did self-conscious authors create a more 'bookish world' parallel to but seemingly better than the real world, with the former composed seamlessly from pronouncements by traditional authors, living and dead, who were now accorded traditionalist treatments.[67]

In this tentative chronology, true authorship – authorship by the standard modern definition – appears relatively late in both civilisations, resulting from successive acts of writing preserved in libraries. The

---

[65] Here I would direct readers to two recent works taking the notion of *xin* (reliability, trustworthiness) seriously: Blitstein 2012; Richter 2012; cf. already Shryock 1937.

[66] For Yang Xiong, for example, we have two early 'lives': the biography or autobiography preserved in Ban Gu's *Writings on the Han* (*Hanshu*, completed c. 92 CE), and a second notice recorded in Chang Qu's (active 265–316) *Record of the Lands South of Mount Hua* (*Huayang guozhi*), plus a host of anecdotes collected by Yang's friends and critics. There are also Yang's three masterworks, the *Fayan* 法言, the *Canon of Supreme Mystery* (*Taixuan jing* 太玄) and the *Fangyan* 方言, and Yang's large corpus of lengthy *fu*, two of which defend Yang's decision to compose his *Taixuan*. The entire curriculum of the late second-century CE Jingzhou 荊州 Academy was supposedly organised around Yang's masterworks. Unfortunately, few details survive, aside from the semi-hagiographic sketches offered by Yang's later admirers. Still, the modern scholar Yan Lingfeng 嚴靈峰 (1904–?) has found enough commentaries upon Yang's philosophical works for brief notices on those works to occupy some eighty printed pages. See Yan Lingfeng 1975–79: V, 319–99. For a reception history of the *Fayan*, see Nylan's 2013 translation of that work; also Nylan 2011.

[67] Silk 2004 emphasises this distinction between tradition and traditionalism.

foregoing hypothesis tallies with the admittedly scanty evidence available to us. The chief advantage of such an evolutionary scheme may be that it will deter premature conclusions about the shadowy past. That the ancient experts acquainted with 'great libraries' spent so little time describing the physical locations where they worked now gains added significance perhaps, since neither patron nor client necessarily saw 'composing' as a special technique or knack apart from oratory and governing, and both preferred to style themselves as immortals transported to antique worlds.

The following section of this chapter hazards the proposition that self-conscious and celebrated authorship, as well as textual criticism, appears in tandem with the formation of the 'great libraries'.[68] Granted, classicists of both East and West have been too ready to inflate the importance of the library inventories produced in Alexandria and in Chang'an, reading into those lists either a massive reorganisation of information or an uncannily accurate reflection of social institutions and formations on the ground.[69] But even if the early precursors to library card catalogues cannot neatly map onto the social realities of the distant past, should not we historians be trying to ascertain the slow processes by which important texts were identified and collated via newly devised methods of textual criticism, then reformulated, and made ready for wider dissemination and perusal?

Chang'an and Alexandria Compared: Literary and Academic Styles

The case of Chang'an

Having established a few baselines before turning to specific manuscript cultures, a more substantive comparison of Alexandria and Chang'an book depositories is in order. I turn first to Chang'an, and manuscript culture at the court of Chengdi (r. 33–7 BCE), not only because that is the example that I know best, but also because there is so much more contemporaneous or nearly contemporaneous evidence about the scholarly activities in that capital. As we will see, five key lessons can be wrested from the case in

---

[68] In Pergamum, Crates, the premier scholar at the library, coined the term *criticus* ('judge') to describe his work. See Pfeiffer 1968: 235–40.

[69] On the side of Alexandria, see Blum 1991 for such tendencies. On the China side, see Queen 2001; Smith 2003; Csikszentmihalyi and Nylan 2003.

early China, lessons with strong parallels in antique Alexandria: (1) a great many of the texts that we think of as Warring States masterworks (the *zhuzi* 諸子) were substantially rewritten and recast during late Western Han – so much so that we should probably date their contents to Chengdi's court, rather than to the pre-Qin period; (2) the development of the full-fledged notion of authorship itself may have depended upon the formation of a new set of imperial libraries (replacing or supplementing the older archives) in the twenty-year period from 26 and 6 BCE, as well as the gradual development of new tools for textual criticism by the same reformers at Chengdi's court; (3) reformers meanwhile proposed a substantially new neoclassical set of reforms, not only in policy matters but also in reading, writing and interpretative practices, thereby paving the way for further developments in classical learning under Wang Mang, Eastern Han and the post-Han periods; (4) a particular intellectual problem, and the search for specific solutions, drove the activities of the 'antiquity-loving' (*haogu* 好古) reformers at Chengdi's court (all of whom belonged to that very small group of scholars assigned to work under imperial patronage in the palace libraries), that problem being, 'How are we to correct the texts of the Classics from the pre-Qin period, if the texts of the Classics and also the traditions inherited from earlier court Academicians are flawed by omissions, misreadings, and interpolations?'; and (5) two of the most interesting solutions to this problem were associated with Liu Xiang and Yang Xiong, who had Liu as his patron. Liu and Yang both hailed the *Erya* 爾雅 as a genuinely old word list mostly authored by the Duke of Zhou, which could be used when 'correcting' old manuscripts. And Yang took to generating lengthy lists of 'obsolete words' and 'regional expressions'. Basically Yang hoped that the outlying lands preserved archaic script types and expressions that could be used in philological research ultimately to produce revised manuscripts of the Classics and masterworks, in line with the latest text critical methods, that would provide better guides to those in power.

In 26 BCE, sixty years after the death of Han Wudi (to whom the birth of Han classicism is wrongly attributed), Chengdi named the members of a commission whose members were to identify lacunae in the imperial collection, locate copies of the missing texts, produce better recensions through collation and editing, and classify all the versions produced for the official imperial collections. An imperial envoy, Chen Nong 陳農, was dispatched from the capital to scour the suburbs and countryside for lost writings. Palace Superintendent Liu Xiang 劉向, a member of the imperial clan, was to oversee the process of substantially revising or reworking earlier transmissions, in such a way as to produce the most authoritative guides to a usable past.[70] He was well chosen. Even before Chengdi came to the throne, Liu had submitted a strongly worded memorial urging Chengdi's father, who was known to be in sympathy with the classicists at court, to restore the antique values espoused in the old manuscripts as a way of shoring up the waning dynastic fortunes.[71] Ren Hong 任宏, an infantry colonel, was to superintend the acquisition and editing of military texts for the imperial collections; the Senior Archivist Yin Xian 尹咸, the technical manuals (*shushu* 數術);[72] and Li Zhuguo 李柱國, a court physician, the medical texts. Liu Xiang, as head of the entire commission, set out to compile an annotated inventory of the imperial collections for the emperor and his staff. So far as we know, this catalogue was the first of its kind. An elegant persuasion piece dating a century later tries to capture the realities of Chengdi's era, when men of 'great talent and vast erudition' were put to work 'collating secret writings' in the four major libraries within the palaces.[73] Several early sources place Yang Xiong in those palace libraries, working under Liu Xiang's direction, which confirms the picture we already have of Liu as one of Yang's patrons.

For nearly twenty years Liu Xiang and his staff busied themselves with the collation and editing and cataloguing of the imperial collections, including illustrated books, charts and maps. Shortly after Chengdi and Liu Xiang died in 7 BCE, Liu Xin, Xiang's son, presented to the new boy emperor Aidi an inventory entitled *Qi lue* 七略 (Seven Summaries),[74] based on his father's work by another title. The *Seven Summaries* groups under seven subject headings a total of 13,296 scrolls in the imperial library collections: (1) the 'Six Arts' or Classics; (2) philosophical masterworks; (3) verse; (4) military works; (5) treatises on the technical and quantitative arts, including divination; (6) medicine; and (7) miscellaneous works.[75] In this inventory, for the first time, so far as we know, texts – not just masters – were treated as experts in their own right.[76] Yang Xiong's own philosophical works resist easy classification under his patron's bibliographic

---

[70] In a few cases, we know that Liu Xiang did not just excise duplicate copies, but also produced 'new texts' (his word) with the intention of making new masterworks (and possibly even new ritual Classics).

[71] The memorial is dated to 42 BCE.

[72] *Shu* generally refers to 'regular changes' that can be predicted and enumerated.

[73] See Ban Gu, 'Two Capitals' *fu*, in *Wenxuan* 1/12a–b; cf. HHS 40.1341. Ban Gu was closely related to the imperial family by marriage.

[74] *Hanshu* 30.1701; *Hanshu* 10.310; cf. *Suishu* 32.905. Van der Loon 1952 judges the *Qi lue* a summary that is base text for the *Hanshu* 30 'abridgement'.

[75] *Tongzhi* 21.1825.   [76] See Queen 2001: 62.

categories,[77] but Yang's writings suggest his wholehearted support for Liu's decision – surely approved by Chengdi himself – to give pride of place to the Classics, above the masterworks, verse and technical manuals.[78] Looking backwards, that decision may have been the first step on a path leading later scholars to conflate library catalogues with 'national history'.[79]

It is easy to overlook the sheer magnitude of the editorial changes wrought by the activist editors working under Liu Xiang's direction, massive changes that ended in the compilation of 'new texts' 新書 (their term). To take just one example, the new edition of the *Liezi* 列子 in eight *juan* (scrolls or chapters) was produced after comparing and collating short works, only one of them a shorter *Liezi*, that once circulated under five separate titles in twenty *juan*. By Liu Xiang's own account, he found many incorrect characters and some duplication among the various recensions. Assuming the old palace editions to be more reliable than those circulating 'among the people', Liu made a new edition, which he hoped showed more internal consistency within chapters (though Liu doubted whether the original chapters 'were by the same hand').[80] Similarly, Liu Xiang made up a 'revised and reduced' *Zhanguo ce* 戰國冊 in thirty-three bamboo bundles from six different manuscripts whose texts he described as a total mishmash.[81] More astonishing still, Liu Xiang rejected as 'duplicates' all but thirty-two of 322 *pian* of the *Xunzi* 荀子, or one-tenth of the originals he had at his disposal, when making his new edition of that masterwork; that tenth he had transcribed in a fair hand on strips of properly seasoned bamboo, in order to minimise future damage.[82] Note that Liu Xiang's own accounts have him tossing out unique material, as well as simply discarding duplicate copies. Like father, like son. Liu Xin's labouring in the imperial library reduced a *Shanhai jing* 山海經 in thirty-two *pian* to a mere eighteen.[83] A clear picture emerges, then: following the legends that claimed that Kongzi/Confucius had pared nine-tenths of the Odes to produce the 305 poems in the *Odes Classic*, and had whittled down the *Documents* (or *Shangshu*) from a thousand-

---

[77] As noted in *Tongzhi* 71/836a, Zheng Qiao (1104–62) applied the 'suoxu' 所序 classification to the *Taixuan*, *Fayan* and *Yuezhen* (Music Admonitions) by Yang Xiong. See Drège 1991: 102 n. 49.

[78] The sevenfold classification scheme was replaced in the third century CE by a different scheme that further privileged the Classics.

[79] Here I repeat an observation in Dudbridge 2000: 4–6.

[80] Liu Xiang, cited in Yan Kejun's *Quan Hanwen*, 37.6a–6b.

[81] One of the titles was *Guo ce*, but none of the six titles matches the new title *Zhanguo ce*. Liu Xiang, in *Quan Hanwen*, 37.1a–2b, compares the texts to taros mashed together.

[82] Activist editing did not begin with Liu Xiang and Liu Xin.

[83] Loewe 1993: cf. Liu Rulin 1935: II, 109.

chapter version to one of barely about a hundred chapters, these latter-day sages at the court of Han Chengdi felt free both to toss out much of the material they had gathered, and to emend texts freely, particularly as this was the tradition by Western Han times anyway, given the frequency of oral transmission. (Here marvellous parallels exist with Alexandria. One of the preoccupations of Callimachus' *Pinakes* was to cull the 'spurious' from genuine works ascribed to an authority.)

In the limited space allowed me, I will attempt to tie the *haogu* ('antiquity-loving' neo-classicising movement) to the establishment of the imperial library at Chang'an during Chengdi's court, and the new manuscripts produced for that library, arguing that new methods of reading and writing emerged in connection with the new imperial collection. Sloppy scholars are apt to insist that the 'Chinese race' from time immemorial has always admired and wanted to imitate the distant past, despite the unabashed exaltation of the new in older imperial discourse. However, those adequately acquainted with old manuscript sources before late Western Han, c. 50 BCE, will observe how few times, relatively speaking, before late Western Han legendary heroes and early events figure as substantive precedents.[84] Arguably, Yang Xiong and his peers in late Western Han, despite their evident delight in more recent narratives like the *Zuozhuan* and *Shiji*, were the first generation to truly 'love antiquity' (*haogu*) in the specific sense of wanting to *restore* a distant past they believed to be significantly better than their own time and organised along dramatically different principles.[85] In that way, Yang and the two Lius, father and son, became the leading advocates of a counter-cultural 'return' to classical learning that really represented – as such 'revivals' often do – a reinvention of the revered past accomplished through a careful selection of usable features. (That does not mean, of course, that Yang and the two Lius saw eye-to-eye on every issue.)[86]

Two millennia later, the chief motivation of the late Western Han reformers seems to stem from their shared preoccupation with 'strange writing'

---

[84] Wang Qicai 2009.

[85] Poo Mu-chou 2010 makes some astute observations on the multiple pasts invoked at the Han court.

[86] Liu Xin and Liu Xiang disagreed over the relative superiority of two traditions to the *Chunqiu*, with Liu Xiang preferring the *Guliang* and Xin, the *Zuo*. Liu Xiang had been patron and supervisor to Yang Xiong, but the relationship between Liu Xin and Yang was considerably more fraught. Yang Xiong disparaged Liu Xin, his rival, and Liu Xin returned the favour, even if *Huayang guozhi*, 10A.533, names Liu Xiang and Xin (father and son) and Huan Tan, 'and others' as admirers of Yang's. Wang Chong, *Lunheng* 13/37/25 has Liu Xin objecting to those who would 'reduce desires' (a slogan Yang borrowed from a Zhanguo master, according to *Fayan* 4/16). See Liu Rulin 1935: II, 109; the 'Letters' translated in Knechtges 1977.

(*qi wen* 奇文) and with a course of study called *xiao xue* 小學, meaning 'philology' in this context. Yang spent roughly half his adult life – some twenty-seven years – compiling a *Fangyan* 方言 word list, which served in some way as basis for or forerunner to Xu Shen's 許慎 (c. 55– c. 149) *Shuowen jiezi* 說文解字, the mid-Eastern Han etymological dictionary.[87] Less well known is the fact that Yang first studied and later taught something called 'strange writing'.[88] Up to now, Han historians have generally assumed that the binome *qizi* 奇字, which appears in *Hanshu* 30 and a few later texts,[89] is merely one of the six calligraphic styles practised by children who are destined for or aspiring to high office. After all, the *Hanshu* 'Treatise on Literature' equates *qizi* with one of the 'eight forms' of writing (*bati* 八體). However, the standard commentary to the *Hanshu* bibliographic 'Treatise' unambiguously defines *qizi* as 'archaic script characters that differ from those found in the writings taken from the wall of Confucius' house' (古文謂孔子壁中書 … 奇字即古文而異者也),[90] and the current evidence suggests that this script represented far more than a mere schoolboy's calligraphic exercise.[91] How are we ever to piece this sparse evidence together, in the view of the *haogu* reformers' intention to offer their preferred mode of special training as a viable alternative and an implicit rebuff to the reigning culture of learning at the court?

The *haogu* reformers were at one in excoriating the Academicians (*boshi* 博士) at court, the very men appointed to be the chief keepers of the main classical traditions. As noted, in Yang's day the Academicians tended to be appointed according to their allegiance to particular explications (*shuo* 說), rather than to particular Classics (*jing* 經), and the *haogu* reformers believed that the correlation between career advancement and expertise in a *shuo* greatly diluted the impact of the 'core' texts on ethical cultivation.[92] Indeed, Yang reserved his sharpest attacks for the unthinking

---

[87] Yang's studies had yielded at least three lexicographical works, the compilation we now know under the title of *Fangyan* 方言 (usually translated as *Dialect Words*, but just as plausibly *Correct Words*); a glossary; and a one-*pian* summary and expansion of the *Cang Jie*. The last two works are now lost.

[88] In 10 CE, Yang was accused of teaching Liu Fen 劉棻, son of Liu Xin, the 'strange scripts', for example. Yang somehow managed to study long years with the master Linlü Wengru 林閭翁孺, said to be proficient in 'strange writing'.

[89] *Hanshu* 30.1721.

[90] *Hanshu* 30.1722, n. 7. For the tale about writings 'found' in the wall of Kongzi's house, see Nylan 1994, 1995.

[91] On recent studies of calligraphic script styles in relation to archaeological finds, cf. Hsing I-t'ien 2010: esp. 437, which agrees that only those with advanced learning could read *qizi*.

[92] Of course, each *shuo* had its own textual history, but, generally speaking, far less was known about the individual histories of the *shuo* than about components of the Five Classics corpus.

court officials who considered the Academicians 'the most broadly learned scholars of the age'.[93] Echoing the complaints levelled by Liu Xin, Yang portrayed the Academicians acting like 'clerks and scribes', wanting at all costs 'to protect the flawed and deficient readings' in order to secure publicity for their own interpretations and retain their court sinecures. From the Qin dynasty onwards, the Academicians had merely 'maintained their own families' theories', Yang charged, neglecting their other duties 'to set out the ritual platters and vessels' for the rites of the Confucian Way.[94] But if the court could be persuaded simply to jettison the Academicians' traditions, how could a dedicated learner ever find a way to be able to interpret the traditions with greater surety and faithfulness to antiquity?

The *haogu* reformers proposed several constructive solutions for this conundrum. Liu Xin asked the court to insist that its Academicians avail themselves of a handful of writings transmitted in earlier script forms, even if newer recensions of the same texts employed modern script.[95] The response from the Academicians was predictably hostile, and Chengdi, sensing their mood, quickly retreated, showing a disinclination to upend long-standing interpretative traditions.[96] Liu Xiang, as noted above, spent the last years of his adult life implementing another strategy, that of activist editing, though we may be appalled at the impetus for expunging passages or even entire texts from the record.[97] Yang Xiong proposed two additional strategies, the first of which was that his followers commit to a set of reading practices capable of fostering a common set of values or orientations.[98] The key thing was to spend more time in reading the Classics, until one became cognisant of the special pleasures that they offered. Yang boasted that there was hardly a book that he had not read,[99] and he thought extraordinarily wide-ranging reading was required for those who would cleanse the pre-Qin writings of the numerous flaws, interpolations and lacunae the texts had acquired as they 'were copied over and over again

---

[93] *Hanshu* 36.1970–1. According to Liu Xin (*Hanshu* 30.1969), only Jia Yi 賈誼 (200–168 BCE) was worthy of the name of 'classicist' (*Ru*). The lowest rung was occupied by the *wenli* 文吏 (the scribes and functionaries who kept the penal system functioning). See Li Qing 2003: 235ff.

[94] See 'Boshi jian', in Li Zhen'ai 2001: 305–8.

[95] For Liu Xin's famous 'Letter Addressed to the Academicians', see *Hanshu* 36.1967–71; this is translated in its entirety in Nylan and Vankeerberghen 2015.

[96] See note 88.

[97] Centuries after Yang, at the end of Eastern Han, Zheng Xuan 鄭玄 (127–200 CE) would attempt to 'correct' the Five Classics corpus by another means. See Wagner 2000: 42.

[98] As Yang explains it, in *Hanshu* 87B.3565, under the troubles when the 'Ding and Fu clans and Dong Xian controlled affairs of state', he kept busy drafting the *Taixuan* 'as a means to keep to myself and remain tranquil' despite misrule. That Yang also had a 'sabbatical' under Chengdi, when he was allowed to forsake his usual duties at court, also speaks volumes.

[99] *Hanshu* 87A.3514: 'I read quickly; there is nothing I have not seen.'

and passed down through the generations'.[100] Consequently, Yang Xiong's ideal lover of antiquity would be well versed in the many 'arts' (*yi* 藝), meaning the Classics, and conversant with the *Erya*, a lexicon organised by synonyms and written, at least partly, in archaic script.[101]

For unless the criteria by which to correct the Classics were found outside the texts of the Classics themselves, contradictory readings would inevitably multiply over time and diverge ever more sharply from the sages' ideas and intentions. Yang's second solution therefore brings us back, to the *Erya* and Yang's early version of the *Fangyan*. As noted, Yang's patron Liu Xiang had once proposed to 'correct' the Classics using the *Erya*,[102] but Liu Xiang had found his emperor Chengdi disinclined to spearhead a project that might call into question old ideas about legitimacy. Evidently,[103] Yang Xiong agreed with both Lius about the seminal importance of the *Erya*, believing that its purportedly ancient origin made it the right text 'to correct the Six Arts [i.e., the Five Classics plus the now-lost Music Classic]'. Nor is it likely to be a coincidence that Yang Xiong devoted some twenty-seven years to compiling lists of 'obsolete expressions' and 'regional languages'[104] – a figure that dwarfs the time he spent on the two philosophical neoclassical works for which he is known today. Yang's own philological endeavours were of a piece, then, with a larger ethnographic impulse in late Western Han holding that local folk traditions in remote places might have preserved earlier forms of learning.[105] Like the graphic symbols found in older texts, expressions from these peripheral places that were presumably more immune to the changing fashions than the polyglot metropolitan areas could conceivably retain older meanings, which might then guide would-be reformers in restoring an Ur-language in its purest and most powerful form. (Paul Kroll has made the astute observation that Yang intended his philological works to function like an *Erya* in reverse: rather than listing the elevated expressions used in literary Chinese – virtually a foreign language to many Han subjects – Yang listed obsolete expressions and

---

[100] A saying from Yan Zhitui's (531–c. 590) *Yanshi jiaxun* 30.305.
[101] See, e.g., *Fayan* 2/9, 5/11, 5/17, 5/21, 5/27. For the citation, see *Han jiu yi buyi* 漢舊儀補遺, by Wei Hong 衛宏 (first century CE), collected in Sun Xingyan, *Han guan liu zhong*, item 4.3 citing *Han guan jiu* yi, item 3.3, where this is said of the ideal Academician. Since the *Erya* was a Han text, during Han it must have included characters in the pre-Qin script forms, if this statement is reliable.
[102] For the letter, see Eva Chung 1982: 482–95. If the exchange of letters by Liu Xin and Yang Xiong is genuine (see above), this is the earliest reference to the *Erya*, which was right then gaining immense stature, as the work of the Duke of Zhou. Cf. Zhang Yi, in *Huang Qing jingjie* 667A/1a–2a.
[103] If the early sixth-century *Xijing zaji* account can be trusted.
[104] See Knechtges 1977; cf. Greatrex 1994; DeWoskin 1982: 57 n. 6; Hua Xuecheng 2006: 4.
[105] See *Hanshu* 36.1970 for Liu Xin's discussion of this at Chengdi's court.

regional patois, in the hopes that they preserved still earlier forms of language anterior to the *Erya* itself.[106]) Assisted by the *Erya* ascribed to the Duke of Zhou and promoted by Liu Xiang, and the 'strange writing' evoking the pre-imperial era and outlying lands, Yang and his peers could aim, on an unprecedented scale at the new imperial library, finally to 'rectify names' in the manner advised by Confucius (aligning social roles with status titles, and ultimately language itself).[107]

What strikes us as particularly new in Yang Xiong's time is the insistence that all the complex processes associated with textual production, textual collection and textual appreciation constitute the most enthralling pleasures – pleasures over and above imperial or royal patronage. Doubtless, many readers of classical Chinese before Chengdi's court must have *experienced* the pleasures of reading, judging from an idle comment in the *Huainanzi*.[108] But to experience a pleasure is hardly the same as to write or theorise about it. Yang Xiong and several of his contemporaries – especially Liu Xiang and Liu Xin – constructed the first serious, sustained and systematic case in writing for the keen pleasures to be had from reading the Classics.[109] In building this case, Yang and his contemporaries started a trend, fashioning parts of pre-existing arguments into a distinctively new mix, which they traced back, on tenuous grounds, as we now see, to the Duke of Zhou and Kongzi, centuries earlier.[110] This new mix, which I have dubbed *haogu* ('love of antiquity') for the sake of convenience, was championed by the most famous writers in the centuries following Yang Xiong, so much so that later literary convention virtually required learned members of the governing elite to express their unbounded delight in reading about antiquity.[111] Echoes of Yang, then, resound in Tao Yuanming's 陶淵明 (365–427) 'There's pleasure to be had in it [the text],/ Pleasure reaching unto the utmost limits', as in Ge Hong's 葛洪 (280–c. 343) line about the Ancients: 'They ... diverted themselves with the Classics.'[112] By now, moderns are so thoroughly sick of

---

[106] Paul Kroll (private communication, August 2010).

[107] Liu Xin says that he has learnt that Yang has gathered 'obsolete words from former dynasties and unusual expressions from strange lands'. See Knechtges 1977, on the 'Letters'.

[108] See *Huainanzi* 21.706; ('Yao lue' 要略), which speaks of writings to 'make oneself happy' (*zile* 自樂).

[109] *Hanshu* 8.272; 36.1929 says that Liu Xiang 'focused all his thoughts on Classics and the arts' (*jing shu* 經術).

[110] See *Liezi* 4.20/18–21/8, especially the last line's description of Zhongni as one who 'would strum and sing, and intone texts, until the end of his life, without stopping'.

[111] The phrase *haogu*, of course, comes from *Analects* 7/1, where Kongzi describes his own love of antiquity.

[112] For Tao, see Tian Xiaofei 2005: 148ff. For Ge Hong's *Baopuzi*, see *Waipian* 50/199/10 (*yi dianji ziyu* 以典籍自娛).

expressions like 'roaming through texts' and 'playing with texts' that we frequently fail to realise how utterly novel the phrases would have seemed to the *haogu* reformers who coined them at Chengdi's court, men who recall the leading figures at Alexandria, especially Callimachus and his ilk.[113] But the early Eastern Han and post-Han readers of works by the three masters at Chengdi's court understood the magnitude of their achievements. Hence Lu Zhaolin's 盧照鄰 (638?–684?) lyrical evocation of an era sadly lost: 'Silent and lonely is the place where Yang Xiong lived/ Over the years, nothing left but a bedful of books.'[114]

The Case of Alexandria, or Callimachus with his Rivals and Friends[115]

Leaving Chengdi's court to examine the comparable case of Ptolemaic Egypt, we find numerous parallels. To recapitulate a few points previously registered by others: the Ptolemaic 'scholars and writers were deeply reliant on written sources, on books from the past, and so on the use of libraries'[116] – just like their Chang'an counterparts.

1. Already by the third century BCE, scholars in Alexandria had begun to compare multiple variants in manuscripts with the aim of establishing a 'better text' than any surviving manuscript.

2. In Alexandria, as in Chang'an, the two collections included quite a few examples of texts originally composed in different scripts and different dialects.[117]

---

[113] Jacob 2013: conclusion, says of Callimachus: 'He was the creator of a new alliance between poetic imagination and book-learning, a man of letters who played to the full the games of culture.' These words could also describe Yang Xiong.

[114] From Lu's 'Chang'an: Ancient Theme' (Chang'an guyi 長安古意), 2.73.

[115] Despite claims to the contrary, there is no evidence that Callimachus was ever 'librarian' or 'director', as P.Oxy. 10.1241 would seem to exclude him. However, Callimachus was the author of what appears to be the first comprehensive bibliography of Greek literature, the *Pinakes* or *Tables*, and this work probably owed something to the collection then being assembled in the library. Barnes 2002: 69. There is no space to give Apollonius of Rhodes the attention he deserves, yet it is worth noting that Callimachus and Apollonius disagreed strongly in many aspects of their classicism, as per Pfeiffer 1968: 145–7. Apollonius was tutor to the crown prince in Callimachus' own day, and one of the foremost 'new poets', along with Theocritus, Nicander, Euphorian and others. See Rodenbeck 2001–2: esp. 529, 536. Jacob 2013: 107 couples their names in his description of the Alexandrian achievements, as do others.

[116] Jacob and de Polignac 2000: 65.

[117] The Jewish 'Letter of Aristeas' tells us that books in different languages were translated at the library, though we are not sure whether the Hebrew Bible was translated at the library, as Johnstone 2014 notes. Homer and Sappho would have been practically a different language to the Greeks living in third-century BCE Alexandria. Pliny the Elder says that Callimachus' student wrote a commentary on Zoroaster's verses in Iranian (or possibly Greek by that time). The pre-Qin seal scripts from the Six Kingdoms could be quite different.

3. Comparison of multiple texts (some in multiple scripts) treating the same topics allowed for an in-depth examination of discrepant accounts.

4. Concentrations of books usually drew scholars in the ancient world (as it does even in the Internet age). This circumstance also invited comparisons which, in turn, prompted the notion of greater 'selectivity', and an abiding interest in classifying and organising information.[118]

5. Textual criticism first emerged in Alexandria, apparently as a natural 'side-effect' of accumulating multiple copies of the same work or related works. Nonetheless, for the scholars gathered together at Alexandria philological questions evidently developed a momentum of their own, spawning new research questions as well as new methods of study,[119] which gradually spurred the development of a well-defined 'science' or technology of textual criticism at Alexandria. It was at Alexandria, after all, that the most authoritative editions were produced of Homer, of Hippocrates, of Aristophanes, and possibly of the Bible and Zoroaster, to note a few famous examples.[120]

6. As a result, 'canons' and 'classics' were demarcated in unprecedented ways, and the distant past nominally valued over the present, in literature and rhetoric as in political models.

7. A love of pithy epigrams arose, Callimachus providing one superb counterpart to Yang Xiong,[121] in company with an evident delight in learning as the 'least perishable' of the pleasures available to those elites 'in the know'.[122]

7. One of the several ways in which 'canons' and 'classics' were privileged over 'lesser' texts less worthy of transmission and emulation was by the massive cumulative inventories produced in Alexandria, as in Chang'an.

8. This process essentially entailed the displacement of 'tradition, memory, and inspiration' as the acknowledged fount of wisdom, learning and intellectual creativity and its replacement by archaising texts and their authoritative textual masters.[123]

Parts of the above scenario remain speculative, given the paucity of evidence for the pre-Roman Alexandrian library. (Remember, we have what looks to be a complete list of the contents of the main Han imperial libraries in its third version, and multiple passages describing citations of its precursors.[124]) To take one example, Rudolph Blum surmises, on the basis of eight short fragments of the original *Pinakes*, that the Alexandrian

---

[118] See Witty 1973 for details.
[119] This is a close paraphrase of Woolf 2013: 18; cf. Hatzimichali 2013.
[120] See Cameron 1995. *The Art of Grammar*, ascribed to Dionysius of Thrace (perhaps dubiously?), is the sole piece of Alexandrian philology to have survived intact.
[121] See Harder 2014.   [122] For Yang, see above; for Callimachus, see Pfeiffer 1968: 125.
[123] See Rodenbeck 2001–2: 527.   [124] I.e., *Hanshu* 30, the 'Yiwen zhi.'

library arranged authors into classes (with subdivisions, if necessary), in alphabetical order; listed under each author's name the titles of his works, with longer poems considered to be single works; cited the opening lines of each work; and supplied the number of lines in each work or, with longer works, the number of rolls needed to transcribe the work. Blum's evidence is sparse; only two of the fragments (nos. 443 and 434) specify the number of lines in a given work, for instance. Blum admits that one cannot even ascertain whether the headings indicated specific classes of authors and their works.[125] Onto remarkably slender threads have giant edifices been built. That said, we can establish the fact that Zenodotus introduced the systematic use of *recensio* and also the systematic comparison of texts before editing; that Callimachus' predecessor, the poet Philitas of Cos, had written a glossary of unusual expressions, Homeric forms and technical terms (shades of Yang Xiong in Chang'an); and that Callimachus compiled the *Pinakes*, an annotated inventory of some collection(s) in 120 papyrus scrolls, which was then reviewed by Aristophanes, pupil of Callimachus.

We glimpse the emergence in Alexandria, as in Western Han Chang'an, not only of a new style of textual criticism, applied to the 'worthy' texts handed down from the distant past, but also of a new style of writing that would prove hugely influential for well over a millennium afterwards – a style devised by some of the very people most closely associated with the libraries. 'Elegance, conciseness, allusiveness, high polish, learning and sophistication' were the 'hallmarks of Alexandria poetry directed at new readers',[126] just as they were the hallmarks of writing at Chang'an, where the three best stylists of the age plunged into their duties in the imperial manuscript collections. The impulse to use multiple citations ('allusiveness') was notably strengthened by participation in this library work, judging from the extant works at our command.[127] While the learned style developed in Alexandria, like the late Western Han style, is now occasionally derided as 'obscure', verging on the overly 'scholastic', it was this very self-conscious 'Alexandrian style', with its unaffected hunger for literature, that the Roman poets imitated,[128] and then the medieval

---

[125] Blum 1991: 150–60. [126] For Yang Xiong's witty epigrams, see Nylan 2013.
[127] Wang Qicai 2009 on memorials.
[128] Horace is influenced more by the epigrammatists than by Sappho or Alcaeus (other Hellenic models). Virgil was inspired by Theocritus in his *Eclogues*, while his *Aeneid* echoes Homer much less than Apollonius. Catullus was inspired by the epigrammatist Phalaecus; Alexandrian Callimachus and 'immortal Sappho', he says. Propertius calls Callimachus and Philitas his inspirations. See Rodenbeck 2001–2: 536, for this paraphrase. The phrase 'unaffected love of literature' is also from *ibid.*, 539.

imitators of Roman poetry. Yet another parallel, then, for in faraway Chang'an the compilations by the *haogu* reformers provided models for historians, poets, essayists and lexicographers for well over a millennium.

Conclusion

While military and political power-holders intent upon advertising their power created the earliest 'great libraries', the foregoing suggests that the mere collection of so many variant editions of Classics and masterworks quickly incited new sorts of 'intellectual' commitments and 'literary' ventures that diverged from their political patrons' conscious design; temporary contacts and shared endeavours may shape the course of learning and inquiry alike.[129] In both capitals halfway round the globe we discern an unprecedented interest in antiquarian and philological pursuits;[130] the revolutionary fashioning of poetic forms novel in idiom, technique and theme, with learned indirection, coded distance, resort to rare dialect words and glittery allusiveness the new stocks-in-trade;[131] the concomitant development of the first 'textual criticism'; the decision to single out the so-called 'canonical' authors for each category, outlined in those definitive compilations known as the *Hanshu* 'Yiwen zhi' and *Pinakes*; a marked preference for *complete* works of *selected* authors; and the gradual subordination of commentarial traditions to 'canonical' works. No longer, given the comparable results in the discrete fields of Classics and East Asian Studies, need we deem the impact of 'great libraries' on writing styles and genres 'disputed and difficult to assess'.[132] After all, the poets and the historians and the textual critics were one and the same people (in this chapter best represented by the polymaths Yang Xiong and Callimachus).[133] These scholars' identity, so inextricably bound up with the recuperation of diverse traditions from much earlier eras, appears both highly self-conscious and proudly instrumental. Moreover, the urgent calls to recapture long-forgotten 'traditions'

---

[129] Fraser 1972: 468.
[130] Veyne 1988 argues, with some exaggeration, that classical Greek and Roman historians typically wrote about their own time; the same is true in China, with Sima Qian the exception rather than the rule.
[131] On this, see Silk 2004.   [132] Maehler 2004: 12.
[133] One could mention others, e.g., the Augustan meta-scholar Didymus, who wrote commentaries on a large number of classical authors, from Homer to Pindar to Demosthenes; and several word lists and miscellanies. He cites a very wide range of earlier authors, including earlier grammarians. For him, see Hatzimichali 2013. The works of the library now were seen as a kind of intellectual heritage.

were thoroughly anti-traditional, in that it was the writers' keenly felt distance from current traditions that elicited those repeated calls for 'renovations' of the recent past. In effect the technical advances associated with textual criticism, as well as the shift in emphasis from oral to written transmissions, however gradual, depended upon invented traditions and induced ruptures.[134] What Yang Xiong, Callimachus and kindred spirits concocted out of the manuscripts before them were bookish worlds in which the distant past could live forever, heedless of the rise and fall of individual dynasties, worlds whose origins and essences would become the stuff of sustained scrutiny, but also of certainty.[135]

This comparative project in my mind's eye took off from a 'zombie claim', if you will,[136] found in recent popular books touting the 'open access' and 'democratic' function of the first 'universal library' at Alexandria, in contrast to the 'closed' and 'secret' character of the libraries in autocratic China, a canard neatly consigning China to Oriental Despotism.[137] The essay was soon propelled by my growing astonishment at the paucity of contemporary evidence for the famous Great Library at Alexandria versus the abundance of contemporary evidence for the Chang'an palace libraries in Chang'an, also a budding awareness that neither antique culture could boast what we call a 'library' in the modern sense. The Chang'an palace manuscript depositories were supervised by ritualists lodged in two ministries, that of the *Taichang* (Commissioner of Ritual) and the *Zongzheng* (Commissioner of the Imperial Clan), and important documents continued to be kept in Chang'an temples. Similarly, at Alexandria, the Great Library (Libraries?)[138] was subordinated to the Temple of the Muses or Museion.

So what? The Stoic Seneca the Younger in the first century CE scoffed at the idea of large libraries, asking, 'What is the point of countless books and

---

[134] Silk 2004: 361 calls this commitment to tradition by those operating outside tradition the 'Alexandrian dilemma'.

[135] For the phrase 'bookish world', see Jacob 2013: 107.

[136] For 'zombie arguments', see the economist Paul Krugman, who defines them as 'arguments that have been proven wrong, should be dead, but keep shambling along because they serve a political purpose'. See Krugman's column in *The New York Times* editorial page for 19 June 2014.

[137] See McNeely 2008. Ironically, as Manning 2010 has shown, within Classics itself, Ptolemaic Egypt is cast in the Oriental Despot mode, when compared with Greece (dubbed 'democratic', despite the many tyrannies). The worst offender here is Polastron 2008: 95–108.

[138] The paucity of reliable early testimony (which contradicts itself on this point, as on others) prevents us from determining how many imperial libraries existed in Alexandria. The classical authors occasionally talk of 'the libraries' but more often of 'the king's library' or the 'great library'. See El-Abbadi 2004: 172 n. 26. Tatemi Sotoshi 2009 reminds us that the *fengchang/taichang* were generally selected from the nobility related to the imperial house.

libraries, whose titles the owner can barely read through in his lifetime? . . . It is better to entrust yourself to a few authors than to wander through many' in monumental works showing off 'the good taste and care of kings'.[139] To Seneca we offer the rejoinder that the large imperial libraries in Alexandria and Chang'an evidently fostered a set of specific ways to forge connections across and within manuscripts, in order to produce better transcriptions and more capacious minds, processes that eventually selected out the 'canonical' writings in prose and in poetry to be preserved at all cost by trained scholars through the ages. Geoffrey Lloyd's own writings, like those of the ancient masters, invite us to hone our powers of discrimination and recast our traditions. I am honoured to dedicate this essay to him.

Bibliography

Classical Greek and Latin Texts and Papyri Cited

Diodorus Siculus, Seneca, Strabo, and Suda are all cited according to standard editions. Except where otherwise noted, papyri are cited according to the standard edition.

Classical Chinese Texts Cited

Baopu zi 抱朴子. Ge Hong 葛洪. See Sun Xingyan 孫星衍. *Xin zheng Baopu zi* 新校正抱朴子 edn of 1885. n.p. (Zhushi Huailu jiashu), indexed in *Baopu zi neipian tongjian* 通檢; *waipian tongjian* 通檢. Paris, 1965; reprint 1969.
Fayan 法言. Yang Xiong 揚雄. See Nylan 2013.
Hanguan jiuyi bu yi 漢官舊儀補遺. Comp. Wei Hong 衛宏 (fl. 25–57). 1 *juan*. In *Hanguan liu zhong* 漢官六種. Reconstituted by Sun Xingyan 孫星衍 (1753–1818) et al., collated and punctuated by Zhou Tianyou 周天遊. Beijing, 1990.
Hanshi waizhuan 韓氏外傳. Han Ying 韓嬰. See the standard paragraphs preserved in the Harvard-Yenching Sinological Institute series.
Huayang guozhi 華陽國志. Chang Qu 常璩 (active 265–316). See *Huayang guozhi*, ed. Ren Naiqiang 任乃強. Chengdu; reprint 1984.
Liezi 列子. See *Liezi zhu zi suo yin* 列子逐字索引. Hong Kong, 1996.
Lu Zhaolin 盧照鄰. See *Lu Zhaolin ji jiao zhu* 盧照鄰集校注. Beijing, 1998.
Lunheng 論衡. Wang Chong 王充. See the *Lunheng zhuzi suoyin* 論衡逐字索引. Hong Kong, 1966.
Quan Han wen 全漢文: See Yan Kejun.

---

[139] Seneca, *On Tranquillity of Mind* 9.4–5, whose phrase 'good taste and care of kings' may come from Livy's *History of Rome*.

Taiping yulan 太平御覽. Li Fang 李昉 et al., in *Siku quanshu* [e-Siku].
Tongzhi 通志. Zheng Qiao 鄭樵 (1104–62). See *Tongzhi er shi lue* 通志二十略, ed. Wang Shumin 王樹民. Beijing, 1995, 2 vols.
Yanshi jiaxun 顏氏家訓. Yan Zhitui 顏之推. See Zhuang Huiming.
Zhang Yi 張揖 (fifth century), Wang Niansun 王念孫 (early eighteenth century). *Guangya shu zheng* 廣雅疏證, *Huang Qing jing jie* 皇清經解, Nanjiang; reprint 2000.

Secondary Literature in Asian Languages

Chen Zhi 陳直 (1973) *Qin Han wadang gaishu* 秦漢瓦當概述. Hong Kong.
Fu Jiayi 傅嘉儀 (2002) *Zhongguo wadang yishu* 中國瓦當藝術. Shanghai, vol. I of 2.
Fu Yuzhang 傅玉璋 (2008) *Zhongguo gudai shixue shi* 中國古代史學史. Hefei.
Guan Xihua 管錫華 (2002) *Zhongguo gudai biaodian fuhao fazhan shi* 中國古代標點符號發展史. Chengdu.
Hsing I-t'ien 邢義田 (2010) 'Handai *Cang Jie, Jijiu*, bati he shishu wenti: zai lun Qin Han guanli rehe xuexi wenzi' 漢代倉頡, 急就, 八體和史書問題: 再論秦漢官吏如何學習文字. In *Paleography and Early Chinese History* 古文字與古代史, no. 2 (December), ed. Li Zong-kun 李宗 (Symposium Series of the Institute of History and Philology), Academia Sinica. Taipei: 429–70.
Hsü Fu-kuan 徐復觀 [Xu Fuguan in *pinyin*] (1966) *Zhongguo yishu jingshen* 中國藝術精神. Taizhong.
Hua Xuecheng 華學誠 (2006) *Yang Xiong Fang yan jiaoshi huizheng* 揚雄方言校釋匯證. Beijing.
Li Qing 李卿 (2003) *Qin Han Wei Jin Nanbei chao shiqi jiazu zongzu guanxi yanjiu* 秦漢魏晉南北朝時期家族宗族關係研究. Shanghai.
Li Yufang 李毓芳 1995 'Han Chang'an cheng de Weiyang gong de kaogu faxian 汉长安城未央宫考古发掘與研究, *Wenbo* 文博 1995: 3, 82–93.
Lin Zhen'ai 林貞愛 (2001) *Yang Xiong ji jiaozhu* 揚雄集校注. Chengdu.
Liu Hong 劉紅 and Li Bilang 李笔浪 (2011) 'Lun Handai de zhongshu cangshu de queli, bianqian yiji yingxiang' 論漢代的中樞藏書的確立, 變図及其影響, *Tangdu Journal* 唐度學刊 27.4: 30–4.
Liu Rulin 劉汝霖 (1935) *Han Jin xueshu biannian* 漢晉學術編年, 2 vols. Shanghai.
Noma Fumachika (1988) *Gokyō seigi no kenkyū: sono seiritsu to tenkai* 五經正義の研究: その成立と展開. Tokyo: 7–38.
Tatemi Satoshi 楯身智志 (2009). 'Kan hatsu kōso koshin I ji ko: zenkan zenhen ki ni okeru sobyo seido no tenkai to koso koshin rekko no suii' 漢初高祖功臣位次考:前漢前半期における宗廟制度の展開と高祖功臣列侯の推移. *Tōyō gakuhō* 90.4: 1–32.
Wang Qicai 王啟才 (2009) *Handai zouyi de wenxue yiyun yu wenhua jingshen* 漢代奏議的文學意蘊與文化精神. Beijing.

Yan Kejun 嚴可均 (1961) *Quan shanggu sandai Qin Han Sanguo Liuchao wen* 全上古三代秦漢三國六朝文, 6 vols. Taipei.

Yan Lingfeng 嚴靈峰 (1975-9) *Zhou Qin Han Wei zhu zi zhi jian shu mu* 周秦漢魏諸子知見書目, 6 vols. Taipei.

Zhuang Huiming 庄輝明 and Zhang Yihe 章義和 (1999) *Yanshi jiaxun yizhu* 顔氏家訓譯注. Tianjin.

Western Bibliography

Bagley, R. W. (2004) 'Anyang writing and the origin of the Chinese writing system', in *The First Writing: Script Invention as History and Process*, ed. S. D. Houston. Cambridge: 190-237.

Bagnall, R. S. (2002) 'Alexandria: library of dreams', *Proceedings of the American Philosophical Society* 146.4: 348-62.

Barnes, R. (2002) 'Cloistered bookworms in the chicken-coop of the muses: the ancient library of Alexandria', in Macleod: 61-79.

Blitstein, P. (2012). 'L'art politique du texts: savoirs lettrés et pouvoir impérial dans la Chine du Sud aux Ve-VIe siècles', PhD thesis, Institute National des Langues et Civilisations Orientales.

Blum, R. (1991) *Kallimachos: The Alexandria Library and the Origins of Bibliography*, trans. from German by Hans H. Wellisch. Madison.

Callmer, C. (1944) 'Antike Bibliotheken', *Opuscula Archaeologica* 3: 145-193 (*Acta Instituti Romani Regni Sueciae* 10).

Cameron, A. (1995) *Callimachus and his Critics*. Princeton.

Cherniack, S. (1994) 'Book culture and textual transmission in Sung China', *Harvard Journal of Asiatic Studies* 54: 5-126.

Chung, E. 1982. 'A study of the *shu* (letters) of the Han dynasty (206 B.C.-A.D. 220)', PhD thesis, University of Washington.

Coqueugniot, G. (2013a) *Archives et bibliothèques dans le monde grec: edifices et organization, Ve siècle avant notre ère – IIe siècle de notre ère*. Oxford.

  (2013b) 'Where was the Royal Library at Pergamum: an institution found and lost again', in König et al.: 109-23.

Cribiore, R. (2005) *Gymnastics of the Mind: Greek Education in Hellenistic and Roman Egypt*. Princeton.

Crone, P. (1989) *Pre-industrial Societies*. Oxford.

Csikszentmihalyi, M. and Nylan, M. (2003) 'Constructing lineages and inventing traditions through exemplary figures in early China', *T'oung pao* 89: 1-41.

Delia, D. (1992) 'From romance to rhetoric: the Alexandrian Library in Classical and Islamic traditions', *American Historical Review* 97.5: 1149-67.

DeWoskin, K. (1982) *A Song for One or Two: Music and the Concept of Art in Early China*. Ann Arbor, MI.

Drège, J-P. (1991) *Les bibliothèques en Chine au temps des manuscrits (jusqu'au Xe siècle)*. Paris.

Dudbridge, G. (2000) *Lost Books of Medieval China*. London.
Durrant, S., Li Waiyee, Nylan, M., Van Ess, H. (2016) *The Letter to Ren An and Sima Qian's Legacy*. Seattle.
Egan, R. (2014). *The Burden of Female Talent*. Cambridge, MA.
El-Abbadi, M. (2004) 'The Alexandria Library in history', in Hirst and Silk: 167–83.
El-Abbadi, M. and Fathallah, O. M. (2008) *What Happened to the Ancient Library of Alexandria?* Leiden.
Feeney, D. (2007) *Caesar's Calendar: Ancient Time and the Beginnings of History*. Berkeley.
Finnegan, R. (1977) *Oral Poetry: Its Nature, Significance and Social Context*. Cambridge.
Fraser, P. M. (1972) *Ptolemaic Alexandria*, vol. I: *Text*. Oxford.
Giele, E. (2005) 'Signatures in early imperial China', *Asiatische Studien/Etudes Asiatiques* 59.1: 353–87.
  (2010) 'Excavated manuscripts: context and methodology' in eds. M. Nylan and M. Loewe, *China's Early Empires: A Re-appraisal*. Cambridge: 114–34.
  (2014) Private communication, 'Sealing Letters', addressed to M. Nylan.
Greatrex, R. (1994) 'An early Western Han synonymicon: the Fuyang copy of the *Cang Jie pian*', in *Outstretched Leaves on his Bamboo Staff: Studies in Honour of Göran Malmqvist on his 70th Birthday*, ed. J. Enwall. Stockholm: 97–113.
Guidobaldi, M. P. and Esposito, D. (2010) 'New archaeological research at the Villa of the Papyri', in *The Villa of the Papyri at Herculaneum*, ed. M. Zarmakoupi. Berlin: 21–62.
Harder, A. (2013) 'From text to text, the impact of the Alexandrian Library on the work of Hellenistic poets', in König et al.: 96–108.
Hatzimichali, M. (2013) 'Ashes to ashes? The library of Alexandria after 48 BC', in König et al.: 167–82.
Hendrickson, T. (2014) 'The invention of the Greek library', *Transactions of the American Philological Association* 144.2: 371–413.
Hightower, J. R. (trans.) (1952) *Han Ying's Illustrations of the Didactic Application of the Classic of Songs*. Cambridge.
Hirst, A. and Silk, M. (eds.) (2004) *Alexandria, Real and Imagined*. Aldershot.
Houston, G. W. (2002) 'The slave and freedman personnel of public libraries in ancient Rome', *Transactions of the American Philological Association* 132: 139–76.
Jacob, C. (2013) 'Fragments of a history of ancient libraries', in König et al.: 57–81.
Jacob, C. and de Polignac, F. (eds.) (2000) *Alexandria, Third Century BC: The Knowledge of the World in a Single City*. Alexandria.
Johnson, L. L. (1984) 'The Hellenistic and Roman library: studies pertaining to their architectural form', PhD thesis, Brown University.

Johnson, W. A. (2004) *Bookrolls and Scribes in Oxyrhynchus*. Toronto.
  (2010) *Readers and Reading Culture in the High Roman Empire: A Study of Elite Communities*. New York.
  (2013) 'Libraries and reading culture in the High Empire', in König et al.: 347–63.
Johnstone, S. (2014) 'A new history of libraries and books in the Hellenistic period', *Classical Antiquity* 33.2: 347–93.
Kaster, R. A. (1988) *Guardians of Language: The Grammarian and Society in Late Antiquity*. Princeton.
Knechtges, D. R. (1977) 'The Liu Hsin/Yang Hsiung correspondence on the *Fang yen*', *Monumenta Serica* 33: 309–25.
König, J., Oikonomopoulou, K. and Woolf, G. (eds.) (2013) *Ancient Libraries*. Cambridge.
Lewis, N. (1963), 'The non-scholar members of the Alexandrian Museum', *Mnemosyne* 16: 257–67.
Loewe, M. (ed.) (1993) *Early Chinese Texts: A Bibliographical Guide*. Berkeley.
Macleod, R. (ed.) (2002) *The Library of Alexandria*. New York.
Maehler, H. (2004) 'Alexandria, the Mouseion, and cultural identity', in Hirst and Silk: 1–14.
Manning, J. G. (2010) *The Last Pharaohs: Egypt under the Ptolemies, 305–30 BC*. Princeton.
McDermott, J. P. (2006) *A Social History of the Chinese Book*. Hong Kong.
McGrath, A. (2004) *The Twilight of Atheism: The Rise and Fall of Disbelief in the Modern World*. New York.
McKenzie, J. (2007) *The Architecture of Alexandria and Egypt: c. 300 B.C. to A.D. 700*. New Haven.
McNeely, I. F. with Wolverton, L. (2008) *Reinventing Knowledge: From Alexandria to the Internet*. New York.
Mielsch, H. (1995) 'Die Bibliothek und die Kunstsammlung der Könige von Pergamon', *Archäologischer Anzeiger*: 765–79.
Montgomery, S. L. (2000) *Science in Translation: Movements of Knowledge through Cultures and Time*. Chicago.
Neudecker, R. (2013) 'Archives, books and sacred space in Rome', in König et al.: 312–31.
Nicholls, M. (2013) 'Roman libraries as public buildings in the cities of the empire', in König et al.: 261–76 (a summary of Nicholls' unpublished thesis, 'Roman public libraries', 2005).
Nylan, M. (1994) 'The *chin wen/ku wen* (New Text/Old Text) controversy in Han', *T'oung pao* 80: 83–145.
  (1995) 'The *ku wen* Documents in Han times', *T'oung pao* 81: 1–27.
  (2008) 'Classics without canonization: reflections on classical learning and authority in Qin (221–210 BC) and Han (206 BC–AD 220)', in *Early*

Chinese Religion, part I: *Shang through Han (1250 BC – AD 220*, eds. J. Lagerwey and M. Kalinowski. Leiden: 721–77.

(2011) *Yang Xiong and the Pleasures of Reading and Classical Learning in Han China*. New Haven.

(2013) *Exemplary Figures: A Complete Translation of Yang Xiong's Fayan*. Seattle.

(2015) 'Han views of the Qin legacy and the late Western Han "classical turn"', *Bulletin of the Museum of Far Eastern Antiquities* 79–80: 47–94.

Nylan, M. and Vankeerberghen, G. (eds.) (2015) *Chang'an 26 BCE: An Augustan Age in China*. Seattle and London.

Olson, D. R. (1994) *The World on Paper: The Conceptual and Cognitive Implications of Writing and Reading*. Cambridge.

Owen, S. (1986). *Remembrances: The Experience of the Past in Classical Chinese Literature*. Cambridge, MA.

Petrain, D. (2013) 'Visual supplementation and metonymy in the Roman public library', in König et al.: 332–46.

Pfeiffer, R. (1968) *History of Classical Scholarship, from the Beginnings to the End of the Hellenistic Age*. Oxford.

Platthy, J. (1968) *Sources on the Earliest Greek Libraries with the Testimonia*. Amsterdam.

Polastron, L. (2008) 'Ce que construisent les ruines', in El-Abbadi: 95–107.

Poo Mu-chou 蒲慕州 (2010) 'Xian Qin Liang Han de zungu siwei yu zhengzhi quanwei 先秦兩漢的尊古思維與政治權威', unpublished conference paper, from International Conference on Institutions and Social Order in the Han Empire, 5–7 May, Chinese University of Hong Kong.

Richter, M. (2012) *Guan Ren* 觀人: *Texte der altchinesischen Literatur zur Charakterkunde und Beamtenrekrutierung*. Berne.

(2013) *Embodied Text: Establishing Textual Identity in Early Chinese Manuscripts*. Leiden.

Rodenbeck, J. (2001–2) 'Literary Alexandria', *Massachusetts Review* 42.4: 542–72.

Queen, S. A. (2001) 'Inventories of the past: rethinking the "school" affiliation of the *Huainanzi*', *Asia Major* 3rd ser. 14: 51–72.

Schwartz, J. (1976) *Papyrus grecs de la Bibliothèque nationale et universitaire de Strasbourg*, vol V. Strasbourg.

Shapin, S. and Schaffer, S. (1985) *Leviathan and the Air-Pump: Hobbes, Boyle, and the Experimental Life*. Princeton.

Shryock, J. K. (1937) *The Study of Human Abilities: The Jen wu chih of Liu Shao*. New Haven.

Sider, D. (2005) *The Library of the Villa dei Papiri at Herculaneum*. Los Angeles.

Silk, M. (2004) 'Alexandrian poetry from Callimachus to Eliot', in Hirst and Silk: 353–72.

Smith, K. (2003) 'Sima Tan and the invention of "Daoism", "Legalism," et cetera', *Journal of Asian Studies* 62.1: 129–56.

Thern, K. L. (1966) *Postface to the* Shuo wen chieh tzu: *The First Comprehensive Chinese Dictionary*. Ann Arbor, MI.
Tian Xiaofei (2005) *Tao Yuanming and Manuscript Culture: The Record of a Dusty Table*. Seattle.
Too, Y. L. (2010) *The Idea of the Library in Classical Antiquity*. Oxford.
Van der Loon, P. (1952) 'On the transmission of the Kuan-tzu', *T'oung pao* 41: 4–5, 357–93.
Vankeerberghen, G. (2010) 'Texts in the *Shiji*', in *China's Early Empires: A Reappraisal*, eds. M. Nylan and M. Loewe. Cambridge: 461–79.
Veyne, P. (1988) *Did the Greeks Believe in their Myths? An Essay on the Constitutive Imagination*, trans. P. Wissing. Chicago.
Wagner, R. G. (2000) *The Craft of a Chinese Commentator: Wang Bi on the Laozi*. Albany.
Witty, F. (1973) 'The other Pinakes and reference works of Callimachus', *Library Quarterly* 43.3: 237–44.
Woolf, G. (2013) 'Introduction: approaching the ancient library', in König et al.: 1–20.
Yates, R. D. S. (2007) 'Soldiers, scribes, and women: literacy among the lower orders in early China', English draft of a *Wenbo* 文博 essay, dated 18 July 2007.

Afterword

MICHAEL LOEWE

By concentrating their research on a particular moment of time, an incident or a personage historians lay the groundwork whereby comparison and contrast with other such incidents may become possible; and as a second stage in their inquiries it may become possible to proceed to do so. In demonstrating the valid ways in which such work may proceed, the contributors to this volume also show that while such comparisons may best start by examining events or situations that occur within one and the same culture, extension to a study of those that pertain to two or more cultures may strengthen and enrich the study of each one. By such means there may well emerge the significance and explanation of issues which may elude comprehension if they are treated as unique occurrences. This book thus opens up a subject and develops a method that can be extended to many other questions beyond those tackled in the preceding chapters. The suggestions and ideas that follow below derive in part from considering the results that have already been attained.

Before embarking on a comparative study historians will be only too well aware of two major dangers that confront them: the one of a rigid insistence on concentrating on the minutiae of a special subject, thus obscuring its inherent pattern of development; the other of bravely asserting a general statement that fails to take account of the inherent differences between two situations. They are also conscious of the ways in which the different natures and extent of their sources and the objectives of their compilers may limit their inquiries. Our sources are never complete and comprehensive, and so may not always allow identification of one and the same historical situation at differing times within one culture, and there may be even less certainty in seeking an identity as between two cultures. Or the type and extent of valid information may preclude examination of the same problem to the same degree. The changing assumptions and attitudes of the compilers of our sources may likewise inhibit immediate comparison. Julius Caesar wrote his histories against the background of the Republic, Tacitus against that of the empire; Sima Qian (?145–?86 BCE) lived at a time when the practice of imperial government was still in its infancy and its concept perhaps open to question; by the time of Ban Gu (32–92 CE) it had become accepted as the norm.

Such difficulties may attend historical investigation within one and the same culture; they become apparent all too quickly in comparison and contrast between two cultures, for example in identifying the concepts of law and examining the conduct of judicial cases in the China of Zhou or Qin times on the one hand, and those we find in Athens or Sparta or Rome on the other. Less general examples may be seen in the arrangements taken to supply and control the consumption of water in the countryside of Italy and Shandong; or the correct deportment of mourners at the funeral of a relative in Rome and Chang'an.

An approach to comparison between two cultures may start by identifying the conditions, problems and conflicts that are of a similar nature in each one, and examining the reactions and attempts made to solve the recurring difficulties, either by individuals or by an established authority. In general terms we might compare the responses evoked in each one by the abnormalities and enormities wrought by nature. We might ask whether social changes and technological innovation necessitated a choice between an adherence to hallowed tradition or the initiation of new means with which to confront newly emerging problems. In political terms we might examine the differing ways whereby criticism or protest could be voiced at times when the government and control of a population gave rise to hardship. Or we might ask how far a prevalence of religious belief might affect the conduct of rulership; or what compromises might follow in a choice between rule by ethical provisions or dependence on stark measures of power and punishment.

All historians will identify the topics that they think would best respond to treatment by comparison and it is possible that such treatment can become more productive for later rather than earlier times. Source materials for the Roman and Chinese empires are more extensive than those for the city states of Greece or the communities of pre-imperial China and may well facilitate a more detailed study of certain subjects. But without corresponding information for earlier periods, the assumptions and motives behind the ideas and actions of later times may fail to be appreciated or remain concealed.

That references to religion were somewhat subdued during the conference whose proceedings are published herewith is perhaps not surprising. It would certainly have been too ambitious to attempt a comparison between the religious beliefs and practices of the Greek cities and those of the kingdoms of the *Zhan guo* period. Major subjects, such as the significance of sacrifice, would demand deep consideration, in both religious and anthropological terms. However, comparison of particular aspects of the services rendered to occult powers, such as the significance of mountain cults, might be possible within a more restricted frame of reference. It may also be thought that religious demands form an important element that cannot be ignored in studying the background against which intellectual activities and social structure develop. There may well be ground for a study of the place of rituals within a social or political structure, or in the provisions for ethical instruction; if the subject may be extended, one may think of the rules laid down in the book of Leviticus, by Hesiod and in the *Liji*.

Comparative studies of whatever type must take account of the motives, attitudes and objectives that lay behind the compilation of historical sources. There is no shortage of scholarly work that has paid attention to this subject, but this has been largely directed to the sources of history within one culture. There may still be a call for a direct comparison of the basic assumptions and aims of the historians of different cultures. We might well learn much about Sima Qian's attitude to causation by comparison with that of Herodotus, or about Ban Gu's view of imperial power with that of Thucydides. In this major subject there may well be reason to extend the comparison even more widely, by investigating the motives that were inherent in the chapters of imperial annals (*ben ji*) of China's dynastic histories and those of the books of Samuel, Kings and Chronicles.

Social and political circumstances may include fruitful ground for comparison and contrast. The appearance of differing problems and conflicts in two cultures may illuminate the basic causes of each one, and here again comparison between China's early empires and the Republic and empire of Rome might well prove to be more legitimate than that between the earlier societies of the West and the East. There is no shortage of major and basic topics here, starting with the two concepts of a *civis Romanus* and a subject of a Qin or Han emperor. Different institutions and practices served to weld a community together, to bring about cooperative rather than divisive efforts and to control the population's activities. One may contrast the function and effects of public oratory with those of persuasion voiced in private, and within the former group between the different types of audience that constituted such a public. From this there may arise a further question: that of how far the orators gave rise to a public opinion and how far public opinion was voiced in China's empires. The sculptures and memorial columns of Rome sang the praises of heroes and encouraged an emulation of their qualities; dedicated shrines and carefully served tombs may have aimed at the same objectives in Chang'an. As against the title of Divus Augustus that a coin bore, the terms of a reign-title, as seen in official documents, could call to mind the achievements of an emperor or the blessed fortune that had come his way.

The contrasts between the unique characteristics of two cultures are equally illuminating. Athens produced the means whereby males, save slaves and metics (resident foreigners), might take part in formulating major decisions of the city. It is difficult to see how such an idea would have appealed to those who ruled in the kingdoms of pre-imperial China. Imperial China produced and fostered a highly privileged class of officials, educated in a scholarly way and imbued with a sense of tradition; Athens chose some of its leaders by lot; Rome some of its officials by popular election. In both the Roman and the Han empires acknowledged social hierarchies lay behind the implementation of a government's decisions.

In practical terms it was evidently sufficient for the government of Rome to rely on a count of the population that was arranged once in five years; the officials of Han China submitted their registers of taxable households and individuals every year. Following up the survey in Chapter 13 it might well be profitable to compare the means adopted to store grain in China and Egypt, subject as these would be as much to ecological conditions as to human administration. Circulation of copies of the year's calendar to distant parts of the Chinese empires depended on a postal service and its strict schedules, and therefore on effective supervision by officials and the energy of their runners; it may be asked whether such a need was necessary in Rome and if so how it was met. Fragments of documents survive both from the Roman wall in Britain and from the military outposts along the protected route in China's north-west. Comparison will surely lead eventually to a deeper understanding of the organisation of the servicemen and their living conditions. Studies of such particular instances in two cultures may well lead to more general considerations; such as where the responsibility or initiative lay in planning a Roman aqueduct or a Chinese canal; or how the necessary labour and materials were provided and on whom the expenses devolved.

In these and other examples comparison starts from particular details of two situations that were generally at the same stage of development and whose sources of evidence are of much the same type. From such considerations it may well be possible to seek the more general and pervasive characteristics of the two or more cultures that are concerned. In all such inquiry, assessment and critical use of the primary sources and their terms must take first place; one may ask, for example, whether it is correct to use the term 'law' in respect of νόμος, *lex, lü* and *ling*. Too easy a dependence on secondary sources may well lead to the imposition of a further difficulty in the exercise of comparison; it may subject a reader to a secondary writer's implicit assumptions or understandings that refer to a particular situation; translations of Greek, Latin or Chinese texts may betray the background and prejudices of the translator, in whatever century he or she was working or works.

Comparison and contrast probably best proceed from the particular to the general, from local situations to abstractions. Some scholars may start by fastening on the facts or problems of a political, social or economic situation and then proceed to explain its intellectual and religious conditions. The day-to-day reports of how men and women lived and worked on the walls of northern Britain and north-western China may point the way to understanding the organisation of the military and administrative services of the two cultures. Others, who are more venturesome, may find it possible to reverse this order of procedures: a study of the religious differences that assailed Byzantium or Buddhist Japan may explain the dynastic or political conflicts of both of these centres of civilisation.

Only in rare cases has a scholar mastered the means of working in two or more cultures. Otherwise, appropriate and valid comparison requires the cooperation of two specialists, working in parallel and independently, on a subject or problem that is of the same type, be it manifest in Delphi and Taishan, or in Rome and Luoyang. Comparative work follows, when they present their conclusions in a form which specialists in other disciplines will follow and to which they may be able to contribute.

The choice of subjects and problems that a historian names as being suitable for comparative study will perforce arise directly from his or her own special field of study. Those that are described below are chosen from a number that have attracted the interest of a writer whose principal concern has been with the early empires of China.

A basic question lies in the religious and intellectual grounds upon which monarchies draw to prove that they are exercising their rule with unquestionable authority and legitimacy. Some, such as those of the kingdom of Judah or Israel, might call on the power of revelation or holy writ, or ordination by a prophet; others, known as constitutional monarchies, may look to an ideal based on theoretical argument; and yet another, such as that of Wang Mang (9–23 CE) or an emperor of Japan, may deliberately create a myth, fanciful perhaps, but sufficiently appealing to be convincing, perhaps for no more than a short time.

These differences bring with them the various ways in which the leaders of a culture portray the past. Some modern scholars have seen this as a process whereby direct intervention or rule by the gods yielded place to the predominance of man. In antiquity many looked back to a golden age that was followed by a retro-active recession. Yet others, like Whig-minded historians of a later age, might think of the past as a set of periods marked by a continual and ennobling progress, whereby mankind has successfully striven to overcome the forces of nature.

Sources of history may be at their most unreliable and frustrating for those who seek to evaluate the part played by an emperor or king in the decisions taken in his realm and in his name. That his powers and functions varied widely both within his own culture and as between others needs little stress; and however erratic our sources may be, all hereditary monarchies gave rise to kings who were either strong or weak, wise or foolish, ascetic or indulgent. A number of questions arise; of the means whereby an incompetent emperor could be removed from his position, whether in Han China or Rome; that of the extent to which he could enforce his personal will, for example as between kings John and Henry VIII of England; or that of his freedom to choose his own advisers, as between a Han emperor such as Jingdi (reigned 157–141 BCE) and a Roman emperor such as Claudius. Where political leaders were subject to a process of election, the situation was very different.

In some cultures, such as Japan and Rome, the emperor was seen as a godhead. Some kings or emperors had proved themselves and reached their pre-eminent position thanks to the personal appeal of their leadership or their success on the field of battle. Elsewhere an infant who found himself sitting on a throne could be no more than a puppet. His function however might be essential. For, whether infant, adult or in his dotage, the king was seen to be the source from which all authority on earth devolved. Without him, officials had no power of compelling obedience.

Emperors and kings ruled over several or many communities whose religious beliefs may be utterly different or even antagonistic, as in India, or sometimes co-existing in amity, as in Japan. The ideas of leadership and social structure that emerge may be in conflict, as in India. The means adopted or the struggle to maintain a livelihood may differ dramatically, as between Roman Gaul and Syria, or the extreme northern and southern parts of a Chinese empire. It is in such circumstances that the leaders of a realm may need to treat their kingdom or empire as a unity, or at least to persuade their subjects that they are all members of one and the same unity, backed by a sense of pride and loyalty. In some instances, and perhaps somewhat rarely, the natural authority or inherent power of leadership of an individual may bring about this result; and in such cases it may be asked how different cultures reacted to the rise or demise of an Alexander, Qin Shi Huang Di, Khubilai Khan or Napoleon.

Conformity with a religion, whether voluntary or imposed, may act as an agency whereby a sense of corporate identification is created and it may exercise its own effect on the conduct of public life and the forms of a nation's institutions. Differences in such conditions may well be apparent in the study of empires whose government, whether nominally or effectively, was subservient to Judaism, Christianity or Islam, or professed adherence to Buddhism.

Compulsion and an imposed discipline may effectively instil a sense of identification as members of a kingdom or empire, but whether such methods would confirm a loyal support or arouse subversive action could not be predicted. Nor may they always have conveyed much more than an obligation to fulfil certain duties, under fear of punishment. It may be asked whether peasants who paid their dues to a Chinese tax collector were really concerned whether he had been appointed by a Han emperor or a king of Wei, Shu or Han. How far did Serbians or Hungarians, Poles or Venetians, pride themselves as being members of one and the same empire, obedient to the orders of officials appointed by a German-speaking emperor? Did it concern the farmers of Norman England that their king had been crowned at Westminster or that his father had been buried at Fontevrault?

A people and its leaders may attribute greater significance either to heredity and the call of kinship or to an individual's character, ability and merits. The preference may vary from period to period, both within a particular culture and as between different cultures. That the non-hereditary monarchies, of Rome, the Papacy and Byzantium, may have lasted with greater continuity than any of the hereditary houses may give rise to fruitful questioning (Japan's claim to unbroken continuity from Jimmu *tennō* can hardly be sustained).

Kings and emperors could not hope to rule without the loyal support of administrators and clerks, military officers and soldiers. The more senior of these, who carried heavy responsibilities, might be chosen for their tasks thanks to favouritism, or their prominence at court, or their intellectual abilities. In the latter case they might be fit to organise the construction of a major building or project for irrigation, that might take decades to complete, or to lead the armed forces in circumstances that were quite unpredictable. At a lower level were the ever present tasks that required routine, systematised service. Officials of the provinces needed numerous copies of essential documents, such as the government's orders and, in China, the calendar; their preparation and distribution depended on the humdrum work of the copyist and the scheduled journeys of the runner who carried the mail. The question always arises of the degree of what we may call professionalisation was expected or attained by officials at different levels of administration.

Different empires adopted different means of recruiting and training their officials and their scribes, and comparison of these procedures would be significant, where sufficient evidence makes it possible. It may however be possible to identify some features with a view to examining whether they were used in several regimes or uniquely in one. Tests in literary ability and learning, based on writings chosen for their lessons in morality, characterised some of the means that emerged and were developed to great complexity in China's empires. It may be asked in what ways other empires, such as that of Byzantium, sought men of ability to serve their needs. The training of the officials and officers of the Japanese empires instilled into them an unquestioned obedience to commands and an immediate readiness for self-sacrifice. It remains open to question whether these results are unmatched elsewhere, and how significant these were in Japan's practice of empire.

Whether they were founded in Europe or Asia, empires rarely resisted the temptation to indulge in territorial expansion. Different motives prevailed, perhaps a search for defensive protection or perhaps for material wealth, as occurred in both the Han and the Tang empires; or perhaps such activities derived from the yearnings of an Alexander or a Napoleon, perhaps of Tang Taizong (r. 626–49), or the Kangxi emperor (r. 1662–1722). The emperors and high officials who served them would need to determine whether the ventures that were being planned would be profitable; how essential the Han or Tang defensive lines to Central Asia, or those in northern Britain, were to the general well-being of the empire; whether the income from gold mines in Spain or Dacia, or the pearls and exotica from southern China and Hainan, was sufficient to warrant the expense of procuring it. The information needed to assess the value of the schemes that might be proposed was by no means always available, nor was it comprehensive.

The task of implementing the proposals of the central government fell on to the shoulders of the provincial governors, who would probably have served as such in the interior of the empire before being posted to its fringe. An official of China could rise to become a governor of a commandery, presiding over the livelihood of perhaps 2 million inhabitants as in Runan (present-day Henan) or 20,000 as in Nanhai (present-day Guangdong). His responsibilities included a number of specialist tasks. Preparation of the annual accounts would require some of the abilities of a mathematician. He would need a full knowledge of legal documents and pronouncements with which to conduct a judicial investigation and treatment of crime. He must have some idea of military strategy and tactics, so as to ensure the protection of the land against marauders, whether from within or without the emperor's territory. His training had not included instruction in these technical skills, and he might well find himself at a loss to solve some of the problems that faced him.

Provincial governors or officials of Rome might face very different situations and problems as they were transferred from one post to another, be it at Volubilis in Africa, Petra in Asia Minor or Eboracum in northern Europe. So too would a Han governor who was posted to the thriving commandery of Shu (present-day Sichuan), or to the bleak expanse of Liaodong (in present-day Liaoning) or to one of the densely populated and highly civilised parts of Shandong. A Roman official might live in comfort, ensconced in his villa on the Isle of Wight; another would direct his government from Alexandria. His colleague from Han China might have been posted to an isolated encampment in modern Korea, while his more fortunate friend might be enjoying the company of the scholarly learned men whose lives centred around the schools of learning in present-day Shandong or Jiangsu. Official or private adventurers of Europe were to establish trading settlements in India, Africa or America. All these men and perhaps their wives faced severe conditions in their livelihood, a threat of violence and the ravages of disease, all encountered in far-off lands of which they knew nothing. Had we more extensive written accounts of their activities and hardships, their feelings of proud independence or abandoned isolation, we might be able to see more clearly how conditions of colonial life varied between different empires.

Many of the governors of the newly penetrated lands would have been ignorant of the conditions that they would soon face; for it is questionable how far a governor of an area that was within the later province of Guangxi, or of Gallia, had been informed of the religious beliefs or way of livelihood of the inhabitants of those lands or their likely attitude to a foreign authority. A governor's tasks or problems lay in imposing an administration and establishing colonial settlements on peoples whose cultural level may have differed widely from his own. They must contrive to carry out their task in such a way that would bring material benefit to the empire that they served while avoiding strife and insurrection, loss of life and financial expense. Rome's colonialists in Africa and European empire builders in India, Africa or America may well have been confronted with somewhat similar problems; they could hardly have taken identical steps to resolve them. A study of the differences could be instructive.

The foregoing thoughts for the expansion of comparative cross-cultural and interdisciplinary studies derive from a writer who has specialised in the history of China's early empires and who is well aware of the advances made by his colleagues who have been working in other periods or aspects of China's history. That it is possible to think in a comparative way now forms a marked contrast with the situation a century or even fifty years previously. Dramatic changes have affected the subject by a concentration on the history of China's imperial dynasties, hardly started until 1945; by the embarrassingly rich extent of archaeological discoveries, including manuscripts of early writings which may require the growth of textual criticism; by the extension of the subject into other disciplines, such as those of literary criticism, anthropology, law or art history; and by the pioneer research of Joseph Needham and those of his colleagues who have striven both to deepen our understanding of China's past and to place those achievements within the context of the world's humanities.

Index

abstract expressions (*kongyan*), 308, 310, 320
abstraction, 45, 290, 299, 300, 301, 302, 303, 307
Academy
  imperial Chinese, 21, 22, 219
  Plato's, 22
Achilles, 161
actuality, 137, 138
acupuncture, 13, 332
administration, 36
advisers, 5, 13, 14, 22, 385, 387, 388
Aelius Aristides, 16
aesthetics, 337, 348
affections, 113, 122
Africa, 368
agalma, agalmata (statue, gift), 198, 201
Agamemnon, 199
agapē (love), 336
agriculture, 2, 9, 10, 18
alchemy, 34
Alcmaeonids, 201
Alexander, 416, 417
Alexandria, 21, 34, 373, 374, 375, 377, 380, 381, 386, 389, 393, 398, 399, 400, 402, 418
algebra, 293
algorithm, 7, 276
alphabet, 20
Amazons, 207
anachronism, 26
Analects. See Lunyu
analogies, 13, 206
anatomy, 12, 333, 347
Anaxagoras, 134
Anaximander, 131, 134, 141
ancestors, 23, 163, 164, 168, 171, 175, 177, 179, 195, 210
animals
  and humans, 131, 343, 347
  as food, 360, 365
  as models, 142
  behaviour of, 24
  common attributes of, 150
  creation of, 134
  lack of speech, 146
  sacrifice, 178
  sharing of, 369
  types of, 147, 149
anonymity, 335
anthropogony, 133, 135, 137, 141
anthropomorphy, 134
antiquity, love of (*haogu*), 390
anxiety, 333
aphrodisia, 326, 328, 331, 341, 342, 344, 345, 348
Aphrodite, 160, 161, 240, 329, 344
Apollo, 15, 74, 160, 179, 203
Apollonius Dyscolus, 63
Apollonius of Perga, 303
Apollonius of Rhodes, 388
appetite, 331, 335
approximation, 284
aqueduct, 413
archaeobotany, 364, 368
archaeology, 47, 48, 328, 360, 380, 381, 383, 419
Archelaus, 135
Archestratus, 330
Archimedes, 259, 262, 265, 268, 271–4, 276, 278, 279, 280, 281, 282, 283, 284, 285, 303
  Conoids and Spheroids, 276, 278, 281, 285
  Method, 259, 267, 268, 281, 285
  Palimpsest, 259, 260, 261
  Quadrature of the Parabola, 265, 285
  Sphere and Cylinder, 267, 276
archives, 374, 380, 385, 386
argument, 286
argumentation, 273
aristocracy, 165, 194, 195, 198, 199, 201, 227
Aristophanes (comic playwright), 399
Aristophanes (pupil of Callimachus), 400
Aristotle, 5, 6, 7, 19, 20, 22, 26, 63, 68, 88, 104, 110–18, 119, 120–3, 126–8, 131, 134, 137, 141, 142, 145, 146, 149, 150, 286, 334, 336
  De Anima, 121, 137, 145–6, 152, 153
  Generation and Corruption, 152
  Generation of Animals, 150, 152
  History of Animals, 137, 151

Metaphysics, 152
Nicomachean Ethics, 19, 113
Parts of Animals, 138, 150
Physics, 63
Posterior Analytics, 150
Prior Analytics, 150
Rhetoric, 111, 113, 115
Topics, 151
army, 53
Arrian, 100
art, 3, 25, 26, 99, 189, 228
artemisia, 341
asceticism, 360
Asclepius, 15, 16
as-if, 177, 180
assassination, 214, 215, 218
assemblies, 7, 9, 84, 228
Assiros, 365
Astarte, 240
astrology, 347
astronomers, 36
astronomy, 23, 297, 340, 347
Athena, 160, 203, 205, 208, 210, 226, 228
Athenaeus, 330, 357, 359
   Deipnosophists, 357, 359
Athenians, 20, 204, 228, 328
Athens, 15, 17, 19, 21, 189, 202, 203, 208, 210, 227, 367, 411, 413
athletic victory, 201
Atomists, 68
Atreus, 199
audience, 412
Augustine, St, 360
Augustus, 413
authority, 38, 91, 97, 104, 225, 238, 241, 286, 332, 344, 345, 376, 377, 379, 384, 387, 393, 399, 411, 414
authorship, 378–9, 386, 388
autocratic rule, 224
autonomy, 101, 178, 179, 182, 287
axial age, 68
axioms, 7

Babylonia, 277
bamboo, 377, 383, 392
Ban Gu, 212, 220, 222, 382, 411, 412
Bao Si, 234, 242, 243, 244, 246, 247, 249, 253
barbarians, 18, 49, 237, 242
beauty, 26, 235, 237, 238, 247, 250, 251, 329, 342
bian (debate, argument), 70, 84
Bible, 399
biomedicine, 11, 35

Biot
   Edouard, 296, 299
   Jean-Baptiste, 297–9, 305
Bloch, Marc, 42
blockages, 13
body, 13, 33, 34, 101, 105, 114, 137, 152, 167, 332, 333, 334, 336, 340, 342, 345, 348
Book of Documents. See *Shangshu*
Book of Rites. See *Liji*
bookish world, 402
books, 374, 378
Box-Lid, 259, 270, 277
breath, 335
Bronze Age, 163, 165, 189, 193, 198, 227, 361, 363, 365, 368
bronzes, 197, 198, 210
Buddhism, 2, 24, 414, 416
bureaucracy, 3, 24, 189, 216, 228, 285
Byzantium, 414, 416

calendar, 18, 413, 417
calligraphy, 66, 394
Callimachus, 204, 375, 388, 393, 398, 399, 400, 401, 402
   Pinakes, 400, 401
canals, 413
canons, 21, 220, 279, 285, 399
Cao Zhi, 225
capriciousness, 160, 169, 171, 173, 174, 175, 176, 178, 179, 182
Caraka samhitā, 331
catalogues, 375, 384, 389, 391
causes, 14, 44, 50, 84, 88, 106, 140, 141, 340
Cavalieri, Bonaventura, 259, 271, 276, 277, 278, 280, 282
censuses, 166
ceramics, 368
Ceres, 9
chance, 136
Chang'an, 373–4, 377, 380, 381, 382, 386, 388, 389, 393, 399, 400, 401, 402
change, 44, 45, 140
chaos
   Chinese, 141, 213
   Greek, 134
character, 114, 250
charlatans, 14
Chasles, Michel, 290, 301, 302
chemistry, 34, 37, 299, 301
Chemla, Karine, 276, 277, 286
Chevreul, Eugène, 299, 301, 302
Chi You, 169, 175
child, 20, 114, 121

choice, 104
Christianity, 2, 22, 24, 360, 416
Chrysippus, 96, 97, 99
Chu Ci (Songs of the South), 358, 359
Chunqiu (Spring and Autumn Annals), 21
Chunqiu fanlu (Luxuriant Dew of the Spring and Autumn Annals), 155
Chunyu Yi, 11
Cicero, 98, 99, 103, 106, 107
  On Fate, 99
  Stoic Paradoxes, 98, 99
cities, 135
citizens, 10, 22, 110
city-states, 193, 202, 411
civil service, 22
Classics, Chinese, 376, 390, 391, 394, 397, 399
classification, 148, 151, 153, 328
Claudius, 415
Cleanthes, 96, 106
Cleon, 208
Cleopatra, 253
clients, 374, 379, 388, 389
climate, 52, 366
Clytemnestra, 239
codex, 375, 377
Cold-hot Disorders, 35
commentaries, 220, 270, 276, 279, 285, 307, 308
comparative literature, 47
comparison, 42, 43, 45, 419
competition, 50, 73, 90, 365, 388
concord, 91
Confucian tradition, 111, 155, 220
Confucius, 5, 19, 86, 111, 171, 176, 220, 225, 387, 392, 394, 397
  as Zhong Ni in the *Zhuangzi*, 73, 86, 89–95
conic sections, 284, 285
consistency, 92, 378
Constantine, 24
constraint, 95, 103
consumption, 332, 355, 357, 359, 361, 363, 364, 366, 368
cooking, 328, 356, 364
cosmetics, 342
cosmology, 141, 153, 155, 162, 180, 346, 347
cosmos, 10, 13, 15, 33, 64, 83, 97, 104, 106, 107, 134, 161, 173, 174, 176, 179, 192, 333
courage, 116
court, 95, 194, 219, 228, 360, 374, 379, 384, 388, 390, 391, 393, 397
Cratylus, 67
Croesus, 201
cross-cultural universals, 26
Cua, Antonio, 111

cuisine, 355, 359
Cullen, William, 36
cultivation, 171
cultural manifolds, 37
curiosities, 375
curses, 337, 338

Da Ji, 234, 242, 243, 244, 245, 253
daemonic man, 88
dao (Way), 6, 8, 71, 78, 83, 87, 90, 93, 124, 140
Daodejing, 21
Daoism, 69, 70, 73, 75
Darwin, Charles, 142
Davidson, Donald, 65
de (virtue, power, force), 87, 90, 197
de Morgan, Augustus, 304
death, 132, 167, 178, 209, 236
debates, 84, 141
Delphi, 202, 414
Demeter, 9
demiurge, 84, 97, 136
democracy, 17, 193, 204, 287
Democritus, 67
demons, 13, 16, 166
demonstrations, 7
demonstrative work, 277
desire, 96, 114, 118, 120, 121, 123, 127, 343
destiny, 131–2, 201
determinism, 83, 97
dicasts, 19
dictionaries, 376
didacticism, 243
differentiae, 151
Diogenes the Cynic, 103
Dionysus, 179, 327
Dioscorides, 344
disciples, 379
Discourses of the States (Guoyu), 242
discovery, 286
diseases, 11, 13, 14, 22, 34, 35, 36, 345
disgrace, 112, 115, 118, 126, 127
disorder, 124
disrepute, 116, 117, 122
divination, 226, 339, 391
divine, 11, 14, 22
doctors, 12, 34
dogmatists, 84
domestication, 170–1, 175, 180, 182
Douglas, Mary, 355, 356, 363
dreams, 16
drugs, 329, 332, 334, 341, 344

Duke
  of Zhou, 164, 221, 222, 224, 390, 397
  Xian, 243
Dunhuang, 330, 340
dushu (universal procedure), 309, 320
dynasty, 172

Earth, 134, 147
earthquakes, 14
East/West, 43, 45, 53
eclipses, 14
ecology, 51
economics, 24, 37, 40, 52, 197
education, 3, 20, 25, 117, 118, 121, 250
efficacy, 26, 340, 341, 342
efficiency, 9
egalitarianism, 199
Egypt, 11, 18, 199, 200, 238, 240, 251, 330, 358, 384, 398
Eion, 206
elements, 12, 136, 141, 155
elites, 20, 21, 54, 166, 189, 199, 202, 216, 219, 227, 228, 286, 300, 374, 378, 397
elitism, 200, 204
emotions, 142, 149, 160, 163, 167, 180, 181, 326, 331, 340
Empedocles, 131, 134, 135, 138
emperors, 10, 23, 375
  Chinese
    Ai, 391
    Cheng, 21, 219, 373, 389, 390, 393, 395, 397
    Gaozu, 169
    Huan, 221
    Huangdi. *See* Yellow Emperor
    Jing, 415
    Kangxi, 23, 417
    Ming, 220
    Qin Shi Huang, 23, 223, 224, 416
    Taizong, 417
    Wu, 21, 222, 390
  Roman. *See* Augustus, Claudius, Julius Caesar
empires, 53, 208, 384
  Chinese, 51, 53, 411
  Roman, 24, 53, 60, 380, 411
empiricism, 326, 328, 341
emptiness, 91–3
energies, 167, 179
engineering, 9
enkratēs (continent man), 122
Enlightenment, 44
entertainment, 250
environments, 139, 171

epamphoterizein (dualise), 151
epic, 234
Epictetus, 83, 84, 85, 96, 100, 101, 104, 105, 106
Epicureans, 5
Epicurus, 22
Epidaurus, 15
epigrams, 399
epistemology, 4, 280
equalising, 314
equality, 10, 50
Eros, 134, 237
erōs, 336
eroticism, 327, 337
errors, 380
erudition, 391
Erya, 147, 390, 396
ethics, 96, 101, 112, 121, 171
ethnocentrism, 34
etymology, 376, 394
Euclid, 8, 274, 282, 285, 286, 291, 293, 303
  Elements, 274, 277, 281, 291, 293, 304, 307, 308, 322
  Elements of Conics, 285
Eudoxus, 275
Eulau, 367
eunuchs, 221, 223, 228, 359
Euripides, 209, 238
Europe, 34, 41, 51, 290, 299, 368
Europeans, 295
evolution, 136, 138, 140, 153
examinations, 285
experience, 114, 209, 334, 347, 348
experimentation, 37, 332, 347
experts, 15, 54, 86, 377

family, 361
famines, 356
Fangyan, 394, 396
farming, 348, 361, 368
fasting, 92, 93, 95, 96, 102
fate, 99, 133
femmes fatales, 234–54
fen (allotments), 131
festivals, 208
fevers, 34, 36
food, 3, 8, 123, 179, 197, 326, 331, 345, 355, 360
foreigners, 49
fossils, 134
France, 42
Frede, Michael, 84, 85, 97, 100, 102, 107
free will, 101
freedom, 83, 85, 88, 95, 96, 98, 100, 103, 105, 106–7, 207, 208

French language, 3, 61
friends, 89, 105, 115
Fu Shan, 36
functions, 12, 16
Funeral Orations, 208
funerals, 210, 221, 236
funerary shrines, 221

Galen, 11, 12, 334, 342, 344
   Simple Remedies, 344
Gaozi, 4
genealogies, 160, 177, 178, 201, 243
generality, 302
gentlemen, 25, 119, 125, 332, 334, 335
geographical factors, 51
geomancy, 10
geometry, 265, 285, 290, 302, 303
German language, 3, 37, 63, 416
ghosts, 160, 165, 166, 167, 168, 170, 171, 173, 174, 175, 176, 179, 182
gifts, 123, 197, 198, 243, 379
gluttony, 333
gods, 14, 16, 22, 24, 75, 77, 83, 97, 101, 105, 107, 131, 132, 133, 136, 141, 154, 160, 165, 168, 178, 181, 203, 210, 237, 347, 415
good, 4, 110, 117, 160
goods, 121, 127
Goody, Jack, 20, 355, 357, 368
Gorgias, 237–8
   Encomium of Helen, 237
Gougu theorem ('Pythagoras' theorem'), 278
government, 5, 13, 18, 36, 37, 221, 387, 389, 413, 417
Graham, Angus, 64, 86, 89, 107, 347
Grand Scribe, 18
Great Divergence, 51
Guanzi, 147, 155
gui. See demons, ghosts
guilt, 120, 128
Guoyu (*Discourses of the States*), 242, 244

habits, 125
habituation, 122
Han dynasty, 21, 36, 54, 55, 214, 224, 331, 339, 390, 412, 417
Hanshu (*Book of Han*), 382, 394, 401
happiness, 5
harm, 120, 124
Harmodios, 205
harmony
   cosmic, 161, 176, 180
   musical, 8, 25
   of cold and heat, 147

of *xing* and *wei*, 123
social, 179, 181, 221, 339
He zun, 162, 194, 197
healing, 334, 348
health, 3, 8, 10, 12, 13, 330, 333, 335
heart, 13, 91, 93, 95, 96, 102, 124
Heaven, 6, 15, 83, 91, 107, 123, 131–2, 143, 144, 147, 160, 162, 163, 164, 167, 168, 170, 171, 173, 177, 178
Hector, 235
Hegel, Georg Wilhelm Friedrich, 3
hegemony, 197, 202, 384
Heidegger, Martin, 3
Helen, 207, 234–41, 250–1
Hephaistos, 198
Hera, 160, 238
Heracles, 161, 179, 205, 208
Heraclitus, 67, 69, 74, 75, 76, 77, 79, 135
herbs, 341, 343, 346
heredity, 173
Hermes, 198
Herodotus, 18, 50, 190, 192, 193, 205, 207, 239, 240, 251, 252, 387, 412
heroes, 203, 205, 393, 412
Hesiod, 131, 141, 178, 412
   Theogony, 133, 178
   Works and Days, 178
heuristics, 65
hierarchy, 83, 133, 144, 145, 154, 194, 199, 334, 355, 357, 359, 363, 365, 368, 369, 413
Hippocrates, 10, 11, 14, 16, 330, 334, 341, 399
   Airs, Waters, Places, 342
   On Generation, 336
   On the Nature of Man, 12
   On the Nature of Women, 336
   On the Sacred Disease, 14
historians, ancient, 17
historiography, 17, 41, 48, 304
history, 36, 40, 44, 189, 192, 235, 378
Homer, 60, 63, 135, 198, 201, 234, 237, 239, 253, 375, 387, 399, 400
   Iliad, 235
homogenising, 314
homophonic translations, 65
honour, 112, 115, 116, 118, 123, 127
housing, 3, 10
Huainanzi, 131, 143, 145, 148, 149, 153, 155, 170, 397
Huan Tan, 14
Huangdi neijing (*Inner Canon of the Yellow Emperor*), 11, 21
Hui Shi, 72
humanities, 37, 47, 419

humans
  are nothing at all, 84
  as lacking essence, 72
  as sensitive to the truth, 107
  creation of, 134, 140
  freedom of, 98
  genealogies of, 160
  highest activity of, 5
  mortality, 78
  nature of, 4, 118
  place of, 10
  privilege of, 97
  relationship with gods, 181
  under constraint, 103
humours, 12
hybrids, 153

iconography, 200, 203, 220
ideals, 113, 286
ideology, 9, 10, 17, 37, 46, 207, 287
imaginary, 179, 182
immortality, 153, 340, 344
impulse, 103, 105
incantation, 338, 340
incommensurability, 20
incomparability, 3
incontrovertible conclusions, 7
India, 11, 330, 415
indivisibles, 259, 261, 266, 271
Indo-European languages, 64, 65
ineffability, 61, 67, 69, 74
infinite, 261, 264, 269, 275, 276, 278, 280, 281
infinitesimal slices, 275
Inner Mongolia, 361
innovation, 348, 411
inquire, 252
inscriptions, 21, 197
intelligence, 131, 133, 154
inter-cultural comparison, 47, 50
Islam, 416
Isocrates, 239, 250
isomorphism, 264, 281
isotope, 362, 363, 367
Italians, 60

Japan, 414, 416
Japanese, 20, 340
Jaspers, Karl, 68
Jesuits, 22, 290
Jia Kui, 220
Jiahu, 361
jing (essence), 335, 348
Jing Ke, 215, 218, 220, 223, 224

Jiuzhang suanshu. See *Nine Chapters*
Joyce, James, 60
Judaism, 416
Julius Africanus, 330
Julius Caesar, 410

Kāma Sūtra, 331
Kant, Immanuel, 88
Kastanas, 366
Keats, John, 65
Khubilai Khan, 36, 416
Kimon, 202, 206
kings, 375
  Cheng, 162, 164, 194, 222, 224
  Jie, 213, 234
  of Huainan, 33
  You, 246, 247, 248
  Zhao, 195
  Zhou, 234, 246
kinship, 50
knowledge, 73, 90, 219, 241, 250, 253, 295, 326, 341, 374, 376
Kongzi. See Confucius
Kongzi Jiayu (*School Sayings of Confucius/Family Sayings of Confucius*), 225
kouros (youth), 199
Kripke, Saul, 3

language, 79, 144, 356, 397
Laozi, 174
law, 3, 17, 18, 19, 48, 83, 97, 135, 411, 414
law-courts, 7, 9, 18
learned men, 348, 395
learning, 6, 112, 118, 125, 374, 376, 379, 384, 390, 400, 417, 418
Legge, James, 291
leisure, 9, 19, 334, 378
Lévi-Strauss, Claude, 356
Leviticus, 412
lexicons, 376, 396
Li Bing, 9
Li Chunfeng, 271, 307, 313–15
Li Ji (daughter of barbarian leader), 242, 244
Li Shanlan, 292, 294, 304, 321
  Explanations on the Four Unknowns, 292
Li Ye, 321
Liar paradox, 62
libraries, 340, 357, 380, 382, 384, 386, 390
Lienü Zhuan (*Arrayed Biographies of Women*), 218, 220, 245
Liezi, 131, 133, 138, 140, 146, 154, 392
life, 85, 104, 132, 134, 139, 152
lifespan, 132, 145

lightning, 14
Liji (Book of Rites), 21, 170, 177, 359, 412
lineage, 21, 179
literacy, 20
literate elite, 10, 24, 189
literature, 48, 399
litigation, 19
Liu Bingzhong, 36
Liu Hui, 259, 269, 270, 274, 275, 277, 278, 280, 281, 284, 307, 308, 318, 320, 321
Liu Xiang, 217, 218, 220, 245, 247, 248, 252, 375, 382, 388, 390–3, 396, 397
Liu Xin, 375, 382, 388, 393, 395, 397
logic, 4, 63
logos, 74, 75
London Missionary Society, 292, 293
longevity, 346
love, 134, 135, 237, 326, 329, 331, 336, 339
lun (ordering), 84
Lunyu (Analects), 155, 176
Luoyang, 414
Lüshi chunqiu (Master Lü's Spring and Autumn Annals), 21, 244
Lyceum, 22
Lycurgus, 209
lyric, 234

magic, 330, 337, 339, 343
magnanimous man, 117
maker of things (*zaowuzhe*), 84, 89
Makriyalos, 364
malaria, 341
Manchus, 36
manuscripts, 373, 376, 377, 379, 384, 389, 393, 398
maps, 375, 385
Marathon, 202, 205, 206, 207, 209, 226
market, 379
marriage, 342, 356
material, 140
materialism, 83, 141
mathematics, 3, 6–8, 17, 26, 36, 290, 301
Mawangdui, 12, 330, 334, 339, 344, 348
meals, 363
meaning, 59, 65, 72, 75
measurement, 260, 265, 270, 276, 278, 284, 345
measures
  created by humans, 144
mechanics, 261, 266, 271, 299, 300
medicine, 3, 24, 35, 41, 48, 326, 334, 340, 345, 391
  texts, 11
Mediterranean, 43, 50, 68, 202, 357, 381, 382, 386
Mei Wending, 36

memory
  ancestral, 199
  historical, 194
  practices, 198
  strategies, 192
Mencius, 4, 68, 111, 171, 172, 330, 360, 363
Menelaus, 238, 240
Meriones, 199
Mesopotamia, 11
metallurgy, 368, 369
metamorphosis, 153
metaphysics, 4, 280
methodology, 2, 241, 260
  of comparison, 38, 43, 111
methods, 275, 276, 277, 282, 410
metics, 413
Metrodora, 343
microcosm, 10
midwives, 12
military texts, 391
Mill, John Stuart, 44
millet, 346, 362, 363, 366
  broomcorn, 367
  foxtail, 367
Miltiades, 203, 204
mind, 135
ming (destiny), 131, 154
Ming dynasty, 36, 359
ministers, 13, 22, 213, 223
mirror, 73
missionaries, 22, 23
mnemonic, 378
Mo Xi, 234, 242, 243, 244, 253
Möbius, August, 300, 302
Mohists, 173–4
monarchy, 19, 49, 173, 414, 416
money, 50
Mongols, 36
monotheism, 22
morality, 4, 24, 86, 155, 417
motives, 254
moxibustion, 12, 13
Mozi, 144, 155, 173, 332
Museion, 402
museums, 380, 384
music, 3, 8, 20, 25
Mycenaeans, 198, 199
myth, 209, 240, 241, 378

nature
  in Aristotle, 137, 153
  in Heraclitus, 70

in Pythagorean tradition, 8
in Stoicism, 83, 97, 107
in Xunzi, 123
necessity, 88, 136
Needham, Joseph, 419
Neolithic, 361, 363, 364, 368
Nicander, 344
Nietzsche, Friedrich, 3, 70
Nine Chapters, 21, 269, 273, 274, 276, 277, 282, 293, 294, 306, 308, 318, 320
nudity, 205
numbers, 6

obeying, 92
obligations, 86, 106
observation, 326, 332, 343, 345
officials, 9, 18, 216, 221, 224, 374, 379, 395, 413, 415, 417, 418
Oinoe, 207
Onomasticon of Amenope, 358
opposites, 12, 77, 140
oppositions, 149
oral transmission, 377, 378, 383, 393, 402
oratory, 387, 412
order, 10, 17, 83, 97, 124, 141, 172
 of Heaven, 174
orders (commands), 101
organisms, 152
orgasm, 333, 336
Ovid, 330

pain, 115, 122, 123
palace, 211, 220, 339, 382, 384, 390, 402
pantheon, 160, 168, 173
paper, 375
Pappus, 303
papyrus, 330, 377, 381, 383
Paracelsus, 342
paradox, 70, 85, 94, 96, 120
parchment, 383
Paris (prince of Troy), 235
Parmenides, 135
passion, 331
patronage, 22, 228, 252, 374, 377, 379, 388, 389, 390, 397
peace, 91
Penelope, 238
penis, 342, 344; *see also* phallus
performance, 67, 164, 358, 360, 378
Pergamum, 15, 381
Pericles, 210
Persian Empire, 18, 205
Persian Wars, 190, 202, 208, 240

personalities, 160, 163, 166, 169, 174, 175, 180
persuasion, 7, 49, 110, 391, 412
petty man, 120, 126
phallus, 327, 328; *see also* penis
phantasia (imagination, impression), 100, 101, 103, 137
pharmacology, 328
phases. *See wuxing*
philia (love, affection), 331
Philitas, 400
philology, 46, 394, 396, 399
philosophers, 14, 36, 103, 106, 110, 330
philosophy, 3–5, 6, 8, 17, 26, 41, 48, 334, 375, 391
physiology, 336, 345
Pindar, 201, 203, 206
Pinker, Steven, 66
placebo, 340
plague, 15
plants, 24, 132, 142, 342, 360
Plato, 7, 14, 20, 22, 25, 131, 136, 141, 142, 226, 239, 387
 Cratylus, 4
 Laws, 20
 Menexenus, 209
 Republic, 104
 Timaeus, 14, 135, 141
pleasure, 113, 114, 116, 120, 121, 122, 123, 125, 127
 in reading, 395, 397
 sexual, 330, 332, 333, 336, 342, 345, 346
Pliny, 330, 343
Plutarch, 253
pneuma (breath), 33
poetry, 60
poets, 237
polemics, 15, 286
polis, 115, 228
Polish language, 63
politics, 84, 85, 102, 110, 377, 387
Poseidon, 160
Positivism, 68
Pound, Ezra, 66
power, 73, 411
powers, 83, 170, 181
prayer, 23, 24
prediction, 24
Presocratic philosophy, 69
Priam, 236
printing, 375, 379
processes, 12, 35
professionalisation, 417
profit, 113, 119, 120, 127
prohairesis (choice, will), 102, 103, 105, 114

Index

Prometheus, 161, 163, 178, 183
proof, 265, 286, 298, 302
proportion, 264, 269, 274, 280, 281, 284, 285
propriety, 119, 120, 127
psychology, 16
Ptolemaic dynasty, 21, 384
Ptolemy Philadelphus, 373
punishment, 13, 117, 127, 411, 416
pupil, 21
purifications, 14
Pyrrhonians, 68
Pythagoras, 5
Pythagoras' theorem, 263, 278
Pythagorean tradition, 8

qi (breath, energy), 13, 33, 87, 133, 138, 141, 142, 143, 146, 147, 148, 155, 332, 335, 341, 344, 345, 348
Qin dynasty, 54, 252, 411, 412
qing (feelings), 123, 132
Qing dynasty, 36, 60
Qu Yuan, 359
Quine, Willard Van Orman, 3, 65

ratio, 281
rationality, 106
   animals, 100
readers, 376, 378
reason, 83, 88, 100, 101, 107, 145
reasoning, 104, 123
recipes, 67, 326, 330, 340, 341, 345, 348
regularities, 132
religion, 9, 14, 22, 23, 48, 146, 328, 365, 411, 414, 416, 418
remedies, 12
remonstration, 246
representations, 26, 193, 234
reproduction, 140, 153, 336, 346
reputation, 113, 115, 123
research, 346
responsibility, 85, 98, 100, 112, 126, 235, 416
revelation, 414
rhetoric, 209, 251, 399
Ricci, Matteo, 22, 293
right and wrong, 4, 114
Rites controversy, 22
ritual, 10, 22, 23, 86, 118, 144, 163, 164, 166, 168, 171, 175, 176, 178, 183, 197, 199, 219, 225, 327, 339, 341, 346, 347, 386, 395
rivals, 11, 15, 16, 398
Rome, 4, 9, 22, 23, 52, 54, 212, 381, 411, 413, 414, 416, 418
root gatherers, 348

Ru, 86
rulers, 19

sacred, 23
sacrifices, 50, 147, 166, 168, 169, 170, 175, 178, 180, 182, 194, 195, 209, 412
sages, 70, 73, 99, 133, 171, 172, 386, 393
   kings, 6, 8, 174
   Shun, 96, 172
   Yao, 172
   Yu, 76, 96, 172
Sahlins, Marshall, 356
Sanzuodian, 361
Sappho, 236, 250
scale of nature, 131, 142, 145, 155
sceptical text, 84
Sceptics, 5
scholars, 21, 221, 384
schooling, 20
science, 37, 41, 48
Scribe Bo, 246
script, 20, 390, 394, 396, 399
Scythians, 342
seasons, 140
secret, 260, 391
seed, 336
self
   confines of, 87
   losing the, 94
   self-cultivation, 6, 126, 146, 333
   self-experimentation, 326, 328, 345, 348
   self-reflection, 125
   understanding of, 167
semantics, 59, 63, 65
semen, 331, 336, 344
semiotics, 67
Seneca the Younger, 402
senses, 137, 326, 333, 334, 335, 341
sexuality, 327
   continence, 334
   passion, 341
   relations, 24
shamans, 14
shame, 101, 110–18, 120, 121, 122, 126–8
Shandong, 227
Shang dynasty, 164, 198, 202, 213, 222, 224, 234, 242
Shangshu (Book of Documents), 21, 245, 392
Shanhaijing (Classic of Mountains and Seas), 169, 392
shen ren (spirit-people), 132
Shennong, 9
Shi Qiang Pan, 194

Shiji, 11, 17, 192, 213, 214, 217, 225, 244, 393
Shijing (Odes/ Book of Poetry/ Classic of Poetry), 21, 191, 246, 253, 359, 392
shrines, 16, 221, 380, 412
Shuowen jiezi, 394
Shuoyuan (Garden of Discourse), 217
Sibyl, 74
signatures, 342
silk, 375, 377, 383
Sima Qian, 17, 50, 190, 193, 213, 214, 217, 223, 225, 244, 245, 247, 248, 252, 387, 410, 412
Sima Tan, 17
simples, 343
sinecures, 395
slavery, 3, 9, 19, 83, 84, 85, 104, 105, 359, 413
small-*N* problem, 45, 51
social sciences, 40, 42, 44
societies, 115, 146
sociology, 40
Socrates, 5, 103, 209, 387
Son of Heaven, 179
Songshan, 215, 222
sophists, 22
soul
 in Aristotle, 112, 137, 145, 146, 152
 in Chinese accounts, 167, 214, 358, 359
 in Epictetus, 104
 in Heraclitus, 77
Spartans, 207, 234, 239, 251, 367, 411
specialism, 37, 38, 44
species, 131, 134, 135, 138, 139, 141, 143, 148, 149, 150, 152, 153
speech, 71, 146
spells, 329, 337, 339
 spellbinding literature, 340
sperm, 336, 337
spirits, 14, 132, 165, 166, 167, 168, 170, 171, 181, 182, 197, 332, 341, 347
spontaneity, 15, 86, 88, 136, 140
state, 13, 17, 33, 228, 285
statues, 201
Stesichorus, 239, 251
Stoa Poikile, 193, 202, 203, 205, 210, 226, 228
Stoics, 5, 83, 85, 88, 95, 99, 101, 106, 107, 402
substances, 12
success, 119
supernatural, 11, 13
superstition, 11
Suśruta samhitā, 331
symbols, 8, 9, 10, 237, 252, 340, 356
symposia, 50
symptoms, 35
syndromes, 35

Tacitus, 410
Taishan, 414
Tang dynasty, 417
Tarski, Alfred, 62
tastes, 26
taxation, 24
taxonomies, 131, 143, 145, 147, 149, 153
teaching, 6, 125
technology, 9, 23, 24, 135, 142, 144, 149
teleology, 136, 141, 142, 155
temples, 168, 194, 208, 210, 226, 228, 380
 medicine, 15
Terquem, Olry, 300, 301
Theocritus, 337
Theophrastus, 328, 330, 341, 342, 343, 344
 Enquiry into Plants, 328
therapy, 35
Theseus, 17, 205, 207
Thucydides, 18, 190, 193, 210, 387, 412
thunder, 14
Thyestes, 199
tian. *See* Heaven
Timon, 68
ting (listen), 92
tombs, 10, 18, 21, 167, 215, 221, 222, 328, 330, 344, 413
touch, 334
trade, 24
traditions, 84, 378, 386, 388, 390, 395, 399, 402, 413
transformation, 131, 133, 135, 138, 139, 153, 155, 179
translation, 59
trial and error, 347
Trojan War, 234, 236, 237, 241
Troy, 235
truth, 5, 59, 69, 74, 102, 107, 239
Tyrannicides, 189, 193, 205, 207, 226
tyrants, 90, 384

understanding, 128
uniqueness, 142
universal procedure. *See dushu*
urbanism, 53, 54, 368
uselessness, 132
utility, 299

values, 6, 38, 101, 112, 120, 198, 238, 239, 301
Vernant, Jean-Pierre, 131
villages, 361
virtue, 112, 116, 117, 213, 245
vote, 7
votives, 200

Wang Chong, 5, 14, 193
Wang Mang, 374, 390, 414
Wang Wenkao, 213
Wang Xishan, 36
war, 24, 53, 75, 77, 166, 169, 210, 234, 237, 242, 243, 247
Warring States, 5, 22, 50, 51, 53, 68, 110, 197, 210, 331, 390, 411
water, 76
Way. See dao
weaving, 236
Weber, Max, 41
wei (artifice, conscious exertion), 123
well-being, 11
Wenzi, 155
Westermarck, Edward, 61
wheat, 364, 367
will, 83, 98, 102, 103, 105, 112, 179
Williams, Bernard, 3, 120
wisdom, 4, 8, 79, 95, 241, 243, 378, 399
wise person, 85, 96, 99, 100, 103, 106
womb, 336
women, 104, 356
  as author, 343
  chaste, 213
  dangerous, 24
  fear about, 234
  formation of, 136
  in medical writing, 336
  kidnappings, 241
  pleasure of, 333
  practitioners, 12
  warriors, 212
world
  in the ritual space, 176, 178
  order of, 85, 97
  physical, political, moral, 34
worship, 10, 23, 24, 163
writing, 170
Wu Liang Shrine, 189, 192, 193, 213–19
wuxing (five phases), 143, 149, 347
Wylie, Alexander, 290, 291, 293–6, 301, 304–7, 320, 321
  Jottings, 293, 294, 305, 321

Xenophanes, 131, 134
Xia dynasty, 76, 213, 224, 234, 242, 246
Xi'an, 381
Xiaotangshan, 210, 214, 226
xing (conduct) 行, 91
xing (nature) 性, 15, 123, 148
Xinglonggou, 361, 362
xu (emptiness), 92
Xu Guangqi, 293
Xu Shen, 394
Xue Fengzuo, 36
Xunzi, 4, 14, 110–11, 113, 118–20, 123–8, 131, 142, 144, 146, 155, 330, 332, 392

Yan Hui, 73, 89–96, 99, 106
Yang Xiong, 375, 388, 390, 393–8, 399, 400, 401, 402
Yellow Emperor, 169, 213
Yi (Changes), 21
yin-yang, 140, 141, 143, 148, 149, 153, 155, 332, 335, 346, 347, 348
young people, 113, 115, 117, 118, 122

Zeno, 22, 33, 96, 106
Zenodotus, 375, 400
Zeus, 63, 79, 83, 97, 100, 101, 103, 104, 106, 134, 160, 163, 178, 179, 183, 198, 203
zhan guo. See Warring States
Zhangjiashan, 18
Zhanguo ce (Strategies of the Warring States), 392
zhi (will), 91, 92
Zhou dynasty, 162, 164, 193–202, 210, 213, 222, 224, 228, 242, 246, 247, 411
Zhoubi suanjing, 8, 21
Zhouli (Rites of Zhou), 147, 155
Zhu Shijie, 292, 294
Zhuangzi, 5, 68–79, 83–96, 99, 102, 106, 131, 132, 138, 139, 144–5, 146, 154, 387
Zhushu jinian (Bamboo Annals), 244
zoogony, 133, 135, 137, 141
Zoroaster, 399
Zu Gengzhi, 259, 269–83
Zuozhuan, 155, 251, 393